Great
Divides

D1372419

Great
Divides

=

Readings in Social Inequality
in the United States

Third Edition

Thomas M. Shapiro

THE HELLER SCHOOL FOR SOCIAL
POLICY AND MANAGEMENT
BRANDEIS UNIVERSITY

Boston   Burr Ridge, IL   Dubuque, IA   Madison, WI   New York
San Francisco   St. Louis   Bangkok   Bogotá   Caracas   Kuala Lumpur
Lisbon   London   Madrid   Mexico City   Milan   Montreal   New Delhi
Santiago   Seoul   Singapore   Sydney   Taipei   Toronto

Higher Education

GREAT DIVIDES: READINGS IN SOCIAL INEQUALITY IN THE UNITED STATES
Published by McGraw-Hill, a business unit of The McGraw-Hill Companies, Inc., 1221
Avenues of the Americas, New York, NY, 10020. Copyright © 2005, 2001, 1998, by The
McGraw-Hill Companies, Inc. All rights reserved. No part of this publication may be reproduced or distributed in any form or by any means, or stored in a database or retrieval system,
without the prior written consent of The McGraw-Hill Companies, Inc., including, but not
limited to, in any network or other electronic storage or transmission, or broadcast for distance
learning.

Some ancillaries, including electronic and print components, may not be available to customers outside the United States.

This book is printed on acid-free paper.

2   3   4   5   6   7   8   9   0   FGR/FGR   0   9   8   7   6   5   4

ISBN 0-07-282584-7

Publisher: *Philip A Butcher*
Sponsoring editor: *Sherith H. Pankratz*
Developmental editor: *Jill Gordon*
Senior marketing manager: *Daniel M. Loch*
Project manager: *Jean R. Starr*
Lead production supervisor: *Randy L. Hurst*
Associate designer: *Srdjan Savanovic*

Photo research coordinator: *Brian Pecko*
Art editor: *Cristin Yancey*
Permissions editor: *Marty Granahan*
Cover photo: © *Illustration Works*
Typeface: *10/12 Electra*
Compositor: *Thompson Type*
Printer: *Quebecor World Fairfield Inc.*

Library of Congress Cataloging-in-Publication Data

Great divides : readings in social inequality in the United States / Thomas M. Shapiro.—
   3rd ed.
     p. cm.
   ISBN 0-07-282584-7 (softcover: alk. paper)
   1. Equality—United States. 2. Marginality, Social—United States. 3. Minorities—
United States—Social conditions. 4. Women—United States—Social conditions.
5. United States—Social conditions. I. Shapiro, Thomas M.
HN90.S6S43 2005
305'.0973—dc22

                                                                          200367465

www.mhhe.com

CONTENTS

Part VI
CLASS, RACE, AND GENDER IN AN INSTITUTIONAL CONTEXT: EDUCATION AND THE ENVIRONMENT   378

PREFACE

AS THE TITLE SUGGESTS, *GREAT DIVIDES* IS about the barriers that keep groups and individuals apart from one another in the United States; the obstacles of social inequality and power that prevent the formation of a stronger, more united whole; and the great possibilities for this society that go unrealized because of artificial structures for maintaining inequality.

Why should there be another edition of another book about social inequality in the United States? Don't we know enough of the dreary details already? Over the past four decades, a number of anthologies have attempted to expose students to the nature, sources, and meanings of inequality. Indeed, at first I was skeptical about the need for yet another reader when an editor first suggested the idea. An examination of available readers quickly changed my mind for two important reasons. First, the existing readers fail to note a host of new, creative, rigorous, and very rich scholarship examining social inequality (e.g., studies of class, race, ethnicity, and gender inequality) that has become available in the past several years. Second, the current readers on social inequality do not reflect the rapidly changing basis of inequality in the United States that has resulted from economic restructuring and globalization of labor and markets.

My goal has been to put together an anthology that blends some of the classic essays on inequality and social stratification together with some of the best exciting, new research in the area. In my own teaching, I feel it is very important for students to read good, challenging scholarship in its original form. Too much of what American students read (in scholarly literature, as well as in the popular culture) is filtered information, watered down for quick consumption. These readings offer a challenging invitation to explore inequality in American society.

CHANGES TO THE THIRD EDITION

With this third edition, I maintain a balance of classical and contemporary readings in social inequality. I have added sixteen new selections of contemporary, cutting-edge sociological research, including recent writings by Maxine Baca Zinn and Stanley Eitzen, Lisa Keister, Glenda Laws, Mary Waters, Marta Tienda, and Haya Stier, Alejandro Portes and Rubén Rumbaut, Bonnie Dill, and Robert Bullard. In addition, a range of new issues are highlighted in the third edition, including the effects of global capitalism, the economic struggles of women on welfare, the widening gap between the wealthy and the poor, "the middle-class squeeze," the effects of deindustrialization on the continuing plight of the poor, and women and work across class and racial lines. The concluding part of this edition also introduces an entirely new section on the intersection of environmental justice and class, race, and gender.

ACKNOWLEDGMENTS

In preparation for this new edition, we solicited and received valuable comments and suggestions from professors who adopted *Great Divides*. A group of sociologists who teach courses on social inequality also were asked to comment on the manuscript at various stages. This high-powered dialogue was funneled through me, and I took their comments and suggestions very seriously. This professional review process was tremendously helpful in sculpting this reader. The common denominator for all participants was the wish to enlighten our students: to create a teaching tool for fostering better understanding of social inequality. I want to salute this group of reviewers as a whole and thank each one individually.

For the third edition, I would like to thank the following team of reviewers: Tom Gerschick, Illinois State University; Ed Hackett, Arizona State University; Michael Miller, University of Texas–San Antonio; and George Wilson, University of Miami.

The third edition has benefited from the creative and patient efforts of a great production team, including the developmental and editorial assistance of Jill Gordon, and Jan Nickels who copyedited the manuscript.

Serina Beauparlant, then of Mayfield Publishing, first suggested this project, cajoled me into doing it, put the team of reviewers together, sweated every detail, and found ways to make it rewarding. When Mayfield was acquired by McGraw-Hill, Sherith Pankratz took on the project, made me feel welcome, and has skillfully guided the new edition.

Many colleagues suggested potential readings for this book. At Northeastern University, I had the fantastic assistance of Yndia Lorick-Wilmot to support me in gathering and organizing the materials.

Most of all, the support, understanding, and love of Ruth Birnberg helped me through yet another project. To Izak, I apologize, once again, for the distractions this reader meant; in addition, I thank him for sharing with me a young man's curiosity about what's fair, which is both challenging and inspiring for our future.

ABOUT THE CONTRIBUTORS

Mathieu Albert (Reading 36) is Assistant Professor in the Department of Psychiatry and Educational Research in the Centre for Research in Education at Université de Montréal. His current research projects include the study of scientific knowledge production in health research. Dr. Albert's work also focuses on the political dimension of knowledge production in the social sciences.

Elijah Anderson (Readings 25 and 30) is the Charles and William L. Day Professor of the Social Sciences, Professor of Sociology, and Director of The Philadelphia Ethnography Project at the University of Pennsylvania. He has authored *A Place on the Corner* (1978), *Streetwise* (1990), and *Code of the Street* (1999). Anderson received the Robert E. Park Award of the American Sociological Association for *Streetwise*.

Joaquín Arango (Reading 16) is Professor at the Instituto Universitario Ortega y Gasset, Spain.

Regina Austin (Reading 46) is the William A. Schnader Professor of Law at the University of Pennsylvania law school. She is a leading authority on economic discrimination and minority legal feminist. Her work on the overlapping burdens of race, gender, and class oppression, widely recognized for its insight and creativity, has been widely reprinted.

Maxine Baca Zinn (Readings 2 and 5) is Professor of Sociology and a Senior Faculty Associate with the Julian Samora Research Institute. She specializes in the sociology of the family, race and ethnic relations, and the sociology of gender. She is recognized nationally as a leading scholar on Latinas and Latino families in the United States.

Richard J. Barnet (Reading 14) is the author of numerous books including *Global Reach, Roots of War: The Men and Institutions Behind U.S. Foreign Policy, The Giants: Russia and America*, and *Who Wants Disarmament?*

Edna Bonacich (Reading 9) is Professor of Sociology and Ethnic Studies at the University of California–Riverside. Her research interests include race and ethnicity and inequality.

Robert D. Bullard (Reading 44) is the pioneer of Environmental Justice, nationally known for his research in the areas of urban land use, housing, community development, industrial facility siting processes, and environmental quality. He is also Ware Professor of Sociology at Clark Atlanta.

Lisa Catanzarite (Reading 20) is Professor of Sociology at the University of California–San Diego and Research Affiliate of the Center for Comparative Immigration Studies. Her areas of interest include the socioeconomic mobility of immigrants in the United States.

John Cavanagh (Reading 14) is the Director and founding fellow of the Institute of Policy Studies in Washington, D.C. He has coauthored numerous books on the world economy.

Peter W. Cookson, Jr. (Reading 1) is Associate Provost at Adelphi University. His research interests focus on education reform and social policy.

Kingsley Davis (Reading 11) was born in Tuxedi, Texas in 1908. He taught at the University of Southern California and University of California–Berkeley. His books include *Human Society* and *Contemporary Marriage*. He died in 1997.

Nancy A. Denton (Reading 28) is Associate Professor of Demography at the SUNY–Albany. She coauthored *American Apartheid* with Douglas Massey, which won the Distinguished Scholarly Publication Award from the American Sociological Association in 1995.

G. William Domhoff (Reading 19) is Professor of Psychology and Sociology at the University of California–Santa Cruz. He has authored and edited several books, including *The Powers That Be*, *The Higher Circles*, and *Who Rules America?*

W. E. B. Du Bois (Reading 22) was born in Great Barrington, Massachusetts, in 1868 and died in 1963. Du Bois was a leading social theorist on race issues who organized the Niagara Movement (1905–1910), which became the NAACP. His classic works include *The Philadelphia Negro*, *Black Reconstruction*, and *Souls of Black Folk.*

Kathryn Edin (Reading 21) is Associate Professor of Sociology at Northwestern University. She is the coauthor of *Making Ends Meet*. Her current research focuses on the social meaning of work and family in poor communities.

D. Stanley Eitzen (Reading 2) is Professor Emeritus of Sociology at Colorado State University. He is a former president of the North American Society for the Sociology of Sport and a Sports Ethics Fellow of the Institute for International Sport.

Friedrich Engels (Reading 6) was born in Barmen, Germany and later moved to Manchester and became a collaborator with Karl Marx. His influential works include *The Germany Ideology*, the *Manifesto of the Communist Party*, and *The Origins of the Family, Private Property and the State.*

Claude S. Fischer (Reading 1) is Professor of Sociology at University of California–Berkeley. His areas of interest are social history, urban sociology, technology, and social networks. His most recent works include *Inequality by Design: Cracking the Bell Curve Myth* with Hout, Lucas, Sánchez Jankowski, Swidler, and Voss (1996) and *America Calling: A Social History of the Telephone to 1940* (1992).

Herbert J. Gans (Reading 12) is the Robert S. Lynd Professor of Sociology at Columbia University. He is the author of more than a dozen books and over 170 articles. His first book was *The Urban Villagers* (1962); his latest is *Democracy and the News* (2002). He is a past president of the Eastern Sociological Society and in 1989 served as president of the American Sociological Association. In 1999, he received the Association's Award for Contributions to the Public Understanding of Sociology.

Heidi Hartmann (Reading 8) is the founder, Director and President of the Institute for Women's Policy Research. She has been awarded a MacArthur Fellowship.

Elizabeth Higginbotham (Reading 38) is Professor of Sociology at the University of Delaware. Her research interests focus on race, class, gender, and employment and mobility issues for professional Black women. She is the author of *Too Much to Ask: Black Women in the Era of Integration* (2001) and coeditor of *Women and Work: Exploring Race, Ethnicity, and Class* (1997).

Michael Hout (Reading 1) is Professor of Sociology at the University of California–Berkeley. He is the author of *Following in Father's Footsteps: Occupational Mobility in Ireland* and *Mobility Tables.*

Graeme Hugo (Reading 16) is professor of the Department of Geographical and Environmental Studies and Director of the National Key Centre in Research and Teaching in Social Applications of Geographical Information Systems at the University of Adelaide. His books include *Australia's Changing Population* (Oxford University Press). In 1987 Professor Hugo was elected a fellow of the Academy of Social Sciences in Australia and has been president of the Australian Population Association and was a member of the National Population Council.

Lisa A. Keister (Reading 5) is Associate Professor of Sociology at the Ohio State University. She is the recipient of the National Science Foundation Faculty Early Career Development Award and author of *Chinese Business Groups* and *Wealth in America: Trends in Wealth Inequality.*

Ali Kouaouci (Reading 16) is a lecturer in the department of demography at the University of Montreal.

Jonathan Kozol (Reading 42) taught public school for several years. He is the award-winning author of many books, including *Death at an Early Age, Illiterate America, Free Schools,* and *Rachael and Her Children.*

Suzanne Laberge (Reading 36) Titular Professeure at Université de Montréal. Her areas of interest include designs of femininity and masculinity and the practice of physical activities and sociology of sport.

Glenda Laws (Reading 15) was an urban social geographer and Associate Professor of Geography at Pennsylvania State University. Her interests included marginalized populations and the political struggles around their well being. She died in June 1996 at age thirty-seven.

Charles Lee (Reading 45) is Director of Research for the Commission for Racial Justice for the United Church of Christ.

Laura Lein (Reading 21) has a dual appointment with the Department of Anthropology and the School of Social Work as Senior Lecturer and Research Scientist at the University of Texas–Austin. She is the coauthor of *Making Ends Meet* (1997).

Frank Levy (Reading 3) is the Rose Professor of Urban Economics at MIT's Department of Urban Studies and Planning. He is the author of *The New Dollars and Dreams,* a history of American incomes and the economy for the last fifty years.

Samuel R. Lucas (Reading 1) is Associate Professor of Sociology at the University of California–Berkeley. His most recent books include *Tracking Inequality: Stratification and Mobility in American High Schools.*

Jay MacLeod (Reading 4) is a Rhodes Scholar, holding degrees in social studies and theology. His latest work is *Ain't No Makin' It* (1995). MacLeod

is currently an Anglican priest in Chesterfield, England.

Karl Marx (Reading 6) was born in 1818 in the Prussian Rhineland and died in 1883. He is known for his immense contributions to philosophy and social theory. Some of his major works are the *Manifesto of the Communist Party,* and the *Economic and Philosophic Manuscripts.*

Douglas S. Massey (Readings 16 and 28) is the Dorothy Swaine Thomas Professor of Sociology and department chair at the University of Pennsylvania. He has coauthored numerous books including *Problem of the Century: Racial Stratification in the United States at Century's* with Elijah Anderson (2001), *Worlds in Motion: International Migration at the End of the Millennium* with Joaquín Arango, Graeme Hugo, Ali Kouaouci, Adela Pellegrino, and J. Edward Taylor (1998), and *American Apartheid* (1993), which won the American Sociological Association's Distinguished Publication Award.

Peggy McIntosh (Reading 34) is Associate Director of the Wellesley College Center for Research on Women. She is a recipient of the Klingenstein Award for Distinguished Educational Leadership from Columbia Teachers College. McIntosh has written many articles on women's studies and curriculum change.

Roslyn Arlin Mickelson (Readings 39 and 43) is Professor of Sociology and Adjunct Professor of Women's Studies at the University of North Carolina–Charlotte. Her research centers on how political economy, race, class, and gender shape educational processes and outcomes. Her most recent book is *Children on the Streets of Americas* (1999).

C. Wright Mills (Reading 17) was born in Waco, Texas, in 1916 and died in 1962. He was Professor of Sociology at Columbia University and author of many books including *The Power Elite, White Collar: The American Middle Classes,* and *The Sociological Imagination.*

Wilbert E. Moore (Reading 11) was Professor of Sociology at Princeton University and former

President of the American Sociological Association.

Melvin L. Oliver (Reading 29) is former Vice President of the Ford Foundation's program for Asset Building and Community Development. He is the Dean of the College of Social Sciences at the University of California–Santa Barbara. He coauthored, with Thomas M. Shapiro, *Black Wealth/White Wealth: a New Perspective on Racial Inequality*, which won the C. Wright Mills Award and the American Sociological Association's Distinguished Scholarly Publication Award.

Michael Omi (Reading 23) is Professor of Ethnic Studies at the University of California–Berkeley. He is the coauthor of *Racial Formation in the United States from the 1960's to the 1980's* (1986). His writings have focused on race, politics, and popular culture. He received Berkeley's Distinguished Teaching Award in 1990.

Vilma Ortiz (Reading 20) is Associate Professor of Sociology at the University of California–Los Angeles. Her areas of interest include race and ethnicity, immigration, and Latina/Latino population studies in the United States. She coauthored *Challenging Fronteras: Structuring Latina and Latino Lives in the U.S.* with Mary Romero and Pierrette Hondagneu-Sotelo (1997) and "Family Income and Migration among Puerto Ricans" In Luis Falcon and Edwin Melendez (editors), *Recasting Puerto Rican Poverty* (forthcoming).

Irene Padavic (Reading 40) is Associate Professor of Sociology at Florida State University. Her areas of interest include gender and work, economic restructuring, and labor-management relations.

Adela Pellegrino (Reading 16) is Professor of the Facultad de Ciencias Sociales, Programa de Poblacion, Uruguay.

Caroline Hodges Persell (Reading 41) is Professor of Sociology at New York University. Her research interests are education and stratification.

Alejandro Portes (Reading 31) is Professor of Sociology at Princeton University and Faculty Associate at the Woodrow Wilson School of Public Affairs. Portes is coauthor of *City on Edge: The Transformation of Miami* (1993) and *Latin Journey: Cuban and Mexican Immigrants in the United States* (1985).

Jeffrey Reiman (Reading 18) is a Criminologist, a William Fraser McDowell Professor of Philosophy, and Director of the Master's Program in Philosophy and Social Policy at American University. He has authored many books, including *The Rich Get Richer and the Poor Get Prison: Ideology, Crime, and Criminal Justice*; *In Defense of Political Philosophy*; and *Justice and Modern Moral Philosophy*. He also has written numerous articles in philosophy and criminal justice journals and anthologies.

Barbara F. Reskin (Reading 40) is Professor of Sociology at Harvard University. She has written six books and several dozen articles and chapters about gender and race inequality in the workplace, sex segregation, discrimination, and affirmative action. Her books include *Job Queues, Gender Queues: Explaining Women's Inroads into Male Occupations* with Patricia Roos.

Barbara J. Risman (Reading 33) is Professor of Sociology at North Carolina State University. She is the author of *Gender Vertigo* (1998) and coeditor of the journal *Contemporary Sociology*.

Rubén G. Rumbaut (Reading 31) is Professor of Sociology at Michigan State University. He is coauthor, with Alejandro Portes, of *Immigrant America: A Portrait* (1996) and coeditor of *Immigration Research for a New Century. Multidisciplinary Perspectives* (2000) and *Origins and Destinies: Immigration, Race, and Ethnicity in America* (1996).

Stephen Samuel Smith (Reading 43) is cochair of the African-American Studies committee and Professor and acting chair of the Department of Political Science at Winthrop University. Smith's research deals with desegregation, educational policy, and urban politics. Recent publications include "Liberty, Equality, and . . . Social Capital?" in *Social Capital: Historical and Theoretical*

Perspectives on Civil Society (2002) with Jessica Kulynych, "Desegregation" in *Education and Sociology: An Encyclopedia* (2001), and *Boom for Whom? Desegregation, Development and Education in Charlotte* (forthcoming, 2003).

Martin Sanchez Jankowski (Reading 1) is Professor of Sociology at the University of California–Berkeley. His areas of interest include urban sociology, political sociology, poverty, race and ethnicity, youth culture, and survey research. He is the author of *City Bound: Urban Life and Political Attitudes among Chicano Youth* and *Islands in the Streets: Gangs and American Urban Poverty.*

Michael H. Schill (Reading 46) is Professor of Law and Urban Planning at the New York University School of Law and Wagner School of Public Service, where he teaches courses in property law, land use regulation, and real estate. He is also the Director of the Furman Center for Real Estate and Urban Policy at NYU. He has written or edited three books and a number of articles on various aspects of housing policy, deregulation, finance, and discrimination.

Thomas M. Shapiro (Reading 29) is the Pokross Professor of Law and Social Policy at the Heller School for Social Policy and Management, Brandeis University. His book, *The Hidden Cost of Being African American: How Wealth Perpetuates Inequality* will publish in 2004. Melvin Oliver and Shapiro have been awarded the C. Wright Mills Award and the American Sociological Association's Distinguished Publication Award for *Black Wealth/White Wealth: A New Perspective on Racial Inequality.*

Mindy Stombler (Reading 37) teaches courses on inequality at Georgia State University. Her current research focuses on gay fraternities. Stombler wrote "Buddies" or "Slutties" as a graduate student in the sociology department at Florida State University.

Haya Stier (Reading 27) is Associate Professor at the Department of Labor Studies and the Department of Sociology at Tel Aviv University. Her areas of interest include labor markets, issues concerning women's market behavior along the life cycle, demography of the labor force, quantitative research methods, and poverty and welfare. Her current research focuses on women's part-time employment and their work behavior along the life cycle in a comparative framework.

Ann Swidler (Reading 1) is Professor of Sociology at the University of California–Berkeley. Her areas of specialization are culture, religion, theory, and political sociology. She recently authored *Meaning and Modernity: Religion, Polity, Self* with Richard Madsen, William Sullivan, and Steven M. Tipton (2001) and *Talk of Love: How Culture Matters* (2001).

Ronald Takaki (Reading 26) is Chair of the Ethnic Studies Department at the University of California–Berkeley. His books include *Strangers from a Different Shore* (1989), *A Different Mirror: A History of Multicultural America* (1993), and *Hiroshima: Why America Dropped the Atomic Bomb* (forthcoming).

J. Edward Taylor (Reading 16) is Professor at the University of California–Davis.

Bonnie Thornton Dill (Reading 35) is Professor of Women's Studies; Director of the Consortium on Race, Gender and Ethnicity; and an affiliate faculty member with the Departments of Sociology, Afro-American Studies, and American Studies at the University of Maryland. Her research focuses on the intersections of race, class, and gender with an emphasis on African American women and families. Dill's recent published works include: *A Better Life for Me and My Children: Low Income Single Mothers' Struggle for Self Sufficiency in the Rural South* (1998); *Valuing Families Differently: Race, Poverty and Welfare Reform* (1998), with Maxine Baca Zinn and Sandra Patton; and *African Americans in the Rural South: The Persistence of Race and Poverty* (1996), with Bruce Williams.

Marta Tienda (Reading 27) is Professor of Sociology at Princeton University and Faculty Associate at the Woodrow Wilson School of Public Policy. Her areas of interest include labor markets, ethnic stratification, immigration, poverty, and social demography. Her current research focuses on race, ethnic, and gender variation in the transition from school to work and the paradox of birth outcomes among immigrants. She is author of numerous papers and several books, including *The Hispanic Population of the United States, Divided Opportunities, Hispanics and the U.S. Economy,* and *The Color of Opportunity.*

Ralph H. Turner (Reading 10) is Emeritus Professor of Sociology at the University of California–Los Angeles. He has written widely about social movements and social theory.

Kim Voss (Reading 1) is Associate Professor of Sociology at the University of California–Berkeley. Her research interests are labor, social movements, and historical sociology. Her most recent publications are *Organize or Die: Labor's New Tactics and Immigrant Workers* (1999), with Rachael Sherman, and *The Making of American Exceptionalism: The Knights of Labor and Class Formation in the Nineteenth Century* (1993).

Mary C. Waters (Reading 24) is Professor and Chair of the Sociology Department at Harvard University. Her areas of interest include race and ethnicity, immigration, and demography. She is currently the codirector (with John Mollenkopf and Philip Kasnitz of City University of New York) of The New York Second Generation Project. Waters is the author and coeditor of numerous articles and books on the subject of race, ethnicity, and immigration. She is the coeditor (with historian Reed Ueda of Tufts University) of *The New Americans: A Handbook to Immigration Since 1965* (forthcoming) and author of *Black Identities: West Indian Immigrant Dreams and American Re-*

alities (1999); *From Many Strands: Ethnic and Racial Groups in Contemporary America* (1998), with Stanley Lieberson; *Ethnic Options: Choosing Identities in America* (1990); and *The New Race Question: How the Census Counts Multi-Racial Individuals* (2002), with Joel Perlmann.

Max Weber (Reading 7) was born in Erfurt, Germany, in 1864 and died in 1920. He is known for his extensive writing on bureaucracies, politics, power, and authority. His most famous works include *The Protestant Ethic* and *The Spirit of Capitalism.*

William Julius Wilson (Reading 32) is Lewis P. and Linda L. Geyser University Professor at Harvard University. He served as past President of the American Sociological Association, and has received several honors including the MacArthur Prize fellowship and the 1998 National Medal of Science. He is the author of numerous award-winning publications, including *The Declining Significance of Race,* winner of the American Sociological Association's Sydney Spivack Award; *The Truly Disadvantaged,* which received the Society for the Study of Social Problems' C. Wright Mills Award; and *When Work Disappears: The World of the New Urban Poor,* which received the Sidney Hillman Foundation Award.

Howard Winant (Reading 23) is Professor of Sociology at the University of California–Santa Barbara. He has authored many books including *Racial Formation in the United States from 1960s to the 1990s* with Michael Omi (1994) and *Racial Conditions* (1994).

Erik Olin Wright (Reading 13) is Professor of Sociology at the University of Wisconsin. He has authored several books including *Class, Crisis and the State.*

INTRODUCTION

—ɯ—

THE AMERICAN DREAM
PAST AND PRESENT

WE ALL KNOW THAT "THE AMERICAN DREAM" means economic opportunity, social mobility, and material success. It means that all of us do better than our parents did, that our standard of living improves over the course of our lifetimes, and that we can own our homes. It also means that regardless of our background or origin, all of us have a chance to succeed. As Americans, we do not favor the idea that background privileges some people or groups while others are systematically blocked from success. Economic opportunity and social equality are thus twin pillars of the American belief system.

In the decades following the end of World War II—from 1945 to the early 1970s—the American Dream became a reality for millions of families and individuals in our society. People were able to buy homes, purchase new automobiles, take vacations, and see their standard of living steadily rise. At the same time, our society made strides toward improved social conditions for minorities and greater equality among groups of people. For these changes, many observers credit pressure from the civil rights movement, the women's movement, labor unions, and other social organizations and movements, along with changes in public policy and a growing, prosperous economy. A better standard of living and a narrowing gap between rich and poor together reinforced vital elements of the American credo. Many Americans assumed that material life would continue to improve indefinitely and that the economic and social gaps among groups would continue to narrow.

In the 1970s, however, the economy slowed down and began to stagnate. The standard of living

began to fall, poverty began to increase, and membership in the middle class became more tenuous. Just to stay in the same place, many families had to adapt, as more women sought work outside the home, living spaces became smaller, and time for leisure activities and for families getting together was reduced as people worked harder for longer hours. The 1980s saw a return to some of the inequalities of the past, as measured by comparisons of the relative material positions of African and European Americans and by comparisons of women's income with men's. Many observers began to feel that the United States was retreating and losing ground in its struggle against social inequality.

The changes we saw in our society during the 1990s and at the beginning of 2000—stagnating living standards, persistent poverty, a precarious middle class, and a growing gap between rich and poor—are probably the result of globalization and the specific way that economic restructuring is taking place in the United States. Economic restructuring is one way in which corporations, businesses, bureaucracies, individuals, and various levels of government respond to the challenge of keeping the United States a preeminent nation in the emerging global economy. Restructuring includes a variety of strategies, policies, and practices, including corporate and government downsizing, deindustrialization, movement of production from the central city to the suburbs, and changes from a permanent to a contingent workforce, from local to global production, from mass assembly line production to more flexible and decentralized production, and from a manufacturing-based to a service-based economy. Together with other factors, including the increasing diversity of the American population, economic restructuring is giving

1

a new shape to social and economic inequality in our society.

To appreciate fully the decisions American families face, we need to understand the extent, causes, and consequences of the vast increase in inequality that has taken place since the early 1970s. Inequality has increased during both Democratic and Republican administrations. Those at the top of the income distribution have increased their share the most. In fact, the slice of the income pie received by the top 1 percent of families is nearly twice as large as it was 30 years ago, and their share now is about as large as the share of the bottom 40 percent. This is not news. President Bush's 2003 tax stimulus package carves 39 percent of the benefits for the wealthiest 1 percent of the population.

An ideology that equated personal gain with benefits to society accompanied the great economic boom of the last part of the twentieth century. Despite loud words, inequality increased in the past 20 years, and due to little action, policies such as affordable housing and equitable school funding that challenged that mindset simply had no chance of getting off the ground. Ironically, historically low unemployment rates went hand-in-hand with rising inequality in an America where hard work no longer means economic success. Success includes harder work, less family time, and probably more stress. The average middle-income, two-parent family now works the equivalent of 16 more weeks than it did in 1979 due to longer hours, second jobs, and working spouses. The years of economic stagnation subsequent to the boom of the late 1990s produced a dramatic increase in the number of working poor, and working homeless families are a growing concern. Since late 2001, in a period marked by a declining stock market and rising unemployment, an abundance of data has provided strong evidence that lower-income households are under severe economic stress. Personal bankruptcies, automobile repossessions, mortgage foreclosures, and other indicators of bad debt all reached records in 2002.

The American economy hit a wall in late 2001 when the stock market bubble burst and the realities of a fragile economy struck home for many families. In a society where a growing economy and job growth is an article of faith, over two million jobs were lost within the first two years of the Bush administration. The tragic events of September 11, accompanied by a renewed emphasis on domestic and national security and coupled with the war in Iraq, worsened already tough economic realities. Economists tell us that the recession officially ended in mid-2003, but job loss was still growing and the standard of living had not improved.

My goal in this third edition is to help you make sense of these changes and understand the basic theories, concepts, and findings associated with inequality in the United States today. Part I, on opportunity and inequality in the United States, explores what has been happening to the American dream and looks particularly at the sources and meanings of this new shape of inequality.

SOCIAL STRATIFICATION

Strata are layers, or hierarchy. Social stratification is a process or system by which groups of people are arranged into a hierarchical social structure. Dimensions of power and powerlessness undergird this hierarchy and influence subsequent opportunities for rewards. Consequently, people have differential access to, and control over, prospects, rewards, and whatever is of value in society based on their hierarchical positions, primarily because of social factors. Social stratification, an expression of social inequality, is so pervasive in American society that an entire field of sociology is devoted to its study.

Social-stratification systems are based primarily on either ascribed status or achieved status. Ascribed status is a social position typically designated or given to each person at birth. In a society with ascribed status, differential opportunities, rewards, privileges, and power are provided to individuals according to criteria fixed at birth. Achieved status is a social position gained as a result of ability or effort. This type of stratification is evident in all industrial societies, including the United States.

Given that social stratification is an expression of social inequality, how does inequality result, in turn, from social stratification? One leading scholar has proposed that inequality is produced by two different kinds of matching processes: "The jobs, occupations, and social roles in society are first matched to 'reward packages' of unequal value"; then, individuals are sorted and matched to particular jobs, occupations, and social roles through training and other institutional processes (Grusky, 1994, p. 3). Both parts of this matching process have been the subject of much investigation in sociology, as many inquiries have probed the following two questions (Fischer et al., 1996, p. 7): (1) What determines how much people get for performing various economic roles and tasks? (2) What social and institutional processes determine who gets ahead and who falls behind in the competition for positions of unequal value?

Other questions sociologists ask about stratification include the following: How is ascribed status constructed over time? What are the institutional processes and practices that shape ascriptive stratification? To what extent does an ascribed status circumscribe people's opportunities and rewards? To what extent is achieved status fixed or open? What determines how and whether individuals are able to move through the occupational and wage structure in a system characterized by achieved status? When people can move through such a structure, how do they move? These and other questions are explored in Part II, on how social stratification is generated.

Social Stratification in the United States

Ascriptive stratification based on gender is found in nearly every society, and racial and ethnic stratification is almost as widespread. Nevertheless, social stratification in the United States is based primarily on achieved status, at least in theory. When this nation was formed, the founders deliberately distinguished it from nations where life

chances and social rank were determined by birth. A core element of the American credo is that talent, skill, hard work, and achievement largely determine life chances. We believe that everyone has a fair shot at whatever is valued or prized and that no individual or group is unfairly advantaged or disadvantaged.

This belief does not mean that we expect everyone to achieve equal results; rather, we expect that everyone is starting with the same opportunities for achieving these different outcomes. Indeed, we tend to see differences in material success as the legitimate result of playing by the agreed-upon rules. Although our national history is ambiguous about our implementation of social inequality, we normally take great exception when systemic and systematic differences in achievement clearly and directly result from public policy, varying or hidden rules, discrimination, or differential rewards for similar accomplishments. These pernicious factors produce what we think of as inequality.

Despite our egalitarian values and beliefs, social inequality has been an enduring fact of life and politics in the United States. Some groups of people have sufficient power—through family, neighborhood, school, or community—to maintain higher economic class positions and higher social status in American society. People in these groups have the ability to get and stay ahead in the competition for success. Further, social inequality has always been integrally bound up with three dimensions of social stratification: socioeconomic class, race and ethnicity, and gender. Divisions based on these three dimensions are deeply embedded in the social structures and institutions that define our lives, so these three constructs must be at the center of any analysis of social inequality. The integration of these constructs is not simple, however, because we lack both a common understanding of them and an agreement as to their significance in the structure of social inequality.

An example illustrates this lack of common ground. Whenever I ask my students what they mean by "class," they say they are sure that classes exist in the United States and that a lot of economic inequality, privilege, and disadvantage results from class structure. However, they become much less certain when I ask them what determines class status. A recent group of students suggested a number of ways to determine class status, including income, wealth, education, job, and neighborhood, as well as how many members of a given family were working. Even when we focused on income—one criterion often used to define class—they could not agree on how much income placed people into which class, much less on how many classes exist. This example suggests the lack of common understanding about class. As this book shows, the difficulties involved in analyzing the influence of ethnicity (and race) and gender on social inequality probably are even greater than those for analyzing class. This analysis is more difficult because there is little agreement regarding the existence or significance of ethnic (and racial) and gender inequality.

DIMENSIONS OF INEQUALITY IN THE UNITED STATES

Class, race and ethnicity, and gender shape the history, experiences, and opportunities of people in the United States. As a leading social theorist indicated, we should view class, race, and gender as different and interrelated, with interlocking levels of domination, not as discrete dimensions of stratification (Collins, 1990). Thus, even though the following discussion introduces class, race and ethnicity, and gender as separate concepts, many of the readings and discussions in this book examine these dimensions as simultaneous, interrelated, and interlocking means of configuring people's social relations and life opportunities.

Class

A class is a group of people who share the same economic or social status, life chances, and outlook on life. A class system is a system of social stratification in which social status is determined by the ownership and control of resources and by the kinds of work people do. The two major sociological explanations of class derive from its two most influential contributors, Karl Marx and Max Weber. In Marx's theory, social classes are defined by their distinct relationship to the means of production—that is, by whether people own the means of production (the capitalists) or sell their labor to earn a living (the workers). People's role in social life and their place in society are fixed by their place in the system of production. In Marx's theoretical perspective, the classes that dominate production also dominate other institutions in society, from schools and the mass media to the institutions that make and enforce rules.

German sociologist Max Weber also believed that divisions between capitalists and workers and their assigned classes were the driving force of social organization. For Weber, however, Marx's theory of social stratification was too strongly driven by the single motor of economics and by where an individual was positioned in the production process. In addition to a person's economic position, Weber included social status and party (i.e., coordinated political action) as different bases of power, independent of (but closely related to) economics. Weber's multidimensional perspective examines wealth, prestige, and power.

In the social sciences, the debate over class has not been whether classes exist, rather, essential theoretical perspectives flow from these two different ways (Marx's or Weber's) of understanding and thinking about class. These two theoretical perspectives on class are fundamental to understanding social stratification and social inequality. Parts II and III of this text, on stratification and class, include selections from the original work of Marx and Weber and also address some of the questions associated with class in the United States.

Race and Ethnicity

Like class, race and ethnicity are important dimensions of social stratification and social inequality. Although the terms race and ethnicity are often used interchangeably, they do not refer to the same thing. Both concepts are complex, and both defy easy definition. In the past, race was usually defined as a category of people sharing genetically transmitted traits deemed significant by society. However, this simple view does not hold up when we take into consideration the complex biology of genetic inheritance, migration, intermarriage, and the resulting wide variation within so-called racial groups. Today, most social scientists view race as a far more subjective (and shifting) social category than the fixed biological definitions of the past, wherein people are labeled by themselves or by others as belonging to a group based on some physical characteristic, such as skin color or facial features. Racial-formation theory, which emphasizes the shifting meanings and power relationships inherent in notions of race, defines race "as a concept that signifies and symbolizes sociopolitical conflicts and interests in reference to different types of human bodies" (Winant, 1994, p. 115). The concept of race, then, has both biological and social components. Examples of racial categories that have been used in the past are Caucasian, Asian, and African.

The concept of ethnicity is closely related to that of race. An ethnic group can be defined as a category of people distinguished by their ancestry, nationality, traditions, or culture. Examples of ethnic groups in the United States are Puerto Ricans, Japanese Americans, Cuban Americans, Irish Americans, and Lebanese Americans. Ethnicity is a cultural and social construct, and people's ethnic categories may be either self-chosen or assigned by outsiders to the group. Because characteristics such as culture, traditions, religion, and language are less visible and more changeable than skin color or facial features, ethnicity is even more arbitrary and subjective than is race.

The distinction between race and ethnicity is important. The basis for the social construction of race is primarily (though not entirely) biological; for ethnicity, it is primarily (though not entirely) cultural and social. Race is usually visible to an observer; ethnicity is usually a guess. The historical discourse about race in the United States is charged with notions of difference, of superiority and inferiority, of domination and subordination. Ideas and practices surrounding race, especially the deeply embedded divisions between African Americans and Caucasian (European) Americans, go to the core of the American experience of social inequality. (Issues of social inequality centered on race and ethnicity are addressed more fully in Part IV of this book.)

Gender

Gender, which is perhaps the oldest and deepest division in social life, may be defined as the set of social and cultural characteristics associated with biological sex—being female or male—in a particular society. Like race and ethnicity, gender is socially constructed, whereas biological sex is not. It is rooted in society's belief that females and males are naturally distinct and opposed social beings. These beliefs are translated into reality when people are assigned to different and often unequal political, social, and economic positions based on their sex. It is common for societies to separate adult work, family, and civic roles by gender and to prepare girls and boys differently for those roles. The result is socially discrete gender roles.

Our society provides a great deal of occupational segregation by gender. The division of labor by gender is hierarchical, with males occupying positions accorded higher prestige and value than females occupy. So-called women's work is matched with inferior reward packages and low status.

Many feminists consider the sexual division of labor to be the primary source of gender stratification, along with the socialization and institutional processes that prepare females and males for different lives. These processes include the institutions of patriarchy that bestow power and privilege on male roles and occupations, thereby allowing men to perpetuate their political, social, and economic advantages. Put another way, patriarchy is the ability of men to control the laws and institutions of society and to command superior status and reward packages. (Part V of this text is devoted to discussing questions of social inequality and gender more fully.)

EXPLORING SOCIAL INEQUALITY IN INSTITUTIONAL CONTEXTS: EDUCATION

We have introduced some basic ideas about the three major dimensions of social inequality and social stratification in the United States—class, race and ethnicity, and gender. Discussing them one at a time is a simple and orderly way to begin, but it is critical to keep in mind that these dimensions do not function in isolation. Rather, their dynamic interaction is highly complex. Class, race and ethnicity, and gender are simultaneous, intersecting, and sometimes crosscutting systems of relationships and meanings.

For example, even though we might use the term middle class to refer to all people of a certain income level (or amount of wealth, or occupation, or educational level), African Americans of that income level—the black middle class—occupy a far more precarious position in our society than do members of the white middle class. In considering these two dimensions, we may ask: Do all middle-class people have the same interests? Is their social status more a function of class or of race? How do they identify themselves—as middle class or as African or European Americans?

Other examples of the intersection of the three dimensions abound. In a study conducted in several nations, employed married women identified their socioeconomic class positions more on the basis of their spouses' jobs than on their own familial or educational backgrounds or their own occupations (Erickson and Goldthorpe, 1992). A different study showed that European American women in the United States tend to mention gender alone when asked how they identify themselves, whereas African American women tend to emphasize both race and gender (Rubin, 1994). A recent study, *Women Without Class*, describes how experience with middle class values and institutions wound Mexican American and white girls coming of age. The study shows how practices of exclusion can produce class and race injuries that, in turn, shape the identities of young women (Bettie, 2003).

Evidence points to growing conflict among different ethnic minorities of the same social class or community in the United States, perhaps because of contracting opportunities and limited resources. For example, in Los Angeles and in New York City, many Korean immigrants run grocery, liquor, produce, and fish retail businesses that are heavily concentrated in ethnic-minority neighbor-

hoods. These Korean American merchants often act as an intermediate ethnic minority interposed between low-income Latino and African American minority consumers and high-income European American owners of large companies. The Korean Americans encounter conflicts with both their ethnic-minority customers and their ethnic-majority suppliers. As a result, intergroup conflicts, tension, misunderstandings, and violence erupt all too often in Los Angeles, New York, and other ethnically diverse cities (Min, 1996).

To explore some of the dynamics of these intersections, Part VI of this text examines class, race and ethnicity, and gender in the institutional contexts of education and the environment. Throughout this book, the readings address such themes as socialization, social roles, institutional processes, cultural capital, hidden curriculum, sorting, and gender bias. Many of these themes come together in the context of education, making it an appropriate arena for integrative discussion and analysis. In addition, the familiarity of this context makes it an excellent lens through which student readers may look at social stratification and social inequality.

Further, education traditionally has been seen as a remedy for inequality in the United States. Americans believe that if society creates more educational opportunities for the disadvantaged, greater equality will eventually result. Thus, people who seek greater social equality often turn to education as an arena in which to institute change. Similarly, those who seek to maintain our society's system of social stratification may also try to manipulate the educational system to preserve the status quo. Hence, education becomes an arena for conflict between groups seeking change toward greater social equality and groups seeking to maintain the current social inequalities.

It seems the media report environmental risks, harmful practices, or calamities almost daily. Our notion about the environment has grown from clean water and healthy trees to a concern about what contributes to and produces conditions of environmental risk. In the twent-first century, environmental protection includes harmful practices in housing, land use, the workplace, industrial planning, health care, and sanitation.

Class, race, and gender are integral to this new understanding of environmental justice. Is it a random occurrence that hazardous waste sites cluster in poor communities, or are they located there because disadvantaged communities cannot protect themselves as well as more affluent communities? Are African-Americans more susceptible to certain diseases because of genetics and biology or living conditions and environmental exposure?

My hope is that the theories, concepts, tools, and findings of the sociological perspective, introduced in Parts I through V, will be valuable in helping you analyze and understand the way social stratification and inequality operate in institutional contexts, as synthesized in Part VI.

REFERENCES

Bettie, Julie, 2003. *Women Without Class: Girls, Race, and Identity.* Berkeley: University of California Press.

Collins, Patricia Hill. 1990. *Black Feminist Thought.* New York: Rutledge.

Erickson, Robert, and John H. Goldthorpe. 1992. "Individual or Family? Results from Two Approaches to Class Assignment." *Acta Sociologica* 35: 95–105.

Fischer, Claude S., Michael Hout, Martin Sanchez Jankowski, Samuel R. Lucas, Ann Swidler, and Kim Voss. 1996. *Inequality by Design: Cracking the Bell Curve Myth.* Princeton, NJ: Princeton University Press.

Grusky, David B., Ed. 1994. *Social Stratification: Class, Race, and Gender in Sociological Perspective.* Boulder, CO: Westview Press.

Min, Pyong Cap. 1996. *Caught in the Middle: Korean Merchants in America's Multiethnic Cities.* Berkeley and Los Angeles: University of California Press.

Rubin, Lillian B. 1994. *Families on the Fault Line.* New York: HarperCollins.

Winant, Howard. 1994. *Racial Conditions.* Minneapolis: University of Minnesota Press.

Part I

OPPORTUNITY AND INEQUALITY
IN THE UNITED STATES

—m—

TO BUILD OUR UNDERSTANDING OF SOCIAL inequality in the United States, we first need to construct a foundation based on knowing its contemporary severity, scope, meaning, direction, and pattern. The selections in Part I map out the contours and direction of inequality in American society and thus provide a common basis for discussion.

A host of significant changes in American life have accompanied the slow growth in living standards and the rising inequality that characterize the past two decades: Wages have stagnated and prices have risen, leading to economic hardship for millions of American families; middle-class status has become increasingly tenuous, with more families needing two incomes to attain and maintain a middle-class standard of living; opportunities for upward mobility have contracted; and more women are working outside the home than ever before. Even those women who would prefer to stay at home feel pressure to find a job outside the home. The increased need for family members to have more than one job also means that families have less time for leisure activities and less time to be together. Both the possibility and the reality of losing a job haunt many Americans, including well-trained and respected professionals. Despite these troubling changes for most Americans, it would be deceptive to portray *all* Americans as tumbling down the economic ladder; millions of Americans are doing better than ever before, especially those with high incomes or considerable assets.

The first reading in this part, "Why Inequality?" by Claude S. Fischer and his colleagues, looks at why inequality exists in American society. *Inequality by Design: Cracking the Bell Curve Myth*, the book from which this selection is taken, compellingly indicts the thesis proposed in *The Bell Curve: Intelligence and Class Structure in American Life* by Richard Herrnstein and Charles Murray. Herrnstein and Murray's controversial 1994 best-seller posited that inequality is the inevitable consequence of genetic endowment. As might be expected, most reviewers harshly criticized *The Bell Curve* and found it to have little scientific merit. In it, Herrnstein and Murray argued that class structure in the United States is largely the predictable outgrowth of natural talent and intelligence within families and communities: Smarter people do better, hold better jobs, and earn more money. *The Bell Curve* also argues that African Americans fare much worse in American society than European Americans because African Americans are not as intelligent as European Americans. In sharp contrast, Fischer and his colleagues argue that social policies and practices, not inherent biological endowments, both cause and perpetuate class and racial inequality in the United States.

In the second selection by Maxine Baca Zinn and D. Stanley Eitzen, "Economic Restructuring and Systems of Inequality," suggests that we need to examine inequality in a new way—through the lens of examining the consequences of a changing economy. They propose that understanding economic trends and directions is important to understanding specific configurations of inequality. This essay raises a main theme of this reader: As old inequalities continue to thrive, new forms of inequality connected to globalization and our restructuring economy are taking hold.

The third selection is by Frank Levy and provides a basic context in which to examine post World War II economic prosperity and trends of inequality in the United States. Levy reveals, by examining incomes, some of the family and job pressures that have resulted from economic restructuring. If families receive less real income, how can they adapt to maintain middle-class living standards?

The selection, from Jay MacLeod's book, *Ain't No Makin' It*, looks at how some teenagers view the openness of American society. Their very different views profoundly affect their aspirations, values, behavior, and performance in school. MacLeod's selection raises a fundamental question: How does class, race, and gender affect something as basic as one's values and aspirations?

The article by Levy provides basic ways of looking at inequality by analyzing income. But income is not the only indicator of inequality. What happens when we examine inequality through the lens of family wealth? Wealth pro-vides an additional perspective on inequality. The final selection in this section is from Lisa Keister's *Wealth in America* and examines trends in wealth inequality, especially rising wealth inequality. She also analyzes why wealth inequality has increased. Why is wealth inequality so much greater than income inequality? Which do you think is a truer measure, or should we examine both?

The readings in Part I set out the basic scope and pattern of inequality in the United States. These five readings were selected both to provide a common basis for discussion and to ignite critical thinking about inequality. When I teach, I like students to distinguish between two conflicting notions of equality to demonstrate the philosophical difficulties in thinking about the concept of "fair play" versus "fair shares." The dominant viewpoint in the United States has been fair play, which emphasizes equal opportunity—each individual's unencumbered right to pursue happiness and to obtain resources and material rewards. The other viewpoint, fair shares, stresses equality of results, with equal rights and access to a reasonable share of society's resources being necessary to sustain a decent standard of living. Whereas the former view of equality emphasizes equitable rules and a level playing field, the latter focuses on a socially equitable distribution of rewards.

1
———

Why Inequality?

Claude S. Fischer, Michael Hout, Martin Sanchez Jankowski, Samuel R. Lucas, Ann Swidler, and Kim Voss

AS WE WRITE, AMERICANS ARE ENGAGED IN A great debate about the inequalities that increasingly divide us. For over twenty years, the economic gaps have widened. As the American Catholic Bishops stated in late 1995, "the U.S. economy sometimes seems to be leading to three nations living side by side, one growing more prosperous and powerful, one squeezed by stagnant incomes and rising economic pressures and one left behind in increasing poverty, dependency and hopelessness."[1] Being prosperous may mean owning a vacation home, purchasing private security services, and having whatever medical care one wants; being squeezed may mean having one modest but heavily mortgaged house, depending on 911 when danger lurks, and delaying medical care because of the expense of copayments; and being left behind may mean barely scraping together each month's rent, relying on oneself for physical safety, and awaiting emergency aid at an overcrowded public clinic. Most Americans in the middle know how fragile their position is. One missed mortgage payment or one chronic injury might be enough to push them into the class that has been left behind.

Few deny that inequality has widened.[2] The debate is over whether anything can be done about it, over whether anything should be done about it. Some voices call for an activist government to sustain the middle class and uplift the poor. Other voices, the ones that hold sway as we write, argue that government ought to do less, not more. They argue for balanced budgets, lower taxes, fewer domestic programs, minimal welfare, and less regulation. These moves, they contend, would energize the economy and in that way help the middle class. They would also help the poor, economically and otherwise. Speaker of the House Newt Gingrich in 1995 said of people on welfare: "The government took away something more important than . . . money. They took away their initiative, . . . their freedom, . . . their morality, their drive, their pride. I want to help them get that back."[3] As to the increasing inequality of our time, some advocates of circumscribed government say it cannot be changed, because inequality is natural; some say it ought not be changed, because inequality drives our economy. At a deeper level, then, the debate is about how to understand inequality—what explains its origin, what explains its growth. That is where we shall engage the debate.

The arguments over policy emerged from almost a quarter century of economic turmoil and disappointment. Middle-class Americans saw the era of seemingly ever-expanding affluence for themselves and ever-expanding opportunities for their children come to an abrupt end in 1973. The cars inching forward in the gasoline lines of the mid-1970s foreshadowed the next twenty years of middle-class experience. Wages stagnated, prices rose, husbands worked longer hours, and even wives who preferred to stay at home felt pressed to find jobs. The horizons for their children seemed to shrink as the opportunities for upward economic mobility contracted.[4] What was going on? What could be done about it?

In the early 1980s, one explanation dominated public discussion and public policy: The cause of the middle-class crisis was government, and its solution was less government. Regulations, taxes, programs for the poor, preferences for minorities, spending on schools—indeed, the very size of government—had wrecked the economy by wasting money and stunting initiative, by rewarding the sluggards and penalizing the talented. The answer was to get government "off the backs" of those who generate economic growth. "Unleash the market" and the result would be a "rising tide that will lift all boats, yachts and rowboats alike."

This explanation for the economic doldrums won enough public support to be enacted. Less regulation, less domestic spending, and more tax cuts for the wealthy followed. By the 1990s, however, the crisis of the middle class had not eased; it had just become more complicated. Figure 1.1 shows the trends in family incomes, adjusted for changes in prices, from 1959 to 1989 (the trends continued into the 1990s). The richest families had soared to new heights of income, the poorest families had sunk after 1970, and the middle-income families had gained slightly. But this slight gain was bitterly misleading. The middle class managed to sustain modest income growth only by mothers taking jobs and fathers working longer hours. Also, the slight gain could not make

From *Inequality by Design: Cracking the Bell Curve Myth,* by Claude S. Fischer, Michael Hout, Martin Sanchez Jankowski, Samuel R. Lucas, Ann Swidler, and Kim Voss. Copyright © 1996 by Princeton University Press. Reprinted by permission of Princeton University Press.

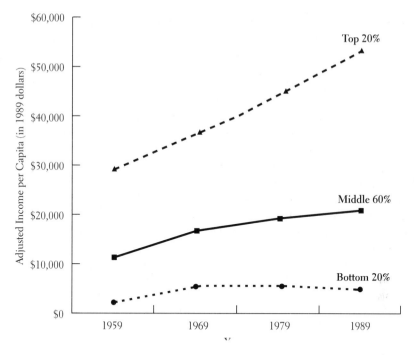

FIGURE 1.1 Changes in Household Incomes, 1959–1989, by Income Class. *Between 1959 and 1969, income per person grew for all households. Since 1970, income per person has continued to grow rapidly for the richest households, grown at a declining rate among middle-income households, and fallen slightly among poor households. The result is significantly more inequality.*(**Note:** Household incomes are adjusted by dividing income per family member by the square root of the household size. **Source:** Karoly and Burtless, "Demographic Change, Rising Earnings Inequality," table 2)

up for growing economic insecurity and parents' anxiety that key elements of the "American Dream"—college education, a stable job, and an affordable home—were slipping beyond the grasp of their children. And so the phrase "the disappearing middle class" began to be heard.

Another puzzle now called for explanation: The 1980s had been a boom decade; overall wealth had grown. But average Americans were working harder to stay even. Why had the gaps between the rich and the middle and between the middle and the poor widened? How do we understand such inequality?

An answer emerged in the public debate, forwarded for the most part by the same voices that had offered the earlier explanation: Inequality is a "natural," almost inevitable, result of an unfettered market. It is the necessary by-product of unleashing talent. The skilled soar and the unskilled sink. Eventually, however, all will gain from the greater efficiency of the free market. The reason such wider benefits have yet to be delivered is that the market has not been freed up enough; we need still less government and then the wealth will flow to middle- and lower-income Americans. Sharp inequality among the classes, these voices suggested, is the necessary trade-off for economic growth.

The strongest recent statement that inequality is the natural result of a free market came in *The Bell Curve: Intelligence and Class Structure in American Life*, published in 1994. Richard Herrnstein and Charles Murray argued that intelligence largely determined how well people did in life. The rich were rich mostly because they were smart, the poor were poor mostly because they were dumb, and middle Americans were middling mostly because they were of middling intelligence. This had long been so but was becoming even more so as new and inescapable economic forces such as global trade and technological development made intelligence more important than ever before. In a more open economy, people rose or sank to the levels largely fixed by their intelligence. Moreover, because intelligence is essentially innate, this expanding inequality cannot be stopped. It might be slowed by government meddling, but only by also doing injustice to the talented and damaging the national economy. Inequality is in these ways "natural," inevitable, and probably desirable.

The Bell Curve also provided an explanation for another troubling aspect of inequality in America—its strong connection to race and ethnicity. Black families, for example, are half as likely to be wealthy and twice as likely to be poor as white families. The questions of how to understand racial disparities and what to do about them have anguished the nation for decades. Now, there was a new answer (actually, a very old answer renewed): Blacks—and Latinos, too—were by nature not as intelligent as whites; that is why they did less well economically, and that is why little can or should be done about racial inequality.

Yet decades of social science research, and further research we will present here, refute the claim that inequality is natural and increasing inequality is fated. Individual intelligence does not satisfactorily explain who ends up in which class; nor does it explain why people in different classes have such disparate standards of living. Instead, what better explains inequality is this: First, individuals' social milieux—family, neighborhood, school, community—provide or withhold the means for attaining higher class positions in American society, in part by providing people with marketable skills. Much of what those milieux have to offer is, in turn, shaped by social

policy. For example, the quality of health care that families provide and the quality of education that schools impart are strongly affected by government action. Second, social policy significantly influences the rewards individuals receive for having attained their positions in society. Circumstances—such as how much money professional or manual workers earn, how much tax they pay, whether their child care or housing is subsidized—determine professionals' versus manual workers' standards of living. In turn, these circumstances are completely or partly determined by government. We do *not* have to suffer such inequalities to sustain or expand our national standard of living.[5] Thus, inequality is not the natural and inevitable consequence of intelligence operating in a free market; in substantial measure it is and will always be the socially constructed and changeable consequence of Americans' political choices.

Our contribution to the debate over growing inequality is to clarify how and why inequality arises and persists. We initiate our argument by first challenging the explanation in *The Bell Curve*, the idea that inequality is natural and fated. Then, we go on to show how social environment and conscious policy mold inequality in America.

If the growing inequality in America is not the inevitable result of free markets operating on natural intelligence, but the aftermath of circumstances that can be altered, then different policy implications follow from those outlined in *The Bell Curve*. We do not have to fatalistically let inequalities mount; we do not have to accept them as the Faustian trade for growth; and we do not have to accept heartlessness as the companion of social analysis. Instead, we can anticipate greater equality of opportunity and equality of outcome and also greater economic growth.

EXPLAINING INEQUALITY

Why do some Americans have a lot more than others? Perhaps, inequality follows inevitably from human nature. Some people are born with more talent than others; the first succeed while the others fail in life's competition. Many people accept this explanation, but it will not suffice. Inequality is not fated by nature, nor even by the "invisible hand" of the market; it is a social construction, a result of our historical acts. *Americans have created the extent and type of inequality we have, and Americans maintain it.*

To answer the question of what explains inequality in America, we must divide it in two. First, who gets ahead and who falls behind in the competition for success? Second, what determines how much people get for being ahead or behind? To see more clearly that the two questions are different, think of a ladder that represents the ranking of affluence in a society. Question one asks why this person rather than that person ended up on a higher or lower rung. Question two asks why some societies have tall and narrowing ladders—ladders that have huge distances between top and bottom rungs and that taper off at the top so that there is room for only a few people—while other societies have short and broad ladders—ladders with little distance between top and bottom and with lots of room for many people all the way to the top.

(Another metaphor is the footrace: One question is who wins and who loses; another question is what are the rules and rewards of the race. Some races are winner-take-all; some award prizes to only the first few finishers; others award prizes to many finishers, even to all participants. To understand the race, we need to understand the rules and rewards.)

The answer to the question of who ends up where is that people's social environments largely influence what rung of the ladder they end up on.[6] The advantages and disadvantages that people inherit from their parents, the resources that their friends can share with them, the quantity and quality of their schooling, and even the historical era into which they are born boost some up and hold others down. The children of professors, our own children, have substantial head starts over children of, say, factory workers. Young men who

graduated from high school in the booming 1950s had greater opportunities than the ones who graduated during the Depression. Context matters tremendously.

The answer to the question of why societies vary in their structure of rewards is more political. In significant measure, societies choose the height and breadth of their "ladders." By loosening markets or regulating them, by providing services to all citizens or rationing them according to income, by subsidizing some groups more than others, societies, through their politics, build their ladders. To be sure, historical and external constraints deny full freedom of action, but a substantial freedom of action remains. . . . In a democracy, this means that the inequality Americans have is, in significant measure, the historical result of policy choices Americans—or, at least, Americans' representatives—have made. In the United States, the result is a society that is distinctively *un*equal. Our ladder is, by the standards of affluent democracies and even by the standards of recent American history, unusually extended and narrow—and becoming more so.

To see how policies shape the structure of rewards (i.e., the equality of outcomes), consider these examples: Laws provide the ground rules for the marketplace—rules covering incorporation, patents, wages, working conditions, unionization, security transactions, taxes, and so on. Some laws widen differences in income and earnings among people in the market; others narrow differences. Also, many government programs affect inequality more directly through, for example, tax deductions, food stamps, social security, Medicare, and corporate subsidies. . . .

To see how policies also affect which particular individuals get to the top and which fall to the bottom of our ladder (i.e., the equality of opportunity), consider these examples: The amount of schooling young Americans receive heavily determines the jobs they get and the income they make. In turn, educational policies—what sorts of schools are provided, the way school resources are distributed (usually according to the community in which children live), teaching methods such as tracking, and so on—strongly affect how much schooling children receive. Similarly, local employment opportunities constrain how well people can do economically. Whether and where governments promote jobs or fail to do so will, in turn, influence who is poised for well-paid employment and who is not.

Claiming that intentional policies have significantly constructed the inequalities we have and that other policies could change those inequalities may seem a novel idea in the current ideological climate. So many voices tell us that inequality is the result of individuals' "natural" talents in a "natural" market. Nature defeats any sentimental efforts by society to reduce inequality, they say; such efforts should therefore be dropped as futile and wasteful. Appeals to nature are common and comforting. As Kenneth Bock wrote in his study of social philosophy, "We have been quick to seek explanations of our problems and failures in what we *are* instead of what we *do*. We seem wedded to the belief that our situation is a consequence of our nature rather than of our historical acts."[7] In this case, appeals to nature are shortsighted.

Arguments from nature are useless for answering the question of what determines the structure of rewards because that question concerns differences in equality *among societies*. Theories of natural inequality cannot tell us why countries with such similar genetic stocks (and economic markets) as the United States, Canada, England, and Sweden can vary so much in the degree of economic inequality their citizens experience. The answer lies in deliberate policies.

Appeals to nature also cannot satisfactorily answer even the first question: Why do some *individuals* get ahead and some fall behind? Certainly, genetic endowment helps. Being tall, slender, good-looking, healthy, male, and white helps in the race for success, and these traits are totally or partly determined genetically. But these traits matter to the degree that society makes them matter—determining how much, for example, good looks or white skin are rewarded. More important yet than these traits are the social milieux in which people grow up and live.

Realizing that intentional policies account for much of our expanding inequality is not only more accurate than theories of natural inequality; it is also more optimistic. We are today more unequal than we have been in seventy years. We are more unequal than any other affluent Western nation. Intentional policies could change those conditions, could reduce and reverse our rush to a polarized society, could bring us closer to the average inequality in the West, could expand both equality of opportunity and equality of result. . . .

OVERVIEW OF THE ARGUMENT

If one asks why some people get ahead and some people fall behind, answers concerning natural differences in ability are woefully inadequate. We can see that by looking closely at "intelligence." One reason inequality in intelligence is a poor explanation of class inequality is that individuals' abilities are much more complex, variable, and changeable than is suggested by the old-fashioned notions of intelligence upon which *The Bell Curve* rests. Concretely, the basic measure of intelligence that Herrnstein and Murray use, the AFQT [Armed Forces Qualifying Test], is actually not a test of genetic capacity or of quick-wittedness. It is instead a test of what people have been taught, especially in high school, of how much they recall, and of how much effort they make in the test. Another reason that intelligence is not an adequate explanation of individual success or failure is that, as social scientists have known for decades, intelligence as measured by such tests is only one among many factors that affect individuals' success or failure. In the NLSY [National Longitudinal Survey of Youth], respondents' AFQT scores in 1980 do not explain well how they ended up at the end of the 1980s. We show that, instead, aspects of respondents' social environments explain the outcomes more fully.

If one asks the more basic question of what determines the pattern of inequality, answers concerning individual intelligence are largely irrelevant. Societies and historical epochs vary greatly in the nature and degree of their inequality; they differ much more than any variations in intelligence, or the market, can account for. Some of that variability lies in technological, economic, and cultural changes. But much of it lies in specific policies concerning matters such as schooling, jobs, and taxes.

In the end, we *can* change inequality. We *have* changed inequality. American policies have reduced inequality in many spheres—for example, improving the economic fortunes of the elderly—and have expanded inequality in others—for example, with tax expenditures that advantage many of the already advantaged. And the experience of other nations shows that there is much more that can be done to reduce inequality if we choose to do so.

Policies also affect where individuals end up on the ladder of inequality. Policies help construct social environments. Policies even alter cognitive skills, particularly in the ways we structure schooling. The leverage here lies not with the episodic compensatory programs over which there has been much debate, but with the everyday structure of schools in America.

Finally, what about race? Arguments that African Americans and Latino Americans have done poorly in the United States because they are less intelligent than whites are completely backward. The experiences of low-caste groups around the world show that subordinate ethnic minorities do worse in schools and on school tests than do dominant groups, whatever the genetic differences or similarities between them. Whether it is Eastern European Jews in 1910 New York, the Irish in England, Koreans in Japan, or Afrikaaners in South Africa, being of lower caste or status makes people seem "dumb." The particular history of blacks and Mexicans in the United States fits the general pattern. *It is not that low intelligence leads to inferior status; it is that inferior status leads to low intelligence test scores.*

NOTES

1. Quoted by the Associated Press, "Bishops Say U.S. Neglects Poor," *San Francisco Chronicle,* November 15, 1995, p. A5.

2. A few do. For discussion of the evidence, see chapter 5 [of *Inequality by Design*].

3. The fuller quotation is:

   "I'm trying to help people on welfare. I'm not hurting them. The government hurt them. The government took away something more important than this money. They [*sic*] took away their initiative, they took away a substantial measure of their freedom, they took away in many cases their morality, their drive, their pride. I want to help them get that back. . . . I want to do it because I love them, because I want them to be Americans. And their children and grandchildren will thank us." Quoted in Frum, "Righter than Newt," p. 84 [1995, March, *Atlantic Monthly*: 81].

4. See, for example, Levy, *Dollars and Dreams* [1987, New York: Russell Sage Foundation]; Levy, "Incomes and Income Inequality" [1995. In Reynolds Farley (Ed.), *State of the Union: America in the 1990s.* New York: Russell Sage Foundation]; Newman, *Declining Fortunes* [1993. New York: Basic Books]; and Schor, *The Overworked American* [1992. New York: Basic Books].

5. For discussion of the point that economic growth does not require inequality—and may perhaps call for more equality—see chapter 5.

6. We know that in statistical models of individual status attainment much, if not most, of the variance is unaccounted for. Of the explained variance, however, the bulk is due to social environment broadly understood. Also, we believe that much of the residual, unexplained variance is attributable to unmeasured social rather than personal factors.

7. Bock, 1994, *Human Nature Mythology*, p. 9, Urbana: University of Illinois Press.

2

Economic Restructuring and Systems of Inequality

Maxine Baca Zinn and D.Stanley Eitzen

THE PRESENT GENERATION IS IN THE MIDST OF economic changes that are more farreaching and are occurring faster than at any other time in human history. While all people in the United States are affected by the technological and economically based reorganization of society, the magnitude of this structural transformation is different throughout society. The old inequalities of class, race, and gender are thriving. New and subtle forms of discrimination are becoming prevalent throughout society as the economic base changes and settles.

Four factors are at work here: (1) new technologies based primarily on the computer chip, (2) global economic interdependence, (3) capital flight, and the (4) dominance of the information and service sectors over basic manufacturing industries. Together these factors have reinforced the unequal placement of individuals and families in the larger society. They have deepened patterns of social inequality, and they have formed new patterns of domination in which the affluent control the poor, whites dominate people of color, and men subjugate women.

The disproportionate effects of economic and industrial change are most visible in three trends: (1) structural unemployment, (2)the changing distribution and organization of jobs, and (3) the low income-generating capacity of jobs. Each of these three trends has significant consequences for the hierarchies of class, race, and gender.

Reprinted by permission of the authors.

CLASS

Two major developments stand out when the emerging class structure is examined. The first is the growing gap between the rich and the poor since 1970. The second is the decline of the middle class.

The distribution of income is very unequal and widening. From 1970 to 1993 the income share of the highest quintile rose from 43.3 to 48.2 percent, while the bottom fifth fell from 4.1 percent to 3.6 percent of all income (U.S. Bureau of the Census 1995:41). While salaries and stock options plus a rising stock market have increased the wealth of those at the top, the wages of the majority have stagnated and benefits (medical and pensions) have declined.

Many Americans have experienced a slow-down of income growth. Since the early 1970s wages have fallen for 80 percent of the workforce, while the richest 20 percent have become richer by far. The following facts demonstrate the contours of this growing disparity:

- "Between 1972 and 1994 the percentage of men aged 25 to 34 with incomes *below* the proverty level for a family of four increased from 14 percent to 32 percent" (Coontz 1997: 139).

- "While 20 million households stayed . . . ahead of inflation from 1991 to 1993 . . . 78 million households lost ground" (Coontz 1997: 126).

- "Between 1973 and 1993 weekly earnings of nonsupervisory workers (adjusted for inflation) fell from $315.38 per week to $254.87, a decline of more than 19 percent" (Kuttner 1995: 5).

- "A young man under 25 years of age employed full time in 1994 earned 31 percent less per week than what his same-aged counterpart earned in 1973" (Sum, Fogg, and Taggert 1996: 83–84).

- "In 1970, the average chief executive officer (CEO) earned about as much as 41 factory workers. In 1992 that CEO made as much as 157 factory workers (Sklar 1995). The gap continues to widen. In 1995 the average compensation for CEOs (salary, bonus, and stock options) increased by 26.9 percent compared to the 2.8 percent increase in wages for the average worker (CNBC 1996). Thus, in 1995 CEOs were earning more than 200 times as much as the average worker (Uchitelle 1996). The gap continues to widen: in 1996 the CEOs for the top 365 corporations received compensation increase averaging 54 percent over the previous year. In a most telling statistic, the CEOs at the 30 corporations with the biggest layoffs averaged increases of 67.3 percent (United for a Fair Economy; reported in Gordon 1997).

In sum, many Americans have experienced a sharp slowdown in income with the advent of corporate downsizing, the increased use of temporary workers (who do not, typically, receive extra benefits such as medical insurance and pension plans), the loss of unions in membership and clout, the decline in the number of well-paid industry jobs, and the emergence of a bipolar wage structure in high tech and service work. These data indicate a shrinkage of the middle class, a trend heretofore unknown in U.S. history. The changing of the economy, in effect, has closed many of the old avenues to social mobility resulting, for the first time, in a rate of downward mobility that exceeds the rate of upward mobility.

RACE

Technology, foreign competition, and the changing distribution of jobs are having devastating effects on minority communities across the United States. The employment status of minorities is falling in all regions. It is worse, however, in areas of industrial decline and in segregated urban cores, where race and class intersect. Sociologist William Julius Wilson provides the data:

In the ghetto census tracts of the nation's one hundred largest central cities, there were only 65.6 employed persons for every hundred adults who did not hold a job in a typical week in 1990. In contrast, the non-poverty areas contained 182.3 employed persons for every hundred of those not working. In other words, the ratio of employed to jobless persons was three times greater in census tracts not marked by poverty (Wilson 1996:19).

Race alone is significant because white job applicants continue to be disproportionately chosen over equally qualified minority ones. A 1991 study by the Urban Institute, for example, using carefully matched and trained pairs of white and black men applying for entry-level jobs, found that discrimination against blacks is "entrenched and widespread" (reported in Sklar 1993: 54). Similarly, studies in Chicago, Tampa, Atlanta, Denver, and other metropolitan areas found consistently that African Americans and Latinos face discrimination in housing, pay more than whites for similar housing, have greater difficulty than whites in receiving business and home loans, pay higher insurance rates, and pay more for consumer goods (Timmer, Eitzen, and Tally 1994: 94–95).

Latinos and African Americans have suffered disproportionately from industrial job loss, declining manufacturing employment, and low-wage production jobs. By every measure including employment rates, occupational standing, and wage rates, the labor market status of racial minorities had deteriorated relative to whites. In 1995, for example, the official unemployment rate for Latinos was 9.4 percent compared with 10 percent for

African Americans and 4.8 percent for whites (Thurm 1995). Not only are minorities twice as likely as whites to be unemployed, they are more likely to work in dead-end jobs. About a quarter of all African Americans and a fifth of all Latinos work at the low end of the occupational ladder, in poorly paid service jobs (Folbre 1995: 4–9).

GENDER

Women and men are affected differently by the transformation of the economy from its manufacturing base to a base in service and high technology. Industrial jobs, traditionally filled by men, are being replaced with service jobs that are increasingly filled by women. Since 1980, women have taken 80 percent of the new jobs created in the economy, but the overall degree of gender segregation has not changed much since 1900 (Herz and Wootton 1996: 56). Unlike other forms of inequality, sexism in U.S.society has not become more intense as a result of the economic transformation. Instead, sexism has taken new forms as women are propelled into the labor market. Women have continued to move from the private sphere (family) to public arenas, but they have done so under conditions of labor market discrimination that have always plagued women. Today, the "typical" job is a non-union, service sector, low-paying job occupied by a woman. Despite the growing feminization of the work force, male domination has been more firmly entrenched in the social organization of work. The rise of the contingent work force (including part-time work, temporary agencies, and subcontracted work) offers many advantages to employers but at considerable cost to women workers.

Women workers do not approach earnings parity with men even when they work in similar occupations and have similar levels of education. Current estimates are that women earn about 72 percent of the wage rate of men (Dunn 1996). The full impact of economic restructuring on women must take into account the relatively low wage levels and limited opportunities for advancement that characterize their work in the new economy.

NEW INTERSECTIONS OF CLASS, RACE, AND GENDER

The hierarchies of class, race, and gender are simultaneous and interlocking systems. For this reason, they frequently operate with and through each other to produce social inequality. Not only are many existing inequalities exacerbated by the structural transformation of the economy, but the combined effects of class, race, and gender are producing new kinds of subordination and exclusion throughout society and especially the workplace. For example, the removal of manufacturing jobs has severely increased African American and Latino job loss. Just how much of this is due to class and how much is due to race remains an important question.

In contrast, many women of color have found their work opportunities expanded, albeit in poorly paid marginal work settings in service and high tech jobs. Does such growth offer traditionally oppressed race/gender groups new mobility opportunities or does the expansion of new kinds of work reproduce existing forms of inequality? The impact of economic restructuring on race and gender varies considerably. In some cases, it generates no jobs at all and displaced minority women workers. In other cases, minority women benefit by the creation of new jobs. Third world immigrant women provide the bulk of the high tech productive labor force in Silicon Valley (Hossfeld 1994,1997). Yet a growing "underclass" in high tech consists of low-paid recent immigrant women form Mexico, Vietnam, Korea, and the Philippines. These examples reveal new labor systems as well as new forms of racial control based on class, race, and gender.

REFERENCES

CNBC. 1996. "Business News" (April 8).

Coontz, Stephanie. 1997. *The Way We Really Are: Coming to Terms with America's Changing Families.* New York: Basic Books.

Dunn, Dana. 1996. "Gender and Earnings." In Paula J. Dubeck and Kathryn Borman (eds.), *Women and Work: A Handbook* (New York: Garland Publishing), pp. 61–63.

Folbre, Nancy. 1995. *The New Field Guide to the U.S. Economy,* New York: New Press.

Gordon, Marcy. 1997. "CEOs Get Layoff-Linked Rewards," Associated Press (May 2).

Herz, Diane E., and Barbara H. Wootton. 1996. "Women in the Workforce: An Overview." In Cynthia Costello and Barbara Kivimae Krimgold (eds.) *The American Woman, 1996–1997* (New York: W. W. Norton), pp. 44–78.

Hossfeld, Karen J. 1994. "Hiring Immigrant Women: Silicon Valley's 'Simple Formula.'" In Maxine Baca Zinn and Bonnie Thornton Dill (eds.), *Women of Color in U.S. Society* (Philadelphia: Temple University Press), pp. 65–93.

Hossfeld, Karen J. 1997. "'Their Logic Against Them': Contradictions in Sex, Race, and Class in Silicon Valley." In Maxine Baca Zinn, Pierrette Hondagneu-Sotelo, and Micheal A. Messner (eds), *Through the Prism of Difference* (Boston: Allyn & Bacon), pp. 388–400.

Kuttner, Robert. 1995. "The Fruits of Our Labor," *Washington Post National Weekly Edition* (September 6–12): 5.

Sklar, Holly. 1993. "Young and Guilty by Stereotype," *Z Magazine* 6 (July/August): 52–61.

Sklar, Holly. 1995. "The Snake Oil of Scapegoating," *Z Magazine* 8 (May): 49–56.

Sum, Andrew, Neal Fogg, and Robert Taggert. 1996. "The Economics of Despair," *The American Prospect,* Number 27 (July/August): 83–88.

Thurm, Scott. 1995. "Hispanic Employment Slips," Denver Post (January 27): E1, E5.

Timmer, Doug A., D. Stanley Eitzen, and Kathryn D. Talley. 1994. *Paths to Homelessness: Extreme Poverty and the Urban Housing Crisis.* Boulder, CO: Westview Press.

Uchitelle, Louis. 1996. "1995 Was Good for Companies, and Better for a Lot of C.E.O.'s," *New York Times* (March 29), A1.

U.S. Bureau of the Census. 1995. "Population Profile of the United States 1995," *Current Population Reports,* Series P23-189. Washington, D.C.: U.S. Government Printing Office.

Wilson, William Julius. 1996. *When Work Disappears: The World of the New Urban Poor.* New York: Alfred A. Knopf.

3

A Half Century of Incomes

Frank Levy

WRITING ABOUT AN ECONOMY IS LIKE WRITing about a river. The backdrop is the motion, a constant evolution with no beginning or end. The stories mix human effort and impersonal forces, sometimes working together, sometimes in opposition.

[I] trace the development of American incomes from the end of World War II through the late 1990s. During this time, our broadest eco-

nomic goals have remained unchanged: a shared prosperity, the opportunity to progress over a career, the opportunity for our children to do better than we have done. In some decades, the economy

From *The New Dollars and Dreams* by Kathryn Edin and Laura Lein. Copyright © 1998 by Russell Sage Foundation. Reprinted by permission Russell Sage Foundation.

has largely delivered these goals. In other decades, it has failed in different ways. When it fails, we develop policies to improve the economy's performance. Since the economy is constantly evolving, we solve existing problems, new problems surface, and the story continues.

The 1998 economy is a case in point. In the spring of 1998, the nation was finishing the second decade of an experiment in free market economics to accelerate economic growth. The economy has always had markets, of course. Over time, better transportation and communication strengthened competition by knitting local U.S. markets into national markets and then into global markets. We also made conscious choices. Through the court-mandated deregulation of telephones, Jimmy Carter's deregulation of airlines, railroads, and trucking, and most powerfully, Ronald Reagan's philosophy of limited government, we embraced free markets as our main economic strategy much as we embraced Keynesian economics as our main strategy in the 1960s.

THREE ECONOMIC STORIES

How well has the free market experiment succeeded? The question has no single answer. In the summer of 1998, we could see three different economic stories. The most visible economic variables—inflation, unemployment, the government deficit—had all improved dramatically. Unemployment stood below 4.5 percent, the lowest in twenty-five years. Despite extremely tight labor

markets, inflation was running at a very modest 2 percent per year. Interest rates were low. The government budget deficit—alarmingly large a decade ago—had temporarily vanished. Consumer confidence and U.S. stock markets were at record highs. All this was part of a business cycle peak—too sweet to last indefinitely—but it was a remarkable achievement.

A second story was the slow growth of average wages. From the close of World War II through 1973, average wages, adjusted for inflation, grew at 2 to 3 percent per year. Rapid wage growth was the basis of a mass upward mobility in which most workers saw big income gains over their careers. After 1973, average wage growth slowed dramatically. It remained slow even in the buoyant economy of the late 1990s.*

The third story was the high level of income inequality, a measure that has traced a long arc through this century. In the 1920s, the richest 5 percent of all families received about 30 percent of all family income.[1] Then, toward the end of the Great Depression, income inequality began a long decline. U.S. Census statistics, which understate the very highest incomes,[†] report that the income share of the richest 5 percent of families fell to 17.5 percent by 1947 and to 15.6 percent in 1969. Inequality stabilized through the mid-1970s but then began to grow. The income share of the richest 5 percent of families rose to 17.9 percent in 1989, and 20.3 percent in 1996—larger than in 1947. To put the matter in different terms, the top one-half percent of federal tax returns—about 560,000 returns out of 116 million—now report almost 11 percent of all adjusted gross income (AGI) tabulated by the Internal Revenue Service.[‡]

When you stand too close to this economy, you get a distorted picture. Think about recent sound bites: "The New Economy"; "An Economy

---

*From April 1997 through March 1998, one measure of hourly wages grew by a respectable 2 percent, adjusted for inflation, but this growth occurred in a labor market that most people judge too tight to sustain.

†Census statistics understate the highest money incomes by not counting income from capital gains and by not counting incomes over fixed reporting limits. In 1996, individual earnings above $1,000,000 were rounded down to $1,000,000 in census inequality calculations. Generally, similar limits apply to family and household incomes. These limits currently affect 75,000 to 100,000 households out of 100 million households.

---

‡In the mid-1990s, there were about 100 million households versus 116 million tax returns but the two populations differ in important respects. Some households file multiple returns. Other households file no tax returns since their income is too low to require payment of federal income taxes—Jim Poterba, personal communication, (1998).

As Good As It Gets"; "A Polarized Economy"; "An Information Economy"; "An Entrepreneurial Economy"; "A Downsized Economy." No one of these phrases tells the story because all of them are more or less true.

When you take a step back and see today's economy in historical perspective, certain facts become clear. In the first quarter-century after World War II—from 1946 to 1973—the economy grew very rapidly and achieved most of the nation's economic goals. In the quarter-century since 1973, the economy's performance has been much weaker. For reasons we will discuss—reasons largely beyond the reach of policy—average wage growth slowed sharply after the early 1970s. As a consequence, many of today's older workers have not seen significant income gains over their careers. If slow average wage growth continues, many young workers—particularly those who have not attended college—will not earn as much as their parents earned.

The conflicting trends we see around us mean that the economy *may* be entering a period in which it can once again generate broadly rising incomes. Whether or not the turning point occurs depends on three factors. One is the growth rate of labor productivity, the increase in output per hour of work. The second is the economy's level of skill bias, the degree to which new production processes, including expanded trade, favor better educated workers over less educated workers. The third is the quality of the nation's equalizing institutions: public and private education, the welfare state, unions, international trade regulations, and the other political structures that blunt the most extreme market outcomes and try to ensure that most people benefit from economic growth.

To anchor the discussion, I will focus on the evolution of the U.S. income distribution. The income distribution is a mirror of economic life, and I will look less at the distribution's statistics than at the stories that explain the statistics—stories about people, places, industries, and jobs. The three abstract factors—productivity growth, skill bias, and equalizing institutions—will help tie the stories together. For example, in the 1950s the continuing mechanization of agriculture both made farming more efficient and displaced large numbers of farm laborers. Often, however, farm laborers could get on a bus to a city where they could find factory jobs at higher pay.[§] In other words, the 1950s economy was not skill-biased: Low-skilled workers displaced in one industry could get good jobs in another industry and so incomes automatically grew throughout the distribution.

Today, the economy favors the better educated over the less educated. When computerization or international trade displaces a semi-skilled worker, the move to a good job means acquiring the training to become a computer repairman or laboratory technician, a much harder move than getting on a bus. If these changes were occurring when productivity and the economy's wage level were growing rapidly, the skill bias would create a benign inequality in which less-educated workers got a little richer and well-educated workers got much richer. Until very recently, productivity and the economy's average wage have grown slowly and so many less-educated workers have taken absolute income losses.[||]

We cannot legislate the rate of productivity growth and we cannot legislate the level of skill bias in technological change and trade. That is why equalizing institutions are important. One of these institutions—quality education—is currently as popular as motherhood. Other institutions including unions and much of the welfare state are frequently described as ideas whose times have passed, obstacles to individual freedom and well-functioning markets. Today, when the unemployment rate is 4.5 percent, arguing against these

---

[§]Kevin Murphy (personal communication in 1993) points out that this was particularly true for blacks. Many of the agricultural jobs held by blacks in the 1940s were ultimately eliminated by mechanization. Yet black incomes rose substantially over the next thirty years as black men and women moved into other industries.

[||]During 1996 to 1997, productivity growth averaged 1.6 percent per year versus 1 percent per year over the previous two decades and 2 to 3 percent per year between 1947 and 1973. In chapter 8, I discuss the consequences if this higher rate is sustained.

institutions is provocative chatter. In the longer run, it is dangerous nonsense. People will not continue to support free market policies if they believe only others benefit. John Gray, a conservative political philosopher who would disagree with much in this book, makes the point well:

[The philosophy of unfettered markets] maintains that only a regime of common rules, perhaps embodying a shared conception of rights, is required for the stability of market institutions and of a liberal civil society. This species of *liberal legalism* overlooks, or denies that market institutions will not be politically stable—at any rate when they are combined with democratic institutions—if they do not accord with widespread conceptions of fairness, if they violate other important cultural norms, or if they have too destructive an effect on established expectations[2] . . .

NOTES

1. The most accessible data on income inequality are series developed by the U.S. Census that begin in 1947. . . .

2. Gray is using the term "liberal" in the nineteenth century meaning of the term, and he would argue, for example, that broadly distributed economic growth is not an unmitigated good. See Gray (1995) p. 102.

REFERENCES

Gray, John. 1995. *Enlightenment's Wake: Politics and Culture at the Close of the Modern Age.* London: Routledge, Inc.

4
———————

Social Immobility in the Land of Opportunity

Jay MacLeod

"ANY CHILD CAN GROW UP TO BE PRESIDENT." so says the achievement ideology, the reigning social perspective that sees American society as open and fair and full of opportunity. In this view, success is based on merit, and economic inequality is due to differences in ambition and ability. Individuals do not inherit their social status; they attain it on their own. Since education ensures equality of opportunity, the ladder of social mobility is there for all to climb. A favorite Hollywood theme, the rags-to-riches story resonates in the psyche of the American people. We never tire of hearing about Andrew Carnegie, for his experience validates much that we hold dear about America, the land

of opportunity. Horatio Alger's accounts of the spectacular mobility achieved by men of humble origins through their own unremitting efforts occupy a treasured place in our national folklore. The American Dream is held out as a genuine prospect for anyone with the drive to achieve it.

"I ain't goin' to college. Who wants to go to college? I'd just end up getting' a shitty job anyway." So says Freddie Piniella,[1] an intelligent

———————

From Ain't No Makin' It: Leveled Aspirations in a Low Income Neighborhood by Jay McLeod. Copyright © 1987 by Westview Press, Inc. Reprinted by permission of Westview Press, a member of Perseus Books, L.L.C.

eleven-year-old boy from Clarendon Heights, a low-income housing development in a northeastern city. This statement, pronounced with certitude and feeling, completely contradicts our achievement ideology. Freddie is pessimistic about his prospects for social mobility and disputes schooling's capacity to "deliver the goods." Such a view offends our sensibilities and seems a rationalization. But Freddie has a point. What of Carnegie's grammar school classmates who labored in factories or pumped gas? For every Andrew Carnegie there are thousands of able and intelligent workers who were left behind to occupy positions in the class structure not much different from those held by their parents. What about the static, nearly permanent element in the working class, whose members consider the chances for mobility remote and thus despair of all hope? These people are shunned, hidden, forgotten—and for good reason—because just as the self-made individual is a testament to certain American ideals, so the very existence of an "underclass" in American society is a living contradiction to those ideals.

Utter hopelessness is the most striking aspect of Freddie's outlook. Erik H. Erikson writes that hope is the basic ingredient of all vitality,[2] stripped of hope, there is little left to lose. How is it that in contemporary America a boy of eleven can feel bereft of a future worth embracing? This is not what the United States is supposed to be. The United States is the nation of hopes and dreams and opportunity. As Ronald Reagan remarked in his 1985 State of the Union Address, citing the accomplishments of a young Vietnamese immigrant, "Anything is possible in America if we have the faith, the will, and the heart."[3] But to Freddie Piniella and many other Clarendon Heights young people who grow up in households where their parents and older siblings are undereducated, unemployed, or imprisoned, Reagan's words ring hollow. For them the American Dream, far from being a genuine prospect, is not even a dream. It is a hallucination.

I first met Freddie Piniella in the summer of 1981 when as a student at a nearby university I worked as a counselor in a youth enrichment program in Clarendon Heights. For ten weeks I lived a few blocks from the housing project and worked intensively with nine boys, aged eleven to thirteen. While engaging them in recreational and educational activities, I was surprised by the modesty of their aspirations. The world of middle-class work was entirely alien to them; they spoke about employment in construction, factories, the armed forces, or, predictably, professional athletics. In an ostensibly open society, they were a group of boys whose occupational aspirations did not even cut across class lines.

The depressed aspirations of Clarendon Heights youngsters are telling. There is a strong relationship between aspirations and occupational outcomes; if individuals do not even aspire to middle-class jobs, then they are unlikely to achieve them. In effect, such individuals disqualify themselves from attaining the American definition of success—the achievement of a prestigious, highly remunerative occupation—before embarking on the quest. Do leveled aspirations represent a quitter's cop-out? Or does this disqualifying mechanism suggest that people of working-class origin encounter significant obstacles to social mobility?

Several decades of quantitative sociological research have demonstrated that the social class into which one is born has a massive influence on where one will end up. Although mobility between classes does take place, the overall structure of class relations from one generation to the next remains largely unchanged. Quantitative mobility studies can establish the extent of this pattern of social reproduction, but they have difficulty demonstrating *how* the pattern comes into being or is sustained. This is an issue of immense complexity and difficulty, and an enduring one in the field of sociology, but it seems to me that we can learn a great deal about this pattern from youngsters like Freddie. Leveled aspirations are a powerful mechanism by which class inequality is reproduced from one generation to the next.

In many ways, the world of these youths is defined by the physical boundaries of the housing development. Like most old "projects" (as low-income public housing developments are known to their residents), Clarendon Heights is architecturally a world unto itself. Although smaller and less dilapidated than many urban housing developments, its plain brick buildings testify that cost efficiency was the overriding consideration in its construction. Walking through Clarendon Heights for the first time in spring 1981, I was struck by the contrast between the project and the sprawling lawns and elegant buildings of the college quadrangle I had left only a half hour earlier. It is little more than a mile from the university to Clarendon Heights, but the transformation that occurs in the course of this mile is startling. Large oak trees, green yards, and impressive family homes give way to ramshackle tenement buildings and closely packed, triple decker, wooden frame dwellings; the ice cream parlors and bookshops are replaced gradually by pawn shops and liquor stores; book-toting students and businesspeople with briefcases in hand are supplanted by tired, middle-aged women lugging bags of laundry and by clusters of elderly, immigrant men loitering on street corners. Even within this typical working-class neighborhood, however, Clarendon Heights is physically and socially set off by itself.

Bordered on two sides by residential neighborhoods and on the other two by a shoe factory, a junkyard, and a large plot of industrial wasteland, Clarendon Heights consists of six large, squat, three-story buildings and one high rise. The architecture is imposing and severe; only the five chimneys atop each building break the harsh symmetry of the structures. Three mornings a week the incinerators in each of the twenty-two entryways burn, spewing thick smoke and ash out of the chimneys. The smoke envelops the stained brick buildings, ash falling on the black macadam that serves as communal front yard, backyard, and courtyard for the project's two hundred families. (A subsequent landscaping effort did result in the planting of grass and trees, the erection of little wire fences to protect the greenery, and the appearance of flower boxes lodged under windows.) Before its renovation, a condemned high-rise building, its doors and windows boarded up, in-

vested the entire project with an ambiance of decay and neglect.

Even at its worst, however, Clarendon Heights is not a bad place to live compared to many inner-city housing projects. This relatively small development, set in a working-class neighborhood, should not be confused with the massive, scarred projects of the nation's largest cities. Nevertheless, the social fabric of Clarendon Heights is marked by problems generally associated with low-income housing developments. Approximately 65 percent of Clarendon Heights' residents are white, 25 percent are black,[4] and 10 percent are other minorities. Few adult males live in Clarendon Heights; approximately 85 percent of the families are headed by single women. Although no precise figures are available, it is acknowledged by the City Housing Authority that significant numbers of tenants are second- and third-generation public housing residents. Social workers estimate that almost 70 percent of the families are on some additional form of public assistance. Overcrowding, unemployment, alcoholism, drug abuse, crime, and racism plague the community.

Clarendon Heights is well known to the city's inhabitants. The site of two riots in the early and mid-1970s and most recently of a gunfight in which two policemen and their assailant were shot, the project is considered a no-go area by most of the public. Even residents of the surrounding Italian and Portuguese neighborhoods tend to shun Clarendon Heights. Social workers consider it a notoriously difficult place in which to work; state and county prison officials are familiar with the project as a source for a disproportionately high number of their inmates. Indeed, considering its relatively small size, Clarendon Heights has acquired quite a reputation.

This notoriety is not entirely deserved, but it is keenly felt by the project's tenants. Subject to the stigma associated with residence in public housing, they are particularly sensitive to the image Clarendon Heights conjures up in the minds of outsiders. When Clarendon Heights residents are asked for their address at a bank, store, or office, their reply often is met with a quick glance of curiosity, pity, superiority, suspicion, or fear. In the United States, residence in public housing is often an emblem of failure, shame, and humiliation.

To many outsiders, Freddie's depressed aspirations are either an indication of laziness or a realistic assessment of his natural assets and attributes (or both). A more sympathetic or penetrating observer would cite the insularity of the project and the limited horizons of its youth as reasons for Freddie's outlook. But to an insider, one who has come of age in Clarendon Heights or at least has access to the thoughts and feelings of those who have, the situation is not so simple. This book, very simply, attempts to understand the aspirations of older boys from Clarendon Heights. It introduces the reader not to modern-day Andrew Carnegies, but to Freddie Piniella's role models, teenage boys from the neighborhood whose stories are less often told and much less heard. These boys provide a poignant account of what the social structure looks like from the bottom. If we let them speak to us and strive to understand them on their own terms, the story that we hear is deeply disturbing. We shall come to see Freddie's outlook not as incomprehensible self-defeatism, but as a perceptive response to the plight in which he finds himself.

Although the general picture that emerges is dreary, its texture is richly varied. The male teenage world of Clarendon Heights is populated by two divergent peer groups. The first group, dubbed the Hallway hangers because of the group's propensity for "hanging" in a particular hallway in the project, consists predominantly of white boys. Their characteristics and attitudes stand in marked contrast to the second group, which is composed almost exclusively of black youths who call themselves the Brothers. Surprisingly, the Brothers speak with relative optimism about their futures, while the Hallway Hangers are despondent about their prospects for social mobility. This dichotomy is illustrated graphically by the responses of Juan (a Brother) and Frankie (a Hallway Hanger) to my query about what their lives will be like in twenty years.

Juan: I'll have a regular house, y'know, with a yard and everything. I'll have a steady job, a good job. I'll be living the good life, the easy life.

Frankie: I don't fucking know. Twenty years. I may be fucking dead. I live a day at a time. I'll probably be in the fucking pen.

Because aspirations mediate what an individual desires and what society can offer, the hopes of these boys are linked inextricably with their assessment of the opportunities available to them. The Hallway Hangers, for example, seem to view equality of opportunity in much the same light as did R. H. Tawney in 1938—that is, as "a heartless jest . . . the impertinent courtesy of an invitation offered to unwelcome guests, in the certainty that circumstances will prevent them from accepting it."[5]

Slick: Out here, there's not the opportunity to make money. That's how you get into stealin' and all that shit. . . . All right, to get a job, first of all, this is a handicap, out here. If you say you're from the projects or anywhere in this area, that can hurt you. Right off the bat: reputation.

The Brothers, in contrast, consistently affirm the actuality of equality of opportunity.

Derek: If you put your mind to it, if you want to make a future for yourself, there's no reason why you can't. It's a question of attitude.

The optimism of the Brothers and the pessimism of the Hallway Hangers stem, at least in part, from their different appraisals of the openness of American society. Slick's belief that "the younger kids have nothing to hope for" obviously influences his own aspirations. Conversely, some of the Brothers aspire to middle-class occupations partly because they do not see significant societal barriers to upward mobility.

NOTES

1. All names of neighborhoods and individuals have been changed to protect the anonymity of the study's subjects.

2. Erik H. Erikson, *Gandhi's Truth* (New York: Norton, 1969), p. 154.

3. Ronald Reagan, "State of the Union Address to Congress," *New York Times*, 6 February 1985, p. 17.

4. Part One, written in 1984, refers to African Americans as "blacks."

5. R. H. Tawney, *Equality* (London: Allen and Unwin, 1938), p. 110.

5

Wealth in America

Trends in Wealth Inequality

Lisa A. Keister

I

WEALTH AND INEQUALITY

The love of wealth is therefore to be traced, as either a principal or accessory motive, at the bottom of all that the Americans do.

(de Tocqueville 1841)

ONE OF THE MOST ASTUTE OBSERVERS OF American life, Alexis de Tocqueville noted that wealth accumulation is perhaps the fundamental motivator of American behavior. At the same time, wealth ownership is thought to be concentrated in the hands of a small minority of the population. It is no secret that wealth ownership has advantages and that these extend beyond the obvious economic benefits to such areas as general social standing and political power. Political influence, for example, is typically exercised indirectly, through lobbying, private funding of research and policy institutes, and campaign financing (Domhoff 1990; Dye 1995; Useem 1984). To the extent to which economic power can be converted into political power, those who own wealth also influence the making of important decisions. As Spencer pointed out more than a century ago, "Even before private landowning begins, quantity of possessions aids in distinguishing the governing from the governed" (Spencer 1882:401). While the nature of the economic and political systems in which wealth is accumulated has changed dramatically since Spencer's time, there is still a strong association between control of material possessions and political influence. Thus those who have wealth have every incentive to maintain that wealth, while those who own little are motivated to acquire wealth. Moreover, the notion of the American dream suggests that such upward mobility is, indeed, possible. Researchers have long suspected, however, that in addition to motivating much of what Americans do wealth ownership is the single dimension on which American families are most persistently unequally distributed. While disparities in income and educational attainment are extreme, disparities in the ownership of wealth are likely worse and apparently more enduring across generations.

Yet information on the distribution of family wealth in the United States has been relatively scarce, and understanding of the processes that lead to wealth inequality has been even more elusive. As a result, knowledge of the role that wealth ownership plays in motivating and constraining behavior has remained relatively limited. Over the last decade, data improvements have allowed researchers to begin outlining a few of the more salient descriptive features of the distribution of wealth, and while the evidence is still preliminary, the picture that has emerged is disquieting. Wealth inequality, already highly concentrated in the early 1960s, became even more so during the 1980s and 1990s. Estimates indicate that the top 1 percent of wealth owners enjoyed two-thirds of all increases in household financial wealth during the 1980s, while the bottom 80 percent actually owned less real financial wealth in 1989 than in 1983 (Wolff 1995b). In the past, Americans smugly assumed that European societies were more stratified than their own, but it now appears that the United States has surpassed all industrial societies in the extent of its family wealth inequality (Wolff 1995b). Interpreting these reports, the press has realized that wealth inequality may be as harmful as income and educational inequality, which have attracted so much more attention. Pondering new wealth distribution estimates in its lead editorial, the *New York Times* worried that "Some inequality is necessary if society wants to reward investors for taking risks and individuals for working hard and well. But excessive inequality can break the spirit of those trapped in society's cellar—and exacerbate social tensions"(4/18/95).

While improvements in wealth data began to cast new light on this fundamental social problem

in the 1980s, understanding of both wealth inequality and its cause remains far from complete. Researchers have begun to create a picture of household wealth distribution, particularly for the years in which surveys were conducted (Wolff 1987b, 1995a, 1995b, 1998; Wolff and Marley 1989). Demographic, social, and financial characteristics of families in various portions of the distribution have also become increasingly clear, again particularly in the years for which survey data are available (Avery, Elliehausen, Canner, and Gustafson 1984b; Avery, Elliehausen, Canner, Gustafson, and Springert 1986; Avery, Elliehausen, and Kennickell 1987; Avery and Kennickell 1990; Kennickell and Shack-Marquez 1992; Kennickell and Starr-McCluer 1994). Yet this research appears in disparate places and has seldom been accumulated into a single story of wealth inequality in America. At the same time, and perhaps more importantly, our understanding of the processes that create these distributional outcomes is limited. Family-level demographics and processes, such as racial differences, aging, and inheritance, are likely to affect wealth accumulation and thus inequality (Ando and Modigliani 1963; Blau and Graham 1990; Danziger, VanDerGaag; Smolensky, and Taussig 1982; Oliver and Shapiro 1995). Likewise, social and economic trends, such as baby booms and stock market fluctuations, are likely to influence distributional outcomes (David and Menchik 1988; Goldsmith 1962; Wolff 1979). While researchers have certainly addressed these subjects, empirical support for arguments has been somewhat limited by the availability of longitudinal data with adequate coverage.

. . .

WHAT IS WEALTH AND WHY SHOULD WE STUDY IT?

When social scientists discuss financial well-being, they usually refer to income. However, I want to make a clear distinction between income and wealth. Wealth is property; it is the value of the things people own. Wealth is measured as net worth, defined as total assets (such as stocks, bonds, checking and savings accounts, the value of the family home, vacation homes, and other real estate) minus total liabilities (such as mortgage debt, the balance on credit cards, student loads, and car loans). Income is a *flow* of financial resources, such as wages or a salary received for work, interest and dividends from investments such as pensions, or transfer payments from the government. In contrast, wealth refers to the *stock* of resources owned at a particular point in time.

Income can, of course, be saved to produce wealth, but the two are not equivalent. Unlike income, wealth is not used directly to buy necessities such as food and clothing, but it can be used to generate income for these purposes. Assets such as stocks and bonds and, to a lesser degree, checking and savings accounts can produce interest and dividend income that can be used to satisfy either short- or long-term consumption needs. In the short term, wealth can be converted wholly or in part to produce income to meet consumption needs or to reduce liabilities. Similarly, wealth can satisfy long-term consumption desires through investment for long-term income streams, as in the accumulation of pension wealth to meet consumption needs after retirement. While there is a clear relationship between wealth and income, having one does not necessarily imply having the other.

In addition to producing income, wealth generates more wealth, allowing the rich to get richer. Because wealth appreciates, saving and reinvesting interest and dividends allow wealth to grow. Wealth can also be used as collateral to secure loans for further investment; many of the wealthiest people leverage their assets this way to produce even greater wealth. Wealth also allows its owner to combine consumption with investment, as in the purchase of houses and other real estate, land, vehicles, paintings, thoroughbred horses, or jewels. Frank (1999) used the term "luxury fever" to highlight the extravagant consumption that is possible, and that was increasingly obvious in the 1980s and 1990s, with great wealth. One of the most famous rich people of the 1990s, Bill Gates, Chairman of the Microsoft Corporation, built a 45,000-square-foot house on

the shores of Lake Washington that cost more than $100 million and included a $6.5-million swimming pool. When new construction is considered "luxury" at $200 per square foot in many regions, the Gates mansion seems even more extravagant given that it cost more than $2,000 per square foot to build. Equally extravagant were the homes of Microsoft cofounder Paul Allen and Oracle CEO Laurence Ellison. Allen's 74,000-square-foot house and Ellison's $40-million, 23-acre complex have drawn nearly as much attention as Gate's new home (Frank 1999:21–22).

In addition to the material luxuries it can buy, there are other more basic advantages of wealth ownership. Wealth not only allows the direct purchase of a home, but it also allows its owner to purchase advantages such as physical protection and a safe and pleasant living environment. Wealth can buy leisure, that is, it can allow its owner to decide whether to work or not. While there may be pressures associated with wealth ownership, it certainly removes the stresses associated with meeting very basic needs. In the words of Rebecca Jacobs, a woman who became rich as an entrepreneur, "Money can't give you health, friends, love. But it can give you peace of mind" (Schervish, Coutsoukis, and Lewis 1994:47). Because assets can be used to lessen the impact of a financial emergency, wealth also provides economic security to its owners. Wealth can be used to indirectly gain advantages such as political influence, social prestige, flexibility, leisure, and improved educational and occupational advantages for oneself and one's children.

Naturally there are also potential disadvantages associated with the ownership of wealth. Excess wealth can attract unwanted media attention and solicitations of various kinds. In some cases, wealth can invite security threats and may produce social isolation. Moreover, wealth ownership may dampen achievement motivation and performance in both those who have created wealth and those who stand to inherit it. A recent investigation provides detailed qualitative accounts of the privileged lives of the American super-rich as well as insights into how the wealthy portray themselves (Schervish, Coutsoukis, and Lewis 1994). the authors attempt to depict both the advantages and disadvantages of wealth ownership. The people they interview do seem to encounter various inconveniences associated with owning great amounts of wealth. However, the authors only succeed in demonstrating that, on balance, the advantages of having wealth far outweigh the potential disadvantages. In the words of Sophie Tucker, a famous entertainer who lived from 1884 to 1996, "I've been rich and I've been poor. Believe me, rich is better."

In the context of these advantages, it seems even more remarkable that the majority of wealth is owned by less than 10 percent of the population. In recent decades, most people have not owned stocks, mutual funds, bonds, or even less-risky assets such as certificates of deposit. Most American families own checking and saving accounts, a vehicle or two, and tend to keep most of their assets in owner-occupied housing. In a common scenario, many middle-class Americans first use their income to make payments on a house to take advantage of tax breaks and the combination of consuming and investing that is available in homeownership. After a mortgage payment, however, there is often little left over to save in other forms. Americans do tend to buy their homes and vehicles with credit, and they finance other expenditures with debt as well. In recent years, in fact, Americans have been willing to accumulate tremendous amounts of such debt, including large amounts of mortgage debt, car loans, loans for vacations, and home improvement loans. While such liabilities may ease short-term financial woes, their long-term effect is to diminish overall wealth along with the advantages associated with wealth.

In many cases, debt accumulation is unavoidable. Many middle-class and poor families are forced to take loans for daily survival and thus erode the small amount of wealth they may have accumulated. In their study of racial inequality in wealth ownership, Oliver and Shapiro interviewed a rather typical American couple. Albert and Robyn are both college graduates, and Albert also has a master's degree. They have been married five and a half years, have a two-year-old daughter, and both are currently employed. They bought a house when their daughter was born to make sure they had a suitable place to raise their child and also to take advantage of tax credits for homeowners. Since the birth of their daughter and the purchase of their home, however, they have been unable to save money. They regularly borrow money at very high interest rates to pay short-term bills. As a result, they have diminished their small savings and have accumulated more debt than they feel comfortable with owning (Oliver and Shapiro 1995:71–72). Like many Americans, Albert and Robyn are at high risk of financial disaster as U.S. society virtually requires two incomes to meet even modest financial obligations. Unlike the wealthy, most Americans could not rely on their assets to replace lost earnings if they were suddenly unemployed. Likewise, most Americans, like Albert and Robyn, are not accumulating assets to pay for potential future expenses such as college educations for their children and a comfortable retirement for themselves.

WEALTH, INCOME, AND INEQUALITY

In this book, I treat wealth as an intrinsically important indicator of family well-being and one quite different from income. When wealth (rather than income) is used as an indicator of family economic well-being, a different picture of advantage and disadvantage emerges; this suggests that our understanding of social inequality and social mobility has been limited by our nearly total focus on income. Moreover, because of the financial security and other advantages associated with wealth ownership, the control of wealth has been an important determinant of well-being throughout history, and the truly advantaged are still signaled by high net worth. Despite the important role wealth plays in stratifying society, however, existing studies of financial well-being generally use income to indicate the relative status of families. Advantage and disadvantage are usually measured in terms of current earned or total income or, less commonly, the present value of potential future income. The recent emphasis on income as an indicator of financial well-being has been the result of empirical convenience because, in the words of one economist, "with the advent of the income tax and the ever widening scope of census questioning, the government began to accumulate vast stores of data concerning the incomes of individuals and families in America" (Winnick 1989:160). Information regarding wealth holdings, in contrast, has not been investigated as successfully by the government, in part because the wealthy have strong incentives to conceal the details of their holdings from such agencies as the Internal Revenue Service.

Using income alone as an indicator of the financial well-being of families would be adequate if income and wealth were highly correlated. In reality, however, the correlation between the two indicators is relatively low. One study found that the correlation coefficient between income and wealth was 0.49 in 1983; while this correlation is already low, much of it is attributable to the inclusion of asset income (income generated by wealth) in the definition of total income. When asset income is removed from total income, the correlation between income and net worth dropped to 0.26 (Lerman and Mikesell 1988:779)! This suggests that the wealthy have rather low earnings, probably because they are able to support current consumption with income derived from assets. It also suggests that studies that focus solely on income miss a large part of the story of advantage and disadvantage in America.

Not only is the correlation between wealth and income low, but there is also substantial dispersion of wealth within income categories (Radner 1989). At all income levels, some families have acquired substantial wealth and own asset and debt portfolios that will maximize future wealth accumulation. Likewise at all income levels, there are those whose wealth is meager and whose portfolios indicate minimal potential for future wealth accumulation. In fact, many families, particularly nonwhite families, with both relatively low and relatively high incomes, have zero or negative net

worth (Radner 1989; Winnick 1989). In contrast, many elderly households have low incomes but substantial net worth because they had years to accumulate assets but no longer have earned income. For these reasons, many families found to be below the poverty line based solely on current income may be living quite comfortably on assets acquired during more prosperous years (Wolff 1990).

Moreover, wealth is even more unequally distributed than income. In 1989, the share of wealth of the top 1 percent of wealth owners was estimated to be 38.9 percent, while the share of the top 1 percent of income recipients was estimated to be 16.4 percent. The top quintile of wealth holders owned almost 85 percent of total household wealth, and the top quintile of income recipients received just over 50 percent of total family income. Another report (based on the Survey of Consumer Finances) found that wealth is more highly concentrated than income (Avery, Elliehausen, Canner, and Gustafson 1984b). This report demonstrated that the top 2 percent of wealth owners owned 28 percent of total wealth in 1983, and the top 10 percent owned 57 percent of wealth. In contrast, in the same year, families with the highest incomes earned 14 percent of total income, and those in the top 10 percent earned 33 percent. Moreover, the Gini coefficient for wealth increased from 0.80 in 1983 to 0.84 in 1989 (Wolff 1994). In contrast, the Gini coefficient for income in 1989 was 0.52. This evidence clearly illustrates that income tells only part of the financial story.[1]

---

[1]The Gini coefficient is an indicator of inequality that is commonly used to indicate levels of income inequality. The Gini coefficient ranges from 0 to 1, with 0 indicating perfect equality and 1 indicating perfect inequality. Conceptually, if a single household were to own all wealth, the Gini coeffient would equal unity. Avery, Elliehausen, Canner, and Gustafson (1984a) compare the Gini coefficient for income to the Gini for wealth ownership. I discuss the Gini coefficient more in Chapter 3.

TABLE 1.1
Total Household Wealth in the United States (trillions of 1990 dollars)

	Total Assets	Total Housing Assets	Home (% of total assets)	Total Stock Assets	Stocks (% of total assets)
1960	$6.6	$1.3	19	$1.6	24
1970	9.3	1.8	20	2.2	24
1980	12.3	3.2	26	1.8	14
1990	13.8	3.6	26	2.5	18
1992	16.6	3.8	23	3.7	22
1995	17.2	3.7	22	5.8	34
1997	17.5	3.8	21	6.2	35

Note: Estimates from the Federal Reserve Board's *Balance Sheets for the U.S. Economy* (Federal Reserve System 1995).

When wealth is used as an indicator of family well-being, a new picture of advantage and disadvantage emerges. For example, studies of income inequality suggest that a black middle class is emerging, and that the gap between the races is closing. Others, however, have argued that when family wealth is included, the existence of a black middle class is highly questionable (Oliver and Shapiro 1995). Oliver and Shapiro's studies of racial differences in wealth ownership, in particular, provided strong evidence that black families have considerably less net worth than white families even when income is controlled. Similar differences are evident when wealth is included in other studies of wealth inequality, including those that focus on such indicators as age and cohort differences in well-being.

In addition to telling a different story about advantage and disadvantage, wealth comes closer both theoretically and empirically to our general understanding of well-being. When we talk about economic well-being, we are referring to how prosperous people are, to how financially secure they are. Income is an indicator of short-term security, a type of security that may be lost if markets change abruptly, if the income earner becomes ill or dies, or if one relocates with a spouse. Wealth implies a more permanent notion of security and an ability to secure advantages in both the short and long terms. It is this later concept that likely

fits our shared conception of well-being. This is also perhaps why most people, including social scientists, use the terms *income* and *wealth* interchangeably. It is the latter concept, however, that we should probably understand if we are to understand how well people are doing and what it really means to be disadvantaged.

How much wealth are we talking about when we refer to family wealth? Table 1-1 provides some indication of the total amount of family wealth outstanding in the United States. The first column in this table indicates the total assets (the sum of all assets such as houses, cars, stocks, bonds, and savings accounts) that families owned between 1960 and 1997. As this table indicates, families owned only $6.6 trillion in 1960 (in 1990 dollars), however, by 1990 this number had risen to nearly $14 trillion dollars. By 1997, total assets had grown to more than $17 trillion, and estimates indicate that continued stock market booms in the late 1990s will push this number even higher by the end of the decade. Just how much money is this? For comparison, in 1990, the Gross Domestic Product (GDP) of the People's Republic of China was only $364 billion, and the GDP of the United States was $5.4 trillion (World Bank 1992). A number that has attracted considerable attention in the United States, the national debt, was $3.2 trillion in 1990. A particularly interesting story told by this table is the change American families have made in this decade in asset ownership. As the tale indicates, in 1990, 26 percent of assets owned by households was in the family home, and only 18 percent was in stocks. By 1997, only 21 percent of assets was in the home and a full 35 percent was in the stock market. Some think that this increase in the relative importance of stocks may be accounted for by the tremendous growth of the stock market that has characterized the 1990s, but it is also true that American families are making fundamental changes in their asset ownership patterns that are reflected in these figures (Norris 1996).

REFERENCES

Ando, A., and Franco Modigliani. 1963. "The Life-Cycle Hypothesis of Saving: Aggregate Implications and Tests." *American Economic Review* 53:55–84

Avery, Robert B., Gregory E. Elliehausen, Glenn B. Canner, and Thomas A. Gustafson. 1984a. "Survey of Consumer Finances, 1983." *Federal Reserve Bulletin* September: 679–692.

Avery, Robert B., Gregory E. Elliehausen, Glenn B. Canner, and Thomas A. Gustafson. 1984b. "Survey of Consumer Finances, 1983: A Second Report." *Federal Reserve Bulletin* December: 857–868.

Avery, Robert B., Gregory E. Elliehausen, Glenn B. Canner, Thomas A. Gustafson, and Julie Springert. 1986. "Financial Characteristics of High-Income Families." *Federal Reserve Bulletin* 72:163–177.

Avery, Robert B., Gregory E. Elliehausen, and Arthur B. Kennickell. 1987. "Changes in Consumer Installment Debt: Evidence from the 1983 and 1986 Surveys of Consumer Finances." *Federal Reserve Bulletin* October: 761–778.

Blau, Francine D., and John W. Graham. 1990. "Black-White Differences in Wealth and Asset Composition." *Quarterly Journal of Economics* May:321–339.

Danziger, Sheldon, Jacques Van DerGaag, Eugene Smolensky, and M. Taussig. 1982. "The Life-Cycle Hypothesis and the Consumption Behavior of the Elderly." *Journal of Post-Keynesian Economics* 5:208–227.

David, Martin, and Paul Menchik. 1988. "Changes in Cohort Wealth over a Generation." *Demography* 25:317–335.

Domhoff, G. William. 1990. *The Power Elite and the State: How Policy Is Made in America.* New York: Aldine de Gruyter.

Dye, Thomas R. 1995. *Who's Running America? The Clinton Years.* Englewood Cliffs, NJ: Prentice-Hall.

Frank, Robert H. 1999. *Luxury Fever: Why Money Fails to Satisfy in an Era of Excess.* New York: The Free Press.

Goldsmith, Raymond W. 1962. *The National Wealth of the United States in the Postwar Period.* Princeton, NJ: Princeton University Press.

Kennickell, Arthur, and Janie Shack-Marquez. 1992. "Changes in Family Finances From 1983 to 1989: Evidence from the Survey of Consumer Finances." *Federal Reserve Bulletin* 78:1–18.

Kennickell, Arthur B., and Martha Starr-McCluer. 1994. "Changes in Family Finances From 1989 to 1992: Evidence from the Survey of Consumer Finances." *Federal Reserve Bulletin* October: 861–882.

Lerman, Donald L., and James J. Mikesell. 1988. "Rural and Urban Poverty: An Income/Net Worth Approach." *Policy Studies Review* 7:765–781.

Norris, Floyd. January 5, 1996. "Flood of Cash to Mutual Funds Helped Fuel '95 Bull Market." P. A1 in *New York Times.*

Oliver, Melvin L., and Thomas M.Shapiro. 1995. *Black Wealth/White Wealth.* New York: Routledge.

Radner, Daniel B. 1989. "Net Worth and Financial Assets of Age Groups in 1984." *Social Security Bulletin* 52:2–15.

Schervish, Paul G., Platon E. Coutsoukis, and Ethan Lewis. 1994. *Gospels of Wealth: How the Rich Portray Their Lives.* Westport, CT: Praeger.

Spencer, Herbert. 1882. *Principles of Sociology*, Volume II, Part V. New York: D. Appleton Press.

Useem, Michael. 1984. *The Inner Circle.* New York: Oxford University Press.

Winnick, Andrew. 1989. *Toward Two Societies: The Changing Distributions of Income and Wealth in the United States Since 1960.* New York: Praeger.

Wolff, Edward N. 1979. "The Distributional Effects of the 1969–75 Inflation on Holdings of Household Wealth in the United States." *Review of Income and Wealth* 2:195–208.

Wolff, Edward N. 1987b. "Estimates of Household Wealth Inequality in the United States, 1962–1983." *Review of Income and Wealth* 33:231–256.

Wolff, Edward N. 1990. "Wealth Holdings and Poverty Status in the United States." *Review of Income and Wealth* 36:143–165.

Wolff, Edward N. 1994. "Trends in Household Wealth in the United States 1962–1983 and 1983–1994." C. V. Starr Center for Applied Economics, New York University, #94-03.

Wolff, Edward N. 1995a. "The Rich Get Increasingly Richer: Latest Data on Household Wealth During the 1980s." Pp. 33–68 in *Research in Politics and Society*, vol. 5, edited by R. E. Ratcliff, M. L. Oliver, and T.M. Shapiro. Greenwich, CT: JAI Press.

Wolff, Edward N. 1995b. *Top Heavy: A Study of the Increasing Inequality of Wealth in America.* New York: Twentieth Century Fund.

Wolff, Edward N. 1998. "Recent Trends in the Size Distribution of Household Wealth." *Journal of Economic Perspectives* 12:131–150.

Wolff, Edward N., and Maria Marley. 1989. "Long Term Trends in U.S. Wealth Inequality: Methodological Issues and Results." Pp. 765–839 in *The Measurement of Saving, Investment, and Wealth*, edited by R. Lipsey and H.S. Tice. Chicago: University of Chicago Press.

World Bank. 1992. *World Development Report.* Washington, DC: World Bank / Oxford University Press.

Part II

HOW SOCIAL STRATIFICATION IS GENERATED

—◊◊◊—

PART II COMPRISES TWO SECTIONS. THE FIRST section introduces both the classic theories of social stratification that anchor any study of social inequality and two relatively contemporary (1970s) theories of ascribed social stratification that are based on gender and race ethnicity. The second section focuses on observations and interpretations of how stratification actually operates in American society.

The first section opens with readings from two major contributors to the field of sociology who proposed classic theories on the foundations of social stratification: Karl Marx (from his Communist manifesto, coauthored with Friedrich Engels, and from his critique of capitalism) and Max Weber (from his analysis of class, status, and party). For Marx, economic class drives social stratification, social divisions, and inequality. Marx defines class in relation to the means of production: owners and workers, haves and have-nots. Weber expands Marxist thought on social stratification and adds the dimensions of power, authority, and prestige ("social honor"). Weber's perspective is probably closer to how Americans think about class because its multidimensional approach includes noneconomic factors.

The first of two readings on theories of ascriptive social stratification, Hartmann's provocative essay "Capitalism, Patriarchy, and Job Segregation by Sex" examines our system of occupational segregation, which rewards females far less than males. Next, Edna Bonacich's "A Theory of Ethnic Antagonism: The Split Labor Market" proposes that a hierarchical labor market split along ethnic lines causes differing degrees of ethnic

conflict. Bonacich analyzes the structural basis of ethnic inequality and conflict; the same type of theoretical analysis is often claimed for race.

The second section of Part II focuses on social mobility and the question of whether stratification is a necessary feature of society. Even in Marxist and Weberian theories of social stratification, classes are not closed systems like the caste system in India or, until recently, the apartheid system in South Africa. Sociologists often use social mobility to indicate the degree of openness of a class system. Most class systems provide the opportunity for people to move up (or down) within the structure to enhance (or diminish) their status, standard of living, and life chances, as well as the prospects for their children. This social mobility can occur intergenerationally—from one generation to the next—or intragenerationally—over the course of a person's career.

The prospect for upward (or downward) social mobility is not solely determined by talent, hard work, education, or luck. The state of the economy—expanding, stable, or contracting—also plays a critical role in each individual's chances for social mobility. In addition, demographic features of a society (such as immigration rates and birth rates) shape a person's chances for social mobility.

Research on social mobility and status attainment has produced very insightful findings that analyze how individuals move within the class, occupational, and wage structures. The first essay, "Sponsored and Contest Mobility and the School System," by Ralph Turner, illustrates some important notions of social mobility. It provides a classic view of two different modes of social mobility, as well as ways in which society attempts to maintain loyalty to its social system and values. In contest mobility, elite status is awarded as a prize of an open contest, said to be characteristic of the public mass educational system in the United States. In sponsored mobility, elite recruits are chosen for sponsorship by the established elites, according to criteria that suit the elite sponsors' interests and ensure that high status is passed along to the sponsors' children. This mode of mobility is more characteristic of private schooling in the United States and of prep schools in England.

Part II closes with an examination of the long-standing sociological debate over whether class based stratification is an inevitable or a desired feature of modern society. This controversy is one of the most enduring debates in contemporary sociology. In "Some Principles of Stratification," Kingsley Davis and Wilbert E. Moore explore the classic social problem of how a society motivates individuals to do tasks necessary for its well-being. Their answer clearly supports the need for stratification and for accepting inequality as necessary, a viewpoint known as functionalist theory. Conflict theory argues that social stratification encourages hostility and distrust among various social strata, limits the talent available to a society, sets artificial limits on productive resources, provides the elite with the political power and ideology to rationalize the status quo, and unequally distributes the motivation to participate. Conflict theorists also maintain that tension and social conflict is endemic to social stratification systems because such systems rely on coercion rather than consensus to promote cooperation with the rules of society.

In their model, Davis and Moore rely primarily on the belief that achievement, rather than ascription, determines occupational status and role. This belief may be subject to question, and their assumptions about human nature and motivation may be erroneous. For example, it is possible that motivation may be based on nonmaterial rewards, such as education and authority. Thus, functionalist theory and conflict theory offer contrasting positions, which ultimately provide antithetical principles, values, and policy agendas.

The final reading in this section is "The Uses of Undeservingness" by Herbert Gans. This essay is included not just because it discusses the important subject of poverty and the underclass but also because it offers a way to think through the theoretical debate on stratification between functionalist and conflict theorists. Gans presents a tightly reasoned rationale for the important functions of poverty in the United States. When you read this article, ask yourself, Does Gans really believe that poverty is a functional necessity in society, or is he actually criticizing America's poverty policy and the functionalist perspective? Is inequality necessary for efficiency and economic growth? If inequality did not exist, what would motivate hard work, ambition, and risk taking?

6

Manifesto of the Communist Party

Karl Marx and Friedrich Engels

A SPECTRE IS HAUNTING EUROPE—THE SPECTRE of Communism. All the Powers of old Europe have entered into a holy alliance to exorcise this spectre: Pope and Czar, Metternich and Guizot, French Radicals and German police-spies.

Where is the party in opposition that has not been decried as Communistic by its opponents in power? Where the Opposition that has not hurled back the branding reproach of Communism, against the more advanced opposition parties, as well as against its reactionary adversaries?

Two things result from this fact.

I. Communism is already acknowledged by all European Powers to be itself a Power.

II. It is high time that Communists should openly, in the face of the whole world, publish their views, their aims, their tendencies, and meet this nursery tale of the Spectre of Communism with a Manifesto of the party itself.

To this end, Communists of various nationalities have assembled in London, and sketched the following Manifesto, to be published in the English, French, German, Italian, Flemish and Danish languages.

I. BOURGEOIS AND PROLETARIANS[1]

The history of all hitherto existing society[2] is the history of class struggles.

Freeman and slave, patrician and plebeian, lord and serf, guild-master[3] and journeyman, in a

---

[1] By bourgeoisie is meant the class of modern Capitalists, owners of the means of social production and employers of wage-labour. By proletariat, the class of modern wage-labourers who, having no means of production of their own, are reduced to selling their labour-power in order to live. [*Note by Engels to the English edition of 1888.*]

[2] That is, all *written* history. In 1847, the pre-history of society, the social organisation existing previous to recorded history, was all but unknown. Since then, Haxthausen discovered common ownership of land in Russia, Maurer proved it to be the social foundation from which all Teutonic races started in history, and by and by village communities were found to be, or to have been the primitive form of society everywhere from India to Ireland. The inner organisation of this primitive Communistic society was laid bare, in its typical form, by Morgan's crowning discovery of the true nature of the *gens* and its relation to the *tribe*. With the dissolution of these primæval communities society begins to be differentiated into separate and finally antagonistic classes. I have attempted to retrace this process of dissolution in: "Der Ursprung der Familie, des Privateigenthums und des Staats" [*The Origin of the Family, Private Property and the State.*—Ed.], 2nd edition, Stuttgart 1886. [*Note by Engels to the English edition of 1888*].

[3] Guild-master, that is, a full member of a guild, a master within, not a head of a guild. [*Note by Engels to the English edition of 1888.*]

word, oppressor and oppressed, stood in constant opposition to one another, carried on an uninterrupted, now hidden, now open fight, a fight that each time ended, either in a revolutionary reconstitution of society at large, or in the common ruin of the contending classes.

In the earlier epochs of history, we find almost everywhere a complicated arrangement of society into various orders, a manifold gradation of social rank. In ancient Rome we have patricians, knights, plebeians, slaves; in the Middle Ages, feudal lords, vassals, guild-masters, journeymen, apprentices, serfs; in almost all of these classes, again, subordinate gradations.

The modern bourgeois society that has sprouted from the ruins of feudal society has not done away with class antagonisms. It has but established new classes, new conditions of oppression, new forms of struggle in place of the old ones.

Our epoch, the epoch of the bourgeoisie, possesses, however, this distinctive feature: it has simplified the class antagonisms. Society as a whole is more and more splitting up into two great hostile camps, into two great classes directly facing each other: Bourgeoisie and Proletariat.

From the serfs of the Middle Ages sprang the chartered burghers of the earliest towns. From these burgesses the first elements of the bourgeoisie were developed.

The discovery of America, the rounding of the Cape, opened up fresh ground for the rising bourgeoisie. The East-Indian and Chinese markets, the colonisation of America, trade with the colonies, the increase in the means of exchange and in commodities generally, gave to commerce, to navigation, to industry, an impulse never before known, and thereby, to the revolutionary element in the tottering feudal society, a rapid development.

The feudal system of industry, under which industrial production was monopolised by closed guilds, now no longer sufficed for the growing wants of the new markets. The manufacturing system took its place. The guild-masters were pushed on one side by the manufacturing middle class; division of labour between the different corporate guilds vanished in the face of division of labour in each single workshop.

Meantime the markets kept ever growing, the demand ever rising. Even manufacture no longer sufficed. Thereupon, steam and machinery revolutionised industrial production. The place of manufacture was taken by the giant, Modern Industry, the place of the industrial middle class, by industrial millionaires, the leaders of whole industrial armies, the modern bourgeois.

Modern industry has established the world-market, for which the discovery of America paved the way. This market has given an immense development to commerce, to navigation, to communication by land. This development has, in its turn, reacted on the extension of industry; and in proportion as industry, commerce, navigation, railways extended, in the same proportion the bourgeoisie developed, increased its capital, and pushed into the background every class handed down from the Middle Ages.

We see, therefore, how the modern bourgeoisie is itself the product of a long course of development, of a series of revolutions in the modes of production and of exchange.

Each step in the development of the bourgeoisie was accompanied by a corresponding political advance of that class. An oppressed class under the sway of the feudal nobility, an armed and self-governing association in the mediæval commune[4]; here independent urban republic

---

[4]"Commune" was the name taken, in France, by the nascent towns even before they had conquered from their feudal lords and masters local self-government and political rights as the "Third Estate." Generally speaking, for the economical development of the bourgeoisie, England is here taken as the typical country; for its political development, France. [*Note by Engels to the English edition of 1888.*]

This was the name given their urban communities by the townsmen of Italy and France, after they had purchased or wrested their initial rights of self-government from their feudal lords. [*Note by Engels to the German edition of 1890.*]

(as in Italy and Germany), there taxable "third estate" of the monarchy (as in France), afterwards, in the period of manufacture proper, serving either the semi-feudal or the absolute monarchy as a counterpoise against the nobility, and, in fact, corner-stone of the great monarchies in general, the bourgeoisie has at last, since the establishment of Modern Industry and of the world-market, conquered for itself, in the modern representative State, exclusive political sway. The executive of the modern State is but a committee for managing the common affairs of the whole bourgeoisie.

The bourgeoisie, historically, has played a most revolutionary part.

The bourgeoisie, wherever it has got the upper hand, has put an end to all feudal, patriarchal, idyllic relations. It has pitilessly torn asunder the motley feudal ties that bound man to his "natural superiors," and has left remaining no other nexus between man and man than naked self-interest, than callous "cash payment." It has drowned the most heavenly ecstasies of religious fervour, of chivalrous enthusiasm, of philistine sentimentalism, in the icy water of egotistical calculation. It has resolved personal worth into exchange value, and in place of the numberless indefeasible chartered freedoms, has set up that single, unconscionable freedom—Free Trade. In one word, for exploitation, veiled by religious and political illusions, it has substituted naked, shameless, direct, brutal exploitation.

The bourgeoisie has stripped of its halo every occupation hitherto honoured and looked up to with reverent awe. It has converted the physician, the lawyer, the priest, the poet, the man of science, into its paid wage-labourers.

The bourgeoisie has torn away from the family its sentimental veil, and has reduced the family relation to a mere money relation.

The bourgeoisie has disclosed how it came to pass that the brutal display of vigour in the Middle Ages, which Reactionists so much admire, found its fitting complement in the most slothful indolence. It has been the first to show what man's activity can bring about. It has accomplished wonders far surpassing Egyptian pyramids, Roman aqueducts, and Gothic cathedrals; it has conducted expeditions that put in the shade all former Exoduses of nations and crusades.

The bourgeoisie cannot exist without constantly revolutionising the instruments of production, and thereby the relations of production, and with them the whole relations of society. Conservation of the old modes of production in unaltered form, was, on the contrary, the first condition of existence for all earlier industrial classes. Constant revolutionising of production, uninterrupted disturbance of all social conditions, everlasting uncertainty and agitation distinguish the bourgeois epoch from all earlier ones. All fixed, fast-frozen relations, with their train of ancient and venerable prejudices and opinions, are swept away, all new-formed ones become antiquated before they can ossify. All that is solid melts into air, all that is holy is profaned, and man is at last compelled to face with sober senses, his real conditions of life, and his relations with his kind.

The need of a constantly expanding market for its products chases the bourgeoisie over the whole surface of the globe. It must nestle everywhere, settle everywhere, establish connexions everywhere.

The bourgeoisie has through its exploitation of the world-market given a cosmopolitan character to production and consumption in every country. To the great chagrin of Reactionists, it has drawn from under the feet of industry the national ground on which it stood. All old-established national industries have been destroyed or are daily being destroyed. They are dislodged by new industries, whose introduction becomes a life and death question for all civilised nations, by industries that no longer work up indigenous raw material, but raw material drawn from the remotest zones; industries whose products are consumed, not only at home, but in every quarter of the globe. In place of the old wants, satisfied by the productions of the country, we find new wants, requiring for their satisfaction the products of distant lands and climes. In place of the old local and national seclusion and self-sufficiency, we have intercourse in every direction, universal inter-dependence of nations. And as in material, so also in intellectual production. The intellectual creations of individual nations become common property. National one-sidedness and narrow-mindedness become more and more impossible, and from the numerous national and local literatures, there arises a world literature.

The bourgeoisie, by the rapid improvement of all instruments of production, by the immensely facilitated means of communication, draws all, even the most barbarian, nations into civilisation. The cheap prices of its commodities are the heavy artillery with which it batters down all Chinese walls, with which it forces the barbarians' intensely obstinate hatred of foreigners to capitulate. It compels all nations, on pain of extinction, to adopt the bourgeois mode of production; it compels them to introduce what it calls civilisation into their midst, i.e., to become bourgeois themselves. In one word, it creates a world after its own image.

The bourgeoisie has subjected the country to the rule of the towns. It has created enormous cities, has greatly increased the urban population as compared with the rural, and has thus rescued a considerable part of the population from the idiocy of rural life. Just as it has made the country dependent on the towns, so it has made barbarian and semi-barbarian countries dependent on the civilised ones, nations of peasants on nations of bourgeois, the East on the West.

The bourgeoisie keeps more and more doing away with the scattered state of the population, of the means of production, and of property. It has agglomerated population, centralised means of production, and has concentrated property in a few hands. The necessary consequence of this was political centralisation. Independent, or but loosely connected provinces, with separate interests, laws, governments and systems of taxation, became lumped together into one nation, with one government, one code of laws, one national class-interest, one frontier and one customs-tariff.

The bourgeoisie, during its rule of scarce one hundred years, has created more massive and more colossal productive forces than have all preceding generations together. Subjection of Nature's forces to man, machinery, application of chemistry to industry and agriculture, steam-navigation, railways, electric telegraphs, clearing of whole continents for cultivation, canalisation of rivers, whole populations conjured out of the ground—what earlier century had even a presentiment that such productive forces slumbered in the lap of social labour?

We see then: the means of production and of exchange, on whose foundation the bourgeoisie built itself up, were generated in feudal society. At a certain stage in the development of these means of production and of exchange, the conditions under which feudal society produced and exchanged, the feudal organisation of agriculture and manufacturing industry, in one word, the feudal relations of property became no longer compatible with the already developed productive forces; they became so many fetters. They had to be burst asunder; they were burst asunder.

Into their place stepped free competition, accompanied by a social and political constitution adapted to it, and by the economical and political sway of the bourgeois class.

A similar movement is going on before our own eyes. Modern bourgeois society with its relations of production, of exchange and of property, a society that has conjured up such gigantic means of production and of exchange, is like the sorcerer, who is no longer able to control the powers of the nether world whom he has called up by his spells. For many a decade past the history of industry and commerce is but the history of the revolt of modern productive forces against modern conditions of production, against the property relations that are the conditions for the existence of the bourgeoisie and of its rule. It is enough to mention the commercial crises that by their periodical return put on its trial, each time more threateningly, the existence of the entire bourgeois society. In these crises a great part not only of the existing products, but also of the previously created productive forces, are periodically destroyed. In these crises there breaks out an epidemic that, in all earlier epochs, would have seemed an absurdity—the epidemic of over-production. Society suddenly finds itself put back into a state of momentary barbarism; it appears as if a famine, a universal war of devastation had cut off the supply of every means of subsistence; industry and commerce seem to be destroyed; and why? Because there is too much civilisation, too much means of subsistence, too much industry, too much commerce. The productive forces at the disposal of society no longer tend to further the development of the conditions of bourgeois property; on the contrary, they have become too powerful for these conditions, by which they are fettered, and so soon as they overcome these fetters, they bring disorder into the whole of bourgeois society, endanger the existence of bourgeois property. The conditions of bourgeois society are too narrow to comprise the wealth created by them. And how does the bourgeoisie get over these crises? On the one hand by enforced destruction of a mass of productive forces; on the other, by the conquest of new markets, and by the more thorough exploitation of the old ones. That is to say, by paving the way for more extensive and more destructive crises, and by diminishing the means whereby crises are prevented.

The weapons with which the bourgeoisie felled feudalism to the ground are now turned against the bourgeoisie itself.

But not only has the bourgeoisie forged the weapons that bring death to itself; it has also called into existence the men who are to wield those weapons—the modern working class—the proletarians.

In proportion as the bourgeoisie, i.e., capital, is developed, in the same proportion is the proletariat, the modern working class, developed—a class of labourers, who live only so long as they find work, and who find work only so long as their labour increases capital. These labourers, who must sell themselves piecemeal, are a commodity, like every other article of commerce, and are consequently exposed to all the vicissitudes of competition, to all the fluctuations of the market.

Owing to the extensive use of machinery and to division of labour, the work of the proletarians has lost all individual character, and, consequently, all charm for the workman. He becomes an appendage of the machine, and it is only the most simple, most monotonous, and most easily acquired knack, that is required of him. Hence, the cost of production of a workman is restricted, almost entirely, to the means of subsistence that he requires for his maintenance, and for the propagation of his race. But the price of a commodity, and therefore also of labour, is equal to its cost of production. In proportion, therefore, as the repulsiveness of the work increases, the wage decreases. Nay more, in proportion as the use of machinery and division of labour increases, in the same proportion the burden of toil also increases, whether by prolongation of the working hours, by increase of the work exacted in a given time or by increased speed of the machinery, etc.

Modern industry has converted the little workshop of the patriarchal master into the great factory of the industrial capitalist. Masses of laborers, crowded into the factory, are organised like soldiers. As privates of the industrial army they are placed under the command of a perfect hierarchy of officers and sergeants. Not only are they slaves of the bourgeois class, and of the bourgeois State; they are daily and hourly enslaved by the machine, by the overlooker, and, above all, by the individual bourgeois manufacturer himself. The more openly this despotism proclaims gain to be its end and aim, the more petty, the more hateful and the more embittering it is.

The less the skill and exertion of strength implied in manual labour, in other words, the more modern industry becomes developed, the more is the labour of men superseded by that of women. Differences of age and sex have no longer any distinctive social validity for the working class. All are instruments of labour, more or less expensive to use, according to their age and sex.

No sooner is the exploitation of the labourer by the manufacturer, so far, at an end, and he receives his wages in cash, than he is set upon by the other portions of the bourgeoisie, the landlord, the shopkeeper, the pawnbroker, etc.

The lower strata of the middle class—the small tradespeople, shopkeepers, and retired tradesmen generally, the handicraftsmen and peasants—all these sink gradually into the proletariat, partly because their diminutive capital does not suffice for the scale on which Modern Industry is carried on, and is swamped in the competition with the large capitalists, partly because their specialised skill is rendered worthless by new methods of production. Thus the proletariat is recruited from all classes of the population.

The proletariat goes through various stages of development. With its birth begins its struggle with the bourgeoisie. At first the contest is carried on by individual labourers, then by the workpeople of a factory, then by the operatives of one trade, in one locality, against the individual bourgeois who directly exploits them. They direct their attacks not against the bourgeois conditions of production, but against the instruments of production themselves; they destroy imported wares that compete with their labour, they smash to pieces machinery, they set factories ablaze, they seek to restore by force the vanished status of the workman of the Middle Ages.

At this stage the labourers still form an incoherent mass scattered over the whole country, and broken up by their mutual competition. If anywhere they unite to form more compact bodies, this is not yet the consequence of their own active union, but of the union of the bourgeoisie, which class, in order to attain its own political ends, is compelled to set the whole proletariat in motion, and is moreover yet, for a time, able to do so. At this stage, therefore, the proletarians do not fight their enemies, but the enemies of their enemies, the remnants of absolute monarchy, the landowners, the non-industrial bourgeois, the petty bourgeoisie. Thus the whole historical movement is concentrated in the hands of the bourgeoisie; every victory so obtained is a victory for the bourgeoisie.

But with the development of industry the proletariat not only increases in number; it becomes concentrated in greater masses, its strength grows, and it feels that strength more. The various interests and conditions of life within the ranks of the proletariat are more and more equalised, in proportion as machinery obliterates all distinctions of labour, and nearly everywhere reduces wages to the same low level. The growing competition among the bourgeois, and the resulting commercial crises, make the wages of the workers ever more fluctuating. The unceasing improvement of machinery, ever more rapidly developing, makes their livelihood more and more precarious; the collisions between individual workmen and individual bourgeois take more and more the character of collisions between two classes. Thereupon the workers begin to form combinations (Trades' Unions) against the bourgeois; they club together in order to keep up the rate of wages; they found permanent associations in order to make provision beforehand for these occasional revolts. Here and there the contest breaks out into riots.

Now and then the workers are victorious, but only for a time. The real fruit of their battles lies, not in the immediate result, but in the ever-expanding union of the workers. This union is helped on by the improved means of communication that are created by modern industry and that place the workers of different localities in contact with one another. It was just this contact that was needed to centralise the numerous local struggles, all of the same character, into one national struggle between classes. But every class struggle is a political struggle. And that union, to attain which the burghers of the Middle Ages, with their miserable highways, required centuries, the modern proletarians, thanks to railways, achieve in a few years.

This organisation of the proletarians into a class, and consequently into a political party, is continually being upset again by the competition between the workers themselves. But it ever rises up again, stronger, firmer, mightier. It compels legislative recognition of particular interests of the workers, by taking advantage of the divisions among the bourgeoisie itself. Thus the ten-hours' bill in England was carried.

Altogether collisions between the classes of the old society further, in many ways, the course of development of the proletariat. The bourgeoisie finds itself involved in a constant battle. At first with the aristocracy; later on, with those portions of the bourgeoisie itself, whose interests have become antagonistic to the progress of industry; at all times, with the bourgeoisie of foreign countries. In all these battles it sees itself compelled to appeal to the proletariat, to ask for its help, and thus, to drag it into the political arena. The bourgeoisie itself, therefore, supplies the proletariat with its own elements of political and general education, in other words, it furnishes the proletariat with weapons for fighting the bourgeoisie.

Further, as we have already seen, entire sections of the ruling classes are, by the advance of industry, precipitated into the proletariat, or are at least threatened in their conditions of existence. These also supply the proletariat with fresh elements of enlightenment and progress.

Finally, in times when the class struggle nears the decisive hour, the process of dissolution going on within the ruling class, in fact within the whole range of old society, assumes such a violent, glaring character, that a small section of the ruling class cuts itself adrift, and joins the revolutionary class, the class that holds the future in its hands. Just as, therefore, at an earlier period, a section of the nobility went over to the bourgeoisie, so now a portion of the bourgeoisie goes over to the proletariat, and in particular, a portion of the bourgeois ideologists, who have raised themselves to the level of comprehending theoretically the historical movement as a whole.

Of all the classes that stand face to face with the bourgeoisie today, the proletariat alone is a really revolutionary class. The other classes decay and finally disappear in the face of Modern Industry; the proletariat is its special and essential product.

The lower middle class, the small manufacturer, the shopkeeper, the artisan, the peasant, all these fight against the bourgeoisie, to save from extinction their existence as fractions of the middle class. They are therefore not revolutionary, but conservative. Nay more, they are reactionary, for they try to roll back the wheel of history. If by chance they are revolutionary, they are so only in view of their impending transfer into the proletariat, they thus defend not their present, but their future interests, they desert their own standpoint to place themselves at that of the proletariat.

The "dangerous class," the social scum, that passively rotting mass thrown off by the lowest layers of old society, may, here and there, be swept into the movement by a proletarian revolution, its conditions of life, however, prepare it far more for the part of a bribed tool of reactionary intrigue.

In the conditions of the proletariat, those of old society at large are already virtually swamped. The proletarian is without property; his relation to his wife and children has no longer anything in common with the bourgeois family-relations; modern industrial labour, modern subjection to capital, the same in England as in France, in America as in Germany, has stripped him of every trace of national character. Law, morality, religion, are to him so many bourgeois prejudices, behind which lurk in ambush just as many bourgeois interests.

All the preceding classes that got the upper hand, sought to fortify their already acquired status by subjecting society at large to their conditions of appropriation. The proletarians cannot become masters of the productive forces of society, except by abolishing their own previous mode of appropriation, and thereby also every other previous mode of appropriation. They have nothing of their own to secure and to fortify; their mission is to destroy all previous securities for, and insurances of, individual property.

All previous historical movements were movements of minorities, or in the interests of minorities. The proletarian movement is the self-conscious, independent movement of the immense majority, in the interests of the immense majority. The proletariat, the lowest stratum of our present society, cannot stir, cannot raise itself up, without the whole superincumbent strata of official society being sprung into the air.

Though not in substance, yet in form, the struggle of the proletariat with the bourgeoisie is at first a national struggle. The proletariat of each country must, of course, first of all settle matters with its own bourgeoisie.

In depicting the most general phases of the development of the proletariat, we traced the more or less veiled civil war, raging within existing society, up to the point where that war breaks out into open revolution, and where the violent overthrow of the bourgeoisie lays the foundation for the sway of the proletariat.

Hitherto, every form of society has been based, as we have already seen, on the antagonism of oppressing and oppressed classes. But in order to oppress a class, certain conditions must be assured to it under which it can, at least, continue its slavish existence. The serf, in the period of serfdom, raised himself to membership in the commune, just as the petty bourgeois, under the yoke of feudal absolutism, managed to develop into a bourgeois. The modern labourer, on the contrary, instead of rising with the progress of industry, sinks deeper and deeper below the conditions of existence of his own class. He becomes a pauper, and pauperism develops more rapidly than population and wealth. And here it becomes evident, that the bourgeoisie is unfit any longer to be the ruling class in society, and to impose its conditions of existence upon society as an over-riding law. It is unfit to rule because it is incompetent to assure an existence to its slave within his slavery, because it cannot help letting him sink into such a state, that it has to feed him, instead of being fed by him. Society can no longer live under this bourgeoisie, in other words, its existence is no longer compatible with society.

The essential condition for the existence, and for the sway of the bourgeois class, is the formation and augmentation of capital; the condition for capital is wage-labour. Wage-labour rests exclusively on competition between the labourers. The advance of industry, whose involuntary promoter is the bourgeoisie, replaces the isolation of the laborers, due to competition, by their revolutionary combination, due to association. The development of Modern Industry, therefore, cuts from under its feet the very foundation on which the bourgeoisie produces and appropriates products. What the bourgeoisie, therefore, produces, above all, is its own grave-diggers. Its fall and the victory of the proletariat are equally inevitable.

7

Class, Status, Party

Max Weber

1. ECONOMICALLY DETERMINED POWER AND THE SOCIAL ORDER

Law exists when there is a probability that an order will be upheld by a specific staff of men who will use physical or psychical compulsion with the in-

From *Essays in Sociology*, edited and translated by H. H. Gerth and C. Wright Mills. Translation copyright © 1946, 1958 by H. H. Gerth and C. Wright Mills. Reproduced by permission of Oxford University Press, Inc.

tention of obtaining conformity with the order, or of inflicting sanctions for infringement of it. The structure of every legal order directly influences the distribution of power, economic or otherwise, within its respective community. This is true of all legal orders and not only that of thee state. In general, we understand by 'power' the chance of a man or of a number of men to realize their own will in a communal action even against the resistance of others who are participating in the action.

'Economically conditioned' power is not, of course, identical with 'power' as such. On the contrary, the emergence of economic power may be the consequence of power existing on other grounds. Man does not strive for power only in order to enrich himself economically. Power, including economic power, may be valued 'for its own sake.' Very frequently the striving for power is also conditioned by the social 'honor' it entails. Not all power, however, entails social honor: The typical American Boss, as well as the typical big speculator, deliberately relinquishes social honor. Quite generally, 'mere economic' power, and especially 'naked' money power, is by no means a recognized basis of social honor. Nor is power the only basis of social honor. Indeed, social honor, or prestige, may even be the basis of political or economic power, and very frequently has been. Power, as well as honor, may be guaranteed by the legal order, but, at least normally, it is not their primary source. The legal order is rather an additional factor that enhances the chance to hold power or honor; but it cannot always secure them.

The way in which social honor is distributed in a community between typical groups participating in this distribution we may call the 'social order.' The social order and the economic order are, of course, similarly related to the 'legal order.' However, the social and the economic order are not identical. The economic order is for us merely the way in which economic goods and services are distributed and used. The social order is of course conditioned by the economic order to a high degree, and in its turn reacts upon it.

Now: 'classes,' 'status groups,' and 'parties' are phenomena of the distribution of power within a community.

2. DETERMINATION OF CLASS-SITUATION BY MARKET-SITUATION

In our terminology, 'classes' are not communities; they merely represent possible, and frequent, bases for communal action. We may speak of a 'class' when (1) a number of people have in common a specific causal component of their life chances, in so far as (2) this component is represented exclusively by economic interests in the possession of goods and opportunities for income, and (3) is represented under the conditions of the commodity or labor markets. [These points refer to 'class situation,' which we may express more briefly as the typical chance for a supply of goods, external living conditions, and personal life experiences, in so far as this chance is determined by the amount and kind of power, or lack of such, to dispose of goods or skills for the sake of income in a given economic order. The term 'class' refers to any group of people that is found in the same class situation.]

It is the most elemental economic fact that the way in which the disposition over material property is distributed among a plurality of people, meeting competitively in the market for the purpose of exchange, in itself creates specific life chances. According to the law of marginal utility this mode of distribution excludes the non-owners from competing for highly valued goods; it favors the owners and, in fact, gives to them a monopoly to acquire such goods. Other things being equal, this mode of distribution monopolizes the opportunities for profitable deals for all those who, provided with goods, do not necessarily have to exchange them. It increases, at least generally, their power in price wars with those who, being propertyless, have nothing to offer but their services in native form or goods in a form constituted through their own labor, and who above all are compelled to get rid of these products in order barely to subsist. This mode of distribution gives to the propertied a monopoly on the possibility of transferring property from the sphere of use as a 'fortune,' to the sphere of 'capital goods'; that is, it gives them the entrepreneurial function and all chances to share directly or indirectly in returns on capital. All this holds true within the area in which pure market conditions prevail. 'Property' and 'lack of property' are, therefore, the basic categories of all class situations. It does not matter whether these two categories become effective in price wars or in competitive struggles.

Within these categories, however, class situations are further differentiated: on the one hand, according to the kind of property that is usable for returns; and, on the other hand, according to the kind of services that can be offered in the market. Ownership of domestic buildings; productive establishments; warehouses; stores; agriculturally usable land, large and small holdings—quantitative differences with possibly qualitative consequences; ownership of mines; cattle; men (slaves); disposition over mobile instruments of production, or capital goods of all sorts, especially money or objects that can be exchanged for money easily and at any time; disposition over products of one's own labor or of others' labor differing according to their various distances from consumability; disposition over transferable monopolies of any kind—all these distinctions differentiate the class situations of the propertied just as does the 'meaning' which they can and do give to the utilization of property, especially to property which has money equivalence. Accordingly, the propertied, for instance, may belong to the class of rentiers or to the class of entrepreneurs.

Those who have no property but who offer services are differentiated just as much according to their kinds of services as according to the way in which they make use of these services, in a continuous or discontinuous relation to a recipient. But always this is the generic connotation of the concept of class: that the kind of chance in the *market* is the decisive moment which presents a common condition for the individual's fate. 'Class situation' is, in this sense, ultimately 'market situation.' The effect of naked possession *per se*, which among cattle breeders gives the nonowning slave or serf into the power of the cattle owner, is only a forerunner of real 'class' formation. However, in the cattle loan and in the naked severity of the law of debts in such communities, for the first time mere 'possession' as such emerges as decisive for the fate of the individual. This is very much in contrast to the agricultural communities based on labor. The creditor–debtor relation becomes the basis of 'class situations' only in those cities where a 'credit market,' however primitive, with rates of interest increasing according to the extent of dearth and a factual monopolization of credits, is developed by a plutocracy. Therewith 'class struggles' begin.

Those men whose fate is not determined by the chance of using goods or services for themselves on the market, e.g. slaves, are not, however, a 'class' in the technical sense of the term. They are, rather, a 'status group.'

3. COMMUNAL ACTION FLOWING FROM CLASS INTEREST

According to our terminology, the factor that creates 'class' is unambiguously economic interest, and indeed, only those interests involved in the existence of the 'market.' Nevertheless, the concept of 'class-interest' is an ambiguous one: even as an empirical concept it is ambiguous as soon as one understands by it something other than the factual direction of interests following with a certain probability from the class situation for a certain 'average' of those people subjected to the class situation. The class situation and other circumstances remaining the same, the direction in which the individual worker, for instance, is likely to pursue his interests may vary widely, according to whether he is constitutionally qualified for the task at hand to a high, to an average, or to a low degree. In the same way, the direction of interests may *vary* according to whether or not a *communal* action of a larger or smaller portion of those commonly affected by the 'class situation,' or even an association among them, e.g. a 'trade union,' has grown out of the class situation from which the individual may or may not expect promising results. [Communal action refers to that action which is oriented to the feeling of the actors that they belong together. Societal action, on the other hand, is oriented to a rationally motivated adjustment of interests.] The rise of societal or even of communal action from a common class situation is by no means a universal phenomenon.

The class situation may be restricted in its effects to the generation of essentially *similar* reactions, that is to say, within our terminology, of 'mass actions.' However, it may not have even this result. Furthermore, often merely an amorphous communal action emerges. For example, the 'murmuring' of the workers known in ancient oriental ethics: the moral disapproval of the work-master's conduct, which in its practical significance was probably equivalent to an increasingly typical phenomenon of precisely the latest industrial development, namely, the 'slow down' (the deliberate limiting of work effort) of laborers by virtue of tacit agreement. The degree in which 'communal action' and possibly 'societal action,' emerges from the 'mass actions' of the members of a class is linked to general cultural conditions, especially to those of an intellectual sort. It is also linked to the extent of the contrasts that have already evolved, and is especially linked to the *transparency* of the connections between the causes and the consequences of the 'class situation.' For however different life chances may be, this fact in itself, according to all experience, by no means gives birth to 'class action' (communal action by the members of a class). The fact of being conditioned and the results of the class situation must be distinctly recognizable. For only then the contrast of life chances can be felt not as an absolutely given fact to be accepted, but as a resultant from either (1) the given distribution of property, or (2) the structure of the concrete economic order. It is only then that people may react against the class structure not only through acts of an intermittent and irrational protest, but in the form of rational association. There have been 'class situations' of the first category (1), of a specifically naked and transparent sort, in the urban centers of Antiquity and during the Middle Ages; especially then, when great fortunes were accumulated by factually monopolized trading in industrial products of these localities or in foodstuffs. Furthermore, under certain circumstances, in the rural economy of the most diverse periods, when agriculture was increasingly exploited in a profit-making manner. The most important historical example of the second category (2) is the class situation of the modern 'proletariat.'

4. TYPES OF 'CLASS STRUGGLE'

Thus every class may be the carrier of any one of the possibly innumerable forms of 'class action,' but this is not necessarily so. In any case, a class does not in itself constitute a community. To treat 'class' conceptually as having the same value as 'community' leads to distortion. That men in the same class situation regularly react in mass actions to such tangible situations as economic ones in the direction of those interests that are most adequate to their average number is an important and after all simple fact for the understanding of historical events. Above all, this fact must not lead to that kind of pseudo-scientific operation with the concepts of 'class' and 'class interests' so frequently found these days, and which has found its most classic expression in the statement of a talented author, that the individual may be in error concerning his interests but that the 'class' is 'infallible' about its interests. Yet, if classes as such are not communities, nevertheless class situations emerge only on the basis of communalization. The communal action that brings forth class situations, however, is not basically action between members of the identical class; it is an action between members of different classes. Communal actions that directly determine the class situation of the worker and the entrepreneur are: the labor market, the commodities market, and the capitalistic enterprise. But, in its turn, the existence of a capitalistic enterprise presupposes that a very specific communal action exists and that it is specifically structured to protect the possession of goods *per se*, and especially the power of individuals to dispose, in principle freely, over the means of production. The existence of a capitalistic enterprise is preconditioned by a specific kind of 'legal order.' Each kind of class situation, and above all when it rests upon the power of property *per se*, will become most clearly efficacious when all other determinants of reciprocal relations are, as far as possible, eliminated in their significance. It is in this way that the utilization of the power of property in the market obtains its most sovereign importance.

Now 'status groups' hinder the strict carrying through of the sheer market principle. In the present context they are of interest to us only from this one point of view. Before we briefly consider them, note that not much of a general nature can be said about the more specific kinds of antagonism between 'classes' (in our meaning of the term). The great shift, which has been going on continuously in the past, and up to our times, may be summarized, although at the cost of some precision: the struggle in which class situations are effective has progressively shifted from consumption credit toward, first, competitive struggles in the commodity market and, then, toward price wars on the labor market. The 'class struggles' of antiquity—to the extent that they were genuine class struggles and not struggles between status groups—were initially carried on by indebted peasants, and perhaps also by artisans threatened by debt bondage and struggling against urban creditors. For debt bondage is the normal result of the differentiation of wealth in commercial cities, especially in seaport cities. A similar situation has existed among cattle breeders. Debt relationships as such produced class action up to the time of Cataline. Along with this, and with an increase in provision of grain for the city by transporting it from the outside, the struggle over the means of sustenance emerged. It centered in the first place around the provision of bread and the determination of the price of bread. It lasted throughout antiquity and the entire Middle Ages. The propertyless as such flocked together against those who actually and supposedly were interested in the dearth of bread. This fight spread until it involved all those commodities essential to the way of life and to handicraft production. There were only incipient discussions of wage disputes in antiquity and in the Middle Ages. But they have been slowly increasing up into modern times. In the earlier periods they were completely secondary to slave rebellions as well as to fights in the commodity market.

The propertyless of antiquity and of the Middle Ages protested against monopolies, preemption, forestalling, and the withholding of goods from the market in order to raise prices. Today the central issue is the determination of the price of labor.

This transition is represented by the fight for access to the market and for the determination of the price of products. Such fights went on between merchants and workers in the putting-out system of domestic handicraft during the transition to modern times. Since it is quite a general phenomenon we must mention here that the class antagonisms that are conditioned through the market situation are usually most bitter between those who actually and directly participate as opponents in price wars. It is not the rentier, the share-holder, and the banker who suffer the ill will of the worker, but almost exclusively the manufacturer and the business executives who are the direct opponents of workers in price wars. This is so in spite of the fact that it is precisely the cash boxes of the rentier, the share-holder, and the banker into which the more or less 'unearned' gains flow, rather than into the pockets of the manufacturers or of the business executives. This simple state of affairs has very frequently been decisive for the role the class situation has played in the formation of political parties. For example, it has made possible the varieties of patriarchal socialism and the frequent attempts—formerly, at least—of threatened status groups to form alliances with the proletariat against the 'bourgeoisie.'

5. STATUS HONOR

In contrast to classes, *status groups* are normally communities. They are, however, often of an amorphous kind. In contrast to the purely economically determined 'class situation' we wish to designate as 'status situation' every typical component of the life fate of men that is determined by a specific, positive or negative, social estimation of *honor*. This honor may be connected with any quality shared by a plurality, and, of course, it can be knit to a class situation: class distinctions are linked in the most varied ways with status distinctions. Property as such is not always recognized as a status qualification, but in the long run it is, and with extraordinary regularity. In the subsistence economy of the organized neighborhood, very often the richest man is simply the chieftain. However, this often means only an honorific preference. For example, in the so-called pure modern 'democracy,' that is, one devoid of any expressly ordered status privileges for individuals, it may be that only the families coming under approximately the same tax class dance with one another. This example is reported of certain smaller Swiss cities. But status honor need not necessarily be linked with a 'class situation.' On the contrary, it normally stands in sharp opposition to the pretensions of sheer property.

Both propertied and propertyless people can belong to the same status group, and frequently they do with very tangible consequences. This 'equality' of social esteem may, however, in the long run become quite precarious. The 'equality' of status among the American 'gentlemen,' for instance, is expressed by the fact that outside the subordination determined by the different functions of 'business,' it would be considered strictly repugnant—wherever the old tradition still prevails—if even the richest 'chief,' while playing billiards or cards in his club in the evening, would not treat his 'clerk' as in every sense fully his equal in birthright. It would be repugnant if the American 'chief' would bestow upon his 'clerk' the condescending 'benevolence' marking a distinction of 'position,' which the German chief can never dissever from his attitude. This is one of the most important reasons why in America the German 'clubby-ness' has never been able to attain the attraction that the American clubs have.

6. GUARANTEES OF STATUS STRATIFICATION

In content, status honor is normally expressed by the fact that above all else a specific *style of life* can be expected from all those who wish to belong to the circle. Linked with this expectation are restrictions on 'social' intercourse (that is, intercourse which is not subservient to economic or any other of business's 'functional' purposes). These restrictions may confine normal marriages to within the status circle and may lead to complete endogamous closure. As soon as there is not a mere individual and socially irrelevant imitation of another style of life, but an agreed-upon communal action of this closing character, the 'status' development is under way.

In its characteristic form, stratification by 'status groups' on the basis of conventional styles of life evolves at the present time in the United States out of the traditional democracy. For example, only the resident of a certain street ('the street') is considered as belonging to 'society,' is qualified for social intercourse, and is visited and invited. Above all, this differentiation evolves in such a way as to make for strict submission to the fashion that is dominant at a given time in society. This submission to fashion also exists among men in America to a degree unknown in Germany. Such submission is considered to be an indication of the fact that a given man *pretends* to qualify as a gentleman. This submission decides, at least *prima facie*, that he will be treated as such. And this recognition becomes just as important for his employment chances in 'swank' establishments, and above all, for social intercourse and marriage with 'esteemed' families, as the qualification for dueling among Germans in the Kaiser's day. As for the rest: certain families resident for a long time, and, of course, correspondingly wealthy, e.g. 'F. F. V., i.e. First Families of Virginia,' or the actual or alleged descendants of the 'Indian Princess' Pocahontas, of the Pilgrim fathers, or of the Knickerbockers, the members of almost inaccessible sects and all sorts of circles setting themselves apart by means of any other characteristics and badges . . . all these elements usurp 'status' honor. The development of status is essentially a question of stratification resting upon usurpation. Such usurpation is the normal origin of almost all status honor. But the road from this purely conventional situation to legal privilege, positive or negative, is easily traveled as soon as a certain stratification of the social order has in fact been 'lived in' and has achieved stability by virtue of a stable distribution of economic power.

7. 'ETHNIC' SEGREGATION AND 'CASTE'

Where the consequences have been realized to their full extent, the status group evolves into a closed 'caste.' Status distinctions are then guaranteed not merely by conventions and laws, but also by *rituals*. This occurs in such a way that every physical contact with a member of any caste that is considered to be 'lower' by the members of a 'higher' caste is considered as making for a ritualistic impurity and to be a stigma which must be expiated by a religious act. Individual castes develop quite distinct cults and gods.

In general, however, the status structure reaches such extreme consequences only where there are underlying differences which are held to be 'ethnic.' The 'caste' is, indeed, the normal form in which ethnic communities usually live side by side in a 'societalized' manner. These ethnic communities believe in blood relationship and exclude exogamous marriage and social intercourse. Such a caste situation is part of the phenomenon of 'pariah' peoples and is found all over the world. These people form communities, acquire specific occupational traditions of handicrafts or of other arts, and cultivate a belief in their ethnic community. They live in a 'diaspora' strictly segregated from all personal intercourse, except that of an unavoidable sort, and their situation is legally precarious. Yet, by virtue of their economic indispensability, they are tolerated, indeed, frequently privileged, and they live in interspersed political communities. The Jews are the most impressive historical example.

A 'status' segregation grown into a 'caste' differs in its structure from a mere 'ethnic' segregation: the caste structure transforms the horizontal and unconnected coexistences of ethnically segregated groups into a vertical social system of super- and subordination. Correctly formulated: a comprehensive societalization integrates the ethnically divided communities into specific political and communal action. In their consequences they differ precisely in this way: ethnic coexistences condition a mutual repulsion and disdain but allow each ethnic community to consider its own honor as the highest one; the caste structure brings about a social subordination and an acknowledgment of 'more honor' in favor of the privileged caste and status groups. This is due to the fact that in the caste structure ethnic distinctions as such have become 'functional' distinctions within the political societalization (warriors, priests, artisans that are politically important for war and for building, and so on). But even pariah people who are most despised are usually apt to continue cultivating in some manner that which is equally peculiar to ethnic and to status communities: the belief in their own specific 'honor.' This is the case with the Jews.

Only with the negatively privileged status groups does the 'sense of dignity' take a specific deviation. A sense of dignity is the precipitation in individuals of social honor and of conventional demands which a positively privileged status group raises for the deportment of its members. The sense of dignity that characterizes positively privileged status groups is naturally related to their 'being' which does not transcend itself, that is, it is to their 'beauty and excellence' ($\kappa\alpha\lambda o$-$\kappa\alpha\,\gamma\alpha\vartheta\iota\alpha$). Their kingdom is 'of this world.' They live for the present and by exploiting their great past. The sense of dignity of the negatively privileged strata naturally refers to a future lying beyond the present, whether it is of this life or of another. In other words, it must be nurtured by the belief in a providential 'mission' and by a belief in a specific honor before God. The 'chosen people's' dignity is nurtured by a belief either that in the beyond 'the last will be the first,' or that in this life a Messiah will appear to bring forth into the light of the world which has cast them out the hidden honor of the pariah people. This simple state of affairs, and not the 'resentment' which is so strongly emphasized in Nietzsche's much admired construction in the *Genealogy of Morals*, is the source of the religiosity cultivated by pariah status groups. In passing, we may note that resentment may be accurately applied only to a limited extent; for one of Nietzsche's main examples, Buddhism, it is not at all applicable.

Incidentally, the development of status groups from ethnic segregations is by no means the normal phenomenon. On the contrary, since objective 'racial differences' are by no means basic to every subjective sentiment of an ethnic community, the ultimately racial foundation of status structure is rightly and absolutely a question of the concrete individual case. Very frequently a status group is instrumental in the production of a thoroughbred anthropological type. Certainly a status group is to a high degree effective in producing extreme types, for they select personally qualified individuals (e.g. the Knighthood selects those who are fit for warfare, physically and psychically). But selection is far from being the only, or the predominant, way in which status groups are formed: political membership or class situation has at all times been at least as frequently decisive. And today the class situation is by far the predominant factor, for of course the possibility of a style of life expected for members of a status group is usually conditioned economically.

8. STATUS PRIVILEGES

For all practical purposes, stratification by status goes hand in hand with a monopolization of ideal and material goods or opportunities, in a manner we have come to know as typical. Besides the specific status honor, which always rests upon distance and exclusiveness, we find all sorts of material monopolies. Such honorific preferences may consist of the privilege of wearing special costumes, of eating special dishes taboo to others, of carrying arms—which is most obvious in its consequences—the right to pursue certain nonprofessional dilettante artistic practices, e.g. to play certain musical instruments. Of course, material monopolies provide the most effective motives for the exclusiveness of a status group; although, in themselves, they are rarely sufficient, almost always they come into play to some extent. Within a status circle there is the question of intermarriage: the interest of the families in the monopolization of potential bridegrooms is at least of equal importance and is parallel to the interest in the monopolization of daughters. The daughters of the circle must be provided for. With an increased inclosure of the status group, the conventional preferential opportunities for special employment grow into a legal monopoly of special offices for the members. Certain goods become objects for monopolization by status groups. In the typical fashion these include 'entailed estates' and frequently also the possessions of serfs or bondsmen and, finally, special trades. This monopolization occurs positively when the status group is exclusively entitled to own and to manage them; and negatively when, in order to maintain its specific way of life, the status group must *not* own and manage them.

The decisive role of a 'style of life' in status 'honor' means that status groups are the specific bearers of all 'conventions.' In whatever way it may be manifest, all 'stylization' of life either originates in status groups or is at least conserved by them. Even if the principles of status conventions differ greatly, they reveal certain typical traits, especially among those strata which are most privileged. Quite generally, among privileged status groups there is a status disqualification that operates against the performance of common physical labor. This disqualification is now 'setting in' in America against the old tradition of esteem for labor. Very frequently every rational economic pursuit, and especially 'entrepreneurial activity,' is looked upon as a disqualification of status. Artistic and literary activity is also considered as degrading work as soon as it is exploited for income, or at least when it is connected with hard physical exertion. An example is the sculptor working like a mason in his dusty smock as over against the painter in his salon-like 'studio' and those forms of musical practice that are acceptable to the status group.

9. ECONOMIC CONDITIONS AND EFFECTS OF STATUS STRATIFICATION

The frequent disqualification of the gainfully employed as such is a direct result of the principle of status stratification peculiar to the social order, and of course, of this principle's opposition to a distribution of power which is regulated exclusively through the market. These two factors operate along with various individual ones, which will be touched upon below.

We have seen above that the market and its processes 'knows no personal distinctions': 'functional' interests dominate it. It knows nothing of 'honor.' The status order means precisely the reverse, viz.: stratification in terms of 'honor' and of styles of life peculiar to status groups as such. If mere economic acquisition and naked economic power still bearing the stigma of its extra-status origin could bestow upon anyone who has won it the same honor as those who are interested in status by virtue of style of life claim for themselves, the status order would be threatened at its very root. This is the more so as, given equality of status honor, property *per se* represents an addition even if it is not overtly acknowledged to be such. Yet if such economic acquisition and power gave the agent any honor at all, his wealth would result in his attaining more honor than those who successfully claim honor by virtue of style of life. Therefore all groups having interests in the status order react with special sharpness precisely against the pretensions of purely economic acquisition. In most cases they react the more vigorously the more they feel themselves threatened. Calderon's respectful treatment of the peasant, for instance, as opposed to Shakespeare's simultaneous and ostensible disdain of the *canaille* illustrates the different way in which a firmly structured status order reacts as compared with a status order that has become economically precarious. This is an example of a state of affairs that recurs everywhere. Precisely because of the rigorous reactions against the claims of property *per se*, the 'parvenu' is never accepted, personally and without reservation, by the privileged status groups, no matter how completely his style of life has been adjusted to theirs. They will only accept his descendants who have been educated in the conventions of their status group and who have never besmirched its honor by their own economic labor.

As to the general *effect* of the status order, only one consequence can be stated, but it is a very important one: the hindrance of the free development of the market occurs first for those goods which status groups directly withheld from free exchange by monopolization. This monopolization may be effected either legally or conventionally. For example, in many Hellenic cities during the epoch of status groups, and also originally in Rome, the inherited estate (as is shown by the old formula for indiction against spendthrifts) was monopolized just as were the estates of knights, peasants, priests, and especially the clientele of the craft and merchant guilds. The market is restricted, and the power of naked property *per se*, which gives its stamp to 'class formation,' is pushed into the background. The results of this process can be most varied. Of course, they do not necessarily weaken the contrasts in the economic situation. Frequently they strengthen these contrasts, and in any case, where stratification by status permeates a community as strongly as was the case in all political communities of antiquity and of the Middle Ages, one can never speak of a genuinely free market competition as we understand it today. There are wider effects than this direct exclusion of special goods from the market. From the contrariety between the status order and the purely economic order mentioned above, it follows that in most instances the notion of honor peculiar to status absolutely abhors that which is essential to the market: higgling [haggling]. Honor abhors higgling among peers and occasionally it taboos higgling for the members of a status group in general. Therefore, everywhere some status groups, and usually the most influential, consider almost any kind of overt participation in economic acquisition as absolutely stigmatizing.

With some oversimplification, one might thus say that 'classes' are stratified according to their relations to the production and acquisition of goods; whereas 'status groups' are stratified according to the principles of their *consumption* of goods as represented by special 'styles of life.'

An 'occupational group' is also a status group. For normally, it successfully claims social honor only by virtue of the special style of life which may be determined by it. The differences between classes and status groups frequently overlap. It is precisely those status communities most strictly segregated in terms of honor (viz. the Indian castes) who today show, although within very rigid limits, a relatively high degree of indifference to pecuniary income. However, the Brahmins seek such income in many different ways.

As to the general economic conditions making for the predominance of stratification by 'status,' only very little can be said. When the bases of the acquisition and distribution of goods are relatively stable, stratification by status is favored. Every technological repercussion and economic transformation threatens stratification by status and pushes the class situation into the foreground. Epochs and countries in which the naked class situation is of predominant significance are regularly the periods of technical and economic transformations. And every slowing down of the shifting of economic stratifications leads, in due course, to the growth of status structures and makes for a resuscitation of the important role of social honor.

10. PARTIES

Whereas the genuine place of 'classes' is within the economic order, the place of 'status groups' is within the social order, that is, within the sphere of the distribution of 'honor.' From within these spheres, classes and status groups influence one another and they influence the legal order and are in turn influenced by it. But 'parties' live in a house of 'power.'

Their action is oriented toward the acquisition of social 'power,' that is to say, toward influencing a communal action no matter what its content may be. In principle, parties may exist in a social 'club' as well as in a 'state.' As over against the actions of classes and status groups, for which this is not necessarily the case, the communal actions of 'parties' always mean a societalization. For party actions are always directed toward a goal which is striven for in planned manner. This goal may be a 'cause' (the party may aim at realizing a program for ideal or material purposes), or the goal may be 'personal' (sinecures, power, and from these, honor for the leader and the followers of the party). Usually the party action aims at all these simultaneously. Parties are, therefore, only possible within communities that are societalized, that is, which have some rational order and a staff of persons available who are ready to enforce it. For parties aim precisely at influencing this staff, and if possible, to recruit it from party followers.

In any individual case, parties may represent interests determined through 'class situation' or 'status situation,' and they may recruit their following respectively from one or the other. But they need be neither purely 'class' nor purely 'status' parties. In most cases they are partly class parties and partly status parties, but sometimes they are neither. They may represent ephemeral or enduring structures. Their means of attaining power may be quite varied, ranging from naked violence of any sort to canvassing for votes with coarse or subtle means: money, social influence, the force of speech, suggestion, clumsy hoax, and so on to the rougher or more artful tactics of obstruction in parliamentary bodies.

The sociological structure of parties differs in a basic way according to the kind of communal action which they struggle to influence. Parties also differ according to whether or not the community is stratified by status or by classes. Above all else, they vary according to the structure of domination within the community. For their leaders normally deal with the conquest of a community. They are, in the general concept which is maintained here, not only products of specially modern forms of domination. We shall also designate as parties the ancient and medieval 'parties,' despite the fact that their structure differs basically from the structure of modern parties. By virtue of these structural differences of domination it is impossible to say anything about the structure of parties without discussing the structural forms of social domination *per se*. Parties, which are always structures struggling for domination, are very frequently organized in a very strict 'authoritarian' fashion. . . .

Concerning 'classes,' 'status groups,' and 'parties,' it must be said in general that they necessarily presuppose a comprehensive societalization, and especially a political framework of communal action, within which they operate. This does not mean that parties would be confined by the frontiers of any individual political community. On the contrary, at all times it has been the order of the day that the societalization (even when it aims at the use of military force in common) reaches beyond the frontiers of politics. This has been the case in the solidarity of interests among the Oligarchs and among the democrats in Hellas, among the Guelfs and among Ghibellines in the Middle Ages, and within the Calvinist party during the period of religious struggles. It has been the case up to the solidarity of the landlords (international congress of agrarian landlords), and has continued among princes (holy alliance, Karlsbad decrees), socialist workers, conservatives (the longing of Prussian conservatives for Russian intervention in 1850). But their aim is not necessarily the establishment of new international political, i.e. *territorial*, dominion. In the main they aim to influence the existing dominion.*

---

*The posthumously published text breaks off here. We omit an incomplete sketch of types of 'warrior estates.'

8

Capitalism, Patriarchy, and Job Segregation by Sex

Heidi Hartmann

THE DIVISION OF LABOR BY SEX APPEARS TO have been universal throughout human history. In our society the sexual division of labor is hierarchical, with men on top and women on the bottom. Anthropology and history suggest, however, that this division was not always a hierarchical one. The development and importance of a sex-ordered division of labor is the subject of this paper. It is my contention that the roots of women's present social status lie in this sex-ordered division of labor. It is my belief that not only must the hierarchical nature of the division of labor between the sexes be eliminated, but the very division of labor between the sexes itself must be eliminated if women are to attain equal social status with men and if women and men are to attain the full development of their human potentials.

The primary questions for investigation would seem to be, then, first, how a more sexually egalitarian division became a less egalitarian one, and second, how this hierarchical division of labor became extended to wage labor in the modern period. Many anthropological studies suggest that the first process, sexual stratification, occurred together with the increasing productiveness, specialization, and complexity of society; for example through the establishment of settled agriculture, private property, or the state. It occurred as human society emerged from the primitive and became "civilized." In this perspective capitalism is a relative latecomer, whereas patriarchy,[1] the hierarchical relation between men and women in which men are dominant and women are subordinate, was an early arrival.

I want to argue that, before capitalism, a patriarchal system was established in which men

Originally published in *Signs: Journal of Women in Culture and Society*, Vol. 1, Number 3, Part 2 (University of Chicago Press, Spring 1977). Reprinted by permission of the University of Chicago Press.

[1] I define patriarchy as a set of social relations which has a material base and in which there are hierarchical relations between men, and solidarity among them, which enable them to control women. Patriarchy is thus the system of male oppression of women. Rubin argues that we should use the term "sex-gender system"

controlled the labor of women and children in the family, and that in so doing men learned the techniques of hierarchical organization and control. With the advent of public–private separations such as those created by the emergence of state apparatus and economic systems based on wider exchange and larger production units, the problem for men became one of maintaining their control over the labor power of women. In other words, a direct personal system of control was translated into an indirect, impersonal system of control, mediated by society-wide institutions. The mechanisms available to men were (1) the traditional division of labor between the sexes, and (2) techniques of hierarchical organization and control. These mechanisms were crucial in the second process, the extension of a sex-ordered division of labor to the wage-labor system, during the period of the emergence of capitalism in Western Europe and the United States.

The emergence of capitalism in the fifteenth to eighteenth centuries threatened patriarchal control based on institutional authority as it destroyed many old institutions and created new ones, such as a "free" market in labor. It threatened to bring all women and children into the labor force and hence to destroy the family and the basis of the power of men over women (i.e., the control over their labor power in the family).[2] If the theoretical tendency of pure capitalism would have been to eradicate all arbitrary differences of status among laborers, to make all laborers equal in the marketplace, why are women still in an inferior position to men in the labor market? The possible answers are legion; they range from neoclassical views that the process is not complete or is hampered by market imperfections to the radical view that production requires hierarchy even if the market nominally requires "equality."[3] All of these explanations, it seems to me, ignore the role

---

to refer to that realm outside the economic system (and not always coordinate with it) where gender stratification based on sex differences is produced and reproduced. Patriarchy is thus only one form, a male-dominant one, of a sex-gender system. Rubin argues further that patriarchy should be reserved for pastoral nomadic societies as described in the Old Testament where male power was synonymous with fatherhood. While I agree with Rubin's first point, I think her second point makes the usage of patriarchy too restrictive. It is a good label for most male-dominant societies (see Gayle Rubin, "The Traffic in Women," in *Toward an Anthropology of Women*, ed. Rayna Reiter [New York: Monthly Review Press, 1975]). Muller offers a broader definition of patriarchy "as a social system in which the status of women is defined primarily as wards of their husbands, fathers, and brothers," where wardship has economic and political dimensions (see Viana Muller, "The Formation of the State and the Oppression of Women: A Case Study in England and Wales," mimeographed [New York: New School for Social Research, 1975], p. 4, n. 2). Muller relies on Karen Sacks, "Engels Revisited: Women, the Organization of Production, and Private Property," in *Woman, Culture and Society*, ed. Michelle Z. Rosaldo and Louise Lamphere (Stanford, Calif.: Stanford University Press, 1974). Patriarchy as a system between and among men as well as between men and women is further explained in a draft paper, "The Unhappy Marriage of Marxism and Feminism: Towards a New Union," by Amy Bridges and Heidi Hartmann.

[2]Marx and Engels perceived the progress of capitalism in this way, that it would bring women and children into the labor market and thus erode the family. Yet despite Engels's acknowledgment in *The Origin of the Family, Private Property, and the State* (New York: International Publishers, 1972), that men oppress women in the family, he did not see that oppression as based on the control of women's labor, and, if anything, he seems to lament the passing of the male-controlled family (see his *The Condition of the Working Class in England* [Stanford, Calif.: Stanford University Press, 1968], esp. pp. 161–64).

[3]See Richard C. Edwards, David M. Gordon, and Michael Reich, "Labor Market Segmentation in American Capitalism," draft essay, and the book they edited, *Labor Market Segmentation* (Lexington, Ky.: Lexington Books, forthcoming) for an explication of this view.

of men—ordinary men, men as men, men as workers—in maintaining women's inferiority in the labor market. The radical view, in particular, emphasizes the role of men as capitalists in creating hierarchies in the production process in order to maintain their power. Capitalists do this by segmenting the labor market (along race, sex, and ethnic lines among others) and playing workers off against each other. In this paper I argue that male workers have played and continue to play a crucial role in maintaining sexual divisions in the labor process.

Job segregation by sex, I will argue, is the primary mechanism in capitalist society that maintains the superiority of men over women, because it enforces lower wages for women in the labor market. Low wages keep women dependent on men because they encourage women to marry. Married women must perform domestic chores for their husbands. Men benefit, then, from both higher wages and the domestic division of labor. This domestic division of labor, in turn, acts to weaken women's position in the labor market. Thus, the hierarchical domestic division of labor is perpetuated by the labor market, and vice versa. This process is the present outcome of the continuing interaction of two interlocking systems, capitalism and patriarchy. Patriarchy, far from being vanquished by capitalism, is still very virile; it shapes the form modern capitalism takes, just as the development of capitalism has transformed patriarchal institutions. The resulting mutual accommodation between patriarchy and capitalism has created a vicious circle for women.

My argument contrasts with the traditional views of both neoclassical and Marxist economists. Both ignore patriarchy, a social system with a material base. The neoclassical economists tend to exonerate the capitalist system, attributing job segregation to exogenous *ideological* factors, like sexist attitudes. Marxist economists tend to attribute job segregation to capitalists, ignoring the part played by male workers and the effect of centuries of patriarchal social relations. In this paper I hope to redress the balance. The line of argument I have outlined here and will develop further below

is perhaps incapable of proof. This paper, I hope, will establish its plausibility rather than its incontrovertibility. . . .

CONCLUSION

The present status of women in the labor market and the current arrangement of sex-segregated jobs is the result of a long process of interaction between patriarchy and capitalism. I have emphasized the actions of male workers throughout this process because I believe that emphasis to be correct. Men will have to be forced to give up their favored positions in the division of labor—in the labor market and at home—both if women's subordination is to end and if men are to begin to escape class oppression and exploitation. [4] Capitalists have indeed used women as unskilled, underpaid labor to undercut male workers, yet this is only a case of the chickens coming home to roost—a case of men's co-optation by and support for patriarchal society, with its hierarchy among men, being turned back on themselves with a vengeance. Capitalism grew on top of patriarchy; patriarchal capitalism is stratified society par excellence. If non-ruling-class men are to be free they will have to recognize their co-optation by patriarchal capitalism and relinquish their patriarchal benefits. If women are to be free, they must fight against both patriarchal power and capitalist organization of society.

Because both the sexual division of labor and male domination are so longstanding, it will be very difficult to eradicate them and impossible to

---

[4]Most Marxist-feminist attempts to deal with the problems in Marxist analysis raised by the social position of women seem to ignore these basic conflicts between the sexes, apparently in the interest of stressing the underlying class solidarity that should obtain among women and men workers. Bridges and Hartmann's draft paper (n. 1) reviews this literature. A few months ago a friend (female) said, "We are much more likely to be able to get Thieu out of Vietnam than we are to get men to do the dishes." She was right.

eradicate the latter without [eradicating] the former. The two are now so inextricably intertwined that it is necessary to eradicate the sexual division of labor itself in order to end male domination.[5] Very basic changes at all levels of society and culture are required to liberate women. In this paper, I have argued that the maintenance of job segregation by sex is a key root of women's status, and I have relied on the operation of society-wide institutions to explain the maintenance of job segregation by sex. But the consequences of that division of labor go very deep, down to the level of the subconscious. The subconscious influences behavior patterns, which form the micro underpinnings (or complements) of social institutions and are in turn reinforced by those social institutions.

I believe we need to investigate these micro phenomena as well as the macro ones I have discussed in this paper. For example, it appears to be a very deeply ingrained behavioral rule that men cannot be subordinate to women of a similar social class. Manifestations of this rule have been noted in restaurants, where waitresses experience difficulty in giving orders to bartenders, unless the bartender can reorganize the situation to allow himself autonomy; among executives, where women executives are seen to be most successful if they have little contact with others at their level and manage small staffs; and among industrial workers, where female factory inspectors cannot successfully correct the work of male production workers.[6] There is also a deeply ingrained fear of being identified with the other sex. As a general rule, men and women must never do anything which is not masculine or feminine (respectively).[7] Male executives, for example, often exchange handshakes with male secretaries, a show of respect which probably works to help preserve their masculinity.

At the next deeper level, we must study the subconscious—both how these behavioral rules are internalized and how they grow out of personality structure.[8] At this level, the formation of personality, there have been several attempts to study the production of gender, the *socially* imposed differentiation of humans based on biological sex dif-

---

[5]In our society, women's jobs are synonymous with low-status, low-paying jobs: ". . . we may replace the familiar statement that women earn less because they are in low paying occupations with the statement that women earn less because they are in *women's jobs.* . . . As long as the labor market is divided on the basis of sex, it is likely that the tasks allocated to women will be ranked as less prestigious or important, reflecting women's lower social status in the society at large" (Francine Blau [Weisskoff], "Women's Place in the Labor Market," *American Economic Review* 62, no. 4 [May 1972]: 161).

[6]Theodore Caplow, *The Sociology of Work* (New York: McGraw-Hill Book Co., 1964), pp. 237 ff., discusses several behavioral rules and their impact. Harold Wilensky, "Women's Work: Economic Growth, Ideology, Structure," *Industrial Relations* 7, no. 3 (May 1968): 235–48, also discusses the implication for labor-market phenomena of several behavioral rules.

[7]"The use of tabooed words, the fostering of sports and other interests which women do not share, and participation in activities which women are intended to disapprove of—hard drinking, gambling, practical jokes, and sexual assays of various kinds—all suggest that the adult male group is to a large extent engaged in a reaction *against* feminine influence, and therefore cannot tolerate the presence of women without changing its character entirely" (Caplow, p. 239). Of course, the lines of division between masculine and feminine are constantly shifting. At various times in the nineteenth century, teaching, selling in retail stores, and office work were each thought to be totally unsuitable for women. This variability of the boundaries between men's jobs and women's jobs is one reason why an effort to locate basic behavioral principles would seem to make sense—though, ultimately, of course, these rules are shaped by the division of labor itself.

[8]Caplow based his rules on the Freudian view that men identify freedom from female dominance with maturity, i.e., they seek to escape their mothers.

ferences.[9] A materialist interpretation of reality, of course, suggests that gender production grows out of the extant division of labor between the sexes,[10]

_____

[9]See Rubin (n. 1), and Juliet Mitchell, *Feminism and Psychoanalysis* (New York: Pantheon Books, 1974), who seek to re-create Freud from a feminist perspective. So does Shulamith Firestone, *The Dialectic of Sex* (New York: Bantam Books, 1971).

[10]For example, the current domestic division of labor in which women nurture children profoundly affects (differentially) the personality structures of girls and boys.

and, in a dialectical process, reinforces that very division of labor itself. In my view, because of these deep ramifications of the sexual division of labor we will not eradicate sex-ordered task division until we eradicate the socially imposed gender differences between us and, therefore, the very sexual division of labor itself.

In attacking both patriarchy and capitalism we will have to find ways to change both society-wide institutions and our most deeply ingrained habits. It will be a long, hard struggle.

—*New School for Social Research*

9

_____

A Theory of Ethnic Antagonism

The Split Labor Market

Edna Bonacich

SOCIETIES VARY CONSIDERABLY IN THEIR DEgree of ethnic and racial antagonism. Such territories as Brazil, Mexico, and Hawaii are generally acknowledged to be relatively low on this dimension; while South Africa, Australia, and the United States are considered especially high. Literally hundreds of variables have been adduced to account for these differences, ranging from religions of dominant groups, to whether the groups who migrate are dominant or subordinate, to degrees of difference in skin color, to an irreducible "tradition" of ethnocentrism. While some writers have

_____

From the *American Sociological Review*, Vol. 37, October 1972, pp. 547–559. Reprinted by permission of the American Sociological Association.

attempted to synthesize or systematize some subset of these (e.g., Lieberson, 1961; Mason, 1970; Noel, 1968; Schermerhorn, 1970; van den Berghe, 1966), one is generally struck by the absence of a developed theory accounting for variations in ethnic antagonism.

One approach to this problem is to consider an apparent anomaly, namely that ethnic antagonism has taken two major, seemingly antithetical forms: exclusion movements, and so-called caste systems.[1] An example of the former is the "white Australia" policy; while South Africa's color bar illustrates the latter. The United States has shown both forms, with a racial caste system in the South and exclusion of Asian and "new" immigrants[2] from the Pacific and eastern seaboards respectively. Apart from manifesting antagonism between ethnic elements, exclusion and caste seem to have little in common. In the one, an effort is made to prevent an ethnically different group from being part of the society. In the other, an ethnically different group is essential to the society: it is an exploited class supporting the entire edifice. The deep south felt it could not survive without its black people; the Pacific coast could not survive without its Japanese. This puzzle may be used as a touchstone for solving the general problem of ethnic antagonism, for to be adequate a theory must be able to explain it.

The theory presented here is, in part, a synthesis of some of the ideas used by Oliver Cox to explain the Japanese–white conflict on the U.S. Pacific coast (Cox, 1948:408–22), and by Marvin Harris to analyze the difference between Brazil and the deep south in rigidity of the "color line" (Harris, 1964:79–94). It stresses the role of a certain kind of economic competition in the development of ethnic antagonism. Economic factors have, of course, not gone unnoticed, though until recently sociological literature has tended to point them out briefly, then move on to more "irrational" factors (even such works as *The Economics of Discrimination*, Becker, 1957). A resurgence of Marxian analysis (e.g. Blauner, 1969; Reich, 1971) has thrust economic considerations to the fore, but I shall argue that even this approach cannot adequately deal with the problem posed by exclusion movements and caste systems. In addition, both Marxist and non-Marxist writers assume that racial and cultural differences in themselves prompt the development of ethnic antagonism. This theory challenges that assumption, suggesting that economic processes are more fundamental.

No effort is made to prove the accuracy of the following model. Such proof depends on a lengthier exposition. Historical illustrations are presented to support it.

ETHNIC ANTAGONISM

"Ethnic" rather than "racial" antagonism was selected as the dependent variable because the former is seen to subsume the latter. Both terms refer to groups defined socially as sharing a common ancestry in which membership is therefore inherited or ascribed, whether or not members are currently physically or culturally distinctive.[3] The difference between race and ethnicity lies in the size of the locale from which a group stems, races generally coming from continents, and ethnicities from national sub-sections of continents. In the past the term "race" has been used to refer to both levels, but general usage today has reversed this practice (e.g. Schermerhorn, 1970; Shibutani and Kwan, 1965). Ethnicity has become the generic term.

Another reason for choosing this term is that exclusion attempts and caste-like arrangements are found among national groupings within a racial category. For example, in 1924 whites (Europeans) attempted to exclude whites of different national backgrounds from the United States by setting up stringent immigration quotas.

The term "antagonism" is intended to encompass all levels of intergroup conflict, including ideologies and beliefs (such as racism and prejudice), behaviors (such as discrimination, lynchings, riots), and institutions (such as laws perpetuating segregation). Exclusion movements and caste systems may be seen as the culmination of many pronouncements, actions, and enactments, and are continuously supported by more of the same. "Antagonism" was chosen over terms like prejudice and discrimination because it carries fewer moralistic and theoretical assumptions (see Schermerhorn, 1970:6–9). For example, both of these terms see conflict as emanating primarily from one side: the dominant group. Antagonism allows for the possibility that conflict is mutual; i.e. a product of interaction.

THE SPLIT LABOR MARKET

The central hypothesis is that ethnic antagonism first germinates in a labor market split along ethnic lines. To be split, a labor market must contain at least two groups of workers whose price of labor differs for the same work, or would differ if they did the same work. The concept "price of labor" refers to labor's total cost to the employer, includ-

TABLE 1

Estimated Cost of Three Types of Labor to Be Shepherds in New South Wales, 1841*

	Free Man (White)			Prisoner (White)			Coolie (Indian)		
	£	s.	d.	£	s.	d.	£	s.	d.
Rations	16	18	0	13	14	4	9	6	4
Clothing	—	—	—	3	3	0	1	1	8
Wages	25	0	0	—	—	—	6	0	0
Passage from India	—	—	—	—	—	—	2	0	0
Total per Annum	41	18	0	16	17	4	18	8	0

*From Yarwood (1968:13).

ing not only wages, but the cost of recruitment, transportation, room and board, education, health care (if the employer must bear these), and the costs of labor unrest. The degree of worker "freedom" does not interfere with this calculus; the cost of a slave can be estimated in the same monetary units as that of a wage earner, from his purchase price, living expenses, policing requirements, and so on.

The price of a group of workers can be roughly calculated in advance and comparisons made even though two groups are not engaged in the same activity at the same time. Thus in 1841 in the colony of New South Wales, the Legislative Council's Committee on Immigration estimated the relative costs of recruiting three groups of laborers to become shepherds. Table 1 shows their findings. The estimate of free white labor, for example, was based on what it would take to attract these men from competing activities.

FACTORS AFFECTING THE INITIAL PRICE OF LABOR

Labor markets that are split by the entrance of a new group develop a dynamic which may in turn affect the price of labor. One must therefore distinguish initial from later price determinants. The initial factors can be divided into two broad categories: resources and motives.

1. Resources

Three types of resources are important price determinants. These are:

a. Level of Living, or Economic Resources The ethnic groups forming the labor market in a contact situation derive from different economic systems, either abroad or within a conquered territory. For members of an ethnic group to be drawn into moving, they must at least raise their wage level. In general, the poorer the economy of the recruits, the less the inducement needed for them to enter the new labor market. Crushing poverty may drive them to sell their labor relatively cheaply. For example, Lind (1968:199) describes the effect of the living level on the wage scale received by immigrant workers to Hawaii:

In every case [of labor importations] the superior opportunities for gaining a livelihood have been broadcast in regions of surplus manpower, transportation facilities have been provided, and finally a monetary return larger than that already received has been offered to the prospective laborer. The monetary inducement has varied considerably, chiefly according to the plane of living of the population being recruited, and the cheapest available labor markets have, of course, been most extensively drawn upon.

Workers need not accept the original wage agreement for long after they have immigrated, since other opportunities may exist; for instance, there may be ample, cheap land available for individual farming. One capitalist device for keeping wages low at least for a time is to bind immigrants to contracts before they leave the old economy. The Indian indenture system, for example, rested on such an arrangement (Gillion, 1962:19–38).

b. Information   Immigrants may be pushed into signing contracts out of ignorance. They may agree to a specific wage in their homeland not knowing the prevailing wage in the new country, or having been beguiled by a false account of life and opportunity there. Williams (1944:11), for example, describes some of the false promises made to draw British and Germans as workers to West Indian sugar plantations before the advent of African slavery. Chinese labor to Australia was similarly "obtained under 'false and specious pretences'" (Willard, 1967:9).

The possibilities for defrauding a population lacking access to the truth are obvious. In general, the more people know about conditions obtaining in the labor market to which they are moving, the better can they protect themselves against disadvantageous wage agreements.

c. Political Resources   By political resources I mean the benefits to a group of organizing. Organization can exist at the level of labor, or it can occur at higher levels, for example, in a government that protects them. These levels are generally related in that a strong government can help organize its emigrants. There are exceptions, however: strong emigrant governments tend not to extend protection to their deported convicts or political exiles; and some highly organized groups, like the Jews in the United States, have not received protection from the old country.

Governments vary in the degree to which they protect their emigrants. Japan kept close watch over the fate of her nationals who migrated to Hawaii and the Pacific coast; and the British colonial government in India tried to guard against abuses of the indenture system (for example, by refusing to permit Natal to import Indian

workers for their sugar plantations until satisfactory terms had been agreed to; cf. Ferguson-Davie, 1952:4–10). In contrast Mexican migrant workers to the United States have received little protection from their government, and African states were unable to intervene on behalf of slaves brought to America. Often the indigenous populations of colonized territories have been politically weak following conquest. Thus African nations in [southern] Africa have been unable to protect their migrant workers in the cities.

In general, the weaker a group politically, the more vulnerable it is to the use of force, hence to an unfavorable wage bargain (or to no wage bargain at all, as with slavery). The price of a labor group varies inversely with the amount of force that can be used against it, which in turn depends on its political resources.

2. Motives

Two motives affect the price of labor, both related to the worker's intention of not remaining permanently in the labor force. Temporary workers tend to cost less than permanent workers for two reasons. First, they are more willing to put up with undesirable work conditions since these need not be endured forever. If they are migrants, this tolerance may extend to the general standard of living. Often migrant temporary workers are males who have left the comforts of home behind and whose employers need not bear the cost of housing and educating their families. Even when families accompany them, such workers tend to be willing to accept a lower standard of living since it is only short term.

Second, temporary workers avoid involvement in lengthy labor disputes. Since they will be in the labor market a short while, their main concern is immediate employment. They may be willing to undercut wage standards if need be to get a job, and are therefore ripe candidates for strikebreaking. Permanent workers also stand to lose from lengthy conflict, but they hope for benefits to their progeny. If temporary workers are from elsewhere, they have no such interest in future business–labor relations. Altogether, temporary workers have little reason to join the organizations and unions of a permanent work force, and tend not to do so.

a. Fixed or Supplementary Income Goal   Some temporary workers enter the market either to supplement family income, or to work toward a specific purchase. The worker's standard of living does not, therefore, depend on his earnings on the job in question, since his central source of employment or income lies elsewhere. Examples of this phenomenon are to be found throughout Africa:

... the characteristic feature of the labor market in most of Africa has always been the massive circulation of Africans between their villages and paid employment outside. In some places villagers engage in wage-earning seasonally. More commonly today they work for continuous though short-term periods of roughly one to three years, after which they return to the villages. ... the African villager, the potential migrant into paid employment, has a relatively low, clearly defined and rigid income goal; he wants money to pay head and hut taxes, to make marriage payments required of prospective bridegrooms, or to purchase some specific consumer durable (a bicycle, a rifle, a sewing machine, a given quantity of clothing or textiles, etc.) (Berg, 1966:116–8).

Such a motive produces the "backward-sloping labor supply function" characteristic of many native peoples in colonized territories. In addition to the general depressing effects on wages of being temporary, this motive leads to a fairly rapid turnover in personnel, making organization more difficult and hindering the development of valuable skills which could be used for bargaining. If wages were to rise, workers would reach their desired income and withdraw more quickly from the market, thereby lessening their chances of developing the political resources necessary to raise their wages further.

b. Fortune Seeking   Many groups, commonly called sojourners (see Siu, 1952), migrate long distances to seek their fortune, with the ultimate intention of improving their position in their homeland. Such was the case with Japanese immigrants on the west coast and Italian immigrants in the east. Such workers stay longer in the labor market, and can develop political resources. However, since they are temporary they have little incentive to join the organizations of the settled population. Instead they tend to create competing organizations composed of people who will play a part in their future in the homeland, i.e. members of the same ethnic group.

Sojourner laborers have at least three features which affect the price of labor: lower wages, longer hours, and convenience to the employer. The Japanese show all three. Millis (1915:45) cites the U.S. Immigration Commission on the question of relative wages:

The Japanese have usually worked for a lower wage than the members of any other race save the Chinese and the Mexican. In the salmon canneries the Chinese have been paid higher wages than the Japanese engaged in the same occupations. In the lumber industry, all races, including the East Indian, have been paid higher wages than the Japanese doing the same kind of work. As section hands and laborers in railway shops they have been paid as much [as] or more than the Mexicans, but as a rule less than the white men of many races.

And so on. The lower wage level of Japanese workers reflects both a lower standard of living, and a desire to get a foothold in the labor market. As Iwata (1962:27) puts it: "Their willingness to accept even lower wages than laborers of other races enabled the Japanese to secure employment readily."

Millis (1915:155) describes a basket factory in Florin, California, where Japanese workers had displaced white female workers because the latter were unwilling to work more than ten hours a day or on weekends. The Japanese, anxious to return to Japan as quickly as possible, were willing to work twelve to fourteen hours per day and on weekends, thereby saving their employers the costs of a special overtime work force.

The Japanese immigrants developed political resources through a high degree of community organization. This could be used for the convenience of the employer, by solving his recruitment problems, seeing that work got done, and providing workers with board and lodging. In the case of seasonal labor, the Japanese community could provide for members during the off-season by various boarding arrangements and clubs, and by transporting labor to areas of demand (Ichihashi, 1932:172–6; Millis, 1915:44–5). These conveniences saved the employer money.[4]

As the reader may have noted, I have omitted a factor usually considered vital in determining the price of labor, i.e. differences in skills. I would contend, however, that this does not in itself lead to that difference in price for the same work which distinguishes a split labor market. While a skilled worker may be able to get a higher paying job, an unskilled laborer of another ethnicity may be trained to fill that job for the same wage. Skills are only indirectly important in that they can be used to develop political resources, which in turn may lead to a difference in wage level for the same work.

PRICE OF LABOR AND ETHNICITY

Ethnic differences need not always produce a price differential. Thus, if several ethnic groups who are approximately equal in resources and/or goals enter the same economic system, a split labor market will not develop. Alternatively, in a two-group contact situation, if one ethnic group occupies the position of a business elite and has no members in the labor force (or in a class that could easily be pushed into the labor force, e.g. low-capital farmers) then regardless of the other group's price, the labor market will not be split. This statement is a generalization of the point made by Harris (1964) that the critical difference in race relations between the deep south and Brazil was that the former had a white yeomanry in direct competition with ex-slaves, while the Portuguese only occupied the role of a business elite (plantation owners).

Conversely, a split labor force does not only stem from ethnic differences. For example, prison and female labor have often been cheaper than free male labor in western societies. Prison labor has been cheap because prisoners lack political resources, while women often labor for supple-

mentary incomes (cf. Hutchinson, 1968:59–61; Heneman and Yoder, 1965:543–4).

That initial price discrepancies in labor should ever fall along ethnic lines is a function of two forces. First, the original wage agreement arrived at between business and new labor often takes place in the labor group's point of origin. This is more obviously a feature of immigrant labor, but also occurs within a territory when conquered peoples enter their conquerors' economy. In other words, the wage agreement is often concluded within a national context, these nationalities coming to comprise the ethnic elements of the new labor market. One would thus expect the initial wages of co-nationals to be similar.

Second, nations or peoples that have lived relatively separately from one another are likely to have developed different employment motives and levels of resources (wealth, organization, communication channels). In other words, the factors that affect the price of labor are likely to differ grossly between nations, even though there may be considerable variation within each nation, and overlap between nations. Color differences in the initial price of labor only seem to be a factor because resources have historically been roughly correlated with color around the world.[5] When color and resources are not correlated in the "expected" way, then I would predict that price follows resources and motives rather than color.

In sum, the prejudices of business do not determine the price of labor, darker skinned or culturally different persons being paid less because of them. Rather, business tries to pay as little as possible for labor, regardless of ethnicity, and is held in check by the resources and motives of labor groups. Since these often vary by ethnicity, it is common to find ethnically split labor markets.

THE DYNAMICS OF SPLIT LABOR MARKETS

In split labor markets, conflict develops between three key classes: business, higher paid labor, and cheaper labor. The chief interests of these classes are as follows:

1. BUSINESS OR EMPLOYERS

This class aims at having as cheap and docile a labor force as possible to compete effectively with other businesses. If labor costs are too high (owing to such price determinants as unions), employers may turn to cheaper sources, importing overseas groups or using indigenous conquered populations. In the colony of Queensland in Australia, for example, it was believed that cotton farming would be the most suitable economic enterprise:

However, such plantations (being too large) could not be worked, much less cleared, by their owners; neither could the work be done by European laborers because sufficient numbers of these were not available—while even had there been an adequate supply, the high rates of wages would have been prohibitive. This was a consideration which assumed vast importance when it was realized that cotton would have to be cultivated in Queensland at a considerably lower cost than in the United States in order to compensate for the heavier freights from Queensland—the more distant country from England. It seemed then that there was no possibility of successful competition with America unless the importation of some form of cheap labor was permitted (Moles, 1968:41).

Cheaper labor may be used to create a new industry having substantially lower labor costs than the rest of the labor market, as in Queensland. Or they may be used as strikebreakers or replacements to undercut a labor force trying to improve its bargaining position with business. If cheap labor is unavailable, business may turn to mechanization, or try to relocate firms in areas of the world where the price of labor is lower.

2. Higher Paid Labor

This class is very threatened by the introduction of cheaper labor into the market, fearing that it will either force them to leave the territory or reduce them to its level. If the labor market is split ethnically, the class antagonism takes the form of ethnic antagonism. It is my contention (following Cox, 1948:411n) that, while much rhetoric of ethnic antagonism concentrates on ethnicity and race, it really in large measure (though probably not entirely) expresses this class conflict.

The group comprising higher paid labor may have two components. First, it may include current employees demanding a greater share of the profits or trying to maintain their position in the face of possible cuts. A second element is the small, independent, entrepreneur, like the subsistence farmer or individual miner. The introduction of cheaper labor into these people's line can undermine their position, since the employer of cheaper labor can produce at lower cost. The independent operator is then driven into the labor market. The following sequence occurs in many colonies: settlement by farmers who work their own land, the introduction of intensive farming using cheaper labor, a rise in land value and a consequent displacement of independent farmers. The displaced class may move on (as occurred in many of the West Indies when African slave labor was introduced to raise sugar), but if it remains, it comes to play the role of higher paid labor.

The presence of cheaper labor in areas of the economy where higher paid labor is not currently employed is also threatening to the latter, since the former attract older industries. The importance of potential competition cannot be overstressed. Oftentimes writers assert the irrationality of ethnic antagonism when direct economic competition is not yet in evidence owing to few competitors having entered the labor market, or to competitors having concentrated in a few industries. Thus Daniels (1966:29) belittles the role of trade unions in the Asiatic Exclusion League by describing one of the major contributors as "an organization whose members, like most trade unionists in California, were never faced with job competition from Japanese." It does not take direct competition for members of a higher priced labor group to see the possible threat to their well-being, and to try to prevent its materializing. If they have reason to believe many more low-priced workers are likely to follow an initial "insignificant trickle" (as Daniels, 1966:1, describes the Japanese immigration, failing to mention that it was insignificant precisely because a larger anticipated flow had been thwarted, and diverted to Brazil), or if they see a large concentration of cheaper labor in a few industries which could easily be used to undercut them in their own, they will attempt to forestall undercutting.

Lest you think this fear misguided, take note that, when business could override the interests of more expensive labor, the latter have indeed been displaced or undercut. In British Guiana the local labor force, composed mainly of African ex-slaves, called a series of strikes in 1842 and 1847 against planters' attempts to reduce their wages. Plantation owners responded by using public funds to import over 50,000 cheaper East Indian indentured workers (Despres, 1969). A similar situation obtained in Mississippi, where Chinese were brought in to undercut freed blacks. Loewen (1971:23) describes the thinking of white landowners: "the 'Chinaman' would not only himself supply a cheaper and less trouble-some work force but in addition his presence as a threatening alternative would intimidate the Negro into resuming his former docile behavior." Such displacement has occurred not only to non-white more expensive labor, but, as the effects of slavery in the West Indies show, to whites by white capitalists.

3. Cheaper Labor

The employer uses this class partly to undermine the position of more expensive labor, through strikebreaking and undercutting. The forces that make the cheaper group cost less permit this to occur. In other words, either they lack the re-sources to resist an offer or use of force by busi-ness, or they seek a quick return to another economic and social base.

With the possible exception of sojourners, cheaper labor does not intentionally undermine more expensive labor; it is paradoxically its weak-ness that makes it so threatening, for business can more thoroughly control it. Cox makes this point (1948:417–8) in analyzing why Pacific coast white and Asian workers could not unite in a coalition against business:

. . . the first generation of Asiatic workers is ordinarily very much under the control of labor contractors and employers, hence it is easier for the employer to frus-trate any plans for their organization. Clearly this cul-tural bar helped antagonize white workers against the Asiatics. The latter were conceived of as being in al-liance with the employer. It would probably have taken two or three generations before, say, the East Indian low-caste worker on the Coast became suffi-ciently Americanized to adjust easily to the policies and aims of organized labor.

Ethnic antagonism is specifically produced by the competition that arises from a price differen-tial. An oversupply of equal-priced labor does not produce such antagonism, though it too threatens people with the loss of their job. However, hiring practices will not necessarily fall along ethnic lines, there being no advantage to the employer in hir-ing workers of one or another ethnicity. All work-ingmen are on the same footing, competing for scarce jobs (cf. Blalock, 1967:84–92, who uses this model of labor competition). When one ethnic group is decidedly cheaper than another (i.e. when the labor market is split) the higher paid worker faces more than the loss of his job; he faces the pos-sibility that the wage standard in all jobs will be un-dermined by cheaper labor.

VICTORY FOR MORE EXPENSIVE LABOR

If an expensive labor group is strong enough (strength generally depending on the same factors that influence price), they may be able to resist being displaced. Both exclusion and caste systems represent such victories for higher paid labor.

1. Exclusion

Exclusion movements generally occur when the majority of a cheaper labor group resides outside a given territory but desires to enter it (often at the request of business groups). The exclusion move-ment tries to prevent the physical presence of cheaper labor in the employment area, thereby preserving a non-split, higher priced labor market.

There are many examples of exclusion attempts around the world. In Australia, for instance, a group of white workers was able to prevent capitalists from importing cheaper labor from India, China, Japan and the Pacific Islands. Attempts at importation were met with strikes, boycotts, petitions and deputations (Willard, 1967:51–7). Ultimately, organized white labor pressed for strong exclusion measures, and vigilantly ensured their enforcement. As Yarwood (1964:151–2) puts it: "A comparison of the records of various governments during our period [1896–1923] leaves no doubt as to the special role of the Labour Party as the guardian of the ports." In other words, a white Australia policy (i.e. the exclusion of Asian and Polynesian immigrants) appears to have sprung from a conflict of interests between employers who wanted to import cheap labor, and a labor force sufficiently organized to ward off such a move.

California's treatment of Chinese and Japanese labor is another example of exclusion. A socialist, Cameron H. King, Jr., articulates the threatened labor group's position:

Unskilled labor has felt this competition [from the Japanese] for some time being compelled to relinquish job after job to the low standard of living it could not endure. The unskilled laborers are largely unorganized and voiceless. But as the tide rises it is reaching the skilled laborers and the small merchants. These are neither unorganized nor voiceless, and viewing the menace to their livelihood they loudly demand protection of their material interests. We of the Pacific Coast certainly know that exclusion is an effective solution. In the seventh decade of the nineteenth century the problem arose of the immigration of Chinese laborers. The Republican and Democratic parties failed to give heed to the necessities of the situation and the Workingman's party arose and swept the state with the campaign cry of "The Chinese must go." Then the two old parties woke up and have since realized that to hold the labor vote they must stand for Asiatic exclusion (King, 1908:665–6).

King wrote this around the time of the Gentlemen's Agreement, an arrangement of the U.S. and Japanese governments to prevent further immigration of Japanese labor to the Pacific Coast (Bailey, 1934). The Agreement was aimed specifically at labor and not other Japanese immigrants, suggesting that economic and not racial factors were at issue.

Exclusion movements clearly serve the interests of higher paid labor. Its standards are protected, while the capitalist class is deprived of cheaper labor.

2. Caste

If cheaper labor is present in the market, and cannot be excluded, then higher paid labor will resort to a caste arrangement, which depends on exclusiveness rather than exclusion. Caste is essentially an aristocracy of labor (a term borrowed from Lenin, e.g. 1964), in which higher paid labor deals with the undercutting potential of cheaper labor by excluding them from certain types of work. The higher paid group controls certain jobs exclusively and gets paid at one scale of wages, while the cheaper group is restricted to another set of jobs and is paid at a lower scale. The labor market split is submerged because the differentially priced workers ideally never occupy the same position.

Ethnically distinct cheaper groups (as opposed to women, for example, who face a caste arrangement in many Western societies) may reside in a territory for two reasons: either they were indigenous or they were imported early in capitalist–labor relations, when the higher paid group could not prevent the move. Two outstanding examples of labor aristocracies based on ethnicity are South Africa, where cheaper labor was primarily indigenous, and the U.S. south, where they were imported as slaves.

Unlike exclusion movements, caste systems retain the underlying reality of a price differential, for if a member of the subordinate group were to occupy the same position as a member of the stronger labor group he would be paid less. Hence, caste systems tend to become rigid and vigilant, developing an elaborate battery of laws, customs and beliefs aimed to prevent undercutting. The victory has three facets. First, the higher paid group tries to ensure its power in relation to business by monopolizing the acquisition of certain essential skills, thereby ensuring the effectiveness of strike action, or by controlling such important resources as purchasing power. Second, it tries to prevent the immediate use of cheaper labor as undercutters and strikebreakers by denying them access to general education thereby making their training as quick replacements more difficult, or by ensuring through such devices as "influx control" that the cheaper group will retain a base in their traditional economies. The latter move ensures a backward-sloping labor supply function (cf. Berg, 1966) undesirable to business. Third, it tries to weaken the cheaper group politically, to prevent their pushing for those resources that would make them useful as undercutters. In other words, the solution to the devastating potential of weak, cheap labor is, paradoxically, to weaken them further, until it is no longer in business's immediate interest to use them as replacements.

South Africa is perhaps the most extreme modern example of an ethnic caste system. A split labor market first appeared there in the mining industry. With the discovery of diamonds in 1869, a white working class emerged.[6] At first individual whites did the searching, but, as with the displacement of small farms by plantations, they were displaced by consolidated, high-capital operations, and became employees of the latter (Doxey, 1961:18). It was this class together with imported skilled miners from Cornwall (lured to Africa by high wages) which fought the capitalists over the use of African labor. Africans were cheaper because they came to the mines with a fixed income goal (e.g. the price of a rifle) and did not view the mines as their main source of livelihood. By contrast, European workers remained in the mines and developed organizations to further their interests.

Clearly, it would have been to the advantage of businessmen, once they knew the skills involved, to train Africans to replace the white miners at a fraction of the cost; but this did not happen. The mining companies accepted a labor

aristocracy, not out of ethnic solidarity with the white workers but:

(as was to be the case throughout the later history of mining) they had little or no choice because of the collective strength of the white miners. . . . The pattern which was to emerge was that of the Europeans showing every sign of preparedness to use their collective strength to ensure their exclusive supremacy in the labour market. Gradually the concept of trade unionism, and, for that matter, of socialism, became accepted in the minds of the European artisans as the means of maintaining their own position against non-white inroads (Doxey, 1961:23–4).

The final showdown between mine owners and white workers occurred in the 1920s when the owners tried to substitute cheaper non-white labor for white labor in certain semi-skilled occupations. This move precipitated the "Rand Revolt," a general strike of white workers on the Witwatersrand, countered by the calling in of troops and the declaration of martial law. The result was a coalition between Afrikaner nationalists (predominantly workers and small-scale farmers being pushed off the land by larger, British owned farms) and the English-speaking Labor Party (Van der Horst, 1965:117–8). The Revolt "showed the lengths to which white labour was prepared to go to defend its privileged position. From that time on, mine managements have never directly challenged the colour-bar in the mining industry" (Van der Horst, 1965:118).

The legislative history of much of South Africa (and of the post-bellum deep south) consists in attempts by higher priced white labor to ward off undercutting by cheaper groups, and to entrench its exclusive control of certain jobs.[7]

This interpretation of caste contrasts with the Marxist argument that the capitalist class purposefully plays off one segment of the working class against the other (e.g. Reich, 1971). Business, I would contend, rather than desiring to protect a segment of the working class supports a liberal or laissez faire ideology that would permit all workers to compete freely in an open market. Such open competition would displace higher paid labor. Only under duress does business yield to labor aristocracy, a point made in *Deep South*, a book written when the depression had caused the displacement of white tenant farmers and industrial workers by blacks:

The economic interests of these groups [employers] would also demand that cheaper colored labor should be employed in the "white collar" jobs in business offices, governmental offices, stores, and banks. In this field, however, the interests of the employer group conflict not only with those of the lower economic group of whites but also with those of the more literate and aggressive middle group of whites. A white store which employed colored clerks, for example, would be boycotted by both these groups. The taboo upon the employment of colored workers in such fields is the result of the political and purchasing power of the white middle and lower groups (Davis, et. al., 1941:480).

In sum, exclusion and caste are similar reactions to a split labor market. They represent victories for higher paid labor. The victory of exclusion is more complete in that cheaper labor is less available to business. For this reason I would hypothesize that a higher paid group prefers exclusion to caste, even though exclusion means they have to do the dirty work. Evidence for this comes from Australia where, in early attempts to import Asian labor, business tried to buy off white labor's opposition by offering to form them into a class of "mechanics" and foremen over the "coolies" (Yarwood, 1968:16, 42). The offer was heartily rejected in favor of exclusion. Apartheid in South Africa can be seen as an attempt to move from caste to the exclusion of the African work force.

Most of our examples have contained a white capitalist class, a higher paid white labor group, and a cheaper, non-white labor group. Conditions in Europe and around the world, and not skin color, yield such models. White capitalists would gladly dispense with and undercut their white working-class brethren if they could, and have done so whenever they had the opportunity. In the words of one agitator for excluding Chinese from the U.S. Pacific coast: "I have seen men . . . American born, who certainly would, if I may use a

strong expression, employ devils from Hell if the devils would work for 25 cents less than a white man" (cited in Daniels and Kitano, 1970:43).

In addition, cases have occurred of white workers playing the role of cheap labor, and facing the same kind of ethnic antagonism as non-white workers. Consider the riots against Italian strikebreakers in the coal fields of Pennsylvania in 1874 (Higham, 1965:47–8). In the words of one writer: "Unions resented the apparently inexhaustible cheap and relatively docile labor supply which was streaming from Europe obviously for the benefit of their employers" (Wittke, 1953:10).

Even when no ethnic differences exist, split labor markets may produce ethnic-like antagonism. Carey McWilliams (1945:82–3) describes an instance:

During the depression years, "Old Stock"—that is, white, Protestant, Anglo-Saxon Americans, from Oklahoma, Arkansas, and Texas—were roundly denounced in California as "interlopers." The same charges were made against them that were made against the Japanese: they were "dirty"; they had "enormous families"; they engaged in unfair competition; they threatened to "invade" the state and to "undermine" its institutions. During these turgid years (1930–1938) California attempted *to exclude*, by various extra-legal devices, those yeoman farmers just as it had excluded the Chinese and Japanese. "Okies" were "inferior" and "immoral." There was much family discord when Okie girl met California boy, and vice versa. . . . The prejudice against the Okies was obviously not "race" prejudice; yet it functioned in much the same manner.

CONCLUSION

Obviously, this type of three-way conflict is not the only important factor in ethnic relations. But it does help explain some puzzles, including, of course, the exclusion–caste anomaly. For example, Philip Mason (1970:64) develops a typology of race relations and finds that it relates to numerical proportions without being able to explain the dynamic behind this correlation. Table 2 presents a modified version of his chart. My theory can explain these relationships. Paternalism arises in situations where the cleavage between business and labor corresponds to an ethnic difference. A small business elite rules a large group of workers who entered the labor market at approximately the same price or strength. No split labor market existed, hence no ethnic caste system arises. The higher proportion of the dominant ethnicity under "Domination" means that part of the dominant group must be working class. A labor element that shares ethnicity with people who have sufficient resources to become the business elite is generally likely to come from a fairly wealthy country and have resources of its own. Such systems are likely to develop split labor markets. Finally, competition has under it societies whose cheaper labor groups have not been a major threat because the indigenous population available as cheap labor has been small and/or exclusion has effectively kept business groups from importing cheap labor in large numbers.

This theory helps elucidate other observations. One is the underlying similarity in the situation of blacks and women. Another is the history of political sympathy between California and the South. And, a third is the conservatism of the American white working class, or what Daniels and Kitano (1970:45) consider to be an "essential paradox of American life: [that] movements for economic democracy have usually been violently opposed to a thorough-going ethnic democracy." Without having to resort to psychological constructs like "authoritarianism," this theory is able to explain the apparent paradox.

In sum, in comparing those countries with the most ethnic antagonism with those having the least, it is evident that the difference does not lie in the fact that the former are Protestant and the latter Catholic: Protestants are found in all three of Mason's types, and Hawaii is a Protestant dominated territory. It does not lie in whether the dominant or subordinate group moves: South Africa and the deep south show opposite patterns of movement. It is evident that some of the most antagonistic territories have been British colonies, but not all British colonies have had this attribute.

TABLE 2

Numerical Proportion of Dominant to Subordinate Ethnic Groups*

	Category	
Domination	Paternalism	Competition
	Situations	
South Africa	Nigeria	Britain
(1960)	(1952)	(1968)
1–4	1–2000	50–1
U.S. South	Nyasaland	U.S. North
(1960)	(1966)	(1960)
4–1	1–570	15–1
Rhodesia	Tanganyika	New Zealand
(1960)		
1–16	1–450	13–1
	Uganda	
	1–650	

*Adapted from Mason (1970:64).

The characteristic that those British colonies and other societies high on ethnic antagonism share is that they all have a powerful white, or more generally higher paid, working class.

NOTES

1. I do not wish to enter the debate over the applicability of the term "caste" to race relations (cf. Cox, 1948; Davis, *et al.*, 1941). It is used here only for convenience and implies no particular theoretical bent.

2. The term "exclusion" has not usually been applied to immigrant quotas imposed on eastern and southern European immigrants; but such restrictions were, in effect, indistinguishable from the restrictions placed on Japanese immigration.

3. This usage contrasts with that of van den Berghe (1967a:9–10) who reserves the term "ethnic" for groups socially defined by cultural differences. In his definition, ethnicity is not necessarily inherited. I would contend that, while persons of mixed ancestry may be problematic and are often

assigned arbitrarily by the societies in which they reside, inheritance is implied in the common application of the word.

4. Sojourners often use their political resources and low price of labor to enter business for themselves. . . . This does not remove the split in the labor market, though it makes the conflict more complex.

5. It is, of course, no accident that color and resources have been historically related. Poverty among non-white nations has in part resulted from European imperialism. Nevertheless, I would argue that the critical factor in the development of ethnic segmentation in a country is the meeting that occurs in the labor market of that country. The larger economic forces help determine the resources of entering parties, but it is not such forces to which workers respond. Rather they react to the immediate conflicts and threats in their daily lives.

6. Such a split was not found in the early Cape Colony, where business was one ethnicity—white, and labor another—non-white. Actually in neither case was the ethnic composition simple or homogeneous; but the important fact is that, among the laborers, who included so-called Hottentots, and slaves from Madagascar, Moçambique and the East Indies (cf. van den Berghe, 1967b:14), no element was significantly more expensive. The early Cape is thus structurally similar, in terms of the variables I consider important, to countries like Brazil and Mexico. And it is also noted for its "softened" tone of race relations as reflected in such practices as intermarriage.

7. Ethnically based labor aristocracies are much less sensitive about cheap labor in any form than are systems that do not arrive at this resolution because they are protected from it. Thus, Sutherland and Cressey (1970:561–2) report that both the deep south and South Africa continue to use various forms of prison contract labor, in contrast to the northern U.S. where the contract system was attacked by rising labor organizations as early as 1880.

REFERENCES

Bailey, Thomas A. 1934. Theodore Roosevelt and the Japanese-American Crises. Stanford: Stanford University Press.

Becker, Gary. 1957. The Economics of Discrimination. Chicago: University of Chicago Press.

Berg, E. J. 1966. "Backward-sloping labor supply functions in dual economies—the Africa case." Pp. 114–36 in Immanuel Wallerstein (ed.), Social Change: The Colonial Situation. New York: Wiley.

Blalock, H. M., Jr. 1967. Toward a Theory of Minority-Group Relations. New York: Wiley.

Blauner, Robert. 1969. "Internal colonialism and ghetto revolt." Social Problems 16 (Spring): 393–408.

Cox, Oliver C. 1948. Caste, Class and Race. New York: Modern Reader.

Daniels, Roger. 1966. The Politics of Prejudice. Gloucester, Massachusetts: Peter Smith.

Daniels, Roger, and Harry H. L. Kitano. 1970. American Racism. Englewood Cliffs: Prentice-Hall.

Davis, Allison W., B. B. Gardner, and M. R. Gardner. 1941. Deep South. Chicago: University of Chicago Press.

Despres, Leo A. 1969. "Differential adaptations and micro-cultural evolution in Guyana." Southwestern Journal of Anthropology 25 (Spring):14–44.

Doxey, G. V. 1961. The Industrial Colour Bar in South Africa. Cape Town: Oxford University Press.

Ferguson-Davie, C. J. 1952. The Early History of Indians in Natal. Johannesburg: South African Institute of Race Relations.

Gillion, K. L. 1962. Fiji's Indian Migrants. Melbourne: Oxford University Press.

Harris, Marvin. 1964. Patterns of Race in the Americas. New York: Walker.

Heneman, H. G., and Dale Yoder. 1965. Labor Economics. Cincinnati: Southwestern.

Higham, John. 1965. Strangers in the Land. New York: Atheneum.

Hutchison, Emilie J. 1968. Women's Wages. New York: Ams Press.

Ichihashi, Yamato. 1932. Japanese in the United States. Stanford: Stanford University Press.

Iwata, Masakazu. 1962. "The Japanese immigrants in California agriculture." Agricultural History 36 (January):25–37.

King, Cameron H., Jr. 1908. "Asiatic exclusion." International Socialist Review 8 (May):661–669.

Lenin, V. I. 1964. "Imperialism and the split in socialism." Pp. 105–120 in Collected Works, Volume 23, August 1916–March 1917. Moscow: Progress.

Lieberson, Stanley. 1961. "A societal theory of race and ethnic relations." American Sociological Review 26 (December):902–910.

Lind, Andrew W. 1968. An Island Community. New York: Greenwood.

Loewen, James W. 1971. The Mississippi Chinese. Cambridge: Harvard University Press.

Mason, Philip. 1970. Patterns of Dominance. London: Oxford University Press.

McWilliams, Carey. 1945. Prejudice: Japanese-Americans. Boston: Little, Brown.

Millis, H. A. 1915. The Japanese Problem in the United States. New York: Macmillan.

Moles, I. N. 1968. "The Indian coolie labour issue." Pp. 40–48 in A. T. Yarwood (ed.), Attitudes to Non-European Immigration. Melbourne: Cassell Australia.

Noel, Donald L. 1968. "A theory of the origin of ethnic stratification." Social Problems 16 (Fall):157–172.

Reich, Michael. 1971. "The economics of racism." Pp. 107–113 in David M. Gordon (ed.), Problems in Political Economy. Lexington, Massachusetts: Heath.

Schermerhorn, R. A. 1970. Comparative Ethnic Relations. New York: Random House.

Shibutani, Tamotsu, and Kian M. Kwan. 1965. Ethnic Stratification. New York: Macmillan.

Siu, Paul C. P. 1952. "The sojourner." American Journal of Sociology 58 (July):34–44.

Sutherland, Edwin H., and Donald R. Cressey. 1970. Criminology. Philadelphia: Lippincott.

van den Berghe, Pierre L. 1966. "Paternalistic versus competitive race relations: an ideal-type approach." Pp. 53–69 in Bernard E. Segal (ed.), Racial and Ethnic Relations. New York: Crowell.

——. 1967a. Race and Racism. New York: Wiley.

——. 1967b. South Africa: A Study in Conflict. Berkeley: University of California Press.

Van der Horst, Sheila T. 1965. "The effects of industrialization on race relations in South Africa." Pp. 97–140 in Guy Hunter (ed.), Industrialization and Race Relations. London: Oxford University Press.

Willard, Myra. 1967. History of the White Australia Policy to 1920. London: Melbourne University Press.

Williams, Eric. 1944. Capitalism and Slavery. Chapel Hill: University of North Carolina Press.

Wittke, Carl. 1953. "Immigration policy prior to World War I." Pp. 1–10 in Benjamin M. Ziegler (ed.), Immigration: An American Dilemma. Boston: Heath.

Yarwood, A. T. 1964. Asian Immigration to Australia. London: Cambridge University Press.

Yarwood, A. T. (ed.). 1968. Attitudes to Non-European Immigration. Melbourne: Cassell Australia.

10

Sponsored and Contest Mobility and the School System

Ralph H. Turner

THIS PAPER SUGGESTS A FRAMEWORK FOR relating certain differences between American and English systems of education to the prevailing norms of upward mobility in each country. Others have noted the tendency of educational systems to support prevailing schemes of stratification, but this discussion concerns specifically the manner in which the *accepted mode of upward mobility* shapes the school system directly and indirectly through its effects on the values which implement social control.

Two ideal-typical normative patterns of upward mobility are described and their ramifications in the general patterns of stratification and social control are suggested. In addition to showing relationships among a number of differences between American and English schooling, the ideal-types have broader implications than those developed in this paper: they suggest a major dimension of stratification which might be profitably incorporated into a variety of studies in social class; and they readily can be applied in further comparisons between other countries.

THE NATURE OF ORGANIZING NORMS

Many investigators have concerned themselves with rates of upward mobility in specific countries or internationally,[1] and with the manner in which

school systems facilitate or impede such mobility.[2] But preoccupation with the *extent* of mobility has precluded equal attention to the predominant *modes* of mobility. The central assumption underlying this paper is that within a formally open class system that provides for mass education the organizing folk norm which defines the accepted mode of upward mobility is a crucial factor in shaping the school system, and may be even more crucial than the extent of upward mobility. In England and the United States there appear to be different organizing folk norms, here termed *sponsored mobility* and *contest mobility*, respectively. *Contest* mobility is a system in which elite[3] status is the prize in an open contest and is taken by the aspirants' own efforts. While the "contest" is governed by some rules of fair play, the contestants have wide latitude in the strategies they may employ. Since the "prize" of successful upward mobility is not in the hands of an established elite to give out, the latter can not determine who shall attain it and who shall not. Under *sponsored* mobility elite recruits are chosen by the established elite or their agents, and elite status is *given* on the basis of some criterion of supposed merit and cannot be *taken* by any amount of effort or strategy. Upward mobility is like entry into a private club where each candidate must be "sponsored" by one or more of the members. Ultimately the members grant or deny upward mobility on the basis of whether they judge the candidate to have those qualities they wish to see in fellow members. . . .

Ralph H. Turner. "Sponsored and Contest Mobility and the School System" from *American Sociological Review* 25, December 1960.

SOCIAL CONTROL AND
THE TWO NORMS

Every society must cope with the problem of maintaining loyalty to its social system and does so in part through norms and values, only some of which vary by class position. Norms and values especially prevalent within a given class must direct behavior into channels that support the total system, while those that transcend strata must support the general class differential. The way in which upward mobility takes place determines in part the kinds of norms and values that serve the indicated purposes of social control in each class and throughout the society.

The most conspicuous control problem is that of ensuring loyalty in the disadvantaged classes toward a system in which their members receive less than a proportional share of society's goods. In a system of contest mobility this is accomplished by a combination of futuristic orientation, the norm of ambition, and a general sense of fellowship with the elite. Each individual is encouraged to think of himself as competing for an elite position so that loyalty to the system and conventional attitudes are cultivated in the process of preparation for this possibility. It is essential that this futuristic orientation be kept alive by delaying a sense of final irreparable failure to reach elite status until attitudes are well established. By thinking of himself in the successful future the elite aspirant forms considerable identification with elitists, and evidence that they are merely ordinary human beings like himself helps to reinforce this identification as well as to keep alive the conviction that he himself may someday succeed in like manner. To forestall rebellion among the disadvantaged majority, then, a contest system must avoid absolute points of selection for mobility and immobility and must delay clear recognition of the realities of the situation until the individual is too committed to the system to change radically. A futuristic orientation cannot, of course, be inculcated successfully in all members of lower strata, but sufficient internalization of a norm of ambition tends to leave the unambitious as individual deviants and to forestall the latter's

formation of a genuine subcultural group able to offer collective threat to the established system. Where this kind of control system operates rather effectively it is notable that organized or gang deviancy is more likely to take the form of an attack upon the conventional or moral order rather than upon the class system itself. Thus the United States has its "beatniks"[4] who repudiate ambition and most worldly values and its delinquent and criminal gangs who try to evade the limitations imposed by conventional means,[5] but very few active revolutionaries.

These social controls are inappropriate in a system of sponsorship since the elite recruits are chosen from above. The principal threat to the system would lie in the existence of a strong group the members of which sought to *take* elite positions themselves. Control under this system is maintained by training the "masses" to regard themselves as relatively incompetent to manage society, by restricting access to the skills and manners of the elite, and by cultivating belief in the superior competence of the elite. The earlier that selection of the elite recruits is made the sooner others can be taught to accept their inferiority and to make "realistic" rather than fantasy plans. Early selection prevents raising the hopes of large numbers of people who might otherwise become the discontented leaders of a class challenging the sovereignty of the established elite. If it is assumed that the difference in competence between masses and elite is seldom so great as to support the usual differences in the advantages accruing to each,[6] then the differences must be artificially augmented by discouraging acquisition of elite skills by the masses. Thus a sense of mystery about the elite is a common device for supporting in the masses the illusion of a much greater hiatus of competence than in fact exists.

While elitists are unlikely to reject a system that benefits them, they must still be restrained from taking such advantage of their favorable situation as to jeopardize the entire elite. Under the sponsorship system the elite recruits—who are selected early, freed from the strain of competitive struggle, and kept under close supervision—may be thoroughly indoctrinated in elite culture. A norm of paternalism toward inferiors may be inculcated, a heightened sensitivity to the good opinion of fellow elitists and elite recruits may be cultivated, and the appreciation of the more complex forms of aesthetic, literary, intellectual, and sporting activities may be taught. Norms of courtesy and altruism easily can be maintained under sponsorship since elite recruits are not required to compete for their standing and since the elite may deny high standing to those who strive for position by "unseemly" methods. The system of sponsorship provides an almost perfect setting for the development of an elite culture characterized by a sense of responsibility for "inferiors" and for preservation of the "finer things" of life.

Elite control in the contest system is more difficult since there is no controlled induction and apprenticeship. The principal regulation seems to lie in the insecurity of elite position. In a sense there is no "final arrival" because each person may be displaced by newcomers throughout his life. The limited control of high standing from above prevents the clear delimitation of levels in the class system, so that success itself becomes relative: each success, rather than an accomplishment, serves to qualify the participant for competition at the next higher level.[7] The restraints upon the behavior of a person of high standing, therefore, are principally those applicable to a contestant who must not risk the "ganging up" of other contestants, and who must pay some attention to the masses who are frequently in a position to impose penalties upon him. But any special norm of paternalism is hard to establish since there is no dependable procedure for examining the means by which one achieves elite credentials. While mass esteem is an effective brake upon over-exploitation of position, it rewards scrupulously ethical and altruistic behavior much less than evidence of fellow-feeling with the masses themselves.

Under both systems, unscrupulous or disreputable persons may become or remain members of the elite, but for different reasons. In contest mobility, popular tolerance of a little craftiness in the successful newcomer, together with the fact that he does not have to undergo the close scrutiny of the old elite, leaves considerable leeway for unscrupulous success. In sponsored mobility, the unpromising recruit reflects unfavorably on the judgments of his sponsors and threatens the myth of elite omniscience; consequently he may be tolerated and others may "cover up" for his deficiencies in order to protect the unified front of the elite to the outer world.

Certain of the general values and norms of any society reflect emulation of elite values by the masses. Under sponsored mobility, a good deal of the protective attitudes toward and interest in classical subjects percolates to the masses. Under contest mobility, however, there is not the same degree of homogeneity of moral, aesthetic, and intellectual values to be emulated, so that the conspicuous attribute of the elite is its high level of material consumption—emulation itself follows this course. There is neither effective incentive nor punishment for the elitist who fails to interest himself in promoting the arts or literary excellence, or who continues to maintain the vulgar manners and mode of speech of his class origin. The elite has relatively less power and the masses relatively more power to punish or reward a man for his adoption or disregard of any special elite culture. The great importance of accent and of grammatical excellence in the attainment of high status in England as contrasted with the twangs and drawls and grammatical ineptitude among American elites is the most striking example of this difference. In a contest system, the class order does not function to support the *quality* of aesthetic, literary, and intellectual activities; only those well versed in such matters are qualified to distinguish authentic products from cheap imitations. Unless those who claim superiority in these areas are forced to submit their credentials to the elite for evaluation, poor quality is often honored equally with high quality and class prestige does not serve to maintain an effective norm of high quality.

This is not to imply that there are no groups in a "contest" society devoted to the protection and fostering of high standards in art, music, literature, and intellectual pursuits, but that such standards lack the support of the class system which is frequently found when sponsored mobility prevails. In California, the selection by official welcoming committees of a torch singer to entertain a visiting king and queen and "can-can" dancers to entertain Mr. Khrushchev illustrates how American elites can assume that high prestige and popular taste go together.

FORMAL EDUCATION

Returning to the conception of an organizing ideal norm, we assume that to the extent to which one such norm of upward mobility is prevalent in a society there are constant strains to shape the educational system into conformity with that norm. These strains operate in two fashions: directly, by blinding people to alternatives and coloring their judgments of successful and unsuccessful solutions to recurring educational problems; indirectly, through the functional interrelationships between school systems and the class structure, systems of social control, and other features of the social structure which are neglected in this paper.

The most obvious application of the distinction between sponsored and contest mobility norms affords a partial explanation for the different policies of student selection in the English and American secondary schools. Although American high school students follow different courses of study and a few attend specialized schools, a major educational preoccupation has been to avoid any sharp social separation between the superior and inferior students and to keep the channels of movement between courses of study as open as possible. Recent criticisms of the way in which superior students may be thereby held back in their development usually are nevertheless qualified by the insistence that these students must not be withdrawn from the mainstream of student life.[8] Such segregation offends the sense of fairness implicit in the contest norm and also arouses the fear that the elite and future elite will lose their sense of fellowship with the masses. Perhaps the most important point, however, is that schooling is presented as an opportunity, and making use of it depends primarily on the student's own initiative and enterprise.

The English system has undergone a succession of liberalizing changes during this century, but all of them have retained the attempt to sort out early in the educational program the promising from the unpromising so that the former may be segregated and given a special form of training to fit them for higher standing in their adult years. Under the Education Act of 1944, a minority of students has been selected each year by means of a battery of examinations popularly known as "eleven plus," supplemented in varying degrees by grade school records and personal interviews, for admission to grammar schools.[9] The remaining students attend secondary modern or technical schools in which the opportunities to prepare for college or to train for the more prestigeful occupations are minimal. The grammar schools supply what by comparative standards is a high quality of college preparatory education. Of course, such a scheme embodies the logic of sponsorship, with early selection of those destined for middle-class and higher-status occupations, and specialized training to prepare each group for its destined class position. This plan facilitates considerable mobility, and recent research reveals surprisingly little bias against children from manual laboring-class families in the selection for grammar school, when related to measured intelligence.[10] It is altogether possible that adequate comparative study would show a closer correlation of school success with measured intelligence and a lesser correlation between school success and family background in England than in the United States. While selection of superior students for mobility opportunity is probably more efficient under such a system, the obstacles for persons not so selected of "making the grade" on the basis of their own initiative or enterprise are probably correspondingly greater. . . .

EFFECTS OF MOBILITY ON PERSONALITY

Brief note may be made of the importance of the distinction between sponsored and contest mobility with relation to the supposed effects of upward mobility on personality development. Not a great deal is yet known about the "mobile personality" nor about the specific features of importance to the personality in the mobility experience.[11] However, today three aspects of this experience are most frequently stressed: first, the stress or tension involved in striving for status higher than that of others under more difficult conditions than they; second, the complication of interpersonal relations introduced by the necessity to abandon lower-level friends in favor of uncertain acceptance into higher-level circles; third, the problem of working out an adequate personal scheme of values in the face of movement between classes marked by somewhat variant or even contradictory value systems.[12] The impact of each of these three mobility problems, it is suggested, differ depending upon whether the pattern is that of the contest or of sponsorship.

Under the sponsorship system, recruits are selected early, segregated from their class peers, grouped with other recruits and with youth from the class to which they are moving, and trained specifically for membership in this class. Since the selection is made early, the mobility experience should be relatively free from the strain that comes with a series of elimination tests and long-extended uncertainty of success. The segregation and the integrated group life of the "public" school or grammar school should help to clarify the mobile person's social ties. (One investigator failed to discover clique formation along lines of social class in a sociometric study of a number of grammar schools.[13]) The problem of a system of values may be largely met when the elite recruit is taken from his parents and peers to be placed in a boarding school, though it may be less well clarified for the grammar school boy who returns each evening to his working-class family. Undoubtedly this latter limitation has something to do with the observed failure of working-class boys to continue through the last years of grammar school and into the universities.[14] In general, then, the factors stressed as affecting personality formation among the upwardly mobile probably are rather specific to the contest system, or to [an] incompletely functioning sponsorship system.

NOTES

This is an expanded version of a paper presented at the Fourth World Congress of Sociology, 1959, and abstracted in the *Transactions* of the Congress. Special indebtedness should be expressed to Jean Floud and Hilde Himmelweit for helping to acquaint the author with the English school system.

1. A comprehensive summary of such studies appears in Seymour M. Lipset and Reinhard Bendix, *Social Mobility in Industrial Society*, Berkeley and Los Angeles: University of California Press, 1959.

2. *Cf.* C. A. Anderson, "The Social Status of University Students in Relation to Type of Economy: An International Comparison," *Transactions of the Third World Congress of Sociology*, London, 1956, Vol. V, pp. 51–63; J. E. Floud, *Social Class and Educational Opportunity*, London: Heinemann, 1956; W. L. Warner, R. J. Havighurst, and M. B. Loeb, *Who Shall Be Educated?* New York: Harper, 1944.

3. Reference is made throughout the paper to "elite" and "masses." The generalizations, however, are intended to apply throughout the stratification continuum to relations between members of a given class and the class or classes above it. Statements about mobility are intended in general to apply to mobility from manual to middle-class levels, lower-middle to upper-middle class, and so on, as well as into the strictly elite groups. The simplified expressions avoid the repeated use of cumbersome and involved statements which might otherwise be required.

4. See, e.g., Lawrence Lipton, *The Holy Barbarians*, New York: Messner, 1959.

5. *Cf.* Albert K. Cohen, *Delinquent Boys: The Culture of the Gang*, Glencoe, Ill.: Free Press, 1955.

6. D. V. Glass, editor, *Social Mobility in Britain*, Glencoe, Ill.: Free Press, 1954, pp. 144–145, reports studies showing only small variations in intelligence between occupational levels.

7. Geoffrey Gorer, *The American People*, New York: Norton, 1948, pp. 172–187.

8. See, e.g., *Los Angeles Times*, May 4, 1959, Part I, p. 24.

9. The nature and operation of the "eleven plus" system are fully reviewed in a report by a committee of the British Psychological Society and in a report of extensive research into the adequacy of selection methods. See P. E. Vernon, editor, *Secondary School Selection: A British Psychological Inquiry*, London: Methuen, 1957; and Alfred Yates and D. A. Pidgeon, *Admission to Grammar Schools*, London: Newnes Educational Publishing Co., 1957.

10. J. E. Floud, A. H. Halsey, and F. M. Martin, *Social Class and Educational Opportunity*, London: Heinemann, 1956.

11. *Cf.* Lipset and Bendix, *op. cit.*, pp. 250 ff.

12. See, e.g., August B. Hollingshead and Frederick C. Redlich, *Social Class and Mental Illness*, New York: Wiley, 1958; W. Lloyd Warner and James C. Abegglen, *Big Business Leaders in America*, New York: Harper, 1955; Warner *et al.*, *Who Shall Be Educated?*, *op. cit.*; Peter M. Blau, "Social Mobility and Interpersonal Relations," *American Sociological Review*, 21 (June, 1956), pp. 290–300.

13. A. N. Oppenheim, "Social Status and Clique Formation among Grammar School Boys," *British Journal of Sociology*, 6 (September, 1955), pp. 228–245. Oppenheim's findings may be compared with A. B. Hollingshead, *Elmtown's Youth*, New York: Wiley, 1949, pp. 204–242. See also Joseph A. Kahl, *The American Class Structure*, New York: Rinehart, 1957, pp. 129–138.

14. Floud *et al.*, *op. cit.*, pp. 115 ff.

11

Some Principles of Stratification

Kingsley Davis and Wilbert E. Moore

IN A PREVIOUS PAPER SOME CONCEPTS FOR HANDLING the phenomena of social inequality were presented.[1] In the present paper a further step in stratification theory is undertaken—an attempt to show the relationship between stratification and the rest of the social order.[2] Starting from the proposition that no society is "classless," or unstratified, an effort is made to explain, in functional terms, the universal necessity which calls forth stratification in any social system. Next, an attempt is made to explain the roughly uniform distribution of prestige as between the major types of positions in every society. Since, however, there occur between one society and another great differences in the degree and kind of stratification, some attention is also given to the varieties of social inequality and the variable factors that give rise to them.

Clearly, the present task requires two different lines of analysis—one to understand the universal, the other to understand the variable features of stratification. Naturally each line of inquiry aids the other and is indispensable, and in the treatment that follows the two will be interwoven, although, because of space limitations, the emphasis will be on the universals.

Kingsley Davis and Wilbert E. Moore. "Some Principles of Stratification" from the *American Sociological Review* 10, April 1945.

Throughout, it will be necessary to keep in mind one thing—namely, that the discussion relates to the system of positions, not to the individuals occupying those positions. It is one thing to ask why different positions carry different degrees of prestige, and quite another to ask how certain individuals get into those positions. Although, as the argument will try to show, both questions are related, it is essential to keep them separate in our thinking. Most of the literature on stratification has tried to answer the second question (particularly with regard to the ease or difficulty of mobility between strata) without tackling the first. The first question, however, is logically prior and, in the case of any particular individual or group, factually prior.

THE FUNCTIONAL NECESSITY OF STRATIFICATION

Curiously the main functional necessity explaining the universal presence of stratification is precisely the requirement faced by any society of placing and motivating individuals in the social structure. As a functioning mechanism a society must somehow distribute its members in social positions and induce them to perform the duties of these positions. It must thus concern itself with motivation at two different levels: to instill in the proper individuals the desire to fill certain positions, and, once in these positions, the desire to perform the duties attached to them. Even though the social order may be relatively static in form, there is a continuous process of metabolism as new individuals are born into it, shift with age, and die off. Their absorption into the positional system must somehow be arranged and motivated. This is true whether the system is competitive or non-competitive. A competitive system gives greater importance to the motivation to achieve positions, whereas a non-competitive system gives perhaps greater importance to the motivation to perform the duties of the positions; but in any system both types of motivation are required.

If the duties associated with the various positions were all equally pleasant to the human organism, all equally important to societal survival, and all equally in need of the same ability or talent, it would make no difference who got into which positions, and the problem of social placement would be greatly reduced. But actually it does make a great deal of difference who gets into which positions, not only because some positions are inherently more agreeable than others, but also because some require special talents or training and some are functionally more important than others. Also, it is essential that the duties of the positions be performed with the diligence that their importance requires. Inevitably, then, a society must have, first, some kind of rewards that it can use as inducements, and, second, some way of distributing these rewards differentially according to positions. The rewards and their distribution become a part of the social order, and thus give rise to stratification.

One may ask what kind of rewards a society has at its disposal in distributing its personnel and securing essential services. It has, first of all, the things that contribute to sustenance and comfort. It has, second, the things that contribute to humor and diversion. And it has, finally, the things that contribute to self respect and ego expansion. The last, because of the peculiarly social character of the self, is largely a function of the opinion of others, but it nonetheless ranks in importance with the first two. In any social system all three kinds of rewards must be dispensed differentially according to positions.

In a sense the rewards are "built into" the position. They consist in the "rights" associated with the position, plus what may be called its accompaniments or perquisites. Often the rights, and sometimes the accompaniments, are functionally related to the duties of the position. (Rights as viewed by the incumbent are usually duties as viewed by other members of the community.) However, there may be a host of subsidiary rights and perquisites that are not essential to the function of the position and have only an indirect and symbolic connection with its duties, but which still may be of considerable importance in inducing people to seek the positions and fulfill the essential duties.

If the rights and perquisites of different positions in a society must be unequal, then the society must be stratified, because that is precisely what stratification means. Social inequality is thus an unconsciously evolved device by which societies insure that the most important positions are conscientiously filled by the most qualified persons. Hence every society, no matter how simple or complex, must differentiate persons in terms of both prestige and esteem, and must therefore possess a certain amount of institutionalized inequality.

It does not follow that the amount or type of inequality need be the same in all societies. This is largely a function of factors that will be discussed presently.

THE TWO DETERMINANTS OF POSITIONAL RANK

Granting the general function that inequality subserves, one can specify the two factors that determine the relative rank of different positions. In general those positions convey the best reward, and hence have the highest rank, which (a) have the greatest importance for the society and (b) require the greatest training or talent. The first factor concerns function and is a matter of relative significance; the second concerns means and is a matter of scarcity.

Differential Functional Importance

Actually a society does not need to reward positions in proportion to their functional importance. It merely needs to give sufficient reward to them to insure that they will be filled competently. In other words, it must see that less essential positions do not compete successfully with more essential ones. If a position is easily filled, it need not be heavily rewarded, even though important. On the other hand, if it is important but hard to fill, the reward must be high enough to get it filled anyway. Functional importance is therefore a necessary but not a sufficient cause of high rank being assigned to a position.[3]

Differential Scarcity of Personnel

Practically all positions, no matter how acquired, require some form of skill or capacity for performance. This is implicit in the very notion of position, which implies that the incumbent must, by virtue of his incumbency, accomplish certain things.

There are, ultimately, only two ways in which a person's qualifications come about: through inherent capacity or through training. Obviously, in concrete activities both are always necessary, but from a practical standpoint the scarcity may lie primarily in one or the other, as well as in both. Some positions require innate talents of such high degree that the persons who fill them are bound to be rare. In many cases, however, talent is fairly abundant in the population but the training process is so long, costly, and elaborate that relatively few can qualify. Modern medicine, for example, is within the mental capacity of most individuals, but a medical education is so burdensome and expensive that virtually none would undertake it if the position of the M.D. did not carry a reward commensurate with the sacrifice.

If the talents required for a position are abundant and the training easy, the method of acquiring the position may have little to do with its duties. There may be, in fact, a virtually accidental relationship. But if the skills required are scarce by reason of the rarity of talent or the costliness of training, the position, if functionally important, must have an attractive power that will draw the necessary skills in competition with other positions. This means, in effect, that the position must be high in the social scale—must command great prestige, high salary, ample leisure, and the like.

How Variations Are to Be Understood

In so far as there is a difference between one system of stratification and another, it is attributable to whatever factors affect the two determinants of differential reward—namely, functional importance and scarcity of personnel. Positions important in one society may not be important in another, because the conditions faced by the societies, or their degree of internal development, may be different. The same conditions, in turn, may affect the question of scarcity; for in some societies the stage of development, or the external situation, may wholly obviate the necessity of certain kinds of skill or talent. Any particular system of stratification, then, can be understood as a product of the special conditions affecting the two aforementioned grounds of differential reward.

MAJOR SOCIETAL FUNCTIONS AND STRATIFICATION

Religion

The reason why religion is necessary is apparently to be found in the fact that human society achieves its unity primarily through the possession by its members of certain ultimate values and ends in common. Although these values and ends are subjective, they influence behavior, and their integration enables the society to operate as a system. Derived neither from inherited nor from external nature, they have evolved as a part of culture by communication and moral pressure. They must, however, appear to the members of the society to have some reality, and it is the role of religious belief and ritual to supply and reinforce this appearance of reality. Through belief and ritual the common ends and values are connected with an imaginary world symbolized by concrete sacred objects, which world in turn is related in a meaningful way to the facts and trials of the individual's life. Through the worship of the sacred objects and the beings they symbolize, and the acceptance of supernatural prescriptions that are at the same time codes of behavior, a powerful control over human conduct is exercised, guiding it along lines sustaining the institutional structure and conforming to the ultimate ends and values.

If this conception of the role of religion is true, one can understand why in every known society the religious activities tend to be under the charge of particular persons, who tend thereby to enjoy greater rewards than the ordinary societal member. Certain of the rewards and special privileges may attach to only the highest religious functionaries, but others usually apply, if such exists, to the entire sacerdotal class.

Moreover, there is a peculiar relation between the duties of the religious official and the special privileges he enjoys. If the supernatural world governs the destinies of men more ultimately than does the real world, its earthly representative, the person through whom one may communicate with the supernatural, must be a powerful individual. He is a keeper of sacred tradition, a skilled performer of the ritual, and an interpreter of lore and myth. He is in such close contact with the gods that he is viewed as possessing some of their characteristics. He is, in short, a bit sacred, and hence free from some of the more vulgar necessities and controls.

It is no accident, therefore, that religious functionaries have been associated with the very highest positions of power, as in theocratic regimes. Indeed, looking at it from this point of view, one may wonder why it is that they do not get *entire* control over their societies. The factors that prevent this are worthy of note.

In the first place, the amount of technical competence necessary for the performance of religious duties is small. Scientific or artistic capacity is not required. Anyone can set himself up as enjoying an intimate relation with deities, and nobody can successfully dispute him. Therefore, the factor of scarcity of personnel does not operate in the technical sense.

One may assert, on the other hand, that religious ritual is often elaborate and religious lore abstruse, and that priestly ministrations require tact, if not intelligence. This is true, but the technical requirements of the profession are for the most part adventitious, not related to the end in the same way that science is related to air travel. The priest can never be free from competition, since the criteria of whether or not one has genuine contact with the supernatural are never strictly clear. It is this competition that debases the priestly position below what might be expected at first glance. That is why priestly prestige is highest in those societies where membership in the profession is rigidly controlled by the priestly guild itself. That is why, in part at least, elaborate devices are utilized to stress the identification of the person with his office — spectacular costume, abnormal conduct, special diet, segregated residence, celibacy, conspicuous leisure, and the like. In fact, the priest is always in danger of becoming somewhat discredited — as happens in a secularized society — because in a world of stubborn fact, ritual and sacred knowledge alone will not grow crops or build houses. Furthermore, unless he is protected by a professional guild, the priest's identification with the supernatural tends to preclude his acquisition of abundant worldly goods.

As between one society and another it seems that the highest general position awarded the priest occurs in the medieval type of social order. Here there is enough economic production to afford a surplus, which can be used to support a numerous and highly organized priesthood; and yet the populace is unlettered and therefore credulous to a high degree. Perhaps the most extreme example is to be found in the Buddhism of Tibet, but others are encountered in the Catholicism of feudal Europe, the Inca regime of Peru, the Brahminism of India, and the Mayan priesthood of Yucatan. On the other hand, if the society is so crude as to have no surplus and little differentiation, so that every priest must be also a cultivator or hunter, the separation of the priestly status from the others has hardly gone far enough for priestly prestige to mean much. When the priest actually has high prestige under these circumstances, it is because he also performs other important functions (usually political and medical).

In an extremely advanced society built on scientific technology, the priesthood tends to lose status, because sacred tradition and supernaturalism drop into the background. The ultimate values and common ends of the society tend to be expressed in less anthropomorphic ways, by officials who occupy fundamentally political, economic, or educational rather than religious positions. Nevertheless, it is easily possible for intellectuals to exaggerate the degree to which the priesthood in a presumably secular milieu has lost prestige. When the matter is closely examined the urban proletariat, as well as the rural citizenry, proves to be surprisingly god-fearing and priest-ridden. No society has become so completely secularized as to liquidate entirely the belief in transcendental ends and supernatural entities. Even in a secularized society some system must exist for the integration of ultimate values, for their ritualistic expression, and for the emotional adjustments required by disappointment, death, and disaster.

Government

Like religion, government plays a unique and indispensable part in society. But in contrast to religion, which provides integration in terms of sentiments, beliefs, and rituals, it organizes the society in terms of law and authority. Furthermore, it orients the society to the actual rather than the unseen world.

The main functions of government are, internally, the ultimate enforcement of norms, the final arbitration of conflicting interests, and the overall planning and direction of society; and externally, the handling of war and diplomacy. To carry out these functions it acts as the agent of the entire people, enjoys a monopoly of force, and controls all individuals within its territory.

Political action, by definition, implies authority. An official can command because he has authority, and the citizen must obey because he is subject to that authority. For this reason stratification is inherent in the nature of political relationships.

So clear is the power embodied in political position that political inequality is sometimes thought to comprise all inequality. But it can be shown that there are other bases of stratification, that the following controls operate in practice to keep political power from becoming complete: (a) The fact that the actual holders of political office, and especially those determining top policy must necessarily be few in number compared to the total population. (b) The fact that the rulers represent the interest of the group rather than of themselves, and are therefore restricted in their behavior by rules and mores designed to enforce this limitation of interest. (c) The fact that the holder of political office has his authority by virtue of his office and nothing else, and therefore any special knowledge, talent, or capacity he may claim is purely incidental, so that he often has to depend upon others for technical assistance.

In view of these limiting factors, it is not strange that the rulers often have less power and prestige than a literal enumeration of their formal rights would lead one to expect.

Wealth, Property, and Labor

Every position that secures for its incumbent a livelihood is, by definition, economically rewarded. For this reason there is an economic aspect to those positions (e.g. political and religious) the main function of which is not economic. It therefore becomes convenient for the society to use unequal economic returns as a principal means of controlling the entrance of persons into positions and stimulating the performance of their duties. The amount of the economic return therefore becomes one of the main indices of social status.

It should be stressed, however, that a position does not bring power and prestige *because* it draws a high income. Rather, it draws a high income because it is functionally important and the available personnel is for one reason or another scarce. It is therefore superficial and erroneous to regard high income as the cause of a man's power and prestige, just as it is erroneous to think that a man's fever is the cause of his disease.[4]

The economic source of power and prestige is not income primarily, but the ownership of capital goods (including patents, good will, and professional reputation). Such ownership should be distinguished from the possession of consumers' goods, which is an index rather than a cause of social standing. In other words, the ownership of producers' goods is properly speaking, a source of income like other positions, the income itself remaining an index. Even in situations where social values are widely commercialized and earnings are the readiest method of judging social position, income does not confer prestige on a position so much as it induces people to compete for the position. It is true that a man who has a high income as a result of one position may find this money helpful in climbing into another position as well, but this again reflects the effect of his initial, economically advantageous status, which exercises its influence through the medium of money.

In a system of private property in productive enterprise, an income above what an individual spends can give rise to possession of capital wealth. Presumably such possession is a reward for the proper management of one's finances originally and of the productive enterprise later. But as social differentiation becomes highly advanced and yet the institution of inheritance persists, the phenomenon of pure ownership, and reward for pure ownership, emerges. In such a case it is difficult to prove that the position is functionally important or that the scarcity involved is anything other than extrinsic and accidental. It is for this reason, doubtless, that the institution of private property in productive goods becomes more subject to criticism as social development proceeds toward industrialization. It is only this pure, that is, strictly legal and functionless ownership, however, that is open to attack; for some form of active ownership, whether private or public, is indispensable.

One kind of ownership of production goods consists in rights over the labor of others. The most extremely concentrated and exclusive of such rights are found in slavery, but the essential principle remains in serfdom, peonage, encomienda, and indenture. Naturally this kind of ownership has the greatest significance for stratification, because it necessarily entails an unequal relationship.

But property in capital goods inevitably introduces a compulsive element even into the nominally free contractual relationship. Indeed, in some respects the authority of the contractual employer is greater than that of the feudal landlord, inasmuch as the latter is more limited by traditional reciprocities. Even the classical economics recognized that competitors would fare unequally, but it did not pursue this fact to its necessary conclusion that, however it might be acquired, unequal control of goods and services must give unequal advantage to the parties to a contract.

Technical Knowledge

The function of finding means to single goals, without any concern with the choice between goals, is the exclusively technical sphere. The explanation of why positions requiring great technical skill receive fairly high rewards is easy to see, for it is the simplest case of the rewards being so distributed as to draw talent and motivate training. Why they seldom if ever receive the highest rewards is also clear: the importance of technical knowledge from a societal point of view is never so great as the integration of goals, which takes place on the religious, political, and economic levels. Since the technological level is concerned solely with means, a purely technical position must ultimately be subordinate to other positions that are religious, political, or economic in character.

Nevertheless, the distinction between expert and layman in any social order is fundamental, and cannot be entirely reduced to other terms. Methods of recruitment, as well as of reward, sometimes lead to the erroneous interpretation that technical positions are economically determined. Actually, however, the acquisition of knowledge and skill cannot be accomplished by purchase, although the opportunity to learn may be. The control of the avenues of training may inhere as a sort of property right in certain families or classes, giving them power and prestige in consequence. Such a situation adds an artificial

scarcity to the natural scarcity of skills and talents. On the other hand, it is possible for an opposite situation to arise. The rewards of technical position may be so great that a condition of excess supply is created, leading to at least temporary devaluation of the rewards. Thus "unemployment in the learned professions" may result in a debasement of the prestige of those positions. Such adjustments and readjustments are constantly occurring in changing societies; and it is always well to bear in mind that the efficiency of a stratified structure may be affected by the modes of recruitment for positions. The social order itself, however, sets limits to the inflation or deflation of the prestige of experts: an over-supply tends to debase the rewards and discourage recruitment or produce revolution, whereas an under-supply tends to increase the rewards or weaken the society in competition with other societies.

Particular systems of stratification show a wide range with respect to the exact position of technically competent persons. This range is perhaps most evident in the degree of specialization. Extreme division of labor tends to create many specialists without high prestige since the training is short and the required native capacity relatively small. On the other hand it also tends to accentuate the high position of the true experts—scientists, engineers, and administrators—by increasing their authority relative to other functionally important positions. But the idea of a technocratic social order or a government or priesthood of engineers or social scientists neglects the limitations of knowledge and skills as a basis for performing social functions. To the extent that the social structure is truly specialized the prestige of the technical person must also be circumscribed.

VARIATION IN STRATIFIED SYSTEMS

The generalized principles of stratification here suggested form a necessary preliminary to a consideration of types of stratified systems, because it is in terms of these principles that the types must be described. This can be seen by trying to delineate types according to certain modes of variation. For instance, some of the most important modes (together with the polar types in terms of them) seem to be as follows:

a. The Degree of Specialization

The degree of specialization affects the fineness and multiplicity of the gradations in power and prestige. It also influences the extent to which particular functions may be emphasized in the invidious system, since a given function cannot receive much emphasis in the hierarchy until it has achieved structural separation from the other functions. Finally, the amount of specialization influences the bases of selection. Polar types: *Specialized, Unspecialized.*

b. The Nature of the Functional Emphasis

In general when emphasis is put on sacred matters, a rigidity is introduced that tends to limit specialization and hence the development of technology. In addition, a brake is placed on social mobility, and on the development of bureaucracy. When the preoccupation with the sacred is withdrawn, leaving greater scope for purely secular preoccupations, a great development, and rise in status, of economic and technological positions seemingly takes place. Curiously, a concomitant rise in political position is not likely, because it has usually been allied with the religious and stands to gain little by the decline of the latter. It is also possible for a society to emphasize family functions—as in relatively undifferentiated societies where high mortality requires high fertility and kinship forms the main basis of social organization. Main types: *Familistic, Authoritarian* (*Theocratic* or sacred, and *Totalitarian* or secular), *Capitalistic.*

c. The Magnitude of Invidious Differences

What may be called the amount of social distance between positions, taking into account the entire scale, is something that should lend itself to quantitative measurement. Considerable differences apparently exist between different societies in this regard, and also between parts of the same society. Polar types: *Equalitarian, Inequalitarian.*

d. The Degree of Opportunity

The familiar question of the amount of mobility is different from the question of the comparative equality or inequality of rewards posed above, because the two criteria may vary independently up to a point. For instance, the tremendous divergences in monetary income in the United States are far greater than those found in primitive societies, yet the equality of opportunity to move from one rung to the other in the social scale may also be greater in the United States than in a hereditary tribal kingdom. Polar types: *Mobile* (open), *Immobile* (closed).

e. The Degree of Stratum Solidarity

Again, the degree of "class solidarity" (or the presence of specific organizations to promote class interests) may vary to some extent independently of the other criteria, and hence is an important principle in classifying systems of stratification. Polar types: *Class organized, Class unorganized.*

EXTERNAL CONDITIONS

What state any particular system of stratification is in with reference to each of these modes of variation depends on two things: (a) its state with reference to the other ranges of variation, and (b) the conditions outside the system of stratification which nevertheless influence that system. Among the latter are the following:

a. The Stage of Cultural Development

As the cultural heritage grows, increased specialization becomes necessary, which in turn contributes to the enhancement of mobility, a decline of stratum solidarity, and a change of functional emphasis.

b. Situation with Respect to Other Societies

The presence or absence of open conflict with other societies, of free trade relations or cultural diffusion, all influence the class structure to some extent. A chronic state of warfare tends to place emphasis upon the military functions, especially when the opponents are more or less equal. Free trade, on the other hand, strengthens the hand of the trader at the expense of the warrior and priest. Free movement of ideas generally has an equalitarian effect. Migration and conquest create special circumstances.

c. Size of the Society

A small society limits the degree to which functional specialization can go, the degree of segregation of different strata, and the magnitude of inequality.

COMPOSITE TYPES

Much of the literature on stratification has attempted to classify concrete systems into a certain number of types. This task is deceptively simple, however, and should come at the end of an analysis of elements and principles, rather than at the beginning. If the preceding discussion has any validity, it indicates that there are a number of modes of variation between different systems, and that any one system is a composite of the society's status with reference to all these modes of variation. The danger of trying to classify whole societies under such rubrics as *caste*, *feudal*, or *open class* is that one or two criteria are selected and others ignored, the result being an unsatisfactory solution to the problem posed. The present discussion has been offered as a possible approach to the more systematic classification of composite types.

NOTES

1. Kingsley Davis, "A Conceptual Analysis of Stratification," *American Sociological Review.* 7:309–321, June, 1942.

2. The writers regret (and beg indulgence) that the present essay, a condensation of a longer study, covers so much in such short space that adequate evidence and qualification cannot be given and that as a result what is actually very tentative is presented in an unfortunately dogmatic manner.

3. Unfortunately, functional importance is difficult to establish. To use the position's prestige to establish it, as is often unconsciously done, constitutes circular reasoning from our point of view. There are, however, two independent clues: (a) the degree to which a position is functionally unique, there being no other positions that can perform the same function satisfactorily; (b) the degree to which other positions are dependent on the one in question. Both clues are best exemplified in organized systems of positions built around one major function. Thus, in most complex societies the religious, political, economic, and educational functions are handled by distinct structures not easily interchangeable. In addition, each structure possesses many different positions, some clearly dependent on, if not subordinate to, others. In sum, when an institutional nucleus becomes differentiated around one main function, and at the same time organizes a large portion of the population into its relationships, the *key* positions in it are of the highest functional importance. The absence of such specialization does not prove functional unimportance, for the whole society may be relatively unspecialized; but it is safe to assume that the more important functions receive the first and clearest structural differentiation.

4. The symbolic rather than intrinsic role of income in social stratification has been succinctly summarized by Talcott Parsons, "An Analytical Approach to the Theory of Social Stratification," *American Journal of Sociology.* 45:841–862, May, 1940.

12

The Uses of Undeservingness[1]

Herbert J. Gans

BETTER-OFF AMERICANS MAY CONSIDER THE poor undeserving because of the threats associated with them and the public funds allocated to them. In fact, however, labeling the poor as undeserving also has some uses, or positive functions, or beneficial consequences, for more fortunate Americans. Strange as it may seem on first thought, these functions are very real, resulting in material and immaterial benefits, even though many are not immediately apparent, particularly to the people who benefit from them.[2] This is because functions are not purposes. They are not what people intend to do, but are the consequences of what they actually do, whatever their initial purposes. Consequently, functions are usually neither intended nor recognized when they first emerge, and some are unintended but unavoidable because they follow from the demands of politically important groups.[3] Whatever their origin, however, once these functions exist and produce benefits, their beneficiaries may develop an interest in them and even establish interest groups to defend them.[4]

Needless to say, that undeservingness has uses does not justify it; the analysis of its functions just helps to explain why it persists. In addition, functions for the better-off often entail, or are accompanied by, dysfunctions for the poor, which become

economic, social, and political costs not only for them but also for some of the non-poor. . . .

Of the many positive functions of labeling the poor, thirteen will be discussed here, classified into five interrelated sets.[5] The first eleven functions are not listed in order of importance, but the final two are of greater importance than the others, because they appear to benefit virtually the entire society of the nonpoor.

TWO MICROSOCIAL FUNCTIONS

Risk Reduction

Perhaps the primary use of the idea of the undeserving poor—primary because it takes place on the microsocial scale of everyday life—is that it distances the labeled from those who label them. By labeling some people as undeserving, label users protect themselves from the risk of getting close to them and being hurt by the encounter. Risk reduction is a way of dealing with threats of all kinds, actual and imagined. The decision to consider a group of people undeserving absolves one of the responsibility to associate with them or even to treat them like morally equal human beings. This absolution can increase feelings of personal safety. All pejorative labels and stereotypes serve this function, which may be why there are so many of them.

Supplying Objects of Revenge and Repulsion

The scapegoating function that the undeserving poor perform has already been discussed in connection with displaced threats, but the poor are

From *The War Against the Poor* by Herbert J. Gans. Copyright © 1995 by Herbert J. Gans. Reprinted by permission of BasicBooks, a member of Perseus Books, L.L.C.

also useful as general objects of revenge. They can become such objects because their undeservingness justifies feelings of superiority on the part of the better-off classes. In a society in which punishment is reserved for legislative, judicial, and penal institutions, the *feelings* of revenge and punitiveness that can be directed toward the undeserving poor may offer at least some emotional satisfaction to those lacking the power to punish.

Since labeling poor people undeserving makes nearly unlimited scapegoating possible, the labeled can also be used for distinctive kinds of displacement. For example, many years ago, James Baldwin argued that the undeserving black poor could provide a locus for displaced feelings of repulsion and self-hate that a majority population may have difficulty admitting to itself. Broadening a point first made by Baldwin in *The Fire Next Time*, Andrew Hacker suggests that whites "need the 'nigger,' because it is the 'nigger' within themselves that they cannot tolerate. . . . Whatever it is that whites feel 'nigger' signifies about blacks—lust and laziness, stupidity or squalor—in fact exists within themselves. . . . By creating such a creature, whites are able to say that because only members of the black race can carry that taint, it follows that none of its attributes will be found in white people."[6]

Baldwin's analysis is easily transferable to "the undeserving poor" within the mainstream American, for a number of the traits Oscar Lewis identified in the culture of poverty could be found in that person: "mistrust of government and those in high position," for example, as well as "widespread belief in male superiority" and "provincialism," among others.[7] Moreover, Lewis himself initially felt that some of the culture of poverty's traits were positive, thus implying that they deserve being copied by better-off Americans. These included what Rigdon described as "family loyalty, generosity and sharing, spontaneity, gaiety, courage and the ability to love."[8] Thus it seems as if the undeserving poor could also perform positive displacement functions, being put forth as role models for the driven and pressured members of the more prosperous classes.

THREE ECONOMIC FUNCTIONS

Creating Jobs for the Better-Off Population

Perhaps the most important contemporary economic function of the undeserving poor is their mere presence, which creates a large and increasing number of jobs for the deserving poor and almost all strata of the better-off classes, including professionals. Since the undeserving poor are thought to be dangerous or improperly socialized, their behavior has to be modified so that they will learn to act in socially approved ways. Alternatively, they have to be policed and controlled, or isolated from the deserving sectors of society. The larger the number of people who are declared undeserving, the larger also the number of people needed to modify, police, control, or guard them. These include the police, judges, lawyers, court probation officers, guards, and others who staff the criminal courts and prisons, as well as the social workers, psychiatrists, doctors, and others—and their support staffs—in "special" schools, drug treatment centers, homeless shelters, mental hospitals, and the like. And they also include the teachers and trainers who try to retrain the undeserving.

Other jobs established to deal with the undeserving poor include those held by professionals, investigators, and clerks who administer welfare. Yet other jobs go to officials who look for poor fathers and the child-support monies they often do not have, as well as to the additional welfare office staff needed to remove recipients in violation of welfare rules from the rolls. It could be argued that some of the rules for handling the undeserving poor are more effective at performing the latent function of creating jobs for the working and middle classes than achieving their stated goals of enforcing the laws.[9]

Further jobs are created in the social sciences, journalism, and literature, to conduct research and to write about the faults of the undeserving poor for the more fortunate who want to read about the actual or imagined misbehaviors of those they have stigmatized. Moreover, the undeserving poor supply work for the "salvation industries," religious and secular, which try to save the souls and alter the behavior of the undeserving. Not all such jobs are paid, for the undeserving poor also constitute objects of charity and thus mean volunteer work for those providing it, as well as paid jobs for the professional fundraisers who pursue charitable funds these days. Among the most visible volunteers are the members of cafe and high society who organize and contribute to benefits. While they seek mainly to help the deserving poor, some hold charity balls or collect money in other ways for the homeless and unmarried mothers.

Supplying Illegal Goods

The undeserving poor who have trouble finding other jobs, even in the informal labor market, are available for work in the manufacture and sale of illegal goods, including drugs. Although it is estimated that 80 percent of all illegal drugs are sold to nonpoor whites, the street sellers are often drug users and others forced out of the formal labor market.[10] Parts of the informal economy that make or sell legal goods or supply legal services but do so under illegal conditions may also attract the undeserving poor, such as welfare recipients or ex-convicts. Garment industry sweatshops and other below-minimum-wage employers often hire illegal immigrants or other people about whose backgrounds they ask no questions.

Staffing the Reserve Army of Labor

Traditionally, the poor, including even the deserving ones, served the function of staffing the "reserve army of labor." As such they were available to be hired as strikebreakers; they were also invisible presences who could be used to break unions, harass unionized workers, or just scare them into working for less, and thus drive down wage rates. Today, however, with a plentiful supply of jobless people, underpaid full-time and involuntary part-time workers, as well as immigrant workers, a reserve army is less often needed—and when it is needed, it can be recruited from other sectors than the undeserving poor.

Welfare recipients may remain in the reserve army, for many work part-time, in some places in "workfare" programs. They are also encouraged to stay out of the official labor market by being eligible to obtain Medicaid only if they remain on welfare, so that many who need extra money have to work "off the books."[11] If future health insurance programs should ever enable welfare recipients to obtain medical care without staying on welfare, or if future welfare reform programs establish minimum-wage workfare programs on a national basis, larger numbers of welfare recipients will be exerting downward pressure on the wages of the employed. The same effects will occur even more frequently, and drastically, if and when poor women lose their eligibility for welfare or if the welfare program should be abolished entirely. In that case, the victims will once more be full members of the reserve army of labor.[12]

THREE NORMATIVE FUNCTIONS[13]

Moral Legitimation

The same laws that determine what is illegal and criminal also define what is law-abiding, if only by implication and elimination. Likewise, the definition of undeservingness indirectly determines the definition of deservingness. As a result, all institutions and social structures that stigmatize and exclude the undeserving concurrently offer moral and political legitimacy to the institutions and structures of the deserving.[14]

Of these, the most important structure is the class hierarchy, for the existence of an undeserving class or stratum legitimates the deserving classes, and much if not all of their class-related behavior. The alleged immorality of the undeserving also surrounds the class hierarchy with a moral atmosphere, which may help to explain why upward mobility itself is morally praiseworthy. The fact that the people assigned to "the underclass" and several earlier labels are thought to be déclassé only emphasizes further the moral and political legitimacy of the rest of the class system.[15]

Value Reinforcement

When the undeserving poor violate, or are imagined to be violating, mainstream behavioral patterns and values, they help to reinforce and reaffirm the desirability of these patterns and values. As Emile Durkheim pointed out nearly a century ago, norm violation is also norm preservation. As a result, a variety of norms, including those sometimes dismissed as "motherhood" values, gain new prestige when they are violated and their violators stigmatized or punished.

If the undeserving poor can be imagined to be lazy, they help to reaffirm the "Protestant work ethic"; if poor single-parent families are officially condemned, the two-parent family is once more legitimated as ideal. In the 1960s, "middle-class morality" was sometimes criticized as culturally narrow, and therefore inappropriate for the poor, but since the 1980s, "mainstream values" have again been considered vital sources of behavioral guidance for them.[16]

Norm reinforcement also facilitates the active preservation of values. Before the undeserving poor can obtain financial help, one of the conventional prerequisites is visible indication of their readiness to practice the mainstream values. These values may include some that members of the mainstream may not practice themselves. Consequently, values that might otherwise die out can be preserved. For example, welfare recipients and the jobless must behave deferentially in government agencies even though public officials can insult them freely. Promptness, dress codes, and other work rules that can no longer be enforced in many parts of the economy can be maintained in the regulations for workfare. Economists like to argue that if the poor want to be deserving, they must help "clear the market"—take any kind of job, regardless of its low pay or demeaning character. The economists' argument reflects a work ethic that they themselves do not have to practice and might object to practicing if they had to do so.

Conversely, the undeserving poor may even be punished for behaving in by now conventional ways that diverge from traditional values. A welfare recipient can now be removed from the rolls if she is found to be living with a man without benefit of marriage, but the social worker who removes her has every right to do so without endangering his or her job. Welfare recipients can also be punished for violating rules of housecleaning and child care that middle-class people are free to ignore without being punished. More correctly, while there are many norms and laws regulating child care, only the poor are monitored to see if they obey them. If they fail to do so, or are perceived as using more physical punishment than social workers consider desirable, they can be charged with child neglect or abuse and could lose their children to foster care. Likewise, in a society in which the advocates of traditional values remain divided about abortions, the poor, but only the poor, can be prevented from obtaining them. In the political controversy around this issue, the fetuses of the poor seem at times to become especially deserving precisely because their mothers are thought undeserving.

In fact, the defenders of such widely preached if not always so widely practiced values as hard work, thrift, monogamy, and moderation need people who can be accused, accurately or not, of being lazy, spendthrift, promiscuous, and dissolute. All in all, the normative need for misbehaving people creates the exaggerated and imagined behavioral threats of which the undeserving are often accused.

Whether or not very many poor people actually behave in this way is irrelevant if they can be imagined as doing so, and once imaginations take over and the poor can then be labeled undeserving, empirical reality becomes superfluous or not credible. By the 1990s, the beliefs that unmarried motherhood caused poverty, or that young men from poor single-parent families were likely to become street criminals, could appear in the news media without requiring an expert's quote to affirm their accuracy.

Actually, most of the time most of the poor do not violate the fundamental moral values; thus the proportion of welfare recipients who cheat is below the percentage of taxpayers who do so.[17] Moreover, survey after survey has shown that the poor, including most criminals, want to work in secure, well-paid, and respectable jobs like everyone else; hope someday to live in the suburbs and generally pursue the same American Dream as most other Americans of their income level.[18]

Popular Culture Villains

The undeserving poor have also played a continual role in supplying America with popular culture villains. For many years before and after the Second World War, Hollywood's crime villains were largely drawn from the ranks of poor European immigrants, particularly Sicilians. Then they were complemented for some decades by Cold War and other Communist enemies who were not poor, but even before the end of the Cold War, these were being replaced by black and Hispanic drug dealers, gang leaders, and random killers.

The primary role of these villains is value-reinforcing, showing that crime and other norm violations do not pay. Street criminals and other lawbreakers are shown dead or alive in the hands of the police on the local television news programs every day, and with fictional exaggeration, in crime and action movies and television series. At the same time, however, the popular culture industry has also found popular culture heroes, and villains from the ranks of the undeserving poor, who supply cultural and political protest that criticizes some mainstream values or their alleged hypocrisy. The protest is limited, however, to that which is particularly marketable among white record buyers, who may be using black performers, especially "rappers," to express what they dare not say themselves.

Whatever the content of popular music, its creators and performers have always been recruited to some extent from the undeserving poor, for some of the blues, country music, cowboy songs, jazz, and most recently "rap" were composed and originally played in prisons, in brothels, and in the bars or on the streets of the slums.[19]

THREE POLITICAL FUNCTIONS

Institutional Scapegoating

Institutions that serve or control the poor also participate in the scapegoating of the undeserving poor, blaming them for the same phenomena as individual blamers. Institutional scapegoating takes some or all of the responsibility off the shoulders of elected and appointed officials who are supposed to deal with these problems. For example, to the extent that educational experts decide that the children of the poor cannot be taught, or that they are "learning disabled," or genetically inferior in intelligence, attempts to improve the schools can be put off or watered down.

Scapegoating by institutions also personalizes the shortcomings of various sectors of American society. As a result, the anger aimed at the alleged laziness of the jobless and beggars takes the heat off the failure of the economy; the derelictions of slum dwellers and the homeless goes some way to absolving the housing industry; and the existence of poor addicts, mentally ill, and others diverts attention from the destruction of the welfare state and its safety-net measures since the late 1970s. When the undeserving poor are blamed for poverty and poverty-related evils, they are also made responsible for the unwillingness of politicians and voters to do anything about these evils.

Conservative Power Shifting

Once poor people are declared undeserving, their already minimal political influence declines even further. Some cannot vote, for example, for lack of a stable address, and many do not choose to vote because politicians do not listen to them. Politicians would probably ignore them even if they did vote, because they cannot possibly satisfy their demands for economic and other kinds of aid. In addition, the undeserving poor make a dangerous constituency. Politicians who say kind words for them, or who act to represent their interests, are likely to be attacked. Jesse Jackson was hardly the first national politician to be criticized for being too favorable to the poor.

Due partly to its ability to ignore the stigmatized poor, the political system can pay greater attention to the white-collar and professional classes. These have enough economic security and political savvy so that their demands on government are not taken to be immoderate. Meanwhile, many people in the working class seem willing to play down demands for their own economic improvement and security as long as the undeserving poor are kept in their place, and out of their neighborhoods. Without accountability to the stigmatized poor and their economic needs, the polity as a whole can concentrate on economically more conservative issues and so shift to the right.

That shift is also ideological. Since the claims of the poor are part of the liberal and Left repertoires, the undeserving poor offer ample opportunity for conservatives to attack their liberal and Left enemies. If liberals can be accused of favoring "criminals" over "victims," their accusers can launch, and legitimate, incursions not only on the civil liberties and rights of the undeserving poor but also on the liberties and rights of those defending the poor.

Likewise, the undeserving poor can be used to justify attacks on the welfare state, which also makes them politically useful, directly and indirectly, to conservatives. Charles Murray understood the essence of this ideological function when he was able to argue for the abolition of welfare and related welfare-state legislation on the grounds that it only increased the number of poor people.[20]

Spatial Stigmatization

Poor areas can be stigmatized as "underclass areas," making them eligible for other uses. They may be used as drug markets for middle-class customers for drugs, from the suburbs and elsewhere, who would not want to be seen buying drugs in their own areas or have such markets located there. City officials can decide that underclass areas will be used for facilities other neighborhoods reject, from homeless shelters and halfway houses for AIDS patients and rehabilitated drug abusers to toxic and other dumps. In fact, municipalities would have difficulties operating if they lacked stigmatized areas in which necessary but unwanted facilities can be located.

TWO MACROSOCIAL FUNCTIONS
Reproduction of Stigma and the Stigmatized

For centuries now, undeservingness has enabled agencies that are established for helping the poor to evade their responsibilities. Indeed, these agencies—and the policies and programs they pursue—prevent many of the stigmatized from shedding their stigma, and also unwittingly manage to see to it that their children face the same hostility and thus grow up poor.[21] In some cases, this pattern works so fast that the offspring of the labeled face "anticipatory stigmatization"; for example, when the children of welfare recipients are expected, even before they have been weaned, to be unable to learn, to work, and to remain on the right side of the law.

If this outcome were engineered deliberately, one could argue that politically and culturally dominant groups are reluctant to give up a badly needed scapegoat.[22] Usually, however, the reproduction function is an unintended effect that follows from other intended and often popular practices. For example, the so-called war on drugs, which has unsuccessfully tried to keep cocaine and heroin from coming into the country but meanwhile offered very little effective drug treatment to addicts seeking it, has thereby aided the continuation of addiction, street crime, and prison building, as well as of the familial and other disasters that often visit the children of addicts. Similarly, discouraging and even preventing the poor from obtaining abortions has helped to increase the future number of poor youngsters. Schemes to eliminate welfare will make sure to increase that number even further, to worsen their poverty, and help see to it that more of them are forced into street crime when they are adolescents.

The other major source of the reproduction of stigma and the stigmatized is the routine activities of the organizations that exist to service welfare recipients, the homeless, and other stigmatized poor. These activities continue to take place partly because the organizations involved lack the funds or power to provide the resources that would help their clients to leave welfare or rejoin the housed population, or for that matter, to escape poverty altogether. One major reason they lack these funds and this power is because the clients are stigmatized, and thus not viewed as deserving of much help.[23]

The workings of this function can best be summarized by two insightful victims of the agencies that deal with the stigmatized poor. A homeless New York woman attempting to obtain welfare pointed out: "I don't get welfare. . . . I hate those people in there. They make you fuckin' sit and sit and ask you questions that don't make any sense. . . . You're homeless but you have to have an address. They want you to get so fuckin' upset that you get up and walk out. They test you. And if you do get up and walk out that means you don't really want it."[24] And a college junior at Grambling State University commented on the attacks on "midnight basketball" during the debate over the 1994 crime legislation: "If they don't fund these kinds of programs, it's like they are saying to us, 'Go out and sell drugs.' It's like they want to see us locked up."[25]

Forcing the Poor Out of the Labor Force

Ultimately, perhaps the most important function of undeservingness is to push the poor completely out of the labor force. People who have been labeled as undeserving may first be banished from the formal labor market and forced into the informal economy and the criminal underworld. Banishing the undeserving poor from that labor market can also be used to reduce the official jobless rate, a useful political function for election campaign purposes. If the economy of the future requires fewer and fewer workers, however, the easiest and cheapest way of reducing the work force and saving the jobs for the deserving poor and the nonpoor population is to make the undeserving poor ineligible for as many jobs as possible in all labor markets.

This goal can be achieved through legislation—in the case of illegal immigrants, for example—or by labeling, as is the case with poor young males who are stereotyped as unable to learn the job skills and cultural requirements of the modern economy.[26] Once people are unable to find jobs, some will be encouraged directly or indirectly to enter criminal occupations, and can subsequently be kept out of the labor force as ex-convicts. Should labeling people as morally ineligible fail to force enough people out of the labor force, it appears possible to declare them genetically lacking in the intelligence to work. Whatever the methods, they will not be eligible for the jobs sought by the more fortunate population, and will thus reduce the competition in both the formal and informal labor markets if and when the erosion of jobs becomes more serious and permanent.[27]

In the longer run, extrusion from the labor force could even be followed by the gradual extermination of the surplus labor.

In earlier times, when the incomes of the poor regularly fell below subsistence levels, they frequently died at an earlier age than everyone else, thus performing the set of functions forever associated with Thomas Malthus. Standards of living, even for the very poor, have risen considerably in the last century, but rates of morbidity and mortality due to hypertension, heart disease, tuberculosis and many other chronic illnesses, homicide, and now AIDS, remain much higher among the poor than among working-class and moderate-income people, not to mention the higher-income groups.[28]

Whether stereotyping and stigmatizing poor people as undeserving also exposes them to more illness and a shorter life expectancy is not yet known. But even displaced workers who lose their jobs when their firms close begin after a period of unsuccessful job hunting to think that their unemployment is their own fault—and thus to treat themselves as undeserving. Eventually many become depressed and begin to share in the illnesses of the stigmatized.[29]

If the present erosion of jobs continues indefinitely and more people have to be banished from the labor force, they too will suffer more of the chronic illnesses of the poor, more dangerous lives, and a shorter life expectancy. The original Malthusian hypothesis has probably been falsified forever, but advanced capitalism may be supplying data for a new one.[30] In the very long run, then, an even more drastic—and deadly—form of reducing competition for jobs might take place.[31]

NOTES

1. This part of the chapter is a revised version of my article "The Positive Functions of the Undeserving Poor: Uses of the Underclass in America," *Politics and Society* 22 (Sept. 1994): 269–83. It is in turn an updated version of my "Über die positiven Funktionen der unwürdingen Armen: Zur Bedeutung der 'Underclass' in den USA," *Kölner Zeitschrift für Soziologie und Sozialpsychologie* (Sonderheft 32, 1992): 48–62, which was published by the Westdeutscher Verlag, Opladen, Germany. The pages that follow can also be read as a sequel to my article "The Positive Functions of Poverty," *American Journal of Sociology* 78 (Sept. 1972): 275–89, which dealt with the poor generally. For earlier functional analyses of the poor, see Arland D. Weeks, "A Conservative's View of Poverty," *American Journal of Sociology* 22 (1917): 779–800; and Frances Fox Piven and Richard A. Cloward, *Regulating the Poor: The Functions of Public Welfare* (New York: Pantheon, 1971; 2d ed. 1993).

    What follows is a straightforward functional analysis based mostly on Robert K. Merton's classic model, which is illustrated with a variety of data. I write it as an empirical analysis, despite its occasionally ironic tone, which is unavoidable given the sometime debunking connotation of the analysis of the functions Robert Merton called latent. Robert K. Merton, "Manifest and Latent Functions," in Robert K. Merton, *Social Theory and Social Structure: Toward the Codification of Social Research* (Glencoe, Ill.: Free Press, 1949), chap. 1.

2. Functions are not immediately apparent *sui generis*, because there is no easy systematic method for identifying them, but many consequences of labeling are apparent even to lay eyes. Some negative functions or dysfunctions of labeling were identified in [another chapter of Gans's book].

3. A good example is the expenditure of large sums to house the homeless in slum hotels instead of cheaper vacant, and decent, dwellings in standard neighborhoods, in order to satisfy the political demands of working- and middle-class people to keep the homeless out of their neighborhoods.

4. Functions are not, however, causes of undeservingness or of poverty. Being consequences, these uses almost always develop after these causes have done their misdeeds, and except in unusual circumstances cannot enable any form of undeservingness to survive once the causes that brought it into being have disappeared. One set of consequences can, however, cause yet other, or secondary, consequences to develop. Thus if the fear of street crime by the poor results in an increase in the police force, that increase can itself have beneficial consequences for the police: for example, increasing its political power in the community, and its ability thereby to lobby for increased budgets in the future.

5. The sets themselves are arbitrary too; they are an appropriate device for grouping the thirteen functions.

6. The quote is from Andrew Hacker (paraphrasing Baldwin) in *Two Nations: Black and White, Separate, Hostile, Unequal* (New York: Scribner's, 1992), p. 61. Whites have invented so many other pejoratives intended solely for blacks that today terms other than "nigger" can be substituted without altering Baldwin's point.

7. Oscar Lewis, "The Culture of Poverty," in Daniel P. Moynihan, ed., *On Understanding Poverty* (New York: Basic Books, 1968), pp. 190, 192, 193.

8. Susan M. Rigdon, *The Culture Facade: Art, Science and Politics in the Work of Oscar Lewis* (Urbana: University of Illinois Press, 1988), p. 91.

9. More suspicious observers even believe that creating jobs for these classes is a major manifest function of all programs to deal with the poor, from prison building, which hires construction workers and then prison guards, to the nearly continuous investigations of welfare recipients, which supply jobs to college graduates and professional social workers.

10. Ron Harris, "Blacks Feel Brunt of Drug War," *Los Angeles Times*, April 22, 1990, p. 1.

11. For the strongest argument that welfare recipients are already a permanent part of the reserve army, see Piven and Cloward, *Regulating the Poor*.

12. Ralf Dahrendorf has suggested the revival of the reserve army implied in Marx's *Lumpenproletariat*. According to Dahrendorf, when Europe's very poor are excluded from full citizenship, they can become "a reserve army for demonstrations and manifestations, including soccer violence, race riots and running battles with the police." Ralf Dahrendorf, *Law and Order* (London: Stevens, 1985), p. 107.

13. "Normative" is used here as a synonym for "value," but "normative functions" sounds better than "value functions."

14. Since political legitimacy is involved, this function could also be listed among the political ones below.

15. Although Marxists might have been expected to complain that the notion of the undeserving poor enables the higher classes to create a split in the lower ones, Marxist theory copied the mainstream pattern. While declaring capitalists, and sometimes the entire bourgeoisie, undeserving, and ennobling the working class, Marx still found it necessary to construct the *Lumpenproletariat*, although some of its behavior was for Marx, if less so for some of his successors, undeserving mainly in relation to Marxist political goals.

16. For a contrary view, in which the behavior of the undeserving poor is seen as becoming norma-

tively acceptable for the mainstream, see Daniel P. Moynihan, "Defining Deviancy Down," *American Scholar* 62 (Winter 1993): 17–30.

17. Nonetheless, finding a "welfare queen" who defrauds the system is always a very newsworthy, even front-page, story, while cheating by businessmen and -women is almost always restricted to the business pages.

18. Mark R. Rank, *Living on the Edge: The Realities of Welfare in America* (New York: Columbia University Press, 1994), chap. 6 and *passim*.

19. It may be no coincidence that as far back as the eighteenth century, English "actors, fencers, jugglers, minstrels and in fact all purveyors of amusements to common folk" were thought undeserving by the higher classes (Sidney and Beatrice Webb, *English Poor Law History* [Hamden, Conn.: Shoe String Press, 1963 (1927)], p. 354).

20. Charles Murray, *Losing Ground: American Social Policy 1950–1980* (New York: Basic Books, 1984).

21. Many policies and agencies—notably the schools—reproduce the positions and statuses of the people whom they are asked to improve.

22. For an analysis that argues that the lobby of gun manufacturers and private prison operators, as well as political conservatives, have established a "criminal–industrial complex" with an interest in the persistence of crime, see Joe Conason, "Why Conservatives are Tough on Criminals but Soft on Crime," *New York Observer* (Aug. 29–Sept. 5, 1994): 2.

23. See also the discussion in Piven and Cloward, *Regulating the Poor*, 2d ed., pp. 445–49.

24. Reported by Gwendolyn Dordick, "Friends among Strangers: Personal Relations among New York City's Homeless," (Ph.D. diss., Department of Sociology, Columbia University, 1994), p. 47.

25. Don Terry, "Basketball at Midnight: 'Hope' on a Summer Eve," *New York Times*, Aug. 19, 1994, A18.

26. Kathryn M. Neckerman and Joleen Kirschenman, "Hiring Strategies, Racial Bias, and Inner-City Workers," *Social Problems* 38 (Nov. 1991): 433–47.

27. At present, this is only a prediction. It is also an extension of Gunnar Myrdal's 1963 analysis of the American economy, in which he introduced the underclass into America's dictionary for the poor (see chap. 2).

28. These rates are almost always higher for substance abusers, street criminals, participants in the drug trade, and the poor black youngsters caught in the violent culture of the streets.

29. See, for example, M. Harvey Brenner, *Mental Illness and the Economy* (Cambridge, Mass.: Harvard University Press, 1973).

30. For an early analysis along this line that focuses on blacks rather than the poor, see Sidney Wilhelm, *Who Needs the Negro?* (New York: Doubleday Anchor, 1971).

31. Killing off the undeserving poor may conflict with the prior function of reproducing them, but the consequences described by functional analysis do not have to be logically consistent. Moreover, since reproducing undeservingness and turning poor people into undeserving ones can be a first step toward eliminating them, functions twelve and thirteen may even be logically consistent.

Part III

CLASS

—ᴍ—

THE TWO SECTIONS OF PART III EXAMINE DIF-ferent aspects of class in contemporary capitalism in the United States: the effects of social and technological change on the formation and dynamics of class structure, the influence of the American upper class on the whole of society, and the outcomes of a shifting economy for people of different socioeconomic classes. The first section highlights how changes in work, technology, the organization of labor and production, and the global economy affect class formation and dynamics. In the first selection, "A General Framework for the Analysis of Class," Erik Olin Wright provides a theoretical account of the historical growth and continuing existence of a middle class. Wright reviews the fundamental failing of Marxist theory to anticipate the large middle class that evolved between the working class and the capitalist class. His work focuses on the development of a large stratum of workers who supervise and monitor other workers, suggesting that their location in the class structure often leads to inherent contradictions regarding their class interests and their experiences of class exploitation. The second reading, "Mass Production in Postmodern Times" by Richard J. Barnet and John Cavanagh, tackles the important question of how the emerging global marketplace affects production jobs in the United States. This piece reviews some of the major consequences of economic restructuring. For instance, the pool of available jobs has been flowing from city to suburb, leaving formerly thriving inner cities in economic blight. Similarly, multinational corporations are increasingly shifting production jobs from nation to nation in pursuit of tariff and tax advantages and cheap labor. Both of these shifts have led to a decrease in high-paying, industrial jobs (the traditional "breadwinner" jobs) and an increase in relatively low-paying service jobs for U.S. workers.

In the next selection, Glenda Laws raises the important question of how globalization and immigration affect social relations and inequality in urban areas. The next reading, "New Migration, New Theories" continues this theme. Douglas Massey and colleagues argue that globalization brings new migrations. Part of the new world order, then, is a different pattern of international migration, which has profound consequences for the United States.

The second section of Part III presents a fundamental debate about the power and importance of an upper class in America. In essence, this debate centers on Marx's contention that the ruling capitalist class dominates society, making the basic decisions about society's direction and its rules. The key question here is whether the particular class interests of capitalists are defined and carried out for the benefit of all classes. According to C. Wright Mills's classic position presented in "The Structure of Power in American Society," power is concentrated among a relatively few people heading three key institutions: giant corporations, the executive branch of government, and the military. The commanders in chief of these three institutions form a cohesive power elite that makes all the important decisions of society, leaving the vast majority of people in the middle and at the bottom only the most trivial of decision-making authority. Mills thus frames the critical post-World War II debate over both who the elite are and how much power they wield.

Jeffrey Reiman explores how class power is used to define whether certain behaviors are deemed legal or illegal as well as how strictly they are enforced. His "Weeding Out the Wealthy" looks at how the behavior of poor people fall under the close scrutiny of the law, while actions of the wealthy are more typically ignored.

C. William Domhoff's "The American Upper Class" contends that the upper class in the United States has a disproportionate share of power and that its social institutions maintain the distinctions between the upper class and the other classes. Domhoff's work emphasizes the role of elite education, clubs, styles, and marriages in creating and maintaining social cohesion among the American upper class.

The next two essays shift the emphasis and highlight how the shifting economy affects the life experiences of different Americans. Partly as result of welfare reform, the face of poverty is no longer the single mom on welfare. One aspect of the changing face of poverty, for example, is that a growing number of Americans are working hard and often work long hours but remain poor. Lisa Catanzarite and Vilma Ortiz in "Family Matters, Work Matters? Poverty Among Women of Color and White Women" examine the increased burden women face. The last piece in this section builds on this theme by focusing on how tough it is to make ends meet. Kathryn Edin and Laura Lein, in "Making Ends Meet at a Low-Wage Job," present powerful evidence that our measures of poverty are quite misleading. They demonstrate how tough it is to work and still be left in poverty. These articles emphasize the importance of women having access to better-paying jobs, especially females currently working in the low-income jobs traditionally filled by women.

IMPACT OF GLOBALIZATION IN THE UNITED STATES

13

A General Framework for the Analysis of Class[1]

Erik Olin Wright

. . . THE CONCEPT OF EXPLOITATION

We observe inequalities in the distribution of incomes, the real consumption bundles available to individuals, families and groups. The concept of

From *Classes* by Erick Olin Wright. Copyright © 1985 Verso. Reprinted by permission of Verso, London.

exploitation is a particular way of analysing such inequalities. To describe an inequality as reflecting exploitation is to make the claim that there exists a particular kind of causal relationship between the incomes of different actors. More concretely, in Roemer's analysis the rich are said to exploit the poor when it can be established that the welfare of the rich causally depends upon the deprivations of the poor — the rich are rich *because* the poor are poor, they are rich at the expense of others.[2]

Note that this need not be the case for all inequalities. Suppose that two subsistence farmers each have land of the same quality, but one is lazy and works minimally on the land while the other is industrious. In this case there is no causal relationship between the affluence of the one and the poverty of the other. The rich farmer would not become worse off if the lazy farmer started working harder. To count as exploitation it must be demonstrated that one person's welfare is obtained at the expense of the other.

The traditional Marxist concept of exploitation is clearly a special case of this general concept. In Marxian exploitation one class appropriates the surplus labour performed by another class through various mechanisms. The income of the exploiting class comes from the labour performed by the exploited class. There is thus a straightforward causal link between the poverty of the exploited and the affluence of the exploiter. The former benefits at the expense of the latter. . . .

CLASS AND EXPLOITATION

The central message of both of Roemer's strategies for analysing exploitation is that the material basis of exploitation lies in inequalities in the distribution of productive assets, usually referred to as property relations. The asset–exploitation nexus depends in each case upon the capacity of asset-holders to deprive others of equal access to that asset, whether it be alienable or inalienable. On the one hand, inequalities of assets are sufficient to account for transfers of surplus labour; on the other hand, different forms of asset inequality specify different systems of exploitation. Classes are then defined as positions within the social relations of production derived from the property relations which determine the patterns of exploitation.

These conclusions have led Roemer to challenge directly the tendency of Marxists like myself to define class relations primarily in terms of relations of domination *within* production. Of course, exploiting classes dominate exploited classes in the

sense of preventing the exploited classes from taking the exploiting class's productive assets (if they are alienable) or redistributing property rights in those assets (if they are inalienable). As we noted above, Roemer has to introduce some notion of dominance even to be able fully to specify exploitation in the game-theory approach. However, domination, in this context, enters the analysis in a way which, clearly, is conceptually subordinate to exploitation. Most importantly for the thrust of much neo-Marxist class structure analysis, domination *within* the production process or within the labour process does not enter into the definition of class relations as such.[3]

In previous work I have criticized Roemer's position on this issue.[4] I argued that class relations intrinsically involved domination *at the point of production*, not simply in the repressive protection of the property relations as such. I now think that Roemer is correct on this point. While the fact that capitalists supervise workers within production is unquestionably an important feature of most historic forms of capitalist production and may play an important role in explaining the forms of class organization and class conflict within production, the *basis* of the capital–labour relation should be identified with the relations of effective control (i.e. real economic ownership) over productive assets as such.

One of the reasons why I resisted Roemer's conceptualization of classes in terms of property relations is that it seemed to blur the difference between Marxist definitions of class and Weberian definitions. Weberian definitions, as I construed them, were 'market-based' definitions of class, whereas Marxist definitions were 'production based'. The reputed advantage of the latter was that production was more 'fundamental' than exchange, and therefore production-based class concepts had more explanatory power than market-based ones.

What now seems clear to me is that definitions of classes in terms of property relations should not be identified with strictly market-based definitions. Property relations accounts of classes do not define classes by income shares, by the results of market transactions, but by the productive assets which classes control, which lead them to adopt certain strategies within exchange relations, and which in turn determine the outcomes of those market transactions. . . . There remain significant differences between the Weberian use of market criteria for defining classes and the Marxist use of property relations, but the distinction is not captured by the simple contrast between 'exchange' and 'production'.

Towards a General Framework of Class Analysis

The heart of Roemer's analysis is the link between the distribution of property rights in productive assets of various sorts on the one hand, and exploitation and class on the other. Different mechanisms of exploitation are defined with respect to different kinds of assets and different class systems are defined by the social relations of production that are built upon property rights in those assets. These insights will provide the basis for elaborating a comprehensive framework for analysing class structures in general and for reconceptualizing the problem of the middle classes in particular.

Before examining this general framework, however, it is necessary to modify and extend Roemer's analysis in several respects: first, it will be helpful to introduce a distinction between economic exploitation and economic oppression; second, we need to recast Roemer's account of feudal exploitation in terms of a distinctive type of productive asset; and third, we need to replace Roemer's concept of status exploitation with a new concept, which I shall label 'organization exploitation'.

ECONOMIC EXPLOITATION AND ECONOMIC OPPRESSION

One of the criticisms that is often raised about Roemer's methodological device of using 'withdrawal rules' from a 'game' to define different forms of exploitation is that it abandons the Marxist identification of exploitation with transfers of labour from one category of actors to another. While Roemer's procedure allows us to assess inequalities that are the result of causal interconnections between actors, it lacks the additional force of the view that the inequalities in question are produced by real transfers from one actor to another.

Roemer himself has come to reject completely all labour-transfer views of exploitation on the ground that situations can occur in which labour transfers occur from the rich to the poor, situations in which we would not want to say that the poor were exploiting the rich.[5] For example, imagine a society with rich and poor peasants in which everyone has the following preferences for the performance of labour relative to the consumption of leisure: the wealthier one is, the less one values leisure relative to labour. Now, suppose that a given rich peasant has performed all necessary work on his or her land and would prefer to rent some more from a poor peasant than to remain idle. Given these preference structures, the poor peasant might prefer to receive the rent and have a great deal of leisure than work the land him/herself. In this situation, the only transfers of labour are from the rich peasant to the poor peasant (in the form of rent). Does it make sense to say that the poor peasant is 'exploiting' the rich peasant in such a situation? Now, one might want to call this a fanciful example, but it does show that simple flows of labour or the products of labour are insufficient to define what we mean by 'exploitation'.

I think that it is possible to restore the central thrust of the traditional Marxist concept of exploitation by making a distinction between what can be called 'economic oppression' and exploitation. I would argue, that in and of itself, the withdrawal rule procedure simply defines a situation of economic oppression. In the example above, the poor peasant is economically oppressed by the rich peasant through the property rights in land. Exploitation, on the other hand, implies more than just economic oppression; it includes both economic oppression and the appropriation of the fruits of the labour of one class by another (which is equivalent to a transfer of the surplus from one class to another).[6] The poor peasants would not exploit the rich peasants in the example, since they do not economically oppress them.

With this usage of terms, we can identify a fairly wide range of inequalities that we might want to condemn on the basis of economic oppression, but which are not examples of exploitation. The poverty of the permanently disabled or of the unemployed, for example, would in general be cases of economic oppression, but not of exploitation. They would surely be better off under the counterfactual conditions of the withdrawal rules, but the fruits of their labour are not appropriated by any class (since they are not producing anything). The same can be said of the children of workers: they may be economically oppressed by capital, but they are not exploited by capital.[7]

Now, it might be argued that the concept of economic oppression would be sufficient to provide the basis for a class concept, since it does define a set of objective material interests. What, then, is added by the distinction between economic oppressions that involve appropriation of the fruits of labour and those that do not? The critical addition is the idea that in the case of exploitation, the welfare of [the] exploiting class *depends upon the work* of the exploited class. In a case of simple economic oppression, the oppressing class only has interests in protecting its own property rights; in the case of exploitation it also has interests in the productive activity and effort of the exploited. In the case of economic oppression, the oppressors' material interests would not be hurt if all of the oppressed simply disappeared or died.[8] In the case of exploitation, on the other hand, the exploiting class needs the exploited class. Exploiters would be hurt if the exploited all disappeared.[9] Exploitation, therefore, binds the exploiter and exploited together in a way that economic oppression need not. It is this peculiar combination of antagonism of material interests

and inter-dependency which gives exploitation its distinctive character and which makes class struggle such a potentially explosive social force.

This notion of exploitation has a relatively straightforward intuitive meaning for feudal exploitation, where feudal lords directly appropriate a surplus produced by serfs, and for capitalist exploitation, where capitalists appropriate the total product out of which they pay the workers a wage. It is much less obvious that what Roemer calls 'socialist exploitation', exploitation rooted in skills, should be viewed as exploitation in this sense. Let us look at skill-based exploitation more closely to see why it should be considered an instance of exploitation defined in the above way.

To appropriate the fruits of someone else's labour is equivalent to saying that a person consumes more than they produce. If the income of a person with skill assets is identical to their 'marginal product', as neo-classical economists like to argue, how can we say that they are consuming 'more' than their own contribution? . . .

A GENERAL TYPOLOGY OF CLASS AND EXPLOITATION

If we add organization assets to the list in Roemer's analysis, we generate the more complex typology presented in Table 3.2. Let us briefly look at each row of this table and examine its logic. Feudalism is a class system based on unequal distribution of ownership rights in labour power. Feudal lords may also have more means of production than serfs, more organizational assets and more productive skills (although this is unlikely) and thus they may be exploiters with respect to these assets as well. What defines the society as 'feudal', however, is the primacy of the distinctively feudal mechanisms of exploitation, and which, accordingly, means that feudal class relations will be the primary structural basis of class struggle.

The bourgeois revolutions radically redistributed productive assets in people: everyone, at least in principle, owns one unit—themselves. This is at the heart of what is meant by 'bourgeois freedoms',

TABLE 3.2
Assets, Exploitation and Classes

Type of Class Structure	Principal Asset That Is Unequally Distributed	Mechanism of Exploitation	Classes
Feudalism	Labour power	Coercive extraction of surplus labour	Lords and serfs
Capitalism	Means of production	Market exchanges of labour power and commodities	Capitalists and workers
Statism	Organization	Planned appropriation and distribution of surplus based on hierarchy	Managers/bureaucrats and non-management
Socialism	Skills	Negotiated redistribution of surplus from workers to experts	Experts and workers

and it is the sense in which capitalism can be regarded as a historically progressive force. But capitalism raises the second type of exploitation, exploitation based on property relations in means of production, to an unprecedented level.[10]

The typical institutional form of capitalist class relations is capitalists having full ownership rights in the means of production and workers none. However, other possibilities have existed historically. Workers in cottage industry in early capitalism owned some of their means of production, but did not have sufficient assets to actually produce commodities without the assistance of capitalists. Such workers were still being capitalistically exploited even though there was no formal labour market with wages, etc. In all capitalist exploitation, the mediating mechanism is market exchanges. Unlike in feudalism, surplus is not directly appropriated from workers in the form of coerced labour or dues. Rather, it is appropriated through market exchanges: workers are paid a wage which covers the costs of production of their labour power; capitalists receive an income from the sale of the commodities produced by workers. The difference in these quantities constitutes the exploitative surplus appropriated by capitalists.[11]

Anti-capitalist revolutions attempt to eliminate the distinctively capitalist form of exploitation, exploitation based on private ownership of the means of production. The nationalization of the principal means of production is, in effect, a radical equalization of ownership of capital: everyone owns one citizen-share. What anti-capitalist revolutions do not necessarily eliminate, and may indeed considerably strengthen and deepen, are inequalities of effective control over organization assets. Whereas in capitalism the control over organization assets does not extend beyond the firm, in statist societies the coordinated integration of the division of labour extends to the whole society through institutions of central state planning. The mechanism by which this generates exploitative transfers of surplus involves the centrally planned bureaucratic appropriation and distribution of the surplus along hierarchical principles. The corresponding class relation is therefore between managers/bureaucrats—people who control organization assets—and non-managers.

The historical task of the revolutionary transformation of statist societies revolves around the equalization of effective economic control over organization assets. What precisely does such equalization mean? It would be utopian to imagine that in any society with a complex division of labour all productive actors would share equally in the actual *use* of organization assets. This would be equivalent to imagining that the equalization of ownership of means of production implied that all such actors would actually use an identical amount of physical capital. Equalization of control over organization assets means essentially the democratization of bureaucratic apparatuses.[12] This need not imply a thoroughgoing direct democracy, where all decisions of any consequence are directly made in democratic assemblies. There will still be delegated responsibilities, and there certainly can be representative forms of democratic control. But it does mean that the basic parameters of planning and co-ordination of social production are made through democratic mechanisms and that the holding of delegated positions of organizational responsibility does not give the delegates any personal claims on the social surplus.

Lenin's original vision of 'soviet' democracy, in which officials would be paid no more than average workers and would be subject to immediate recall, and in which the basic contours of social planning would be debated and decided through democratic participation, embodied such principles of radical equalization of organization assets. Once in power, as we know, the Bolsheviks were either unable or unwilling seriously to attempt the elimination of organization exploitation. Upon that failure, a new class structure emerged and was consolidated.[13]

The equalization of organization assets and the eradication of class relations rooted in organization exploitation would not in and of itself eliminate exploitation based on skills/credentials. Such exploitation would remain a central feature of socialism.

In this conceptualization of socialism, a socialist society is essentially a kind of nonbureaucratic technocracy. Experts control their own skills or knowledge within production, and by virtue of such control are able to appropriate some of the surplus from production. However, because of the democratization of organization assets, the actual making of planning decisions would not be under the direct control of experts but would be made through some kind of democratic procedure (this is in effect what democratization of organization assets means: equalizing control over the planning and co-ordination of social production). This implies that the actual class power of a socialist technocratic-exploiting class will be much weaker than the class power of exploiting classes in previous class systems. Their ownership rights extend to only a limited part of the social surplus.

This much more limited basis of *domination* implied by skill-based exploitation is consistent with the classical claim in Marxism that the working class—the direct producers—are the 'ruling' class in socialism.[14] The democratization of organization assets necessarily means that workers effectively control social planning. Another way of describing socialism, then, is that it is a society within which the ruling class and the exploiting classes are distinct.

Indeed, one might even want to make a stronger claim, namely that 'experts' in socialism are not really a proper class at all. Unlike in the cases of capital assets, labour power assets and organization assets, it is not at all clear that one can derive any relational properties from the ownership of skill assets as such.[15] To be sure, if skill assets are a criterion for recruitment into positions within organizational hierarchies, then individuals with skills or credentials may be in a particular relation to people without such credentials, but this is because of the link between skill and organization assets, not because of skill assets themselves. The most one can say here is that experts and non-experts exist in a kind of diffuse relation of dependence of the latter on the former. This is a considerably weaker sense of 'social relation' than is the case for the other three types of class relations.

It seems therefore that, while skills or credentials may be a basis for exploitation, this asset is not really the basis of a class relation, at least not in the same sense as labour power, capital and organization assets. In these terms socialism (in contrast to statism) could be viewed as a society with exploitation but without fully constituted classes.[16] Such a characterization of socialism is also consistent with the spirit, if not the letter, of Marx's claim that socialism is the 'lower stage' of communism, since classes are already in a partial state of dissolution in a society with only skill-based exploitation.

'Communism' itself would be understood as a society within which skill-based exploitation had itself 'withered away', i.e., in which ownership rights in skills had been equalized. This does not mean, it must be stressed, that all individuals would actually *possess* the same skills as each other in communism. It is ownership rights in the skills that are equalized. This is quite parallel to what it means to equalize ownership over physical assets: different workers may continue to work in factories with different capital intensities, productivities, amounts of physical assets. Equalization does not mean that everyone physically uses the same means of production, but simply that there are no longer any ownership rights that are differentially distributed with respect to those means of production. No one receives a higher income (or controls a larger part of the social surplus) by virtue of using more physical assets. Similarly the equalization of ownership rights in skills implies that differential incomes and control over the social surplus cease to be linked to differential skills.[17]

THE MIDDLE CLASSES
AND CONTRADICTORY LOCATIONS

The point of elaborating the rather complex inventory of forms of exploitation and corresponding class relations in Table 3.2 was not primarily to be able to give more precision to the abstract mode of production concepts (feudalism, capitalism, statism, etc.), but rather to provide the conceptual tools for analysing the class structures of contemporary capitalism at a more concrete level of analysis. In particular, . . . this means providing

a more coherent and compelling way of theorizing the class character of the 'middle classes'.

Two different kinds of non-polarized class locations can be defined in the logic of this framework:

1. There are class locations that are neither exploiters nor exploited, i.e. people who have precisely the per capita level of the relevant asset. A petty-bourgeois, self-employed producer with average capital stock, for example, would be neither exploiter nor exploited within capitalist relations.[18] These kinds of positions are what can be called the 'traditional' or 'old' middle class of a particular kind of class system.

2. Since concrete societies are rarely, if ever, characterized by a single mode of production, the actual class structures of given societies will be characterized by complex patterns of intersecting exploitation relations. There will therefore tend to be some positions which are exploiting along one dimension of exploitation relations, while on another are exploited. Highly skilled wage-earners (e.g. professionals) in capitalism are a good example: they are capitalistically exploited because they lack assets in capital and yet are skillexploiters. Such positions are what are typically referred to as the 'new middle class' of a given class system.

Table 3.3 presents a schematic typology of such complex class locations for capitalism. The typology is divided into two segments: one for owners of the means of production and one for non-owners. Within the wage-earner section of the typology, locations are distinguished by the two subordinate relations of exploitation characteristic of capitalist society—organization assets and skill/credential assets. It is thus possible to distinguish within this framework a whole terrain of class-locations in capitalist *society* that are distinct from the polarized classes of the capitalist *mode of production*: expert managers, non-managerial experts, non-expert managers, etc.

TABLE 3.3

Typology of Class Locations in Capitalist Society

Assets in the means of production

	Owners of Means of Production	Non-Owners [Wage Labourers]			Organization assets
Owns sufficient capital to hire workers and not work	1 Bourgeoisie	4 Expert Managers	7 Semi-Credentialled Managers	10 Uncredentialled Managers	+
Owns sufficient capital to hire workers but must work	2 Small Employers	5 Expert Supervisors	8 Semi-Credentialled Supervisors	11 Uncredentialled Supervisors	>0
Owns sufficient capital to work for self but not to hire workers	3 Petty Bourgeoisie	6 Expert Non-Managers	9 Semi-Credentialled Workers	11 Proletarians	−
		+	>0	−	

Skill/credential assets

What is the relationship between this heterogeneous exploitation definition of the middle class and my previous conceptualization of such positions as contradictory locations within class relations? There is still a sense in which such positions could be characterized as 'contradictory locations', for they will typically hold contradictory interests with respect to the primary forms of class struggle in capitalist society, the struggle between labour and capital. On the one hand, they are like workers in being excluded from ownership of the means of production;[19] on the other, they have interests opposed to workers because of their effective control of organization and skill assets. Within the struggles of capitalism, therefore, these 'new' middle classes do constitute contradictory locations, or more precisely, contradictory locations within exploitation relations.

This conceptualization of the middle classes also suggests that the principle forms of contradictory locations will vary historically depending upon the particular combinations of exploitation relations in a given society. The historical pattern of principal contradictory locations is presented in Table 3.4. In feudalism, the critical contradictory location is constituted by the bourgeoisie, the rising class of the successor mode of production.[20] Within capitalism, the central contradictory location within exploitation relations is constituted by managers and state bureaucrats. They embody a principle of class organization which is quite distinct from capitalism and which potentially poses an alternative to capitalist relations. This is particularly true for state managers who, unlike corporate managers, are less likely to have their careers tightly integrated with the interests of the capitalist class. Finally, in statist societies, the 'intelligentsia' broadly defined constitutes the pivotal contradictory location.[21]

One of the consequences of this reconceptualization of the middle class is that it is no longer axiomatic that the proletariat is the unique, or perhaps even universally the central, rival to the capitalist class for class power in capitalist society.

TABLE 3.4

Basic Classes and Contradictory Locations in Successive Modes
of Production

Mode of Production	Basic Classes	Principal Contradictory Location
Feudalism	Lords and serfs	Bourgeoisie
Capitalism	Bourgeoisie and proletariat	Managers/bureaucrats
State bureaucratic socialism	Bureaucrats and workers	Intelligentsia/experts

That classical Marxist assumption depended upon the thesis that there were no other classes within capitalism that could be viewed as the 'bearers' of a historical alternative to capitalism. Socialism (as the transition to communism) was the only possible future to capitalism. What Table 3.4 suggests is that there are other class forces within capitalism that have the potential to pose an alternative to capitalism.

Alvin Gouldner and others have argued that the beneficiaries of social revolutions in history have not been the oppressed classes of the prior mode of production, but 'third classes'. Most notably, it was not the peasantry who became the ruling class with the demise of feudalism, but the bourgeoisie, a class that was located outside the principal exploitation relation of feudalism. A similar argument could be extended to manager-bureaucrats with respect to capitalism and experts with respect to state bureaucratic socialism: in each case these constitute potential rivals to the existing ruling class.

In the case of capitalism, it might seem rather far-fetched to claim that managers and state bureaucrats constitute potential challenges to the class power of the bourgeoisie. At least in the advanced capitalist countries, corporate managers are so closely integrated into the logic of private capital accumulation that it seems quite implausible that they would ever oppose capitalism in favour of some sort of statist organization of production. As critics of the 'managerial revolution' thesis have often argued, whatever special interests or motives corporate managers have, the realization of those interests is contingent upon the profitability of their firms and they will therefore adopt strategies consistent with the interests of capital. And even for state managers, who arguably have a power base that is at least partially independent of capital, it still seems very unlikely that they would ever become consistently anti-capitalist because of the multiple ways in which the interests of the state are subordinated to and co-ordinated with the interests of capital. Since in a capitalist society state revenues depend upon privately generated profits (because the state itself does not organize production), the state is systematically constrained to act in a way that supports the profitability of capital and thus capitalist exploitation. Regardless of their personal preferences, therefore, state managers cannot afford to act in anti-capitalist ways.[22] It therefore seems completely unrealistic to treat managers and bureaucrats as even potential class rivals to the bourgeoisie.

Behind each of these claims about the effective integration of managers and bureaucrats into the capitalist social order is the assumption that capitalism is successful as a system of exploitation and accumulation. So long as firms, in general, are able to make profits, they are able to integrate their managers into a logic of capital accumulation; and so long as capitalism reproduces a revenue base for the state, state managers will have their interests tied to the interests of capital. But what happens to these interests and strategies if capitalism permanently stagnates? If profits can no longer be assured in the long-run? If the career prospects for large numbers of managers became very insecure and precarious? Would statist appeals for greater direct state involvement in controlling investments and flows of capital become more attractive to corporate management? Would statist options be seen as more realistic for state managers? I do not want to suggest that statist solutions that undermine the power of the capitalist class would automatically be pursued by managers and bureaucrats under such economic conditions. There would also have to be a range of political and ideological conditions to make such strategies viable, and there is no necessary reason why such political and ideological conditions would be forthcoming even in situations of chronic stagnation.[23] The important point in the present context is not that there be any inevitability to the emergence of such conditions, but that one can imagine historical conditions under which managers and bureaucrats even in the advanced capitalist countries (let alone third world countries) would find anti-capitalist, statist solutions attractive.

The historical typology of contradictory locations in Table 3.4 does not imply that there is any inevitability to the sequence feudalism-capitalism-statism-socialism-communism. There is nothing which implies that state bureaucrats are destined to be the future ruling class of present-day capitalisms. But it does suggest that the process of class formation and class struggle is considerably more complex and indeterminate than the traditional Marxist story has allowed.

This way of understanding contradictory class locations has several advantages over my previous conceptualization:

1. Certain of the specific conceptual problems of the earlier analysis of contradictory loca-

tions within class relations disappear: the problem of autonomy, the anomalous situations where positions like pilots are considered more proletarianized than many unskilled workers, etc.

2. Treating contradictory locations in terms of relations of exploitation generalizes the concept across modes of production. The concept now has a specific theoretical status in all class systems, and has furthermore a much more focused historical thrust as represented in Table 3.4.

3. This way of conceptualizing 'middle-class' locations makes the problem of their class interests much clearer than before. Their location within class relations is defined by the nature of their material optimizing strategies given the specific kinds of assets they own/control. Their specific class location helps to specify their interests both within the existing capitalist society and with respect to various kinds of alternative games (societies) to which they might want to withdraw. In the previous conceptualization it was problematic to specify precisely the material interests of certain contradictory locations. In particular, there was no consistent reason for treating the material interests of 'semi-autonomous employees' as necessarily distinct from those of workers.

4. This exploitation-based strategy helps to clarify the problems of class alliances in a much more systematic way than the previous approach. In the case of contradictory locations it was never clear how to assess the tendencies for contradictory locations to ally themselves with workers or non-workers. I made claims that such alliance tendencies were politically and ideologically determined, but I was not able to put more content into such notions. In contrast, . . . the exploitation-based concept of contradictory locations helps to provide a much clearer material basis for analysing the problem of alliances.

Once Again, Unresolved Problems

The process of concept formation is a continual process of concept transformation. New solutions pose new problems, and the efforts at resolving those problems in turn generate new solutions. Thus, the conceptual apparatus elaborated in this chapter has generated a new set of difficulties. Ultimately, of course, these difficulties may prove 'fatal' to the proposed concept; at a minimum they call for further clarifications and refinements.

Four such problems seem particularly pressing: (1) the status of 'organization' in organization assets; (2) the relationship between skill exploitation and classes; (3) causal interactions among forms of exploitation; (4) non-asset-based mechanisms of exploitation. . . .

NON-ASSET BASES OF EXPLOITATION

. . . I have self-consciously limited the discussion to exploitation rooted in control or ownership of productive forces, i.e. the various kinds of inputs used in production. But there may be other mechanisms through which individuals or groups may be able to appropriate part of the social surplus. Control over the means of salvation may give churches an ability to exploit believers. Control over military violence may give the state an ability to appropriate part of the surplus whether or not it is also involved in controlling aspects of the forces of production. Male domination within the family may enable men to appropriate surplus labour in the form of domestic services from their wives. Racial domination may enable whites as such, regardless of economic class, to exploit blacks.

The issue then becomes: why should property relations be privileged in the analysis of classes? Why should the analysis revolve around ownership/control of the productive forces and the exploitation and class relations that are built on that ownership? Why not talk about religious classes, or military classes, or sex classes, or race classes?

To begin with, it should be noted that if the mechanism which allows priests, officers, men or whites to exploit others is their ownership/control over productive assets, then there is no particular challenge posed to the strategy of analysis proposed in this chapter. While these non-asset social criteria would be important in explaining the social distribution of productive assets, it would remain the case that class and exploitation would remain defined in terms of property relations.

The difficulties arise when various kinds of non-productive categories have direct, enforcable claims on the surplus, unmediated by their relationship to the system of production. Men, for example, may appropriate surplus labour from women simply by virtue of being men within the gender relations of the family and not by virtue of the gender distribution of productive assets. Such possibilities pose a more serious challenge to the approach I have been pursuing.

There are basically two reasons why I think the concept of class should be restricted to exploitation rooted in production relations and not extended to encompass all possible social relations within which exploitation occurs. First, the concept of class is meant to figure centrally in epochal theories of social change, theories of the overall trajectory of historical development. In such epochal theories, the development of the productive forces—of technology and other sources of productivity—play a pivotal role.[24] Even if we do not accord the development of the productive forces an autonomous, trans-historical, dynamic role in a theory of history, nevertheless it can be argued that whatever directionality historical development has is the result of the development of the productive forces.[25] If we grant this, then the effective control over the productive forces and the exploitation which such control generates has a particularly important strategic significance in the theory of history. Such control—property relations broadly conceived—defines the basic terrain of interests with respect to historical development. For this reason, it can be argued, it is appropriate to restrict the concept of class to property relations.

Even if we reject the thesis that the productive forces play a pivotal role in the theory of history, there is still a second argument for restricting the concept of class to production relations. If exploitation rooted in production relations has a distinct logic from exploitation rooted in other relations, then one would be justified in treating property-based exploitation and the associated social relations as a distinct category, that of a 'class'.

What is this 'distinct logic'? Above all, production relations are a distinctive basis for exploitation because of the way they are systematically implicated in the basic subsistence of the exploited. Property relations not only determine mechanisms by which surplus is appropriated; they simultaneously determine mechanisms by which the exploited gain access to subsistence, to their means of existence. Other mechanisms of exploitation are essentially *redistributive* of a social product already produced within a set of property relations; property-based exploitation is directly bound up with the social production of that product in the first place. We are justified, therefore, in considering production-based exploitation a distinct category from non-production exploitations because of the specific type of interdependency it creates between the exploited and the exploiter.

This distinctiveness does not, in and of itself, say anything about the relative importance of class exploitation over other forms of exploitation. Military exploitation or gender exploitation could be more fundamental for understanding social conflict than class exploitation (although I do not in fact think that this is the case). The distinctive form of interdependency constituted by production based exploitation, however, does provide a rationale for restricting the usage of the concept of 'class' to that kind of exploitation. . . .

CONCLUSION

The Exploitation-Centred Concept of Class

My earlier work on class structure suffered, I have argued, from the tendency to displace the concept of exploitation from the centre of class analysis. This weakened the sense in which class relations were intrinsically relations of objectively opposed interests, and posed a series of specific conceptual difficulties.

These difficulties, combined with my empirical research on class structure and my encounter with the theoretical work of John Roemer, have precipitated the reconceptualization of class relations in terms of the multidimensional view of exploitation elaborated [herein]. Classes in capitalist society, I now argue, should be seen as rooted in the complex intersection of three forms of exploitation: exploitation based on the ownership of capital assets, the control of organization assets and the possession of skill or credential assets. While I have some reservations about the class character of the third of these categories, this reconceptualization nevertheless resolved many of the difficulties I had encountered with my previous approach to class structure.

The empirical investigations we have explored add considerable credibility to this reconceptualization. First, . . . when we formally compared the exploitation-centred concept to two rivals—the manual-labour definition of the working class and the productive-labour definition—the exploitation-centred concept fared considerably better. While the results were not without some ambiguities and are thus subject to alternative interpretations, in general where the alternative definitions disagreed about the class of particular positions, the data supported their class placement according to the logic and criteria of the exploitation-based concept.

Second, when we examined the relationship between class structure and income inequality . . . , the results were almost exactly as predicted by the exploitation-centred concept. This was a complex prediction, since it involved specifying the way income would vary across the three dimensions of the class structure matrix. The patterns followed these expectations very closely: income increased essentially monotonically as we moved along all of the dimensions of exploitation taken singly or together.

Finally, . . . the investigation of the relationship between class structure and class consciousness has added further to the credibility of the reconceptualization. The patterns of variation of consciousness across positions in the class structure matrix conform closely to the theoretical expectations. The results seem to be relatively robust and, at least on the basis of the variables we have considered, do not appear to be artifacts of certain possible sources of spuriousness. Furthermore, the same basic pattern is observed in two countries which are dramatically different in their general political complexion.

Taken together, these diverse empirical results lend considerable support to the new conceptualization of class structure. Empirical results of this sort, however, can never provide definitive judgements. Alternative explanations of the observed patterns are always available and the conclusions I have drawn are inevitably open to both theoretical and methodological question. But until a more compelling rival conception of class enters the fray of theoretical and empirical adjudication, there are compelling reasons to adopt some variant of the approach proposed here.

The Class Structure of Contemporary Capitalism

Using this new conceptualization of class structure, we have systematically explored the contours of the American and Swedish class structures. Leaving aside all of the details of that analysis, there are two broad generalizations that we can make.

First, in both countries, in spite of the technical and social changes of contemporary capitalism, the working class remains by far the largest class in the labour force. Even if we adopt a narrow specification of the working class, which excludes various holders of 'marginal' exploitation assets, around forty per cent of the labour force is in this class. If these marginal categories are added—and there are good reasons to do so, particularly in the case of the 'semi-credentialled employee' category—then the working class becomes a clear majority in both countries.

Second, and equally important, while the working class is the largest class, a substantial pro-

portion of the labour force occupies exploitative locations within the class structure. Even if, again, we exclude all possessors of marginal exploitation assets from this designation, somewhere around one quarter of the labour force in Sweden and the United States are exploiters. Looked at in terms of families rather than individuals, an even higher proportion of families have at least one person in an exploiting class within them, probably around forty per cent of all households. This is not to say that such individuals and families are *net* exploiters. The central argument in the reconceptualization of the 'middle class' is that such positions are *simultaneously* exploiters and exploited. This is precisely what defines the complexity of their class interests and puts them into what I have called 'contradictory locations within exploitation relations'. My guess is that most of these individuals and families are still more capitalistically exploited than they are exploiters through other mechanisms. Nevertheless, this does not obliterate the fact that they are exploiters and that, as a result, they have material interests which are fundamentally different from those of workers.

Class Structure and Politics

Class structure is of pervasive importance in contemporary social life. The control over society's productive assets determines the fundamental material interests of actors and heavily shapes the capacities of both individuals and collectivities to pursue their interests. The fact that a substantial portion of the population may be relatively comfortable materially does not negate the fact that their capacities and interests remain bound up with property relations and the associated processes of exploitation.

Nevertheless, in spite of this importance, the effects of class structure are mediated by politics. Class relations may define the terrain upon which interests are formed and collective capacities forged, but the outcome of that process of class formation cannot be 'read off' the class structure itself.

NOTES

1. I would like to express my particular thanks to Robbie Manchin for an intense Sunday afternoon's discussion of the problem of class and exploitation which led to development of the core ideas in this chapter. His ideas in that discussion were particularly important for developing the concept of 'organization assets' discussed below.

2. If the poor are able to force a partial redistribution of income from the rich through political means it might seem that by this definition this could be construed as a situation of the poor exploiting the rich: the poor become less poor at the expense of the rich. It is important, therefore, to examine the total causal context before assessing exploitation relations. In the case in question, *if* the rich obtained their incomes through exploitation, then a redistribution should be viewed as a reduction in exploitation rather than counterexploitation. . . .

3. This is not to imply that domination in the labour process is *institutionally* unimportant, or indeed, that such domination does not in practice intensify capitalist exploitation and reinforce the capital–labour class relation. Roemer's point is simply that it is not the actual criterion for class relations; that criterion is strictly based on property relations as such.

4. See Erik Olin Wright, 'The Status of the Political in the Concept of Class Structure', *Politics & Society*, vol. 11, no. 3, 1982.

5. This position is most forcefully staked out in Roemer's essay, 'Why Should Marxists be Interested in Exploitation?' [University of California, Davis, Department of Economics, working paper no. 221, 1983.] The illustrative example discussed here comes from this essay.

6. Two technical points: first, I use the expression 'the fruits of labour' rather than 'labour' since the definition is meant to be independent of the tenets of the labour theory of value. (For a spe-cific discussion of the distinction between viewing exploitation as appropriation of the fruits of labour rather than the appropriation of labour values, see G. A. Cohen, 'The Labour Theory of Value and the Concept of Exploitation', in *The Value Controversy*, Steedman et al., London 1981). Second, 'surplus' is notoriously hard to define rigorously once the labour theory of value is abandoned, since its magnitude (i.e. its 'value') can no longer be defined independently of prices. Throughout this discussion, when I refer to transfers of surplus or claims on the surplus I am referring to the surplus *product* which will be appropriated by an exploiting class.

7. Roemer has recognized that there is a difference in capitalism between the exploitation of workers and the exploitation of the unemployed. He has captured this difference by introducing the additional criterion . . . capitalists would be worse off if workers stopped producing, but not if the unemployed stopped producing. When Roemer introduces this additional criterion, he refers to the unemployed as 'unfairly treated' rather than exploited, where unfair treatment is essentially equivalent to what I am here calling 'economic oppression'. While I cannot prove this formally, I believe that the criterion Roemer adopts in this instance is equivalent to what I term 'appropriation of the fruits of labour by the exploited': to say that capitalists would be worse off if workers stopped producing (or, equivalently, if they left the game of capitalism with their personal assets, which in this case would only be their labour power) is the same as saying that in fact there is a transfer of surplus occurring from workers to capitalists.

8. Indeed, in many practical cases, the oppressor would be better off if the oppressed died, since oppression typically imposes costs on the oppressor in the form of social-control expenses, and sometimes even subsidies to the oppressed (as in the welfare-state provisions of minimum standards of living for the poor). In the example of the rich and poor peasant above, the rent paid to

the poor peasant is like a welfare-state payment by the rich peasant: the rich peasant would be better off if he simply killed the poor peasant and took over the poor peasant's land.

9. It follows from this that, except under peculiar circumstances, exploiters would not have material interests in the genocide of the exploited, whereas non-exploiting oppressors might. . . .

10. It is because capitalism at one and the same time both largely eliminates one form of exploitation and accentuates another that it is difficult to say whether or not in the transition from feudalism to capitalism overall exploitation increased or decreased.

11. It should be noted that this claim is logically independent of the labour theory of value. There is no assumption that commodities exchange in proportions regulated by the amount of socially necessary labour embodied in them. What is claimed is that the income of capitalists constitutes the monetary value of the surplus produced by workers. That is sufficient for their income to be treated as exploitative. . . .

12. This, it should be noted, is precisely what leftist critics within 'actually existing socialist societies' say is the core problem on the political agenda of radical change in those countries.

13. For a discussion of the problem of the democratization of organizational control in the context of the Russian Revolution and other attempts at workers democracy, see Carmen Sirianni, *Workers Control and Socialist Democracy*, London, 1982.

14. Or, to use the expression that is no longer in favour in 'polite' Marxist circles, that socialism is the 'dictatorship of the proletariat'.

15. Stated somewhat differently, a table of correspondences between asset ownership and relational location could be constructed for both labour-power assets and organization assets, but not skill assets. Although the form of the derivations involved would be different from the one for capi-

tal assets, in each case it would be possible to 'derive' a set of relational properties directly from the ownership of the assets. In the case of organization assets the derivation would be of the authority relations that would be attached to positions by virtue of the organizational assets controlled by incumbents of the position; in the case of feudal assets there would be a direct correspondence between ownership of a labour-power asset and personal control over the biological possessor of that asset.

16. In the case of capitalist societies this might imply that skill or credential differences should be regarded as the basis for class segments or fractions among workers and among manager–bureaucrats, rather than a proper dimension of the class structure. I will continue in the rest of this book to treat credential-exploitation as the basis of a class relation, as reflected in Table 3.2, but this characterization should be treated cautiously.

17. One can imagine three possible degrees of equalization: (1) equalization of actual possession of an asset; (2) equalization of the control over the acquisition and use of the asset; (3) equalization of the income generated by the asset. Eliminating exploitation requires, at a minimum, the satisfaction of (3) for each asset. It may or may not require (1). In the case of the transition from feudalism to capitalism, for example, actual possession of labour power was basically equalized as well as effective control. In the transition from socialism to communism it seems implausible that actual possession of skills could be equalized, but probably control over the use of socially productive skills could be.

18. Note that *some* petty bourgeois, in this formulation, will actually be exploited by capital (through unequal exchange on the market) because they own such minimal means of production, and some will be capitalistic exploiters because they own a great deal of capital even though they may not hire any wage-earners. Exploitation status, therefore, cannot strictly be equated with self-employment/wage-earner status.

19. This is not to deny that many professionals and managers become significant owners of capital assets through savings out of high incomes. To the extent that this happens, however, their class location begins to shift objectively and they move into a bourgeois location. Here I am talking only about those professional and managerial positions which are not vehicles for entry into the bourgeoisie itself.

20. The old middle class in feudalism, on the other hand, is defined by the freed peasants (yeoman farmers), the peasant who, within a system of unequally distributed assets in labour power own their per capita share of the asset (i.e. they are 'free').

21. Theorists who have attempted to analyse the class structures of 'actually existing socialism' in terms of concept of a 'new class' generally tend to amalgamate state bureaucrats and experts into a single dominant class location, rather than seeing them as essentially vying for class power. Some theorists, such as G. Konrad and I. Szelenyi, *Intellectuals on the Road to Class Power*, and Alvin Gouldner, *The Future of Intellectuals . . .* , do recognize this division, although they do not theorize the problem in precisely the way posed here.

22. For discussions of the ways in which the capitalist state is systematically tied to the interests of the bourgeoisie, see Claus Offe, 'Structural Problems of the Capitalist State: Class rule and the political system', in C. von Beyme ed., *German Political Studies*, vol. 1, Russel Sage, 1974; Göran Therborn, *What Does the Ruling Class Do When It Rules?*, London 1978. For a contrasting view which gives the state much greater potential autonomy from capital, see Theda Skocpol, 'Political Response to Capitalist Crisis: neo-Marxist Theories of the State and the Case of the New Deal', *Politics & Society*, vol. 10, no. 2, 1980.

23. While it has become very fashionable on the left to criticize any hint of 'economism' in social theory, I nevertheless believe that the emergence of the kinds of political and ideological conditions necessary for the development of anti-capitalist postures by managers and state bureaucrats are more likely under conditions of chronic stagnation and decline than under conditions of capitalist expansion and growth. . . .

24. This is not the place to enter the debates on the theory of history in general, or the role of the productive forces in such a theory in particular. For a discussion of these problems, see Andrew Levine and Erik Olin Wright, 'Rationality and Class Struggle', *New Left Review*, 123, 1980, and Erik Olin Wright, 'Giddens's Critique of Marxism', *New Left Review*, 139, 1983.

25. The argument is basically that technical change creates a kind of 'ratchet' in which movement 'backward' (regressions) becomes less likely than either stasis or movement 'forward'. Even if the occurrence of technical change is random and sporadic, therefore, it will generate weak tendencies for historical change to have direction.

14

Mass Production in Postmodern Times

Richard J. Barnet and John Cavanagh

I.

In the second half of the twentieth century the global productive system was transformed. The appearance of the factory floor, the sex, race, and nationality of the work force, changes in labor-management relations, and the ever increasing numbers of foreign flags flying in front of corporate headquarters around the world heralded a new era in the history of work. Mammoth assembly plants of the sort that thrilled Henry Ford and Joseph Stalin are still in evidence, many of them now in out-of-the-way places, a few bigger than ever, but less and less of the world's work is done there. One reason is that the production of goods is dispersed to smaller facilities around the world, to subcontractors, suppliers, and casual workers, many of whom cut, sew, and punch data at home. But the main reason is that more and more of the world's work is not in manufacturing.

Vast numbers of workers around the world are engaged in producing, marketing, and distributing paper and electronic data of symbolic value. All sorts of marketable information such as insurance policies, bond offerings, investment tips, legal opinions, and shopping guides are pouring forth into the world marketplace. Word-processed promises, advice, and opinions now figure among the world's most profitable products. Even more workers are engaged in feeding people all over the world, curing, comforting, and entertaining them, or picking up after them in their houses, hotels, and other public places. Armies of service-providers of all sorts are employed by large global networks—ad agencies, law firms, investment houses, airlines, restaurants, hotels, hospitals, clinics, media complexes, and waste-removal companies. According to the *Random House Dictionary*, "any place producing a uniform product, without concern for individuality" is a factory. By this definition more and more of us are factory workers.

The Ford Motor Company ushered in the era of mass production. Indeed, modern capitalism is sometimes described as "Fordism," a word that connotes the marriage of mass production based on well-paid jobs on the assembly line and mass consumption of affordable, standardized products. In 1903, when Henry Ford started making cars, each assembler was responsible for putting the whole car together himself, and it took 514 minutes, almost nine hours, to turn one out. For five years the young mechanic experimented with ways to speed up the assembly process. In 1908 he hit upon a new way to make an automobile. . . .

II.

It fell to the Japanese to modify the mass-production process, and their reward was to take over a third of the U.S. car market. In this they had considerable American help of all sorts. By reducing much of Japanese prewar industry to rubble, American bombs forced the Japanese to conceive a new production system. There was no money to buy factory technology from abroad. It had to be invented, and it was. Americans, notably the quality-control expert W. Edwards Deming, were influential contributors to this process.

From *Global Dreams Imperial Corporation and the New World Order* by Richard J. Barnet and John Cavanagh. Reprinted with permission of Simon & Schuster.

Japanese carmakers, trying to rebuild their plants, made a virtue out of necessity. In the prewar years the Toyota Motor Company, founded in 1937 by a wealthy family that had been in the textile business, specialized in military trucks. Since its prewar factories lay in ruins and hardly anyone was in a position to buy a car in 1945, Toyota and its competitors were forced to develop a new production system. The Japanese combined innovations in engineering with innovations in social organization that fit the new technology and Japanese culture.

The International Motor Vehicle Program at MIT conducted a five-year study of the system Toyota developed, which it calls "lean production."[1] The first element in the process was to develop ways to stamp auto parts in very small batches. Toyota needed a production system that did not create large inventories. In 1950 it was making only 2,685 automobiles a year; Ford was producing 7,000 a day in just one plant. Taiichi Ochno, the engineering chief at Toyota, had by the late 1950s succeeded in reducing the time needed to change dies used for stamping and forming metal parts from a day to three minutes. Dies are metal mold halves held in huge stamping presses. Sheet metal is inserted between the mold halves, which are then brought together to form the distinctive shapes of fenders, hoods, and the nearly 300 other metal stampings that go into an automobile. Changing dies often and quickly meant that defects showed up quickly and much waste was eliminated. Instead of employing specialists to change the dies as in Detroit, he trained the production workers to do it themselves, thus both saving labor costs and making the workers' jobs more interesting.[2]

Douglas MacArthur, the conservative American general in charge of the Japanese occupation, had introduced into Japan a series of labor laws prepared by his liberal advisers that were far more stringent—and for Japanese companies far more expensive—than anything that had been enacted in the United States during the New Deal. Strengthening unions was part of the American program of democratization and reeducation to destroy militarism in Japan. The right to lay off workers was limited, and powerful unions exacted many concessions, including profit sharing. (In the United States, by contrast, the Taft-Hartley law, enacted in 1946, severely cut back labor's bargaining power.)

MacArthur also instituted draconian austerity policies designed to squeeze inflation out of the postwar Japanese economy. There was tremendous pressure on corporations to cut costs. Kiichiro Toyoda, the president of Toyota, attempted this by firing a quarter of his labor force. The workers occupied the factory. But from the settlement of this strike the postwar Japanese labor compact was born. A quarter of the workers were indeed dismissed, but the rest received the promise of lifetime employment. As the summary of the MIT study, *The Machine That Changed the World*, puts it:

In short, they became members of the Toyota community with a full set of rights, including the guarantee of lifetime employment and access to Toyota facilities (housing, recreation, and so forth), that went far beyond what most unions had been able to negotiate for mass-production employees in the West. . . . Thus in every plant workers became as much a fixed cost as the machinery, but, unlike machines, workers gained in skill over their working life.

When Taiichi Ochno, the chief engineer at Toyota, visited Ford's Rouge plant in Detroit in 1950 he was astonished by both the expanse of the plant, which could never be duplicated in the squeezed cities of Japan, and by the waste. Even in the 1980s auto plants using traditional mass-production methods had to dedicate 20 percent of plant area and 25 percent of man-hours to fixing mistakes.[3] Ochno discovered that assembly workers had a much lower status than the specialists who were employed to discover and correct their mistakes. On his return to Japan he organized workers into teams, gradually gave assembly workers additional responsibilities such as tool repair and quality checking. The emphasis was on collaborative team effort. In U.S. plants only the line manager could pull the cord that brought everything to a halt so that the "rework" specialists could undo the damage done days earlier. In Toyota plants, Ochno decided, any worker should be able to stop the line. This emphasis on preventing errors and solving problems early in the production process resulted in a dramatic increase in productivity and quality.

The most famous aspect of post-mass-production manufacturing is the "just in time" supply chain, known as *kanban* in Japan and JIT in the United States. The idea was to calibrate the flow of supplies so that large inventories became unnecessary. The parts would arrive at the time they were needed in the production process. This would eliminate the need for storage space and the costs of idle time on the production line as a result of supplier delays. The production of parts would be dictated by the immediate requirements of the next stage in the production process. Each container of parts was returned to the supplier as soon as the parts were used up, and this was the signal to send more.

Lean production also seeks to reduce production costs by introducing a flexibility that enables producers to adjust to changes in consumer tastes. Toyota is half as big as GM but offers as many models. The average Japanese model is kept in production for only four years while U.S. and European companies keep them almost ten years; production runs are half the size. This greater facility in adapting models to changing customer tastes is backed up by a sophisticated marketing system.

In the American system, dealers have served historically as "shock absorbers" for the carmakers. In slow periods the manufacturers would reduce their factory inventory by forcing dealers to take more cars on their lots than they could sell. In contrast, Toyota and other Japanese companies made much greater efforts to adjust the production process to the market and to develop the market by aggressive monitoring of the shifting attitudes of customers and assiduous cultivation of the best prospects. In Japan, Toyota sales representatives made house calls to drum up business. In the United States, Toyota, Honda, and the other

Japanese manufacturers devoted substantial resources to building up a large data base on customer tastes and preferences. Old customers were treated as members of the "Toyota family."[4]

The Ford Motor Company became the pioneer U.S. automaker to revamp its production line using Japanese models and experience. Lean production was no more dependent on Japanese culture, Ford executives came to believe, than old-fashioned mass production depended on growing up in Detroit. To be sure, Japanese practices had to be modified. The manager of Ford's Wixom plant, which is the largest manufacturing facility in North America, told us he had observed Japanese workers running from one work station to another, something American workers will not do. But Ford has adapted many Japanese techniques to its North American plants, and these are almost as productive as the average Japanese plant. One Ford factory in Mexico, according to the MIT study, had the best assembly-plant quality of the entire global sample, better than the best of the Japanese auto plants.[5]

In 1985 Donald E. Petersen became chairman of the Ford Motor Company, the first engineer to head it since the founder. It was a difficult period for the U.S. auto industry, but Ford surged ahead of its American competitors and for several years it was the most profitable American automaker. Understanding the extent and chronic nature of the global overcapacity of the industry more quickly than its competitors, Ford cut payrolls, closed factories, and figured out how to make attractive and reliable cars more cheaply.

Ford had already carried out a major retooling of its production facilities all over the world, investing $28 billion to automate production and to eliminate excess capacity. The company's global work force was cut from 506,500 to 390,000. Most of the cuts were in the United States. Over a nine-year period, the number of robots in the North American plants rose from 236 to 1,300, and more than 80,000 hourly workers and 16,000 salaried white-collar workers were discharged.[6] The number of hourly workers fell by 47 percent and productivity increased by 57 percent; labor costs per car were now $800 less than at GM.[7]

Computer-driven machines to weld, stamp out parts, and schedule, control, and monitor production were introduced into Ford plants in Europe as well as in North America. Ford also adopted "just in time" production, enabling the company to reduce its inventories from three weeks to one week; in just one engine plant this innovation resulted in a $30-million saving. In Spain, a complete production line for Escorts was installed in a space previously used to store parts. . . .

V.

Because of the size and importance of the industry, the loss of American jobs in auto production has been front-page news for many years. But the same pressures and incentives operate in virtually all other industries and in many other industrial countries. The financial rewards in closing factories in the home country and opening them in low-wage enclaves of Latin America and Asia have been especially irresistible for U.S. companies, however, because of a variety of government policies — credits, tax breaks, tariff exemptions, and insurance against overseas losses — that have accelerated the deindustrialization of the United States.

Poor countries with unorganized work forces are attractive production sites for global companies, whatever flag they fly. Higher profits, labor peace, access to natural resources of the region and to local markets are powerful incentives to relocate factories. The countries spread across the planet along what professors like to call the "periphery" of the world economy and most people still call the Third World have little in common beyond rapidly growing nonwhite populations, histories of colonialism, hot weather, and tenacious poverty. In the years 1962–71 imports of manufactured goods from underdeveloped countries into the United States increased by almost 18 percent a year.

However, a large share of the imports were from U.S.-owned factories in the former colonial world.[8] Bulova, for example, began to manufacture its watch movements in Switzerland and ship them to Pago Pago in American Samoa, where they were assembled for the U.S. market. The cost of transportation was more than offset by the happy circumstance that goods from American Samoa enter the United States free of tariff. "We are able to beat the foreign competition," Bulova president Harry B. Henshel explained, "because we *are* the foreign competition."[9] By 1991 more than half of all U.S. exports and imports were transfers of components and services within the same global corporation, most of them flying the American flag.[10]

European companies such as Philips, Nestlé, and Siemens, all based in small countries like Holland, Switzerland, and the former West Germany, outgrew their home markets years ago and began deriving ever greater shares of their profits from foreign sales. It made economic as well as political sense to locate factories close to new expanding markets to save transportation costs. France encouraged its corporations to establish operations in its former colonial possessions in West Africa. British corporations gravitated to the more promising newly independent countries of once-British East Africa, notably Kenya.

Then the Japanese joined the exodus, although at a slower pace. In the 1960s, as wages at home rose and pollution problems became an issue, textile manufacturers and apparel makers shifted operations from the home islands to East Asia, particularly Hong Kong. In the next decade a sizable chunk of the electronics industry moved offshore. According to the Japanese Electrical Machinery Industry Association, 193,000 workers were employed in the 1980s by Japanese electrical-equipment affiliates throughout the world, and of these 134,000 were in East Asia.[11]

These transformations in the geography of production changed the face of all industrial countries, but the changes have been especially dramatic in the United States. In 1950 about a third of all American jobs were in manufacturing; by the mid-1980s factory employment accounted for only 20 percent of the work force, and by the early 1990s only 16 percent.[12] During the 1970s, to give two examples of a widely imitated cost-cutting strategy, General Electric added 30,000 foreign jobs and eliminated 25,000 American workers from its payroll; RCA laid off 14,000 workers in the United States and hired 19,000 abroad. In the 1990s workers in Australia, Ireland, and the United Kingdom can be hired for 60 percent of a U.S. hourly wage, and Mexicans, Brazilians, and South Koreans still work for 10 to 15 percent of U.S. labor costs. Fiber-optic systems, regional telecommunications, satellite teleports, telefax, microwave communications, and specially wired "smart" buildings make it possible for world headquarters of global corporations to adapt some of the technologies of command and control developed for the military to their commercial and financial operations spread across the globe.[13]

Although the loss of industrial jobs is most pronounced in the United States, the same trends are evident in other great manufacturing centers in the industrial world. In the United Kingdom there was a net decline of more than a million manufacturing jobs between 1966 and 1976. Employment in the motor-vehicle, shipbuilding, metal-manufacturing, mechanical-engineering, and electrical-engineering industries fell from 10 to 20 percent in that decade alone. In the West Midlands, a leading industrial region, 151,117 more manufacturing jobs were lost than were created in just three bad years, 1978–81. In Lancashire the textile industry lost a half-million jobs. In the industrial areas of northeast France and western Belgium unemployment rates shot up from 1 to 2 percent in 1973 to a range of 8 to 12 percent by the mid-1980s. Traditional industrial regions in northern England, Northern Ireland, Wales, Hamburg, Nordrhein-Westfalen, Saarland, Auvergne, and the Paris basin became pockets of severe and chronic unemployment.[14]

The closing of factories that had been located in or near the heart of America's industrial cities caused an exodus from what came to be known as the "inner city." The term dates from the early 1960s. A generation before, many of these same blocks and census tracts were the heart of the city; now people spoke of them as if they were abscesses. Not all the downtown factory closings were prompted by decisions to move out of the country altogether; corporate flight to the suburbs also played a role. In the postwar boom years, huge suburban housing tracts sprouted all across the country, and women (who typically earned 60 percent of what a male earned for equivalent work) entered the labor market in droves. This new labor market, along with cheap land and lower taxes, attracted corporations out of the older urban industrial regions into the surrounding rural areas where clean, safe "bedroom communities" were sprouting.

The result was that virtually all the older cities developed "inner-city problems"—50-percent unemployment rates for undereducated youth, crime, declining educational facilities, inadequate health facilities—and, as cities became increasingly expensive, unpleasant, and dangerous places to work and live, the exodus of large corporations accelerated. As stories of inanities and violence in the schoolroom, traffic jams, soaring real-estate assessments, and random killings were becoming staple dinner-party talk among their executives, a number of top manufacturing companies resolved to relocate their world headquarters to less stressful surroundings.

As firms scanned the globe for the best places to relocate their production facilities, countries and regions all over the world, including the Sunbelt in the United States, hungrily competed for jobs with offers of tax holidays and other benefits that cost-conscious companies could not pass up. What was still being produced in the advanced industrial countries, what neighborhoods, cities, and regions were attracting the production, and what the work force was coming to look like were all caught up in a vortex of change.

As the great corporations merged, automated, exported jobs, and relied increasingly on subcontractors and temporary employees, the Global

Workplace took on a new look. Old jobs were lost by the millions, but new manufacturing and related jobs in substantially lower numbers were created in high-technology industries—aerospace, robotics, synthetics, chemicals, and ceramics—in the technology of sophisticated assembly, and in the fashion industry—clothes, furniture, specialized fittings of all sorts for the upscale market. All this changed the way cities looked. Right next to row on row of dilapidated buildings where former factory workers waited for government checks and young men without hope of jobs supported themselves running drugs or by violent crime, there rose gleaming miracle miles of shopping malls, hotels, and globally connected offices.

For some workers, regions, and city blocks around the world, this shift in production brought unparalleled prosperity and for others crushing poverty. Everywhere the gap between neighborhoods with a future and those with memories of a once-prosperous past widened. As the 1980s began, local politicians in the United States with presidential ambitions claimed that the economic surges in Massachusetts and other parts of the country based on the influx of advanced high-tech hardware factories and information software companies were models for the renewal of the American economy as a whole. But by the end of the decade many of these "miracles" had lost their luster. California and the East Coast industrial corridor were hit hard in the recession of the early 1990s, while enclaves within the old Midwest "Rustbelt" that had diversified their manufacturing bases and were now producing specialized industrial products for export were doing better than the rest of the country.[15] As the impact of the new global production system began to be felt, the fissures dividing the winners and losers grew deeper. The "gales of creative destruction," as the economist Joseph Schumpeter termed the processes of capitalist change, could sweep through a neighborhood as a gentle breeze or an ill wind, depending on whether people who lived or worked there found themselves in or out of the prospering sectors of the global economy.

Arcane matters of trade suddenly became highly charged political issues. As hundreds of thousands of American autoworkers lost their jobs, a few vented their anger by kicking in Honda fenders. Matt Darcy, a Chevrolet salesman from Garden City, Michigan, was interviewed on *60 Minutes* and said he had qualms about urging customers to buy American products when they were inferior to what foreign competitors were offering. He was summarily fired for disloyalty to his car and country.[16] Some U.S. politicians attempted to capitalize on public anger about the loss of American jobs by resorting to voodoo; one congressman took a sledgehammer to a Toshiba television set, and the picture flashed across the world via CNN.

From Japan came return fire, some from prominent political personalities who raised the decibel level: The world's sole remaining superpower was suffering from a lazy, illiterate, mongrelized work force run by avaricious executives who paid themselves fat salaries for producing shoddy products. Such America-bashing remarks circulating in Japan had a good chance of being instantly picked up in the United States, and on one occasion when this happened Senator Ernest F. Hollings of South Carolina told a group of cheering American factory workers to send the Japanese a picture of a mushroom cloud with the message underneath it: "Made in America by lazy and illiterate Americans and tested in Japan."[17] Just as the mayor of Chicago in the 1920s used to run against King George V, now White House aspirants ran against Toyotas. "Buy American" became the cry of the 1990s as the president, the Republican Party, and some prominent American companies took the pledge.

The trouble was that, however heartfelt the patriotic desire to patronize American products, the pledge could not be kept. In the age of globalization, insistence on purity of lineage in cars, radios, indeed most products in international commerce, makes about as much sense as notions of racial purity. There is little of either in the world today, and the illusion of purity of origin, whatever form it takes, can drive human beings to irrational, indeed murderous behavior. What is an "American" car? A Geo Prizm, which is really a Toyota Corolla made in California? A Geo Metro, marketed by GM but made by Suzuki and Isuzu? What is a "foreign" car? A Jaguar made in England by a wholly owned Ford subsidiary? A Mazda Navaho, which is really a Ford Explorer made in Kentucky?[18]

Some companies, including Monsanto, promised to pay as much as $1,000 to any of their employees who bought an "American" car. But all had different definitions of what an American car was. (Franklin Bank of Southfield, Michigan, devised a Buy American plan for its employees under which it rejected Hondas made in Ohio but allowed Chrysler minivans made in Canada.) As the 1992 presidential election campaign got under way, the Bush–Quayle campaign announced its Buy American plan and boasted that its fax machines came from Texas and its computers from San Jose. But one company was Japanese and the other Korean. A spokesperson explained, "We did try very hard to get American-made PCs, but the ones available were way out of our price range."[19]

A key to the American strategy to save jobs in the United States once U.S.-based manufacturers had fled American shores was to insist that foreign companies manufacturing in the United States include substantial "local content." But the concept leads inexorably into a thicket of legal complexity and logical confusion. For example, Hondas made in Canada, according to the Customs Service, do not qualify for tariff-free treatment because they fall short of the required 50-percent "North American content." It is not that Canada is not North American, but that too many parts can be traced back to a network of Japanese suppliers. The Japanese government maintains that more than 60 percent of 931 Japanese-owned companies in the United States obtain "two-thirds of their materials in America," but many of these "American" suppliers are Japanese-owned. Moreover, legal legerdemain and accounting alchemy can turn American parts into Japanese parts and vice versa. Robert Reich, who became secretary of labor in

the Clinton administration, gives a graphic illustration of some of the problems of basing a nation's employment policy on the pedigrees of globally produced machines:

When an American buys a Pontiac Le Mans from General Motors, for example, he engages unwittingly in an international transaction. Of the $10,000 paid to GM, about $3,000 goes to South Korea for routine labor and assembly operations, $1,850 to Japan for advanced components (engines, transaxles, and electronics), $700 to the former West Germany for styling and design engineering, $400 to Taiwan, Singapore, and Japan for small components, $250 to Britain for advertising and marketing services, and about $50 to Ireland and Barbados for data processing. The rest—less than $4,000—goes to strategists in Detroit, lawyers, bankers in New York, lobbyists in Washington, insurance and health care workers all over the country, and to General Motors shareholders all over the world.[20]

It is now a fact of global life that multinationals, whatever flag they fly, can use overseas subsidiaries, joint ventures, licensing agreements, and strategic alliances to assume foreign identities when it suits their purposes—either to help them slip under tariff walls or to take advantage of some law of another country. Thus the American subsidiaries of Japanese and European global companies are going into American courts as zealous protectors of American jobs, bringing antidumping suits against low-wage Korean and Taiwanese competitors. "When we go to Brussels, we're a member state [of the European Community]," an executive of the U.S. pharmaceutical firm SmithKline (now merged with the British-based drug company Beecham) explains. "And when we go to Washington, we're an American company, too."[21]

To look like a "stateless corporation" is becoming more and more of a corporate goal, and to a limited extent the goal is achieved. "IBM, to some degree, has successfully lost its American identity," according to C. Michael Armstrong, senior vice-president in charge of IBM World Trade Corp. The *Economist* puts it more strongly. "One of the secrets of IBM's success is that IBM Europe is a European company just as IBM Japan is a Japanese one." IBM Japan is Japan's biggest exporter of computers.[22] There are no more American-sounding brand names than General Electric and RCA, but a French firm with an English name, Thomson, owns these famous trademarks for its consumer-electronics line.[23] The Japanese government observes the Arab embargo of Israel. Japanese cars are banned by the Taiwanese and South Korean governments to protect local industry. But by the miracle of globalization "Japanese" cars are transformed into "American" cars as Honda ships its Accords to Taiwan, Korea, and Israel from its Ohio plant. The rise of regional trading blocs in Europe, North America, and East Asia is encouraging a number of world corporations to develop what *Business Week* calls "chameleon-like abilities to resemble insiders no matter where they operate."[24]

VI.

As the global market becomes more important for American firms, the less invested they become in the territory of the United States. Reich has argued that these firms "are rapidly becoming global entities with no special relationship to the United States economy."[25] He says that foreign-owned companies willing to employ, train, and offer job security and good working conditions to American workers by locating production plants and advanced research facilities in Ohio or Tennessee are more "us" than nominally American companies that have fled American shores.

There is truth to his proposition, but it is not the whole truth. The problem of defining corporate identity in a world of nation-states and transnational markets is not a new one. In 1972 Carl A. Gerstacker, chairman of the Dow Chemical Company, confided to the White House Conference on the Industrial World Ahead that he dreamed of buying "an island owned by no nation" and on "such truly neutral ground" he would locate the world headquarters of the Dow company so that "we could then really operate in the United States

as U.S. citizens, in Japan as Japanese citizens, and in Brazil as Brazilians rather than being governed in prime by the laws of the United States." (He promised to pay any natives handsomely to move elsewhere and was promptly offered a Pacific atoll.) Corporations dream of escaping the laws of any nations that restrict the free movement of goods, information, and profits.

But at the same time global companies everywhere look to their home governments to protect their existing markets and to provide muscle for penetrating new markets, to keep labor and environmental costs down, and to subsidize their operations in various ways. The relationship between large corporations and the governments of their home countries varies. In Japanese culture an arms-length, not to say adversarial, relationship between the government and big business is considered bizarre. In the United States the relationship is not as intimate as in Japan, but thanks to the deep involvement of corporations in the political process, it is hardly as adversarial as corporate executives often claim. Theoretically, the leverage federal and local governments have over global companies flying the American flag is greater than over foreign-owned companies since U.S.-based corporations are creations of U.S. laws and they are usually more dependent on the American market than are foreign corporations.

Government treatment of their home-based corporations can result in competitive advantages or disadvantages. The Japanese government does not offer its corporations the same tax incentives to abandon the home country as are available in U.S. law. Thanks to a clearer consensus on the national interest with respect to economic matters than exists in the United States, the Japanese government employs a heavier hand over its corporations to ensure that the long-range needs of Japanese are met. How much home governments are willing to spend on health, education, ports, roads, and other public-infrastructure needs and how they spend it can translate into competitive advantages or disadvantages for their home-based corporations. Clearly, Japanese corporations have benefitted from the decisions of Japanese governments to invest in primary and secondary education. In this sense the playing field is never quite level. The national origin of a global business corporation matters less than it once did, but in a world of nation-states it still matters.

NOTES

1. James P. Womack et al., *The Machine That Changed the World* (New York: Rawson Associates, 1990), pp. 17–18.

2. *Ibid.*, pp. 51–53.

3. *Ibid.*, p. 57.

4. *Ibid.*, pp. 67–68.

5. *Ibid.*, p. 87.

6. Carl H. A. Dassbach, *Global Enterprises and the World Economy* (New York: Garland, 1988), p.406.

7. Based on figures in *Automotive News Market Data Book* 1979, 1987; *Automotive Industries*, November 1987, quoted in Mike Parker and Jane Slaughter, *Choosing Sides: Unions and the Team Concept* (Boston: South End Press, 1988), p. 11. . . .

8. Barnet and Müller, *Global Reach: The Power of the Multinational Corporations* (New York: Simon & Schuster, 1974), notes, p. 420.

9. *Ibid.*, p. 305.

10. *Wall Street Journal*, July 5, 1991.

11. Joseph Grunwald and Kenneth Flamm, *Global Factory: Foreign Assembly and International Trade* (Washington, D.C.: Brookings Institution, 1985), p. 30n.

12. Stephen S. Cohen and John Zysman, *Manufacturing Matters* (New York: Basic Books, 1987), p. 4; Council of Economic Advisers, *Economic Report of the President 1992* (Washington, D.C.: U.S. Government Printing Office, 1992), p. 344.

13. Paul Knox and John Agnew, *The Geography of the World Economy* (London: Edward Arnold, 1989), p. 180.

14. *Ibid.*, pp. 182–184.

15. *Wall Street Journal*, July 30, 1991.

16. *New York Times*, Feb. 23, 1992.

17. *New York Times*, Mar. 8, 1992.

18. *Washington Post*, Jan. 21, 1992.

19. *Wall Street Journal*, Jan. 24, 1992.

20. *Wall Street Journal*, July 5, 1991.

21. William J. Holstein, "The Stateless Corporation," *Business Week*, May 14, 1990, p. 100.

22. Larry Reynolds, "Has Globalization Hurt America?" *Management Review*, September 1989, pp. 16–17.

23. Holstein, "Stateless Corporation," p. 99.

24. *Ibid.*, p. 98.

25. Robert B. Reich, *The Work of Nations* (New York: Knopf, 1991).

15

Globalization, Immigration, and Changing Social Relations in U.S. Cities

Glenda Laws

GLOBALIZATION HAS A SOCIAL AND CULTURAL impact on the lives of various social groups in several different ways. It is not simply an economic process.

Some people, including investors who have seen their profits grow and workers who have been employed because of expanding business opportunities, have benefited from the growth of global markets, while others have not. Consequently, relations between people living and working in U.S. cities have changed during the latest round of global restructuring. Immigrant groups have been particularly affected. That is because, in many respects, immigrants and immigration levels are directly related to the globalization of the economy. People, for the most part, migrate in search of economic opportunities (for example, work or investments), and as the economy has globalized, people from around the world find that opportunities attractive to them might well cross international boundaries. Once arrived at their destination, however, immigrants often experience various forms of segregation. Before turning

Glenda Laws was an associate professor of geography at the Pennsylvania State University. She was an urban social geographer with an interest in marginalized populations and political struggles around their well-being. Throughout her career, Dr. Laws focused on, among others, the mentally ill, the homeless, the poor, immigrant women, and the elderly. She was interested in social and economic restructuring and, specifically, the spatial implications of restructuring for those marginalized groups in urban areas. Dr. Laws died in June 1996, aged 37.

to discussion of some of the ways globalization has contributed to the economic, social, political, and spatial segregation of immigrants, I want to start with several preliminary observations.

First, despite much attention being given to the idea of globalization as if it were a recent phenomenon, it would be naive to suggest that U.S. cities have only recently entered a global political economy. Ever since the first European settlements, cities in North America have been linked, to a greater or lesser degree, to the machinations of a global system. The term "globalization," as it is currently used, suggests that linkages between places around the world are now more numerous and more intense than hitherto and that supranational organizations are assuming an ever greater importance. In the context of economic activity, this involves the growth over the last few decades of multinational corporations, the expansion of international capital markets, and related changes in patterns of international trade. Each of these elements of globalization, however, has a history measured in centuries rather than decades. Because of its long historical antecedents, perhaps it is best to think of the current round of globalization, in its economic, political, and sociocultural guise, as a round of qualitatively different international relations, usefully characterized by Jan Nederveen Pieterse[1] as inherently fluid, indeterminate, and open-ended.

Although these new and multiple forms of global interdependence have implications for localities (for example, U.S. cities and their suburbs), the global and the local, or globalization and localization, do not stand in simple opposition to one another. Rather, they are intimately related and it is not particularly useful to discuss either without the other.

Second, we should note the importance of focusing upon the political and sociocultural dimensions of globalization—in terms of both causes and effects. We witness, for example, the growth of international governing bodies such as the United Nations and the World Bank and of advocacy groups such as Amnesty International and the increasingly important role such organizations play in political decision making and developments in the global economy.[2] Further, in terms of sociocultural relations, globalization involves the migration of people and customs. In some instances, large-scale migrations have resulted in the loss or marginalization of some cultures as some immigrants come to dominate indigenous populations (for example, migrations from the so-called Old to the New World under colonial expansions). In other instances, the immigrants themselves are ostracized and segregated in their new locations. Such, in fact, is the situation in many U.S. cities as the twentieth century draws to a close.

Transformations in the global political economy have had a significant impact on relations between residents of U.S. cities. Since the social problem of residential segregation in U.S. cities has been around for some time, it is certainly not a product of the latest round of globalization. Likewise, it would be difficult to argue with any certainty that poverty among inner-city residents is directly related to globalization or that violence directed at minority groups is an outcome of globalization processes. However, the form and function of segregation under globalization might changing. We need to ask what role urban or local segregation plays in a global economy that (seemingly) increasingly looks to supranational organizations. We must, however, bear in mind that if globalization could be used to explain everything, its analytical value for understanding specific manifestations of social problems would need to be questioned. Despite such caveats, I do believe that transformations in the global political econ-

omy have had a significant impact on social problems in U.S. cities, and I hope to tease out some of these links in the ensuing discussion. My focus here is on immigrants who have relocated as a result of changing conditions associated with globalization. Although a comprehensive examination of this topic would include consideration of the conditions in the places from which immigrants move, space does not permit coverage here. I will therefore concentrate on the experiences of and attitudes toward immigrants who have settled in the United States. To organize what follows, I begin by reviewing the links between globalization, immigration, and urban social relations. Then, at the risk of oversimplification, I consider some of the economic, social, and political experiences of recent immigrants living in U.S. cities. Finally, I will explore the implications of continued globalization for residents of U.S. cities.

GLOBALIZATION, IMMIGRATION, AND URBAN SOCIAL RELATIONS

In the contemporary global political economy, some countries function as labor-exporting nodes, for both long-and short-term migrants, while others act as labor-importing countries. Saskia Sassen describes "migration as a global labor supply system"[3] that provides workers to both urban and rural labor markets in developed industrialized economies. This implies that both capital and, to a lesser extent, labor are mobile on a global scale. For both capital and labor, a "sentimental attachment to some geographic part of the world is not part of the [global economic] system."[4] Of course, many businesses (especially small firms) and people do find themselves attached, whether by choice or circumstance, to a particular place and, as a result, may find that they are not competitive in the global market. At various spatial scales, whether international, national, or local, some regions lose workers and capital investment while others gain.

Explanations for large-scale movements of workers and their families between nation-states are rooted in long and complex histories that surround the diffusion of capitalism. Colonial expansions prior to World War I depended on such migrations between the Old and New Worlds. With rapid economic growth since World War II, immigrant workers form less developed countries have become an increasingly important component of the labor forces of most developed countries. Sassen describes current trends as follows:

Two features characterize labor migration: the growing use of immigrant labor in the tertiary sector of developed countries and the growing use of foreign and native migrants in the secondary sector of developing countries. . . . Unlike other labor-intensivecomponents of industrialized economies, service jobs cannot easily be exported. Thus, the growing concentration of immigrant labor in the service sector of highly industrialized countries may be pointing to constraints in the historical transformation of the international division of labor, insofar as most service jobs must be performed *in situ*. This growing concentration of immigrant labor in service jobs in developed countries can be viewed as the correlate of the export of [manufacturing] jobs to the Third World.[5]

At the local scale, U.S. cities, along with their counterparts in other developed economies, have played an important role in the global labor market. The hierarchical organization of multinational corporations has designated some cities as headquarters locations that act as sites for leadership, research and development, and interaction with politicians. These command points watch over the global empires of the largest corporations. More routine functions, like manufacturing, have moved offshore, taking with them many relatively well-paid blue-collar jobs.[6] However, the loss of some, indeed many, manufacturing jobs has not seen the eradication of low-wage positions in U.S. cities. Although increasingly challenged by Japan and other Asian economies, the postwar dominance of the U.S. economy has created (and continues to create) incomes and consumption opportunities that require minimally paid positions. The following description of the local social geography and economy of one neighborhood,

Lennox, near the Los Angeles international airport captures the links between globalization and the low-wage workforce:

The proximity of [the airport] is not coincidental. Many [immigrants] were drawn by the lure of work in area hotels and restaurants, the low-wage service jobs now largely the domain of immigrants. Indeed Lennox is a kind of late-20th Century company town, housing a Third World servant class of maids, waiters and others whose cheap labor sustains an international transportation and tourism hub.[7]

Left behind, too, are those manufacturing activities that can find a cheap enough labor force within the United States to make them competitive in the international market (as well as those manufacturers who require a relatively skilled labor force that cannot as yet readily be found outside the developed economies). Sweatshops (and other institutionalized forms of low wages), then, represent one way of maintaining competitiveness. In addition, those employed in the headquarters offices of multinational corporations require support staff (such as accounting and legal expertise, clerical assistants, and janitorial services), and this has created demands for a whole range of business and personal services. That is, multinational corporations, and the ancillary services that are generated in a region by their presence, are very much dependent on a large, international labor market. The domestic side of that labor market includes a significant number of immigrants.

Of course, this is not an especially new development in the evolution of the U.S. space economy. In the first decade of the twentieth century, nearly 8.8 million people moved from abroad to major U.S. industrial cities. This number translates into a rate of 10.4 immigrants for every 1000 people living in the United States. Both the number and the rate fell off until the post-World War II economic boom, which created renewed demand for immigrant labor. In addition, changes to immigration laws in 1965 resulted in higher levels of migration related to family reunification. The new legislation also led to a change in the countries of origin of migrants, from mainly European sites to regions in Central and South America and Asia. Between 1981 and 1990, 7.34 million immigrants entered at a rate of 3.1 per 1000 population. Between 1991 and 1993, amid growing calls for a slowdown in immigration, the rate had reached 4.8 per 1000, and some 3.71 million immigrants were admitted. In addition, the Bureau of the Census estimates that there may be as many as 4.00 million undocumented immigrants.[8] In 1994, 8.7 percent of the U.S. population was foreign born, the majority of whom live in cities. More than 18 million foreign-born individuals lived in metropolitan areas in 1990, while only 1.3 million resided in nonmetropolitan areas.

Migrants change the character of the places in which they settle. They establish businesses, invest in housing and together aspects of neighborhood infrastructure, celebrate cultural festivals, and bring with them a variety of cultural practices. Sometimes this multicultural aspect of migration is greeted enthusiastically by host communities; more often it is welcomed with ambivalence. However, it takes only the most casual attention to the popular media to realize that there is a groundswell of opposition to continued immigration at what is popularly perceived to be a large scale. Despite this opposition, there remains a persistent demand for both legal and illegal migrant labor. Undocumented immigrants are able to find work in U.S. cities as local manufacturers meet the demand for cheaply produced goods. The products of sweatshops find markets in the United States. And these markets are not only found among struggling small businesses or in the informal economy. Large retailers purchase (knowingly or otherwise) and then sell clothing produced by illegal aliens in Los Angeles sweatshops.[9] Furthermore, affluence in the United States has created a demand among relatively well-off families for housekeepers and gardeners, many of whom are immigrants.[10] Rural regions, too, exhibit a "dependence on an imported peasantry."[11]

Domestic labor markets, then, offer opportunities for global migrants, even while simultaneously there is an almost continuous call for immigration reform. Despite such calls, there are, of course, many supporters of liberal immigration policies. Advocacy groups are joined by business interests that see migrant labor as one means of maintaining competitiveness. A recent advertisement on the Internet asked, "Will immigration damage your business?" and argued that a reduction in the number of employment-based immigrants and restrictions on the length of time temporary workers could stay in the country would be problematic for businesses.[12] Tensions between those who support and those who oppose immigration is indicative of how globalization affects relations between urban residents.

Sassen, in a study of "the global city," examines the increasing social polarization evident in New York City, London, and Tokyo as economic restructuring not only widens the income gap between rich and poor but also accentuates the contrasts between the gentrified commercial and residential settings used by the most privileged urban residents and the sweatshops and crowded houses where poor people work and live.[13] She demonstrates that globalization has invoked not only new economic geographies but also new social geographies. Spatial segregation of different social groups has persisted under globalization even at the same time that it has promoted international, interethnic, and interracial contacts through global migration. Increasing social polarization is a question of social justice, and it begs the questions of how some groups are privileged by social processes and how others might be disadvantaged by those same processes.[14]

In what follows, I will focus primarily on discussions of the economic experiences of immigrants based on their labor force attachment; then I will turn to a consideration of some sociocultural experiences including the assimilation-versus-multiculturalism debate and the violence that sometimes arises from intolerance of cultural difference. I also consider the political powerlessness of immigrants. To illustrate the discussion, I draw upon popular sources, especially reports from newspapers, because these are the sites from which many people gather information to develop their opinions about the merits of, or problems associated with, immigration policy and immigrants.

Economic Segregation: Labor Market Positions and Experiences

"Economic segregation of immigrants" refers to the fact that many simply do not have access to the same resources as the U.S.-born population. One of the most important determinants of both individual and household resources is the positions that workers hold in labor markets. Occupational and sectoral concentrations mean that some groups of immigrants receive, on average, very low wages. Income levels clearly have implications for opportunities and experiences outside the workplace, such as housing, health care, and leisure. For both advocates and opponents, then, the links between immigration and domestic labor markets are critical.

Opponents suggest that by accepting low wages (because they are often high compared to those that immigrants received in their home countries), immigrants have two important potential impacts on local labor markets. First, wage rates are driven down. Second, immigrants are employed in jobs that would otherwise be filled by unskilled or low-skilled U.S.-born workers. For immigrants who had been in the United States for less than five years in 1990, average wages were almost 32 percent below those of U.S.-born workers.[15] It may seem unclear why immigrants should be castigated for the unfairness of this situation if we assume that employers should pay fair and reasonable wages to all workers, regardless of their immigrant status.

The sweatshop conditions in which many immigrant workers find themselves are also indicative of the intensity of exploitation found in some urban areas. On 2 August 1995, a raid on a factory in El Monte, California, exposed a "workshop that held immigrant workers in 'slave labor' conditions inside a barbed-wire compound and forced them to work seven days a week for as little as 50 cents an hour.[16] In February 1996, the factory's operators pleaded guilty to a number of charges including indentured servitude. In this particular case, the majority of workers were described as "illegal aliens," but a suit filed in April 1996 claimed that the operators were paying legal Latino immigrant workers only $1.63 per hour for as many as 13 hours of work per day in another two factories in Los Angeles.[17] Textile and clothing sweatshops seem to be especially exploitative in their treatment of workers—and, importantly, women. At least part of the explanation for the atrocious conditions such workers find themselves in must relate to the erosion of organized labor with respect to its important watchdog role. Globalization has seen many textile activities move offshore. There has been a parallel decline in the number of unionized employees. The Garment Workers Unions suffered a serious membership loss from 314,000 members in 1979 down to 133,000 in 1993.[18] Unions need, for the sake of all workers, to ensure that foreign-born workers are paid wages equal to those of U.S.-born employees.

In September 1995, a letter to the editor of the *New York Times* by the president of the National Association of Manufacturers reveals an interesting business perspective on the links between attitudes toward immigration and the structure of labor markets:

American manufacturing no longer has an interest in maintaining a mass influx of unskilled, low-wage immigrants. While a large number of unskilled laborers helped fuel the Industrial Revolution, the technology-driven plants and offices of today's competitive global economy require the expertise of skilled workers. . . . The National Association of Manufacturers is interested in the immigration issue, but only to maintain the employment-based immigration that provides American companies with the essential technical expertise in short supply in the United States. The shortage of available expert workers is a growing concern of American business.[19]

The distinction drawn here between unskilled and expert workers means that Schlosser's "imported peasantry"[20] is less valued than the class of "high-tech itinerants wandering the globe."[21] Interestingly, the representative of the National

Association of Manufacturers does not note that the service and agricultural sectors seemingly still rely on low-skilled immigrants. Lobbyists for the agriculture industry, for example, recently sought federal legislation that would have granted visas to 250,000 temporary foreign farm workers.[22] Furthermore, this perspective does not help us understand the persistence of sweatshop forms of manufacturing in those areas that are not so much "technology driven" as they are labor intensive.

Iris Marion Young argues that exploitation in the U.S wage labor market may be at its most extreme in the case of the menial work performed by members (especially those classified as "minorities") from the so-called new service class.[23] Newspaper reports suggest that migrant workers, sometimes unaware of their legal rights, are especially susceptible to poor treatment. For example, in January 1996, the Service Employees' International Union charged that three immigrant workers were cheated out of wages to which they were entitled by a contractor with the Massachusetts Bay Transportation Authority. The landscape and property management contractor was accused of claiming that "the three full-time workers [were] part-time employees to avoid paying prevailing wages."[24]

Some immigrants simply cannot find a way into the labor market, especially the legal market, and constitute part of the category of people Young describes as suffering from marginalization; they are "people the system of labor cannot or will not use."[25] Exclusion from the labor force then leads to deprivation in a number of areas of everyday life since a life of poverty does not allow individuals to find adequate housing, health care, and other resources for themselves and their families. This situation has been a cause of some of the most heated political debates over the last decade or so. Immigrants are accused of burdening an already overstretched welfare system in calling upon public assistance programs for basic goods and services. Although illegal immigrants are especially vulnerable to such accusations, the anti-immigrant rhetoric used tends to extend the debate to all foreigners. At times this demands that legal immigrants be denied Social Security and other benefits unless they take out U.S. citizenship.

But is it clear that immigrants are as much of a drain on public assistance as might be thought? According to George Borjas, the relative position of immigrants in the U.S. economy deteriorated between 1970 and 1990. During those two decades, the percentage of immigrants receiving welfare increased from less than 6 percent to just over 9 percent.[26] Importantly, these figure reveal that more than 90 percent of immigrants do not receive welfare. Fix, Passel, and Zimmermann further note that immigrants use welfare programs at about the same rate as U.S.-born residents, although there may be significantly higher usage among particular subsets of immigrants (such as refugees and elderly people).[27] Wages for immigrants have not kept up with those of U.S.-born workers.

Whereas in 1970, immigrants and U.S.-born workers were, on average, receiving almost equal wages, the wage differential in 1990 showed immigrants earning more than 15 percent less than the U.S.-born. Perhaps the growing visibility of the poverty experienced by some segments of the immigrant population over the last two decades might account for some of the opposition to continued migration. The degree to which immigrants might be a drain on a particular pool of resources, however, really depends on the spatial scale of analysis being discussed. Researchers at the Urban Institute in Washington, D.C., argue, for example, that "while immigrants generate a net fiscal surplus, the bulk of the taxes they pay are federal, while the obligations for providing them services remains with local and state governments. Hence, in some communities, immigrants generate a net deficit at the local level.[28] That is, in the overall operation of the U.S. economy, immigrants are a positive force; however, in particular communities and neighborhoods, immigrants might draw upon public resources more heavily than U.S-born residents do.

Naturally, the restructuring of the U.S. economy, as noted in the letter from the representative of the manufacturer's association cited earlier, has created demands for highly skilled immigrant labor. The latest cohorts of immigrants tend to be more highly educated than either earlier immigrants or U.S.-born residents of comparable age.[29] In 1994, 147, 012 employment-based immigrants were admitted to the United States. More than 40,000 of these were classified as priority workers or professionals with advanced degrees.[30] While there is evidence that these workers do relatively well when it comes to wages, in some cases even highly skilled immigrant workers find themselves in exploitative situations. One *Los Angeles Times* report describes the creation of high technology sweatshops staffed by "skilled—and cheap—programmers" from abroad: "Legions of programmers, many working on dubious visas, are hacking away right now in cheap motel rooms, guarded hideaways and corporate computer centers throughout America." The relationships to globalization are made explicit in the following description:

These new high-tech itinerants wandering the globe in search of work are mirrored by a new breed of work wandering the globe in search of cheap labor. Linked to the United States by satellite and electronic mail often backed by government subsidies, overseas workers are providing quality programming at prices far below what it would cost here.[31]

Despite their very high skill levels, then, foreign programmers often enter the United States (on short-term visas) to be paid less than the prevailing wage. Opponents have criticized the immigrants, saying they lower wages, but at least one anti-immigrant group has placed the blame on the corporations that allow their contractors to pay these low wages. Such a strategy places pressure on U.S. firms to pay immigrant workers at prevailing rates so that they are not as competitive with local workers.

The longer immigrants reside in the United States, the better their wages and labor market position are likely to be. Immigrant labor markets are, however, polarized between the low wages of the unskilled who often find work only through informal contacts, and the highly paid positions held by in-migrating individuals whose professional skills are in high demand. Both segments of the immigrant labor market are the target of efforts to restrict the number of people migrating into this country. But where does that leave immigrants who are outside the labor market, and what, then, are their experiences?

Sociospatial Segregation

Accompanying globalization and the influx of migrants has been the growth in anti-immigrant sentiment, evident in any number of sources, including print media, talk radio, and political campaign speeches. By deliberate choice, many of the phrases used here (and elsewhere in this article) come from newspaper reports. It is such popular representations as these that fuel many of the debates about immigration and immigrants. They are the sources from which many people gather information to develop their opinions about the merits of, or problems associated with, immigration policy and immigrants. The extent of the necessity of migrant labor is not clear in the minds of many residents of the United States. Opponents to large-scale immigration complain that because of their supposed heavy use of public services, immigrants, especially (though not exclusively) undocumented workers and their families, are burden to an economy that already has too large a deficit. At a time when politicians grapple with how to balance budgets at federal, state, and local levels, and when unemployment among some segments of the working-age population is very high, questions are asked about why more people are allowed to enter the country. Advocates of immigration argue that immigrants and their families contribute to both the cultural and economic development of the nation.[32] These debates about the relative merits of legal and illegal migration create tensions not only in federal policy debates but also in communities and neighborhoods where there are large concentrations of immigrants.

One suburban Los Angeles resident told a *Los Angeles Times* reporter, "What we have in Southern California is not assimilation—it's annexation by Mexico."[33] In another case, a man charged with assaulting an immigrant reportedly told an arresting officer in Glendale, California, "All of them should go back where they came from. . . . They take our homes, our jobs, they buy up everything, and look at me. I was born here. They don't belong here."[34] U.S.-born (and some immigrant) residents argue that there are simply too many immigrants entering the country who have rejected assimilationist models and who favor a multicultural society that preserves cultural differences.

At the center of many debates is the resistance or inability of some immigrants to adopt English as their primary language. In some cases, immigrants, especially older people and recently arrived migrants, have limited English skills, and thus there has been a growing trend for government services to be provided in other languages. For example, to avoid claims of anti-Hispanic bias, the Chicago Housing Authority introduced a range of Spanish-language services.[35] Opposition to this trend has resulted in greater visibility for the English-only movement.[36] Supporters of English-only initiatives—such as Arizonans for Official English, U.S. English, and English First—lobby at various levels of government for legislation that makes it illegal for government services to be provided in another language. By spring 1996, 23 states had adopted some measure that makes English the "official" language, and the Supreme Court agreed to take another look at the issue.[37] Immigrant parents themselves are not always supportive of bilingual education. For example, a group of Latino parents in Los Angeles demanded that their children be placed in English-only classes because they want them to learn the dominant language.[38]

There is clear evidence that proficiency in English makes a difference to the range of job possibilities open to many immigrants. This in turn can affect the types of housing and other social necessities that are available to immigrant workers and their families. For the poorest immigrants housing is a major problem. *Los Angeles Times* writer David Freed describes "cramped, decaying hovels" that "have slid into filthy disrepair over the years" and that have "crumbling walls

and dripping ceilings." These are the homes of some of the least-skilled immigrants from Asia, Mexico, and South America.[39] It is not just housing but also the communities in which immigrants live that face problems when low wages predominate. First-generation immigrants, especially those with low skills and thus low wages, often find themselves in communities where basic infrastructure is deteriorating. The situation in Washington Heights, a neighborhood of Dominican immigrants in New York City, exemplifies the material hardships faced by immigrant communities in the midst of global affluence:

Washington Heights still has movie theaters and florists and other strong life signs gone from neighborhoods that have succumbed to urban blight, but it also has wall murals that serve as memorials to young men killed in the neighborhood's drug wars. Factory workers see jobs disappearing. Small-business owners are struggling to stay ahead of their rents and debts. Community organizations built on publicly funded programs are groaning under government budget cuts. Neighborhood community centers are threatened with closures and curtailed hours.[40]

Related to the backlash against migrants are hate crimes in which they and their families are subject to violence targeted at individuals and the property they own. Hate crimes are directed at people on the basis of their immigrant status, race, ethnicity, or other attributes ascribed to a social group.[41] Specific statistical data are unreliable because of serious underreporting not only by the victims but also due to the reluctance of some agencies who are supposed to be reporting to the federal government to do so fully. Because of its racialized nature, violence directed toward immigrants spills over onto U.S. citizens and U.S.-born people who appear to be immigrants. The National Asian Pacific American League Consortium released a report in 1995 that found that often Asian Americans were told to "go home . . . as if they were not Americans."[42] Violence, as many people have noted, is an expression of perceived power relations. Immigrants are often the target of abuse and violence because they are believed to be receiving more than they deserve and at the expense of others. Perpetrators, for example, might believe that immigrants are taking jobs or using up resources to which they themselves are more entitled. This raises questions about perceptions of citizenship and what it means to be a citizen in one place but not in another.

. . .

CONCLUSION: POLITICAL AND POLICY IMPLICATIONS

Rhetorical and often inflammatory statements about immigration and immigrants often have little relationship to the reality of the situation. The veracity of claims from both opponents and advocates of immigration is not easily determined. Despite the isolationist rhetoric of some conservative politicians in the United States, it is unlikely that the country can uncouple itself from the global political and economic structures that are now in place. Globalization gives businesses the choice of importing workers or exporting employment and production to other countries. Both create competition for U.S.-born workers living and working at home. Both also encourage, if not rely upon, significant global migration. Thus, despite calls for reform (read "restrictions") of federal immigration policy, it is unlikely that the United States can close its doors to all foreigners—even while immigration to the United States is not as open as some critics would claim.

While globalization is often defined in economic terms, its social consequences are great. This is not to imply that some global economic processes determine local social conditions without any reciprocity. Around the world, concern has been expressed about the extent to which global economic processes might be eradicating some local cultures. However, immigrants to U.S. cities also modify the social and cultural geographies of the places in which they live and work.

Just as more obviously multinational corporations and governments at all levels have developed strategies that simultaneously respond to and promote globalization, so groups of less privileged people also develop such strategies. Globalization has been described as a "new spatial geopolitics."[43] The new urban geopolitics of U.S. cities pits localities against one another as they engage in bidding wars for foreign investment; social groups against one another as each group attempts to stake out a territory of its own; and businesses and the state against communities.

NOTES

1. Jan Nederveen Pieterse, "Globalization as Hybridization," in *Global Modernities, ed. Mike Featherstone, Scott Lash, and Roland Robertson (Thousand Oaks, CA: Sage, 1995), p.46.

2. See Commission on Global Governance, *Our Global Neighborhood* (New York: Oxford University Press, 1995).

3. Saskia Sassen, *The Mobility of Labor and Capital: A Study of International Investment and Labor Flow* (New York: Cambridge University Press, 1988), pp.31–36.

4. Lester C. Thurow, *The Future of Capitalism: How Today's Economic Forces Shape Tomorrow's World* (New York: William Morrow, 1996), p.115.

5. Sassen, *Mobility of Labor and Capital*, p. 53.

6. Stephen Hymer, *The Multinational Corporation: A Radical Approach*, ed. Robert B. Cohen, Morley Nikosi, and Jaap van Liere, with the assistance of Noel Dennis (New York: Cambridge University Press, 1979).

7. Patrick J. McDonnell, "Economic Shocks South of Border in Lennox; Jobs: Like Other Immigrant Areas, It Has Inexorable Ties to Mexico," *Los Angeles Times*, 20 June 1995.

8. U.S., Department of Commerce, Bureau of the Census, *Statistical Abstract of the United States: 1995*, 115th ed. (Washington, DC: Department of Commerce, 1995), tabs. 5, 10.

9. Frank Swoboda and Margaret Webb Pressler, "US Targets Slave Labor Sweatshop; Back Wages

Sought from Clothing Makers," *Washington Post*, 16 Aug. 1995.

10. See, for example, Lynda Natali, "Wealthy Enclaves in O.C. [Orange County] Hide 'Household Slaves,'" *Los Angeles Times*, 1 June 1991.

11. Eric Schlosser, "In the Strawberry Fields," *Atlantic Monthly*, p.80 (Nov. 1993).

12. Heather Hartung and Pamela A. McKnight, "Will Immigration Reform Damage Your Business?" (Advertisement of Brown, Todd & Heyburn PLLC at http://www.bth-pllc.com/legalpad/immrefrm.html).

13. Saskia Sassen, *The Global City: New York, London, Tokyo* (Princeton, NJ: Princeton University Press, 1991).

14. See Iris Marion Young, *Justice and the Politics of Difference* (Princeton, NJ: Princeton University Press, 1992).

15. George J. Borjas, "The Economic Benefit of Immigration," *Journal of Economic Perspectives* (1995); Michael Fix, Jeffrey S. Passel and Wendy Zimmermann, "The Use of SSI and Other Welfare Programs by Immigrants" (Testimony before U.S., Congress, House, Ways and Means Committee, 23 May 1996, copy available from the authors at the Urban Institute, Washington, DC).

16. Swoboda and Pressler, "US Targets Slave Labor Sweatshop."

17. See "39 Garment Workers File Suit to Recover $1.8 Million in Wages," *Los Angeles Times*, 5 Apr. 1996. See also Diane E. Lewis, "Sweatshop Workers Get Early Holiday Gift," *Boston Globe*, 10 Dec. 1995; *Sweatshops in New York City, A Local Example of a Nationwide Problem* (Washington, DC: General Accounting Office, 1989); *Garment Industry, Efforts to Address the Prevalence and Conditions of Sweatshops* (Washington, DC: General Accounting Office, 1994).

18. Bureau of the Census, *Statistical Abstract*, tab. 696. There is little doubt that globalization has eroded the power of unions in the United States.

Businesses can escape union demands by moving operations to a foreign location. Increasing numbers of part-part and other nonunion jobs have undermined traditional sources of union membership. These trends have seen "unions do a u-turn on immigrant worker issue" as "an emerging generation of California Labor leaders envisions poorly paid foreign-born workers—regardless of their immigrant status—as becoming a booming new base of support of U.S. unions." See Stuart Silverstein, "Unions for a U-turn on Immigrant Worker Issue," *Los Angeles Times*, 3 Nov. 1994.

19. Jerry J. Jasinowski, "What U.S. Business Wants From Immigration" (Letter to the editor) *New York Times*, 13 Sept. 1995.

20. Schlosser, "In the Strawberry Fields," p.30.

21. Leslie Helm, "Creating High-Tech Workshops: US Firms Find Skilled—and Cheap—Programmers Abroad," *Los Angeles Times*, 15 Nov. 1993.

22. The proposal was rejected by the U.S. House of Representatives on 21 Mar. 1996.

23. Young, *Justice and the Politics of Difference*.

24. Diane E. Lewis, "MBTA Contractor Sued by Union over Wages," *Boston Globe*, 12 Jan. 1996.

25. Young, *Justice and the Politics of Difference*, p.53.

26. Borjas, "Economic Benefit of Immigration."

27. Fix, Passel, and Zimmermann, "Use of SSI."

28. Michael Fix and Jeffrey S. Passel, "Perspective on Immigration: Balancing the Ledger on Jobs, Taxes," *Los Angeles Times*, 2 Aug.1994.

29. "Foreign-born Residents Highest Percentage of US Population Since World War II, Census Bureau Reports" (Press release, CB95-155, U.S. Department of Commerce, Bureau of the Census, 25 Aug. 1995).

30. Bureau of the Census, *Statistical Abstract*, tab. 5.

31. Helm, "Creating High-Tech Sweatshops."

32. Advocacy groups like the Federation for American Immigration Reform (FAIR) are especially visible

opponents of immigration. For details of the arguments against immigration, see Roy Beck, *The Case Against Immigration: The Moral, Economic, Social and Environmental Reasons for Reducing Immigration Back to Traditional Levels* (New York: W.W. Norton, 1996). See also V. Briggs, Jr., *Mass Immigration and the National Labor Market* (Armonk, NY: M.E. Sharpe, 1992); P. Brimelow, "Time to Rethink Immigration?" *National Review*, 22 June 1992, pp. 30–46. For a very brief overview of the benefits of immigration, see Fix and Passel, "Perspective on Immigration." The full study by Fix and Passel is reported in their *Immigration and Immigrants: Setting the Record Straight* (Washington, DC: Urban Institute, 1995).

33. Quoted in Patrick J. McDonnell, "Study Disputes Immigrant Stereotypes, Cites Gains," *Los Angeles Times*, 3 Nov. 1995.

34. Quoted in Ed Bond, "Man Faces Hate Crime Charge in Assault," *Los Angeles Times*, 8 Apr. 1994.

35. "Hispanics and Housing Subsidies" (editorial), *Chicago Tribune*, 24 Apr. 1996.

36. Bill Piatt, *Only English? Law and Language Policy in the United States* (Albuquerque: University of New Mexico Press, 1990); Raymond Tatalovich, *Nativism Reborn: The Official English Language Movement and the American States* (Lexington: University Press of Kentucky, 1995); James Crawford, *Hold Your Tongue: Bilingualism and the Politics of English Only* (Reading, MA:Addison-Wesley, 1992).

37. See Joan Biskupic, "English-Only Case to Get Court Review: Arizona Law Covers Government Business," *Washington Post*, 26 Mar. 1996.

38. Amy Pyle, "80 Students Stay out of School in Latino Boycott," *Los Angeles Times*, 14 Feb. 1996.

39. David Freed, "Web of Misery: The 'Bricks': Big Profit in Slum Decay," *Los Angeles Times*, 30 July 1989.

40. Roberto Suro, "They Came to Improve But Just Try to Survive; Poverty Threatens the Community Dominicans Built in New York," *Washington Post*, 19 June 1995.

41. See Los Angeles County Commission on Human Relations, *Hate Crime in Los Angeles County 1992: A Report to the Los Angeles County Board of Supervisors* (Los Angeles: Los Angeles County Commission on Human Relations, 1993); Anna Cekola, "Attack on Vietnamese Immigrant Called a Hate Crime," *Los Angeles Times*, 2 May 1994; Art Barnum, "Vietnamese Church's Scars Are Only Outside." *Chicago Tribune*, 18 Apr. 1994; Bond, "Man Faces Hate Crime Charges"; "Arson Fire Destroys House of an Iraqi-American Family," *New York Times*, 22 Feb. 1991; "Racial and Religious Hate Crimes," *Los Angeles Times*, 24 Mar. 1998.

42. Lena H. Sun, "Hate Crimes Against Asian Americans Increase," *Washington Post*, 1 Aug. 1995.

43. Mike Featherstone and Scott Lash, "Globalization, Modernity and the Spatialization of Social Theory: An Introduction," *Global Modernities*, ed. Featherstone, Last, and Robertson, p.3.

16

New Migrations, New Theories

Douglas S. Massey, Joaquín Arango, Graeme Hugo, Ali Kouaouci, Adela Pellegrino, and J. Edward Taylor

LIKE MANY BIRDS, BUT UNLIKE MOST OTHER animals, humans are a migratory species. Indeed, migration is as old as humanity itself. Of this fact there is no better proof than the spread of human beings to all corners of the earth from their initial ecological niche in sub-Saharan Africa (Davis 1974: 53). A careful examination of virtually any historical era reveals a consistent propensity towards geographic mobility among men and women, who are driven to wander by diverse motives, but nearly always with some idea of material improvement.

The modern history of international migration can be divided roughly into four periods. During the *mercantile period*, from 1500 to 1800, world immigration was dominated by flows out of Europe and stemmed from processes of colonization and economic growth under mercantilist capitalism. Over the course of 300 years, Europeans inhabited large portions of the Americas, Africa, Asia, and Oceania (Altman 1995; Heffernan 1995; Lucassen 1995; Tinker 1995). Although the exact number of colonizing emigrants is unknown, the outflow was sufficient to establish Europe's dominion over large parts of the world. During this period, emigrants generally fell into four classes: a relatively large number of agrarian settlers, a smaller number of administrators and artisans, an even smaller num-

ber of entrepreneurs who founded plantations to produce raw materials for Europe's growing mercantilist economies, and in a very few cases, convict migrants sent to penal colonies overseas.

Although the number of Europeans involved in plantation production was small, this sector had a profound impact on the size and composition of population in the Americas. Given a preindustrial technology, plantations required large amounts of cheap labour, a demand met partially by indentured workers from East Asia (Gemery and Horn 1992; Hui 1995; Kritz 1992; Tinker 1977; Twaddle 1995; Vertovec 1995). The most important source of plantation labour, however, was the forced migration of African slaves (Palmer 1992). Over three centuries, nearly 10 million African slaves were imported into the Americas (Curtain 1969) and together with European colonists, they radically transformed the racial and ethnic composition of the New World.

The second, *industrial period* of emigration begins early in the nineteenth century and stemmed from the economic development of Europe and the spread of industrialism to former colonies in the New World (Hatton and Williamson 1994b). From 1800 to 1925, more than 48 million people left the industrializing countries of Europe in search of new lives in the Americas and Oceania. Of these emigrants, 85 per cent went to just five destinations: Argentina, Australia, Canada, New Zealand, and the USA, with the latter receiving 60 per cent all by itself (Ferenczi 1929). Key sending nations were Britain, Italy, Norway, Portugal, Spain, and Sweden, each of which exported a large share of its potential population in the course of industrializing (Massey 1988).

From *Worlds in Motion: Understanding International Migration at the End of the Millennium* by Douglas S. Massey, Joaquín Arango, Graeme Hugo, Ali Kouaouci, Adela Pellegrino, and J. Edward Taylor. Copyright © 1998 IUSSP. Reprinted by permission of Oxford University Press.

The period of large-scale European emigration faltered with the outbreak of the First World War, which brought European emigration to an abrupt halt and ushered in a four-decade *period of limited migration* (Massey 1995). Although emigration revived somewhat during the early 1920s, by then several important receiving countries (most notably the USA) had passed restrictive immigration laws. The onset of the Great Depression stopped virtually all international movement in 1929, and except for a small amount of return migration, there was little movement during the 1930s. During the 1940s, international migration was checked by the Second World War. What mobility there was consisted largely of refugees and displaced persons and was not tied strongly to the rhythms of economic growth and development (Holmes 1995; Noiriel 1995; Sword 1995; Kay 1995), a pattern that persisted well into the subsequent decade.

The period of *post-industrial migration* emerged during the 1960s and constituted a sharp break with the past. Rather than being dominated by outflows from Europe to a handful of former colonies, immigration became a truly global phenomenon, as the number and variety of both sending and receiving countries steadily increased and the global supply of immigrants shifted from Europe to the developing countries of the Third World (Castles and Miller 1993). Whereas migration during the industrial era brought people from densely settled, rapidly industrializing areas to sparsely settled, rapidly industrializing regions, migration in the post-industrial era brought people from densely settled countries in the earliest stages of industrialization to densely settled post-industrial societies.

Before 1925, 85 percent of all international migrants originated in Europe (Ferenczi 1929); but since 1960, Europeans have comprised an increasingly small fraction of world immigrant flows, and emigration from Africa, Asia, and Latin America has increased dramatically (Kritz *et al.* 1981; Stalker 1994). The variety of destination countries has also grown. In addition to traditional immigrant-receiving nations such as Canada,

the USA, Australia, New Zealand, and Argentina, countries throughout Western Europe now attract significant numbers of immigrants—notably Germany, France, Belgium, Switzerland, Sweden, and the Netherlands (Abadan-Unat 1995; Anwar 1995; Hammar 1995; Hoffman-Nowotny 1995; Ogden 1995).

During the 1970s, even long-time nations of emigration such as Italy, Spain, and Portugal began receiving immigrants from the Mediterranean basin and Africa (Fakiolas 1995; Solé 1995); and after the rapid escalation of oil prices in 1973, several less developed but capital-rich nations in the Gulf region also began to sponsor massive labour migration at about the same time (Birks and Sinclair 1980; Abella 1995b). By the 1980s, international migration had spread into Asia, not just to Japan but also to newly industrialized countries such as Korea, Taiwan, Hong Kong, Singapore, Malaysia, and Thailand (Bun 1995; Fee 1995; Hugo 1995; Loiskandl 1995). . . .

A NEW LOOK AT AN OLD PHENOMENON

Human migration is rooted in specific historical conditions that define a particular social and economic context. Historically specific explanations for international migration are frequently *ad hoc* and unsystematic rather than general. Nonetheless, ahistorical frameworks that offer universal explanations, immutable laws, and timeless regularities are not very helpful in trying to understand new patterns of international movement. The theoretical concepts now employed by social scientists to analyse and explain international migration were forged primarily during the industrial era and reflect its particular economic arrangements, social institutions, technology, demography, and politics.

. . .

THE NEW FACE OF INTERNATIONAL MIGRATION

The emblematic international migrant of the late nineteenth and early twentieth centuries was a

European crossing the ocean in search of a better life, exchanging an industrializing region intensive in labour for another industrializing region intensive in land (Hatton and Williamson 1994b). Traditional countries of immigration such as the USA, Canada, Australia, and Argentina had vast, sparsely inhabited territories as well as rapidly growing cities, whereas Europe's countryside was densely settled and the absorptive capacity of its crowded urban centres was often strained beyond practical limits (D. S. Thomas 1941; B. Thomas 1973; Lowell 1987).

Europe's passage through the initial and intermediate stages of economic development was accompanied by a demographic boom that, although small by contemporary Third World standards, was large enough to affect rates of emigration. Ebbs and flows in the volume of out-migration from Europe were closely tied to oscillating cohort sizes caused by earlier fluctuations in period fertility, which were themselves responses to prior economic cycles (D. S. Thomas 1941; Easterlin 1961; Germani 1966a; B. Thomas 1973; Hatton and Williamson 1994a). The tonic of demographic growth continued well into the present century, and even witnessed a fleeting revival after the Second World War.

International migration into the countries of Western Europe began during the second half of the twentieth century (Rose 1969; Castles and Kosack 1973; Power 1979; Stalker 1994). During the third quarter of the century much of the movement was intracontinental. Workers left nations in southern Europe that were still relatively intensive in labour—Italy, Spain, Portugal, and Greece—for nations in the north and west that had become intensive in capital but scarce in labour—Germany, France, Belgium, the Netherlands, Sweden (Martin and Miller 1980; Schierup 1995). Although it was not clear at the time, by the late 1960s, southern Europe was itself on the verge of achieving the long-desired state of capital abundance and labour scarcity, and during the 1970s, Italy, Spain, and Portugal also began importing migrant workers, mainly from the Middle East and North Africa.

The European shift from exporting to importing labour was notable because it involved, for the first time, the widespread movement of migrants to countries that were not intensive in land. Another distinctive feature lay in the *way* European labour migrants were brought in. Faced with rapid economic growth, tight labour markets, and a demand for workers that was impossible to fill from domestic sources (see Kindleberger 1967), but lacking an indigenous tradition of immigration or an ideology that favoured permanent settlement, European governments sought to recruit 'temporary' migrants—*Gastarbeiter* or 'guestworkers' in the language coined at the time—who would return to their countries of origin when the economic conditions that made their recruitment necessary disappeared (Martin 1991a).

When this moment finally arrived, however, the 'guests' failed to take the not-so-subtle hints of their 'hosts' and return home as anticipated. On the contrary, large numbers opted to settle permanently in Europe and began petitioning for the entry of their spouses, children, and other relatives. Although the number of immigrant *workers* stopped growing, foreign *populations* continued to swell (Martin and Miller 1980). In response, countries adopted more restrictive admissions policies after the mid-1970s, but by then the cow was out of the barn and European governments faced the prospect of integrating growing populations of immigrants and their descendants (Rose 1969; Castles and Kosack 1973). Without any popular referendum or explicit decision on the matter, Western Europe had become a multiracial, multi-ethnic society (Castles and Miller 1993).

It was only during the last quarter of the twentieth century, after the watershed event of the 1973 oil shock and the ensuing worldwide recession, that the outlines of the new post-industrial migratory order came into clear view, not just in Europe, but throughout the globe. The sudden infusion of petrodollars transformed the Persian Gulf into a capital-rich, labour-scarce region, and as in Europe, political leaders in the Gulf countries sought to recruit 'temporary' workers to fill the resulting demand for labour, this time from labour-rich, capital-poor States elsewhere in the Middle East and in Asia (Birks and Sinclair 1980). With even weaker traditions of immigration and pluralism than in Europe, the Gulf States placed harsher restrictions on migrant workers in an effort to keep them temporary (Dib 1988). Despite the restrictive nature of these policies, however, immigrants have become a permanent structural feature of economic and social life in the Gulf region.

By the 1980s, several 'Asian Tigers' had joined the ranks of wealthy, industrialized nations. In addition to Japan, which in some ways had become the world's dominant economic power, Taiwan, South Korea, Hong Kong, Singapore, Thailand, and Malaysia achieved stunning rates of economic growth during the 1970s; and by the 1980s, these nations also had become intensive in capital but poor in labour (Hugo 1995). Like the countries of southern Europe during the 1970s, many switched from exporting to importing labour, while others continued simultaneously to import and export workers. Throughout Asia and the Pacific, efforts were made to keep the new labour migration temporary to avoid the problems and tensions of racial and ethnic diversity created by permanent settlement.

Finally, traditional immigrant-receiving nations also experienced a transformation in their migratory patterns after the mid-1960s. Not only did the number of immigrants rise sharply, but the sources shifted from Europe to Asia and Latin America (Massey 1981, 1995). As in other migration systems, international migrants going to Argentina, Australia, Canada, and the USA generally came from labour-rich but capital-poor countries. As these receiving countries imposed new restrictions on immigration to limit and regulate the expanding flows, undocumented migration began to grow, and over time it came to comprise a larger share of the total.

Although experiences may differ across the world's contemporary migration systems, several common denominators stand out. First, most immigrants today come from countries characterized by a limited supply of capital, low rates of job creation, and abundant reserves of labour. Indeed, the imbalance between labour supply and demand in the Third World today far exceeds that which prevailed in Europe during its period of industrialization. This imbalance stems not only from a relative scarcity of capital and investment, but from a disarticulation between demographic conditions and economic limits that in earlier periods had constrained them. Whereas public health measures were readily imported into poor developing countries to lower mortality, social and economic conditions within those countries did not change rapidly enough to stimulate a corresponding decline in fertility, yielding an unprecedented demographic boom. Variation from country to country in the timing and pace of fertility decline thus emerges as a significant factor explaining widening of intercountry differences in labour availability.

Second, today's immigrant-receiving societies are far more intensive in capital and much less intensive in land than destination countries of the past. In fact, nations such as Germany, Japan, Korea, Taiwan, Kuwait, and the USA are so intensive in capital and technology that they have been shedding workers in many sectors (particularly manufacturing) and full employment has become a serious social and political issue. Under present technological conditions, farms and factories today can produce the same output as earlier with a fraction of their earlier labour force (Rifkin 1995). While high rates of unemployment have been the most visible outcome of this process in Europe, low wages and a growing class of working poor have been its principal manifestation in the USA. Rather than comprising a basic input for core sectors of the economy, international migrants now fill marginal niches within a labour market that is highly segmented (Piore 1979).

The economic marginalization of immigrants is associated with another characteristic of the post-industrial period: immigrants are no longer perceived as wanted or even needed, despite the persistence of a demand for their services (see Espenshade and Calhoun 1993; Espenshade and Hemstead 1996; Espenshade 1997). Whereas officials in destination countries of the past saw immigration as necessary for industrialization and a vital part of nation building, today's political leaders view immigrants as a social and political problem to be managed. Received societies increasingly have implemented restrictive admissions policies designed to limit the number of immigrants, confine their activities to the labour market, discourage the entry of dependants, and deter or prevent ultimate settlement.

Some new destination countries such as Japan, Germany, and Kuwait have become *de facto* countries of immigration without ever considering themselves as such, and they continue to maintain *de jure* systems that deny this reality. Meanwhile, traditional immigrant-receiving societies such as the USA, Canada, Australia, and Argentina, have sought to change their *de facto* status as countries of immigration by adopting more restrictive *de jure* policies (Kubat 1979; Stalker 1994). Although governments in capital-rich countries may acknowledge a need for migrant workers, citizens express discomfort at the rising tide of immigration and the growing ethnic diversity that it brings, yielding a fundamental contradiction that politicians seek somehow to finesse.

The last distinctive characteristic of contemporary international migration is the sheer size of the disparities that exist between sending and receiving societies—in wealth, income, power, size, growth, and culture. Presently, there are five principal migratory systems clustered around well-defined regions: North America, Western Europe, Asia and the Pacific, the Gulf region, and the Southern Cone of South America. The specific countries feeding into these zones are diverse and depend on historical ties of colonization, trade, politics, and culture; but generally they are located in the south and are relatively poor.

Considering the great disparities in wealth, power, and population that prevail within these systems, the actual size of the migratory flows is really rather modest, only a fraction of what might potentially result if the systems were left to operate without state interference. It is not so much the *actual* size of flows that accounts for developed countries' current obsessive interest in immigration, but the *potential* size of the flows, as well as the conflicting interests that sending and receiving nations have in perpetuating them.

Thus, the panorama of international migration in the last quarter of the twentieth century is characterized by distinctive features that set it apart from the earlier industrial era: within sending nations there is a sharp imbalance between labour supply and demand; within receiving nations low birth rates and aging populations produce a limited supply of workers while capital-intensive technologies yield a stratified demand producing plentiful opportunities for natives with skills and education, unemployment for those who lack schooling or special skills, and a segmented demand for immigrant workers. The continuing demand for immigrants, combined with high native unemployment and growing unease with ethnic diversity, yields a contradiction that governments seek to manage through restrictive polices that confine migrants to the labour market, limit the entry of dependants, discourage long-term settlement, and repatriate those who enter outside authorized channels. Compared to the earlier industrial era, contemporary patterns and processes of international migration are far more complex.

REFERENCES

Abad-Unat, Nermin (1995), 'Turkish migration to Europe', in Robin Cohen (ed.), *The Cambridge Survey of World Migration*, Cambridge University Press, Cambridge: 274–8.

Abella, Manolo I. (1995a), 'Asian migrant and contract workers in the Middle East', in Robin Cohen (ed.), *The Cambridge Survey of World Migration*, Cambridge University Press, Cambridge: 418–23.

—— (1995b), 'Asian labour migration: past, present and future', ASEAN *Economic Bulletin*, 12: 125–138.

Altman, Ida (1995), 'Spanish migration to the Americas' in Robin Cohen (ed.), *The Cambridge Survey of World Migration*, Cambridge University Press, Cambridge: 28–32.

Anwar, Muhammad (1995), 'New Commonwealth migration to the UK', in Robin Cohen (ed.), *The Cambridge Survey of World Migration*, Cambridge University Press, Cambridge: 271–3.

Birks, J. S., and A. Sinclair (1980), *International Migration and Development in the Arab Region*, International Labour Office, Geneva.

Bun, Chan Kwok (1995), 'The Vietnamese boat people in Hong Kong', in Robin Cohen (ed.), *The Cambridge Survey of World Migration*, Cambridge University Press, Cambridge: 380–5.

Castles, Stephen and Godula Kosack (1973), *Immigrant Workers and Class Structure in Western Europe*, Oxford University Press. London.

—— and Mark J. Miller (1993), *The Age of Migration: International Population Movements in the Modern World*, Guilford Press, New York.

Curtin, Philip D. (1969), *The Atlantic Slave Trade: A Census*, University of Wisconsin Press, Madison.

Davis, Kingsley (1974), 'The migrations of human populations', in *The Human Population*, W. H. Freeman, San Francisco: 53–65.

Dib, George (1988), 'Laws governing migration in some Arab countries', in Reginald T. Appleyard (ed.), *International Migration Today, I: Trends and Prospects*, University of Western Australia for the United Nations Educational, Scientific, and Cultural Organization, Perth: 168–79.

Easterlin, Richard A. (1961), 'Influences on European overseas emigration before World War I', *Economic Development and Cultural Changes*, 9: 331–51.

Espenshade, Thomas J. and Maryann Belanger (1997), 'US public perceptions and reactions to Mexican migration', in Frank D. Bean, Rodolfo O. de la Garza, Bryan R. Roberts, and Sidney Weintraub (eds.), *At the Crossroads: Mexico and US Immigration Policy*, Rowman & Littlefield, Lanham, Md.: 227–64.

—— and Charles A. Calhoun (1993), 'An analysis of public opinion toward undocumented immigration', *Population Research and Policy Review*, 12: 189–224.

—— and Katherine Hempstead (1996), 'Contemporary American attitudes toward US immigration', *International Migration Review*, 30: 535–70.

Fakiolas, Rossettos (1995), 'Italy and Greece: from emigrants to immigrants', in Robin Cohen (ed.), *The Cambridge Survey of World Migration*, Cambridge University Press, Cambridge: 313–15.

Fee, Lian Kwen (1995), 'Migration and the formation of Malaysia and Singapore', in Robin Cohen (ed.), *The Cambridge Survey of World Migration*, Cambridge University Press, Cambridge: 392–6.

Ferenczi, Imre (1929), *International Migrations, I: Statistics*, National Bureau of Economic Research, New York.

Gemery, Henry A., and James Horn (1992), 'British and French indentured servant migration to the Caribbean: a comparative study of seventeenth century emigration and labor markets', in *Proceedings of the Conference on the Peopling of the Americas, I*, International Union for the Scientific Study of Population, Liège: 283–300.

Germani, Gino (1966*a*), 'Mass immigration and modernization in Argentina', *Studies in Comparative International Development*, 2: 165–82.

—— (1966*b*), *Política y Sociedad en una Epoca de Transici;aaon: de la Sociedad Tradicional a la Sociedad de Masas*, Editorial Paidós, Buenos Aires.

Hammar, Tomas (1995), 'Labour migration to Sweden: the Finnish case', in Robin Cohen (ed.), *The Cambridge Survey of World Migration*, Cambridge University Press, Cambridge: 297–301.

Hatton, Timothy J., and Jeffrey G. Williamson (1994*a*), 'What drove the mass migrations from Europe in the late nineteenth century?', *Population and Development Review*, 20: 533–60.

—— (1994*b*), 'International migration 1850–1939: an economic survey', in Timothy J. Hatton and Jeffrey G. Williamson (eds.), *Migration and the International Labour Market: 1850–1939*, Routledge, London: 3–32.

Heffernan, Michael (1995), 'French colonial migration', in Robin Cohen (ed.), *The Cambridge Survey of World Migration*, Cambridge University Press, Cambridge: 33–8.

Hoffmann-Nowotny, Hans-Joachim (1995), 'Switzerland: a non-immigration immigration country', in Robin Cohen (ed.), *The Cambridge Survey of*

World Migration, Cambridge University Press, Cambridge: 302–7.

Holmes, Colin (1995), 'Jewish economic and refugee migrations, 1880–1950', in Robin Cohen (ed.), *The Cambridge Survey of World Migration*, Cambridge University Press, Cambridge: 148–52.

Hugo, Graeme J. (1995), 'Illegal migration in Asia', in Robin Cohen (ed.), *Cambridge Survey of World Migration*, Cambridge University Press, Cambridge: 397–402.

Hui, Ong Jin (1995), 'Chinese indentured labour: coolies and colonies', in Robin Cohen (ed.), *The Cambridge Survey of World Migration*, Cambridge University Press, Cambridge: 51–6.

Kay, Diana (1995), 'The resettlement of displaced persons in Europe, 1946–1951', in Robin Cohen (ed.), *The Cambridge Survey of World Migration*, Cambridge University Press, Cambridge: 154–8.

Kindleberger, Charles P. (1967), *Europe's Postwar Growth: The Role of Labor Supply*, Oxford University Press, New York.

Kritz, Mary M. (1992), 'The British and Spanish migration systems in the colonial era: a policy framework', in *Proceedings of the Conference on the Peopling of the Americas, I*, International Union for the Scientific Study of Population, Liège: 263–82.

——Charles B. Keely, and Silvano M. Tomasi (1981), *Global Trends in Migration: Theory and Research on International Population Movements*, Center for Migration Studies, Staten Island, NY.

Kubat, Daniel (1979), 'Canada', in Daniel Kubat (ed.), *The Politics of Migration Policies*, Center for Migration Studies, Staten Island, NY: 19–36.

Loiskandl, Helmut (1995), 'Illegal migrant workers in Japan', in Robin Cohen (ed.), *The Cambridge Survey of World Migration*, Cambridge University Press, Cambridge: 371–5.

Lowell, B. Lindsay (1987), *Scandinavian Exodus: Demography and Social Development of 19th-Century Rural Communities*, Westview Press, Boulder, Colo.

Lucassen, Jan (1995), 'Emigration to the Dutch colonies and the USA', in Robin Cohen (ed.), *The*

Cambridge Survey of World Migration, Cambridge University Press, Cambridge: 21–7.

Martin, Philip L. (1991*a*), *The Unfinished Story: Turkish Labour Migration to Western Europe*, International Labour Office, Geneva.

Martin, Philip L. and Mark J. Miller (1980), 'Guestworkers: lessons from Western Europe', *Industrial and Labor Relations Review*, 33: 315–30.

Massey, Douglas S. (1981), 'New Immigrants to the United States and the Prospects for Assimilation', *Annual Review of Sociology*, 7: 57–85.

—— (1988), 'International migration and economic development in comparative perspective', *Population and Development Review*, 14: 383–414.

—— (1995), 'The new immigration and the meaning of ethnicity in the United States', *Population and Development Review*, 21: 631–52.

Noiriel, Gérard (1995), 'Italians and Poles in France, 1880–1945', in Robin Cohen (ed.), *The Cambridge Survey of World Migration*, Cambridge University Press, Cambridge: 142–5.

Ogden, Philip E. (1995), 'Labour migration to France', in Robin Cohen (ed.), *The Cambridge Survey of World Migration*, Cambridge University Press, Cambridge: 289–97.

Palmer, Colin (1992), 'The human dimensions of the British Company trade to the Americas, 1672–1739: questions of African Phenotype, age, gender, and health', in *Proceedings of the Conference on the Peopling of the Americas, I*, International Union for the Scientific Study of Population, Liège: 161–82.

Piore, Michael J. (1979), *Birds of Passage: Migrant Labor in Industrial Societies*, Cambridge University Press, New York.

Power, Jonathan (1979), *Migrant Workers in Western Europe and the United States*, Pergamon Press, Oxford.

Rose, Arnold M. (1969), *Migrants in Europe: Problems of Acceptance and Adjustment*, University of Minnesota Press, Minneapolis.

Solé, Carlota (1995), 'Portugal and Spain: from exporters to importers of labour', in Robin Cohen (ed.), *The Cambridge Survey of World Migration*, Cambridge University Press, Cambridge: 316–20.

Stalker, Peter (1994), *The Work of Strangers: A Survey of International Labour Migration*, International Labour Office, Geneva.

Sword, Keith (1995), 'The repatriation of Soviet citizens at the end of the Second World War', in Robin Cohen (ed.), *The Cambridge Survey of World Migration*, Cambridge University Press, Cambridge: 323–6.

Thomas, Brinley (1973), *Migration and Economic Growth: A Study of Great Britain and the Atlantic Economy*, Cambridge University Press, Cambridge.

Thomas, Dorothy S. (1941), *Social and Economic Aspects of Swedish Population Movements: 1750–1933*, Macmillan, New York.

Tinker, Hugh (1977), *The Banyan Tree: Overseas Emigrants from India, Pakistan, and Bangladesh*, Oxford University Press, Oxford.

——(1995), 'The British colonies of settlement', in Robin Cohen (ed.), *The Cambridge Survey of World Migration*, Cambridge University Press: 14–20.

Twaddle, Michael (1995), 'The settlement of South Asians in East Africa', in Robin Cohen (ed.), *The Cambridge Survey of World Migration*, Cambridge University Press: 74–7.

Vertovec, Steven (1995), 'Indian indentured migration to the Caribbean', in Robin Cohen (ed.), *The Cambridge Survey of World Migration*, Cambridge University Press, Cambridge: 57–62.

POWER, DIVISION, AND CLASS

17

The Structure of Power in American Society

C. Wright Mills

POWER HAS TO DO WITH WHATEVER DECISIONS men make about the arrangements under which they live, and about the events which make up the history of their times. Events that are beyond human decision do happen; social arrangements do change without benefit of explicit decision. But in so far as such decisions are made, the problem of who is involved in making them is the basic problem of power. In so far as they could be made but are not, the problem becomes who fails to make them ....

How large a role any explicit decisions do play in the making of history is itself an historical problem. For how large that role may be depends very much upon the means of power that are available at any given time in any given society. In some societies, the innumerable actions of innumerable men modify their milieux, and so gradually modify the structure itself. These modifications—the course of history—go on behind the backs of men. History is

From *British Journal of Sociology* 9 March 1958, pp. 29–41. Reprinted by permission of Taylor & Francis Ltd., 11 New Fetter Lane, London EC4P 4EE, U.K.

drift, although in total "men make it." Thus, innumerable entrepreneurs and innumerable consumers by ten-thousand decisions per minute may shape and re-shape the free-market economy. Perhaps this was the chief kind of limitation Marx had in mind when he wrote, in *The 18th Brumaire*, that "Men make their own history, but they do not make it just as they please; they do not make it under circumstances chosen by themselves."

But in other societies—certainly in the United States and in the Soviet Union today—a few men may be so placed within the structure that by their decisions they modify the milieux of many other men, and in fact nowadays the structural conditions under which most men live. Such elites of power also make history under circumstances not chosen altogether by themselves, yet compared with other men, and compared with other periods of world history, these circumstances do indeed seem less limiting.

I should contend that "men are free to make history," but that some men are indeed much freer than others. For such freedom requires access to the means of decision and of power by which history can now be made. It has not always been so made; but in the later phases of the modern epoch it is. It is with reference to this epoch that I am contending that if men do not make history, they tend increasingly to become the utensils of history-makers as well as the mere objects of history.

The history of modern society may readily be understood as the story of the enlargement and the centralization of the means of power—in economic, in political, and in military institutions. The rise of industrial society has involved these developments in the means of economic production. The rise of the nation state has involved these developments in the means of violence and in those of political administration. . . .

The power to make decisions of national and international consequence is now so clearly seated in political, military, and economic institutions that other areas of society seem off to the side and, on occasion, readily subordinated to these. The scattered institutions of religion, education, and family are increasingly shaped by the big three, in which history-making decisions now regularly occur. . . . There is no longer, on the one hand, an economy, and, on the other, a political order, containing a military establishment unimportant to politics and to money-making. There is a political economy numerously linked with military order and decision. This triangle of power is now a structural fact, and it is the key to any understanding of the higher circles in America today. For as each of these domains has coincided with the others, as decisions in each have become broader, the leading men of each—the high military, the corporation executives, the political directorate—have tended to come together to form the power elite of America.

The political order, once composed of several dozen states with a weak federal-center, has become an executive apparatus which has taken up into itself many powers previously scattered, legislative as well as administrative, and which now reach into all parts of the social structure. The long-time tendency of business and government to become more closely connected has since World War II reached a new point of explicitness. Neither can now be seen clearly as a distinct world. The growth of executive government does not mean merely the "enlargement of government" as some kind of autonomous bureaucracy: under American conditions, it has also meant the ascendancy of the corporation man into political eminence. Already during the New Deal, such men had joined the political directorate; as of World War II they came to dominate it. . . .

The economy, once a great scatter of small productive units in somewhat automatic balance, has become internally dominated by a few hundred corporations, administratively and politically interrelated, which together hold the keys to economic decision. This economy is at once a permanent-war economy and a private-corporation economy. The most important relations of the corporation to the state now rest on the coincidence between military and corporate interests, as defined by the military and the corporate rich, and accepted by politicians and public. Within the elite as a whole, this coincidence of military domain and corporate realm strengthens both of them and further subordinates the merely political man. Not the party politician, but the corporation executive, is now more likely to sit with the military to answer the question: what is to be done?

The military order, once a slim establishment in a context of civilian distrust, has become the largest and most expensive feature of government; behind smiling public relations, it has all the grim and clumsy efficiency of a great and sprawling bureaucracy. The high military have gained decisive political and economic relevance. The seemingly permanent military threat places a premium upon them and virtually all political and economic actions are now judged in terms of military definitions of reality: the higher military have ascended to a firm position within the power elite of our time. . . .

1. To understand the unity of this power elite, we must pay attention to the psychology of its several members in their respective milieux. In so far as the power elite is composed of men of similar origin and education, of similar career and style of life, their unity may be said to rest upon the fact that they are of similar social type, and to lead to the fact of their easy intermingling. This kind of unity reaches its frothier apex in the sharing of that prestige which is to be had in the world of the celebrity. It achieves a more solid culmination in the fact of the interchangeability of positions between the three dominant institutional orders. It is revealed by considerable traffic of personnel within and between these three, as well as by the rise of specialized go-betweens as in the new style high-level lobbying.

2. Behind such psychological and social unity are the structure and the mechanics of those institutional hierarchies over which the political directorate, the corporate rich, and the high military now preside. How each of these hierarchies is shaped and what relations it has with the others determine in large part the relations of their rulers. Were these hierarchies scattered and disjointed, then their respective elites might tend to be scattered and disjointed; but if they have many

interconnections and points of coinciding interest, then their elites tend to form a coherent kind of grouping. The unity of the elite is not a simple reflection of the unity of institutions; but men and institutions are always related; that is why we must understand the elite today in connection with such institutional trends as the development of a permanent-war establishment, alongside a privately incorporated economy, inside a virtual political vacuum. For the men at the top have been selected and formed by such institutional trends.

3. Their unity, however, does not rest solely upon psychological similarity and social intermingling, nor entirely upon the structural blending or commanding positions and common interests. At times it is the unity of a more explicit co-ordination.

To say that these higher circles are increasingly co-ordinated, that this is *one* basis of their unity, and that at times—as during open war—such co-ordination is quite willful, is not to say that the co-ordination is total or continuous, or even that it is very surefooted. Much less is it to say that the power elite has emerged as the realization of a plot. Its rise cannot be adequately explained in any psychological terms. . . .

There are of course other interpretations of the American system of power. The most usual is that it is a moving balance of many competing interests. The image of balance, at least in America, is derived from the idea of the economic market: in the nineteenth century, the balance was thought to occur between a great scatter of individuals and enterprises; in the twentieth century, it is thought to occur between great interest blocs. In both views, the politician is the key man of power because he is the broker of many conflicting powers.

I believe that the balance and the compromise in American society—the "countervailing powers" and the "veto groups," of parties and associations, of strata and unions—must now be seen as having mainly to do with the middle levels of power. It is these middle levels that the political journalist and the scholar of politics are most likely to understand and to write about—if only because being mainly middle class themselves, they are closer to them. Moreover these levels provide the noisy content of most "political" news and gossip; the images of these levels are more or less in accord with the folklore of how democracy works; and, if the master-image of balance is accepted, many intellectuals, especially in their current patrioteering, are readily able to satisfy such political optimism as they wish to feel. Accordingly, liberal interpretations of what is happening in the United States are now virtually the only interpretations that are widely distributed.

But to believe that the power system reflects a balancing society is, I think, to confuse the present era with earlier times, and to confuse its top and bottom with its middle levels.

By the top levels, as distinguished from the middle, I intend to refer, first of all, to the scope of the decisions that are made. At the top today, these decisions have to do with all the issues of war and peace. They have also to do with slump and poverty which are now so very much problems of international scope. I intend also to refer to whether or not the groups that struggle politically have a chance to gain the positions from which such top decisions are made, and indeed whether their members do usually hope for such top national command. Most of the competing interests which make up the clang and clash of American politics are strictly concerned with their slice of the existing pie. Labor unions, for example, certainly have no policies of an international sort other than those which given unions adopt for the strict economic protection of their members. Neither do farm organizations. The actions of such middle-level powers may indeed have consequence for top-level policy; certainly at times they hamper these policies. But they are not truly concerned with them, which means of course that their influence tends to be quite irresponsible.

The facts of the middle levels may in part be understood in terms of the rise of the power elite. The expanded and centralized and interlocked hierarchies over which the power elite preside have encroached upon the old balance and relegated it to the middle level. But there are also independent developments of the middle levels. These, it seems to me, are better understood as an affair of entrenched and provincial demands than as a center of national decision. As such, the middle level often seems much more of a stalemate than a moving balance.

1. The middle level of politics is not a forum in which there are debated the big decisions of national and international life. Such debate is not carried on by nationally responsible parties representing and clarifying alternative policies. There are no such parties in the United States. More and more, fundamental issues never come to any point or decision before Congress, much less before the electorate in party campaigns. . . .

The American political campaign distracts attention from national and international issues, but that is not to say that there are no issues in these campaigns. In each district and state, issues are set up and watched by organized interests of sovereign local importance. The professional politician is of course a party politician, and the two parties are semi-feudal organizations: they trade patronage and other favors for votes and for protection. The differences between them, so far as national issues are concerned, are very narrow and very mixed up. Often each seems to be fifty parties, one to each state; and accordingly, the politician as campaigner and as Congressman is not concerned with national party lines, if any are discernible. Often he is not subject to any effective national party discipline. He speaks for the interests of his own constituency, and he is concerned with national issues only in so far as they affect the interests effectively organized there, and hence his chances of reelection. That is why, when he does speak of national matters, the result is so often such an empty rhetoric. Seated in his sovereign locality, the politician is not at the national summit. He is on and of the middle levels of power.

2. Politics is not an arena in which free and independent organizations truly connect the lower and middle levels of society with the top

levels of decision. Such organizations are not an effective and major part of American life today. As more people are drawn into the political arena, their associations become mass in scale, and the power of the individual becomes dependent upon them; to the extent that they are effective, they have become larger, and to that extent they have become less accessible to the influence of the individual. This is a central fact about associations in any mass society; it is of most consequence for political parties and for trade unions.

In the 'thirties, it often seemed that labor would become an insurgent power independent of corporation and state. Organized labor was then emerging for the first time on an American scale, and the only political sense of direction it needed was the slogan, "organize the unorganized." Now without the mandate of the slump, labor remains without political direction. Instead of economic and political struggles it has become deeply entangled in administrative routines with both corporation and state. One of its major functions, as a vested interest of the new society, is the regulation of such irregular tendencies as may occur among the rank and file.

There is nothing, it seems to me, in the make-up of the current labor leadership to allow us to expect that it can or that it will lead, rather than merely react. In so far as it fights at all it fights over a share of the goods of a single way of life and not over that way of life itself. The typical labor leader in the U.S.A. today is better understood as an adaptive creature of the main business drift than as an independent actor in a truly national context.

3. The idea that this society is a balance of powers requires us to assume that the units in balance are of more or less equal power and that they are truly independent of one another. These assumptions have rested, it seems clear, upon the historical importance of a large and independent middle class. In the latter nineteenth century and during the Progressive Era, such a class of farmers and small businessmen fought politically—and lost—their last struggle for a paramount role

in national decision. Even then, their aspirations seemed bound to their own imagined past.

This old, independent middle class has of course declined. On the most generous count, it is now 40 percent of the total middle class (at most 20 percent of the total labor force). Moreover, it has become politically as well as economically dependent upon the state, most notably in the case of the subsidized farmer.

The *new* middle class of white-collar employees is certainly not the political pivot of any balancing society. It is in no way politically unified. Its unions, such as they are, often serve merely to incorporate it as hanger-on of the labor interest. For a considerable period, the old middle class *was* an independent base of power; the new middle class cannot be. Political freedom and economic security *were* anchored in small and independent properties; they are not anchored in the worlds of the white-collar job. Scattered property holders were economically united by more or less free markets; the jobs of the new middle class are integrated by corporate authority. Economically, the white-collar classes are in the same condition as wage workers; politically, they are in a worse condition, for they are not organized. They are no vanguard of historic change; they are at best a rearguard of the welfare state. . . .

Fifty years ago many observers thought of the American state as a mask behind which an invisible government operated. But nowadays, much of what was called the old lobby, visible or invisible, is part of the quite visible government. The "governmentalization of the lobby" has proceeded in both the legislative and the executive domain, as well as between them. The executive bureaucracy becomes not only the center of decision but also the arena within [which] major conflicts of power are resolved or denied resolution. "Administration" replaces electoral politics: the maneuvering of cliques (which include leading Senators as well as civil servants) replaces the open clash of parties.

The shift of corporation men into the political directorate has accelerated the decline of the politicians in the Congress to the middle levels of power; the formation of the power elite rests in part upon this relegation. It rests also upon the semi-organized stalemate of the interest of sovereign localities, into which the legislative function has so largely fallen; upon the virtually complete absence of a civil service that is a politically neutral but politically relevant depository of brainpower and executive skill; and it rests upon the increased official secrecy behind which great decisions are made without benefit of public or even of Congressional debate.

There is one last belief upon which liberal observers everywhere base their interpretations and rest their hopes. That is the idea of the public and the associated idea of public opinion. Conservative thinkers, since the French Revolution, have of course Viewed With Alarm the rise of the public, which they have usually called the masses, or something to that effect. "The populace is sovereign," wrote Gustave Le Bon, "and the tide of barbarism mounts." But surely those who have supposed the masses to be well on their way to triumph are mistaken. In our time, the influence of publics or of masses within political life is in fact decreasing, and such influence as on occasion they do have tends, to an unknown but increasing degree, to be guided by the means of mass communication.

In a society of publics, discussion is the ascendant means of communication, and the mass media, if they exist, simply enlarge and animate this discussion, linking one face-to-face public with the discussions of another. In a mass society, the dominant type of communication is the formal media, and the publics become mere markets for these media: the "public" of a radio program consists of all those exposed to it. When we try to look upon the United States today as a society of publics, we realize that it has moved a considerable distance along the road to the mass society.

In official circles, the very term, "the public," has come to have a phantom meaning, which dramatically reveals its eclipse. The deciding elite can identify some of those who clamour publicly as "Labor," others as "Business," still others as "Farmer." But these are not the public. "The

public" consists of the unidentified and the non-partisan in a world of defined and partisan interests. In this faint echo of the classic notion, the public is composed of those remnants of the old and new middle classes whose interests are not explicitly defined, organized, or clamorous. In a curious adaptation, "the public" often becomes, in administrative fact, "the disengaged expert," who, although ever so well informed, has never taken a clear-cut and public stand on controversial issues. He is the "public" member of the board, the commission, the committee. What "the public" stands for, accordingly, is often a vagueness of policy (called "open-mindedness"), a lack of involvement in public affairs (known as "reasonableness"), and a professional disinterest (known as "tolerance").

All this is indeed far removed from the eighteenth-century idea of the public of public opinion. That idea parallels the economic idea of the magical market. Here is the market composed of freely competing entrepreneurs; there is the public composed of circles of people in discussion. As price is the result of anonymous, equally weighted, bargaining individuals, so public opinion is the result of each man's having thought things out for himself and then contributing his voice to the great chorus. To be sure, some may have more influence on the state of opinion than others, but no one group monopolizes the discussion, or by itself determines the opinions that prevail.

In this classic image, the people are presented with problems. They discuss them. They formulate viewpoints. These viewpoints are organized, and they compete. One viewpoint "wins out." Then the people act out this view, or their representatives are instructed to act it out, and this they promptly do.

Such are the images of democracy which are still used as working justifications of power in America. We must now recognize this description as more a fairy tale than a useful approximation. The issues that now shape man's fate are neither raised nor decided by any public at large. The idea of a society that is at bottom composed of publics is not a matter of fact; it is the proclamation of an ideal, [as well as] the assertion of a legitimation masquerading as fact.

I cannot here describe the several great forces within American society . . . which have been at work in the debilitation of the public. I want only to remind you that publics, like free associations, can be deliberately and suddenly smashed, or they can more slowly wither away. But whether smashed in a week or withered in a generation, the demise of the public must be seen in connection with the rise of centralized organizations, with all their new means of power, including those of the mass media of distraction. These, we now know, often seem to expropriate the rationality and the will of the terrorized or—as the case may be—the voluntarily indifferent society of masses. In the more democratic process of indifference the remnants of such publics as remain may only occasionally be intimidated by fanatics in search of "disloyalty." But regardless of that, they lose their will for decisions because they do not possess the instruments for decision: they lose their sense of political belonging because they do not belong; they lose their political will because they see no way to realize it.

The political structure of a modern democratic state requires that such a public as is projected by democratic theorists not only exists but that it be the very forum within which a politics of real issues is enacted.

It requires a civil service that is firmly linked with the world of knowledge and sensibility, and which is composed of skilled men who, in their careers and in their aspirations, are truly independent of any private, which is to say, corporation, interests.

It requires nationally responsible parties which debate openly and clearly the issues which the nation, and indeed the world, now so rigidly confront.

It requires an intelligentsia, inside as well as outside the universities, who carry on the big discourse of the western world, and whose work is relevant to and influential among parties and movements and publics.

And it certainly requires, as a fact of power, that there be free associations standing between families and smaller communities and publics, on the one hand, and the state, the military, the corporation, on the other. For unless these do exist, there are no vehicles for reasoned opinion, no instruments for the rational exertion of public will.

Such democratic formations are not now ascendant in the power structure of the United States, and accordingly the men of decision are not men selected and formed by careers within such associations and by their performance before such publics. The top of modern American society is increasingly unified, and often seems willfully coordinated: at the top there has emerged an elite whose power probably exceeds that of any small group of men in world history. The middle levels are often a drifting set of stalemated forces: the middle does not link the bottom with the top. The bottom of this society is politically fragmented, and even as a passive fact, increasingly powerless: at the bottom there is emerging a mass society.

These developments, I believe, can be correctly understood neither in terms of the liberal nor the Marxian interpretation of politics and history. Both of these ways of thought arose as guidelines to reflection about a type of society which does not now exist in the United States. We confront there a new kind of social structure, which embodies elements and tendencies of all modern society, but in which they assumed a more naked and flamboyant prominence.

That does not mean that we must give up the ideals of these classic political expectations. I believe that both have been concerned with the problem of rationality and of freedom: liberalism, with freedom and rationality as supreme facts about the individual; Marxism, as supreme facts about man's role in the political making of history. What I have said here, I suppose, may be taken as an attempt to make evident why the ideas of freedom and of rationality now so often seem so ambiguous in the new society of the United States of America.

18

Weeding Out the Wealthy

Jeffrey Reiman

The offender at the end of the road in prison is likely to be a member of the lowest social and economic groups in the country.[1]

THIS STATEMENT IN THE *REPORT OF THE PRESIDENT'S Commission on Law Enforcement and Administration of Justice* is as true today as it was over three decades ago when it was written. Our prisons are indeed, as Ronald Goldfarb has called them, the "national poorhouse."[2] To most citizens this comes as no surprise—recall the Typical Criminal and the Typical Crime. Dangerous crimes, they think, are mainly committed by poor people. Seeing that prison populations are made up primarily of the poor only makes them surer of this. They think, in other words, that the criminal justice system gives a true reflection of the dangers that threaten them.

In my view, it also comes as no surprise that our prisons and jails predominantly confine the poor. This is not because these are the individuals who most threaten us. It is because the criminal justice system effectively weeds out the well-to-do, so that at *the end of the road in prison*, the vast majority of those we find there come from the lower classes. This weeding out process starts before the agents of law enforcement go into action. . . . I [have] argued that our very definition of crime *excludes* a wide variety of actions [as being] at least as dangerous as those included and often worse. Is it any accident that the kinds of dangerous actions excluded are

the kinds most likely to be performed by the affluent in America? Even before we mobilize our troops in the war on crime, we have already guaranteed that large numbers of upper-class individuals will never come within their sights.

This process does not stop at the definition of crime. It continues throughout each level of the criminal justice system. At each step, from arresting to sentencing, the likelihood of being ignored or released or lightly treated by the system is greater the better off one is economically. As the late U.S. Senator Philip Hart wrote:

> Justice has two transmission belts, one for the rich and one for the poor. The low-income transmission belt is easier to ride without falling off and it gets to prison in shorter order.
>
> The transmission belt for the affluent is a little slower and it passes innumerable stations where exits are temptingly convenient.[3]

This means that the criminal justice system functions from start to finish in a way that makes certain that "the offender at the end of the road in prison is likely to be a member of the lowest social and economic groups in the country."

For the same criminal behavior, the poor are more likely to be arrested; if arrested, they are more likely to be charged; if charged, more likely to be convicted; if convicted, more likely to be sentenced to prison; and if sentenced, more likely to be given longer prison terms than members of the middle and upper classes.[4] In other words, the

From *The Rich Get Richer and the Poor Get Prison: Ideology, Class, and Criminal Justice*, 5th edition, by Jeffrey Reiman. Copyright © 1998 by Allyn & Bacon. Reprinted by permission.

image of the criminal population one sees in our nation's jails and prisons is distorted by the shape of the criminal justice system itself. It is the face of evil reflected in a carnival mirror, but it is no laughing matter.

. . .

ARREST AND CHARGING

The problem with most official records of who commits crime is that they are really statistics on who gets arrested and convicted. If, as I will show, the police are more likely to arrest some people than others, these official statistics may tell us more about police than about criminals. In any event, they give us little reliable data about those who commit crime and do not get caught. Some social scientists, suspicious of the bias built into official records, have tried to devise other methods of determining who has committed a crime. Most often, these methods involve an interview or questionnaire in which the respondent is assured of anonymity and asked to reveal whether he or she has committed any offenses for which he or she could be arrested and convicted. Techniques to check reliability of these self-reports also have been devised; however, if their reliability is still in doubt, common sense would dictate that they would understate rather than overstate the number of individuals who have committed crimes and never come to official notice. In light of this, the conclusions of these studies are rather astounding. It would seem that crime is the national pastime. The President's Crime Commission conducted a survey of 10,000 households and discovered that "91 percent of all Americans have violated laws that could have subjected them to a term of imprisonment at one time in their lives."[5]

A number of other studies support the conclusion that serious criminal behavior is widespread among middle- and upper-class individuals, although these individuals are rarely, if ever, arrested. Some of the studies show that there are no significant differences between economic classes in the incidence of criminal behavior.[6] The au-

thors of a recent review of literature on class and delinquency conclude that "Research published since 1978, using both official and self-reported data suggests . . . that there is no pervasive relationship between SES [socioeconomic status] and delinquency."[7] This conclusion is echoed by Jensen and Thompson, who argue that

The safest conclusion concerning class structure and delinquency is the same one that has been proposed for several decades: class, no matter how defined, contributes little to explaining variation in self-reports of common delinquency.[8]

Others conclude that while lower-class individuals do commit more than their share of crime, arrest records overstate their share and understate that of the middle and upper classes.[9] Still other studies suggest that some forms of serious crime—forms usually associated with lower-class youth—show up *more frequently* among higher-class persons than among lower.[10] For instance, Empey and Erikson interviewed 180 white males aged 15 to 17 who were drawn from different economic strata. They found that "virtually all respondents reported having committed not one but a variety of different offenses." Although youngsters from the middle classes constituted 55 percent of the group interviewed, they admitted to 67 percent of the instances of breaking and entering, 70 percent of the instances of property destruction, and an astounding 87 percent of all the armed robberies admitted to by the entire sample.[11] Williams and Gold studied a national sample of 847 males and females between the ages of 13 and 16.[12] Of these, 88 percent admitted to at least one delinquent offense.

Even those who conclude "that more lower status youngsters commit delinquent acts more frequently than do higher status youngsters"[13] also recognize that lower-class youth are significantly overrepresented in official records. Gold writes that "about five times more lowest than highest status boys appear in the official records; if records were complete and unselective, we estimate "that the ratio would be closer to 1.5:1."[14] The simple fact is that for the same offense, *a poor person is more likely to be arrested and, if arrested charged, than a middle- or upper-class person.*[15]

This means, first of all, that poor people are more likely to come to the attention of the police. Furthermore, even when apprehended, the police are more likely to formally charge a poor person and release a higher-class person *for the same offense.* Gold writes that

boys who live in poorer parts of town and are apprehended by police for delinquency are four to five times more likely to appear in some official record than boys from wealthier sections who commit the same kinds of offenses. These same data show that, at each stage in the legal process from charging a boy with an offense to some sort of disposition in court, boys from different socioeconomic backgrounds are treated differently, so that those eventually incarcerated in public institutions, that site of most of the research on delinquency, are selectively poorer boys.[16]

From a study of self-reported delinquent behavior, Gold finds that when individuals were apprehended, "if the offender came from a higher status family, police were more likely to handle the matter themselves without referring it to the court."[17]

Terence Thornberry reached a similar conclusion in his study of 3,475 delinquent boys in Philadelphia. Thornberry found that among boys arrested *for equally serious offenses* and who had *similar prior offense records,* police were more likely to refer the lower-class youths than the more affluent ones to juvenile court. The police were more likely to deal with the wealthier youngsters informally, for example, by holding them in the station house until their parents came rather than instituting formal procedures. Of those referred to juvenile court, Thornberry found further that for *equally serious offenses* and with *similar prior records,* the poorer youngsters were more likely to be institutionalized than were the affluent ones. The wealthier youths were more likely to receive probation than the poorer ones. As might be expected, Thornberry found the same relationships when comparing the treatment of black and white youths apprehended for equally serious offenses.[18]

Recent studies continue to show similar effects. For example, Sampson found that, for the same crimes, juveniles in lower-class neighborhoods were more likely to have some police record than those in better-off neighborhoods. Again, for similar crimes, lower-class juveniles were more likely to be referred to court than better-off juveniles. If you think these differences are not so important because they are true only of young offenders, remember that this group accounts for much of the crime problem. Moreover, other studies not limited to the young tend to show the same economic bias. McCarthy found that, in metropolitan areas, for similar suspected crimes, unemployed people were more likely to be arrested than employed.[19]

As I indicated above, racial bias is but another form in which the bias against the poor works. And blacks are more likely to be suspected or arrested than whites. A 1988 *Harvard Law Review* overview of studies on race and the criminal process concludes that "most studies . . . reveal what many police officers freely admit: that police use race as an independently significant, if not determinative, factor in deciding whom to follow, detain, search, or arrest."[20] "A 1994 study of juvenile detention decisions found that African American and Hispanic youths were more likely to be detained at each decision point, even after controlling for the influence of offense seriousness and social factors (e.g., single-parent home). Decisions by both police and the courts to detain a youngster were highly influenced by race."[21] The study states that, "[n]ot only were there direct effects of race, but indirectly, socioeconomic status was related to detention, thus putting youth of color again at risk for differential treatment."[22] Reporting the results of University of Missouri criminologist Kimberly Kempf's study of juvenile justice in fourteen Pennsylvania counties, Jerome Miller says that "Black teenagers were more likely to be detained, to be handled formally, to be waived to adult court, and to be adjudicated delinquent."[23] And the greater likelihood of arrest that minorities face is matched by a greater likelihood of being charged with a serious offense. For example, Huizinga and Elliott report that: "Minorities appear to be at greater risk for being charged with more serious offenses than whites when involved in comparable levels of delinquent behavior."[24] Bear in mind that once an individual has a criminal record, it becomes harder for that person to get employment thus increasing the likelihood of future criminal involvement and more serious criminal charges.

For reasons mentioned earlier, a disproportionately large percentage of the casualties in the recent War on Drugs are poor inner-city minority males. Michael Tonry writes that, "according to National Institute on Drug Abuse (1991) surveys of Americans' drug use, [Blacks] are not more likely than Whites ever to have used most drugs of abuse. Nonetheless, the . . . number of drug arrests of Blacks more than doubled between 1985 and 1989, whereas White drug arrests increased only by 27 percent."[25] A study conducted by the Sentencing Project, based mainly on Justice Department statistics, indicates that "Blacks make up 12 percent of the United States' population and constitute 13 percent of all monthly drug users . . . , but represent 35 percent of those arrested for drug possession, 55 percent of those convicted of drug possession and 74 percent of those sentenced to prison for drug possession."[26]

Numerous studies of police use of deadly force show that blacks are considerably more likely than whites or Hispanics to be shot by the police. For example, using data from Memphis, Tennessee, covering the years from 1969 through 1974, James Fyfe found that blacks were "10 times more likely than whites to have been shot at unsuccessfully by police, 18 times more likely to have been wounded, and 5 times more likely to have been killed."[27] A nation that has watched the brutal treatment meted out to Rodney King by California police officers will not find this surprising. Does anyone think this would have happened if King were a white man?

Any number of reasons can be offered to account for the differences in police treatment of poor versus well-off citizens. Some argue that they reflect that the poor have less privacy.[28] What others can do in their living rooms or backyards the

poor do on the street. Others argue that a police officer's decision to book a poor youth and release a middle-class youth reflects either the officer's judgment that the higher-class youngster's family will be more likely and more able to discipline him or her than the lower-class youngster's, or differences in the degree to which poor and middle-class complainants demand arrest. Others argue that police training and police work condition police officers to be suspicious of certain kinds of people, such as lower-class youth, blacks, Mexicans, and so on,[29] and thus more likely to detect their criminality. Still others hold that police mainly arrest those with the least political clout,[30] those who are least able to focus public attention on police practices or bring political influence to bear, and these happen to be the members of the lowest social and economic classes.

Regardless of which view one takes, and probably all have some truth in them, one conclusion is inescapable: One of the reasons the offender "at the end of the road in prison is likely to be a member of the lowest social and economic groups in the country" is that the police officers who guard the access to the road to prison make sure that more poor people make the trip than well-to-do people.

Likewise for prosecutors. A recent study of prosecutors' decisions shows that lower-class individuals are more likely to have charges pressed against them than upper-class individuals.[31] Racial discrimination also characterizes prosecutors' decisions to charge. The *Harvard Law Review* overview of studies on race and the criminal process asserts, "Statistical studies indicate that prosecutors are more likely to pursue full prosecution, file more severe charges, and seek more stringent penalties in cases involving minority defendants than in cases involving nonminority defendants."[32] One study of whites, blacks, and Hispanics arrested in Los Angeles on suspicion of having committed a felony found that, among defendants with equally serious charges and prior records, 59 percent of whites had their charges dropped at the initial screening, compared with 40 percent of blacks and 37 percent of Hispanics.[33]

The *weeding out of the wealthy* starts at the very entrance to the criminal justice system: The decision about whom to investigate, arrest, or charge is not made simply on the basis of the offense committed or the danger posed. It is a decision distorted by a systematic economic bias that works to the disadvantage of the poor.

This economic bias is a two-edged sword. Not only are the poor arrested and charged out of proportion to their numbers for the kinds of crimes poor people generally commit—burglary, robbery, assault, and so forth—but when we reach the kinds of crimes poor people almost never have the opportunity to commit, such as antitrust violations, industrial safety violations, embezzlement, and serious tax evasion, the criminal justice system shows an increasingly benign and merciful face. The more likely that a crime is the type committed by middle- and upper-class people, the less likely that it will be treated as a criminal offense. When it comes to crime in the streets, where the perpetrator is apt to be poor, he or she is even more likely to be arrested and formally charged. When it comes to crime in the suites, where the offender is apt to be affluent, the system is most likely to deal with the crime noncriminally, that is, by civil litigation or informal settlement. Where it does choose to proceed criminally, . . . it rarely goes beyond a slap on the wrist. Not only is the main entry to the road to prison held wide open to the poor but the access routes for the wealthy are largely sealed off. Once again, we should not be surprised at whom we find in our prisons.

Many writers have commented on the extent and seriousness of "white-collar crime," so I will keep my remarks to a minimum. Nevertheless, for those of us trying to understand how the image of crime is created, four points should be noted.

1. White-collar crime is costly; it takes far more dollars from our pockets than all the FBI Index crimes combined.

2. White-collar crime is widespread, probably much more so than the crimes of the poor.

3. White-collar criminals are rarely arrested or charged; the system has developed kindlier ways of dealing with the more delicate sensibilities of its higher-class clientele.

4. When the white-collar criminals are prosecuted and convicted, their sentences are either suspended or very light when judged by the cost their crimes have imposed on society.

The first three points will be discussed here . . . .

Everyone agrees that the cost of white-collar crime is enormous. In 1985, *U.S. News and World Report* reported that "Experts estimate that white-collar criminals rake in a minimum of $200 billion annually."[34] Marshall Clinard also cites the $200 billion estimate in his recent book, *Corporate Corruption: The Abuse of Corporate Power.*[35] Nonetheless, $200 billion probably understates the actual cost. Tax evasion alone has been estimated to cost from 5 to 7 percent of the gross national product. For 1994, that would be between $336 and $470 billion.[36]. . .

This . . . with the modifications . . . gives us an estimate total cost of white-collar crime in 1994 of *$208.5 billion* (about five times higher than the Chamber's 1974 estimated total cost of $41.78 billion). (See Table 3.1 for the total cost and the breakdown into costs per category of white-collar crime.) The figure $208.5 billion jibes with the estimates of $200 billion quoted earlier, but it is surely on the conservative side. Nonetheless, it is more than *7,000 times* the total amount taken in all bank robberies in the United States in 1994 and more than *thirteen times* the total amount stolen in all thefts reported in the FBI *Uniform Crime Reports* for that year.[37]

Nevertheless, corporate executives almost never end up in jail, where they would find themselves sharing cells with poorer persons who had stolen less from their fellow citizens. What Sutherland found in 1949 continues up to the present. In his 1990 book, *Corporate Corruption: The Abuse of Power*, Marshall Clinard writes:

TABLE 3.1
The Cost of White-Collar Crime (in Billions of Dollars)

Bankruptcy fraud		$ 0.30
Bribery, kickbacks, and payoffs		11.28
Computer-related crime		3.00
Consumer fraud, illegal competition, deceptive practices		83.84
Consumer victims	$20.68	
Business victims	13.16	
Government revenue loss	50.00	
Credit card and check fraud		4.76
Credit card	1.00	
Check	3.76	
Embezzlement and pilferage		31.28
Embezzlement (cash, goods, services)	11.28	
Pilferage	20.00	
Insurance fraud		19.88
Insurer victims	18.00	
Policyholder victims	1.88	
Receiving stolen property		13.16
Securities thefts and frauds		40.00
Cellular phone fraud		1.00
	Total (billions)	$208.5

Source: Chamber of Commerce of the United States. *A Handbook on White-Collar Crime*, 1974 (figures adjusted for inflation and population growth through 1994, and supplemented from other sources documented in text).

Many government investigations, both federal and state, have revealed extensive law violations in such industries as oil, autos, and pharmaceuticals . . . . [O]ver one two-year period, the federal government charged nearly two-thirds of the Fortune 500 corporations with law violations; half were charged with a serious violation. . . . According to a 1982 *U.S. News and World Report* study, more than one out of five of the Fortune 500 companies had been convicted of at least one major crime or had paid civil penalties for serious illegal behavior between 1970 and 1979.[38]

A . . . study of offenders convicted of federal white-collar crimes found "that white-collar criminals are often repeat offenders."[39] As for the treatment of these repeat offenders, Clinard says "a large-scale study of sanctions imposed for corporate law violations found that administrative [that is, non-

criminal] penalties were employed in two-thirds of serious corporate law violations, and that slightly more than two-fifths of the sanctions . . . consisted simply of a warning to the corporation not to commit the offense again."[40]

The continued prevalence of these practices is confirmed in a recent study of white-collar crime prosecutions by Susan Shapiro, titled "The Road Not Taken: The Elusive Path to Criminal Prosecution for White-Collar Offenders." Focusing on the enforcement practices of the Securities and Exchange Commission (SEC), Shapiro writes that,

. . . while criminal dispositions are often appropriate, they are rarely pursued to the sentencing stage. Out of every 100 suspects investigated by the SEC, 93 have committed securities violations that carry criminal penalties. Legal action is taken against 46 of them, but only 11 are selected for criminal treatment. Six of these are indicted; 5 will be convicted and 3 sentenced to prison. Thus, for Securities and Exchange Commission enforcement, criminal prosecution most often represents the road not taken. Of those found to have engaged in securities fraud, 88 percent never have to contend with the criminal justice system at all.[41]

With upper-class lawbreakers, the authorities prefer to sue in civil court for damages or for an injunction rather than treat the wealthy as common criminals. Judges have on occasion stated in open court that they would not make criminals of reputable businessmen. One would think it would be up to the businessmen to make criminals of themselves by their actions, but alas, this privilege is reserved for the lower classes.

Examples of reluctance to use the full force of the criminal process for crimes not generally committed by the poor can be multiplied ad infinitum. . . . A large number of potential criminal cases arising out of the savings and loan scandals have been dismissed by Federal law enforcement agencies because they lack the labor power to pursue them—even as we hire 100,000 new police officers to fight street crime.

Let me close with one final example that typifies this particular distortion of criminal justice policy. Embezzlement is the crime of misappropriating money or property entrusted to one's care, custody, or control. Because the poor are rarely entrusted with tempting sums of money or valuable property, this is predominantly a crime of the middle and upper classes. The U.S. Chamber of Commerce estimate of the annual economic cost of embezzlement, adjusted for inflation, is $11.28 billion—more than two-thirds the total value of all property and money stolen in all FBI Index property crimes in 1995. (Don't be fooled into thinking that this cost is imposed only on the rich or on big companies with lots of resources. They pass on their losses—and their increased insurance costs—to consumers in the form of higher prices. Embezzlers take money

out of the very same pockets that muggers do: yours!) Nevertheless, the FBI reports that in 1995, when there were 2,128,600 arrests for property crimes, there were 15,200 arrests for embezzlement nationwide.[42] Although their cost to society is comparable, the number of arrests for property crimes was *140 times greater* than the number of arrests for embezzlement. Roughly, this means there was one property crime arrest for every $7,000 stolen, and one embezzlement arrest for every $742,000 "misappropriated": Note that even the language becomes more delicate as we deal with a "better" class of crook.

The clientele of the criminal justice system forms an exclusive club. Entry is largely a privilege of the poor. The crimes they commit are the crimes that qualify one for admission—and they are admitted in greater proportion than their share of those crimes. Curiously enough, the crimes the affluent commit are not the kind that easily qualify one for membership in the club.

. . .

NOTES

1. *The Challenge of Crime in a Free Society: A Report by the President's Commission* (Washington, DC: U.S. Government Printing Office, 1967), p. 44.

2. Ronald Goldfarb, "Prisons: The National Poorhouse," *New Republic*, November 1, 1969, pp. 15–17.

3. Philip A. Hart, "Swindling and Knavery, Inc.," *Playboy*, August 1972, p. 158.

4. Compare the statement, written more than half a century ago, by Professor Edwin H. Sutherland, one of the major luminaries of twentieth-century criminology:

   First, the administrative processes are more favorable to persons in economic comfort than to those in poverty, so that if two persons on different economic levels are equally guilty of the same offense, the one on the lower level is more likely to be arrested, convicted, and committed to an institution. Second, the laws are written, administered, and implemented primarily with reference to the types of crimes committed by people of lower economic levels. [E. H. Sutherland, *Principles of Criminology* (Philadelphia: Lippincott, 1939), p. 179].

5. Isidore Silver, "Introduction" to the Avon edition of *The Challenge of Crime in a Free Society* (New York: Avon, 1968), p. 31.

6. This is the conclusion of Austin L. Porterfield, *Youth in Trouble* (Fort Worth: Leo Potishman Foundation, 1946); Fred J. Murphy, M. Shirley, and H. L. Witmer, "The Incidence of Hidden Delinquency," *American Journal of Orthopsychiatry* 16 (October 1946), pp. 686–96; James F. Short Jr., "A Report on the Incidence of Criminal Behavior, Arrests, and Convictions in Selected Groups," *Proceedings of the Pacific Sociological Society*, 1954, pp. 110–18, published as vol. 22, no. 2 of *Research Studies of the State College of Washington* (Pullman: State College of Washington, 1954); F. Ivan Nye, James F. Short Jr., and Virgil J. Olson, "Socioeconomic Status and Delinquent Behavior," *American Journal of Sociology* 63 (January 1958), pp. 381–89; Maynard L. Erickson and Lamar T. Empey, "Class Position, Peers and Delinquency," *Sociology and Social Research* 49 (April 1965), pp. 268–82; William J. Chambliss and Richard H. Nagasawa, "On the Validity of Official Statistics; A Comparative Study of White, Black, and Japanese High-School Boys," *Journal of Research in Crime and Delinquency* 6 (January 1969), pp. 71–77; Eugene Doleschal, "Hidden Crime," *Crime and Delinquency Literature* 2, no. 5 (October 1970), pp. 546–72; Nanci Koser Wilson, *Risk Ratios in Juvenile Delinquency* (Ann Arbor, Mich.: University Microfilms, 1972); and Maynard L. Erikson, "Group Violations, Socioeconomic Status, and Official Delinquency," *Social Forces* 52, no. 1 (September 1973), pp. 41–52.

7. Charles R. Tittle and Robert F. Meier, "Specifying the SES/Delinquency Relationship," *Criminology* 28, no. 2 (1990), p. 292.

8. Gary F. Jensen and Kevin Thompson, "What's Class Got to Do with It? A Further Examination of Power-Control Theory," *American Journal of Sociology* 95, no. 4 (January 1990), p. 1021.

9. This is the conclusion of Martin Gold, "Undetected Delinquent Behavior," *Journal of Research in Crime and Delinquency* 3, no. 1 (1966), pp. 27–46; and of Sutherland and Cressey, *Criminology*, pp. 137, 220.

10. Cf. Larry Karacki and Jackson Toby, "The Uncommitted Adolescent: Candidate for Gang Socialization," *Sociological Inquiry* 32 (1962), pp. 203–15; William R. Arnold, "Continuities in Research — Scaling Delinquent Behavior," *Social Problems* 13, no. 1 (1965), pp. 59–66; Harwin L. Voss, "Socio-economic Status and Reported Delinquent Behavior," *Social Problems*, 13, no. 3 (1966), pp. 314–24; LaMar Empey and Maynard L. Erikson, "Hidden Delinquency and Social Status," *Social Forces* 44, no. 4 (1966), pp. 546–54; Fred J. Shanley, "Middle-class Delinquency As a Social Problem," *Sociology and Social Research* 51 (1967), pp. 185–98; Jay R. Williams and Martin Gold, "From Delinquent Behavior to Official Delinquency," *Social Problems* 20, no. 2 (1972), pp. 209–29.

11. Empey and Erikson, "Hidden Delinquency and Social Status," pp. 549, 551. Nye, Short, and Olson also found destruction of property to be committed most frequently by upper-class boys and girls, "Socioeconomic Status and Delinquent Behavior," p. 385.

12. Williams and Gold, "From Delinquent Behavior to Official Delinquency," *Social Problems* 20, no. 2 (1972), pp. 209–29.

13. Gold, "Undetected Delinquent Behavior," p. 37.

14. Ibid., p. 44.

15. Comparing socioeconomic status categories "scant evidence is found that would support the contention that group delinquency is more characteristic of the lower-status levels than other socioeconomic status levels. In fact, only arrests seem to be more characteristic of the low-status category than the other categories." Erikson, "Group Violations, Socioeconomic Status and Official Delinquency," p. 15.

16. Gold, "Undetected Delinquent Behavior," p. 28 (emphasis added).

17. Ibid., p. 38.

18. Terence P. Thornberry, "Race, Socioeconomic Status and Sentencing in the Juvenile Justice System," *Journal of Criminal Law and Criminology* 64, no. 1 (1973), pp. 90–98.

19. Robert Sampson, "Effects of Socioeconomic Context on Official Reaction to Juvenile Delinquency," *American Sociological Review* 51 (December 1986), pp. 876–85; Belinda R. McCarthy, "Social Structure, Crime, and Social Control: An Examination of Factors Influencing Rates and Probabilities of Arrest," *Journal of Criminal Justice* 19, (1991), pp. 19–29.

20. Note, "Developments in the Law—Race and the Criminal Process," *Harvard Law Review* 101 (1988), p. 1496.

21. Jerome Miller, *Search and Destroy: African American Males in the Criminal Justice System* (Cambridge: Cambridge University Press, 1996), p. 76. The study reported is M. Wordes, T. Bynum, and C. Corley, "Locking Up Youth: The Impact of Race on Detention Decisions," *Journal of Research in Crime and Delinquency* 31, no. 2 (May 1994).

22. M. Wordes et al., "Locking Up Youth," p. 164; quoted in Miller, *Search and Destroy*, pp. 76–77.

23. Miller, *Search and Destroy*, p. 72. The study reported is Kimberly L. Kempf, *The Role of Race in Juvenile Justice Processing in Pennsylvania*, Study Grant #89–90/J/01/3615, Pennsylvania Commission on Crime and Delinquency, August 1992.

24. David Huizinga and Delbert Elliott, "Juvenile Offenders: Prevalence, Offender Incidence and Arrest Rates by Race," paper presented at Meeting on Race and the Incarceration of Juveniles, Racine, Wisconsin, December 1986, University of Colorado, Boulder, Institute of Behavioral Science, National Youth Survey; reported in Miller, *Search and Destroy*, p. 73.

25. Michael Tonry, "Racial Politics, Racial Disparities, and the War on Crime," *Crime & Delinquency* 40, no. 4 (October 1994), p. 483.

26. Fox Butterfield, "More Blacks in Their 20s Have Trouble With the Law," *New York Times*, October 5, 1995, p. A8.

27. James Fyfe, "Blind Justice: Police Shootings in Memphis," *Journal of Criminal Law and Criminology* 73 (1982), pp. 707, 718–20.

28. See, for example, D. Chapman, "The Stereotype of the Criminal and the Social Consequences," *International Journal of Criminology and Penology* 1 (1973), p. 24.

29. This view is widely held, although the degree to which it functions as a self-fulfilling prophecy is less widely recognized. Versions of this view can be seen in *Challenge*, p. 79; Jerome Skolnick, *Justice Without Trial* (New York: Wiley, 1966), pp. 45–48, 217–218; and Jessica Mitford, *Kind and Usual Punishment*, p. 53. Piliavin and Briar write in "Police Encounters with Juveniles":

Compared to other youths, Negroes and boys whose appearance matched the delinquent stereotype were more frequently stopped and interrogated by patrolmen—often even in the absence of evidence that an offense had been committed—usually were given more severe dispositions for the same violations. Our data suggest, however, that these selective apprehension and disposition practices resulted not only from the intrusion of long-held prejudices of individual police officers but also from certain job-related experiences of law-enforcement personnel. First, the tendency of police to give more severe dispositions to Negroes and to youths whose appearance correspond to that which police associated with delinquents partly reflected the fact, observed in this study, that these youths also were much more likely than were other types of boys to exhibit the sort of recalcitrant demeanor which police construed as a sign of the confirmed delinquent. Further, officers assumed, partly on the basis of departmental statistics, that Negroes and juveniles who "look tough" (e.g., who wear chinos, leather jackets, boots, etc.) commit crimes more frequently than do other types of youths. [p. 212]

Cf. Albert Reiss, *The Police and the Public* (New Haven, Conn.: Yale University Press, 1971). Reiss attributes the differences to the differences in the actions of complainants.

30. Richard J. Lundman, for example, found higher arrest rates to be associated with "offender powerlessness," "Routine Police Arrest Practices: A Commonweal Perspective," *Social Problems* 22, no. 1 (October 1974), pp. 127–41.

31. William Bales, "Race and Class Effects on Criminal Justice Prosecution and Punishment Decisions," (unpublished Ph.D. dissertation, Florida State University, 1987).

32. Note, "Developments in the Law—Race and the Criminal Process," *Harvard Law Review* 101 (1988), p. 1520.

33. Spohn, Gruhl, and Welch, "The Impact of the Ethnicity and Gender of Defendants on the Decision to Reject or Dismiss Felony Charges," *Criminology* 25 (1987), pp. 175, 180, 185.

34. "Stealing $200 Billion the Respectable Way," *U.S. News and World Report*, May 20, 1985, p. 83.

35. Marshall B. Clinard, *Corporate Corruption: The Abuse of Corporate Power* (New York: Praeger, 1990), p. 15.

36. Michael Levi, *Regulating Fraud: White-Collar Crime and the Criminal Process* (London: Tavistock, 1987), p. 33; *StatAbst-1995*, p. 456, Table no. 705.

37. *UCR-1995*, pp. 35, 36, 196.

38. Marshall B. Clinard, *Corporate Corruption: The Abuse of Power* (New York: Praeger, 1990), p. 15.

39. David Weisburd, Ellen F. Chayet, and Elin J. Waring, "White-Collar Crime and Criminal Careers: Some Preliminary Findings," *Crime & Delinquency* 36, no. 3 (July 1990) p. 352.

40. Clinard, *Corporate Corruption: The Abuse of Power*, p. 15.

41. Susan Shapiro, "The Road Not Taken: The Elusive Path to Criminal Prosecution for White-Collar Offenders," *Law and Society Review* 19, no. 2 (1985), p. 182.

42. *UCR-1994*, pp. 27, 205.

19

The American Upper Class

G. William Domhoff

INTRODUCTION

If there is an American upper class, it must exist not merely as a collection of families who feel comfortable with each other and tend to exclude outsiders from their social activities. It must exist as a set of interrelated social institutions. That is, there must be patterned ways of organizing the lives of its members from infancy to old age, and there must be mechanisms for socializing both the younger generation and new adult members who have risen from lower social levels. If the class is a reality, the names and faces may change somewhat over the years, but the social institutions that underlie the upper class must persist with remarkably little change over several generations. . . .

TRAINING THE YOUNG

From infancy through young adulthood, members of the upper class receive a distinctive education. This education begins early in life in preschools that frequently are attached to a neighborhood church of high social status. Schooling continues during the elementary years at a local private school called a day school. The adolescent years may see the student remain at day school, but there is a strong chance that at least one or two years will be spent away from home at a boarding school in a quiet rural setting. Higher education will be obtained at one of a small number of heavily endowed private universities. Harvard, Yale,

From *Who Rules America Now* by G. William Domhoff (Simon & Schuster 1983). Copyright © 1983 by G. William Domhoff. Reprinted by permission of the author.

Princeton, and Stanford head the list, followed by smaller Ivy League schools in the East and a handful of other small private schools in other parts of the country. Although some upper-class children may attend public high school if they live in a secluded suburban setting, or go to a state university if there is one of great esteem and tradition in their home state, the system of formal schooling is so insulated that many upper-class students never see the inside of a public school in all their years of education.

This separate educational system is important evidence for the distinctiveness of the mentality and lifestyle that exists within the upper class, for schools play a large role in transmitting the class structure to their students. Surveying and summarizing a great many studies on schools in general, sociologist Randall Collins concludes: "Schools primarily teach vocabulary and inflection, styles of dress, aesthetic tastes, values and manners."[1]

The training of upper-class children is not restricted to the formal school setting, however. Special classes and even tutors are a regular part of their extracurricular education. This informal education usually begins with dancing classes in the elementary years, which are seen as more important for learning proper manners and the social graces than for learning to dance. Tutoring in a foreign language may begin in the elementary years, and there are often lessons in horseback riding and music as well. The teen years find the children of the upper class in summer camps or on special travel tours, broadening their perspectives and polishing their social skills.

The linchpins in the upper-class educational system are the dozens of boarding schools that were developed in the last half of the nineteenth and the early part of the twentieth centuries, with the rise of a nationwide upper class whose members desired to insulate themselves from an inner city that was becoming populated by lower-class immigrants. Baltzell concludes that these schools became "surrogate families" that played a major role "in creating an upper-class subculture on almost a national scale in America."[2] The role of boarding schools in providing connections to other upper-class social institutions is also important. As one informant explained to Ostrander in her interview study of upper-class women: "Where I went to boarding school, there were girls from all over the country, so I know people from all over. It's helpful when you move to a new city and want to get invited into the local social clubs."[3]

Consciously molded after their older and more austere British counterparts, it is within these several hundred schools that a unique style of life is inculcated through such traditions as the initiatory hazing of beginning students, the wearing of school blazers or ties, compulsory attendance at chapel services, and participation in esoteric sports such as lacrosse, squash, and crew. Even a different language is adopted to distinguish these schools from public schools. The principal is a headmaster or rector, the teachers are sometimes called masters, and the students are in forms, not grades. Great emphasis is placed upon the building of "character." The role of the school in preparing the future leaders of America is emphasized through the speeches of the headmaster and the frequent mention of successful alumni.* . . .

---

* The Episcopal priest who served as headmaster at Choate from 1908 to 1947 often exhorted his students: "Ask not what your school can do for you, but what you can do for your school." This line was adapted slightly by one of this students, John F. Kennedy, who in 1961 as president of the United States asked his fellow citizens in a stirring patriotic speech: "Ask not what your country can do for you, but what you can do for your country."

Whatever university upper-class students attend, they tend to socialize together as members of a small number of fraternities, sororities, eating clubs, and secret societies, perpetuating to some extent the separate existence of a day or boarding school. As sociologist C. Wright Mills explained, it is not merely a matter of going to a Harvard or a Yale but to the right Harvard or Yale.

That is why in the upper social classes, it does not by itself mean much merely to have a degree from an Ivy League college. That is assumed: the point is not Harvard, but which Harvard? By Harvard, one means Porcellian, Fly, or A.D.: by Yale, one means Zeta Psi or Fence or Delta Kappa Epsilon: by Princeton, Cottage, Tifer, Cap and Gown or Ivy.[4]

From kindergarten through college, then, schooling is very different for members of the upper class from what it is for most Americans, and it teaches them to be distinctive in many ways. In a country where education is highly valued and the overwhelming majority attend public schools, less than one student in a hundred is part of this private system that primarily benefits members of the upper class and provides one of the foundations for the old-boy and old-girl networks that will be with them throughout their lives.

SOCIAL CLUBS

Just as private schools are a pervasive feature in the lives of upper-class children, so, too, are private social clubs a major point of orientation in the lives of upper-class adults. These clubs also play a role in differentiating members of the upper class from other members of society. According to Baltzell, "the club serves to place the adult members of society and their families within the social hierarchy." He quotes with approval the suggestion by historian Crane Brinton that the club "may perhaps be regarded as taking the place of those extensions of the family, such as the clan and the brotherhood, which have disappeared from advanced societies."[5] Conclusions similar to Baltzell's resulted from an interview study in Kansas City: "Ultimately, say upper-class Kansas Citians, social standing in their world reduces to one issue: Where does an individual or family rank on the scale of private club memberships and informal cliques."[6]

The clubs of the upper class are many and varied, ranging from family-oriented country clubs and downtown men's and women's clubs to highly specialized clubs for yachtsmen, sportsmen, gardening enthusiasts, and fox hunters. Many families have memberships in several different types of clubs, but the days when most of the men by themselves were in a half dozen or more clubs faded before World War II. Downtown men's clubs originally were places for having lunch and dinner, and occasionally for attending an evening performance or a weekend party. But as upper-class families deserted the city for large suburban estates, a new kind of club, the country club, gradually took over some of these functions. The downtown club became almost entirely a luncheon club, a site to hold meetings, or a place to relax on a free afternoon. The country club, by contrast, became a haven for all members of the family. It offered social and sporting activities ranging from dances, parties, and banquets to golf, swimming, and tennis. Special group dinners were often arranged for all members on Thursday night, the traditional maid's night off across the United States. . . .

Initiation fees, annual dues, and expenses vary from a few thousand dollars in downtown clubs to tens of thousands of dollars in some country clubs, but money is not the primary barrier in gaining membership to a club. Each club has a very rigorous screening process before accepting new members. Most require nomination by one or more active members, letters of recommendation from three to six members, and interviews with at least some members of the membership committee. Names of prospective members are sometimes posted in the clubhouse, so all members have an opportunity to make their feelings known to the membership committee. Negative votes by two or three members of what is typically a 10-to-20 person committee often are enough to deny admission to the candidate.

The carefulness with which new members are selected extends to a guarding of club membership lists, which are usually available only to club members. Older membership lists are sometimes given to libraries by members or their surviving spouses, and some members will give lists to individual researchers, but for most clubs there are no membership lists in the public domain. Our request to 15 clubs in 1981 for membership lists for research purposes was refused by 12 of the clubs and left unanswered by the other three.

Not every club member is an enthusiastic participant in the life of the club. Some belong out of tradition or a feeling of social necessity. One woman told Ostrander the following about her country club: "We don't feel we should withdraw our support even though we don't go much." Others mentioned a feeling of social pressure: "I've only been to [the club] once this year. I'm really a loner, but I feel I have to go and be pleasant even though I don't want to." Another volunteered: "I think half the members go because they like it and half because they think it's a social necessity."[7]

People of the upper class often belong to clubs in several cities, creating a nationwide pattern of overlapping memberships. These overlaps provide further evidence for the social cohesion within the upper class. An indication of the nature and extent of this overlapping is revealed by our study of membership lists for 20 clubs in several major cities across the country, including the Links in New York, the Century Association in New York, the Duquesne in Pittsburgh, the Chicago in Chicago, the Pacific Union in San Francisco, and the California in Los Angeles. Using a clustering technique based on Boolean algebra, the study revealed there was sufficient overlap among 18 of the 20 clubs to form three regional groupings and a fourth group that provided a bridge between the two largest regional groups. The several dozen men who were in three or more of the clubs were especially important in creating the overall pattern. At the same time, the fact that these clubs often have from 1,000 to 2,000 members makes the percentage of overlap within this small number of clubs relatively small, ranging from a high of 20 to 30 percent between clubs in the same city to as low as 1 or 2 percent in clubs at opposite ends of the country.[8]

One of the most central clubs in this network, the Bohemian Club of San Francisco, is also the most unusual and widely known club of the upper class. Its annual two-week encampment in its 2,700-acre Bohemian Grove 75 miles north of San Francisco brings together the social elite, celebrities, and government officials for relaxation and entertainment. A description of this gathering provides the best possible insight into the role of clubs in uniting the upper class.[9]

The huge forest retreat called the Bohemian Grove was purchased by the club in the 1890s. Bohemians and their guests number anywhere from 1,500 to 2,000 for the three weekends in the encampment, which is always held during the last two weeks in July, when it almost never rains in northern California. However, there may be as few as 400 men in residence in the middle of the week, for most return to their homes and jobs after the weekends. During their stay the campers are treated to plays, symphonies, concerts, lectures, and political commentaries by entertainers, musicians, scholars, and government officials. They also trapshoot, canoe, swim, drop by the Grove art gallery, and take guided tours into the outer fringe of the mountain forest. But a stay at the Bohemian Grove is mostly a time for relaxation and drinking in the modest lodges, bunkhouses, and even teepees that fit unobtrusively into the landscape along the two or three macadam roads that join the few "developed" acres within the Grove. It is like a summer camp for the power elite and their entertainers.

The men gather in little camps of about 10 to 30 members during their stay. Each of the approximately 120 camps has its own pet name, such as Sons of Toil, Cave Man, Mandalay, Toyland, Owl's Nest, Hill Billies, and Parsonage. A group of men from Los Angeles named their camp Lost Angels, and the men in the Bohemian chorus call their camp Aviary. Some camps are noted for special drinks, brunches, or luncheons, to which they invite members from other camps. The camps are a fraternity system within the larger fraternity.

There are many traditional events during the encampment, including plays called the High Jinx and the Low Jinx. But the most memorable event, celebrated every consecutive year since 1880, is the opening ceremony, called the Cremation of Care. This ceremony takes place at the base of a 40-foot Owl Shrine constructed out of poured concrete and made even more resplendent by the mottled forest mosses that cover much of it. The Owl Shrine is only one of many owl symbols and insignias to be found in the Grove and the downtown clubhouse, for the owl was adopted early in the club's history as its mascot or totem animal.

The opening ceremony is called the Cremation of Care because it involves the burning of an effigy named Dull Care, who symbolizes the burdens and responsibilities that these busy Bohemians now wish to shed temporarily. More than 60 Bohemians take part in the ceremony as priests, acolytes, torch bearers, brazier bearers, boatmen, and woodland voices. After many flowery speeches and a long conversation with Dull Care, the high priest lights the fire with the flame from the Lamp of Fellowship, located on the "Altar of Bohemia" at the base of the shrine. The ceremony, which has the same initiatory functions as those of any fraternal or tribal group, ends with fireworks, shooting, and the playing of "There'll Be a Hot Time in the Old Town Tonight." The attempt to create a sense of cohesion and solidarity among the assembled is complete.

As the case of the Bohemian Grove and its symbolic ceremonies rather dramatically illustrate, there seems to be a great deal of truth to the earlier-cited suggestion by Crane Brinton that clubs may have the function within the upper class that the clan or brotherhood has in tribal societies. With their restrictive membership policies, initiatory rituals, private ceremonials, and great emphasis on tradition, clubs carry on the heritage of primitive secret societies. They create within their members an attitude of prideful exclusiveness that contributes greatly to an in-group feeling and a sense of fraternity within the upper class. . . .

MARRIAGE AND FAMILY CONTINUITY

The institution of marriage is as important in the upper class as it is in any level of American society, and it does not differ greatly from other levels in its patterns and rituals. Only the exclusive site of the occasion and the lavishness of the reception distinguish upper-class marriages.

The prevailing wisdom within the upper class is that children marry someone of their own social class. The women interviewed by Ostrander, for example, felt that marriage was difficult enough without differences in "interests" and "background," which seemed to be the code words for class in discussions of marriage. Marriages outside the class were seen as likely to end in divorce.[10] . . .

The general picture for social class and marriage in the United States is suggested in a statistical study of neighborhoods and marriage patterns in the San Francisco area. Its results are very similar to the Philadelphia study using the *Social Register.* Of 80 grooms randomly selected from the highest-level neighborhoods, court records showed that 51 percent married brides of a comparable level. The rest married women from middle-level neighborhoods; only one or two married women from lower-level residential areas. Conversely, 63 percent of 81 grooms from the lowest-level neighborhoods married women from comparable areas, with under 3 percent having brides from even the lower end of the group of top neighborhoods. Completing the picture, most of the 82 men from middle-level areas married women from the same types of neighborhoods, but about 10 percent married into higher-level neighborhoods. Patterns of intermarriage, then, suggest both stability and some upward mobility through marriage into the upper class.[11] . . .

It seems likely, then, that the American upper class is a mixture of old and new members. There is both continuity and social mobility, with the newer members being assimilated into the lifestyle of the class through participation in the schools, clubs, and other social institutions described in this chapter. There may be some ten-sions between those newly arrived and those of established status, as novelists and journalists love to point out, but what they have in common soon outweighs their differences. This point is well demonstrated in the social affiliations and attitudes of highly successful Jewish businessmen who become part of the upper class as they rise in the corporate community.[12]

THE PREOCCUPATIONS OF THE UPPER CLASS

Members of the upper class do not spend all their time in social activities. Contrary to stereotypes, most members of the upper class are and have been hardworking people, even at the richest levels. In a study of the 90 richest men for 1950, for example, Mills found that only 26 percent were men of leisure.[13]

By far the most frequent preoccupation of men of the upper class is business and finance. This point is most clearly demonstrated through studying the occupations of boarding school alumni. A classification of the occupations of a sample of the graduates of four private schools— Saint Mark's, Groton, Hotchkiss, and Andover— for the years 1906 and 1926 showed that the most frequent occupation for all but the Andover graduates was some facet of finance and banking. Others became presidents of medium-size businesses or practiced corporation law with a large firm. Only a small handful went to work as executives for major national corporations. Andover, with a more open curriculum and a far greater number of scholarship students at the time, produced many more people who ended up in middle management, particularly in 1926, when 44 percent of the graduates were in such positions. The second area of concentration for the Andover alumni was as owners or presidents of medium-size businesses. Only 8 percent went into banking and finance, and only 4 percent into law.[14] . . .

Although finance, business, and law are the most typical occupations of upper-class males, there is no absence of physicians, architects, museum officials, and other professional occupations. This fact was demonstrated most systematically in Baltzell's study of the Philadelphians listed in *Who's Who in America* for 1940; 39 percent of the Philadelphian architects and physicians listed in *Who's Who* for that year were also listed in the *Social Register*, as were 35 percent of the museum officials. These figures are close to the 51 percent for lawyers and the 42 percent for businessmen, although they are far below the 75 percent for bankers, clearly the most elite profession in Philadelphia at that time.[15]

Less systematic studies also suggest this wide range of professional occupations. Our classification of the occupations listed by Saint Paul's alumni in the spring 1965 issue of the alumni journal found 7 physicians, 7 academic scholars, and 4 authors in addition to the 20 financiers and 16 businessmen, which were once again the most frequent occupations. The remainder of the sample was divided among small numbers of ministers (5), government officials (4), private school teachers (4), military officers (2), architects (2), playwrights (1), and lawyers (1). Although this study can be considered no more than a set of examples, it is consistent with the findings of Baltzell on Philadelphia 25 years earlier.

The feminine half of the upper class has different preoccupations than those of men. Our study of a large sample of the upper-class women included in *Who's Who in American Women* for 1965 showed the most frequent activity of upper-class women to be that of civic worker or volunteer, which includes a wide range of welfare, cultural, and civic activities. Second on the list was author or artist followed by a career in journalism, where upper-class women are involved in both the management and writing of newspapers and magazines. Finally, women of the upper class were found in academic positions as teachers, administrators, and trustees at leading boarding schools and colleges for women.[16]

The most informative and intimate look at the preoccupations of the feminine half of the upper class is provided in Ostrander's interview study. It revealed the women to be people of both power and subservience, playing decision-making roles in numerous cultural and civic organizations, but also accepting traditional roles at home vis-à-vis their husbands and children. By asking the women to describe a typical day and to explain which activities were most important to them, Ostrander found that the role of community volunteer is a central preoccupation of upper-class women, having significance as a family tradition and as an opportunity to fulfill an obligation to the community. One elderly woman involved for several decades in both the arts and human services explained: "If you're privileged, you have a certain responsibility. This was part of my upbringing; it's a tradition, a pattern of life that my brothers and sisters do too."[17] . . .

Despite this emphasis on volunteer work, the women placed high value on family life. They arranged their schedules to be home when children came home from school (30 of the 38 had three or more children), and they emphasized that their primary concern was to provide a good home for their husbands. Several of them wanted to have greater decision-making power over their inherited wealth, but almost all of them wanted to be in the traditional roles of wife and mother, at least until their children were grown. . . .

Numerous anecdotal examples also show that some members of the upper class even lead lives of failure, despite all the opportunities available to them. Although members of the upper class are trained for leadership and given every opportunity to develop feelings of self-confidence, there are some who fail in school, become involved with drugs and alcohol, or become mentally disturbed. Once again, however, this cannot be seen as evidence for a lack of cohesion in the upper class, for there are bound to be individual failures of this nature in any group.

Deviants and failures do exist within the upper class, then, but it seems likely that a majority of its male members are at work in business, finance, and corporate law, and that most of the female members are equally busy as civic volunteers and homemakers. Members of both sexes have plenty of time for clubs, vacations, and party going, but their major preoccupations are in the world of work. . . .

CONCLUSION

The evidence [here] suggests that there is an interacting and intermarrying upper social stratum or social elite in America that is distinctive enough in its institutions, source and amount of income, and lifestyle to be called an "upper class." This upper class makes up about 0.5 percent of the population, a rough estimate that is based upon the number of students attending independent private schools, the number of listings in past *Social Registers* for several cities, and detailed interview studies in Kansas City and Boston.[18]

Not everyone in this nationwide upper class knows everyone else, but everybody knows somebody who knows someone in other areas of the country thanks to a common school experience, a summer at the same resort, or membership in the same social club. With the social institutions described in this [article] as the undergirding, the upper class at any given historical moment consists of a complex network of overlapping social circles that are knit together by the members they have in common and by the numerous signs of equal social status that emerge from a similar lifestyle. Viewed from the standpoint of social psychology, the upper class is made up of innumerable face-to-face small groups that are constantly changing in their composition as people move from one social setting to another.

Research work in both sociology and social psychology demonstrates that constant interaction in small-group settings leads to the social cohesion that is considered to be an important dimension of a social class.[19] This social cohesion does not in and of itself demonstrate that members of the upper class are able to agree among themselves on general issues of economic and governmental policy. But it is important to stress that social cohesion is one of the factors that makes it possible for policy coordination to

develop. Indeed, research in social psychology demonstrates that members of socially cohesive groups are eager to reach agreement on issues of common concern to them. They are more receptive to what other members are saying, more likely to trust each other, and more willing to compromise, which are no small matters in any collection of human beings trying to get something accomplished.[20]

The more extravagant social activities of the upper class—the debutante balls, the expensive parties, the jet-setting to spas and vacation spots all over the world, the involvement with exotic entertainers—are often viewed by pluralists and Marxists alike as superfluous trivialities best left to society page writers. However, there is reason to believe that these activities play a role both in solidifying the upper class and in maintaining the class structure. Within the class, these occasions provide an opportunity for members to show each other that they are similar to each other and superior to the average citizen. As political scientist Gabriel Almond suggested in his 1941 study of the New York upper class and its involvement in city politics: "The elaborate private life of the plutocracy serves in considerable measure to separate them out in their own consciousness as a superior, more refined element."[21] Then, too, the values upon which the class system is based are conveyed to the rest of the population in this conspicuous consumption. Such activities make clear that there is a gulf between members of the upper class and ordinary citizens, reminding everyone of the hierarchical nature of the society. Social extravaganzas bring home to everyone that there are great rewards for success, helping to stir up the personal envy that can be a goad to competitive striving.

In sociological terms, the upper class comes to serve as a "reference group." Sociologist Harold Hodges, in a discussion of his findings concerning social classes in the suburban areas south of San Francisco, expresses the power of the upper class as a reference group in the following way: "Numerically insignificant—less than one in every 500 Peninsula families is listed in the pages of the

Social Register—the upper class is nonetheless highly influential as a 'reference group': a membership to which many aspire and which infinitely more consciously or unconsciously imitate."[22]

Exhibiting high social status, in other words, is a way of exercising power. It is a form of power rooted in fascination and enchantment. It operates by creating respect, envy, and deference in others. Considered less important than force or economic power by social scientists who regard themselves as tough-minded and realistic, its role as a method of control in modern society goes relatively unnoticed despite the fact that power was originally in the domain of the sacred and the magical.[23]

Whatever the importance that is attached to prestige and social status as mechanisms of power, this [reading] has demonstrated the power of the upper class through the disproportionate amount of wealth and income that its members possess. As [has been] argued [elsewhere] . . . such disparities are evidence for class power if it is assumed that wealth and income are highly valued in American society. However, the case for the hypothesis that the American upper class is a ruling class will not rest solely on reference group power and inequalities in the wealth and income distributions.

NOTES

1. Randall Collins, "Functional and Conflict Theories of Educational Stratification," *American Sociological Review* 36 (1971): 1010.

2. E. Digby Baltzell, *Philadelphia Gentlemen: The Making of a National Upper Class* (Glencoe, IL: Free Press, 1958), p. 160.

3. Susan Ostrander, *A Study of Upper Class Women* ([Philadelphia, PA:] Temple University Press, 1984), p. 174; Steven B. Levine, "The Rise of the American Boarding Schools" (senior honors thesis, Harvard University, 1978), pp. 5–6; "Boys' Schools," *Fortune*, January 1936; Erving Goffman, *Asylums* (Chicago: Aldine, 1961); Michael Gordon, "Changing Patterns of Prep School Placements," *Pacific Sociological Review*, Spring 1969; Jack Trumpbour, "Private Schools" (research memo, 1980); Peter J. Nelligan, "The Cate School and the Upper Class" (term paper, University of California at Santa Barbara, 1971); G. William Domhoff, "The Women's Page as a Window on the Ruling Class," in *Hearth and Home: Images of Women in the Mass Media*, ed. Gaye Tuchman, Arlene K. Daniels, and James Benet (New York: Oxford University Press, 1978).

4. C. Wright Mills, *The Power Elite* (New York: Oxford University Press, 1956), p. 67.

5. Baltzell, *Philadelphia Gentlemen*, p. 373.

6. Richard P. Coleman and Lee Rainwater, *Social Standing in America* (New York: Basic Books, 1978), p. 144; Sophy Burnham, *The Landed Gentry* (New York: G. P. Putnam's Sons, 1978).

7. Ostrander, "A Study of Upper Class Women," p. 204.

8. Philip Bonacich and G. William Domhoff, " Latent Classes and Group Membership," *Social Networks* 3 (1981). . . . For an earlier analysis of this matrix using a technique developed by Bonacich that is based on matrix algebra, see G. William Domhoff, "Social Clubs, Political Groups, and Corporations: A Network Study of Ruling-Class Cohesiveness," *The Insurgent Sociologist*, Spring 1975.

9. G. William Domhoff, *The Bohemian Grove and Other Retreats* (New York: Harper & Row, 1974); G. William Domhoff, "Politics among the Redwoods," *The Progressive*, January 1981.

10. Ostrander, "A Study of Upper Class Women," p. 169.

11. Robert C. Tryon, "Identification of Social Areas by Cluster Analysis: A General Method with an Application to the San Francisco Bay Area," *University of California Publications in Psychology* 8 (1955); Robert C. Tryon, "Predicting Group Differences in Cluster Analysis: The Social Areas

Problem," *Multivariate Behavioral Research* 2 (1967).

12. Richard L. Zweigenhaft and G. William Domhoff, *Jews in the Protestant Establishment* (New York: Praeger, 1982).

13. Mills, *Power Elite*, p. 108.

14. Levine, "Rise of the American Boarding Schools," pp. 128–30.

15. Baltzell, *Philadelphia Gentlemen*, pp. 51–65.

16. G. William Domhoff, *The Higher Circles* (New York: Random House, 1970), pp. 41–43.

17. Ostrander, "A Study of Upper Class Women," p. *xx*.

18. G. William Domhoff, *Who Rules America?* (Englewood Cliffs, NJ: Prentice-Hall, 1967), pp. 7n–8n; "Private Schools Search for a New Social Role," *National Observer*, August 26, 1968, p. 5; Coleman and Rainwater, *Social Standing in America*, p. 148. For a summary of many studies that concludes that "Capital S Society" in the United States includes "probably no more than four-tenths of one percent in large cities, and even a smaller proportion in smaller communities," see Richard P. Coleman and Bernice L. Neugarten, *Social Status in the City* (San Francisco: Jossey-Bass, 1971), p. 270.

19. Domhoff, *Bohemian Grove*, pp. 89–90, for a summary of this research.

20. Dorwin Cartwright and Alvin Zander, *Group Dynamics* (New York: Harper & Row, 1960), p. 89; Albert J. Lott and Bernice E. Lott, "Group Cohesiveness as Interpersonal Attraction," *Psychological Bulletin* 64 (1965): 291–96; Michael Argyle, *Social Interaction* (Chicago: Aldine, 1969), pp. 220–23.

21. Gabriel Almond, "Plutocracy and Politics in New York City" (Ph.D. dissertation, University of Chicago, 1941), p. 108.

22. Harold M. Hodges, Jr., "Peninsula People: Social Stratification in a Metropolitan Complex," in *Education and Society*, ed. Warren Kallenbach and Harold M. Hodges, Jr. (Columbus, OH: Merrill, 1963), p. 414. .

23. See Norman O. Brown, *Life against Death* (London: Routledge & Kegan Paul, 1959), pp. 242, 249–52, for a breathtaking argument on the roots of power in the sacred and the psychological. For one attempt to apply the argument to the class structure, see G. William Domhoff, "Historical Materialism, Cultural Determinism, and the Origin of the Ruling Classes," *Psychoanalytical Review*, no. 2 (1969). For a discussion that rightly announces itself as "the first extensive treatise on prestige as a social control system," see William J. Goode, *The Celebration of Heroes: Prestige as a Social Control System* (Berkeley, CA: University of California Press, 1978).

20

Family Matters, Work Matters?

Poverty Among Women of Color and White Women

Lis Catanzarite and Vilma Ortiz

WOMEN'S POVERTY IS AT THE CENTER OF THE current welfare reform debate. Women and their children do make up an increasing proportion of the population of poor people in the United States, and female-headed families are on the rise. The ample attention is also because of suspicion among some public policymakers that the welfare system itself may have exacerbated these trends (and this emphasis is consistent with the increasing popularity of "less government"). As a result, much of the discussion of policy innovations focuses on getting poor mothers off Aid to Families with Dependent Children (AFDC) and into the labor force. Additionally, a great deal of rhetoric has been devoted to "family values." Poor women (and perhaps women in general) are targeted with messages meant to reform behavior deemed inappropriate. The word is: Get married or stay married; moreover, if you aren't married or won't stay married, then *do not* have children.

Female poverty, however, is complex. African American and Latina women are more likely to be poor than are white women, and are likely to stay poor for longer stretches of time than are whites. Poverty policy will thus have a potentially greater effect on minority women and their children than on white women. In order to adequately design public policies that will help all poor women, we need a better understanding of the differences that are most important for poverty reduction and prevention. The key questions we address in this chapter are: Do work and family matter in the same way for different ethnic groups? Are working white women less likely to be poor than working Latinas with similar backgrounds? Does marriage reduce the likelihood of poverty more for white women than for comparable African Americans? How can public policy successfully address the critical issues that poor and working-poor women face?

FAMILY COMPOSITION, POVERTY, AND RACE/ETHNICITY

A number of factors are important in understanding poverty conditions among black, Latina, and white women. For example, minority women are more likely to have *grown up* poor than are whites. Lower socioeconomic backgrounds have a number of ramifications for upward mobility, such as depressed levels of educational attainment and (relatedly, in these days of rising college costs) fewer resources of the extended family network. Further, among some groups, particularly Latina immigrants, larger families are liable to contribute to higher poverty rates. Collective differences in

From: Diane Dujon and Ann Withorn, eds., *For Crying Out Loud: Women's Poverty in the United States* (Boston: South End Press, 1996), pp. 121–39.

This piece is an extension of a more technical article, "Racial/Ethnic Differences in the Impact of Work and Family on Women's Poverty," *Research in Politics and Society*, 1995 (5): 217–37. Reprinted by permission.

poverty backgrounds of differing racial/ethnic groups result in part from underlying disparities in class background, family composition, English proficiency, and other characteristics. In order to get a clear understanding of racial and ethnic differences in poverty risk, we need to compare individuals of different ethnic groups who are otherwise similar. That is, we need to understand better whether racial and ethnic differences are due solely to factors such as education levels, work behavior, and the like, or whether such differences persist without these factors. Moreover, we must ask whether certain key poverty "prevention" strategies are more effective for whites than for women of color.

One reason commonly thought to explain higher poverty rates for minority women is their marital status and family composition, particularly their higher rates of family dissolution and female headship. Yet marital disruption is most significant in causing poverty for white women. Marital breakups are less likely to *cause* poverty for minority than for white women, since the women of color are more likely to be poor *within* marriages. Bane (1986) demonstrates that, among women who were impoverished after a transition from a male-headed to a female-headed household, only 24 percent of whites were indigent prior to the transition vs. a full 62 percent of African Americans. Leaving marriages is less of an economic disaster for black women than for white women because black women's economic status within marriages is already relatively poor. This is due in part to the lower average material resources of black than white men. While we expect that the same is true for Latinas, this has not been examined empirically. We expect that being married (vs. single) is less economically advantageous to African American and Latina women than to whites. Conversely, being in a disrupted family (vs. being married) should be more harmful for whites than for minority women.

The discussion of black women's poverty has focused largely on the decline of nuclear families in the African-American community. A number of prominent authors have cited the rise in marital dissolution and female-headed families and connected these increases with the problem of minority male joblessness (Moynihan 1965; Garfinkel and McLanahan 1986) and the scarcity of "marriageable men" (Wilson and Neckerman 1986; Wilson 1987). Minority male joblessness and underemployment certainly contribute to indigence among minority women. Improving the employment opportunities of minority men will help to reduce women's poverty, but only indirectly, by providing women with better marriage prospects and male family heads. The underlying assumptions of these prescriptions are clearly patriarchal in nature. If women could only attach themselves to well-paid men, women's (and children's) poverty would be reduced. The reality, however, is that women, especially minority women, increasingly head families. And, they do so for a variety of reasons, only one of which is the employment status of minority men. Individual women may or may not prefer to be married. Rather than prescribing what should be the ideal family (as in recent Republican platforms) or lamenting changing patterns of family composition, discussion and policy concerning women's poverty should shift focus.

WORK, POVERTY, AND RACE/ETHNICITY

Given the reality of female-headed families, as well as the importance of women's earnings in poor two-parent and other families, we need greater attention to the conditions of women's employment—in particular, their jobs and wages. Certainly, much of the current debate about welfare—but not poverty—centers on forcing women to work more and receive lower AFDC benefits (see, Mead, 1986; more recently, California Governor Pete Wilson's 1996 State of the State address and proposed budget). But this policy, without a concomitant commitment to improving women's labor market locations and earnings, will not alleviate poverty, even if it does reduce welfare. In fact, it would surely worsen poverty for most recipients, as many women and children would be forced to forego medical insurance and scramble for childcare. Both welfare policy and labor market policy must recognize the increasing extent to which many women, especially lower-class women, have become critically important and often the primary economic providers for their families. Moreover, policymakers must begin to address the fact that women continue to be at a severe labor market disadvantage, their vital economic role notwithstanding.

Women's employment and earnings are critically important, both for married and unmarried women. The male "family wage" is no longer a reality (despite the fact that men's wages continue to be much higher than women's). With economic restructuring and the decline in real wages that began in the 1970s, most men now do not earn a wage sufficient to support a wife and children. For this and other reasons, the majority of married women, even those with infants under the age of one, are in the labor force.[1] Further, because of the rise in female-headed families, and the abysmal levels of child support payments, women are increasingly responsible not only for their own support, but also for that of their children. The problems of such families are heightened, as women face much worse prospects than men of securing a "family wage." Of course, this is even more important for African-American women than whites, since black women are much less likely to be married, and when married, contribute a higher proportion of family income than do white women.

Female and feminist scholars have argued that women's wages and labor market locations are critical to reducing poverty among female-headed families (see Smith 1984; Pearce 1987; Peterson 1987). A number of such authors have cited the problem of occupational segregation as a contributor to women's poverty (see Ehrenreich 1986; Pearce 1986; Amott and Matthaei 1986). And, while women in general are disadvantaged in the labor market, the disadvantage is more severe for minority women. However, the extent to which work effort has a greater impact on reducing indigence for white as opposed to minority women has not received sufficient attention. If a

minority woman and a white woman (who "look" alike in every way except ethnicity) work the same number of hours, do they have the same chances of staying out of poverty? Further, the impact of occupational segregation on individual poverty has not been tested. If women work in low-level occupations with an overrepresentation of minority women, do they earn less than similar women in other occupations?

Certainly, work effort—working longer hours—improves earnings, and therefore lowers the likelihood of poverty. But, we expect that minority women get a lower payoff for their efforts than do white women. Wilson (1987) has argued that large scale economic changes have lessened opportunities for some segments of the minority population, particularly inner-city blacks. While traditional sociological theory predicts a direct relationship between level of work and economic status, we expect that this relationship is weaker among black and Latina women than among white women. More specifically, since minority women are likely to receive lower hourly wages than are white women with similar individual characteristics (for example, education and work experience), working longer hours will have a smaller payoff for minority than for white women as a poverty prevention strategy.

In addition, we think that minority women's heavier concentration than white women in marginal, female-dominated occupations contributes to their disadvantage at work.[2] Earnings tend to be lowest in occupations where minority women, particularly black, Latina, and Native American women, prevail (Dill, Cannon, and Vanneman 1987) Indeed, Dill et al. (1987) demonstrate that the wage disadvantages, relative to workers' education and experience, are greater in occupations with a large contingent of minority women than in white-female-dominated occupations. Thus, concentration in poorly paid occupations contributes to the labor market disadvantage that minority women face. We expect that, among similar workers (those with similar hours, education, etc.), being in an occupation with a heavy concentration of minority women carries an increased risk of poverty, primarily because of low remuneration in such occupations.

OVERVIEW

In order to investigate these questions, we analyzed the incidence of poverty for black, Mexican-origin, "other" Latina, and white women in the Los Angeles Metropolitan area using the 1980 census.[3] We focused only on women with 12 years of education or less because this is the population most at risk of impoverishment. The analysis had two main parts. First, we examined racial and ethnic differences in the impact of work and marital status on the probability of being needy. Then we looked only at employed women and asked whether or not working in a low-level, minority female occupation increases the likelihood poverty. We looked for *net effects*, that is, we took into account other individual and occupational characteristics in estimating the effects of marital status, work effort, and occupational segregation. . . .

RESULTS

. . . [Poverty] is much more prevalent among African American women and recent immigrant Latinas (both Mexican and "other") than among whites and earlier-immigrant native Latinas. In our sample, black women and recent immigrant Latinas had poverty rates of 42–45 percent, while 15 percent of white women were impoverished. Earlier-immigrant native Latinas had poverty levels that fell between these two extremes (28 percent of Mexicans and 24 percent of other Latinas were poor). Hence, black women were almost 3 times as likely to be poor as whites; Mexicans had poverty rates between 2 and 3 times those for white women; and other Latinas had rates of impoverishment that were approximately 1.5 to 3 times higher than for whites. . . .[4]

These differences in poverty rates among women of different groups are due, in part, to divergences in other characteristics (for example,

lower educational levels, more children among minority than white women). . . .

Recent immigrant Latinas had a large educational disadvantage. Not having completed high school was most common for these women (Mexicans, 87 percent; other Latinas, 70 percent). Native-born, earlier-immigrant Latinas did somewhat better (58 percent of Mexicans and 44 percent of other Latinas) than recent immigrants. Whites had far and away the highest rates of high school completion: only 26 percent had less than 12 years of education. And, black women were a distant second, with 40 percent (of those with 12 years of education or less) being high school dropouts.

Most women were in the labor force, and this was true for all groups. Not working was most common among Mexicans (49 percent of recent immigrants and 44 percent of other Mexicans were not in the Labor force) and blacks (44 percent didn't work); staying out of the labor force was least common for other Latinas and white women (37–38 percent). The pattern of full-time work was the converse of this: rates of full-time work were lowest for Mexicans (18 percent among recent immigrants and 21 percent for natives/earlier immigrants), then blacks (23 percent), other Latinas (23–25 percent), and whites (26 percent). So, while working was the norm among these less-educated women, full-time employment was uncommon. Even among white women, only about one-fourth worked full-time.

The youngest group in the sample was Mexicans, followed by recent-immigrant other Latinas, African Americans, earlier-immigrant native other Latinas, and, finally, whites. The population of recent-immigrant Mexican women was overwhelmingly under 40 years old (81 percent), while just under half of white women (46 percent) were in this younger age group.[5]

African Americans were, by far, the least likely to be married—less than half of black women in our sample were wed (41 percent). Among all other groups, being married was the norm. For other Latinas, the prevalence of marriage was

59–62 percent (lower for recent immigrants); among whites, two-thirds were married; among Mexicans, 65 percent of earlier immigrants/natives and 71 percent of recent immigrants were married. In conjunction with high marriage rates, Mexican women had the highest number of children (an average of 2 for recent immigrants, 1.4 among other Mexicans); next were other Latinas and blacks (just over 1 child), then whites (with an average of 0.7 children).

These descriptive statistics show large variations by ethnic/immigrant group. With respect to most characteristics thought to contribute to keeping women out of poverty, white women appear to enjoy an advantage. (The only exception is that marriage rates are higher among one group—recent-immigrant Mexicans—than among whites). Given these differences in background characteristics, it is perhaps no surprise that white women show lower rates of poverty than do minority women. But, are the racial and ethic differences in poverty due solely to these differences, or are women of color still more likely to be impoverished? We now turn to the following questions:

1. Among women with similar characteristics (education, etc.), are minority women more likely to be poor than white women?

2. Do white women obtain greater economic benefits from marriage than do similarly situated minority women? Conversely, is marital disruption more economically damaging to whites than to women of color?

3. Do white women derive greater economic gains from work than do similarly situated minority women?

4. Among working women, does location in an occupation identified as minority, female contribute to poverty?

Black women were just over twice as likely to be poor as were similarly situated white women. Mexicans were 1.4 times as likely to live in poverty as their white counterparts, and other Latinas had indigence rates that were 1.6 times those for comparable whites. As expected, white women were considerable less likely to be impoverished than minority women with similar backgrounds, family composition, and work effort. . . .

. . . [S]ingle white women had poverty rates 8 times as high as their married counterparts, while single minority women were (only) 4 times as likely to be poor as married minorities. So getting married offered greater financial benefits for whites than for comparable African Americans and Latinas, as predicted.

Poverty risk was highest for separated women, and the divergence between whites and minorities was greatest for this group. White women who were separated had predicted poverty rates 11 times the rates for married whites; the contrast for minorities is a factor of 5. The same pattern holds, but is less pronounced, for divorced women. As we posited, the economic disadvantage that comes with a disrupted marriage is much greater for whites than for black or Latina women. This is presumably because the difference in family income resulting from a marital breakup is greater for whites than for women of color. The literature on the feminization of poverty has emphasized the devastating impact of separation and divorce on women's poverty. Our findings clearly suggest that this phenomenon is more pronounced for white than minority women. . . .

White women who were out of the labor force were 11 times more likely to live in poverty than whites who worked full-time, while relative risk for minorities was only 5 times that of their full-time counterparts. While the risk of poverty was strongly related to employment for both whites and minorities, the effect of working less than full-time (vs. full-time) was always higher for white women than for minorities. As predicted, white women's work effort had a greater impact on reducing the risk of poverty than was true for African American and Latina women.

We also found that, among working women, the likelihood of being poor was higher for women in occupations with a prevalence of African

American women, without these factors. Additionally, women employed in occupations that are white-female-dominated were *less likely* to be needy than other, similarly situated women.

SUMMARY

Neither the marriage nor the labor market offers the same rewards to women of color as to white women. While family and work clearly matter a great deal for women's poverty, they matter *differently* for black and Latina women than for whites. In point of fact, they matter *less*. Minority women are more likely to be poor than are comparable whites of the same marital status at every level of work effort.

We found that marital status had less relevance in determining whether or not minority women were poor than was true for similar whites. Being married (vs. single) reduces indigence less for women of color than for white women. The smaller advantage of being married for blacks and Latinas is doubtlessly due largely to the fact that the earnings of minority husbands are generally lower than white men's pay. Similarly, because the change in family income resulting from a marital breakup tends to be less pronounced for minority than white women, we found that being separated or divorced (vs. being married) was less financially damaging for African American and Latina women.

In addition to these differences in the relative advantages of marriage, we found that work effort was more effective in reducing the risk of privation for white women than for similar women of color, as predicted. The benefits of time spent working were clearly greater for white than minority women at every level of work effort.

Above and beyond individual-level factors, the occupational locations of different groups of women contributed to racial and ethnic differences in poverty risk. Working in an occupation with a large percentage of black women increased the likelihood of impoverishment, while being in a white-female-dominated occupation lowered this risk.

CONCLUSIONS

The two major routes out of poverty for women are work and marriage. Should it come as a surprise that the labor market is not a "level playing field" for women of color and white women? We think not. And, though we may not often conceptualize the *marriage* market in these terms, it appears that this market also is not a level field for women of different racial/ethnic groups.

Our findings underscore the importance of these differences. While marital status is related to privation for all women, the emphasis on marriage in discussions of women's poverty is less relevant to black women and Latinas than to white women. Accordingly, as a poverty prevention "strategy," getting married is less beneficial for African American and Latina women than for whites. Further, popular claims that every woman is "just a divorce away" from penury are particularly misplaced for minority women, who experience relatively high rates of poverty even within marriages, and whose risk of indigence increases less dramatically with a family breakup than is true for whites.

Perhaps of greater importance, given the heavy emphasis on women's work in the current welfare reform debate, are our results regarding work effort: we find that minority women profit less from hours expended at work than do white women. Further, the occupational locations of women contribute to differences in poverty: women who work in heavily black female occupations have a higher risk of indigence than do similar women in comparable occupations. Occupational segregation contributes to minority women's disadvantage (in addition to lower returns to work effort for minorities). The fact that renumeration varies across occupations and tends to be depressed in low-level, minority female occupations highlights our contention that occupational segregation is a significant *poverty* issue for less-educated women.

Although seemingly paradoxical, working is of monumental importance to the economic standing of women of color—despite the fact that minorities derive less gain from time spent working than whites. This is precisely because *marriage* offers less monetary benefit to women of color than to white women. Particularly for less-educated African American women—who are relatively unlikely to be married—work is a critical poverty prevention strategy.

Attention to the conditions of women's work is of utmost significance, particularly in the current environment, where pundits across the political spectrum emphasize work as the panacea for women's poverty. Our results strongly suggest that public policymakers concerned with indigence among working-age women and their children cannot simply focus on pushing women into the labor market and reducing dependency on public assistance. By doing so, they would simply replace an inadequate *welfare* check with an inadequate *pay* check. This would be further compounded by increased responsibility for medical insurance and childcare, the costs of which are prohibitive for at-risk women. Clearly, any antipoverty policy that has women's work as its cornerstone must give attention to adequate childcare and affordable health care.

First and foremost, however, in order to be efficacious, an antipoverty strategy grounded on female employment should focus on *making women's work pay.* In the current climate, where the future of affirmative action is uncertain and employment discrimination legislation is being redefined and narrowed, we must not lose sight of the employment disadvantages encountered by women, particularly women of color. In order to effectively reduce poverty, it is essential that policymakers direct their attention to the labor market. Pivotal to the success of antipoverty efforts will be policies that break down occupational segregation; increase the minimum wage; reduce the financial penalty in marginal, female-dominated occupations; and increase women's—especially minority women's—access to jobs that offer better pay in return for women's work effort.

NOTES

1. By 1988, labor force participation (LFP) rates of married women with children under one were already 50.5 percent for whites and 71.5 percent for blacks (51.9 percent overall) (*Statistical Abstract of the United States*, 1990, p. 385). In light of recent data on the rising trend in LFP for this group (the latest historically to enter the labor force), rates are certainly higher now. Working has become the norm.

2. The heavy concentration of black women in female-dominated occupations is discussed in Malveaux and Wallace (1987) and Malveaux (1985). Catanzarite's (1990) analysis of national data for the 1970s suggests that Latinas may have occupied an intermediate position between black and white women in occupational segregation; that is, they appear to have been concentrated in better jobs than black women, but worse positions than whites. The relative positions of blacks and Latinas may have flipped with the recent increase in immigration.

3. The area includes Los Angeles, Orange, Riverside, San Bernardino, and Ventura counties. The Census file is the 5 percent Public Use Microdata Sample. The sample is comprised of 98,896 women, ages 20–64.

4. These figures are obtained by dividing minority women's poverty rates by those for white women.

5. Recall that the sample is limited to working-age women: 20- to 64-year-olds.

REFERENCES

Amott, Teresa, and Julie Matthaei. 1986. "Comparable Worth, Incomparable Pay" in Rochelle Lefkowitz and Ann Withorn (eds.), *For Crying Out Loud: Women and Poverty in the United States.* New York: Pilgrim Press, pp. 314–23.

Bane, Mary Jo. 1986. "Household Composition and Poverty" in Sheldon Danziger and Daniel Weinberg (eds.), *Fighting Poverty: What Works and What Doesn't.* Cambridge: Harvard University Press, pp. 209–31.

Catanzarite, Lisa. 1990. *Job Characteristics and Occupational Segregation by Gender and Race/*

Ethnicity. Ph.D. Dissertation, Department of Sociology, Stanford University, Stanford, California.

Catanzarite, Lisa, and Vilma Ortiz. 1995. "Racial/Ethnic Differences in the Impact of Work and Family on Women's Poverty." *Research in Politics and Society.* vol. 5, pp. 217–37.

Dill, Bonnie Thornton, Lynn Weber Cannon, and Reeve Vanneman. 1987. "Race and Gender in Occupational Segregation" in "National Committee on Pay Equity," *Pay Equity: An Issue of Race, Ethnicity and Sex.* Washington, D.C.: National Committee on Pay Equity, pp. 11–70.

Ehrenreich, Barbara. 1986. "What Makes Women Poor?" in Rochelle Lefkowitz and Ann Withorn (eds.), *For Crying Out Loud: Women and Poverty in the United States.* New York: Pilgrim Press, pp. 18–28.

Garfinkel, Irwin, and Sara S. McLanahan. 1986. *Single Mothers and Their Children: A New American Dilemma.* Washington, D.C.: The Urban Institute.

Malveaux, Julianne. 1985. "The Economic Interests of Black and White Women: Are They Similar?" *Review of Black Political Economy.* vol. 14 (Summer): pp. 5–28.

Malveaux, Julianne, and Phyllis Wallace. 1987. "Minority Women in the Workplace," in Karen S. Koziara, Michael H. Moskow and Lucretia D. Tanner (eds.), *Working Women: Past, Present and Future.* Washington, D.C.: Bureau of National Affairs, IRRA Series.

Mead, Lawrence. 1986. *Beyond Entitlement: The Social Obligations of Citizenship.* New York: Free Press.

Moynihan, Daniel P. 1965. *The Negro Family: The Case for National Action.* Washington, D.C.: U.S. Department of Labor, Office of Policy Planning and Research.

Pearce, Diana. 1986. "The Feminization of Poverty: Women, Work and Welfare" in Rochelle Lefkowitz and Ann Withorn (eds.), *For Crying Out Loud: Women and Poverty in the United States.* New York: Pilgrim Press, pp. 29–46.

Pearce, Diana. 1987. "On the Edge: Marginal Women Workers and Employment Policy" in Christine Bose and Glenna Spitze (eds.), *Ingredients for Women's Employment Policy.* Albany: State University of New York Press, pp. 197–210.

Petersen, Trond. 1985. "A Comment on Presenting Results from Logit and Probit Models." *American Sociological Review.* vol. 509 (1) pp. 130–31.

Peterson, Janice. 1987. "The Feminization of Poverty," *Journal of Economic Issues.* vol. 21(1): pp. 329–37.

Security Pacific National Bank, 1979. *The Sixty Mile Circle.* Los Angeles: Security Pacific National Bank.

Smith, Joan. 1984. "The Paradox of Women's Poverty: Wage-Earning Women and Economic Transformation." *Signs* (special issue on Women and Poverty), vol. 10 (2): pp. 291–310.

Wilson, William Julius, and Kathryn M. Neckerman. 1986. "Poverty and Family Structure: The Widening Gap Between Evidence and Public Policy Issues" in Sheldon Danziger and Daniel Weinberg (eds.), *Fighting Poverty: What Works and What Doesn't.* Cambridge: Harvard University Press, pp. 232–59.

Wilson, William Julius. 1987. *The Truly Disadvantaged: The Inner City, The Underclass, and Public Policy.* Chicago: University of Chicago Press.

21

Making Ends Meet at a Low-Wage Job

Kathryn Edin and Laura Lein

IN 1992, ALEXANDRIA GONZALEZ—A WHITE woman of twenty-three who lived in San Antonio with her three preschool-aged children—had been off welfare and working for over a year. Of her job as a receptionist she said,

I really like my work, but the money is not enough. People work me really hard, and there's nowhere to be promoted to unless I get more school. So sometimes it's depressing. I feel like I do a good job though, and I like to have contact with all these people.

Gonzalez's budget was tight. Although she made more from working than she had gotten from the state of Texas in welfare payments, some of her expenses rose when she went to work: she spent $110 a month more for child care (with a federal subsidy covering most of the cost) and $125 more a month to insure and maintain an older car. Her welfare benefits were also reduced: she lost her AFDC and Medicaid eligibility; the housing authority increased her rent from about $50 to $230 a month; and the food stamp program reduced her allotment from $274 to $175 a month. She took home roughly $800 a month from her job, but spent just over $1,000. Her mother, who lived nearby, provided the money she needed to bridge the gap between her income and expenses. If her children were not in subsidized child care or if she had lost her subsidized apartment, her expenses would have more than doubled, leaving a short-fall she could not have covered even with the support of her mother.

From *Making Ends Meet: How Single Mothers Survive Welfare and Low-Wage Work* by Kathryn Edin and Laura Lein. Copyright © 1997 by Russell Sage Foundation. Used with permission of Russell Sage Foundation.

Meanwhile, Gonzalez worried about how her busy schedule was affecting her children. She worked forty hours a week and commuted one hour each way, for a total of fifty hours away from home. She brought the children to day care at 8:00 A.M. and picked them up at 6:00 P.M. After arriving home, she had just enough time to feed and bathe her children before she put them to bed. Not surprisingly, Gonzalez worried that her children were spending too much time away from her.

Some readers might wonder why the fathers of her children did not help out.[1] Gonzalez told us that she conceived her first child as a result of rape, and the father was incarcerated as a result. The second child's father was a military man stationed in Hawaii, who had threatened to sue for custody if she attempted to get a child support order:

I'm going to tell you something you should write down about single mothers. They are afraid to try to make the fathers pay support sometimes because they might decide they want custody and try to take them away. I talked to the father of my two-year-old girl. He is in Hawaii, in the service. He didn't care or help or anything, until [I tried to get child support]. All of a sudden, he tells me he wants her. I said no. I told him he couldn't have her. I stopped trying to get him to pay support, but I still worry he might try to get her, and I'd just die.

The father of her third child had broken up with her as soon as he found out she was pregnant. She was planning to take him to court for child support but did not think she would get much as he was only episodically employed.

Based on our analysis . . . we would expect mothers like Alexandria Gonzalez, who traded their federal welfare benefits for low-wage work in the early 1990s, to be disadvantaged in three ways. First, full-time work would bring them no closer to balancing their budgets than federal welfare benefits would have, because they would have to spend more in order to work. Second, they would have less time in which to generate supplemental income. (This was not a problem for Gonzalez, since her only source of supplementary income was her mother.) Finally, their children would have less parental contact and supervision after school and during the summer.

When one considers how much these mothers could lose by taking a job, it is easy to understand why mothers choose welfare over work. Yet, . . . national data amply illustrate that many single mothers have chosen to work rather than to take government money and that even single mothers who accept welfare at a given point in time typically leave the program for a low-wage job within two years. Most of them return to welfare, but a majority then cycle back into the low-wage labor market. Kathleen Harris's (1997) tabulations using PSID data show that among all mothers who received any public assistance between 1968 and 1988, the typical mother in the late 1980s reported receiving welfare in only four of these twenty years. The median number of years mothers reported labor-market earnings was over ten years. In other words, over time single mothers who received federal welfare benefits spent over two-and-a-half times more years in the low-wage workforce than they did on welfare.[2] That most welfare recipients receive benefits for relatively brief periods suggests they prefer low-wage work over welfare when they can manage it.

In order to fully understand how mothers choose between welfare and work, we must know more about how mothers with low-wage jobs get by. We interviewed 165 single mothers who did not get any cash welfare but chose to work instead at low-wage jobs, those paying less than $8 an hour. We show how much low-wage working mothers in the early 1990s spent each month to pay their bills and keep their families together. We also discuss how much they earned from their

wages, the earned income tax credit, and the benefits available from various government programs including food stamps, Medicaid, and housing subsidies. We then compare earnings with expenditures and show that a mother's wages from a low-wage job typically covered only two-thirds of her expenditures. We show that working mothers relied on various strategies for bridging the gap between their incomes and necessary expenditures. Finally, we attempt to assess whether the expenditures working mothers reported were necessary for their families' well-being.[3]

HOW MUCH MUST WORKING MOTHERS SPEND?

Table 4.1 shows that the 165 wage-reliant mothers we interviewed spent nearly 50 percent more than our welfare-reliant mothers in a typical month. However, they did not spend substantially more on food, telephone bills, toiletries, appliances and furniture, cigarettes and alcohol, or the lottery—which suggests that in these areas the working mothers practiced the same frugal consumption patterns and money-saving strategies as the welfare-reliant mothers we interviewed. Working mothers did spend significantly more, however, on housing, medical care, clothing, transportation, child care, school supplies, and miscellaneous expenses, and a little more on some nonessentials.

The similarities and differences in spending between the groups make a good deal of sense. We would expect wage-reliant mothers to have more work-related expenses—that is, higher costs for transportation, child care, medical care, and clothing. Moreover, we would expect housing costs to increase for working mothers living in subsidized housing because their higher cash incomes would reduce their rent subsidies. In another area—miscellaneous items—working mothers' added expenses were largely for haircuts and cosmetics, which could also be construed as work-related. Finally, working mothers tended to have older children than welfare-reliant mothers, so they spent more on school supplies, but less on baby care.

TABLE 4.1

Average Monthly Expenses of 214 Welfare- and 165 Wage-Reliant Mothers

	214 Welfare-Reliant Mothers	165 Wage-Reliant Mothers	Sig.
Housing costs	$213	$341	***
Food costs	262	249	
Other necessities	336	569	***
Medical	18	56	***
Clothing	69	95	***
Transportation	62	129	***
Child care	7	66	***
Phone	31	35	
Laundry/toiletries/cleaning supplies	52	53	
Baby care	18	10	**
School supplies and fees	14	25	*
Appliance and furniture	17	22	
Miscellaneous	47	78	***
Nonessentials	64	84	***
Entertainment	20	27	**
Cable TV	6	9	**
Cigarettes and alcohol	22	22	
Eat out	13	25	***
Lottery costs	3	1	*
TOTAL EXPENSES	876	1,243	***

Source: Authors' calculations using Edin and Lein survival strategies data.
Note: Two-tailed test for significance of differences in means between welfare- and wage-reliant mothers given by * > .10; ** > .05; *** > .01.

To this point, the differences in the budgets of welfare- and wage-reliant mothers largely offset one another. This leaves only one area, nonessentials, in which working mothers actually enjoyed additional consumption of goods and services that were not related to working. Working mothers spent about $20 more a month on entertainment, cable television, and eating out than welfare-reliant mothers did.

Housing Expenses

Overall, our wage-reliant mothers spent $128 more on housing each month than our welfare-reliant mothers. As with the welfare recipients, the amount of rent each mother paid depended heavily on whether she paid market rent, had a housing subsidy in either a public housing project or a private complex, or shared housing with a relative or friend.

Wage-reliant families with project-based subsidies had the lowest rents. Because the Department of Housing and Urban Development (HUD) requires local housing authorities to set rents at 30 percent of all cash income, these families spent an average of $243 for rent or mortgage payments, utilities, taxes, water and sewer, and garbage collection each month—twice as much as our welfare-reliant mothers paid for such housing. Families who received Section 8 subsidies also had low housing expenses ($292 a month, on average), again nearly twice what welfare recipients spent for similar housing. Since cash income makes up a higher proportion of working mothers' total budgets and food stamps make up a smaller proportion, working mothers' rents are higher.

Wage-reliant mothers who shared housing with a relative or friend spent an average of $247 a month for rent and utilities, $100 more than our welfare-reliant mothers paid for shared housing. Two factors explain this difference. First, working mothers who were doubled up told us that their relatives expected them to pay more when they took a full-time job than when they were on welfare. Second, some of the doubled-up working mothers we interviewed were actually better off than their roommates (who were sometimes on welfare, SSI, or living off meager social security pensions). Because of this, they felt they could not ask these roommates to contribute their full share of the housing expenses.

Of all the mothers we interviewed, privately housed wage-reliant mothers spent the most for housing—$446 a month. This amount was nearly identical to what the welfare-reliant group spent when they paid market rent. Although this rent still could seldom buy housing in a "good" neighborhood, these wage-reliant mothers—like their welfare-reliant counterparts in private housing—thought they were better off than those families living in the projects.

Transportation Expenses

Monthly transportation costs averaged $129 for wage-reliant families, more than twice what our welfare group paid. Yet transportation expenses were rather low when one considers that mothers who owned cars had to cover car payments, insurance, taxes, licensing and registration, gasoline, maintenance and repairs, and parking. For those who did not own a car, we included all expenditures for public transportation and taxi cabs, as well as what mothers chipped in for car pools.

All the states we studied had mandatory insurance laws, and even the least expensive liability in-

surance cost families roughly $50 each month. South Carolina and Texas also taxed the value of a family's automobile, while Chicago and Boston residents had to purchase city stickers each year. Like their welfare-reliant counterparts, wage-reliant mothers living in Charleston spent the most on transportation because they had less access to public transportation and had to maintain automobiles. Mothers living on the outskirts of each city also paid more because of a lack of public transit services.

Child Care Expenses

Although the working mothers we interviewed spent far more on child care than welfare-reliant mothers ($66 versus $7), they spent less than one might expect. This was partly because most mothers who worked had both fewer children and older children than their welfare-reliant counterparts and partly because they seldom paid market rate for child care. In our wage-reliant group, 5 percent of the mothers told us they paid market rate for child care, 23 percent received child care subsidies or had found an unlicensed provider who accepted less than the market rate, 18 percent had a friend or relative who watched their children for little or no cash, and the rest worked at home, worked only during their children's school hours, or felt their children were responsible enough to be left home alone. It was their ability to find low-cost child care that allowed our wage-reliant mothers to remain at their jobs. (Conversely . . . the absence of such low-cost care was one of several factors that kept mothers in our welfare-reliant group out of the workforce.)

Mothers who paid market rates reported child care expenditures averaging $331 a month. Mothers with subsidies, however, paid only $83 in a typical month. Estimates drawn from the Survey of Income and Program Participation show that U.S. mothers who made any cash payments for child care services in 1991 (35 percent of all mothers) paid about $270 a month.[4] Interestingly, the SIPP data show that when poor mothers pay for child care they have to spend as much as nonpoor mothers do for care, so that child care ends up constituting a much larger portion of a poor mother's total monthly budget (27 percent versus 7 percent of a nonpoor mother's budget).[5]

Child care not only makes working more expensive; the limited hours offered by most child care providers can interfere with a mother's ability to move up in her job. One of our respondents worked evenings and weekends at a fast food restaurant because her mother, who worked a full-time day job, was able to care for her infant son during those hours. She told us,

I don't think [I could accept a promotion]. I mean, they have talked to me before about being a manager, but I need the availability. See, I can only work weekday nights and weekends. They need someone to be there [whenever they need them]. If I could get her into a [subsidized] day care I would take a promotion.

In addition, concerns about child care can interfere with mothers' plans to advance professionally through increased education and training. One mother planned to return to school to obtain certification as a licensed practical nurse. She would not enroll, however, unless she could find someone who was willing to keep an eye on her children after school. In her words, "They're [school-age], but they still need someone to keep an eye on them, you know." In sum, working mothers often found that childrearing and jobholding conflicted in ways that limited their ability to get ahead.

Medical Care Expenses

Health care premiums, prescription drugs, over-the-counter medicines, and other medical services constituted another $56 of an average wage-reliant mother's monthly budget. Although some of these mothers received Medicaid for their children, most had no insurance for either their children or themselves. Their employers seldom offered health benefits, and those that did usually required large copayments. National data show that 15 percent of all Americans went without any health insurance in 1993. Among the officially poor, the figure was 29 percent, despite the existence of

Medicaid and Medicare. Among poor workers only, this figure rises to nearly 50 percent. The figure is also higher for persons living in southern states like South Carolina and Texas (states with weak labor unions and few unionized workers) than in northern states like Illinois and Massachusetts (U.S. Bureau of the Census 1994c).[6] One mother told us,

We don't have any health insurance except for the baby. He's on his father's plan. When someone gets sick we go to the doctor and pay for it. Christmas day, my daughter had a high fever, so I took her to the doctor. I had to pay $175 and she was in there only fifteen minues. Health insurance would cost $250 to $300 a month for the whole family.

The copayment problem was particularly salient for mothers whose children were not covered by Medicaid. Although employers sometimes covered all or part of an employee's health care premiums, they almost always required the mother to pay the additional premiums for the children. Not surprisingly, this meant that some children of insured wage-reliant mothers had no health insurance. One mother said,

I'm not making that much. I started at $4.50. I've been working there almost a year now and I make $5. I have good benefits, . . . insurance, but it's just basically for me. I can't really afford to get the family insured. It would be $100 a month for my kids too.

Mothers' concerns about going without health benefits were so powerful that a few mothers we interviewed actually left jobs paying between $6 and $7 an hour for jobs that paid less but had better benefits. One mother left a job as a bookkeeper at a neighborhood health clinic for a minimum-wage job at a retail chain store for precisely this reason. Although she had worked at the clinic for seven years and had gotten several promotions, she had never been eligible for individual or family health benefits. One year prior to our interviews, an emergency appendectomy had left her deeply in debt. After she returned to work, she immediately began looking for a job that offered benefits. When she switched jobs, she had to take a $1 an hour cut in pay. In her own words, "I rely on my benefits. I don't know what I would do without my benefits."

Another mother worked for several years at a "letter shop" (a business that specializes in preparing bulk mailings) and had worked her way up to an hourly wage of $7. She told us, "I'm leaving that job because my employer can no longer afford to insure me. I'm taking a new job housecleaning. It pays only $6 but has some health benefits, and I get $2 for gas between houses."

Women without health benefits can get into serious debt if a health emergency occurs. Melinda Brown, a working mother in San Antonio, told us that over the last year she had run up nearly $1,000 in unpaid medical bills: "I am paying off various doctor bills at the rate of $5 or $10 a month. I owe the dentist $440 and a pediatrician $353. Then I owe another $68 for a doctor visit." Over time, unpaid medical debt can damage credit ratings, making it harder for mothers to obtain credit cards, automobiles, or homes.

Clothing Expenses

Working mothers spent an average of $95 a month on clothing (or $26 more than the average welfare-reliant mother). Most of this increase was in mothers' expenditures for work clothes. Mothers in the fast food and health care industries had to purchase uniforms for work, and others, particularly those in clerical jobs, had to meet dress codes. Even so, these women shopped at discount stores, bought used clothing at garage sales and thrift stores, wore hand-me-downs from sisters and friends, and sometimes sewed their own clothing.

Miscellaneous

Miscellaneous items in the working mothers' budgets included checking account fees, credit card fees, burial or life insurance . . . haircuts and cosmetics, and payments on existing debt. These items totaled $78 in the average month. Most of the difference between working and welfare-reliant mothers' expenditures in this catch-all category were for haircuts and cosmetics. Mothers

explained that they needed to maintain a professional image at work to keep their jobs and to be considered, if a chance ever arose, for promotion.

Nonessentials

. . . Entertainment for wage-reliant families—which cost them $27 each month—was usually limited to video rentals and an occasional movie.[7] Wage-reliant mothers spent an additional $22 for cigarettes, $25 to eat out, $9 for cable television, and $1 for the lottery in a typical month. All told, the typical wage-reliant family spent $84 a month on these nonessential items, or about 7 percent of their total budget.

Variations in Expenditures by Site

. . . The averages given in the preceding section mask some variation across the four cities in our study. Housing cost Charleston and Boston mothers roughly $400 a month. Although Charleston rents were cheaper, more Boston wage-reliant mothers had doubled up, so their average rent payments were similar. In Chicago, where working mothers were even more likely to be doubled up than in Boston, mothers' rent averaged $328 a month. In San Antonio, where housing was least expensive, mothers who worked paid less than $250 in an average month for rent and utilities (see Table 4.2).

Food expenses did not vary much by site, but expenses for other necessity items did, including medical care and child care. Overall, mothers' expenditures for nonfood necessities in Charleston, Chicago, and Boston averaged around $600 a month, while San Antonio mothers spent less than $500 a month for these items. San Antonians spent significantly less on medical care and child care than mothers in other sites. They were able to economize because their hourly wages, weekly working hours, and opportunities for overtime work were far lower than in any other site. As a result, their children more often qualified for Medicaid and child card subsidies. The working mothers in this site made ends meet because they

TABLE 4.2

Average Monthly Expenses of 165 Low-Wage Workers by Site

	Charleston	San Antonio	Chicago	Boston	Sig.
Family size	2.83	3.27	2.56	2.94	***
Housing costs	$404	$241	$328	$388	***
% paying market rent	60%	44%	44%	18%	***
Food costs	$235	$236	$257	$272	
Food per person	88	72	106	96	***
Other necessities	615	476	572	615	**
Medical	72	39	63	44	
Clothing	84	97	103	98	
Transportation	192	100	101	110	***
Child care	76	33	90	63	
Phone[a]	39	28	32	45	*
Laundry/toiletries/cleaning supplies	47	50	60	58	
Baby care	4	16	19	2	***
School supplies	24	15	8	61	***
Appliances/furniture	20	26	16	28	
Miscellaneous[b]	58	73	82	106	**
Nonessentials	76	73	85	107	
Entertainment	32	20	25	32	
Cable TV	8	12	2	19	***
Cigarettes and alcohol	17	16	36	18	*
Eat out	19	25	21	38	**
Lottery costs	0	1	2	1	
TOTAL EXPENSES	1,330	1,027	1,243	1,383	***

Source: Authors' calculations using Edin and Lein survival strategies data.

[a]Basic line charges varied from about $12 in San Antonio to $20 in Chicago, and more than $25 in Charleston and the Boston area.

[b]Includes monthly payments for burial insurance, haircuts, unspecified credit payments, and check-cashing fees.

Note: Two-tailed tests for significance of differences in means between cities given by * > .10; ** > .05; *** > .01.

received more noncash benefits, not because they were better at managing their money.

Half of the wage-reliant mothers interviewed in Charleston, San Antonio, and Boston, and one-third of those in Chicago, lived in subsidized housing. Since most of this housing was federally funded, these mothers usually paid about 30 percent of their declared incomes for rent. The remaining wage-reliant mothers lived in private housing, either on their own or with another family. . . . Private housing costs varied dramatically by site in the early 1990s, with Boston being the most expensive, followed by Chicago, Charleston, and San Antonio. San Antonio residents paid about half as much as Boston-area residents for a market-rent apartment.

Transportation costs also varied by city. Because public transportation was relatively good in

TABLE 4.6
Survival Strategies of 165 Wage-Reliant Mothers

Variable	Amount of Income Generated Through Each Survival Strategy	Percentage of Total Budget	Percent of Mothers Engaging in Each Survival Strategy
TOTAL EXPENSES	$1,243	100%	N/A
Housing costs	341	24	N/A
Food costs	249	30	N/A
Other necessities	569	39	N/A
Nonessentials	84	7	N/A
TOTAL INCOME	1,226	100	N/A
Main job	777	63	100
Food stamps	57	5	28
SSI	3	0	2
EITC	25	2	28
Work-based strategies	88	7	39
Reported work	27	2	12
Unreported work	59	5	28
Underground work	2	0	1
Network-based strategies	253	21	82
Family and friends	65	5	47
Boyfriends	60	5	27
Absent fathers	127	10	42
Agency-based strategies	36	3	22

Source: Authors' calculations using Edin and Lein survival strategies data.

Chicago and Boston, most working mothers in those two cities were able to limit their transportation expenses to about $100 each month. Like their welfare counterparts, Charleston workers spent the most on transportation, averaging $192 a month, because they were more likely to have cars. San Antonio mothers were also ill-served by public transportation, but the labor market was so slack and wages for women so low that few mothers could afford to take jobs that required commuting by car. San Antonio mothers were usually restricted to jobs within or near their immediate neighborhoods, often in light manufacturing or to jobs within the central city, which they could

reach by bus if they were willing to walk a significant distance to a bus stop.

Finally, Boston mothers, who earned the highest wages on average, spent roughly $25 more each month for nonessential items than mothers in other sites, although this difference was not statistically significant.

HOW DO WAGE-RELIANT MOTHERS MAKE ENDS MEET?

We found during our interviews that many low-wage working mothers were able to keep their families afloat because they had an unusually

TABLE 4.7

Income Generated Through Each Survival Strategy, Percent of Total Budget, and Percent of Welfare-Reliant and Wage-Reliant Mothers Engaging in Each Survival Strategy

	% of Welfare-Reliant Mothers Engaging in Strategy	% of Wage-Reliant Mothers Engaging in Strategy	Sig. of F.	Average Amount — Welfare-Reliant Mothers	Average Amount — Wage-Reliant Mothers	Sig.
N	214	165	N/A	214	165	N/A
Total % work-based strategies	46%	39%		$128	$ 88	**
Total network-based strategies	77	82		157	253	***
Total agency-based strategies	31	22	**	37	36	
Food Stamps	95	28	***	222	57	***
SSI	9	2	***	36	3	***
EITC	7	28	***	3	25	***

Source: Authors' calculations using Edin and Lein survival strategies data.
Note: Two-tailed tests for significance of differences in means between welfare recipients and workers given by * > .10; ** > .05; *** > .01.

generous parent or boyfriend, worked substantial overtime, took a second job, or got a lot of help from an agency. . . . Table 4.6 shows that, on average, mothers' earnings from their main jobs covered only 63 percent of their monthly expenses. Another 7 percent came from food stamps, SSI, and the EITC. Earnings from other legal and illegal work made up 7 percent of their total monthly income. The remainder came from family and friends (5 percent), boyfriends (5 percent), absent fathers (10 percent), and cash or vouchers from public or private agencies (3 percent).[8] Like their welfare counterparts, wage-reliant mothers made up the remaining gap in three ways: generating cash, garnering in-kind contributions, and purchasing stolen goods at below market value. Table 4.6 shows only cash income and expenditures, so it is quite conservative in estimating working mothers' total needs.

We can get a clearer sense of working mothers' income-generating strategies by looking at the percentage of workers who relied on each source of income in a typical month. By definition, none of these mothers received anything from AFDC. However, Table 4.6 shows that 28 percent received food stamps, 2 percent received SSI for a disabled child, and 28 percent reported benefits from the EITC during the previous year. Two-fifths worked at second jobs, and four-fifths got help from family and friends, boyfriends, or absent fathers. When we compare welfare- and wage-reliant mothers' strategies (Table 4.7), we see that working mothers were more likely to get large contributions from members of their personal networks.

TABLE 4.8

Average Expenses of Welfare-Reliant and Wage-Reliant Mothers Compared with Those of Poor Households in the Consumer Expenditure Survey

	Mean for 214 Welfare-Reliant Mothers	Mean for 165 Wage-Reliant Mothers	CES 90-91 One-Parent Households with at Least One Child Under 18	CES 90-91 Two or More Person Households with Very Low Incomes (less than $5,000 per year)
TOTAL EXPENSES	$876	$1,243	$1,804	$1,563
Size	3.17	2.9	2.9	3.0
Housing	213	341	469	394
Food	275	274	303	289
Food (at home)	262	249	217	193
Food (eat out)	13	25	88	97
Medical	18	56	65	97
Clothing	69	95	147	103
Transportation	62	129	260	247
Phone	31	35	51	44
Laundry/toiletries/cleaning	52	53	45	42
School supplies	14	25	22	23
Appliances/furniture	17	22	61	64
Entertainment	26	36	81	86
Cigarettes/alcohol	22	22	32	42
Miscellaneous	47	78	259	130

Sources: Column 1, Edin and Lein survival strategies data. Column 2, extracted from U.S. Bureau of Labor Statistics (1993), pp. 146–47, table 34. Column 3, extracted from U.S. Bureau of Labor Statistics (1993), pp. 30–33, table 5. Although we include child care, baby care, and lottery expenses in the total, we do not itemize them, because they were not included in CES categories. The family site is rounded to match the CES figures.

Some readers may still suspect that single mothers could get by on a low-wage job alone if they managed their money more carefully. Yet when we compare our respondents' reported expenses with the poorest income group interviewed by the CES, we see that the expenses these mothers reported were, in virtually all cases, substantially lower than those reported by other very poor families. Table 4.8 divides our mothers' expenditures into categories that are roughly comparable with those the CES uses. Columns 1 and 2 show what our two groups of mothers spent; columns 3 and 4 show how much the CES's very

low-income families spent in these same categories. As with the welfare-reliant mothers, our wage-reliant families spent far less than the CES families for both necessary and nonnecessary items. This again suggests that our working mothers' expenses reflect the very low end of national consumption norms.

Work and Material Hardship

Despite their higher monthly incomes, the working mothers we interviewed were having a very difficult time coping financially. Indeed, they reported experiencing somewhat more material hardships than our welfare-reliant mothers. One woman who had left welfare for work said,

I received welfare for a few years in the '80s, but once I got off I wasn't going back. But since I have been working I have gone to work in the winter without a coat because I had to give it to my daughter to wear, and we have lit candles because we didn't have any lights. I have even gone a full year without a phone.

Another woman told us,

[Although I go to work every day] I have had to have the telephone turned off at different times. Before I qualified for Section 8, I lived without electricity for a week or two. I did get emergency assistance to help, but without that help, we would have a lot of hardship.

Yet another woman recounted,

Since I have been on the job, there was a couple [of] times where I really thought I was going to have a nervous breakdown. It was just really hard. I mean, because you worry about your children, you care about them, and you see all these other children, and there's these times where they need new shoes, well I don't even have the extra $20 to go to the store and buy a pair of shoes. I have to try to go to the thrift shop and hope that I can find a decent pair for $3, and my son just went down there and he found a decent pair for $4. He had a [pair of shoes] that he had worn so long that the soles had a hole in them. And I'm not talking money to party with or anything like that, because that's not where my money goes. I just don't have it. I didn't have any money to buy any Christmas [presents] for my children. This Christmas, that was another time I thought I was getting out of control. I just knew that they weren't going to get anything. Nothing.

. . .

HARDSHIP MEASURES

When we compare the material well-being of welfare- and wage-reliant mothers, we find that, on balance, working mothers were worse off than those who received welfare, although they did do

better on some individual measures . . . .[9] Of course, mothers' assessments of which hardships were the worst varied. Although no one wanted to run out of food at the end of the month, some mothers believed it preferable to going without needed medical attention. Others were willing to go without medical coverage if they could avoid living in the projects. These rankings often played a key role in a given mother's choice of whether to work or receive welfare. . . .

. . . No matter which hardship index we use, wage-reliant mothers had more hardships than welfare-reliant mothers. Yet even these indices underestimate the differences between the two groups because the wage-reliant mothers had fewer children than the welfare-reliant group: theoretically, smaller families should have fewer hardships than larger families. If we control for differences in family size and for our sample selection criteria, working mothers had 1.5 times more hardship than comparable welfare recipients using the unweighted core hardship scale and 1.3 times more hardship using the weighted version of this scale. These differences were due entirely to differences in health care. The third scale (hardship I) shows that the fact that working mothers lived in slightly more desirable housing partly offset their health care disadvantage.

Using the weighted core hardship scale, working mothers would have needed to spend roughly $9,000 more a year than their welfare counterparts to be equally well off in the early 1990s. Using the weighted hardship I scale lowers the figure to roughly $6,500. In both cases, using the unweighted scales yields even higher estimates.

We also used these summary measures to assess whether there were differences among wage-reliant mothers by site (see Table 4.10). Using the unweighted core hardship scale, site differences are not statistically reliable. The weighted version of this measure does show variations, but they are due almost entirely to the differences in housing quality discussed previously. The hardship I measure again shows no important differences among sites, but adding weights reveals that the differences are due to a combination of housing quality

TABLE 4.10

Measures of Material Hardship for 165 Wage-Reliant Mothers by Site

Hardship	Charleston	San Antonio	Chicago	Boston	Sig.
N	47	41	43	34	
1. No food	15%	27%	28%	26%	
2. Hungry	9	5	5	18	
3. Doctor[a]	40	39	33	47	
4. No health benefits	55	41	65	44	
5. Utilities off	21	12	21	12	
6. At least two housing-quality problems	19	39	7	38	**
7. Public housing	6	22	5	26	***
8. Shared housing	15	22	43	18	**
Phone off or no phone	30	42	40	29	
Winter clothes	13	12	14	24	
Evicted	15	7	7	0	
Homeless	15	7	19	6	
Core hardships (1 to 6)[b]	1.57	1.78	1.37	1.85	
Weighted core hardships	.82	1.04	.56	1.08	**
Hardship I (1 to 8)	1.79	2.22	1.84	2.29	
Weighted hardship I	.88	1.89	.72	1.22	***

Source: Authors' calculations using Edin and Lein survival strategies data.

[a]Includes medical and eye doctors, but does not include dentists or mental health professionals.

[b]Unweighted scores are the sum of individual hardships.

Note: Two-tailed tests for significance of differences in means between cities given by * > .10; ** > .05; *** > .01.

and the number of mothers living in the projects. Again, it seems that San Antonio and Boston working mothers were the least able to purchase adequate housing in the early 1990s.

. . .

NOTES

1. Others might wonder why none of them was living with her. Still others might wonder why she had had three children. These questions, while important, were not the focus of our study.

2. Because of the limitations imposed by the twenty-year window, Harris's estimates are somewhat right-censored. In some cases, spells of work and welfare overlapped. The 5.5 years the typical respondent reported neither working nor earning income were generally spent married and/or in school (Harris 1997).

3. Formal-sector work and welfare are not always mutually exclusive. Very low earners and part-time workers can retain some of their welfare benefits.

4. This average includes the cash payments of mothers who had child care subsidies.

5. SIPP respondents with preschool-aged children paid more than mothers with older children: $312 versus $173 a week (U.S. Bureau of the Census 1994e).

6. Unionized workers are more likely to have health insurance than nonunionized workers.

7. In terms of nonnecessary spending, more than a third of families spent nothing whatsoever on entertainment during the previous year; two-thirds never ate out; nearly half spent nothing on cigarettes or alcohol during the year; and four-fifths went without cable television.

8. The agency figure includes the portion of student grants and loans left over after paying for tuition and books.

9. For example, working mothers were less likely to run out of food or go hungry and less likely to live in the projects, but they were far more likely to say they had untreated medical problems.

REFERENCES

Harris, Kathleen Mullan. 1997. Unpublished Calculations. Chapel Hill, NC: Carolina Population Center, University of North Carolina at Chapel Hill.

Part IV

RACE AND ETHNICITY

—⚏—

PART IV ADDRESSES THE IMPORTANT ISSUES OF race and ethnicity. We Americans think of the United States as a nation where people from diverse cultures, lands, and languages successfully unite into one nation. America's diversity is unquestionable. In fact, America is more ethnically diverse today than it was when we initially began thinking of ourselves as the first new nation composed of immigrants.

The current wave of immigration has dramatically changed the face of American society. The proportion of Asian Americans and Hispanic Americans in the U.S. population is growing rapidly, whereas the number of African Americans is growing at a slower rate. Non-Hispanic European Americans are declining in relative proportion to other groups, so that less than 75 percent of the U.S. population today is non-Hispanic European American. It should not be surprising, then, that various ethnically and racially charged issues have become hot topics for political discussion and action, including immigration policy, interethnic conflict and violence, language-related policies (e.g., multilingual and Ebonics movements versus English-only and standard-English initiatives), and public education (e.g., multicultural vs. majoritarian instruction).

The introduction to this book outlined how race and ethnicity are sociohistorical-political conceptions. It also noted the importance of power relationships in determining how societies construct the meaning of the terms "race" and "ethnicity." An important consideration is how people define a group as being either a minority or part of a majority. The sociological term "minority group" is somewhat misleading because a group does not have to be numerically small to be called a "minority." Rather, power and discrimination are the points of departure from which we derive any meaning of the term minority group. A minority group is a group that is disadvantaged and subjected to unequal treatment, status, power, and rewards. A minority group is also usually distinguished by one or more visibly identifiable characteristics; for instance, women, African Americans, and Latinos fit this conception. A majority group is one that controls superior resources and rights in society and thus is advantaged by its power, not necessarily its numbers. The terms "subordinate group and dominant group are often used synonymously with minority and majority groups, respectively.

The first section of this part focuses on current problems of racial equality by placing them within a historical context. This part opens with W. E. B. Du Bois's landmark statement about the importance of race in American history, "The Problem of the Twentieth Century Is the Problem of the Color Line." Du Bois reviewed racial apartheid in the United States and the progress made in the first half of the twentieth century, proposing that our ideals about social equality and modern democracy be measured against the objective conditions of African Americans in an economy dominated by corporate wealth. He urged all Americans to pursue social equality, reminding African Americans not to abandon their egalitarian goals once they have gained some economic, political, and social advantages.

Going then to the end of the twentieth century, Michael Omi and Howard Winant examine the complexities of simply asking, What is race? In "Racial Formation" they reveal the shortcomings of traditional biological answers and propose that our categories of race be historical and social constructions. The theme of race and identity continues in the next essay. In "Optional Ethnicities," Mary Waters takes up the intriguing question of whether individuals can choose their identities. Is this an option more available to whites?

The next selection, entitled "Campaigning for Respect," is from Elijah Anderson's *Code of the Streets*, an ethnographic look at one urban African American teenager and how he understands the streets and the idea of respect. While Tyree's outlook may be disquieting for many, Anderson invites us to walk the streets in this young man's shoes.

In "A History of Multicultural America," Ronald Takaki recounts this history through the voices of all of America's peoples. In examining what it means to be an American, Takaki argues that we must use "a different mirror"—one that reflects reality—so we can see an undistorted view of our past. Once we truly appreciate and understand our tradition of diversity, we can realistically discuss race and ethnicity in American history and in contemporary experience.

The second group of readings in this part focuses on distinctions between race and ethnicity, highlighting various dimensions of racial and ethnic stratification. In the first essay, "The Wages of Race: Color and Employment Opportunity in Chicago's Inner City," Marta Tienda and Haya Stier examine whether color matters in employment opportunities and wages. The results they present demonstrate that discriminatory attitudes often produce inequality.

Douglas S. Massey's and Nancy A. Denton's "The Continuing Causes of Segregation" investigates residential segregation, its causes, and its consequences. If residential segregation is the linchpin of American race relations, then Massey and Denton's findings are quite sobering. Three quarters of African Americans or European Americans would have to move to substantially differ-

ent neighborhoods to achieve racially balanced communities. These authors' data demonstrate persistent and profound degrees of racial isolation in major cities in the United States.

In "Black Wealth/White Wealth," Melvin L. Oliver and Thomas M. Shapiro use wealth as a significant measure of financial security and well-being, to demonstrate crucial differences between European Americans and African Americans. Oliver and Shapiro show that equally achieving, equally educated, and even equally earning European Americans and African Americans possess markedly different assets and life chances. These findings pose a serious challenge to the way we have thought about inequality in the United States. Equal opportunity and even equal achievement do not necessarily produce equal rewards for African Americans, as compared with other Americans. To personalize their objective data, these authors tell of Carol's fall from middle-class grace. Carol's story offers readers an opportunity to explore one way in which class interacts with race and gender to affect a person's financial well-being and security. Similarly, the authors describe how the Dobbs family illustrates the often precarious middle-class status of many African American families.

The melting pot is the chief metaphor for American race and ethnic relations. Besides the assumptions a melting pot implies, we do not often question whether different ethnicities and races have blended together. The next piece by Elijah Anderson, "Beyond the Melting Pot Reconsidered," asks us to examine the implications of contemporary discrimination, like profiling, for the ideal of assimilation. The selection by Alejandro Portes and Rubén Rumbaut examines the melting pot and assimilation ideas from a different direction. In "Not Everyone is Chosen," they consider the experience of a foreign minority coming to America and how it "fits" in. They consider the case history of a Nicaraguan immigrant family living in Miami. The parents become dependent upon their children's acquired language, cultural, and social skills, losing their ability to guide their future in the bargain. The last reading in this section, William Julius Wilson's "Racial Antagonisms and Race-Based Social Policy," moves our discussion from analyzing inequality to remedying it. In this piece, Wilson proposes policy ideas and strategies for alleviating poverty. His policy ideas are both influential and controversial. How should public policy respond to longstanding inequities? Universal or targeted, specific policies? Should inner city policies focus on the class or racial basis of stratification?

RACE IN OUR TIME

22

The Problem of the Twentieth Century Is the Problem of the Color Line

W. E. B. Du Bois

WE ARE JUST FINISHING THE FIRST HALF OF THE twentieth century. I remember its birth in 1901. There was the usual discussion as to whether the century began in 1900 or 1901; but, of course, 1901 was correct. We expected great things . . . peace; the season of war among nations had passed; progress was the order . . . everything going forward to bigger and better things. And then, not so openly expressed, but even more firmly believed, the rule of white Europe and America over black, brown, and yellow peoples.

I was 32 years of age in 1901, married, and a father, and teaching at Atlanta University with a program covering a hundred years of study and investigation into the condition of American Negroes. Our subject of study at that time was

education: the college-bred Negro in 1900, the Negro common school in 1901. My own attitude toward the twentieth century was expressed in an article which I wrote in the *Atlantic Monthly* in 1901. It said:

The problem of the Twentieth Century is the problem of the color-line. . . . I have seen a land right merry with the sun, where children sing, and rolling hills lie like passioned women wanton with harvest. And there in the King's Highway sat, and sits, a figure veiled and bowed, by which the Traveler's footsteps hasten as they go. On the tainted air broods fair. Three centuries' thought have been the raising and unveiling of that bowed human soul; and now behold, my fellows, a century now for the duty and the deed! The problem of the Twentieth Century is the problem of the color-line.

This is what we hoped, to this we Negroes looked forward; peace, progress, and the breaking of the color line. What has been the result? We know it all too well . . . war, hate, the revolt of the colored peoples and the fear of more war.

From January 14, 1950 issue of *The Pittsburgh Courier.* Copyright © 1950 by the Pittsburgh Courier: copyright renewed 1978 by The New Pittsburgh Courier. Reprinted by permission of GRM Associates, Inc., Agents for The New Pittsburgh Courier.

In the meantime, where are we; those 15,000,000 citizens of the United States who are descended from the slaves, brought here between 1600 and 1900? We formed in 1901, a separate group because of legal enslavement and emancipation into caste conditions, with the attendant poverty, ignorance, disease, and crime. We were an inner group and not an integral part of the American nation; but we were exerting ourselves to fight for integration.

The burden of our fight was in seven different lines. We wanted education; we wanted particularly the right to vote and civil rights; we wanted work with adequate wage; housing, without segregation or slums; a free press to fight our battles, and (although in those days we dare not say it) social equality.

In 1901 our education was in perilous condition, despite what we and our white friends had done for 30 years. The Atlanta University Conference said in its resolutions of 1901:

We call the attention of the nation to the fact that less than one million of the three million Negro children of school age are at present regularly attending school, and these attend a session which lasts only a few months. We are today deliberately rearing millions of our citizens in ignorance and at the same time limiting the rights of citizenship by educational qualifications. This is unjust.

More particularly in civil rights, we were oppressed. We not only did not get justice in the courts, but we were subject to peculiar and galling sorts of injustice in daily life. In the latter half of the nineteenth century, where we first get something like statistics, no less than 3,000 Negroes were lynched without trial. And in addition to that we were subject continuously to mob violence and judicial lynching.

In political life we had, for 25 years, been disfranchised by violence, law, and public opinion. The 14th and 15th amendments were deliberately violated and the literature of the day in book, pamphlet, and daily press, was widely of opinion that the Negro was not ready for the ballot, could not use it intelligently, and that no action was

called for to stop his political power from being exercised by Southern whites. . . .

We did not have the right or opportunity to work at an income which would sustain a decent and modern standard of life. Because of a past of chattel slavery, we were for the most part common laborers and servants, and a very considerable proportion were still unable to leave the plantations where they worked all their lives for next to nothing.

There were a few who were educated for the professions and we had many good artisans; that number was not increasing as it should have been, nor were new artisans being adequately trained. Industrial training was popular, but funds to implement it were too limited, and we were excluded from unions and the new mass industry.

We were housed in slums and segregated districts where crime and disease multiplied, and when we tried to move to better and healthier quarters we were met by segregation ordinance if not by mobs. We not only had no social equality, but we did not openly ask for it. It seemed a shameful thing to beg people to receive us as equals and as human beings; that was something we argued "that came and could not be fetched." And that meant not simply that we could not marry white women or legitimize mulatto bastards, but we could not stop in a decent hotel, nor eat in a public restaurant nor attend the theater, nor accept an invitation to a private white home, nor travel in a decent railway coach. When the "public" was invited, this did not include us and admission to colleges often involved special consideration if not blunt refusal.

Finally we had poor press . . . a few struggling papers with little news and inadequately expressed opinion, with small circulation or influence and almost no advertising.

This was our plight in 1901. It was discouraging, but not hopeless. There is no question but that we had made progress, and there also was no doubt but [that] that progress was not enough to satisfy us or to settle our problems.

We could look back on a quarter century of struggle which had its results. We had schools;

we had teachers; a few had forced themselves into the leading colleges and were tolerated if not welcomed. We voted in Northern cities, owned many decent homes, and were fighting for further progress. Leaders like Booker Washington had perceived wide popular approval and a Negro literature had begun to appear.

But what we needed was organized effort along the whole front, based on broad lines of complete emancipation. This came with the Niagara Movement in 1906 and the NAACP in 1909. In 1910 came the *Crisis* magazine and the real battle was on.

What have we gained and accomplished? The advance has not been equal on all fronts, nor complete on any. We have not progressed with closed ranks like a trained army, but rather with serried and broken ranks, with wide gaps and even temporary retreats. But we have advanced. Of that there can be no atom of doubt.

First of all in education; most Negro children today are in school and most adults can read and write. Unfortunately this literacy is not as great as the census says. The draft showed that at least a third of our youth are illiterate. But education is steadily rising. Six thousand bachelor degrees are awarded to Negroes each year and doctorates in philosophy and medicine are not uncommon. Nevertheless as a group, American Negroes are still in the lower ranks of learning and adaptability to modern conditions. They do not read widely, their travel is limited, and their experience through contact with the modern world is curtailed by law and custom.

Secondly, in civil rights, the Negro has perhaps made his greatest advance. Mob violence and lynching have markedly decreased. Three thousand Negroes were lynched in the last half of the nineteenth century and five hundred in the first half of the twentieth. Today lynching is comparatively rare. Mob violence also has decreased, but is still in evidence, and summary and unjust court proceedings have taken the place of open and illegal acts. But the Negro has established, in the courts, his legal citizenship and his right to be included in the Bill of Rights. The question still remains of "equal but separate" public accommodations, and that is being attacked. Even the institution of "jim-crow" in travel is tottering. The infraction of the marriage situation by law and custom is yet to be brought before the courts and public opinion in a forcible way.

Third, the right to vote on the part of the Negro is being gradually established under the 14th and 15th amendments. It was not really until 1915 that the Supreme Court upheld this right of Negro citizens and even today the penalties of the 14th amendment have never been enforced. There are 7,000,000 possible voters among American Negroes and of these it is a question if more than 2,000,000 actually cast their votes. This is partly from the national inertia, which keeps half of all American voters away from the polls; but even more from the question as to what practical ends the Negro shall cast his vote.

He is thinking usually in terms of what he can do by voting to better his condition and he seldom gets a chance to vote on this matter. On the wider implications of political democracy he has not yet entered; particularly he does not see the economic foundations of present civilization and the necessity of his attacking the rule of corporate wealth in order to free the labor group to which he belongs.

Fourth, there is the question of occupation. There are our submerged classes of farm labor and tenants: our city laborers, washerwomen, and scrubwomen and the mass of lower-paid servants. These classes still form a majority of American Negroes and they are on the edge of poverty, with the ignorance, disease, and crime that always accompany such poverty.

If we measure the median income of Americans, it is $3,000 for whites and $2,000 for Negroes. In Southern cities, seven percent of the white families and 30 percent of the colored families receive less than $1,000 a year. On the other hand, the class differentiation by income among Negroes is notable: the number of semiskilled and skilled artisans has increased as will membership in labor unions. Professional men have increased, especially teachers and less notably, physicians, dentists, and lawyers.

The number of Negroes in business has increased; mostly in small retail businesses, but to a considerable extent in enterprises like insurance, real estate, and small banking, where the color line gives Negroes certain advantages and where, too, there is a certain element of gambling. Also beyond the line of gambling, numbers of Negroes have made small fortunes in antisocial enterprises. All this means that there has arisen in the Negro group a distinct stratification from poor to rich. Recently I polled 450 Negro families belonging to a select organization 45 years old. Of these families, 127 received over $10,000 a year and a score of these over $25,000; 200 families received from $5,000 to $10,000 a year and 86 less than $5,000.

This is the start of a tendency which will grow; we are beginning to follow the American pattern of accumulating individual wealth and of considering that this will eventually settle the race problem. On the other hand, the whole trend of the thought of our age is toward social welfare; the prevention of poverty by more equitable distribution of wealth, and business for general welfare rather than private profit. There are few signs that these ideals are guiding Negro development today. We seem to be adopting increasingly the ideal of American culture.

Housing has, of course, been a point of bitter pressure among Negroes, because the attempt to segregate the race in its living conditions has not only kept the more fortunate ones from progress, but it has confined vast numbers of Negro people to the very parts of cities and country districts where they have fewest opportunities and least social contacts. They must live largely in slums, in contact with criminals, and with fewest of the social advantages of government and human contact. The fight against segregation has been carried on in the courts and shows much progress against city ordinances, against covenants which make segregation hereditary.

Literature and art have made progress among Negroes, but with curious handicaps. An art expression is normally evoked by the conscious and unconscious demand of people for portrayal of their own emotion and experience. But in the case of the American Negroes, the audience, which embodies the demand and which pays sometimes enormous price for satisfaction, is not the Negro group, but the white group. And the pattern of what the white group wants does not necessarily agree with the natural desire of Negroes.

The whole of Negro literature is therefore curiously divided. We have writers who have written, not really about Negroes, but about the things which white people, and not the highest class of whites, like to hear about Negroes. And those who have expressed what the Negro himself thinks and feels, are those whose books sell to few, even of their own people; and whom most folk do not know. This has not made for the authentic literature which the early part of this century seemed to promise. To be sure, it can be said that American literature today has a considerable amount of Negro expression and influence, although not as much as once we hoped.

Despite all this we have an increasing number of excellent Negro writers who make the promise for the future great by their real accomplishment. We have done something in sculpture and painting, but in drama and music we have markedly advanced. All the world listens to our singers, sings our music, and dances to our rhythms.

In science, our handicaps are still great. Turner, a great entomologist, was worked to death for lack of laboratory, just never had the recognition he richly deserved; and Carver was prisoner of his inferiority complex. Notwithstanding this, our real accomplishment in biology and medicine; in history and law; and in the social sciences has been notable and widely acclaimed. To this in no little degree is due our physical survival, our falling death rate, and our increased confidence in our selves and in our destiny.

The expression of Negro wish and desire through a free press has greatly improved as compared with 1900. We have a half dozen large weekly papers with circulations of a hundred thousand or more. Their news coverage is immense, even if not discriminating. But here again, the influence of the American press on us has been devastating. The predominance of advertising over opinion, the desire for income rather than literary excellence and the use of deliberate propaganda, had made our press less of a power than it could be, and leaves wide chance for improvement in the future.

In comparison with other institutions, the Negro church during the twentieth century has lost ground. It is no longer the dominating influence that it used to be, the center of social activity and of economic experiment. Nevertheless, it is still a powerful institution in the lives of a numerical majority of American Negroes if not upon the dominant intellectual classes. There has been a considerable increase in organized work for social progress through the church, but there has also been a large increase of expenditure for buildings, furnishings, and salaries; and it is not easy to find any increase in moral stamina or conscientious discrimination within church circles.

The scandal of deliberate bribery in election of bishops and in the holding of positions in the churches without a hierarchy has been widespread. It is a critical problem now as to just what part in the future the church among Negroes is going to hold.

Finally there comes the question of social equality, which, despite efforts on the part of thinkers, white and black, is after all the main and fundamental problem of race in the United States. Unless a human being is going to have all human rights, including not only work, but friendship, and if mutually desired, marriage and children, unless these avenues are open and free, there can be no real equality and no cultural integration.

It has hitherto seemed utterly impossible that any such solution of the Negro problem in America could take place. The situation was quite similar to the problem of the lower classes of laborers, serfs and servants in European nations during the sixteenth, seventeenth, and eighteenth centuries.

All nations had to consist of two separate parts and the only relations between them was employment and philanthropy.

That problem has been partly solved by modern democracy, but modern democracy cannot succeed unless the peoples of different races and religions are also integrated into the democratic whole. Against this, large numbers of Americans have always fought and are still fighting, but the progress despite this has been notable. There are places in the United States, especially in large cities like New York and Chicago, where the social differences between the races has, to a large extent, been nullified and there is a meeting on terms of equality which would have been thought impossible a half century ago.

On the other hand, in the South, despite religion, education, and reason, the color line, although perhaps shaken, still stands, stark and unbending, and to the minds of most good people, eternal. Here lies the area of the last battle for the complete rights of American Negroes.

Within the race itself today there are disquieting signs. The effort of Negroes to become Americans of equal status with other Americans is leading them to a state of mind by which they not only accept what is good in America, but what is bad and threatening so long as the Negro can share equally. This is peculiarly dangerous at this epoch in the development of world culture.

After two world wars of unprecedented loss of life, cruelty, and destruction, we are faced by the fact that the industrial organization of our present civilization has in it something fundamentally wrong. It went to pieces in the first world war because of the determination of certain great powers excluded from world rule to share in that rule, by acquisition of the labor and materials of colonial peoples. The attempt to recover from the cataclysm resulted in the collapse of our industrial system, and a second world war.

In spite of the propaganda which has gone on, which represents America as the leading democratic state, we Negroes know perfectly well, and ought to know even better than most, that America is not a successful democracy and that until it is, it is going to drag down the world. This nation is ruled by corporate wealth to a degree which is frightening. One thousand persons own the United States and their power outweighs the voice of the mass of American citizens. This must be cured, not by revolution, not by war and violence, but by reason and knowledge.

Most of the world is today turning toward the welfare state; turning against the idea of production for individual profit toward the idea of production for use and for the welfare of the mass of citizens. No matter how difficult such a course is, it is the only course that is going to save the world and this we American Negroes have got to realize.

We may find it easy now to get publicity, reward, and attention by going along with the reactionary propaganda and war hysteria which is convulsing this nation, but in the long run America will not thank its black children if they help it go the wrong way, or retard its progress.

23

Racial Formation

Michael Omi and Howard Winant

IN 1983 SUSIE GUILLORY PHIPPS UNSUCCESS-fully sued the Louisiana Bureau of Vital Records to change her racial classification from black to white. The descendant of an 18th-century white planter and a black slave, Phipps was designated "black" in her birth certificate in accordance with a 1970 state law which declared anyone with at least 1/32nd "Negro blood" to be black.

The Phipps case raised intriguing questions about the concept of race, its meaning in contemporary society, and its use (and abuse) in public policy. Assistant Attorney General Ron Davis defended the law by pointing out that some type of racial classification was necessary to comply with federal record-keeping requirements and to facili-

tate programs for the prevention of genetic diseases. Phipps's attorney, Brian Begue, argued that the assignment of racial categories on birth certificates was unconstitutional and that the 1/32nd designation was inaccurate. He called on a retired Tulane University professor who cited research indicating that most Louisiana whites have at least 1/20th "Negro" ancestry.

In the end, Philpps lost. The court upheld the state's right to classify and quantify racial identity.[1]

Phipps's problematic racial identity, and her effort to resolve it through state action, is in many ways a parable of America's unsolved racial dilemma. It illustrates the difficulties of defining race and assigning individuals or groups to racial categories. It shows how the racial legacies of the past—slavery and bigotry—continue to shape the present. It reveals both the deep involvement of the state in the organization and interpretation of race, and the inadequacy of state institutions to carry out these functions. It demonstrates how deeply Americans both as individuals and as a civilization are shaped, and indeed haunted, by race.

From *Racial Formation in the United States: From the 1960s to the 1990s*, Second Edition, by Michael Omi and Howard Winant. Copyright © 1994 by Michael Omi and Howard Winant. Reproduced by permission of Taylor & Francis, Inc., Routledge, Inc., http://www.routledge-ny.com.

Having lived her whole life thinking that she was white, Phipps suddenly discovers that by legal definition she is not. In U.S. society, such an event is indeed catastrophic.[2] But if she is not white, of what race is she? The *state* claims that she is black, based on its rules of classification,[3] and another state agency, the court, upholds this judgment. But despite these classificatory standards which have imposed an either-or logic on racial identity, Phipps will not in fact "change color." Unlike what would have happened during slavery times if one's claim to whiteness was successfully challenged, we can assume that despite the outcome of her legal challenge, Phipps will remain in most of the social relationships she had occupied before the trial. Her socialization, her familial and friendship networks, her cultural orientation, will not change. She will simply have to wrestle with her newly acquired "hybridized" condition. She will have to confront the "Other" within.

The designation of racial categories and the determination of racial identity is no simple task. For centuries, this question has precipitated intense debates and conflicts, particularly in the U.S.—disputes over natural and legal rights, over the distribution of resources, and indeed, over who shall live and who shall die.

A crucial dimension of the Phipps case is that it illustrates the inadequacy of claims that race is a mere matter of variations in human physiognomy, that it is simply a matter of skin color. But if race cannot be understood in this manner, how *can* it be understood? We cannot fully hope to address this topic—no less than the meaning of race, its role in society, and the forces which shape it—in one chapter, nor indeed in one book. Our goal in this chapter, however, is far from modest: we wish to offer at least the outlines of a theory of race and racism.

WHAT IS RACE?

There is a continuous temptation to think of race as an *essence*, as something fixed, concrete, and objective. And there is also an opposite temptation: to imagine race as a mere *illusion*, a purely ideological construct which some ideal non-racist social order would eliminate. It is necessary to challenge both these positions, to disrupt and reframe the rigid and bipolar manner in which they are posed and debated, and to transcend the presumably irreconcilable relationship between them.

The effort must be made to understand race as an unstable and "decentered" complex of social meanings constantly being transformed by political struggle. With this in mind, let us propose a definition: *race is a concept which signifies and symbolizes social conflicts and interests by referring to different types of human bodies.* Although the concept of race invokes biologically based human characteristics (so-called "phenotypes"), selection of these particular human features for purposes of racial signification is always and necessarily a social and historical process. In contrast to the other major distinction of this type, that of gender, there is no biological basis for distinguishing among human groups along the lines of race.[4] Indeed, the categories employed to differentiate among human groups along racial lines reveal themselves, upon serious examination, to be at best imprecise, and at worst completely arbitrary.

If the concept of race is so nebulous, can we not dispense with it? Can we not "do without" race, at least in the "enlightened" present? This question has been posed often, and with greater frequency in recent years.[5] An affirmative answer would of course present obvious practical difficulties: it is rather difficult to jettison widely held beliefs, beliefs which moreover are central to everyone's identity and understanding of the social world. So the attempt to banish the concept as an archaism is at best counterintuitive. But a deeper difficulty, we believe, is inherent in the very formulation of this schema, in its way of posing race as a *problem*, a misconception left over from the past, and suitable now only for the dustbin of history.

A more effective starting point is the recognition that despite its uncertainties and contradictions, the concept of race continues to play a fundamental role in structuring and representing the social world. The task for theory is to explain this situation. It is to avoid both the utopian framework which sees race as an illusion we can somehow "get beyond," and also the essentialist formulation which sees race as something objective and fixed, a biological datum.[6] Thus we should think of race as an element of social structure rather than as an irregularity within it; we should see race as a dimension of human representation rather than as an illusion. These perspectives inform the theoretical approach we call racial formation.

RACIAL FORMATION

We define *racial formation* as the sociohistorical process by which racial categories are created, inhabited, transformed, and destroyed. Our attempt to elaborate a theory of racial formation will proceed in two steps. First, we argue that racial formation is a process of historically situated *projects* in which human bodies and social structures are represented and organized. Next we link racial formation to the evolution of hegemony, the way in which society is organized and ruled. Such an approach, we believe, can facilitate understanding of a whole range of contemporary controversies and dilemmas involving race, including the nature of racism, the relationship of race to other forms of differences, inequalities, and oppression such as sexism and nationalism, and the dilemmas of racial identity today.

From a racial formation perspective, race is a matter of both social structure and cultural representation. Too often, the attempt is made to understand race simply or primarily in terms of only one of these two analytical dimensions.[7] For example, efforts to explain racial inequality as a purely social structural phenomenon are unable to account for the origins, patterning, and transformation of racial difference.

Conversely, many examinations of racial difference—understood as a matter of cultural attributes *à la* ethnicity theory, or as a society-wide

signification system, *à la* some poststructuralist accounts—cannot comprehend such structural phenomena as racial stratification in the labor market or patterns of residential segregation.

An alternative approach is to think of racial formation processes as occurring through a linkage between structure and representation. Racial *projects* do the ideological "work" of making these links. *A racial project is simultaneously an interpretation, representation, or explanation of racial dynamics, and an effort to reorganize and redistribute resources along particular racial lines.* Racial projects connect what race *means* in a particular discursive practice and the ways in which both social structures and everyday experiences are racially *organized*, based upon that meaning. Let us consider this proposition, first in terms of large-scale or macro-level social processes, and then in terms of other dimensions of the racial formation process.

Racial Formation as a Macro-Level Social Process

To *interpret the meaning of race is to frame it socially structurally.* Consider for example, this statement by Charles Murray on welfare reform:

My proposal for dealing with the racial issue in social welfare is to repeal every bit of legislation and reverse every court decision that in any way requires, recommends, or awards differential treatment according to race, and thereby put us back onto the track that we left in 1965. We may argue about the appropriate limits of government intervention in trying to enforce the ideal, but at least it should be possible to identify the ideal: Race is not a morally admissible reason for treating one person differently from another. Period.[8]

Here there is a partial but significant analysis of the meaning of race: it is not a morally valid basis upon which to treat people "differently from one another." We may notice someone's race, but we cannot act upon that awareness. We must act in a "color-blind" fashion. This analysis of the meaning of race is immediately linked to a specific conception of the role of race in the social structure: it can play no part in government action, save in "the enforcement of the ideal." No state policy can legitimately require, recommend, or award different status according to race. This example can be classified as a particular type of racial project in the present-day U.S.—a "neoconservative" one.

Conversely, *to recognize the racial dimension in social structure is to interpret the meaning of race.* Consider the following statement by the late Supreme Court Justice Thurgood Marshall on minority "set-aside" programs:

A profound difference separates governmental actions that themselves are racist, and governmental actions that seek to remedy the effects of prior racism or to prevent neutral government activity from perpetuating the effects of such racism.[9]

Here the focus is on the racial dimensions of *social structure*—in this case of state activity and policy. The argument is that state actions in the past and present have treated people in very different ways according to their race, and thus the government cannot retreat from its policy responsibilities in this area. It cannot suddenly declare itself "color-blind" without in fact perpetuating the same type of differential, racist treatment.[10] Thus, race continues to signify difference and structure inequality. Here, racialized social structure is immediately linked to an interpretation of the meaning of race. This example too can be classified as a particular type of racial project in the present-day U.S.—a "liberal" one.

To be sure, such political labels as "neoconservative" or "liberal" cannot fully capture the complexity of racial projects, for these are always multiply determined, politically contested, and deeply shaped by their historical context. Thus, encapsulated within the neoconservative example cited here are certain egalitarian commitments which derive from a previous historical context in which they played a very different role, and which are rearticulated in neoconservative racial discourse precisely to oppose a more open-ended, more capacious conception of the meaning of equality. Similarly, in the liberal example, Justice

Marshall recognizes that the contemporary state, which was formerly the architect of segregation and the chief enforcer of racial difference, has a tendency to reproduce those patterns of inequality in a new guise. Thus he admonishes it (in dissent, significantly) to fulfill its responsibilities to uphold a robust conception of equality. These particular instances, then, demonstrate how racial projects are always concretely framed, and thus are always contested and unstable. The social structures they uphold or attack, and the representations of race they articulate, are never invented out of the air, but exist in a definite historical context, having descended from previous conflicts. This contestation appears to be permanent in respect to race.

These two examples of contemporary racial projects are drawn from mainstream political debate; they may be characterized as center-right and center-left expressions of contemporary racial politics.[11] We can, however, expand the discussion of racial formation processes far beyond these familiar examples. In fact, we can identify racial projects in at least three other analytical dimensions: first, the political spectrum can be broadened to include radical projects, on both the left and right, as well as along other political axes. Second, analysis of racial projects can take place not only at the macro-level of racial policy-making, state activity, and collective action, but also at the micro-level of everyday experience. Third, the concept of racial projects can be applied across historical time, to identify racial formation dynamics in the past. We shall now offer examples of each of these types of racial projects.

The Political Spectrum of Racial Formation

We have encountered examples of a neoconservative racial project, in which the significance of race is denied, leading to a "color-blind" racial politics and "hands off" policy orientation; and of a "liberal" racial project, in which the significance of race is affirmed, leading to an egalitarian and "activist" state policy. But these by no means exhaust the political possibilities. Other racial projects can be readily identified on the contemporary U.S.

scene. For example, "far right" projects, which uphold biologistic and racist views of difference, explicitly argue for white supremacist policies. "New right" projects overtly claim to hold "color-blind" views, but covertly manipulate racial fears in order to achieve political gains.[12] On the left, "radical democratic" projects invoke notions of racial "difference" in combination with egalitarian politics and policy.

Further variations can also be noted. For example, "nationalist" projects, both conservative and radical, stress the incompatibility of racially defined group identity with the legacy of white supremacy, and therefore advocate a social structural solution of separation, either complete or partial.[13] . . . Nationalist currents represent a profound legacy of the centuries of racial absolutism that initially defined the meaning of race in the U.S. Nationalist concerns continue to influence racial debate in the form of Afrocentrism and other expressions of identity politics.

Taking the range of politically organized racial projects as a whole, we can "map" the current pattern of racial formation at the level of the public sphere, the "macro-level" in which public debate and mobilization takes place.[14] But important as this is, the terrain on which racial formation occurs is broader yet.

Racial Formation as Everyday Experience

At the micro-social level, racial projects also link signification and structure, not so much as efforts to shape policy or define large-scale meaning, but as the applications of "common sense." To see racial projects operating at the level of everyday life, we have only to examine the many ways in which, often unconsciously, we "notice" race.

One of the first things we notice about people when we meet them (along with their sex) is their race. We utilize race to provide clues about *who* a person is. This fact is made painfully obvious when we encounter someone whom we cannot conveniently racially categorize—someone who is, for example, racially "mixed" or of an ethnic/racial group we are not familiar with. Such an encounter becomes a source of discomfort and momentarily a crisis of racial meaning.

Our ability to interpret racial meanings depends on preconceived notions of a racialized social structure. Comments such as, "Funny, you don't look black," betray an underlying image of what black should be. We expect people to act out their apparent racial identities; indeed we become disoriented when they do not. The black banker harassed by police while walking in casual clothes through his own well-off neighborhood, the Latino or white kid rapping in perfect Afro patois, the unending *faux pas* committed by whites who assume that the non-whites they encounter are servants or tradespeople, the belief that non-white colleagues are less qualified persons hired to fulfill affirmative action guidelines, indeed the whole gamut of racial stereotypes—that "white men can't jump," that Asians can't dance, etc., etc.—all testify to the way a racialized social structure shapes racial experience and conditions meaning. Analysis of such stereotypes reveals the always present, already active link between our view of the social structure—its demography, its laws, its customs, its threats—and our conception of what race means.

Conversely, our ongoing interpretation of our experience in racial terms shapes our relations to the institutions and organizations through which we are imbedded in social structure. Thus we expect differences in skin color, or other racially coded characteristics, to explain social differences. Temperament, sexuality, intelligence, athletic ability, aesthetic preferences, and so on are presumed to be fixed and discernible from the palpable mark of race. Such diverse questions as our confidence and trust in others (for example, clerks or salespeople, media figures, neighbors), our sexual preferences and romantic images, our tastes in music, films, dance, or sports, and our very ways of talking, walking, eating, and dreaming become racially coded simply because we live in a society where racial awareness is so pervasive. Thus in ways too comprehensive even to monitor consciously, and despite periodic calls—neoconservative and otherwise—for us to ignore race and adopt "color-blind" racial attitudes, skin color "differences" continue to rationalize distinct treatment of racially identified individuals and groups.

To summarize the argument so far: the theory of racial formation suggests that society is suffused with racial projects, large and small, to which all are subjected. This racial "subjection" is quintessentially ideological. Everybody learns some combination, some version, of the rules of racial classification, and of her own racial identity, often without obvious teaching or conscious inculcation. Thus are we inserted in a comprehensively racialized social structure. Race becomes "common sense"—a way of comprehending, explaining, and acting in the world. A vast web of racial projects mediates between the discursive or representational means in which race is identified and signified on the one hand, and the institutional and organizational forms in which it is routinized and standardized on the other. These projects are the heart of the racial formation process.

Under such circumstances, it is not possible to represent race discursively without simultaneously locating it, explicitly or implicitly, in a social structural (and historical) context. Nor is it possible to organize, maintain, or transform social structures without simultaneously engaging, once more either explicitly or implicitly, in racial signification. Racial formation, therefore, is a kind of synthesis, an outcome, of the interaction of racial projects on a society-wide level. These projects are, of course, vastly different in scope and effect. They include large-scale public action, state activities, and interpretations of racial conditions in artistic, journalistic, or academic fora,[15] as well as the seemingly infinite number of racial judgments and practices we carry out at the level of individual experience.

Since racial formation is always historically situated, our understanding of the significance of race, and of the way race structures society, has changed enormously over time. The processes of racial formation we encounter today, the racial projects large and small which structure U.S. society in so many ways, are merely the present-day outcomes of a complex historical evolution. The contemporary racial order remains transient. By knowing something of how it evolved, we can perhaps better discern where it is heading.

NOTES

1. *San Francisco Chronicle*, 14 September 1982, 19 May 1983. Ironically, the 1970 Louisiana law was enacted to supersede an old Jim Crow statute which relied on the idea of "common report" in determining an infant's race. Following Phipps' unsuccessful attempt to change her classification and have the law declared unconstitutional, a legislative effort arose which culminated in the repeal of the law. See *San Francisco Chronicle*, 23 June 1983.

2. Compare the Phipps case to Andrew Hacker's well-known "parable" in which a white person is informed by a mysterious official that "the organization he represents has made a mistake" and that ". . . [a]ccording to their records . . . , you were to have been born black: to another set of parents, far from where you were raised." How much compensation, Hacker's official asks, would "you" require to undo the damage of this unfortunate error? See Hacker, *Two Nations: Black and White, Separate, Hostile, Unequal* (New York: Charles Scribner's Sons, 1992) pp. 31–32.

3. On the evolution of Louisiana's racial classification system, see Virginia Dominguez, *White By Definition: Social Classification in Creole Louisiana* (New Brunswick, NJ: Rutgers University Press, 1986).

4. This is not to suggest that gender is a biological category while race is not. Gender, like race, is a social construct. However, the biological division of humans into sexes—two at least, and possibly intermediate ones as well—is not in dispute. This provides a basis for argument over gender divisions—how "natural," etc.—which does not exist with regard to race. To ground an argument

for the "natural" existence of race, one must resort to philosophical anthropology.

5. "The truth is that there are no races, there is nothing in the world that can do all we ask race to do for us. . . . The evil that is done is done by the concept, and by easy—yet impossible—assumptions as to its application." (Kwame Anthony Appiah, *In My Father's House: Africa in the Philosophy of Culture* [New York: Oxford University Press, 1992].) Appiah's eloquent and learned book fails, in our view, to dispense with the race concept, despite its anguished attempt to do so; this indeed is the source of its author's anguish. We agree with him as to the non-objective character of race, but fail to see how this recognition justifies its abandonment. This argument is developed below.

6. We understand essentialism as *belief in real, true human, essences, existing outside or impervious to social and historical context*. We draw this definition, with some small modifications, from Diana Fuss, *Essentially Speaking: Feminism, Nature, & Difference* (New York: Routledge, 1989) p. xi.

7. Michael Omi and Howard Winant, "On the Theoretical Status of the Concept of Race" in Warren Crichlow and Cameron McCarthy, eds., *Race, Identity, and Representation in Education* (New York: Routledge, 1993).

8. Charles Murray, *Losing Ground: American Social Policy, 1950–1980* (New York: Basic Books, 1984) p. 223.

9. Justice Thurgood Marshall, dissenting in *City of Richmond v. J. A. Croson Co.*, 488 U.S. 469 (1989).

10. See, for example, Derrick Bell, "Remembrances of Racism Past: Getting Past the Civil Rights Decline," in Herbert Hill and James E. Jones, Jr., eds., *Race in America: The Struggle for Equality* (Madison: The University of Wisconsin Press, 1993) pp. 75–76; Gertrude Ezorsky, *Racism and Justice: The Case for Affirmative Action* (Ithaca: Cornell University Press, 1991) pp. 109–111; David Kairys, *With Liberty and Justice for Some: A Critique of the Conservative Supreme Court* (New York: The New Press, 1993) pp. 138–41.

11. Howard Winant has developed a tentative "map" of the system of racial hegemony in the U.S. circa 1990, which focuses on the spectrum of racial projects running from the political right to the political left. See Winant, "Where Culture Meets Structure: Race in the 1990s," in idem, *Racial Conditions: Politics, Theory, Comparisons* (Minneapolis: University of Minnesota Press, 1994).

12. A familiar example is use of racial "code words." Recall George Bush's manipulations of racial fear in the 1988 "Willie Horton" ads, or Jesse Helms's use of the coded term "quota" in his 1990 campaign against Harvey Gantt.

13. From this perspective, far right racial projects can also be interpreted as "nationalist." See Ronald Walters, "White Racial Nationalism in the United States," *Without Prejudice* Vol. 1, no. 1 (Fall 1987).

14. To be sure, any effort to divide racial formation patterns according to social structural location—"macro" vs. "micro," for example—is necessarily an analytic device. In the concrete, there is no such dividing line. See Winant, "Where Culture Meets Structure."

15. We are not unaware, for example, that publishing this work is in itself a racial project.

24

Optional Ethnicities

For Whites Only?

Mary C. Waters

WHAT DOES IT MEAN TO TALK ABOUT ETHNIC-ity as an option for an individual? To argue that an individual has some degree of choice in their ethnic identity flies in the face of the common sense notion of ethnicity many of us believe in— that one's ethnic identity is a fixed characteristic, reflective of blood ties and given at birth. However, social scientists who study ethnicity have long concluded that while ethnicity is based on a *belief* in a common ancestry, ethnicity is primarily a *social* phenomenon, not a biological one (Alba 1985, 1990; Barth 1969; Weber [1921] 1968, p. 389). The belief that members of an ethnic group have that they share a common ancestry may not be a fact. There is a great deal of change in ethnic identities across generations through intermarriage, changing allegiances, and changing social categories. There is also a much larger amount of change in the identities of individuals over their lives than is commonly believed. While most people are aware of the phenomenon known as "passing"—people raised as one race who change at some point and claim a different race as their identity—there are similar life course changes in ethnicity that happen all the time and are not given the same degree of attention as "racial passing."

From Silvia Pedraza and Rubén G. Rumbaut, eds. *Origins and Destinies: Immigration, Race and Ethnicity in America* (Belmmont, CA: Wadsworth, 1996), pp. 444–54. Reprinted by permission.

White Americans of European ancestry can be described a having a great deal of choice in terms of their ethnic identities. The two major types of options White Americans can exercise are (1) the option of whether to claim any specific ancestry, or to just be "White" or American, [Lieberson (1985) called these people "unhyphenated Whites"] and (2) the choice of which of their European ancestries to choose to include in their description of their own identities. In both cases, the option of choosing how to present yourself on surveys and in everyday social interactions exists for Whites because of social changes and societal conditions that have created a great deal of social mobility, immigrant assimilation, and political and economic power for Whites in the United states. Specifically, the option of being able to not claim any ethnic identity exists for Whites of European background in the United States because they are the majority group—in terms of holding political and social power, as well as being a numerical majority. The option of choosing among different ethnicities in their family backgrounds exists because the degree of discrimination and social distance attached to specific European backgrounds has diminished over time. . . .

SYMBOLIC ETHNICITIES FOR WHITE AMERICANS

What do these ethnic identities mean to people and why do they cling to them rather than just abandoning the tie and calling themselves American? My own field research with suburban Whites in California and Pennsylvania found that later-generation descendants of European origin maintain what are called "symbolic ethnicities." *Symbolic ethnicity is a term coined by Herbert Gans* (1979) to refer to ethnicity that is individualistic in nature and without real social cost for the individual. These symbolic identifications are essentially leisure-time activities, rooted in nuclear family traditions and reinforced by the voluntary enjoyable aspects of being ethnic (Waters 1990). Richard Alba (1990) also found later-generation Whites in Albany, New York, who chose to keep a tie with an ethnic identity because of the enjoyable and voluntary aspects to those identities, along with the feelings of specialness they entailed. An example of symbolic ethnicity is individuals who identify as Irish, for example, on occasions such as Saint Patrick's Day, on family holidays, or for vacations. They do not usually belong to Irish American organizations, live in Irish neighborhoods, work in Irish jobs, or marry other Irish people. The symbolic meaning of being Irish American can be constructed by individuals from mass media images, family traditions, or other intermittent social activities. In other words, for later-generation White ethnics, ethnicity is not something that influences their lives unless they want it to. In the world of work and school and neighborhood, individuals do not have to admit to being ethnic unless they choose to. And for an increasing number of European-origin individuals whose parents and grandparents have intermarried, the ethnicity they claim is largely a matter of personal choice as they sort through all of the possible combinations of groups in their genealogies. . . .

RACE RELATIONS AND SYMBOLIC ETHNICITY

However much symbolic ethnicity is without cost for the individual, there is a cost associated with symbolic ethnicity for the society. That is because symbolic ethnicities of the type described here are confined to White Americans of European origin.

Black Americans, Hispanic Americans, Asian Americans, and American Indians do not have the option of a symbolic ethnicity at present in the United States. For all of the ways in which ethnicity does not matter for White Americans, it does matter for non-Whites. Who your ancestors are does affect your choice of spouse, where you live, what job you have, who your friends are, and what your chances are for success in American society, if those ancestors happen not to be from Europe. The reality is that White ethnics have a lot more choice and room for maneuver than they themselves think they do. The situation is very different for members of racial minorities, whose lives are strongly influenced by their race or national origin regardless of how much they may choose not to identify themselves in terms of their ancestries.

When White Americans learn the stories of how their grandparents and great-grandparents triumphed in the United States over adversity, they are usually told in terms of their individual efforts and triumphs. The important role of labor unions and other organized political and economic factors in their social and economic successes are left out of the story in favor of a generational story of individual Americans rising up against communitarian, Old World intolerance, and New World resistance. As a result, the "individualized" voluntary, cultural view of ethnicity for whites is what is remembered.

One important implication of these identities is that they tend to be very individualistic. There is a tendency to view valuing diversity in a pluralist environment as equating all groups. The symbolic ethnic tends to think that all groups are equal; everyone has a background that is their right to celebrate and pass on to their children. This leads to the conclusion that all identities are equal and all identities in some sense are interchangeable—"I'm Italian American, you're Polish American. I'm Irish American, you're African American." The important thing is to treat people as individuals and all equally. However, this assumption ignores the very big difference between an individualistic symbolic ethnic identity and a socially enforced and imposed racial identity.

My favorite example of how this type of thinking can lead to some severe misunderstandings between people of different backgrounds is from the *Dear Abby* advise column. A few years back a person wrote in who had asked an acquaintance of Asian background where his family was from. His acquaintance answered that this was a rude question and he would not reply. The bewildered White asked Abby why it was rude, since he thought it was a sign of respect to wonder where people were from, and he certainly would not mind anyone asking HIM about where his family was from. Abby asked her readers to write in to say whether it was rude to ask about a person's ethnic background. She reported that she got a large response, that most non-Whites thought it was a sign of disrespect, and Whites thought it was flattering:

Dear Abby,

I am 100 percent American and because I am of Asian ancestry I am often asked "What are you" It's not the personal nature of this question that bothers me it's the question itself. This query seems to question my very humanity. "What am I? Why I am a person like everyone else!"

Signed, A REAL AMERICAN

Dear Abby,

Why do people resent being asked what they are? The Irish are so proud of being Irish, they tell you before you even ask. Tip O'Neill has never tried to hide his Irish ancestry.

Signed, JIMMY

In this exchange Jimmy cannot understand why Asians are not as happy to be asked about their ethnicity as he is, because he understands his ethnicity and theirs to be separate but equal. Everyone has to come from somewhere—his family from Ireland, another's family from Asia—each has a history and each should be proud of it. But the reason he cannot understand the perspective of the Asian American is that all ethnicities are not equal; all are not symbolic, costless, and voluntary. When White Americans equate their own symbolic ethnicities with the socially enforced identities of non-White Americans, they obscure the fact that the experiences of Whites and non-Whites have been qualitatively different in the United States and that the current identities of individuals partly reflect that unequal history.

In the next section I describe how relations between Black and White students on college campuses reflect some of these asymmetries in the understanding of what a racial or ethnic identity means. While I focus on Black and White students in the following discussion, you should be aware that the myriad other groups in the United States—Mexican Americans, American Indians, Japanese Americans—all have some degree of social and individual influences on their identities, which reflect the group's social and economic history and present circumstance.

RELATIONS ON COLLEGE CAMPUSES

Both Black and White students face the task of developing their race and ethnic identities. Sociologists and psychologists note that at the time people leave home and begin to live independently from their parents, often ages eighteen to twenty-two, they report a heightened sense of racial and ethnic identity as they sort through how much of their beliefs and behaviors are idiosyncratic to their families and how much are shared with other people. It is not until one comes in close contact with many people who are different from oneself that individuals realize the ways in which their backgrounds may influence their individual personality. This involves coming into contact with people who are different in terms of their ethnicity, class, religion, region, and race. For White students, the ethnicity they claim is more often than not a symbolic one—with all of the voluntary, enjoyable, and intermittent characteristics I have described above.

Black students at the university are also developing identities through interactions with others who are different from them. Their identity development is more complicated than that of Whites because of the added element of racial discrimination and racism, along with the "ethnic" developments of finding others who share their background. Thus Black students have the positive attraction of being around other Black students who share some cultural elements, as well as the need to band together with other students in a reactive and oppositional way in the face of racist incidents on campus.

Colleges and universities across the country have been increasing diversity among their student bodies in the last few decades. This has led in many cases to strained relations among students from different racial and ethnic backgrounds. The 1980s and 1990s produced a great number of racial incidents and high racial tensions on campuses. While there were a number of racial incidents that were due to bigotry, unlawful behavior, and violent or vicious attacks, much of what happens among students on campuses involves a low level of tension and awkwardness in social interactions.

Many Black students experience racism personally for the first time on campus. The upper-middle-class students from White suburbs were often isolated enough that their presence was not threatening to racists in their high schools. Also, their class background was known by their residence and this may have prevented attacks being directed at them. Often Black students at the university who begin talking with other students and recognizing racial slights will remember incidents that happened to them earlier that they might not have thought were related to race.

Black college students across the country experience a sizable number of incidents that are clearly the result of racism. Many of the most blatant ones that occur between students are the result of drinking. Sometimes late at night, drunken groups of White students coming home from parties will yell slurs at single Black students on the street. The other types of incidents that happen include being singled out for special treatment by employees, such as being followed when shopping at the campus bookstore, or going to the art museum with your class and the guard stops you and asks for your I.D. Others involve impersonal encounters on the street—being called a nigger by a

truck driver while crossing the street, or seeing old ladies clutch their pocketbooks and shake in terror as you pass them on the street. For the most part these incidents are not specific to the university environment, they are the types of incidents middle-class Blacks face every day throughout American society, and they have been documented by sociologists (Feagin 1991).

In such a climate, however, with students experiencing these types of incidents and talking with each other about them, Black students do experience a tension and a feeling of being singled out. It is unfair that this is part of their college experience and not that of White students. Dealing with incidents like this, or the ever-present threat of such incidents, is an ongoing developmental task for Black students that takes energy, attention, and strength of character. It should be clearly understood that this is an asymmetry in the "college experience" for Black and White students. It is one of the unfair aspects of life that results from living in a society with ongoing racial prejudice and discrimination. It is also very understandable that it makes some students angry at the unfairness of it all, even if there is no one to blame specifically. It is also very troubling because, while most Whites do not create these incidents, some do, and it is never clear until you know someone well whether they are the type of person who could do something like this. So one of the reactions of Black students to these incidents is to band together.

In some sense then, as Blauner (1992) has argued, you can see Black students coming together on campus as both an "ethnic" pull of wanting to be together to share common experiences and community, and a "racial" push of banding together defensively because of perceived rejection and tension from Whites. In this way the ethnic identities of Black students are in some sense similar to, say, Korean students wanting to be together to share experiences. And it is an ethnicity that is generally much stronger than, say, Italian Americans. But for Koreans who come together there is generally a definition of themselves as "different from" Whites. For Blacks reacting to exclusion, there is a tendency for the coming together to involve both being "different from" but also "opposed to" Whites.

The anthropologist John Ogbu (1990) has documented the tendency of minorities in a variety of societies around the world, who have experienced severe blocked mobility for long periods of time, to develop such oppositional identities. An important component of having such an identity is to describe others of your group who do not join in the group solidarity as devaluing and denying their very core identity. This is why it is not common for successful Asians to be accused by others of "acting White" in the United States, but it is quite common for such a term to be used by Blacks and Latinos. The oppositional component of a Black identity also explains how Black people can question whether others are acting "Black enough." On campus, it explains some of the intense pressures felt by Black students who do not make their racial identity central and who choose to hang out primarily with non-Blacks. This pressure from the group, which is partly defining itself by not being White, is exacerbated by the fact that race is a physical marker in American society. No one immediately notices the Jewish students sitting together in the dining hall, or the one Jewish student sitting surrounded by non-Jews, or the Texan sitting with the Californians, but everyone notices the Black student who is or is not at the "Black table" in the cafeteria.

An example of the kinds of misunderstandings that can arise because of different understandings of the meanings and implications of symbolic versus oppositional identities concerns questions students ask one another in the dorms about personal appearances and customs. A very common type of interaction in the dorm concerns questions Whites ask Blacks about their hair. Because Whites tend to know little about Blacks, and Blacks know a lot about Whites, there is a general asymmetry in the level of curiosity people have about one another. Whites, as the numerical majority, have had little contact with Black culture; Blacks, especially whose who are in college, have

had to develop bicultural skills—knowledge about the social worlds of both Whites and Blacks. Miscommunication and hurt feelings about White students' questions about Black students' hair illustrate this point. One of the things that happens freshman year is that White students are around Black students as they fix their hair. White students are generally quite curious about Black students' hair—they have basic questions such as how often Blacks wash their hair, how they get it straightened or curled, what products they use on their hair, how they comb it, etc. Whites often wonder to themselves whether they should ask these questions. One thought experiment Whites perform is to ask themselves whether a particular question would upset them. Adopting the "do unto others" rule, they ask themselves, "If a Black person was curious about my hair would I get upset?" The answer usually is "No, I would be happy to tell them." Another example is an Italian American student wondering to herself, "Would I be upset if someone asked me about calamari?" The answer is no, so she asks her Black roommate about collard greens, and the roommate explodes with an angry response such as, "Do you think all Black people eat watermelon too?" Note that if this Italian American knew her friend was Trinidadian American and asked about peas and rice the situation would be more similar and would not necessarily ignite underlying tensions.

Like the debate in *Dear Abby*, these innocent questions are likely to lead to resentment. The issue of stereotypes about Black Americans and the assumption that all Blacks are alike and have the same stereotypical cultural traits has more power to hurt or offend a Black person than vice versa. The innocent questions about Black hair also bring up a number of asymmetries between the Black and White experience. Because Blacks tend to have more knowledge about Whites than vice versa, there is not an even exchange going on, the Black freshman is likely to have fewer basic questions about his White roommate than his White roommate has about him. Because of the differences historically in the group experiences of

Blacks and Whites there are some connotations to Black hair that don't exist about White hair. (For instance, is straightening your hair a form of assimilation, do some people distinguish between women having "good hair" and "bad hair" in terms of beauty and how is that related to looking "White"?) Finally, even a Black freshman who cheerfully disregards or is unaware that there are these asymmetries will soon slam into another asymmetry if she willingly answers every innocent question asked of her. In a situation where Blacks make up only 10 percent of the student body, if every non-Black needs to be educated about hair, she will have to explain it to nine other students. As one Black student explained to me, after you've been asked a couple of times about something so personal you begin to feel like you are an attraction in a zoo, that you are at the university for the education of the White students.

INSTITUTIONAL RESPONSES

Our society asks a lot of young people. We ask young people to do something that no one else does as successfully on such a wide scale—that is to live together with people from very different backgrounds, to respect one another, to appreciate one another, and to enjoy and learn from one another. The successes that occur every day in this endeavor are many, and they are too often overlooked. However, the problems and tensions are also real, and they will not vanish on their own. We tend to see pluralism working in the United States in much the same way some people expect capitalism to work. If you put together people with various interests and abilities and resources, the "invisible hand" of capitalism is supposed to make all the parts work together in an economy for the common good.

There is much to be said for such a model—the invisible hand of the market can solve complicated problems of production and distribution better than any "visible hand" of a state plan. However, we have learned that unequal power relations among the actors in the capitalist market-

place, as well as "externalities" that the market cannot account for, such as long-term pollution, or collusion between corporations, or the exploitation of child labor, means that state regulation is often needed. Pluralism and the relations between groups are very similar. There is a lot to be said for the idea that bringing people who belong to different ethnic or racial groups together in institutions with no interference will have good consequences. Students from different backgrounds will make friends if they share a dorm room or corridor, and there is no need for the institution to do any more than provide the locale. But like capitalism, the invisible hand of pluralism does not do well when power relations and externalities are ignored. When you bring together individuals from groups that are differentially valued in the wider society and provide no guidance, there will be problems. In these cases the "invisible hand" of pluralist relations does not work, and tensions and disagreements can arise without any particular individual or group of individuals being "to blame." On college campuses in the 1990s some of the tensions between students are of this sort. They arise from honest misunderstandings, lack of a common background, and very different experiences of what race and ethnicity mean to the individual.

The implications of symbolic ethnicities for thinking about race relations are subtle but consequential. If your understanding of your own ethnicity and its relationship to society and politics is one of individual choice, it becomes harder to understand the need for programs like affirmative action, which recognize the ongoing need for group struggle and group recognition, in order to bring about social change. It also is hard for a White college student to understand the need that minority students feel to band together against discrimination. It also is easy, on the individual level, to expect everyone else to be able to turn their ethnicity on and off at will, the way you are able to, without understanding that ongoing discrimination and social attention to minority status makes that impossible for individuals from minority groups to do. The paradox of symbolic ethnicity is that it depends upon the ultimate goal of a pluralist society, and at the same time makes it more difficult to achieve that ultimate goal. It is dependent upon the concept that all ethnicities mean the same thing, that enjoying the traditions of one's heritage is an option available to a group or an individual, but that such a heritage should not have any social costs associated with it.

As the Asian Americans who wrote to *Dear Abby* make clear, there are many societal issues and involuntary ascriptions associated with non-White identities. The developments necessary for this to change are not individual but societal in nature. Social mobility and declining racial and ethnic sensitivity are closely associated. The legacy and the present reality of discrimination on the basis of race or ethnicity must be overcome before the ideal of a pluralist society, where all heritages are treated equally and are equally available for individuals to choose or discard at will, is realized.

REFERENCES

Alba, Richard D. 1985. *Italian Americans: Into the Twilight of Ethnicity.* Englewood Cliffs, NJ: Prentice-Hall.

———. 1990. *Ethnic Identity: The Transformation of White America.* New Haven: Yale University Press.

Barth, Frederick. 1969. *Ethnic Groups and Boundaries.* Boston: Little, Brown.

Blauner, Robert. 1992 "Talking Past Each Other: Black and White Languages of Race." *American Prospect* (Summer): 55–64.

Feagin, Joe R. 1991. "The Continuing Significance of Race: Anti-Black Discrimination in Public Places." *American Sociological Review* 56: 101–17.

Gans, Herbert. 1979. "Symbolic Ethnicity: The Future of Ethnic Groups and Cultures in America." *Ethnic and Racial Studies* 2: 1–20.

Lieberson, Stanley. 1985. "Unhyphenated Whites in the United States." *Ethnic and Racial Studies* 8: 159–180.

Ogbu, John. 1990. "Minority Status and Literacy in Comparative Perspective." *Daedalus* 119: 141–69.

Waters, Mary C. 1990. *Ethnic Options: Choosing Identities in America.* Berkeley: University of California Press.

Weber, Max. [1921]/1968. *Economy and Society: An Outline of Interpretive Sociology*, Eds. Guenther Roth and Claus Wittich, trans. Ephraim Fischoff. New York: Bedminister Press.

25

Campaigning for Respect

Elijah Anderson

TYREE'S STORY*

Tyree is a young black man of fifteen, a high school student, and his story illustrates the intricacy of the rules of the code. Until recently, he lived in a poor section of South Philadelphia with his mother, Rose, a nurse's aide at a local hospital. Then their house burned down, and they lost much of what they owned. Tyree never knew his father, but his mother has had a number of boyfriends who have served as a male presence in his life. These men have come and gone, leaving a bit of themselves here and there. He has known Richard, a man who worked as a security guard; Reece, a parking lot attendant who sold drugs on the side; and Mike, who worked as a janitor at the hospital. Mike continues to come around, and at this point he is Tyree's mom's "main squeeze," the man with whom she keeps company the most. Tyree likes Mike the best. Mike has taken Tyree to Eagles games in the fall and Seventy-sixers games in the winter. Steady and decent, Mike has been most like a real father to Tyree.

After the fire Tyree and Rose moved in with his grandmother, who lives in Southwest Philadelphia, one of the most distressed neighborhoods in the city. Along Fifty-eighth in Southwest, a local staging area, small groups of teenage boys hang out, talking, milling, and passing the time. On the side of a dilapidated building is a graffiti memorial reading, "Barry, we love you, RIP." Particularly at night, prostitutes hustle their wares on the corners. A drug dealer hangs near the pay telephone, standing there as though this is his corner, which for all intents and purposes it is. Public, open-air drug marketing goes on here—in broad daylight or at night. Buyers, some with out-of-town license plates, stop their cars, seeming not to care who might be looking on. Some are white, others are black, but they have one thing in mind—to "cop" their drugs and go on about their business.

Drug dealing is big business here. The trade is carried out in public, but also in the homes of certain proprietors, who charge dealers to sell in the house and rent rooms to whores or johns who want to get "tightened up." There are also crack houses, where people simply go to buy or smoke their drugs. The neighbors are aware of this situation, but they are often demoralized, feeling there is little they can do about it. They sometimes call the police, but the police require proof that the place is what the neighbors know it to be. But such proof is not easy for the police to gather. It is sometimes easier, though frustrating, for the residents simply to "see but don't see," trying their best to ignore what is much more than a nuisance.

This is the neighborhood Tyree has moved into, and he has been here only a few days. His major concern at this point in his young life is "to get cool" with the boys who run the neighborhood. He refers to these boys as "bols." He refuses to call them boys. Part of this may have to do with

---

From *Code of the Street: Decency, Violence, and the Moral Life of the Inner City* by Elijah Anderson. Copyright © 1999 by Elijah Anderson. Used by permission of W. W. Norton and Comapany.

---

*This account of "Tyree's Story" is base on an extended ethnographic interview. It is dramatized in places to represent vividly the intricacies of the code of the street.

the fact that for so long the term "boy" was so demeaning that young black men replaced the term with one considered to be "cool" from the standpoint of the code. At any rate, Tyree says "bols," spelling it "b-o-l-s" and pronouncing it "bulls." A particular meaning of the term is "friend." On the streets of his new neighborhood, Tyree's biggest problem now is to get cool with these bols.

What does that entail? Here, as in almost any working-class to impoverished inner-city neighborhood, the bols are known to run the neighborhood. Tyree understands what the deal is. He used to run with the bols from his old neighborhood, where he himself was in charge, where he had established himself as a main bol of the neighborhood. The task before him now is to get to know the new bols—but also to allow them to get to know him. They must be able to take his "measure" up close, to see what he will or will not stand in his dealings with others, how much nerve and heart he possesses, whether he will defend what he claims is his. Tyree has a general idea of what he has to do here to survive or to have any semblance of a decent existence.

On Saturday, while his mom is at work, Tyree's grandmom quite innocently asks him to run to the store for her.

"Yeah, Grandmom. What you want?"

"I need a loaf of bread and a quart of milk."

Tyree dutifully takes the money and heads out the door. It is two o'clock on a nice, sunny afternoon. He leaves the house and begins to walk up the street toward the store. He can't help being somewhat tense, given his familiarity with the code of the street. He knows that eventually he will encounter the bols. And sure enough, after about five minutes, he spies about twenty bols walking up the street toward him. He sees them, and they see him. Their eyes meet. It is too late to turn back, for that would mean he would lose face, that he had acted scared, and his sense of manhood will not allow him to do that. He must face this situation.

As he approaches the bols, he feels himself tensing up even more, but he continues. As they come face-to-face, they stop and begin to talk. He knows they want to know what his business is. What is he doing here? Where does he come from? What gang is he from? Even before the questions are fully asked, Tyree tries to respond, "Well, uh, my grandmom, uh . . ." But the bols do not really want an answer. They want to roll on him (beat him up). Before he realizes it, the bols begin to punch him out, allowing most of the group to "get a piece." One boy punches—then another and another.

It is important to understand that these are almost ritual punches, with "good licks" and some kicking, pushing, and slapping "upside the head." Soon Tyree loses his balance and falls to the ground. "[This] really scared me," he said. Falling in such a fight is very risky, for then the worst can happen: someone "could really get messed up." There is an important distinction between rolling on someone and messing someone up. To roll is simply to take advantage of someone, to act as the aggressor in the fight. To mess someone up is actually to hurt him physically to the point where blood is spilled and he might have to go to the hospital. In this instance, the bols are not out to mess Tyree up.

The bols leave Tyree lying on the ground in a fetal position. As they move away, they smirk and say things like, "Who do he think he is?" and "We showed the motherfucker, think he gon' come up in here bigger than shit!" Tyree is bruised and hurt, but his pride is hurt much more than his body. For Tyree is a man, and it is extremely important not to let people do this to you. But there was really little that he could do to prevent this. He has been rolled on and utterly dissed. He is very angry, but also sad and dejected. He knows that they could have seriously hurt him. They wanted to put something on his mind, to show him whose turf this is. And Tyree understands the profound meaning of this incident, for he understands the code and has himself lived by it.

Tyree picks himself up and, without completing his errand, walks back to his grandmom's house with his head down. He is angry, for he has been violated. When he arrives at his grandmom's house, she says, "Where you been? Where are the groceries?" He mumbles a reply and goes to sit on the living room stairs and peer out the window. "What's wrong, boy?" she asks.

"Aw, nothin'," he says.

"Wha—you been fightin'?" she presses.

With this, he mumbles, "I met some bols."

"You hurt!? I'll call the police!" she exclaims.

"Naw, don't call the police."

"But you hurt."

"Don't call no police, I'll take care of it myself," he pleads.

This is something of a revelation to his grandmom. She hadn't known that the young men on the streets were this way, because she has never had Tyree with her for so long. She's an elderly woman, and old people are sometimes deferred to and protected by the same bols who violated Tyree. This is part of the code. She had never been aware that Tyree was so vulnerable, so she now worries about what to do.

Tyree goes to the bathroom to clean himself up. He showers and then sits and mopes around the house. He knows his grandmom still needs her groceries, and pretty soon, without saying a word, he leaves for the store. As he travels the distance to the store, he is somewhat edgy, circumspect, trying to watch his back, peeping around the corners and hoping to see any of the bols *before* they see him. He makes it up the two blocks to the store, walks in, and looks around. And over by the ice cream freezer he spies one of the bols who rolled on him earlier. The bol sees him. What does Tyree do now? Full of nerve, he rushes over to the bol and punches him in the face. Tyree gets in a couple of licks before the boy's nose begins to bleed, which was really all Tyree wanted to do; he wanted to pay him back, to let him know he has been punched and violated back. At that point the bol looks at Tyree and acknowledges aloud, "You got me that time, but I'll be back!"

Tyree looks in the bol's eyes and says, "Yeah, you and yo' mama." And with that he exits the store, without getting what he came for. He walks away. Tyree now feels good, as though he is getting his respect back.

With all the punches and hits, and particularly the public dissing he underwent at the hands of the bols, Tyree suffered a serious loss of respect. To settle scores as he did with the bol at the store is to begin to get his respect back. He retrieves self-esteem at the expense of another, in this case, the bol he publicly punched out. Tyree feels so good, in fact, that he walks (with some care) on to another store—through the turf of the bols—to get his grandmom's groceries. He buys what he wants and heads home carefully, watching out for the bols. Tyree feels under some obligation to punch out every bol he sees until he can avenge himself and regain his respect.

This is the code of the street. The code is not new. It is as old as the world, going back to Roman times or the world of the shogun warriors or the early American Old South.[1] And it can be observed in working-class Scotch-Irish or Italian or Hispanic communities. But profound economic dislocation and the simultaneous emergence of an underground economy that thrives on the "law of the jungle" implicit in the code have exacerbated conditions in many communities. Equally important, the proliferation and availability of guns have further exacerbated such conditions. Tyree could easily acquire a gun. Most of the young boys he knows from his old neighborhood know where they can get a gun without too much trouble.

Tyree arrives home with the groceries, and his grandmom is pleased. Although relieved that Tyree hasn't gotten into more trouble, she now has a new worry—how Tyree will get along with the young men of her neighborhood. She asks him more about his altercation, and he tries to assure her that he can take care of himself. But when he leaves the house, his grandmother worries, and this worry is shared by his mother. Increasingly, given the local news reports of street crime, shootings, and drugs, Tyree's mother questions her decision to move in with her own mother, although she really had little choice; the alternative would have been homelessness. Now Tyree spends much of his energy trying to persuade his mother and grandmother not to worry about him as he ventures outside in the streets. And while he tries to reassure them, he is really not very sure himself. For he knows that when he leaves the house he must watch his back.

The young men are very aware of Tyree's presence in the neighborhood; they are much more sensitive to the presence of interlopers than are the adults. (This fact is relevant to an understanding of Tyree's mother's and grandmother's ignorance of or indifference to the implications of their move into the new neighborhood.) When leaving home, Tyree steps from his house into the street and then looks up and down, trying to spot a bol before the bol spots him. His orientation is one of studied defensiveness. He wants to avoid contact with those who might be inclined to roll on him. He peeks around corners, travels through alleys, and basically does what he feels he must do—lie low.

There is pressure on Tyree to get cool with these bols, if only in the interest of safety. A few weeks later, on a Saturday afternoon, he is again walking down a street in his new neighborhood, heading to Center City to meet some friends from his old neighborhood. As he approaches the bus stop, he sees a group of bols coming up the street. They are about a block and a half away, and Tyree thus has a choice of running or staying. But something inside him—his concern about being manly, his quest to be defined as a person with nerve, heart, or simply street knowledge—makes him hesitate. They see him, and now it is too late. They know that he sees them. Now he can't run or dodge them; he must meet this situation head-on. Tyree must do what a man has to do. He knows he must deal with them, because the situation has been building for a while. He tenses up, for he feels caught in the wrong place, but he is unable to flee. He knows that if he runs today, he'll always be running. His manhood is on the line. Therefore he goes and meets the bols. But it is almost as though both parties have been expecting this day. He knew it was coming eventually. They knew it was com-

ing, and all the while they have been keeping tabs on him, maybe even keeping score on him, particularly noting the way he rolled on the bol in the convenience store (whose name he later found out was Tiny). This is a showdown.

As they come face-to-face, Tyree says, "What's up!"

They return his greeting, "Hey!" The situation is tense. Tyree says, "Look, y'all. I can't fight no twenty bols." There is a short silence. Then he says, "Can we be bols? Can I be bols with y'all?"

Summoned by Calvin, who seems to be the leader, the group huddles. A few talk to one another, while the others remain quiet. Calvin soon emerges and says, "You gotta fight J C." J C steps forward. He is about six one, eighteen years old, and weighs about 180 pounds. Though Tyree is daunted by the prospect of fighting J C, he tries not to display any signs of fear. He has been expecting to have to fight someone, and he has been dreading this for four weeks; he just didn't know how this would work out—when it would be, whom he would fight, or whether he could trust that others would not jump in. The showdown, therefore, is something of a relief. So he doesn't hesitate. He simply and quickly agrees, saying, "All right," trying to disabuse others of the notion that he is scared.

Calvin says, "Let's go behind this building." So the group of young men go behind a building on Walton Street for what promises to be a fair fight. Tyree is only five seven and weighs about 140 pounds, but he is muscular and quick, and he knows how to hold his hands in a pose to block any shots. J C does the same, and they begin to spar, dancing around, swinging now and then. Their eyes are riveted, following each other's every move. They watch each other's hands, looking for weaknesses and trying not to show any of their own. Much is at stake here. They spar and keep their eyes on each other but also on the audience that eggs them on. J C, of course, is the favorite, but Tyree seems not to care.

They begin to fight. Tyree lands the first punch to J C's midsection, breaking the tension. J C feints and swings at Tyree with a right cross.

Finally J C grabs Tyree and begins to pummel him. But Tyree hangs in there, swinging, punching, scratching, even biting. This is supposed to be a "fair fight," but the distinction soon gets blurred. J C is clearly getting the best of Tyree, and Tyree becomes increasingly angry, while feelings of humiliation loom. Yet, in addition to the nerve he showed in taking J C on, he shows just as much heart by hanging in there with the larger boy, for J C is not only larger but also quick with his hands and quite agile. What Tyree lacks in strength and ability, he makes up for in guts. And this is on display for everyone to observe.

After about twenty minutes, the fight ends, and apparently J C has won. "The bol was just too big and too fast, but I showed them that I had heart," says Tyree. He might have added that J C also had much at stake in this fight; he had a lot to lose if he had gotten whipped, particularly in front of his bols. It is also clear that J C knows he has been in a fight. He has lost a shoe, and his eye is badly bruised. Tyree's shirt collar is almost completely torn off, his arms and neck now bear deep scratches and scrapes, and his nose is bleeding. He put up a very good fight, which was impressive to all. He lost, but he lost to a worthy opponent.

Tyree has now won the respect of the bols, and he is thus allowed to be—in a limited way—a member of the group. The fight with J C has been a step in a long process that will allow him to get cool with the bols and to establish himself in the neighborhood. In the next few days and weeks, people will talk about the fight and how Tyree, though he did not win, gave a good account of himself. And since J C had such a strong reputation or "name" in the neighborhood, Tyree benefits from the encounter. So Tyree gets known around the 'hood. The bols will now greet him on the streets and not bother him, at least on certain conditions. Tyree may be carrying a box of chicken, and if a bol says, "Hey, Tyree, what's up. Gimme some of that," Tyree is obligated to share it. This is true not just for food but for virtually anything Tyree displays as his own. If he is wearing a nice jacket or a nice pair of sneaks, he must be ready to "loan" them. If he has money, he is expected to be generous with the others. And

as he does so, he negotiates his place in the group. This is the code.

As he meets the demands of his new role, he gets cool with the others, establishing, maintaining, and controlling his share of respect. As the young men learn to relate to others, they learn, in effect, their place. But in an environment of such deprivation, respect is in short supply and cannot be taken for granted; trials and contests continue, day in, day out. Status in the group is continually being adjusted, and this dynamic allows bols who are cool with one another to live in relative peace.

I GOT YO' BACK

In the process of working his way up in the group, Tyree makes friends with Malik. Malik is Tyree's age, fifteen, and is physically about the same size; they are pretty evenly matched. Both young men are marginal to the group, not yet completely established as members. Both have fought other boys but have never fought each other. This observation is significant because fighting is such an important part of residing in the neighborhood, of being a part of the neighborhood groups that dominate the public spaces. Physical prowess and ultimately respect itself are in large part the coin of the social order. Certain boys appoint themselves as defenders and protectors of their turf—of their neighborhood—against bols from other neighborhoods; in so doing, they claim the area as their domain, making it known that anyone and anything going down in the neighborhood is their business, particularly in matters involving young women.

Malik and Tyree hang together. They traverse the city together, occasionally going downtown to the Gallery, to Thirtieth Street Station, or to one of the staging areas dominated by other bols; in these other areas of the city, people might jump them without a moment's hesitation, mainly because if someone is not in his own neighborhood, there may be a virtual price on his head. This means that anyone out to make a name for himself might jump outsiders for the honor of it, or simply on "GP"—general principle. So in order to travel in peace, or to believe they are traveling in peace, Malik and Tyree often dress to look mean or cool, as though they are "not for foolishness"—not to be messed with. They try to be ready, working to impress others with the notion that they are deadly serious, "that we don't play." When they travel out of the 'hood, they charge each other with watching their backs, and by taking on these critical responsibilities, they bond and become "tight," at times "going for brothers," or "cousins."[2]

These fictive kinship relationships involve a close connection between the two boys, so close that they are ready and willing not only to watch each other's back but to take up for the other in time of need. But this is not always an easy relationship.

For instance, one day Malik and Tyree are walking down a street in the neighborhood and encounter a group of young women. In his characteristic way, Tyree begins to "rap" or "hit on" one of the young women, trying out his conversational game. As so often happens when young women are present, the boys can become downright silly, acting out in ways that at times surprise both themselves and their companions. The girls giggle and laugh at Tyree, and Malik, too, laughs at his "silly" conversation in front of the young women. Tyree's "jaws get tight"—that is, he becomes perturbed by Malik's show of disrespect.

As they leave the girls and walk about a block down the street, Tyree stops and confronts Malik. "Say, man. Why you always squarin' me off. You always dissin' me. I'm tired of yo' shit, man."

"Aw, man. I didn't do nothin'," responds Malik.

"Yes you did. You always gettin' on my case, and I'm tired of yo' shit. Put up yo' hands, man. Put up yo' hands," challenges Tyree.

"Aw, man. I don't wanta fight you, man," responds Malik.

"Naw, man. I ain't bullshittin'. Put up yo' hands," presses Tyree.

"Well, I ain't gon' fight you here, let's go behind this building," offers Malik, finally accepting Tyree's challenge.

The two young men walk behind the building they are standing next to and begin to square off. Almost on cue, the two friends put up their hands in the fighting position in an attempt to settle their differences in the man-to-man manner they know. With no audience present, they commence battle, sparring and dancing about.

Tyree and Malik have agreed to a contest that is somewhere between a fair fight and a real fight. Such fights are part of a long and honorable tradition of settling disputes between men, and this tradition has a justice that is its own result, effectively settling things for the time being. The fights are characterized by elaborate rules, including "no hitting in the face," "you got to use just your hands," and "no double-teaming." No one can tell beforehand, however, whether a fight will remain "fair" or change in the course of battle. A change can result simply from audience reaction, which serves to interpret each blow and indicate who is winning or who is beating whom. Audience reaction can sometimes tilt the scale from fair to unfair, and it can determine who wins and loses and thus who must then get even. For instance, a loud slap to the face, even if accidental and quickly followed by apologies, can alter the character of the contest. Young boys can start off joking and wind up fighting to the death, all because of a reaction to a miscalculation that pushed the contest hopelessly off-balance.

Malik and Tyree dance and spar, huffing and puffing, dodging and feinting. To the onlooker, it appears to be a game, for real blows seem hardly to be exchanged. But suddenly Malik lands a blow to Tyree's shoulder and another to his stomach, and he follows this up with this taunt: "I gotcha." Dropping his guard, Tyree acknowledges this, but then he quickly resumes his fighting stance, again putting up his hands. They go at it again, punching, dancing, dodging. Tyree lands a good punch to Malik's stomach and then, with a right cross, catches him on the chest, but Malik counters with a kidney punch and a knee to the crotch. Tyree checks his opponent with, "Watch that shit, man." They continue trading punches, hits, and feints. They are getting tired. Tyree, hands up, accidentally lets an open hand to Malik's face with the sound of a slap. Tyree knows instinctively what he has done, that he has seriously violated the rules of the fair fight, and just as quickly he says, "Aw, 'cuse me, man." The apology must come quickly and must be sincere, otherwise such a blow can escalate the fight to the point of a serious exchange. Malik responds, "Watch yourself, man. Watch yourself."

They continue their dancing and sparring for about twenty minutes and then stop. They have fought and, for the moment, settled their differences. But, actually, something much more profound has occurred as well. To be sure, the two boys can now smile at each other again, knowing that if they have a disagreement, they can settle it man to man. Through this little fight, they have bonded socially. They have tested each other's mettle, discerned important limits, and gained an abiding sense of what each one will "take" from the other. With this in mind they adjust their behavior in each other's presence, giving the other his "props," or respect. In this context they learn to accept each other, or pay the consequences; in effect, they learn the rules of their relationship. After consummating their bond through a fight, they can now walk together again, while expecting that

if someone was to try to jump Malik, Tyree would likely be there to defend his friend, or vice versa. They informally agree to watch each other's back. When this very strong—and necessary in the inner city—expectation is met, powerful bonds of trust are formed and, with repeated supportive exchanges, ever more firmly established. Essentially, this is what it means to "get cool" with someone, and when the story gets out, each is now more cool with the wider group of bols as well.

NOTES

1. See Fox Butterfield, *All God's Children* (New York: Knopf, 1995).

2. See Elliot Liebow, *Tally's Corner: A Study of Negro Streetcorner Men* (Boston: Little, Brown, 1967); Elijah Anderson, *A Place on the Corner* (Chicago: University of Chicago Press, 1978); and Martin Sánchez Jankowski, *Islands in the Street: Gangs and American Urban Society* (Berkeley: University of California Press, 1991).

26

A History of Multicultural America

Ronald Takaki

A DIFFERENT MIRROR

I had flown from San Francisco to Norfolk and was riding in a taxi to my hotel to attend a conference on multiculturalism. Hundreds of educators from across the country were meeting to discuss the need for greater cultural diversity in the cur-

From *A Different Mirror* by Ronald Takaki. Copyright © 1993 by Ronald Takaki. Reprinted by Permission of Little, Brown and Company.

riculum. My driver and I chatted about the weather and the tourists. The sky was cloudy, and Virginia Beach was twenty minutes away. The rearview mirror reflected a white man in his forties. "How long have you been in this country?" he asked. "All my life," I replied, wincing. "I was born in the United States." With a strong southern drawl, he remarked: "I was wondering because your English is excellent!" Then, as I had many times before, I explained: "My grandfather came here from Japan in the 1880s. My family has been here, in America, for over a hundred years." He glanced at me in the mirror. Somehow I did not look "American" to him; my eyes and complexion looked foreign.

Suddenly, we both became uncomfortably conscious of a racial divide separating us. An awkward silence turned my gaze from the mirror to the passing landscape, the shore where the English and the Powhatan Indians first encountered each other. Our highway was on land that Sir Walter Raleigh had renamed "Virginia" in honor of Elizabeth I, the Virgin Queen. In the English cultural appropriation of America, the indigenous peoples themselves would become outsiders in their native land. Here, at the eastern edge of the continent, I mused, was the site of the beginning of multicultural America. Jamestown, the English settlement founded in 1607, was nearby: the first twenty Africans were brought here a year before the Pilgrims arrived at Plymouth Rock. Several hundred miles offshore was Bermuda, the "Bermoothes" where William Shakespeare's Prospero had landed and met the native Caliban in *The Tempest.* Earlier, another voyager had made an Atlantic crossing and unexpectedly bumped into some islands to the south. Thinking he had reached Asia, Christopher Columbus mistakenly identified one of the islands as "Cipango" (Japan). In the wake of the admiral, many peoples would come to America from different shores, not only from Europe but also Africa and Asia. One of them would be my grandfather. My mental wandering across terrain and time ended abruptly as we arrived at my destination. I said good-bye to my driver and went into the hotel, carrying a vivid reminder of why I was attending this conference.

Questions like the one my taxi driver asked me are always jarring, but I can understand why he could not see me as American. He had a narrow but widely shared sense of the past—a history that has viewed American as European in ancestry. "Race," Toni Morrison explained, has functioned as a "metaphor" necessary to the "construction of Americanness": in the creation of our national identity, "American" has been defined as "white."[1]

But America has been racially diverse since our very beginning on the Virginia shore, and this reality is increasingly becoming visible and ubiquitous. Currently, one-third of the American people do not trace their origins to Europe; in California, minorities are fast becoming a majority. They already predominate in major cities across the country—New York, Chicago, Atlanta, Detroit, Philadelphia, San Francisco, and Los Angeles.

This emerging demographic diversity has raised fundamental questions about America's identity and culture. In 1990, *Time* published a cover story on "America's Changing Colors." "Someday soon," the magazine announced, "white Americans will become a minority group." How soon? By 2056, most Americans will trace their descent to "Africa, Asia, the Hispanic world, the Pacific Islands, Arabia—almost anywhere but white Europe." This dramatic change in our nation's ethnic composition is altering the way we think about ourselves. "The deeper significance of America's becoming a majority nonwhite society is what it means to the national psyche, to individuals' sense of themselves and their nation—their idea of what it is to be American."[2]

Indeed, more than ever before, as we approach the time when whites become a minority, many of us are perplexed about our national identity and our future as one people. This uncertainty has provoked Allan Bloom to reaffirm the preeminence of Western civilization. Author of *The Closing of the American Mind,* he has emerged as a leader of an intellectual backlash against cultural diversity. In his view, students entering the university are "uncivilized," and the university has the responsibility to "civilize" them. Bloom claims he knows what their "hungers" are and "what they can digest." Eating is one of his favorite metaphors. Noting the "large black presence" in major universities, he laments the "one failure" in race relations—black students have proven to be "indigestible." They do not "melt as have *all* other groups." The problem, he contends, is that "blacks have become blacks": they have become "ethnic." This separatism has been reinforced by an academic permissiveness that has befouled the curriculum with "Black Studies" along with "Learn Another Culture." The only solution, Bloom insists, is "the good old Great Books approach."[3]

Similarly, E. D. Hirsch worries that America is becoming a "tower of Babel," and that this multiplicity of cultures is threatening to rend our social fabric. He, too, longs for a more cohesive culture and a more homogeneous America: "If we *had* to make a choice between the *one* and the *many*, most Americans would choose the principle of unity, since we cannot function as a nation without it." The way to correct this fragmentization, Hirsch argues, is to acculturate "disadvantaged children." What do they need to know? "Only by accumulating shared symbols, and the shared information that symbols represent," Hirsch answers, "can we learn to communicate effectively with one another in our national community." Though he concedes the value of multicultural education, he quickly dismisses it by insisting that it "should not be allowed to supplant or interfere with our schools' responsibility to ensure our children's mastery of American literate culture." In *Cultural Literacy: What Every American Needs to Know*, Hirsch offers a long list of terms that excludes much of the history of minority groups.[4]

While Bloom and Hirsch are reacting defensively to what they regard as a vexatious balkanization of America, many other educators are responding to our diversity as an opportunity to open American minds. In 1990, the Task Force on Minorities for New York emphasized the importance of a culturally diverse education. "Essentially," the *New York Times* commented, "the issue is how to deal with both dimensions of the nation's motto: 'E pluribus unum' — 'Out of many, one.'" Universities from New Hampshire to Berkeley have established American cultural diversity graduation requirements. "Every student needs to know," explained University of Wisconsin's chancellor Donna Shalala, "much more about the origins and history of the particular cultures which, as Americans, we will encounter during our lives." Even the University of Minnesota, located in a state that is 98 percent white, requires its students to take ethnic studies courses. Asked why multiculturalism is so important, Dean Fred Lukermann answered: As a national university, Minnesota has to offer a national curriculum — one that includes all of the peoples of America. He added that after graduation many students move to cities like Chicago and Los Angeles and thus need to know about racial diversity. Moreover, many educators stress, multiculturalism has an intellectual purpose. By allowing us to see events from the viewpoints of different groups, a multicultural curriculum enables us to reach toward a more comprehensive understanding of American history.[5]

What is fueling this debate over our national identity and the content of our curriculum is America's intensifying racial crisis. The alarming signs and symptoms seem to be everywhere — the killing of Vincent Chin in Detroit, the black boycott of a Korean grocery store in Flatbush, the hysteria in Boston over the Carol Stuart murder, the battle between white sportsmen and Indians over tribal fishing rights in Wisconsin, the Jewish–black clashes in Brooklyn's Crown Heights, the black–Hispanic competition for jobs and educational resources in Dallas, which *Newsweek* described as "a conflict of the have-nots," and the Willie Horton campaign commercials, which widened the divide between the suburbs and the inner cities.[6]

This reality of racial tension rudely woke America like a fire bell in the night on April 29, 1992. Immediately after four Los Angeles police officers were found not guilty of brutality against Rodney King, rage exploded in Los Angeles. Race relations reached a new nadir. During the nightmarish rampage, scores of people were killed, over two thousand injured, twelve thousand arrested, and almost a billion dollars' worth of property destroyed. The live televised images mesmerized America. The rioting and the murderous melee on the streets resembled the fighting in Beirut and the West Bank. The thousands of fires burning out of control and the dark smoke filling the skies brought back images of the burning oil fields of Kuwait during Desert Storm. Entire sections of

Los Angeles looked like a bombed city. "Is this America?" many shocked viewers asked. "Please, can we get along here," pleaded Rodney King, calling for calm. "We all can get along. I mean, we're all stuck here for a while. Let's try to work it out."[7]

But how should "we" be defined? Who are the people "stuck here" in America? One of the lessons of the Los Angeles explosion is the recognition of the fact that we are a multiracial society and that race can no longer be defined in the binary terms of white and black. "We" will have to include Hispanics and Asians. While blacks currently constitute 13 percent of the Los Angeles population, Hispanics represent 40 percent. The 1990 census revealed that South Central Los Angeles, which was predominantly black in 1965 when the Watts rebellion occurred, is now 45 percent Hispanic. A majority of the first 5,438 people arrested were Hispanic, while 37 percent were black. Of the fifty-eight people who died in the riot, more than a third were Hispanic, and about 40 percent of the businesses destroyed were Hispanic-owned. Most of the other shops were Korean-owned. The dreams of many Korean immigrants went up in smoke during the riot: two thousand Korean-owned businesses were damaged or demolished, totaling about $400 million in losses. There is evidence indicating they were targeted. "After all," explained a black gang member, "we didn't burn our community, just *their* stores."[8]

"I don't feel like I'm in America anymore," said Denisse Bustamente as she watched the police protecting the firefighters. "I feel like I am far away." Indeed, Americans have been witnessing ethnic strife erupting around the world—the rise of neo-Nazism and the murder of Turks in Germany, the ugly "ethnic cleansing" in Bosnia, the terrible and bloody clashes between Muslims and Hindus in India. Is the situation here different, we have been nervously wondering, or do ethnic conflicts elsewhere represent a prologue for America? What is the nature of malevolence? Is there a deep, perhaps primordial, need for group identity rooted in hatred for the other? Is ethnic pluralism possible in America? But answers have been limited. Television reports have been little more than thirty-second sound bites. Newspaper articles have been mostly superficial descriptions of racial antagonisms and the current urban malaise. What is lacking is historical context; consequently, we are left feeling bewildered.[9]

How did we get to this point, Americans everywhere are anxiously asking. What does our diversity mean, and where is it leading us? *How* do we work it out in the post–Rodney King era?

Certainly one crucial way is for our society's various ethnic groups to develop a greater understanding of each other. For example, how can African Americans and Korean Americans work it out unless they learn about each other's cultures, histories, and also economic situations? This need to share knowledge about our ethnic diversity has acquired new importance and has given new urgency to the pursuit for a more accurate history.

More than ever before, there is a growing realization that the established scholarship has tended to define America too narrowly. For example, in his prize-winning study *The Uprooted*, Harvard historian Oscar Handlin presented—to use the book's subtitle—"The Epic Story of the Great Migrations That Made the American People." But Handlin's "epic story" excluded the "uprooted" from Africa, Asia, and Latin America—the other "Great Migrations" that also helped to make "the American People." Similarly, in *The Age of Jackson*, Arthur M. Schlesinger, Jr., left out blacks and Indians. There is not even a mention of two marker events—the Nat Turner insurrection and Indian removal, which Andrew Jackson himself would have been surprised to find omitted from a history of his era.[10]

Still, Schlesinger and Handlin offered us a refreshing revisionism, paving the way for the study of common people rather than princes and presidents. They inspired the next generation of historians to examine groups such as the artisan laborers of Philadelphia and the Irish immigrants of Boston. "Once I thought to write a history of the immigrants in America," Handlin confided in his introduction to *The Uprooted*. "I discovered that the immigrants *were* American history." This door, once opened, led to the flowering of a more inclusive scholarship as we began to recognize that ethnic history was American history. Suddenly, there was a proliferation of seminal works such as Irving Howe's *World of Our Fathers: The Journey of the East European Jews to America*, Dee Brown's *Bury My Heart at Wounded Knee: An Indian History of the American West*, Albert Camarillo's *Chicanos in a Changing Society*, Lawrence Levine's *Black Culture and Black Consciousness*, Yuji Ichioka's *The Issei: The World of the First Generation Japanese Immigrants*, and Kerby Miller's *Emigrants and Exiles: Ireland and the Irish Exodus to North America.*[11]

But even this new scholarship, while it has given us a more expanded understanding of the mosaic called America, does not address our needs in the post–Rodney King era. These books and others like them fragment American society, studying each group separately, in isolation from the other groups and the whole. While scrutinizing our specific pieces, we have to step back in order to see the rich and complex portrait they compose. What is needed is a fresh angle, a study of the American past from a comparative perspective.

While all of America's many groups cannot be covered in one book, the English immigrants and their descendants require attention, for they possessed inordinate power to define American culture and make public policy. What men like John Winthrop, Thomas Jefferson, and Andrew Jackson thought as well as did mattered greatly to all of us and was consequential for everyone. A broad range of groups has been selected: African Americans, Asian Americans, Chicanos, Irish, Jews, and Indians. While together they help to explain general patterns in our society, each has contributed to the making of the United States.

African Americans have been the central minority throughout our country's history. They were initially brought here on a slave ship in 1619. Actually, these first twenty Africans might not have been slaves; rather, like most of the white laborers, they were probably indentured servants. The transformation of Africans into slaves is the story of the "hidden" origins of slavery. How and when was it decided to institute a system of bonded black labor? What happened, while freighted with racial significance, was actually conditioned by class conflicts within white society. Once established, the "peculiar institution" would have consequences for centuries to come. During the nineteenth century, the political storm over slavery almost destroyed the nation. Since the Civil War and emancipation, race has continued to be largely defined in relation to African Americans—segregation, civil rights, the underclass, and affirmative action. Constituting the largest minority group in our society, they have been at the cutting edge of the Civil Rights Movement. Indeed, their struggle has been a constant reminder of America's moral vision as a country committed to the principle of liberty. Martin Luther King clearly understood this truth when he wrote from a jail cell: "We will reach the goal of freedom in Birmingham and all over the nation, because the goal of America is freedom. Abused and scorned though we may be, our destiny is tied up with America's destiny."[12]

Asian Americans have been here for over one hundred and fifty years, before many European immigrant groups. But as "strangers" coming from a "different shore," they have been stereotyped as "heathen," exotic, and unassimilable. Seeking "Gold Mountain," the Chinese arrived first, and what happened to them influenced the reception of the Japanese, Koreans, Filipinos, and Asian Indians as well as the Southeast Asian refugees like the Vietnamese and the Hmong. The 1882 Chinese Exclusion Act was the first law that prohibited the entry of immigrants on the basis of nationality. The Chinese condemned this restriction as racist and tyrannical. "They call us 'Chink,'" complained a Chinese immigrant, cursing the "white demons." "They think we no good! America cuts us off. No more come now, too bad!" This precedent later provided a basis for the restriction of European immigrant groups such as Italians, Russians, Poles, and Greeks. The Japanese painfully discovered that their accomplishments in America did not lead to acceptance, for during World War II, unlike Italian Americans and German Americans, they were placed in internment camps. Two-thirds of them were citizens by birth. "How could I as a 6-month-old child born in this country," asked Congressman Robert Matsui years later, "be declared by my own Government to be an enemy alien?" Today, Asian Americans represent the fastest-growing ethnic group. They have also become the focus of much mass media attention as "the Model Minority" not only for blacks and Chicanos, but also for whites on welfare and even middle-class whites experiencing economic difficulties.[13]

Chicanos represent the largest group among the Hispanic population, which is projected to outnumber African Americans. They have been in the United States for a long time, initially incorporated by the war against Mexico. The treaty had moved the border between the two countries, and the people of "occupied" Mexico suddenly found themselves "foreigners" in their "native land." As historian Albert Camarillo pointed out, the Chicano past is an integral part of America's westward expansion, also known as "manifest destiny." But while the early Chicanos were a colonized people, most of them today have immigrant roots. Many began the trek to El Norte in the early twentieth century. "As I had heard a lot about the United States," Jesus Garza recalled, "it was my dream to come here." "We came to know families from Chihuahua, Sonora, Jalisco, and Durango," stated Ernesto Galarza. "Like ourselves, our Mexican neighbors had come this far moving step by step, working and waiting, as if they were feeling their way up a ladder." Nevertheless, the Chicano experience has been unique, for most of them have lived close to their homeland—a proximity that has helped reinforce their language, identity, and culture. This migration to El Norte has continued to the present. Los Angeles has more people of Mexican origin than any other city in the world, except Mexico City. A mostly mestizo people of Indian as well as African and Spanish ancestries, Chicanos currently represent the largest minority group in the Southwest, where they have been visibly transforming culture and society.[14]

The Irish came here in greater numbers than most immigrant groups. Their history has been tied to America's past from the very beginning. Ireland represented the earliest English frontier: the conquest of Ireland occurred before the colonization of America, and the Irish were the first group that the English called "savages." In this context, the Irish past foreshadowed the Indian future. During the nineteenth century, the Irish, like the Chinese, were victims of British colonialism. While the Chinese fled from the ravages of the Opium Wars, the Irish were pushed from their homeland by "English tyranny." Here they became construction workers and factory operatives as well as the "maids" of America. Representing a Catholic group seeking to settle in a fiercely Protestant society, the Irish immigrants were targets of American nativist hostility. They were also what historian Lawrence J. McCaffrey called "the pioneers of the American urban ghetto," "previewing" experiences that would later be shared by the Italians, Poles, and other groups from southern and eastern Europe. Furthermore, they offer contrast to the immigrants from Asia. The Irish came about the same time as the Chinese, but they had a distinct advantage: the Naturalization Law of 1790 had reserved citizenship for "whites" only. Their compatible complexion allowed them to assimilate by blending into American society. In making their journey successfully into the mainstream, however, these immigrants from Erin pursued an Irish "ethnic" strategy: they promoted "Irish" solidarity in order to gain political power and also to dominate the skilled blue-collar occupations, often at the expense of the Chinese and blacks.[15]

Fleeing pogroms and religious persecution in Russia, the Jews were driven from what John Cuddihy described as the "Middle Ages into the Anglo-American world of the *goyim* 'beyond the pale.'" To them, America represented the Promised Land. This vision led Jews to struggle not only for themselves but also for other oppressed groups, especially blacks. After the 1917 East St. Louis race riot, the Yiddish *Forward* of New York compared this anti-black violence to a 1903 pogrom in Russia: "Kishinev and St. Louis—the same soil, the same people." Jews cheered when Jackie Robinson broke into the Brooklyn Dodgers in 1947. "He was adopted as the surrogate hero by many of us growing up at the time," recalled Jack Greenberg of the NAACP Legal Defense Fund. "He was the way we saw ourselves triumphing against the forces of bigotry and ignorance." Jews stood shoulder to shoulder with blacks in the Civil Rights Movement: two-thirds of the white volunteers who went south during the 1964 Freedom Summer were Jewish. Today Jews are considered a highly successful "ethnic" group. How did they make such great socioeconomic strides? This question is often reframed by neoconservative intellectuals like Irving Kristol and Nathan Glazer to read: if Jewish immigrants were able to lift themselves from poverty into the mainstream through self-help and education without welfare and affirmative action, why can't blacks? But what this thinking overlooks is the unique history of Jewish immigrants, especially the initial advantages of many of them as literate and skilled. Moreover, it minimizes the virulence of racial prejudice rooted in American slavery.[16]

Indians represent a critical contrast, for theirs was not an immigrant experience. The Wampanoags were on the shore as the first English strangers arrived in what would be called "New England." The encounters between Indians and whites not only shaped the course of race relations, but also influenced the very culture and identity of the general society. The architect of Indian removal, President Andrew Jackson told Congress: "Our conduct toward these people is deeply interesting to the national character." Frederick Jackson Turner understood the meaning of this observation when he identified the frontier as our transforming crucible. At first, the European newcomers had to wear Indian moccasins and shout the war cry. "Little by little," as they subdued the wilderness, the pioneers became "a new product" that was "American." But Indians have had a different view of this entire process. "The white man," Luther Standing Bear of the Sioux explained, "does not understand the Indian for the reason that he does not understand America." Continuing to be "troubled with primitive fears," he has "in his consciousness the perils of this frontier continent. . . . The man from Europe is still a foreigner and an alien. And he still hates the man who questioned his path across the continent." Indians questioned what Jackson and Turner trum-

peted as "progress." For them, the frontier had a different "significance": their history was how the West was lost. But their story has also been one of resistance. As Vine Deloria declared, "Custer died for your sins."[17]

By looking at these groups from a multicultural perspective, we can comparatively analyze their experiences in order to develop an understanding of their differences and similarities. Race, we will see, has been a social construction that has historically set apart racial minorities from European immigrant groups. Contrary to the notions of scholars like Nathan Glazer and Thomas Sowell, race in America has not been the same as ethnicity. A broad comparative focus also allows us to see how the varied experiences of different racial and ethnic groups occurred within shared contexts.

During the nineteenth century, for example, the Market Revolution employed Irish immigrant laborers in New England factories as it expanded cotton fields worked by enslaved blacks across Indian lands toward Mexico. Like blacks, the Irish newcomers were stereotyped as "savages," ruled by passions rather than "civilized" virtues such as self-control and hard work. The Irish saw themselves as the "slaves" of British oppressors, and during a visit to Ireland in the 1840s, Frederick Douglass found that the "wailing notes" of the Irish ballads reminded him of the "wild notes" of slave songs. The United States annexation of California, while incorporating Mexicans, led to trade with Asia and the migration of "strangers" from Pacific shores. In 1870, Chinese immigrant laborers were transported to Massachusetts as scabs to break an Irish immigrant strike; in response, the Irish recognized the need for interethnic working-class solidarity and tried to organize a Chinese lodge of the Knights of St. Crispin. After the Civil War, Mississippi planters recruited Chinese immigrants to discipline the newly freed blacks. During the debate over an immigration exclusion bill in 1882, a senator asked: If Indians could be located on reservations, why not the Chinese?[18]

Other instances of our connectedness abound. In 1903, Mexican and Japanese farm laborers went on strike together in California: their union officers had names like Yamaguchi and Lizarras, and strike meetings were conducted in Japanese and Spanish. The Mexican strikers declared that they were standing in solidarity with their "Japanese brothers" because the two groups had toiled together in the fields and were now fighting together for a fair wage. Speaking in impassioned Yiddish during the 1909 "uprising of twenty thousand" strikers in New York, the charismatic Clara Lemlich compared the abuse of Jewish female garment workers to the experience of blacks: "[The bosses] yell at the girls and 'call them down' even worse than I imagine the Negro slaves were in the South." During the 1920s, elite universities like Harvard worried about the increasing numbers of Jewish students, and new admissions criteria were instituted to curb their enrollment. Jewish students were scorned for their studiousness and criticized for their "clannishness." Recently, Asian-American students have been the targets of similar complaints: they have been called "nerds" and told there are "too many" of them on campus.[19]

Indians were already here, while blacks were forcibly transported to America, and Mexicans were initially enclosed by America's expanding border. The other groups came here as immigrants: for them, America represented liminality — a new world where they could pursue extravagant urges and do things they had thought beyond their capabilities. Like the land itself, they found themselves "betwixt and between all fixed points of classification." No longer fastened as fiercely to their old countries, they felt a stirring to become new people in a society still being defined and formed.[20] . . .

Through their narratives about their lives and circumstances, the people of America's diverse groups are able to see themselves and each other in our common past. They celebrate what Ishmael Reed has described as a society "unique" in the world because "the world is here" — a place "where the cultures of the world crisscross." Much of America's past, they point out, has been riddled with racism. At the same time, these people offer hope, affirming the struggle for equality as a central theme in our country's history. At its conception, our nation was dedicated to the proposition of equality. What has given concreteness to this powerful national principle has been our coming together in the creation of a new society. "Stuck here" together, workers of different backgrounds have attempted to get along with each other.

People harvesting
Work together unaware
Of racial problems,

wrote a Japanese immigrant describing a lesson learned by Mexican and Asian farm laborers in California.[21]

Finally, how do we see our prospects for "working out" America's racial crisis? Do we see it as through a glass darkly? Do the televised images of racial hatred and violence that riveted us in 1992 during the days of rage in Los Angeles frame a future of divisive race relations — what Arthur Schlesinger, Jr., has fearfully denounced as the "disuniting of America"? Or will Americans of diverse races and ethnicities be able to connect themselves to a larger narrative? Whatever happens, we can be certain that much of our society's future will be influenced by which "mirror" we choose to see ourselves. America does not belong to one race or one group, the people in this study remind us, and Americans have been constantly redefining their national identity from the moment of first contact on the Virginia shore. By sharing their stories, they invite us to see ourselves in a different mirror.[22] . . .

THROUGH A GLASS DARKLY

. . . By viewing ourselves in a mirror which reflects reality, we can see our past as undistorted and no longer have to peer into our future as through a glass darkly. The face of our cultural future can be found on the western edge of the continent. "California, and especially Los Angeles, a gateway to both Asia and Latin America," Carlos Fuentes observed, "poses the universal question of the coming century: how do we deal with the

Other?" Asked whether California, especially with its multiethnic society, represented the America of the twenty-first century, Alice Walker replied: "If that's not the future reality of the United States, there won't be any United States, because that's who we are." Walker's own ancestry is a combination of Native American, African American, and European American. Paula Gunn Allen also has diverse ethnic roots—American Indian, Scotch, Jewish, and Lebanese. "Just people from everywhere are related to me by blood," she explained, "and so that's why I say I'm a multicultural event. . . . It's beautiful, it's a rainbow. . . . It reflects light, and I think that's what a person like me can do." Imagine what "light" a "multicultural event" called America can reflect. America has been settled by "the people of all nations," Herman Melville observed over a century ago, "all nations may claim her for their own. You can not spill a drop of American blood, without spilling the blood of the whole world." Americans are not "a narrow tribe"; they are not a nation, "so much as a world." In this new society, Melville optimistically declared, the "prejudices of national dislikes" could be "forever extinguish[ed]."[23]

But, as it has turned out, Melville was too sanguine. As our diversity is increasingly recognized today, it is accompanied by even more defensive denial, grim jeremiads of the Allan Blooms about the "closing of the American mind," and demagogic urgings of the Patrick Buchanans to take back "our cities, our culture, and our country." But who, in this case, are "we"? Such a backlash is defining our diversity as a "cultural war," a conflict between "us" and "them." Reflecting a traditional Eurocentrism that remains culturally hegemonic, this resistance is what is really driving the "disuniting of America."[24]

America's dilemma has been our resistance to ourselves—our denial of our immensely varied selves. But we have nothing to fear but our fear of our own diversity. "We can get along," Rodney King reassured us during an agonizing moment of racial hate and violence. To get along with each other, however, requires self-recognition as well as self-acceptance. Asked whether she had a specific proposal for improving the current racial climate in America, Toni Morrison answered: "Everybody remembers the first time they were taught that part of the human race was Other. That's a trauma. It's as though I told you that your left hand is not part of your body." In his vision of the "whole hoop of the world," Black Elk of the Sioux saw "in a sacred manner the shapes of all things in the spirit, and the shape of all shapes as they must live together like one being." And he saw that the "sacred hoop" of his people was "one of many hoops that made one circle, wide as daylight and as starlight, and in the center grew one mighty flowering tree to shelter all the children of one mother and one father." Today, what we need to do is to stop denying our wholeness as members of humanity as well as one nation.[25]

As Americans, we originally came from many different shores, and our diversity has been at the center of the making of America. While our stories contain the memories of different communities, together they inscribe a larger narrative. Filled with what Walt Whitman celebrated as the "varied carols" of America, our history generously gives all of us our "mystic chords of memory." Throughout our past of oppressions and struggles for equality, Americans of different races and ethnicities have been "singing with open mouths their strong melodious songs" in the textile mills of Lowell, the cotton fields of Mississippi, on the Indian reservations of South Dakota, the railroad tracks high in the Sierras of California, in the garment factories of the Lower East Side, the canefields of Hawaii, and a thousand other places across the country. Our denied history "bursts with telling." As we hear America singing, we find ourselves invited to bring our rich cultural diversity on deck, to accept ourselves. "Of every hue and caste am I," sang Whitman. "I resist any thing better than my own diversity."[26]

NOTES

1. Toni Morrison, *Playing in the Dark: Whiteness in the Literary Imagination* (Cambridge, Mass., 1992), p. 47.

2. William A. Henry III, "Beyond the Melting Pot," in "America's Changing Colors," *Time*, vol. 135, no. 15 (April 9, 1990), pp. 28–31.

3. Allan Bloom, *The Closing of the American Mind: How Higher Education Has Failed Democracy and Impoverished the Souls of Today's Students* (New York, 1987), pp. 19, 91–93, 340–341, 344.

4. E. D. Hirsch, Jr., *Cultural Literacy: What Every American Needs to Know* (Boston, 1987), pp. xiii, xvii, 2, 18, 96. See also "The List," pp. 152–215.

5. Edward Fiske, "Lessons," *New York Times*, February 7, 1990; "University of Wisconsin-Madison: The Madison Plan," February 9, 1988; interview with Dean Fred Lukermann, University of Minnesota, 1987.

6. "A Conflict of the Have-Nots," *Newsweek*, December 12, 1988, pp. 28–29.

7. Rodney King's statement to the press, *New York Times*, May 2, 1992, p. 6.

8. Tim Rutten, "A New Kind of Riot," *New York Review of Books*, June 11, 1992, pp. 52–53; Maria Newman, "Riots Bring Attention to Growing Hispanic Presence in South-Central Area," *New York Times*, May 11, 1992, p. A10; Mike Davis, "In L.A. Burning All Illusions," *The Nation*, June 1, 1992, pp. 744–745; Jack Viets and Peter Fimrite, "S.F. Mayor Visits Riot-Torn Area to Buoy Businesses," *San Francisco Chronicle*, May 6, 1992, p. A6.

9. Rick DelVecchio, Suzanne Espinosa, and Carl Nolte, "Bradley Ready to Lift Curfew," *San Francisco Chronicle*, May 4, 1992, p. A1.

10. Oscar Handlin, *The Uprooted: The Epic Story of the Great Migrations That Made the American People* (New York, 1951); Arthur M. Schlesinger, Jr., *The Age of Jackson* (Boston, 1945).

11. Handlin, *The Uprooted*, p. 3; Irving Howe, *World of Our Fathers: The Journey of the East European Jews to America and the Life They Found and Made* (New York, 1983); Dee Brown, *Bury My Heart at Wounded Knee: An Indian History of the American West* (New York, 1970); Albert Camar-illo, *Chicanos in a Changing Society: From Mexican Pueblos to American Barrios in Santa Barbara and Southern California, 1848–1930* (Cambridge, Mass., 1979); Lawrence W. Levine, *Black Culture and Black Consciousness: Afro-American Folk Thought from Slavery to Freedom* (New York, 1977); Yuji Ichioka, *The Issei: The World of the First Generation Japanese Immigrants* (New York, 1988); Kerby A. Miller, *Emigrants and Exiles: Ireland and the Irish Exodus to North America* (New York, 1985).

12. Abraham Lincoln, "The Gettysburg Address," in *The Annals of America*, vol. 9, *1863–1865: The Crisis of the Union* (Chicago, 1968), pp. 462–463; Martin Luther King, *Why We Can't Wait* (New York, 1964), pp. 92–93.

13. Interview with old laundryman, in "Interviews with Two Chinese," circa 1924, Box 326, folder 325, Survey of Race Relations, Stanford University, Hoover Institution Archives; Congressman Robert Matsui, speech in the House of Representatives on the 442 bill for redress and reparations, September 17, 1987, *Congressional Record* (Washington, D.C., 1987), p. 7584.

14. Camarillo, *Chicanos in a Changing Society*, p. 2; Juan Nepomuceno Seguín, in David J. Weber (ed.), *Foreigners in Their Native Land: Historical Roots of the Mexican Americans* (Albuquerque, N. Mex., 1973), p. vi; Jesus Garza, in Manuel Gamio, *The Mexican Immigrant: His Life Story* (Chicago, 1931), p. 15; Ernesto Galarza, *Barrio Boy: The Story of a Boy's Acculturation* (Notre Dame, Ind., 1986), p. 200.

15. Lawrence J. McCaffrey, *The Irish Diaspora in America* (Washington, D.C., 1984), pp. 6, 62.

16. John Murray Cuddihy, *The Ordeal of Civility: Freud, Marx, Levi Strauss, and the Jewish Struggle with Modernity* (Boston, 1987), p. 165; Jonathan Kaufman, *Broken Alliance: The Turbulent Times between Blacks and Jews in America* (New York, 1989), pp. 28, 82, 83–84, 91, 93, 106.

17. Andrew Jackson, First Annual Message to Congress, December 8, 1829, in James D. Richardson

(ed.), *A Compilation of the Messages and Papers of the Presidents, 1789–1897* (Washington, D.C., 1897), vol. 2, p. 457; Frederick Jackson Turner, "The Significance of the Frontier in American History," in *The Early Writings of Frederick Jackson Turner* (Madison, Wis., 1938), pp. 185ff.; Luther Standing Bear, "What the Indian Means to America," in Wayne Moquin (ed.), *Great Documents in American Indian History* (New York, 1973), p. 307; Vine Deloria, Jr., *Custer Died for Your Sins: An Indian Manifesto* (New York, 1969).

18. Nathan Glazer, *Affirmative Discrimination: Ethnic Inequality and Public Policy* (New York, 1978); Thomas Sowell, *Ethnic America: A History* (New York, 1981); David R. Roediger, *The Wages of Whiteness: Race and the Making of the American Working Class* (London, 1991), pp. 134–136; Dan Caldwell, "The Negroization of the Chinese Stereotype in California," *Southern California Quarterly*, vol. 33 (June 1971), pp. 123–131.

19. Tomas Almaguer, "Racial Domination and Class Conflict in Capitalist Agriculture: The Oxnard Sugar Beet Workers' Strike of 1903," *Labor History*, vol. 25, no. 3 (summer 1984), p. 347; Howard M. Sachar, *A History of the Jews in America* (New York, 1992), p. 183.

20. For the concept of liminality, see Victor Turner, *Dramas, Fields, and Metaphors: Symbolic Action in Human Society* (Ithaca, N.Y., 1974), pp. 232, 237; and Arnold Van Gennep, *The Rites of Passage* (Chicago, 1960). What I try to do is to apply liminality to the land called America.

21. Ishmael Reed, "America: The Multinational Society," in Rick Simonson and Scott Walker (eds.), *Multi-cultural Literacy* (St. Paul, 1988), p. 160; Ito, *Issei*, p. 497.

22. Arthur M. Schlesinger, Jr., *The Disuniting of America: Reflections on a Multicultural Society*

(Knoxville, Tenn., 1991); Carlos Bulosan, *America Is in the Heart: A Personal History* (Seattle, 1981), pp. 188–189.

23. Carlos Fuentes, *The Buried Mirror: Reflections on Spain and the New World* (Boston, 1992), p. 348; Reese Erlich, "Alice's Wonderland," an interview with Alice Walker, *Image, San Francisco Examiner*, July 19, 1992, p. 12; Paula Gunn Allen, interview, in Laura Coltelli (ed.), *Winged Words: American Indian Writers Speak* (Lincoln, Nebr., 1990), p. 17; Herman Melville, *Redburn* (Chicago, 1969; originally published in 1849), p. 169, also quoted in Gates, *Loose Canons*, pp. 116–117, and Michael Paul Rogin, *Subversive Genealogy: The Politics and Art of Herman Melville* (New York, 1983), p. 69.

24. Allan Bloom, *The Closing of the American Mind: How Higher Education Has Failed Democracy and Impoverished the Souls of Today's Students* (New York, 1987); Patrick Buchanan, speech at the National Republican Convention, 1992, quoted in Garry Wills, "The Born-Again Republicans," *New York Review of Books*, September 24, 1992; Arthur M. Schlesinger, Jr., *The Disuniting of America: Reflections on a Multicultural Society* (Knoxville, Tenn. 1991).

25. Rodney King's statement to the press, *New York Times*, May 2, 1992, p. 6; interview with Toni Morrison, *Time*, May 22, 1989, p. 121; Black Elk, *Black Elk Speaks: Being the Life Story of a Holy Man of the Oglala Sioux*, as told to John G. Neihardt (Lincoln, Nebr., 1988), p. 43.

26. Joy Kogawa, *Obasan* (Boston, 1982), opening page; Lincoln, "First Inaugural Address," *The Annals of America*, vol. 9, *1863–65: The Crisis of the Union* (Chicago, 1968), p. 255; Walt Whitman, *Leaves of Grass* (New York, 1958), pp. 9, 10, 38.

27

The Wages of Race

Color and Employment Opportunity in Chicago's Inner City

Marta Tienda and Haya Stier

AS THE SECOND LARGEST U.S. CITY AT THE turn of the century, Chicago was a booming industrial center on its way to becoming a major distribution center as well. Rapid industrial growth meant job growth—employment opportunities—which served as a magnet for southern and eastern European immigrants and northbound Blacks seeking better destinies than their southern origins had yielded. The dimensions of the "Great Migration" which relocated thousands of unskilled laborers from southern plantations to northern

This research was supported by grants from the Rockefeller Foundation and from ASPE of the Department of Health and Human Services to the Institute for Research on Poverty of the University of Wisconsin. Our work was also supported by a fellowship at the Center for Advanced Study in the Behavioral Sciences, and we appreciate the generous support of the John D. and Catharine T. MacArthur Foundation for this opportunity. We gratefully acknowledge comments from Ronald Mincy, Christopher Tilly, and Harry Holzer. We appreciate technical assistance from Adelle Hinojosa, Safia Khan, and Frank Norfleet in preparing the final manuscript.

The data on which this article is based were collected under the auspices of the Urban Poverty and Family Structure Project of Chicago conducted under the direction of William J. Wilson, who provided generous access to the Urban Poverty and Family Life Survey of Chicago and the Social Opportunity Survey.

ghettos have been amply documented. Suffice it to recall that between 1916 and 1920 approximately 60,000 southern-born Blacks migrated to Chicago (Grossman 1991; Johnson and Campbell 1981). Chicago's ethnic landscape during the roaring twenties and the depression years provided the substance for Robert Park's (1914) classical notions about the cycle of race relations, assimilation, and along with his colleagues Burgess (1923) and Wirth (1938), the very conception of the city. Before the Depression, Chicago was Carl Sandburg's "City of Big Shoulders"—the "stormy, brawling, husky" place where the world's butchers, toolmakers, wheat stackers, railroad and freight handlers lived and labored.

As the end of the century approaches, Chicago is a different city—a place where opportunity has been dimmed as industrial restructuring eliminated thousands of semiskilled and unskilled jobs that paid family wages. Like other northern cities (that is, Detroit, Cleveland, Philadelphia, New York, and St. Louis), Chicago's industrial decline is mirrored in its demographic decline; the city has lost nearly 1 million people since mid-century. During the 1980s Chicago fell from second to third largest city, surpassed by Los Angeles. Yet Chicago remains a destination for thousands of immigrants who continue to diversify the ethnic terrain. Contemporary immigrants destined for Chicago and other major cities originate from Mexico, Central America, Korea, and other parts of Asia rather than Europe. The 1990 census indicated that Blacks comprised nearly two-fifths of the city's population; Hispanics (overwhelmingly Mexican and Puerto Rican) another fifth; and Whites, many of them European ethnics, most of the remaining two-fifths.

Against this backdrop, it is unsurprising that Chicago was a core city for the Civil Rights movement, for Jessie Jackson's Operation PUSH, and for William J. Wilson's (1987) *"Truly Disadvantaged."* That poverty and joblessness has become more concentrated and devastating for Chicago's Black population suggests that race matters as much at the close of the century as it did at the beginning. This study is an investigation of just that question—how does color influence job opportunities in the city of "Big Shoulders?" Accordingly, in this chapter we examine differences in labor force activity among parents residing in economically and ethnically diverse neighborhoods. Our general aim is to identify and evaluate the circumstances that sustain inequities in employment opportunities within a single labor market. Comparisons among Blacks, Whites, Mexicans, and Puerto Ricans who resided in Chicago's inner-city neighborhoods, and between the inner-city sample and a national sample of parents with similar background characteristics, serves several objectives that have been neglected in prior research.

First, we broaden the population at risk of exclusion from the labor market to include Hispanics. This is an important extension in light of recent evidence that Hispanic poverty has been less responsive to economic recovery than White and Black poverty, and theoretical arguments about possibly distinct mechanisms undergirding persisting poverty among Blacks and Hispanics (Moore 1989; Tienda 1989; Tienda and Jensen 1988). Second, we provide a national benchmark against which to compare the allegedly deviant labor force behavior of inner-city residents. Finally, we evaluate the relative merits of structural and individual explanations for the pervasiveness of joblessness in inner-city neighborhoods while appraising the salience of color in shaping employment opportunity in Chicago.

A brief overview of relevant theoretical considerations serves to frame the empirical analyses of race and ethnic differences in labor force activity. Following a description of the data sources, we first compare rates of labor force activity among race and gender groups for samples of Chicago and U.S. parents. Subsequently we evaluate how color and opportunity influence employment experiences in Chicago by assessing empirically the relative importance of individual and structural factors on labor force activity. We supplement our statistical analyses of labor force activity and wages with a textual analysis about social opportunity in Chicago, emphasizing race and ethnic differences in perceptions of opportunity and competition along color lines as voiced by inner-city residents themselves.

THEORETICAL CONSIDERATIONS

Various perspectives have been marshaled to explain widened race and ethnic economic inequities. One set of explanations focuses on the opportunities to work, including inequities produced by employer discrimination, while others emphasize individual differences in skills or willingness to work. Although these explanations of race and ethnic differences in inner-city joblessness have limitations and they are not mutually exclusive, it is instructive to discuss them separately for heuristic purposes. Evaluating their relative merits can provide useful insights about why race and ethnic differences in labor force activity have widened.

OPPORTUNITIES AND ETHNIC INEQUALITY

A dominant structural explanation for the rise of inner-city joblessness focuses on the decline of well-paying manufacturing jobs in old industrial centers (see Kasarda 1985: Wilson 1987). Wilson proposed that "social isolation" from mainstream work norms and behavior sustains chronic labor market inactivity in ghetto poverty neighborhoods. Yet this explanation does not resolve the puzzle of large race and ethnic differences in employment behavior among inner-city populations residing in a single labor market.

"Queuing theory" provides another structural perspective of ethnic differentials in employment (Hodge 1973). Simply stated, when job opportunities requiring low to moderate skills (education) decline, ethnic employment competition intensifies for two reasons. First, employers can be more "choosy" about which workers to hire, allowing their preferences and prejudices to play themselves out differently from a situation of labor scarcity. Second, the changing ethnic composition of neighborhoods resulting from differential migration of minority workers can reconfigure the extent and nature of job competition along color lines (Hodge 1973; Tienda, Donato, and Cordero-Guzmán 1992).

Several studies have documented that immigrants participate in the labor force at a higher rate than natives (Borjas and Tienda 1987), but researchers do not agree whether immigrants displace native minority workers. Aggregate econometric evidence indicates that the labor market impacts of recent immigrants are benign, but studies of specific firms and communities reveal intense competition between immigrants and native minorities (Tienda and Liang 1993). At issue for the contemporary debates about pervasive inner-city joblessness is whether native minorities both perceive competition from immigrants and experience lower employment rates than comparably or less-skilled immigrants.

Finally, discrimination against people of color could also give rise to race and ethnic differences in joblessness even in the absence of skill differences because it implies unequal treatment of entire groups. For example, a recent study showed that the employment returns to education came to depend increasingly on race and ethnicity between 1960 and 1985, particularly among women with less than a high school degree (Tienda, Donato, and Cordero-Guzmán 1992). However, this study did not consider whether higher minority joblessness was associated with group differences in willingness to work.

INDIVIDUAL DIFFERENCES AND ETHNIC INEQUALITY

The human capital explanation for the disadvantaged labor market standing of minority workers is essentially one that focuses on workers' differences in skills. Assuming that education has uniform exchange value, then the highest labor force participation rates should correspond to groups with the most education. The skill deficit explanation of rising inner-city joblessness also has been tied to the "spatial mismatch hypothesis" (Holzer 1991; Kasarda 1985). Simply put, the rapid decline of unskilled and semi-skilled jobs from old industrial centers has produced a major imbalance between the supply of workers available and the demand for a highly educated workforce. Stated as a variant of the spatial mismatch hypothesis, the skill deficit interpretation maintains that increased inequities between White and non-White workers reflect the failure of minorities to keep pace with the rising educational requisites of new jobs.

An alternative individualistic explanation for pervasive inner-city joblessness suggests that weak labor force attachment is coupled with a preference for welfare (Murray 1984). Although several critics have challenged this interpretation, few studies have investigated the willingness of inner-city dwellers to work (Tienda and Stier 1991; Van Haitsma 1989). One variant of the weak attachment explanation is that jobless inner-city residents require higher wage rates than employers are willing to pay, given their skills and prior employment experience. Reservation wage refers to the minimum hourly pay required by workers in order to accept a job offer. Applied to race and ethnic differences in labor force activity, this implies that jobless minority workers demand higher compensation as a condition of accepting a job than similarly skilled nonminority workers. This argument has been summoned to explain the anomaly of high minority unemployment coupled with high rates of labor force activity among undocumented workers. However, few studies have examined empirically whether people of color actually demand

TABLE 1

Labor Force Participation and Unemployment Rates of Parents Ages 18 to 44 by Ethnicity and Gender: Chicago's Inner City and United States, 1987.

				Chicago								*United States*		
				Mixed Poverty Neighborhoods		*Ghetto Poverty Neighborhoods*								*Non-Core City*
		Total Inner City							*Total*		*Core City*			
Sex and Ethnicity	[N]	LFP	UNEM	LFP	UNEM	LFP	UNEM	[N]	LFP	UNEM	LFP	UNEM	LFP	UNEM
Men	[811]	86.1	9.4	91.0	7.0	78.9	13.0	[1796]	96.2	3.2	96.1	4.1	96.4	2.3
Black	[308]	82.6	12.9	88.4	10.0	76.5	15.9	[334]	94.1	8.4	94.3	11.8	93.7	2.6
White	[127]	91.3	4.3	93.0	5.5	84.9	0.0[a]	[1321]	96.6	2.3	96.3	2.2	96.8	2.3
Mexican	[228]	94.8	1.7	96.5	1.7	89.6	1.8	[118]	97.1	4.5	98.3	5.1	—[b]	—[b]
Puerto Rican	[148]	84.4	7.6	85.6	7.3	82.1	8.2	[23]	90.1	13.3	91.5	14.5[b]	—[b]	—[b]
Women	[1523]	50.0	5.1	56.0	4.5	42.9	5.8	[3387]	65.8	4.5	66.5	4.7	65.0	4.1
Black	[719]	50.5	6.4	59.8	6.2	42.8	6.5	[793]	73.7	10.3	72.5	10.2	76.4	10.4
White	[237]	55.9	3.3	58.4	4.1	45.7	0.0[a]	[2296]	65.2	2.9	67.2	2.3	63.4	3.4
Mexican	[261]	52.8	1.9	52.4	1.5	54.2	3.7	[227]	60.0	9.9	58.0	9.5	77.1[c]	13.1[c]
Puerto Rican	[306]	35.4	1.3	37.4	1.6	31.9	0.6	[71]	34.8	4.6	32.9	5.1	—[b]	—[b]

[a] Based on unweighted cell sizes of 30 men and 58 women.

[b] Based on unweighted cell sizes of 20 or less observations.

[c] Based on weighted cell size of 30 or less observations.

Source: UPFLS (1987) and NSFH (1987).

higher wages than their skill characteristics warrant. We evaluate this claim in some detail below.

. . .

RACE AND ETHNIC DIFFERENCES IN LABOR FORCE ACTIVITY

Table 1 compares labor force participation rates for Chicago and the United States. The "core city" refers to residence within city boundaries, as in accordance with U.S. census guidelines, while the noncore city refers to suburban fringes and nonmetropolitan areas. Within Chicago, separate tabulations for "mixed poverty" and "ghetto poverty" neighborhoods, respectively, refer to census tracts with family poverty rates of 5 to 20 and 30 percent or more.

These tabulations show that the labor force activity of parents depends on ethnicity and gender, and within Chicago's inner city, neighborhood context as well. Three broad generalizations are warranted from these results. First, in the aggregate, labor force participation rates are uniformly lower among Chicago parents than parents nationally, with gaps approaching 10 percent for men, and exceeding 15 percent for women. Likewise, unemployment rates also were appreciable higher in Chicago than in the nation as a whole, 9.4 versus 3.2 percent for men, and 5.1 versus 4.5 percent for women.

Second, while race and ethnic differences in labor force activity are clearly evident in both samples, Chicago's Blacks and Puerto Ricans experience extreme labor market hardships.[1] Chicago's Black inner-city men participated in the labor force at a rate 11 percent below Black men nationally, compared to a 5 percent point difference for White men and a 2.3 percent gap for Mexican-origin fathers. The narrow labor force activity gap for Mexican-origin men reflects the high immigrant composition of the Chicago sample relative to the national sample, combined with the higher labor force participation rates of immigrant compared to native-born men (Bean and Tienda 1987).[2] Among mothers, the lowest rates of labor activity correspond to Puerto Ricans, whose rates hovered around 35 percent in both samples.

Racial disparities in unemployment were also apparent in both samples. Black parents experienced the highest unemployment rates. Chicago's Black fathers were three times more likely than White fathers to be unemployed in 1987, but this compared favorably with the national Black-White unemployment ratio of 3.6. For Women, the ratio of Black-White unemployment was approximately 2 in Chicago, compared to 3.5 nationally.

Third, residence-specific differentials in labor force activity rates were substantial between mixed and ghetto poverty neighborhoods in Chicago. In the mixed poverty neighborhoods, 91 percent of fathers were in the labor force compared to 79 percent in ghetto poverty neighborhoods. Black fathers are largely responsible for the low average male participation rate in ghetto poverty areas. Mothers residing in mixed poverty neighborhoods participated in the labor force at a rate of 56 percent compared to 43 percent among those residing in ghetto poverty neighborhoods. Furthermore, in mixed poverty neighborhoods, Black and White women exhibited the highest rate of labor force activity, but in ghetto poverty areas, Mexican origin women did. Unemployment rates of Black fathers were 50 percent higher in ghetto versus mixed poverty areas, but employment rates of Hispanic fathers did not vary appreciably from neighborhood poverty status.

MAKING SENSE OF ETHNIC INEQUALITY: VOICES FROM THE INNER CITY

Robert Hodge's (1973) conception of the labor market as an ethnic queue is helpful in under-

standing race and ethnic differences in employment statuses and provides some insight into the emergence of wage inequities. The basic principle of queuing is that in the process of matching workers to jobs, the most desirable workers are hired first and the least desirable workers are hired last. Thus, when labor demand shrinks, increases in joblessness will be greatest for workers at the bottom than for workers ranked higher in the queue (Hodge 1973; Lieberson 1980; Reskin and Roos 1990). In a totally meritocratic society, skills would be the primary basis for determining individuals' rank in a hiring queue; in practice, gender, race, and national origin are also decisive. Distortions in rankings based purely on skills result because employers have imperfect information about prospective workers productivity, organizational procedures often protect and reward others with seniority, and employers discriminate against entire groups of workers (Hodge 1973).

We believe that the worsened labor market position of Black and Puerto Rican inner-city workers results partly from displacement through competition with new sources of labor. Responses to the open-ended interviews from the Social Opportunity Survey led support to this interpretation, and reinforce our contention that the significance of color increases when the supply of jobs at a given skill level contracts and the supply of immigrant workers increases. These responses provide richly textured substance about how opportunity depends on race and national origin.

Jack's comments in response to a question about who gets ahead are especially illuminating about how color shapes opportunity in Chicago.[3] Jack is married, Black, and forty-four years old. He has five kids to support. He lives in an extremely poor, all-Black neighborhood and has never been on welfare, though he lost his house when the steel mill shut down. To the question on who gets ahead, he responded:

It's still the same old thing: Whites get ahead much quicker than Blacks. Still the same, that hasn't changed, 'cause on this job right now, I can see that. But there's nothing you can do about it if you want keep your job, you gotta just lay dead and try to make it. . . . I can say this much: a man gotta do what he gotta do. If he gotta work, he gotta work: it's as simple as that. (emphatically) *You got to work.* If you don't do that, you gonna rob, and steal and I can't do that, 'cause what would I do in jail with five kids and a wife, you know? So I *have to work.*

When probed about who is least likely to get ahead, he replied:

It would go between the Puerto Ricans and the Blacks. They, they catch hell too. 'Cause a lot of them work out there with me. I don't know why, I don't know: I wish I knew why. I don't know why it's like that. They're just saying "that's the way it is." It's like a set pattern.

A Mexican respondent was equally blunt in linking job opportunities to ethnicity. Says he: "The good jobs go to the gringos!"

Many respondents—too numerous to report—spontaneously answered questions about opportunity and access to good and bad jobs with references to race and ethnicity. Some acknowledged that color could be used to reserve slots for minorities, but there was general agreement that the best jobs go to Whites, and especially educated Whites, while the worst jobs go to Blacks and Latinos. "Someone has to do the dirty work," replied a White woman in response to several questions about employment opportunities. Having networks and connections was another recurrent theme in responses to questions about access to good and bad jobs, but no one clarified how one gets connections in the first place, except that the rich and White folks have them.

Belinda, a thirty-nine-year-old, married, Black woman with six kids who is on public aid, sees this quite clearly:

Well, like, I've been here all my life, you know, and it's a White-ruled system, you know. If you're White, you've got a better chance. And I've personally experienced that as far as moving. . . . You know, I've went on jobs and seen a White person get hired and I was

told there was no job. The job wasn't even, didn't even require skills, you know, things like that.

Several respondents, especially Blacks, lamented the better times they experienced in the past. Letonya, a forty-one-year-old mother of two, legally separated, and on strike from a certified nurse's aid job, articulated this position:

Now they don't have the jobs that they had, even back in the sixties . . . before, I don't think it's as many people are from other countries was over here like it is now, you know. And it seems to me they're sort of moving out the Americans (laughs). I mean taking up the jobs where the peoples, Americans used to have. 'Cause I had worked for quite a few in my life, I worked in a hospital until four years ago and they laid us off. And it was a lot of foreigners over here you know. And when they come over here, they work for little or nothing, you know what I'm saying. . . . *Americans understand that they couldn't live off with what little money they were paying.* (authors' emphasis)

Some would say Letonya had a higher reservation wage than immigrants, meaning that she demanded higher wages than other workers with similar characteristics. However, a more perceptive interpretation, particularly in light of the empirical evidence provided below showing that Blacks have lower reservation wages than similarly skilled Hispanics or Whites, is that Letonya understands what it takes to live in Chicago, and appropriately questions a decline in her economic status.

Letonya was not the only respondent who blamed her weakened labor market position on illegal immigrants. Several respondents implicated immigration as a major reason for the narrowing of economic opportunities among Chicago's native residents. In contrast to several econometric studies based on national data which show little competition between native minorities and recent immigrants, Chicago's inner-city parents perceived acute competition and job displacement from recent immigrants, and especially undocumented immigrants.

According to Sabrina, a forty-two-year-old widow in a visiting union, who has seven kids and a history of chronic unemployment, opportunity is lessened by the presence of immigrants:

NO. They're bringing too many foreigners over here from other countries for any of us to get ahead or do what it's our right to do, and that's put us down.[4]

Jane, a married mother of four who holds a GED and has been on welfare since 1972, thinks only the bad jobs go to illegals. Her response supports the view that undocumented migrants take the jobs U.S. natives refuse:

Well, the bad jobs are usually for the poor Spanish people that come here illegally and they'll work for 2 dollars an hour . . . because they're afraid, you know, that they're . . . and they get mistreated and . . . stuff. Wetbacks they call 'em, which I don't see why they do. Call 'em Spanish or whatever, but . . .[5]

Yet other respondents felt that unauthorized immigrants were taking both good and bad jobs. For example, Ann, a thirty-year-old mother of four who has never been on welfare and is currently married, doesn't believe there are enough good jobs for everybody:

'cause the illegal aliens . . . they're taking all the jobs, 'cause its cheap labor. They can work for $3.00 an hour, whereas they're looking for $8 or $9 an hour. . . . I'm not prejudiced against any illegal alien, but they shouldn't come here, and be taking our jobs and what belong to us.

Susan, a disabled welfare mother of three, also agrees:

I don't know, I might sound . . . like I'm prejudice or something, but I think they should go back to where they belong and let the White people work and make a living. . . . The Mexicans should go to Mexico and the Puerto Ricans should go back to Puerto Rico and the Blacks to Africa.[6]

These responses from Chicago's inner-city poor illustrate that competition for jobs is not simply a matter of Blacks versus Whites, or undocumented migrants versus native minorities. We

were particularly struck by the responses of Puerto Ricans and Mexicans indicating job competition between them, intense discrimination against Puerto Ricans, and more generally, perceived rankings of Mexicans as workers preferred over Puerto Ricans. Dolores, a forty-two-year-old Puerto Rican welfare mother of four, has never been married and has been on public aid since 1969, following a highly unstable employment history between the ages of fifteen and twenty-four. She has lived in Chicago thirty-three years, and in her current neighborhood sixteen years. It is not lack of effort that keeps her jobless:

I go down to . . . I would love to work there, you make good money there. Every time I go they say they are not hiring. Every time I go I sign an application. They tell me I already have a lot of them there, but I say give me another. . . . I go down to the next factory where they make plastic flowers and apply there too. And to the next one and like that. . . . My daughters tell me they see help wanted signs, but when I go over they say no. My daughters tell me they want Mexicans and that I should just say I'm Mexican. Because they'll work for less and all that. But I say, "But they'll ask me for my papers!" But if you want the job, maybe you have to do that. Because I have some Mexican friends they go and get the job just like that. Because it's a $5 an hour job but they would only pay the Mexicans like $3.50.

When probed if she would work for $3.50, she replied:

I wouldn't mind. I used to work for less, for eighty cents an hour. I wouldn't mind, but then when I go they say they aren't hiring. But the other ones get the jobs and then I don't want to go back, you know.

While argument about differences in the labor market standing of Mexicans and Puerto Ricans based on national data lend themselves quite readily to structural interpretations that emphasize the decline of blue-collar operative jobs as being responsible for the declining economic status of Puerto Ricans, this is only part of the story. In particular, it is difficult to argue that geography is a major factor in the differential labor force activity of Mexicans and Puerto Ricans living in poor

Chicago neighborhoods. Also, a recent study provided strong evidence that the position of Puerto Ricans in New York was undermined by recent immigrants (Tienda and Donato 1993). Therefore, we wish to emphasize the importance of intense discrimination as a factor responsible for the declining labor market status of Puerto Ricans.

EXPLAINING RACE AND ETHNIC INEQUALITY IN LABOR FORCE PARTICIPATION

Our theoretical discussion identified differences in skill and willingness to work as two plausible reasons for race and ethnic variation in labor force activity. If educational deficits were the primary reason for high joblessness among inner-city minorities, we would expect lower education levels in Chicago than the United States, and among ethnic groups, the lowest educational levels for Blacks. In fact, as Table 2 shows, the educational characteristics of Chicago's Blacks and Whites are generally similar to those of their national counterparts. Hispanic parents were far more educationally disadvantaged than Black inner-city parents, averaging seven to ten years for Mexicans and Puerto Ricans, respectively. Yet the highest labor force activity rate (and lowest unemployment rate) corresponds to Mexican, not White or Black fathers.

Despite the similar mean levels of completed schooling among the Chicago and the national samples, the proportion of high school graduates revealed greater discrepancies. For example, between 55 and 58 percent of Chicago's Black parents were high school graduates, compared to about 80 percent of the Black parents nationally. Among Mexicans, 35 to 38 percent of Chicago parents reported having graduated from high school, compared to 43 to 63 percent of mothers and fathers nationally. The greatest discrepancy in high school graduation rates corresponds to Whites, as over 90 percent of the national sample compared to two-thirds of the inner-city sample claimed high school diplomas.

Race and ethnic differences in receipt of transfer income (that is, public aid) show relatively low rates of welfare utilization among White and Mexican parents, particularly when contrasted with the welfare participation rates of Black and Puerto Rican parents. Less than 10 percent of White mothers nationally were on public aid at the time of the survey, compared to 30 percent of White mothers in Chicago. By contrast, over half of Chicago's Black and Puerto Rican mothers were on aid in 1987, compared to between one-quarter and one-third of their national counterparts. Despite their severe educational disadvantages, Chicago's Mexican parents made relatively low use of transfer income. Ineligibility for means-tested benefits (because of immigrant status) may partly explain the low rates of welfare utilization among Mexicans, but their high rates of labor force activity, even at low wages, also may obviate their need for transfer income.

Skill, Color, and Labor Force Activity

A more succinct assessment of the relationship between ethnicity, education, and work activity is possible by examining simultaneously several determinants of labor force participation. For this we estimated a model that allowed us to evaluate the unique influence of individual, family, and neighborhood characteristics on the likelihood that respondents obtained a job. These results are illuminating and we summarize their lessons below. First, there are striking similarities in the determinants of labor force activity for both mother and fathers, despite some noteworthy differences. For example, marriage increases the probability of labor force participation for both men and women, and the presence of young children has no influence on labor force activity of either mothers or fathers. Also, disability lowers the odds of labor force participation for both mothers and fathers. However, the presence of other adults increases the probability that mothers will work, but not fathers. This result has a parallel based on national populations (Tienda and Glass 1985).

TABLE 2

Selected Demographic and Socio-economic Characteristics of Respondents by Ethnicity and Gender: Chicago's Inner City and United States, 1987 (Means and Percents)

	Blacks		Whites		Mexicans		Puerto Ricans	
	Men	Women	Men	Women	Men	Women	Men	Women
Chicago								
x̄ Education	12.1	11.9	13.1	12.1	7.0	7.2	9.7	9.9
(s.d.)	(2.1)	(1.9)	(2.9)	(2.6)	(3.6)	(3.8)	(3.0)	(2.8)
High School Graduates (%)	54.8	58.0	67.1	63.6	38.3	35.6	31.0	38.7
Employment								
Never worked (%)	9.9	20.7	0.0	8.6	0.9	17.0	5.4	28.6
Currently working (%)	69.7	44.1	87.0	52.6	93.1	50.9	76.8	34.1
Transfer income								
Ever received aid (%)	46.1	81.3	13.6	45.3	9.6	29.6	35.5	75.3
Currently on aid (%)	22.3	52.0	6.2	29.7	2.6	13.6	11.6	53.7
[N]	[338]	[689]	[126]	[238]	[229]	[260]	[145]	[309]
U.S. cities								
x̄ Education	12.7	12.5	13.8	13.3	10.9	9.6	—[a]	9.9
(s.d.)	(2.5)	(1.9)	(2.6)	(2.4)	(3.6)	(3.5)	—[a]	(3.2)
High School Graduates (%)	79.7	79.7	91.7	90.2	63.6	43.1	—[a]	39.3
Employment								
Never worked (%)	0.0	12.5	0.0	4.8	0.0	19.2	—[a]	40.5
Currently working (%)	83.3	62.1	94.0	65.3	90.6	48.9	—[a]	27.7
Transfer income								
Ever received aid[b] (%)	9.2	36.1	7.3	15.3	8.6	31.6	—[a]	46.2
Currently on aid (%)	3.6	27.5	1.7	7.4	2.9	16.4	—[a]	34.0
[N]	[213]	[529]	[613]	[1095]	[101]	[201]	[20]	[62]

[a] Too few cases.

[b] Received since 1982.

Source: UPFLS (1987) and NSFH (1987).

Second, two findings are particularly noteworthy for our hypothesis about the relative importance of color and skill in determining labor force outcomes. One is that high school graduation status significantly increased the labor market activity of inner-city mothers, but had no influence on the market activity of inner-city fathers. This indicates that education is a necessary, albeit insufficient condition for labor market success. Another key finding is that race and ethnic differences in labor force activity persist, even after standardizing our sample for differences in education, family status, and neighborhood characteristics. Specifically, Black fathers were significantly less likely, and Mexican fathers more likely, to participate in the labor force than their statistically equivalent White counterparts. Among mothers, significant ethnic differences were obtained only for Mexican-origin women, whose labor force activity exceeded that of White mothers with similar educational, family, and personal characteristics.

Finally, consistent with prior theorizing about the pervasiveness of joblessness in ghetto poverty areas, our results clearly show that labor force activity is significantly lower in neighborhoods with poverty rates in excess of 39 percent. It is unclear whether this result is obtained because residents of ghetto poverty area refuse to work, or because they experience greater barriers obtaining jobs. This possibility is addressed next.

. . .

CONCLUSION

Our emphasis on discrimination is not intended to discount the importance of explanations of persisting race and ethnic differences in wages which emphasize the surplus of laborers willing to work at low wages. Although we have taken into account individual differences in education and experience, there probably remain unmeasured skill differences (English proficiency, for example) among the groups. Ultimately, shifts in both supply and demand curves set wages, hence the various individual and structural interpretations reviewed at the outset are pertinent for understanding persisting wage disparities along color lines (Holzer 1993). Our approach considered both supply and demand factors that have been summoned to explain increased labor market inequities along race and ethnic lines.

By the way of a tentative conclusion we propose that discrimination against people of color residing in the inner city, but especially Blacks, was heightened during the 1980s as the share of low-skill jobs declined. Even though Black jobless parents reported the lowest reservation wage rates and received the lowest wages among those with a job, employers are increasingly reluctant to hire them, particularly when alternative sources of immigrant labor are readily available. Stated differently, employers seem to prefer Mexican and White workers over Blacks, and to a somewhat lesser extent Puerto Ricans. Not only does color matter, but it has an exchange value that fluctuates according to general economic conditions and the availability of alternative sources of unskilled labor. But we want to be clear that, while the market may very well set prices, it is employers, not the market, who discriminate.

NOTES

1. Unfortunately, it is not possible to tabulate separately Puerto Rican men in the NSFH. Although the participation rates for Puerto Rican women are lower than those of other minority women (Bean and Tienda 1987; Tienda 1989; Tienda, Donato, and Cordero-Guzmán 1992), the small number of Puerto Ricans in the national sample warrants caution in interpreting the actual estimates.

2. The Chicago sample is approximately 85 percent foreign-born versus approximately 25 to 30 percent for the national population, depending on the enumeration of undocumented immigrants. The over-representation of immigrant Mexicans in the Chicago sample reflects the higher residential concentration of recent arrivals in poorer ethnic neighborhoods compared to native-born persons of Mexican descent.

3. All names used are fictive.

4. This was in response to a question about opportunity in Chicago.

5. This was in response to a question about who gets the bad jobs in Chicago.

6. Apparently the GED she received didn't provide a balanced account of U.S. labor history.

REFERENCES

Bean, Frank D., and Marta Tienda. 1987. *The Hispanic Population of the United States*. New York: Russell Sage.

Borjas, George J., and Marta Tienda. 1987. "The Economic Consequences of Immigration." *Science* 235 (February 6): 613–620.

Burgess, Ernest W. 1923. "The Growth of the City: An Introduction to a Research Project." *Publications of the American Sociological Society* 18: 85–97.

Grossman, James. 1991. "The White Man's Union: The Great Migration and the Resonance of Race and Class in Chicago, 1916–1922." Pp. 83–105 in *The Great Migration in Historical Perspective: New Dimensions of Race, Class and Gender*, ed. Joe W. Trotter, Jr. Bloomington: Indiana University Press.

Hodge, Robert W. 1973. "Toward a Theory of Racial Differences in Employment." *Social Forces* 52 (1): 16–31.

Holzer, Harry J. 1991. "The Spatial Mismatch Hypothesis: What has the evidence Shown?" *Urban Studies* 28 (1): 105–122.

——— . 1993. "Black Employment Problems: New Evidence, Old Questions." Unpublished paper, Department of Economics, Michigan State University.

Johnson, Daniel M., and Rex R. Campbell. 1981. *Black Migration in America: A Social Demographic History.* Durham, N.C.: Duke University Press.

Kasarda, John P. 1985. Urban Change and Minority Opportunities." In *The New Urban Reality*, ed. Paul E. Peterson. Washington D.C.: Brookings Institution.

Lieberson, Stanley. 1980. *A Piece of the Pie: Blacks and White Immigrants Since 1880.* Berkeley and Los Angeles: University of California Press.

Moore, Joan. 1989. "Is there a Hispanic Underclass?" *Social Science Quarterly* 70 (2): 265–284.

Murray, Charles. 1984. *Losing Ground.* New York: Basic Books.

Park, Robert E. 1914. "Racial Assimilation in Secondary Groups." *American Journal of Sociology* 19: 606–623.

Reskin, Barbara, and Patricia A. Roos. 1990. *Job Queues, Gender Queues: Explaining Women's Inroads into Male Occupations.* Philadelphia: Temple University Press.

Tienda, Marta. 1989. "Puerto Ricans and the Underclass Debate." *Annals of the American Academy of Political and Social Science* 501 (January): 105–119.

Tienda, Marta, Katharine Donato, and Héctor Cordero-Guzmán. 1992. "Schooling. Color and Labor Force Activity of Women." *Social Forces* 71 (2): 365–395.

Tienda, Marta, and Jennifer Glass. 1985. "Household Structure and Labor Force Participation of Black, Hispanic and White Mothers." *Demography* 22 (3): 381–394.

Tienda, Marta, and Leif Jensen. 1988. "Poverty and Minorities: A Quarter Century Profile of Color Socioeconomic Disadvantage." Pp. 23–61 in *Divided Opportunities*, ed. Gary D. Sandefur and Marta Tienda. New York: Plenum Publishers.

Tienda, Marta, and Zai Liang. 1963. "Poverty and Immigration in Policy Perspective." In *Poverty and Public Policy*, ed. Sheldon H. Danziger, Gary D. Sandefur, and Daniel H. Weinberg. Cambridge: Harvard University Press.

Tienda, Marta, and Haya Stier. 1991. "Joblessness or Shiftlessness: Labor Force Activity in Chicago's Inner City." In *The Urban Underclass*, ed. Christopher Jencks and Paul Peterson. Washington D.C.: Brookings Institution.

Van Haitsma, Martha. 1989. "A Contextual Definition of the Underclass." *Focus* 12 (spring/summer): 27–31.

Wilson, William Julius. 1987. *The Truly Disadvantaged: The Inner City, the Underclass, and Public Policy.* Chicago: University of Chicago Press.

Wirth, Louis. 1938. "Urbanism as a Way of Life." *American Journal of Sociology* 44 (1): 3–24.

28

The Continuing Causes of Segregation

Douglas S. Massey and Nancy A. Denton

Residential segregation has proved to be the most resistant to change of all realms—perhaps because it is so critical to racial change in general.

Thomas Pettigrew, 1966,
review of *Negroes in Cities*
by Karl and Alma Taeuber

THE SPATIAL ISOLATION OF BLACK AMERICANS was achieved by a conjunction of racist attitudes, private behaviors, and institutional practices that disenfranchised blacks from urban housing markets and led to the creation of the ghetto.[1] Discrimination in employment exacerbated black poverty and limited the economic potential for integration, and black residential mobility was systematically blocked by pervasive discrimination and white avoidance of neighborhoods containing blacks. The walls of the ghetto were buttressed after 1950 by government programs that promoted slum clearance and relocated displaced ghetto residents into multi-story, high-density housing projects.

In theory, this self-reinforcing cycle of prejudice, discrimination, and segregation was broken during the 1960s by a growing rejection of racist sentiments by whites and a series of court decisions and federal laws that banned discrimination in public life. The Civil Rights Act of 1964 out-lawed racial discrimination in employment, the Fair Housing Act of 1968 banned discrimination in housing, and the *Gautreaux* and *Shannon* court decisions prohibited public authorities from placing housing projects exclusively in black neighborhoods. Despite these changes, however, the nation's largest black communities remained as segregated as ever in 1980. Indeed, many urban areas displayed a pattern of intense racial isolation that could only be described as hypersegregation.

Although the racial climate of the United States improved outwardly during the 1970s, racism still restricted the residential freedom of black Americans; it just did so in less blatant ways. In the aftermath of the civil rights revolution, few whites voiced openly racist sentiments; realtors no longer refused outright to rent or sell to blacks; and few local governments went on record to oppose public housing projects because they would contain blacks. This lack of overt racism, however, did not mean that prejudice and discrimination had ended; although racist attitudes and behaviors went underground, they did not disappear. Despite whites' endorsement of racial equality in principle, prejudice against blacks continued in subtle ways; in spite of the provisions of the Fair Housing Act, real estate agents continued to practice surreptitious but widespread discrimination;

From *American Apartheid: Segregation and the Making of the Underclass* by Douglas S. Massey and Nancy A. Denton. Copyright © 1993 by the President and Fellows of Harvard College. Reprinted by permission of Harvard University Press.

and rather than conform to court decrees, local authorities stopped building projects.

RACE VERSUS CLASS: AN UNEQUAL CONTEST

Before exploring the continuing causes of segregation, we assess the extent to which the geographic separation of blacks and whites may be attributed to economic differences between the two groups. In the market-driven, status-conscious society of [the] United States, affluent families live in different neighborhoods than poor families, and to the extent that blacks are poor and whites are affluent, the two groups will tend to be physically separated from one another. Is what appears to be racial segregation actually segregation on the basis of social class?

Economic arguments can be invoked to explain why levels of black–white segregation changed so little during the 1970s. After decades of steady improvement, black economic progress stalled in 1973, bringing about a rise in black poverty and an increase in income inequality.[2] As the black income distribution bifurcated, middle-class families experienced downward mobility and fewer households possessed the socioeconomic resources necessary to sustain residential mobility and, hence, integration. If the economic progress of the 1950s and 1960s had been sustained into the 1970s, segregation levels might have fallen more significantly. William Clark estimates that 30%–70% of racial segregation is attributable to economic factors, which, together with urban structure and neighborhood preferences, "bear much of the explanatory weight for present residential patterns."[3]

Arguments about whether racial segregation stems from white racism or from economic disadvantages are part of a larger debate on the relative importance of race and class in American society. Some observers hold that black social and economic problems now stem from the unusually disadvantaged class position of African Americans; they argue that black poverty has become divorced from race per se and is now perpetuated by a complex set of factors, such as joblessness, poor schooling, and family instability, that follow from the transformation of cities from manufacturing to service centers.[4] Other investigators place greater emphasis on racism; they argue that because white prejudice and discrimination have persisted in a variety of forms, both overt and subtle, skin color remains a powerful basis of stratification in the United States.[5]

Since the mid-1970s, the race–class debate has gone on without definitive resolution with respect to a variety of socioeconomic outcomes: employment, wealth, family stability, education, crime. But when one considers residential segregation, the argument is easily and forcefully settled: race clearly predominates. Indeed, race predominates to such an extent that speculations about what would have happened if black economic progress had continued become moot. Even if black incomes had continued to rise through the 1970s, segregation would not have declined: no matter how much blacks earned they remained spatially separated from whites. In 1980, as in the past, money did not buy entry into white neighborhoods of American cities.

The dominance of race over class is illustrated by Table 4.1, which presents black–white dissimilarity indices for three income groups within the thirty largest black communities of the United States. These data show the degree of residential segregation that blacks experience as their family income rises from under $2,500 per year to more than $50,000 per year. Although we computed segregation indices for all income categories between these two extremes, in the interest of brevity we only show one middle category ($25,000–$27,500). Little is added by including other income groups, because black segregation does not vary by affluence.[6]

Among northern metropolitan areas, for example, blacks, no matter what their income, remain very highly segregated from whites. As of 1980, black families earning under $2,500 per year experienced an average segregation index of 86, whereas those earning more than $50,000 had an average score of 83; blacks in the middle category

TABLE 4.1

Segregation by Income in Thirty Metropolitan Areas with the Largest Black Populations, 1970–1980

Metropolitan Area	Income Category		
	Under $2,500	$25,000–$27,500	$50,000 +
Northern Areas			
Boston	85.1	83.9	89.1
Buffalo	85.2	80.0	90.0
Chicago	91.1	85.8	86.3
Cincinnati	81.7	70.9	74.2
Cleveland	91.6	87.1	86.4
Columbus	80.3	74.6	83.4
Detroit	88.6	85.0	86.4
Gary–Hammond–E. Chicago	90.6	89.5	90.9
Indianapolis	80.8	76.6	80.0
Kansas City	86.1	79.3	84.2
Los Angeles–Long Beach	85.4	79.8	78.9
Milwaukee	91.3	87.9	86.3
New York	86.2	81.2	78.6
Newark	85.8	79.0	77.5
Philadelphia	84.9	78.6	81.9
Pittsburgh	82.1	80.6	87.9
St. Louis	87.3	78.4	83.2
San Francisco–Oakland	79.9	73.7	72.1
Average	85.8	80.7	83.2
Southern Areas			
Atlanta	82.2	77.3	78.2
Baltimore	82.4	72.3	76.8
Birmingham	46.1	40.8	45.2
Dallas–Ft. Worth	83.1	74.7	82.4
Greensboro–Winston-Salem	63.2	55.1	70.8
Houston	73.8	65.5	72.7
Memphis	73.8	66.8	69.8
Miami	81.6	78.4	76.5
New Orleans	75.8	63.1	77.8
Norfolk–Virginia Beach	70.1	63.3	72.4
Tampa–St. Petersburg	81.8	76.0	85.7
Washington, D.C.	79.2	67.0	65.4
Average	74.4	66.7	72.8

Source: Nancy A. Denton and Douglas S. Massey, "Residential Segregation of Blacks, Hispanics, and Asians by Socioeconomic Status and Generation," *Social Science Quarterly* 69 (1988):811. Reprinted by permission of the University of Texas Press and the authors.

displayed a score of 81. This pattern of constant, high segregation was replicated in virtually all northern urban areas. In Chicago, for example, the poorest blacks displayed an index of 91; the most affluent blacks had an index of 86. In New York, the respective figures were 86 and 79; and in Los Angeles they were 85 and 79. In no northern metropolitan area did blacks earning more than $50,000 per year display a segregation index lower than 72.

Although southern areas generally evinced lower levels of racial segregation, the basic pattern by income was the same: rising economic status had little or no effect on the level of segregation that blacks experienced. On average, segregation moved from 74 in the lowest income category to 73 in the highest, with a value of 67 in between. Segregation was particularly high and resistant to change in Atlanta, Baltimore, Dallas, Miami, and Tampa; but even in southern cities with relatively low levels of segregation, there was little evidence of a meaningful differential by income: the poorest blacks in Birmingham, Alabama, displayed a segregation index of 46, whereas the most affluent black families had a segregation index of 45.

One possible explanation for this pattern of constant segregation irrespective of income is that affluent blacks are not well informed about the cost and availability of housing opportunities in white neighborhoods. Reynolds Farley examined this possibility using special data collected in the University of Michigan's Detroit Area Survey. He found that blacks were quite knowledgeable about housing costs throughout the metropolitan area, even in distant white suburbs, and were well aware that they could afford to live outside the ghetto.[7] Whatever was keeping affluent blacks out of white areas, it was not ignorance.

The uniqueness of this pattern of invariant high segregation is starkly revealed when blacks are compared with Hispanics or Asians. In the Los Angeles metropolitan area, for example, the segregation index for Hispanics earning under $2,500 in 1979 was 64, and it declined to a moderate value of 50 among those earning $50,000 or more. In the

largest Latino barrio in the United States, therefore, the *poorest* Hispanics were less segregated than the *most affluent* blacks (whose score was 79). Similarly, in the San Francisco–Oakland metropolitan area, which contains the largest concentration of Asians in the United States, the Asian–white segregation index fell from 64 in the lowest income category to 52 in the highest (compared with respective black–white indices of 86 and 79). These contrasts were repeated in cities throughout the United States: Hispanic and Asian segregation generally begins at a relatively modest level among the poor and falls steadily as income rises.[8]

Similar patterns are observed when segregation is examined by education and occupation. No matter how socioeconomic status is measured, therefore, black segregation remains universally high while that of Hispanics and Asians falls progressively as status rises. Only blacks experience a pattern of constant, high segregation that is impervious to socioeconomic influences. The persistence of racial segregation in American cities, therefore, is a matter of race and not class. The residential segregation of African Americans cannot be attributed in any meaningful way to the socioeconomic disadvantages they experience, however serious these may be.[9]

ATTITUDES IN BLACK AND WHITE

Even if the segregation of African Americans cannot be linked to black socioeconomic disadvantages, it does not necessarily follow that current residential patterns are involuntary. It is conceivable, for example, that high levels of segregation reflect black preferences for racial separation, and that these desires for residential homogeneity are merely expressed through urban housing markets. If most black people prefer to live in neighborhoods that are largely black, then high levels of racial segregation may correspond to black desires for self-segregation and not discrimination or prejudice.[10]

This line of reasoning does not square with survey evidence, however. The vast majority of

TABLE 4.2

Neighborhood Preferences of Black Respondents to Detroit Area Survey, 1976

Neighborhood Composition	Preference Ranking					
	First Choice	*Second Choice*	*Third Choice*	*Fourth Choice*	*Last Choice*	*Percentage Willing to Enter Such a Neighborhood*
All black	12%	5%	21%	35%	27%	69%
70% black	14	55	18	10	2	99
50% black	63	20	14	2	1	99
15% black	8	17	40	32	3	95
All white	2	3	7	21	66	38
Total	100%	100%	100%	100%	100%	

Sources: Reynolds Farley, Suzanne Bianchi, and Diane Colasanto, "Barriers to the Racial Integration of Neighborhoods: The Detroit Case," *Annals of the American Academy of Political and Social Science* 441 (1979):104; Reynolds Farley, Howard Schuman, Suzanne Bianchi, Diane Colasanto, and Shirley Hatchett, "'Chocolate City, Vanilla Suburbs': Will the Trend toward Racially Separate Communities Continue?" *Social Science Research* 7 (1978):330–335.

black Americans express strong support for the ideal of integration, and when asked on national surveys whether they favor "desegregation, strict segregation, or something in-between" they generally answer "desegregation" in large numbers. Although support for the "in-between" option rose during the 1970s, an average of 68% favored desegregation across the decade.[11] Moreover, 98% of black respondents have consistently agreed that "black people have a right to live wherever they can afford to," and in 1978 71% said they would be willing to vote for a community-wide law to ban racial discrimination in housing.[12]

In both principle and action, therefore, blacks strongly favor the desegregation of American society. They endorse the ideal of integration, they unanimously state that people should be able to move wherever they want to regardless of skin color, and they support the passage of laws to enforce these principles. But the endorsement of abstract principles and laws does not really get at the kinds of neighborhoods that blacks actually prefer to live in, or the degree of neighborhood

integration they find attractive and comfortable. The most widely cited source of information on this issue is the Detroit Area Survey.

Respondents to the survey were shown drawings of hypothetical neighborhoods with homes colored in either black or white. The percentage of black homes was systematically varied and respondents were asked how they felt about different racial compositions. Blacks expressed a strong preference for racial parity in neighborhoods: 63% chose a neighborhood that was half-black and half-white as most desirable, and 20% selected this option as their second choice (see Table 4.2). Virtually all blacks (99%) said they would be willing to live in such a neighborhood. At the same time, blacks appeared to resist strongly complete segregation: nearly a third would not be willing to move into a neighborhood that was all black, and 62% would be unwilling to enter an area that was all white. Nearly 90% ranked all-white neighborhoods as their fourth or fifth preference, and 62% placed all-black neighborhoods into one of these rankings.

Among racially mixed neighborhoods, blacks seem to prefer those with a relatively higher black percentage, other things equal. Thus the second choice of most blacks (55%) was a neighborhood that was 70% black, and only 17% selected an area where whites clearly predominated; neighborhoods that were 15% black were generally chosen as the third most desirable neighborhood. Even though blacks prefer a racial mixture of 50% black or higher, however, they are comfortable with almost any level of integration: 95% would be willing to live in any neighborhood with a black percentage lying between 15% and 70%.

These expressed preferences for integrated living coincide with comments made by black respondents to survey interviewers, which suggest that blacks not only favor integration but are motivated by an ideological commitment to racial harmony: "When you have different kinds of people around, children understand better"; "I'd rather live in a neighborhood that is mixed — don't have any trouble, no hostility"; "It might make it better to get along with white people."[13] Thus black support for residential desegregation comes not simply from a desire to achieve the social and economic benefits associated with residence in a white neighborhood, which are very real, but from a real commitment to the ideal of racial integration.

Despite this ideological stance, however, blacks express considerable reluctance about entering all-white neighborhoods. On the Detroit Area Survey, for example, 66% listed this racial mixture as their last choice, and only 38% were willing to move into such an area. This apprehension does not reflect a rejection of whites or white neighborhoods per se, but stems from fears of white hostility, rejection, or even worse. Among blacks who said they would not consider moving into a white area, 34% thought that white neighbors would be unfriendly and make them feel unwelcome, 37% said they would be made to feel uncomfortable, and 17% expressed a fear of violence.[14] Moreover, four-fifths of black respondents rejected the view that moving into a white neighborhood constituted a desertion of the black community.[15]

Although the level of antiblack violence has declined since the 1920s, black apprehensions about entering white neighborhoods are by no means unfounded. Some 213 racial "hate crimes" were reported in Chicago during 1990, about half directed at blacks. These crimes included 57 incidents of battery, 18 cases of vandalism, and 28 reports of threats or racial harassment. As in the past, these incidents occurred mainly along the color line: of 1,129 hate crimes reported in Chicago during 1985–1990, half were located in ten community areas undergoing racial change.[16] The Los Angeles Commission on Human Relations reported 167 racially motivated hate crimes during 1989, representing an increase of 78% over the prior year. About 60% of the crimes were directed against blacks and about 70% occurred at the victim's residence. The specific complaints included 54 instances of racist graffiti or literature, 53 assaults, 34 acts of vandalism, 19 threats, 6 cross-burnings, and one case of arson.[17]

Blacks moving into white neighborhoods in other cities encounter similar treatment. In Philadelphia, for example, an interracial couple made national headlines in 1985 when they moved into a white working-class neighborhood and were met by an angry mob and fire bombs.[18] When Otis and Alva Debnam became the first blacks to buy a home in an Irish neighborhood of Boston, they experienced a sustained campaign of racial intimidation, violence, and vandalism that culminated in a pitched battle with white youths on the eve of the nation's bicentennial in 1976.[19] In New York City, an Italian American told the sociologist Jonathan Rieder about the treatment he and his friends gave to Puerto Rican and black families who invaded their turf: "We got them out of Canarsie. We ran into the house and kicked the shit out of every one of them."[20]

This evidence suggests that the high degree of segregation blacks experience in urban America is not voluntary. By large majorities, blacks support the ideal of integration and express a preference for integrated living, and 95% are willing to live in neighborhoods that are anywhere between 15% and 70% black. Those who express a reluctance to enter all-white areas do so because of realistic fears of violence and harassment. If it were solely up to them, blacks would live primarily in racially mixed neighborhoods and levels of racial segregation would be markedly lower than they presently are.

The issue is not solely up to blacks to decide, however, because their preferences interact with those of whites to produce the residential outcomes we actually observe. Even though blacks may prefer neighborhoods with a 50–50 racial mixture, desegregation will not occur if most whites find this level of racial contact unacceptable. The smaller the percentage of blacks that whites are willing to tolerate, the less likely integration becomes.

On the surface, whites seem to share this ideological commitment to open housing. According to one national survey, the percentage of whites who agree that "black people have a right to live wherever they can afford to" rose from 76% in 1970 to 88% in 1978.[21] The percentage of whites on another national survey who disagreed with the statement that "white people have a right to keep blacks out of their neighborhoods if they want to" increased from 53% in 1970 to 67% in 1980.[22] By 1978, only 5% of whites called for the strict segregation of American society.[23]

Clearly, by the end of the 1970s most whites had come to acknowledge the legitimacy of integration as a social goal and supported open housing as a basic principle. This ideological stance logically implies an acceptance of residential desegregation, because, given black preferences, an open housing market will yield substantial racial mixing within neighborhoods. But surveys also reveal inconsistencies in white attitudes. Although whites may accept open housing in principle, they remain uncomfortable about its implications in practice and are reluctant to support legislation to implement it. Moreover, negative stereotypes about black neighbors remain firmly entrenched in white psyches.

Unlike blacks, whites are more committed to open housing and residential integration in principle than in practice. Although 88% of whites in 1978 agreed that blacks have a right to live wherever they want to, only 40% in 1980 were willing

to vote for a community-wide law stating that "a homeowner cannot refuse to sell to someone because of their race or skin color."[24] That is, as recently as 1980, 60% of whites would have voted against a fair housing law, even though one had been on the federal books for a dozen years.

Although whites may support fair housing in the abstract, their willingness to act on this ideal generally declines as the number of blacks increases. Whereas 86% of whites in 1978 said they would not move if "a black person came to live next door," only 46% stated they would not move if "black people came to live in large numbers."[25] Only 28% of whites in 1978 were willing to live in a neighborhood whose population was half black.[26]

Again, however, these questions about broad ideals and abstract principles do not really get at how whites feel about living with blacks, or how comfortable they are with different racial mixtures. When they are asked detailed questions about specific neighborhood racial compositions, it becomes very clear that whites still harbor substantial prejudice against blacks as potential neighbors, and that their tolerance for racial mixing is really quite limited.

We may summarize white neighborhood preferences using data from the Detroit Area Survey (see Table 4.3). As with blacks, whites were asked how they felt about hypothetical neighborhoods that contained black and white homes in different proportions. In their responses, whites indicated they were still quite uncomfortable with the prospect of black neighbors in practice, despite their endorsement of open housing in principle. Roughly a fourth of whites said they would feel uncomfortable in a neighborhood where 8% of the residents were black, and about the same percentage would be unwilling to enter such an area. When the black percentage reached 21%, half of all whites said they would be unwilling to enter, 42% would feel uncomfortable, and 24% would seek to leave. Once a neighborhood reached about one-third black, the limits of racial tolerance were reached for the majority of whites: 73% would be unwilling to enter, 57% would feel uncomfortable, and 41% would try to leave. At

TABLE 4.3

Neighborhood Preferences of White Respondents to Detroit Area Survey, 1976

Neighborhood Composition	Percentage Who Would Feel Uncomfortable in Neighborhood	Percentage Who Would Try to Move Out of Neighborhood	Percentage Unwilling to Move into Neighborhood
8% black	24%	7%	27%
21% black	42	24	50
36% black	57	41	73
57% black	72	64	84

Source: Reynolds Farley, Howard Schuman, Suzanne Bianchi, Diane Colasanto, and Shirley Hatchett, "'Chocolate City, Vanilla Suburbs': Will the Trend toward Racially Separate Communities Continue?" *Social Science Research* 7 (1978):330–335. Copyright 1978 by Academic Press. Reproduced by permission of the publisher.

the 50–50 threshold, a neighborhood became unacceptable to all but a small minority of whites: 84% said they would not wish to enter a neighborhood that was 57% black, 64% would try to leave, and 72% would feel uncomfortable.

Whereas 63% of blacks picked a 50–50 racial mixture as the most desirable, the great majority of whites would not be willing to enter such a neighborhood and most would try to leave. Although blacks and whites may share a common commitment to "integration" in principle, this word connotes very different things to people in the two racial groups. For blacks, integration means racial mixing in the range of 15% to 70% black, with 50% being most desirable; for whites, it signifies much smaller black percentages.

This fundamental disparity between blacks and whites has been confirmed by surveys conducted in Milwaukee, Omaha, Cincinnati, Kansas City, and Los Angeles, all of which show that blacks strongly prefer a 50–50 mixture and that whites have little tolerance for racial mixtures beyond 20% black.[27] When the New York newspaper *Newsday* asked whites and blacks on suburban Long Island what "integration" meant to them, 64% of black respondents chose a neighborhood composition that was 40% black or higher, whereas 52% of whites selected a mixture that was 40% black or lower.[28] On a nationwide survey carried out by Lou Harris in

1988, 69% of blacks said the races were better off living next to each other "in the long run," but only 53% of whites shared this sentiment.[29]

White apprehensions about racial mixing are associated with the belief that having black neighbors undermines property values and reduces neighborhood safety. According to the *Newsday* poll, 58% of Long Island's whites believe that property values fall once blacks enter a neighborhood[30] (in fact, evidence suggests the opposite, at least during the transition process[31]). Likewise, among whites in Detroit who said they would leave if blacks moved into their neighborhoods, 40% believed that property values would decrease after black entry, and 17% believed that the crime rate would rise.[32]

Given that a home is widely viewed as a symbol of a person's worth,[33] these views imply that whites perceive blacks to be a direct threat to their social status.[34] This interpretation is underscored by a 1985 study of white voters commissioned by the Michigan state Democratic Party. After carrying out a series of focus-group interviews in blue-collar suburbs of Detroit, the study concluded that working-class whites "express a profound distaste for blacks, a sentiment that pervades almost everything they think about government and politics . . . Blacks constitute the explanation for their vulnerability and for almost everything that has gone wrong in their lives; not being black is what constitutes being middle class; not living with blacks is what makes a neighborhood a decent place to live."[35]

The belief that blacks have deleterious effects on neighborhoods is consistent with a broader set of pejorative racial stereotypes. Among whites surveyed in the San Francisco area in 1973, for example, 41% believed that blacks were less likely to take care of their homes than whites, 24% said that blacks were more likely to cheat or steal, and 14% said that blacks were more prone to commit sex crimes.[36] Similar results were uncovered in the Detroit Area Survey: 70% of whites believed that blacks were less likely to take good care of their house and yard, 59% believed that blacks were prone to violence, 50% felt that blacks were not as quiet as whites, and nearly half believed that blacks were less moral than whites.[37]

When respondents in these samples were queried about the racial beliefs of others, moreover, they saw their fellow citizens as even more racially prejudiced than themselves (or at least more prejudiced than they acknowledged themselves to be). Whereas 56% of whites in Detroit said they would be willing to sell their house to a black family even if their neighbors objected, only 31% thought their neighbors would do the same.[38] Of whites in the San Francisco area, 70% said that "most Americans" believed blacks were likely to cheat or steal, and 60% said they thought that most Americans believed blacks were prone to commit sex crimes.[39]

These pejorative racial stereotypes are not local aberrations of San Francisco or Detroit; they are consistent with findings from recent national surveys. When Tom Smith of the University of Chicago's National Opinion Research Center asked respondents to compare blacks and other ethnic groups on a variety of personal traits in 1990, he found that 62% of nonblack respondents thought that blacks were lazier than other groups, 56% felt they were more prone to violence, 53% saw them as less intelligent, and 78% thought they were less self-supporting and more likely to live off welfare.[40] A 1988 survey by Lou Harris asked

whites to evaluate blacks more directly, and 36% stated that blacks have less ambition than whites, 17% said they were less intelligent, 21% thought they were more likely to commit crimes, and 26% felt blacks were unable to get equal work at equal pay because they lacked a work ethic.[41]

Although overt expressions of racism are now publicly unacceptable, when questioned more specifically most white Americans still admit to holding a host of antiblack stereotypes. They continue to believe that blacks do not keep up their homes and are more prone to violence, and these negative images lead directly to fears that black neighbors lower property values and increase crime rates. These beliefs promote white resistance to black entry and avoidance of residential areas that contain black residents. Whites also display considerable aversion to the intimate contacts that inevitably grow out of residential proximity: 70% of whites in a 1978 national survey rejected interracial marriage on principle.[42] Perhaps for this reason, the negative view that whites have of black neighbors holds up even when one controls for neighborhood location, crime rate, upkeep, and cleanliness.[43]

The contrasting attitudes of blacks and whites create a huge disparity in the demand for housing in racially mixed neighborhoods. Given the harassment that historically has followed their entry into white areas, blacks express considerable reluctance at being the first to cross the color line. Once one or two black families have entered a neighborhood, however, black demand grows rapidly given the high value placed on integrated housing. This demand escalates as the black percentage rises toward 50%, the most preferred neighborhood configuration; beyond this point, black demand stabilizes until the neighborhood reaches 70% black, after which demand falls off.

The pattern of white demand for housing in racially mixed areas follows precisely the opposite trajectory. Demand is strong for homes in all-white areas, but once one or two black families enter a neighborhood, white demand begins to falter as some white families leave and others refuse to move in. The acceleration in residential turnover coincides with the expansion of black demand, making it very likely that outgoing white households will be replaced disproportionately with black families. As the black percentage goes up, white demand drops ever more steeply as black demand rises at an increasing rate. By the time black demand peaks at the 50% mark, practically no whites are willing to enter and the majority (64%) are trying to leave. It is no surprise, therefore, that most black households relocate within areas that are at least 50% black, whereas most white families move into neighborhoods that are overwhelmingly white.[44] As in the past, segregation is created by a process of racial turnover fueled by the persistence of significant antiblack prejudice.

. . .

THE CONTINUING SIGNIFICANCE OF RACE

Putting together the trends in segregation . . . with the evidence on prejudice and discrimination reviewed here leads to three conclusions. First, residential segregation continues unabated in the nation's largest metropolitan black communities, and this spatial isolation cannot be attributed to class. Second, although whites now accept open housing in principle, they have not yet come to terms with its implications in practice. Whites still harbor strong antiblack sentiments and they are unwilling to tolerate more than a small percentage of blacks in their neighborhoods. Third, discrimination against blacks is widespread and continues at very high levels in urban housing markets.

Although these conclusions may provide a damning indictment of theoretically "color-blind" markets, they do not conclusively prove that prejudice and discrimination cause segregation. The persistence of prejudice, discrimination, and segregation in American cities strongly suggests a possible causal connection, but a mere coincidence of trends does not necessarily link racist attitudes and behaviors to segregation. We have shown only that three conceptually related conditions persist across time, not that they are causally connected.

Fortunately, several studies have been carried out to document and quantify the link between discrimination, prejudice, and segregation. Using data from the 1977 HUD [Department of Housing and Urban Development] audit study, George Galster related cross-metropolitan variation in housing discrimination to the degree of racial segregation in different urban areas.[45] He confirmed the empirical link between discrimination and segregation, and he also discovered that segregation itself has important feedback effects on socioeconomic status.[46] Not only does discrimination lead to segregation, but segregation, by restricting economic opportunities for blacks, produces interracial economic disparities that incite further discrimination and more segregation.

Galster has also shown that white prejudice and discrimination are connected to patterns of racial change within neighborhoods. In a detailed study of census tracts in the Cleveland area, he found that neighborhoods that were all white or racially changing evinced much higher rates of discrimination than areas that were stably integrated or predominantly black.[47] The pace of racial change was also strongly predicted by the percentage of whites who agreed with the statement that "white people have a right to keep blacks out of their neighborhoods." Areas with a high degree of racist sentiment experienced systematic white population loss after only a few blacks had entered, and the speed of transition accelerated rapidly after the population became only 3% black. Tracts where whites expressed a low degree of racist sentiment, however, showed little tendency for white flight up to a population composition of around 40% black.[48]

These studies confirm a strong link between levels of prejudice and discrimination and the degree of segregation and spatial isolation that blacks experience. The accumulated information on the persistence of prejudice, the continuation of discrimination, and their close connection to racial segregation underscore the continued salience of race in American society and suggest that race remains the dominant organizing principle of U.S. urban housing markets. When it comes to determining where, and with whom, Americans live, race overwhelms all other considerations.

This conclusion, however, may appear to be challenged by certain trends in segregation we have not fully explored here. By focusing on the largest black communities in the United States, does our analysis overstate the persistence of racial segregation? By concentrating on large, older industrial areas in the northeast and midwest, we fail to mention a substantial and marked decline in black segregation that occurred in some small and mid-sized metropolitan areas in the south and west. In fact, the level of black–white segregation fell by more than 10 points in twenty-two of the sixty largest metropolitan areas between 1970 and 1980.[49] Consistent with this finding, Barrett Lee and his colleagues report that, by the 1980s, racial turnover was relatively unlikely in the neighborhoods of smaller southern and western cities.[50]

Such large and widespread declines in segregation are unprecedented in urban America, and they led Reynolds Farley to conclude that they are "indicative of declining racism."[51] Scott McKinney has similarly concluded that "the decade of the 1970s witnessed substantial progress in integrating residential neighborhoods in metropolitan areas."[52] We believe, however, that rather than indicating significant racial progress, these declines in segregation paradoxically confirm the persisting significance of race in the United States. Instead of indicating an end to prejudice, they more accurately reveal the new character that prejudice has assumed.

As we discussed earlier, although large majorities of whites agree that people should be free to live wherever they want to regardless of skin color, most would not vote for a community law to implement this principle, and most would not want to live in a neighborhood where more than a small percentage of the families were black. This ambivalent attitude implies entirely different behaviors and outcomes in urban areas with large and small black populations.[53]

If whites accept integration on principle but remain fearful of living with blacks in practice, then blacks are more likely to be tolerated as neighbors when they constitute a small share of the population than when they are a relatively large proportion. When the number of blacks is small, an open housing market yields neighborhood racial compositions that are within the limits of white tolerance, and fears of resegregation are muted by the small number of potential black in-migrants. In a city with a large black population, however, an open market generates neighborhood racial compositions that are unacceptable to the vast majority of whites, and fears of resegregation are strong because the number of blacks seeking entry is potentially very large.

As the proportion of blacks in an urban area rises, therefore, progressively higher levels of racial segregation must be imposed in order to keep the probability of white–black contact within levels that are tolerable to whites.[54] In urban areas where racial composition is such that open housing can be implemented without threatening white preferences for limited contact with blacks, desegregation should occur; but in areas where relatively large numbers of blacks imply a high degree of black–white mixing under an open market, racial segregation will be maintained.[55]

This is precisely what happened in American metropolitan areas during the 1970s. Virtually all of the areas that experienced sharp declines in segregation had small black percentages, so that in spite of rapid desegregation, the probability of white–black contact within neighborhoods did not increase noticeably. In Tucson, for example, the level of black–white segregation fell by 24 points between 1970 and 1980 (from 71 to 47), but because the percentage of blacks in the metropolitan area was so small (under 3%), the probability of white–black contact rose only from .017 to .021.[56] Despite the massive desegregation of Tucson's black community, in other words, the percentage of blacks in the neighborhood of the average white resident moved only from 1.7% to 2.1%.

In U.S. metropolitan areas, the likelihood of white–black contact rarely exceeds 5% no matter what the trends in segregation have been. Douglas Massey and Andrew Gross have derived a formula that computes the degree of segregation that is required to keep neighborhood racial mixtures at 5% black or less.[57] Their formula depends primarily on the relative number of blacks in the metropolitan area: when the black percentage is low, little or no segregation needs to be applied to keep white–black contact within limits tolerable to most whites; but as the black percentage increases, progressively higher levels of segregation must be enforced to keep neighborhood racial compositions within these bounds.

According to their calculations, essentially no residential segregation needed to be imposed on blacks to keep the likelihood of white–black contact under 5% in areas such as Denver, Seattle, Tucson, and Phoenix, where large declines did take place, but levels of 85 or above were required in Chicago, Cleveland, Detroit, Philadelphia, and New York, precisely those areas where little change occurred. In statistical terms, the hypothetical level of segregation required to keep white–black contact low strongly predicted whether or not a decline, in fact, occurred, and the extent of the decline was strongly correlated with the size of the shift.[58] Desegregation only occurred in those metropolitan areas where the number of blacks was relatively small and where an open housing market would not lead to significant racial mixing within neighborhoods.

The persisting significance of race can be demonstrated in one final way: by considering patterns of segregation among Caribbean Hispanics. In the United States, this group consists mainly of Puerto Ricans and Cubans, but also includes Dominicans, Panamanians, and others. Caribbean Hispanics are distinguished from native whites by their use of the Spanish language, their common Spanish colonial heritage, their Latin Catholicism, and their remarkable racial diversity. Owing to a unique history of slavery and miscegenation quite distinct from that in the United States, Hispanics originating in the Caribbean region display a wide variety of racial characteristics and identities: some consider themselves black, others call themselves white, and large numbers identify themselves as something in-between black and white, a mixture of European and African origins.[59]

This racial diversity creates a natural experiment that allows us to examine the effects of race on segregation while holding ethnicity constant. Caribbean Hispanics of all races entered the United States under similar conditions and have the same cultural background, class composition, and family characteristics. Indeed, dark-skinned and light-skinned Hispanics are frequently members of the same family; what differentiates them is race and the way that it is treated in U.S. housing markets. If black and racially mixed Hispanics prove to be more segregated than white Hispanics, this fact cannot easily be attributed to different preferences or tastes. Rather, the segregation of African-origin Hispanics provides strong proof of the crucial role of race in determining residential outcomes.

We compiled segregation indices for Hispanics in ten metropolitan areas where Latinos of Caribbean origin predominate (see Table 4.6). Hispanic–white dissimilarity indices are calculated for three different Hispanic racial groups: those who said they were white, those who said they were black, and those who identified themselves as something in-between. From these figures, it is apparent that race is a powerful determinant of segregation, even among an otherwise homogeneous ethnic group. The average level of segregation increases steadily as one moves from white Hispanics, with an index of 52, to mixed-race Hispanics, with an index of 72, to black Hispanics, whose index of 80 is comparable to that observed for black Americans.

The New York metropolitan area houses the largest single concentration of Caribbeans in the United States. Here white Hispanics are moderately segregated from whites at 57, whereas those who are black or racially mixed are highly segregated at 81 and 77, respectively. Similar patterns are replicated in all of the other metropolitan areas, a contrast that persists even when adjustments are made for socioeconomic differences between the racial categories.[60] And John Yinger has shown, using 1988 HDS audit data, that dark-skinned Hispanics are significantly more likely to encounter discriminatory treatment in metropolitan housing

TABLE 4.6

Indices of Segregation of Hispanics in Three Racial Groups from Whites in Ten Metropolitan Areas, 1980

Metropolitan Area	White Hispanics	Mixed-Race Hispanics	Black Hispanics
Boston	44.8	79.0	85.1
Chicago	57.0	74.0	85.2
Jersey City	49.0	54.3	68.1
Los Angeles	53.2	64.0	77.0
Miami	51.9	66.2	71.5
Nassau–Suffolk	31.7	63.2	79.4
New York	56.7	76.8	81.1
Newark	61.8	78.1	84.2
Paterson	67.4	80.0	83.8
Philadelphia	45.7	83.4	84.4
Average	51.9	71.9	80.0

Source: Nancy A. Denton and Douglas S. Massey, "Racial Identity among Caribbean Hispanics: The Effect of Double Minority Status on Residential Segregation," *American Sociological Review* 54 (1980):803. Reprinted by permission of American Sociological Association.

markets than are those with light skin, a finding that has been replicated in at least one local study.[61]

When it comes to housing and residential patterns, therefore, race is the dominant organizing principle. No matter what their ethnic origin, economic status, social background, or personal characteristics, African Americans continue to be denied full access to U.S. housing markets. Through a series of exclusionary tactics, realtors limit the likelihood of black entry into white neighborhoods and channel black demand for housing into areas that are within or near existing ghettos. White prejudice is such that when black entry into a neighborhood is achieved, that area becomes unattractive to further white settlement and whites begin departing at an accelerated pace. This segmentation of black and white housing demand is encouraged by pervasive discrimination in the allocation of mortgages and home improvement loans, which systematically channel money away from integrated areas. The end result is that blacks remain the most spatially isolated population in U.S. history.

NOTES

1. Epigraph from Thomas Pettigrew, Book Review of *Negroes in Cities: Residential Segregation and Neighborhood Change. American Journal of Sociology* 82 (1966): 112–13.

2. Douglas S. Massey and Mitchell L. Eggers, "The Ecology of Inequality: Minorities and the Concentration of Poverty, 1970–1980," *American Journal of Sociology* 95 (1990):1153–89.

3. William A. V. Clark, "Residential Segregation in American Cities: A Review and Interpretation," *Population Research and Policy Review* 5 (1986):95–127.

4. The most forceful exposition of the argument is by William Julius Wilson, *The Declining Significance*

of Race: Blacks and Changing American Institutions (Chicago: University of Chicago Press, 1978); see also William Julius Wilson, *The Truly Disadvantaged: The Inner City, the Underclass, and Public Policy* (Chicago: University of Chicago Press, 1987).

5. See Douglas S. Glasgow, *The Black Underclass: Poverty, Unemployment, and the Entrapment of Ghetto Youth* (New York: Vintage, 1980); Alphonso Pinkney, *The Myth of Black Progress* (Cambridge: Cambridge University Press, 1984); Bettylou Valentine, *Hustling and Other Hard Work* (New York: Macmillan, 1978); Charles V. Willie, "The Inclining Significance of Race," *Society* 15 (1978):10–15.

6. Nancy A. Denton and Douglas S. Massey, "Residential Segregation of Blacks, Hispanics, and Asians by Socioeconomic Status and Generation," *Social Science Quarterly* 69 (1988):797–818.

7. Reynolds Farley, "Can Blacks Afford to Live in White Residential Areas? A Test of the Hypothesis That Subjective Economic Variables Account for Racial Residential Segregation," paper presented at the annual meeting of the Population Association of America, Philadelphia, April 1979.

8. Denton and Massey, "Residential Segregation . . . by Socioeconomic Status and Generation"; Douglas S. Massey, "Effects of Socioeconomic Factors on the Residential Segregation of Blacks and Spanish Americans in United States Urbanized Areas," *American Sociological Review* 44 (1979):1015–22.

9. Socioeconomic variables have also been entered into multivariate regression equations in an effort to explain away intergroup differences in segregation, but the very high degree of black segregation persists even when education, income, and occupational status are controlled statistically; see Douglas S. Massey and Nancy A. Denton, "Trends in the Residential Segregation of Blacks, Hispanics, and Asians: 1970–1980," *American Sociological*

Review 52 (1987):802–25; and Douglas S. Massey and Nancy A. Denton, "Suburbanization and Segregation in U.S. Metropolitan Areas," *American Journal of Sociology* 94 (1988):592–626.

10. See the arguments in Clark, "Residential Segregation in American Cities"; and Stanley Lieberson and Donna K. Carter, "A Model for Inferring the Voluntary and Involuntary Causes of Residential Segregation," *Demography* 19 (1982):511–26.

11. Howard Schuman, Charlotte Steeh, and Lawrence Bobo, *Racial Attitudes in America: Trends and Interpretations* (Cambridge: Harvard University Press, 1985), pp. 144–45.

12. Lawrence Bobo, Howard Schuman, and Charlotte Steeh, "Changing Racial Attitudes toward Residential Integration," in John M. Goering, ed., *Housing Desegregation and Federal Policy* (Chapel Hill: University of North Carolina Press, 1986), pp. 152–69.

13. Reynolds Farley, Howard Schuman, Suzanne Bianchi, Diane Colasanto, and Shirley Hatchett, "'Chocolate City, Vanilla Suburbs': Will the Trend toward Racially Separate Communities Continue?" *Social Science Research* 7 (1978): 319–44.

14. Reynolds Farley, Suzanne Bianchi, and Diane Colasanto, "Barriers to the Racial Integration of Neighborhoods: The Detroit Case," *Annals of the American Academy of Political and Social Science* 441 (1979):97–113.

15. Ibid.

16. Chicago Commission on Human Relations, *1990 Hate Crime Report* (Chicago: City of Chicago Commission on Human Relations, 1991).

17. Los Angeles Commission on Human Relations, *Hate Crime in the 1980s: A Decade of Bigotry*, report to the Los Angeles County Board of Supervisors (Los Angeles: Los Angeles Commission on Human Relations, 1990).

18. Julia Cass, "The Elmwood Incident," *Philadelphia Inquirer Magazine,* Sunday, May 4, 1986.

19. J. Anthony Lukas, *Common Ground: A Turbulent Decade in the Lives of Three American Families* (New York: Vintage, 1985), pp. 509–535.

20. Jonathan Rieder, *Canarsie: The Jews and Italians of Brooklyn against Liberalism* (Cambridge: Harvard University Press, 1985), p. 201.

21. Schuman, Steeh, and Bobo, *Racial Attitudes in America,* pp. 74–75.

22. Ibid.

23. Ibid.

24. Ibid., pp. 88–89; see also Howard Schuman and Lawrence Bobo, "Survey-Based Experiments on White Racial Attitudes toward Residential Integration," *American Journal of Sociology* 2 (1988): 273–99.

25. Schuman, Steeh, and Bobo, *Racial Attitudes in America,* pp. 106–107.

26. Ibid.; see also Clark, "Residential Segregation in American Cities," p. 109.

27. William A. V. Clark, "Residential Preferences and Neighborhood Racial Segregation: A Test of the Schelling Segregation Model," *Demography* 28 (1991):1–19.

28. "A World Apart: Segregation on Long Island," *Newsday,* Monday, September 24, 1990.

29. Louis Harris and Associates, *The Unfinished Agenda on Race in America* (New York: NAACP Legal Defense and Education Fund, 1989).

30. "A World Apart."

31. Brian J. L. Berry, "Ghetto Expansion and Single-Family Housing Prices: Chicago, 1968–1972," *Journal of Urban Economics* 3 (1976):397–423; Harvey L. Molotch, *Managed Integration: The Dilemmas of Doing Good in the City* (Berkeley: University of California Press, 1972), pp. 22–37.

32. Farley, Bianchi, and Colasanto, "Barriers to the Racial Integration of Neighborhoods," pp. 106–107.

33. Brian J. L. Berry, *The Human Consequences of Urbanization* (New York: St. Martin's, 1973), p. 50.

34. Brian J. L. Berry, Carole A. Goodwin, Robert W. Lake, and Katherine B. Smith, "Attitudes toward Integration: The Role of Status in Community Response to Racial Change," in Barry Schwartz, ed., *The Changing Face of the Suburbs* (Chicago: University of Chicago Press, 1976), pp. 221–64; Brian J. L. Berry, *The Open Housing Question: Race and Housing in Chicago, 1966–76* (Cambridge, Mass.: Ballinger, 1979), pp. 375–99.

35. Stanley B. Greenberg, *Report on Democratic Defection* (Washington, D.C.: Analysis Group, 1985), pp. 13–18, 28, cited in Thomas B. Edsall and Mary D. Edsall, *Chain Reaction: The Impact of Race, Rights, and Taxes on American Politics* (New York: Norton, 1991), p. 182.

36. Richard A. Apostle, Charles Y. Glock, Thomas Piazza, and Marijean Suelzle, *The Anatomy of Racial Attitudes* (Berkeley: University of California Press, 1983), pp. 120–21.

37. Farley, Bianchi, and Colasanto, "Barriers to the Racial Integration of Neighborhoods," pp. 106–107.

38. Ibid.

39. Apostle, Glock, Piazza, and Suelzle, *The Anatomy of Racial Attitudes,* p. 120.

40. Tom W. Smith, "Ethnic Images," *GSS Technical Report No. 19,* National Opinion Research Center, Chicago, January 1991.

41. Harris and Associates, *The Unfinished Agenda.*

42. Schuman, Steeh, and Bobo, *Racial Attitudes in America,* pp. 74–75.

43. Craig St. John and Nancy A. Bates, "Racial Composition and Neighborhood Evaluation," *Social Science Research* 19 (1990):47–61.

44. William A. V. Clark, "Residential Mobility and Neighborhood Change: Some Implications for Racial Residential Segregation," *Urban Geography* 1 (1980):95–117; William A. V. Clark, "Racial Transition in Metropolitan Suburbs: Evidence from Atlanta," *Urban Geography* 3 (1988):269–82. . . .

45. George C. Galster, "More than Skin Deep: The Effect of Housing Discrimination on the Extent and Pattern of Racial Residential Segregation in the United States," in John M. Goering, ed., *Housing Discrimination and Federal Policy* (Chapel Hill: University of North Carolina Press, 1986), pp. 119–38.

46. George C. Galster and W. Mark Keeney, "Race, Residence, Discrimination, and Economic Opportunity: Modeling the Nexus of Urban Racial Phenomena," *Urban Affairs Quarterly* 24 (1988):87–117.

47. George C. Galster, "The Ecology of Racial Discrimination in Housing: An Exploratory Model," *Urban Affairs Quarterly* 23 (1987):84–107.

48. George C. Galster, "White Flight from Racially Integrated Neighbourhoods in the 1970s: The Cleveland Experience," *Urban Studies* 27 (1990):385–99; George C. Galster, "Neighborhood Racial Change, Segregationist Sentiments, and Affirmative Marketing Policies," *Journal of Urban Economics* 27 (1990):344–61.

49. Massey and Denton, "Trends in Residential Segregation."

50. Barrett A. Lee, "Racially Mixed Neighborhoods during the 1970s: Change or Stability?" *Social Science Quarterly* 66 (1985):346–64; Barrett A. Lee, "Is Neighborhood Racial Succession Place-Specific?" *Demography* 28 (1991):21–40.

51. Reynolds Farley, "After the Starting Line: Blacks and Women in an Uphill Race," *Demography* 25 (1988):476–96.

52. Scott McKinney, "Change in Metropolitan Area Residential Integration, 1970–1980," *Population Research and Policy Review* 8 (1989):143–64.

53. Douglas S. Massey and Andrew B. Gross, "Explaining Trends in Residential Segregation, 1970–1980," *Urban Affairs Quarterly* 27 (1991):13–15.

54. Ibid.

55. Ibid.

56. Ibid.; see also Massey and Denton, "Trends in Segregation."

57. The formula is: $E(D_{.05}) = (q - .05)/(q - q^2)$, where $E(D_{.05})$ is the level of residential dissimilarity required to keep the probability of white–black contact $(_wP^*_b)$ at .05 or less and q is the proportion of blacks in the urban area; see Massey and Gross, "Explaining Trends in Residential Segregation."

58. Ibid.

59. Clara E. Rodriguez, "Racial Classification among Puerto Rican Men and Women in New York," *Hispanic Journal of Behavioral Sciences* 12 (1990):366–80; Nancy A. Denton and Douglas S. Massey, "Racial Identity among Caribbean Hispanics: The Effect of Double Minority Status on Residential Segregation," *American Sociological Review* 54 (1980):790–808.

60. Denton and Massey, "Racial Identity among Caribbean Hispanics."

61. Yinger, *Housing Discrimination Study: Incidence of Discrimination and Variations in Discriminatory Behavior*, Table 32; see also John Hakken, *Discrimination against Chicanos in the Dallas Rental Housing Market: An Experimental Extension of the Housing Market Practices Survey* (Washington, D.C.: Office of Policy Development and Research, U.S. Department of Housing and Urban Development, 1979).

29

Black Wealth/White Wealth

Melvin L. Oliver and Thomas M. Shapiro

THE GREAT RACIAL WEALTH DIVIDE

. . . African Americans have not shared equally in the nation's prosperity. They earn less than whites, and they possess far less wealth, whatever measure one may use. Table 4.4 presents data on income along with median wealth figures. The black-to-white median income ratio has hovered in the mid-50 to mid-60 percentage range for the past twenty years or so. Fluctuations have been relatively minor, measured in tenths of a percent, and in many ways American society became accustomed to this standard of inequality. In 1988 results from SIPP [Survey on Income and Program Participation] showed that for every dollar earned by white households black households earned sixty-two cents. The median wealth data expose even deeper inequalities. Whites possess nearly twelve times as much median net worth as blacks, or $43,800 versus $3,700. In an even starker contrast, perhaps, the average white household controls $6,999 in net financial assets [NFA] while the average black household retains no NFA nest egg whatsoever.

ACCESS TO ASSETS

The potential for assets to expand or inhibit choices, horizons, and opportunities for children emerged as the most consistent and strongest common theme in our interviews. Since parents want to invest in their children, to give them whatever advantages they can, we wondered about the ability of the average American household to expend assets on their children. This section thus delves deeper into the assets households command by (1) considering the importance of home and vehicle equity in relation to other kinds of assets; (2) inspecting available financial assets for various groups of the population; and (3) looking at children growing up in resource-deficient households. We found a strong relationship between the amount of wealth and the composition of assets. Households with large amounts of total net worth control wealth portfolios composed mostly of financial assets. Financial investments make up about four-fifths of the assets of the richest households. Conversely, home and vehicle equity represents over 70 percent of the asset portfolio among the poorest one-fifth of American households, one in three of which possesses zero or negative financial assets.

Table 4.5 reports households with zero or negative net financial assets for various racial, age, education, and family groups. It shows that one-quarter of white households, 61 percent of black households, and 54 percent of Hispanic households are without financial resources. A similar absence of financial assets affects nearly one-half of young households; circumstances steadily improve with age, however, leaving only 15 percent of those households headed by seniors in a state of resource deficiency. The educational achievement of householders also connects directly with access to resources, as 40 percent of poorly educated household heads control no financial assets while over 80 percent of households headed by a

From *Black Wealth/White Wealth: A New Perspective on Racial Inequality* by Melvin L. Oliver and Thomas M. Shapiro. Reproduced by permission of Taylor & Francis, Inc., Routledge, Inc., http://www.routledge-ny.com.

TABLE 4.4
Wealth and Race

Race	Median Income	Median NW[a]	Mean NW[a]	Median NFA[b]	Mean NFA[b]
White	$25,384	$43,800	$95,667	$6,999	$47,347
Black	$15,630	3,700	23,818	0	5,209
Ratio	0.62	0.08	0.25	0.0	0.11

[a]Net worth
[b]Net financial assets

college graduate control some NFA. Findings reported in this table also demonstrate deeply embedded disparities in resource command between single and married-couple parents. Resource deprivation characterizes 62 percent of single-parent households in comparison to 37 percent of married couples raising children.

Besides looking at resource deprivation, Table 4.5 also sets criteria for "precarious-resource" circumstances. Households without enough NFA reserves to survive three months at the poverty line ($2,904) meet these criteria. Nearly 80 percent of single-parent households fit this description. Likewise 38 percent of white households and 79 percent of black households live in precarious-resource circumstances.

Among our interviewees, parents with ample assets planned to use them to create a better world for their children. Those without them strategized about acquiring some and talked about their "wish list." Parents talked about ballet lessons, camp, trips for cultural enrichment or even to Disney World, staying home more often with the children, affording full-time day care, allowing a parent to be home after day care. The parents discussed using assets to provide better educational opportunities for their children. Kevin takes great pride in paying for his son's college and being able to offer him advanced training. Stacie wants to be able to afford private school for Carrie. Ed and Alicia told us about the private school choices and dilemmas facing their children.

Figure 4.2 looks at the percentage of children in resource-poor households by race. It provides information both on households with no net financial assets and on those with just enough assets to survive above the poverty line for at least three months. Close to one-half of all children live in households with no financial assets and 63 percent live in households with precarious resources, scarcely enough NFA to cushion three months of interrupted income.

A further analysis of this already disturbing data discloses imposing and powerful racial and ethnic cleavages. For example, 40 percent of all white children grow up in households without financial resources in comparison to 73 percent of all black children. Most telling of all perhaps, only 11 percent of black children grow up in households with enough net financial assets to weather three months of no income at the poverty level. Three times as many white kids live in such households.

According to Richard Steckel and Jayanthi Krishnan, cross-sectional measures of wealth acquisition and inequality may disguise underlying changes in wealth status. Analyzing surveys from 1966 and 1976, Steckel and Krishnan found that changes in marital status were associated with changes in wealth. The largest increase in wealth occurred for single women who later married. Other groups who experienced increases in wealth included households headed by the young, those with at least twelve years of schooling, and individuals who married. The greatest loss of wealth occurred among households headed by older individuals, single men, and those experiencing marital disruption. . . .

TABLE 4.5
Who Is on the Edge?

	Households with 0 or Negative NFA[a]	Households Without NFA[a] for 3 Months[b]	Households Without NFA[a] for 6 Months[b]
Sample	31.0%	44.9%	49.9%
Race			
White	25.3	38.1	43.2
Black	60.9	78.9	83.1
Hispanic	54.0	72.5	77.2
Age of Householder			
15–35	48.0	67.0	72.8
36–49	31.7	45.2	50.7
50–64	22.1	32.0	36.2
65 or older	15.1	26.4	30.6
Education			
Less than high school	40.3	55.5	60.0
High school degree	32.2	48.0	63.2
Some college	29.9	45.3	61.4
College degree	18.9	26.8	31.2
Family Type[c]			
Single parent	61.9	79.2	83.2
Married couple	36.9	53.8	59.9

[a]Net financial worth

[b]NFA reserves to survive at the poverty line of $968 per month

[c]Includes only households with children

Financial wealth is the buried fault line of the American social system. The wealth distribution portrait drawn in this chapter has disclosed the existence of highly concentrated wealth at the top; a pattern of steep resource inequality; the disproportionate asset reserves held by various demographic groups; the precarious economic foundation of middle-class life; and how few financial assets most American households can call upon. . . . At one level, income makes up the largest component of potential wealth. At the same time, however, distinctive patterns of income and wealth inequality exist. Put another way, substituting what is known about income inequality for what is not known about wealth inequality limits, and even biases, our understanding of inequality. A thorough understanding of inequality must therefore pay more attention to resources than has been paid in the past.

Perhaps no single piece of information conveys the sense of fragility common to those on the lowest rungs of the economic ladder as the proportion of children who grow up in households without assets. Reducing all life's chances for success to economic circumstances no doubt overlooks much, but resources nonetheless provide an accurate measure of differential access to educational, career, health, cultural, and social opportunities. In poignantly reciting the hopes they have for their children, parents recognize the importance of resources. Our interviews show how parents use assets to bring these hopes to life, or wish they had ample assets so they could bring them to life. Nearly three-quarters of all black

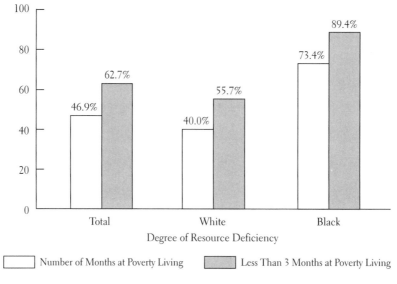

FIGURE 4.2
Percentage of Children in Resource-Deficient Households by Race

children, 1.8 times the rate for whites, grow up in households possessing no financial assets. Nine in ten black children come of age in households that lack sufficient financial reserves to endure three months of no income at the poverty line, about four times the rate for whites. . . .

THE BLACK MIDDLE CLASS

One of the most heated scholarly controversies in the area of racial equality and social justice over the past two decades concerns the dispute over the nature, causes, and meaning of economic changes occurring within the black community. The way in which one views these changes has enormous inherent implications for social policy. In essence, commentators argue that the black community has become increasingly differentiated economically, dividing into a growing underclass trapped in urban misery and an improving middle class bent on escaping the ghetto. While the condition of the most disadvantaged African Americans deteriorated rapidly after 1970, the middle class grew, becoming substantially better off and less burdened by the effects of race.

The economic status of the black middle class[1] is a vital factor in ongoing debates in the field of racial equity. A frequent question that arises concerns what one means by "the black middle class." Some demark the limits simply in terms of income; others include education or occupation in the definition. Most scholars embrace a class conception based on the work of Karl Marx or Max Weber and make occupation their central focus. [We consider] all these bases—educational achievement, earnings, and occupation. . . . Middle class means working in a white-collar occupation or being self-employed. In using several different indicators of class status, we confirm that the economic foundation of the black middle class is not dependent upon any one way of thinking about class. The point of this exercise is to show that an accurate and realistic appraisal of the economic footing of the black middle class reveals its precariousness, marginality, and fragility. The case for this characterization rests not only on an inspection of the resources available to the black middle class but on the relative position of the latter with respect to the white middle class.

Carol illustrates the fragility of the black middle class. She and her husband seemed to have found financial security in the American middle class. Her husband was a sales manager, earning about $60,000 a year in salary and bonuses. He had acquired stock in the growing company he worked for, put money aside in a 401(k) retirement account, and invested in some treasury bills; he was also vested in the company's pension plan. Carol and her husband owned a home, as well as a rental property next door, and had invested some money in an apartment building. Carol raised the couple's three children, earned her college degree, and then began working full time after the children went off to college. Carol and her husband put their kids through private schools and college. Today they are divorced and Carol works as a receptionist for eight dollars an hour. In the divorce settlement she kept the home and the property next door as her share of the couple's joint assets.

Sometime after the divorce she went to work as the assistant director of a private elementary school run by her sister. The school became insolvent because her sister grew "sick and everybody else was tied up." Carol felt it was her familial responsibility to close the school for her sister. For seven months she continued as the school's unpaid assistant director while closing it down and settling accounts out of her personal funds. Carol's only income during this seven-month period consisted of unemployment compensation from the government. Her savings depleted, Carol had to sell the house next door in order to pay her own bills. Her total loss was on the order of $50,000.

As Carol's experience demonstrates, even the most seemingly secure financial status can be changed by unforeseen circumstances. For Carol the fall from middle-class grace is a story of divorce, family obligations, and low-paid work. She feels both lucky and vastly underpaid. Lucky, because unemployment had run out, she needed a job badly, and a friend she once worked for found her a job. Vastly underpaid, because she went "from making about $18 an hour down to $8," from $36,000 to $16,000 a year. "And that's where I am now." At fifty, she owns her home, with a handsome $85,000 worth of equity, as well as an insurance policy; but she has no liquid assets, not even a savings account. The limits of home equity as a source of ready cash became painfully clear to Carol when, during a recent drop in interest rates, she attempted to borrow some money by refinancing her home. Even though a new mortgage would have lowered her monthly payments, the bank refused to restructure her loan because she was unemployed at the time. It had taken years of hard work to gain entry into the middle class and a divorce and family financial crisis to jeopardize Carol's middle-class status. Even with ample "paper assets" in the home, Carol is no longer secure because a failure to meet her mortgage payments or some other financial crisis might force her to put her house up for sale.

Carol's story shows how a middle-class standard of living rests on the twin pillars of income and wealth. The two together create a solid economic foundation that simultaneously safeguards a secure standard of living and enhances future life chances. When either one is lacking, middle-class status is jeopardized. Without ample income, families must draw on their available wealth reserves, which, as Carol learned, can be rapidly depleted. In the absence of wealth resources, especially liquid assets, middle-class living standards become dependent on an uninterrupted source of earnings, or rock-solid job security. Table 5.1 displays the resources that middle-class whites and blacks command. This table incorporates the three ways in which we have previously defined the middle class: first, those earnings between $25,000 and $50,000; second, those with college degrees; and third, those working at white-collar jobs, including the self-employed.

The figures in Table 5.1 vividly demonstrate our contention that the black middle class stands on very shaky footing, no matter how one determines middle-class status. Most significant, we believe, is that blacks' claim to middle-class status is based on income and not assets. The net worth middle-class blacks command, ranging from $8,000 for white-collar workers to $17,000 for college graduates, largely represents housing equity, because neither the middle-income earners nor the well educated nor white-collar workers

TABLE 5.1
Race, Wealth, and Various Conceptions of "The Middle Class"

	Income	Net Worth	Net Financial Assets
White			
Middle Income	$25,000–50,000	$44,069$	$ 6,988
College-degree	38,700	74,922	19,823
White-collar	33,765	56,487	11,952
Black			
Middle Income	$25,000–50,000	$15,250	$290
College-degree	29,440	17,437	175
White-collar	23,799	8,299	0

control anything other than petty net financial assets. Without wealth reserves, especially liquid assets, the black middle class depends on income for its standard of living. Without the asset pillar, in particular, income and job security shoulder a greater part of the burden.

Recalling the overall black-to-white income ratio of 0.62, we may note that the gap for white-collar workers narrows to 0.7, and further tapers to 0.76 for college graduates. Turning to net worth, we see in Table 5.1 that the least amount of inequality occurs among middle-income earners, where the ratio registers 0.35; but even among households with similar income flows the difference amounts to over $28,000. White-collar occupations disclose the most inequality: the black middle class owns fifteen cents for every dollar owned by the white middle class. We have already observed the trivial net financial assets of the black middle class; comparing them to the net financial assets available to the white middle class makes the plight of blacks even starker. When one defines the middle class as those with college degrees, the most numerically restrictive definition, one finds that the white middle class commands $19,000 more NFA; using the broadest definition, white-collar occupations, the white middle class controls nearly $12,000 more.

In *The New Black Middle Class* Bart Landry highlights the importance of dual wage-earning

couples in explaining how black families attain middle-class living standards. The loss of breadwinner jobs that support a whole family has had a great impact on American life over the last two decades, pushing more family members into the paid labor force. Following Landry's lead, first using SIPP data from 1984, we inspected all middle-income earning households to see how many full-time wage earners were needed to attain middle-class living standards. One full-time breadwinner supported 57 percent of white and 42 percent of black middle-income earning households. Most black households attaining a middle-class standard of living managed to do so only because both partners earned a wage (58 percent for black versus 43 percent for white households).

Results from 1988 strengthen and extend Landry's argument. To sustain a middle-class living standard in 1988, two-thirds of white and close to three-quarters of all black households needed more than one worker. Among married couples enjoying a middle-class standard of living, both partners worked in 78 percent of black households versus 62 percent for whites. These figures represent those spending any time in the paid labor force, not necessarily in a full-time job. Looking only at full-time workers, one arrives at a fuller understanding of the work commitments and family sacrifice necessary for middle-class existence. Among married couples it takes two

TABLE 5.2
Race, "Middle Class" Families, Work, and Wealth

	Income	Net Worth	Net Financial Assets
Married			
White	$32,400	$65,024	$11,500
Black	25,848	17,437	0
Ratio	0.80	0.27	—
Two-Earner Couple			
White	40,865	56,046	8,612
Black	34,700	17,375	0
Ratio	0.85	0.31	—
Two-Earner Young Couple[a]			
White	36,435	23,165	1,150
Black	29,377	4,124	0
Ratio	0.81	0.18	—
White-Collar[b]			
White	34,821	48,310	8,680
Black	34,320	7,697	0
Ratio	0.70	0.16	—

[a]Twenty-five- to thirty-five-year-olds
[b]Self-employed not included

full-time workers in 60 percent of black homes to earn between $25,000 and $50,000 yearly; the same is true for only 37 percent of white homes.

Gerald Jaynes and Robin Williams in *A Common Destiny* and Bart Landry in *The New Black Middle Class* noted that two-parent black and white families have relatively equal incomes. They have also observed that black families need more wage earners to approach the living standard of white families. We expect to find that black married couples fare better than other kinds of household units, both within the context of all types of black households and in comparison to their white counterparts. We also expect that households in which both partners work manage better still. Table 5.2 reviews the income and wealth resources that various kinds of black and white households govern. Fresh data are presented in this table concerning the resources of young couples, twenty-five to thirty-five years old, in which both husband and wife earn a living. Optimistic observers point to this group as typifying blacks' best chance for income equality. The typical young, two-earner black couple brings in four-fifths of the earnings of analogous white couples, leaving only a [$7,058] income gap. This breach appears relatively small, but the net worth of these young black couples amounts to less than one-fifth that of their white counterparts, which puts them at a $19,000 disadvantage. Finally, young white couples have already accumulated $1,150 in net financial assets, of which blacks have none.

The lack of financial reserves among young two-earner couples heralds the fragility of black middle-class living standards more generally. To gauge the precariousness of the black middle class, we calculated the number of months a household could survive without a steady stream of income, asking how far wealth reserves would stretch in a crisis or emergency. We discovered that the occupationally defined white middle class could support its present middle-class standard of living (the median middle-class income being $2,750 per month) for four and one-third months. . . . The typical black middle-class household would not make it to the end of the first month. Whites' reserves allow them to survive at the poverty level ($968 per month) for over a year, while most blacks, yet again, would not make it through the first month. Put another way, just 65 percent of white middle-class households possess a large enough nest egg to maintain their present living standard for at least one month, and 55 percent could last at least three months. In unmistakable contrast, only 27 percent of the black middle class has enough NFA to keep up present living standards for one month, and less than one in five households could sustain their lifestyles for three months. At poverty living standards, 35 percent of the black middle class might last one month, and 27 percent might hold out for three.

A WEALTH COMPARISON

Previous studies comparing the wealth of blacks and whites have found that blacks have anywhere from $8 to $19 of wealth for every $100 that whites possess.[2] Andrew Brimmer points out in his "Income, Wealth, and Investment Behavior in the Black Community" that blacks owned only 3 percent of all accumulated wealth in the United States in 1984, even though they received 7.6 percent of the total money earned that year and made up 11 percent of all households. Francine Blau and John Graham reported that young black families (twenty-four to thirty-four years of age) in 1976 held only about 18 percent of the wealth of young white families.[3] Looking at preliminary wealth data from the SIPP survey, Billy Tidwell characterizes the economic status of blacks as "very marginal" in his 1987 book *Beyond the Margin.* . . . The 1988 ratio of black-to-white median household income reached 0.62, but the median net worth ratio stood at 0.08. Moreover, a comparison of net finan-

cial assets shows the enormity of blacks' wealth disadvantage—white households households possess nearly ten times as much mean NFA as black households. Half of all white households have at least $6,999 in an NFA nest egg, whereas nearly two-thirds of all black households have zero or negative NFA. Of course these are averages; many whites as well as blacks command larger wealth portfolios than these figures suggest, just as many also control fewer resources. However, the asset deprivation to which blacks are subject, both absolutely and in relation to whites, reverberates throughout their economic circumstances and thus forms the focus of this analysis.

Eva and Clarence Dobbs and their three children live in a neat two-story craftsman home that architectural purists want to preserve. In this working-class area of South Central Los Angeles known as the Crenshaw District, historical preservation of homes takes a backseat to "struggling" and "surviving." The Dobbs family is a perfect example. Both adults are full-time workers who together bring in close to $50,000 annually but who are asset-poor and, in fact, live in the shadow of debt. Clarence works as an occupational therapist with stroke patients for a number of hospitals. The work is not steady, nor does it pay much. Eva is a personnel assistant in a Fortune 500 company. While she has been on a career ladder and done well, the corporation is in the midst of outsourcing their personnel functions, and her job may last for only a couple more years. The Dobbses' lives are organized around church and the children. The kids all go to a private Christian school to "protect them from the streets" and to give them the kind of education that will "teach their souls as well as their minds." For Eva the $3,000 cost is high but not excessive "if you think about clothes they need if they were in public school." Their rented home, which they have only moved into recently, is sparsely furnished. They have two cars, which they need to get around in a city whose public transportation is notoriously poor. Eva and Clarence are very proud of their oldest son, who has received a scholarship to go to a private university in the Midwest, but they are some-

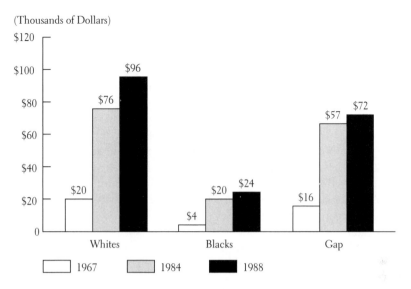

(Thousands of Dollars)

FIGURE 5.1   Gains and Gaps in Racial Wealth Accumulation[a], 1967–1988
Sources: Terrell 1971; Oliver and Shapiro (1989); SIPP, 1987 Panel, Wave 4
[a]Mean net worth

what concerned about finding the money they will need to help him out. But this is a family that will survive.

In their everyday struggle to make ends meet there is little left over to save. Eva and Clarence have no savings account. They once had about $1,500 in savings, but "emergencies" and "nickel and dime" withdrawals for little things soon depleted these reserves. Their most fervent hope is to save enough money to be able to purchase a home. The housing market in Los Angeles, however, plays havoc with that desire. A median-priced home in Los Angeles costs $220,000, and the 20 percent down payment seems way beyond the Dobbses' reach. Furthermore, years of struggle have left a trail of bad credit that will hurt their chances of even qualifying for a home loan.

What few assets they have come from Eva's 401(k) account at the company for which she works. For the past couple of years Eva has been regularly making deposits that have earned a 50 percent company match. She now has about $4,000 in this fund. The high penalties for early

withdrawal have prevented the Dobbses from drawing on these assets in their battle to survive.

The Dobbses have begun to attack their credit woes. A $2,500 loan from the credit union helped consolidate Eva's credit card debt. Unfortunately, however, Eva owes another $1,600 that she borrowed to help pay her auto insurance ("which is usually about $1,400 for the one car [the other car is not insured], because of the area I live in"), her state income taxes, and her son's college-related expenses. While both Eva and Clarence come from very poor backgrounds and have no family assets to draw on, Eva's mother bought her her car for $6,000, a sum that Eva is determined to pay back. Thus, when the ledger is balanced, the Dobbses have no assets and are, in fact, in debt.

The Dobbses' asset poverty is well represented in the data from SIPP. SIPP provides a yardstick with which to measure absolute gains in wealth accumulation. As shown in Figure 5.1, Henry Terrell reports in his "Wealth Accumulation of Black and White Families" that the average black family held $3,779 in mean net worth in 1967, a figure that by 1984 had risen to $19,736. In 1988 the average black family's net worth had increased to $23,818. Yet this impressive progress among blacks pales somewhat when matched with wealth gains among whites. The average white family's mean net worth in 1967 stood at $20,153 and rose to $76,297 in 1984. By 1988 it had increased to $95,667. Although there were impressive absolute gains for blacks between 1967 and 1984, the wealth divide widened by $40,000 during those years, and by 1988 it had reached a gaping $71,849.[4]

Theories of wealth accumulation emphasize income as the preeminent factor in wealth differentials. Indeed, . . . there is a clear relationship between income inequality and wealth accumulation: wealth accrues with increasing income. Since black households earn less than two-thirds as much as the average white household, it only makes sense to ask, to what extent can the gross wealth disparities that we have noted be explained by the well-known income inequality between whites and blacks? Examining blacks' and whites' wealth at similar income levels provides a clear and direct way to respond to this question. Standardizing for income permits us to test whether the black–white disparity in wealth holding emanates from income differences. Henry Terrell reported in his 1971 study that black families owned less than one-fifth the accumulated (mean) wealth of white families; furthermore, keeping income constant, he noted that black families held less than one-half the wealth of whites in similar income brackets. Thus, he concluded that racial differences in income alone are not sufficient to account for black–white wealth disparities. Francine Blau and John Graham conclude that while "income difference is the largest single factor explaining racial differences in wealth," even after one controls for income as much as three-quarters of the wealth gap remains.[5]

We standardized SIPP wealth data into four income brackets. *Poverty*-level households earn $11,611 or less. *Moderate*-level incomes range from $11,612 to $24,999. *Middle*-level household incomes fall between $25,000 and $50,000.

High-income households bring in over $50,000. This data only represents households headed by those under age sixty-five, because we did not want . . . age effects . . . to cloud the relationship between income, wealth, and race. . . .

The data are very convincing in one simple respect: differences in observed income levels are not nearly sufficient to explain the large racial wealth gap. . . . The black-to-white wealth ratio comes closest to equality among prosperous households earning $50,000 or more. Even here where the wealth gap is narrowest, however, blacks possess barely one-half (0.52) the median net worth of their high-earning white counterparts. For net financial assets, the mean ratio . . . ranges from 0.006 to 0.33. The highest earning black households possess twenty-three cents of median net financial assets for every dollar held by high-income white households. One startling comparison reveals that poverty-level whites control nearly as many mean net financial assets as the highest-earning blacks, $26,683 to $28,310. For those surviving at or below the poverty level, this table indicates quite clearly that poverty means one thing for whites and another for blacks. The general conclusion to be drawn from these straightforward yet very revealing tabulations is that the long-term life prospects of black households are substantially poorer than those of whites in similar income brackets. This analysis of wealth leaves no doubt regarding the serious misrepresentation of economic disparity that occurs when one relies exclusively on income data. Blacks and whites with equal incomes possess very unequal shares of wealth. More so than income, wealth holding remains very sensitive to the historically sedimenting effects of race.

Figure 5.2 examines resource distribution within racial groups. Starting with income for whites, this figure shows that one in five households falls below the poverty line and over 15 percent earn more than $50,000. Almost twice as many black households (39 percent) survive on poverty-level incomes, and only 6 percent make their way into the highest income bracket. In the [middle row of pie graphs] of Figure 5.2, we find

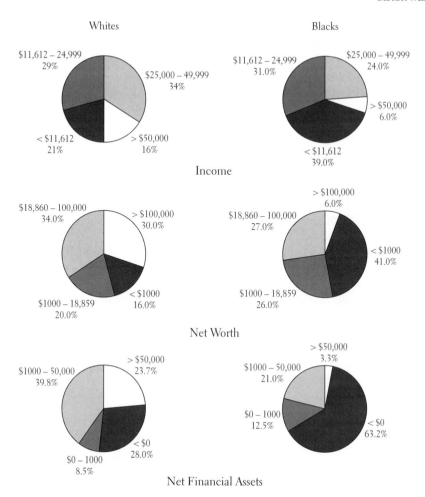

Whites

Blacks

$11,612 – 24,999
29%

$25,000 – 49,999
34%

< $11,612
21%

> $50,000
16%

$11,612 – 24,999
31.0%

$25,000 – 49,999
24.0%

> $50,000
6.0%

< $11,612
39.0%

Income

$18,860 – 100,000
34.0%

> $100,000
30.0%

$1000 – 18,859
20.0%

< $1000
16.0%

> $100,000
6.0%

$18,860 – 100,000
27.0%

< $1000
41.0%

$1000 – 18,859
26.0%

Net Worth

$1000 – 50,000
39.8%

> $50,000
23.7%

$0 – 1000
8.5%

< $0
28.0%

> $50,000
3.3%

$1000 – 50,000
21.0%

$0 – 1000
12.5%

< $0
63.2%

Net Financial Assets

FIGURE 5.2   Shares of Income and Wealth Held by Whites and Blacks

that 16 percent of white households possess less than $1,000 and nearly three in ten control over $100,000 in net worth. On the black side of the ledger, over four in ten households (41 percent) hold less than $1,000 in net worth and only about one in twenty (6 percent) controls over $100,000. The [bottom two pie graphs] of Figure 5.2 reveals that over 28 percent of white households possess zero or negative net financial assets and almost one-quarter (24 percent) have amassed more than $50,000 in these valuable financial resources. Nearly two-thirds (63.2 percent) of all black households possess no net financial assets and

only 3.3 percent make it into the $50,000-plus category.

The meager asset accumulation of black households clearly contributes to blacks' economic deprivation vis-à-vis whites in American society. While the contention that whites control the financial resources of American society is strongly supported when one examines their disproportionate control of all types of economic resources, their advantage is particularly obvious when it comes to accumulated assets. We examined the proportion of the nation's total income and wealth held by various racial groups. Using the percentage of blacks represented in the SIPP survey (9.2 percent) as an indicator of their relative numbers in the population, it is clear that blacks control a less than proportionate share of the nation's economic resources. The "black progress" narrative is most evident in blacks' share of total income, which amounts to 7.4 percent. This figure nonetheless reflects a 20 percent deficit between their slice of the income pie and their numbers in the population. The "no progress" narrative, moreover, is represented in blacks' meager portion of the nation's net worth, a portion amounting to a mere 2.9 percent and leaving blacks with 320 percent less net worth than their numbers would appear to entitle them to. Black net worth would have to increase more than threefold to reach parity with whites. However, it is their paltry share of the financial assets pie that is most distressing. Blacks control only 1.3 percent of the nation's financial assets. Whites, by contrast, who make up 82.5 percent of the population according to our SIPP data, are in total command of the nation's NFA: 95 percent of the net financial assets pie rests on their plate.

These statistical portrayals of the distribution of economic resources at the command of black and white households help us to understand the dual economic fortunes of blacks and whites in American society. While income figures clearly show that progress was made in the post–civil rights era, the distribution of wealth paints a picture of two nations on diverging tracks labeled "black progress" and "no progress."

An examination of wealth concentration compares the wealth distribution within black and white communities. Henry Terrell presented evidence showing greater inequality in blacks' wealth distribution. He explains, however, that a substantial amount of the difference in relative wealth concentrations exists because "a large portion of the black population simply did not report any wealth accumulation at all."[6]

When the wealth pies are placed on the table, very few black households are served. Sixty-three percent of black households retain zero or negative net financial assets, in comparison to 28 per-

cent of white households. Thus massive inequalities arise in wealth concentration: one in twenty households controls 46 percent of aggregated white net financial assets and 87 percent of those of blacks. One-fifth of all households owns two-thirds of white net worth and three-quarters of the net worth of blacks.[7]

Removing households with zero wealth assets from the mix, William Bradford reports similar wealth distributions in the white and black populations. It would seem that the wealth stratification among blacks who have wealth is as egalitarian as it is because the few blacks who have wealth have so little of it.[8]

Many authors, led by William J. Wilson in *The Truly Disadvantaged*, correctly point to increasing economic differentiation as the reason for growing economic inequality in the black community, but a comparison with white households provides a different perspective. In our analysis $43,000 in net worth situates a household smack in the middle of the white community's wealth distribution but a household with the same net worth in the black community ranks among the wealthiest one-fifth. Similarly, a small nest egg of $2,000 in net financial assets places a black household in the richest one-fifth of the black community, whereas the same amount puts a household only in the fortieth percentile among whites.

NOTES

1. On definitions of the black middle class (see Landry 1987).

2. $8 to $19. Several factors accounting for this range have already been discussed or will be discussed in fuller detail later in this chapter. First, the use of differing wealth definitions . . . yields dissimilar results. Second, some studies report means and others use medians as summary statistics. As with income data, wealth means, because of their sensitivity to extreme values, reveal greater inequality. Third, the studies we cite report wealth statistics from different years, databases, or subsamples.

3. Young black families in 1976 held only about 18 percent of the wealth (see Blau and Graham 1990).

4. Mean net worth is used in our asset comparison because it is the statistic most often used in previous studies on racial wealth differences.

5. "Income difference . . ." The quote is from Blau and Graham 1990, 321.

6. "A large portion of the black population . . ." The quote is from Terrell 1971, 370.

7. On wealth concentration in the black community (see Jaynes and Williams 1989).

8. On similar wealth distributions in the white and black populations (see Bradford 1987).

REFERENCES

Blau, Francine D., and John W. Graham. 1990. "Black–White Differences in Wealth and Asset Composition." *Quarterly Journal of Economics,* May, 321–39.

Bradford, William D. 1987. "Wealth, Assets, and Income of Black Households." Paper prepared for the Committee on the Status of Black Americans, National Research Council, Washington, D.C.

Brimmer, Andrew. 1988. "Income, Wealth, and Investment Behavior in the Black Community." *American Economic Review Papers and Proceedings,* 15 May, 1–5.

Jaynes, Gerald D., and Robin M. Williams, eds. 1989. *A Common Destiny: Blacks and American Society.* Washington, D.C.: National Academy Press.

Landry, Bart. 1987. *The New Black Middle Class.* Berkeley: University of California Press.

O'Hare, William P. 1983. *Wealth and Economic Status: A Perspective on Racial Inequality.* Washington, D.C.: Joint Center for Political Studies.

Steckel, Richard H., and Jayanthi Krishnan. 1992. "Wealth Mobility in America." *National Bureau of Economic Research Working Paper,* no. 4137. Cambridge, MA: National Bureau of Economic Research.

Terrell, Henry S. 1971. "Wealth Accumulation of Black and White Families: The Empirical Evidence." *Journal of Finance* 26:363–77.

Tidwell, Billy. 1987. *Beyond the Margin: Toward Economic Well-being for Black Americans.* Washington, D.C.: National Urban League.

Wilson, William Julius. 1987. *The Truly Disadvantaged.* Chicago: University of Chicago Press.

30

Beyond the Melting Pot Reconsidered

Elijah Anderson

IN 1963, GLAZER AND MOYNIHAN MADE A BOLD and optimistic statement about American race and ethnic relations to the effect that one day we would resolve the divisive issue of different ethnicities, and be melded into one in the melting pot of American society. As an idea, this can be traced to Robert Park and the beginnings of urban sociology (Park, 1950), but Glazer and Moynihan felt that they were documenting the realization of this concept in the New York City of the late 1950s and early 1960s. Indeed, the black and Puerto Rican populations seemed not to be keeping pace with the process of assimilation, but even they had made progress. The message of *Beyond the Melting Pot* was that it was only a matter of time, perhaps a generation or two, until the process would change the face of American society. Yet today, thirty-five years later, we see that this has not occurred. Why?

In 1999, we have more of a salad bowl than a melting pot. Rather than giving it up, racial and ethnic groups appear to embrace their particularism. In public and to an extent in private life, there is more mixing of people of various groups than there was a generation ago, but at the same time people tend to retain more of their ethnic particularity within these interactions. An important reason for this has been the continuation of racial and ethnic competition, especially in the wake of the

From: *International Migration Review*, Spring 2000 v34 i1 p262

Copyright © 2000 Center for Migration Studies of New York, Inc.

civil rights movement that—while its goal was the incorporation of blacks into mainstream society—encouraged racial pride among African Americans. This in turn prompted other groups to do the same. At the same time, the U.S. experienced an influx of immigration, especially of people of color, who have likewise retained their particularity. As all these people compete for place and position, they do so from the base of their own particular ethnic identities. The main argument of *Beyond the Melting Pot* is that ethnicity declines in importance as groups become middle class and that at the time this was rapidly occurring with the Jews, the Italians, and the Irish. Replacing ethnicity was religious identification. Because blacks and Puerto Ricans were not moving into the middle class according to the patterns of the white immigrant groups, their ethnicity remained salient. However, for blacks ethnicity is in fact race and for the Puerto Ricans it is becoming a permanent subculture that includes the use of Spanish as an official language. The major obstacles to assimilation into the American mainstream are seen to be the legacy of slavery for blacks and the continuing close ties with the island for Puerto Ricans. A loose black family structure and lack of economic initiative are seen to derive from slavery, whereas because Puerto Ricans go back and forth between the U.S. and Puerto Rico, they maintain their dysfunctional social and cultural patterns.

Glazer and Moynihan's belief was that even though skin color and the unique history of blacks in America made their assimilation more problematic than that of white immigrant groups, eventually it would occur. Yet today there has been some but not nearly as much as the authors expected: in fact, at the present time, the rate of assimilation seems to be actually slowing down (Glazer, 1997; Schlesinger, 1999). What happened?

A large part of the answer lies in the occurrence of developments that Glazer and Moynihan could not have anticipated: changes in the economic structure and in immigration. For the past thirty years, the U.S. has been undergoing deindustrialization—the change from a manufacturing to a service and high-tech economy—in the context of an increasingly global economy (Suro, 1998; Taylor, 1997). As a result, jobs that inner-city residents could perform are being sent to the suburbs and to third world countries, leaving the inner city virtually jobless. This has obvious economic implications for the black lower classes, but it also has implications for relations between them and the black middle classes. As many of the unemployed poor have become mired in an underclass, the middle class, having taken advantage of affirmative action programs and other efforts to incorporate blacks into the mainstream, has grown, and the split between the two is becoming increasingly visible. At the same time, all blacks are currently under siege due to a withdrawal of responsibility by the wider society. In the inner-city communities, this has occurred in terms of policing, public welfare, and employment. For the middle class and those who aspire to it, it has been through cutbacks in the programs and policies that made the middle class possible.

A further stressor has been the huge influx during this period of immigrants of color, the result of the Immigration act of 1965. These people often move into underclass areas and effectively compete with blacks for place and position. In addition, many of these new immigrants are already middle class and feel less pressured to give up their particularism, thus helping to fuel the revival of ethnic particularism just at the time that, as Glazer and Moynihan found, it seemed about to fade away. This has had a profound effect on American blacks, for whom particularism already played a different role than it had for the white immigrant groups.

The situation of blacks is complicated by the civil rights movement and the rise of black cultural nationalism. In the process of forming a cohesive block that could successfully challenge the white mainstream society from which they were excluded, blacks were encouraged to become highly particularistic. An unfortunate byproduct of that particularism, however, has been the development of a certain stance among whites that views blacks as a monolith, apart, often alienated and angry. The interplay of these two viewpoints has led to the current situation in which even blacks who rise into the middle or upper class now tend to live in self-segregated communities, such as Prince George's County, Maryland and Teaneck, New Jersey (Massey and Denton, 1993). But buying into such a limited housing market has implications for the ability of blacks to build up long-term financial capital (Oliver and Shapiro, 1997).

The divisive racial atmosphere in which we live makes such a seemingly contradictory stance entirely predictable. We now have an increasingly diverse black middle class in the midst of a black working class that has seen its fortunes decline rapidly with the industry that supported it. In turn, the weakest members of the working class find themselves slipping into the growing underclass. The Republican Right stirs up the latent racism of those who are inclined to see black people as incompetent, at best, and, at worst, freeloaders who are getting something for nothing. At the same time, black leaders, such as Louis Farrakhan and the Reverend Al Sharpton, fan the flames of separatism, challenging blacks with the question of whether whites are really worthy of integration.

This places the middle class black in a bind: If he leaves behind his ethnic particularism, he may be seen by blacks as a sellout and therefore something of a failure even though he has achieved success in white society; but if he embraces particularism, his chances for success may be adversely affected. This dilemma, previously unknown to whites, was thrust into the public spotlight in the O.J. Simpson trial, particularly with regard to Christopher Darden. Regardless of the merits of the case, many blacks found themselves disgusted with a black man who would prosecute another.

Darden's dilemma is one that many blacks in professional positions are experiencing in the 1990s but that could not have been foreseen in the 1960s when Glazer was considering the issue of assimilation. Many of these blacks face the dual pressures and expectations of being "professionals" in a white world and of dealing with what it means to be African American in the context of a reanimated racial pride. The choice of coming to terms with their situations as blacks or as professionals, as the example of Darden shows, is not always left up to them and is made all the more painful by those who see racial loyalty as an either/or proposition—you're either for us or against us, a race man or a sellout.

The idea of the race man goes back to the segregated black community, in fact, all the way back to the time of slavery. The term itself comes from the classic ethnographic study of the black community in Chicago, Black Metropolis, carried out in the 1940s by two sociologists at the University of Chicago, Horace Cayton and St. Clair Drake. By Cayton and Drake's definition, the race man (or woman) was a particular kind of black leader who lived in a segregated society and felt strongly responsible to the black race, especially in front of whites or outsiders to the community. Such a person was intent on "advancing the race" by working as a role model, both to uplift the ghetto community and to disabuse the wider society of its often negative view of blacks. Implicit in this belief was a kind of racial solidarity, a peculiar celebration of racial "particularism," of putting matters of race above all other issues. For a long time, there was a critical mass of race men and women in the black community.

However, over the past several decades, the wider system has been pressured to treat blacks as full citizens. At the impetus of the civil rights movement and the insurgencies and civil disorders of the 1960s, the white system began the process of granting blacks civil rights and incorporating blacks more fully into the economic system. By the 1970s, a black middle class was developing, increasingly assimilated with the wider society, particularly in terms of education, employment, residence, and lifestyle. But one of the costs of becoming a trusted member of this system is to divest oneself, to some extent, of one's own ethnic particularity, to display a commitment to the values of the dominant culture. Adopting this posture works against the ideology of the race man; the more his people are assimilated, the less important is his role. Thus, the process we've been witnessing on a large scale in the past quarter century is the emergence of a new type of black professional who, even though he or she often experiences divided loyalties, appears as interested in his or her class or profession as in his or her race.

As described by Glazer and Moynihan, this process is, in many respects, similar to what the Irish, Jews, Italians, and other ethnic groups have undergone. All these groups have had their race men at certain times in their histories, but as the groups' fortunes have risen, the need for their respective race men has declined and other individuals have emerged who are increasingly more interested in their professions and class positions. These individuals don't necessarily forget their roots, but often the requirements of their profession win out, and class issues take precedence over public displays of ethnic and racial particularism. This is what we have come to expect as a normal consequence of upward mobility in the United States. The exception is that of race and the nature and complexity of racism that blacks face.

In the 1990s, after this age of integration and the gradual loss of traditional race men and women, we have seen the emergence of Farrakhan, Al Sharpton, the Rodney King beating and its aftermath, the Simpson case, the Million Man March, and the implicit marginalization of people like Jesse Jackson, Coretta Scott King, and other moderate black leaders who actively supported integration. A concomitant, parallel development has been the emergence of an oppositional culture among black youths, especially in the inner cities (Anderson, 1999). Unlike many of their parents and grandparents, these young people often pride themselves on being racially particularistic and identifying with an ideology that is often diametrically opposed to "white" conventions, the norms of the wider society, an attitude that appears to be spreading. Fueled by an increasingly resistant white system, it is one of the most dramatic developments in the black community today.

In this context, at a time of heightened feelings by blacks of being persecuted by the society at large, the race man has reemerged to defend and serve the group. But this time it is a new race man. The former race men were integrationists, striving to attain the same rights, duties, and privileges for blacks that were claimed by whites. In contrast, Farrakhan and others like him promote separatism. Their goals for the black society—such as self-reliance and stable families—are largely shared by the white society, but they see the ideal black society as parallel to, rather than an integrated part of, the white society. Several factors have been at work to bring this situation about, some obvious and well documented and some perhaps more subtle.

One element is the growing trend toward ethnicity and particularism among groups throughout the wider society (and the world), including the newer waves of immigrants. Many are educated and already middle class and thus are under less pressure than previous immigrants to divest themselves of their ethnic identities in exchange for upward mobility. In contrast, they are encouraged to hold on to their particularities and even to celebrate them as cultural diversity, and with heightened ethnic consciousness, groups from previous waves join that trend. Blacks, having always been apart from the wider society to a large extent, have a real and justified interest in more fully embracing their own ethnicity, celebrating it, becoming ethnocentric. And many do.

Strongly related to these considerations are the many forces that are pressing on the inner-city black population today. Repeatedly, blacks have witnessed the precipitous rise and fall in their fortunes through slavery, emancipation, segregation, the civil rights movement, affirmative action, and now political retrenchment as politicians are gaining political clout by proving themselves hostile to the advancement of blacks. Today, we are experiencing the transformation of American cities from centers of manufacturing to centers

of service and high technology. The loss of well-paying manufacturing jobs in the cities as U.S. corporations have sent their low-skill jobs to Third World countries and nonmetropolitan areas of this country has devastated the black working class (Bluestone and Harrison, 1982; Reich, 1992; Wilson, 1996; Rifkin, 1996). The resulting poverty has created a social breakdown in our inner cities on a huge scale—witness the all-too familiar and escalating problems of alienation, drug abuse, violence, teenage pregnancy, family disintegration, record rates of arrest and incarceration, AIDS, homelessness, and endemic joblessness.

At the heart of the matter, and of the rise in the fortunes of this new generation of more separatist race men, is the dominant culture's denigration of the character and competence of black men. Because men are considered to be responsible for providing for the welfare of their families and communities in our society, many people who are confronted with the widespread unemployment of black people have reached a simple conclusion: There is something terribly wrong with the black man. His moral fiber, his common decency, his very masculinity are being called into question. In any discussion of prisons, welfare, joblessness, family desertion, crime, violence, or drugs, his name is invoked. Shopkeepers fear him. Taxi drivers refuse to pick him up. And policemen "profile" him or sometimes shoot him dead. It has become easy to grumble that he is the reason for our nation's problems. And some politicians have responded by slashing welfare and ignoring economic and structural realities, such as the aforementioned devastation of the inner cities, threatening to turn back a generation of racial gains. In addition, in public interactions, blacks' images of themselves may be called into question by the set of negative stereotypes that emerge from the mass media's reports on the plight of the underclass.

The young inner-city black man has not failed to respond to this state of affairs. Resigned to a society that does not include him in the American Dream, he comes of age realizing the hard truths that American society is not there for him, that a racially stratified system is in place, and that his place, fortified through acts of prejudice and discrimination, is at the bottom of it. This creates in him a profound sense of alienation and forces him to adapt (Anderson, 1990, 1999). That resignation can be observed in the young men's looks, in their actions, and in their tendency to disparage white people except for those who can be used to attain an immediate goal. Life has taught the young black man that he can do certain things but cannot go beyond his limited situation; dreams are simply never fulfilled. He knows the dream that says people will "judge you not by the color of your skin, but by the content of your character," but he also knows "the real deal"—that he must always pay a tax for being black in America. A common response is to embrace the profound alienation represented by the oppositional culture of the street.

Even the black men who win—"make it" in mainstream society—must have a certain distrust of the prize: Their own success alienates them from the black masses but fails to win them true acceptance by the wider system. Those young middle class black men who acquire the resources to negotiate the wider system and who, in the process, have worked so hard to eliminate any potential confusion between themselves and their inner-city counterparts feel eternally in limbo between two extremes: the drug-dealing, gold-wearing street hustler who "disses" the conventions of the wider society, on the one hand, and the successful mainstream professional, on the other hand. Therefore, black professionals must constantly struggle to define themselves on their own terms, in the context of a society that both demonizes and celebrates them (O.J. Simpson being a good case in point). All this contributes to a certain precariousness of place that results from people's presuppositions with regard to the black man. The black man's color and maleness become his master status, putting into question anything else he may claim to be. Darden's dilemma, therefore, is one he shares with many African Americans. He was trying to serve two basically contradictory gods, that of black racial particularism and that of meritocracy and universalism.

Blacks often see these events as reflecting the racism of a white population that has always discouraged their demands for fuller inclusion and participation in the wider society's economic, political, and social life, and they respond by embracing their own ethnic particularism. Unfortunately, the line between ethnocentrism and alienation can be blurry. Whether young blacks are of the street or of the middle class, it is hard for them to see themselves as part of the wider society. At black colleges and other black institutions, young people display elements of the street culture simply to prove to others that they're truly black and haven't sold out, that they haven't forgotten their roots. Most young African Americans ultimately come to terms with these feelings of alienation. Those with fewer resources, however, may express it through drug abuse and violence. Only one of the resulting tragedies of this alienation is the tendency of some whites to discriminate against all blacks because to do otherwise simply requires too much energy and an understanding that they do not possess.

This is the hand blacks have been dealt by the circumstances of history, particularly such recent events as the Rodney King affair and a whole host of grievances toward the police that had been building up in the black community—the hand from which Johnnie Cochran extracted the "race card." Cochran's defense was to transform Simpson into a symbol of black persecution in a white judicial system that is already distrusted by a large number of blacks. In these times, when the black community is seen to be under assault by the wider society, the community is coming together around the defense of black victims at the same time as it is searching for race men, leaders of the race.

A disturbing implication of all this for American society is that as a result, Christopher Darden found himself out of style because the prevailing racial atmosphere is one in which the ultimate value of integration and conformity with the larger society is increasingly being called into question. This is a situation that Glazer and Moynihan's *Beyond the Melting Pot* did not anticipate or expect, but Glazer's most recent book, *We Are All*

Multiculturalists Now, is consistent with this reality and is testimony to how much things have changed—and how they don't remain the same.

REFERENCES

Alba, R. 1999. "Immigration and the American Realities of Assimilation and Multiculturalism," *Sociological Forum,* 14:3–25.

———. 1990. *Ethnic Identity: The Transformation of White America.* New Haven: Yale University Press.

———. 1985. *Italian Americans: Into the Twilight of Ethnicity.* Englewood Cliffs: Prentice Hall.

Alba, R. and V. Nee. 1997. "Rethinking Assimilation Theory for a New Era of Immigration," *International Migration Review,* 31(4):826–874.

Anderson, E. 1999. *Code of the Street: Decency, Violence, and the Moral Life of the Inner City.* New York: W.W. Norton.

———. 1990. *Streetwise: Race Class, and Change in an Urban Community.* Chicago: University of Chicago Press.

Bluestone, B. and B. Harrison. 1982. *The Deindustrialization of America: Plant Closings, Community Abandonment, and the Dismantling of Basic Industry.* New York: Basic Books.

Cordero-Guzmán, H. and R. Grosfoguel. 1998. The Demographic and Socio-Economic Characteristics of Post-1965 Immigrants to New York City," Unpublished paper.

Crowder, K. 1999. "Residential Segregation of West Indians in the New York/New Jersey Metropolitan Area: The Roles of Race and Ethnicity," *International Migration Review,* 33(1):79–113.

DeWind, J. and P. Kasinitz. 1997. "Everything Old is New Again? Processes and Theories of Immigrant Incorporation," *International Migration Review,* 31(4):1096–1111.

Foner, N. Forthcoming *From Ellis Island to JFK: New York's Two Great Waves of Immigration.* New Haven and New York: Yale University Press and Russell Sage Foundation.

———. 1987. "The Jamaicans: Race and Ethnicity among Migrants in New York City." In *New Immigrants in New York.* Ed. N. Foner. New York: Columbia University Press.

———. 1973. *Status and Power in Rural Jamaica: A Study of Educational and Political Change.* New York: Teachers College Press, Columbia University.

Gans, H. 1979. "Symbolic Ethnicity: The Future of Ethnic Groups and Cultures in America," *Ethnic and Racial Studies,* 2:1–20.

Glazer, N. 1997. *We are All Multiculturalists Now.* Cambridge: Harvard University Press.

———. 1993. "Is Assimilation Dead?" *The Annals of the American Academy of Political and Social Science,* 530:122–136.

———. 1988. "The New New Yorkers." In *New York Unbound.* Ed. P. Salins. New York: Basil Blackwell.

Glazer, N. and D. P. Moynihan. [1963] 1970. *Beyond the Melting Pot: The Negroes, Puerto Ricans, Jews, Italians and Irish of New York City.* Cambridge: MIT Press.

Gorelick, S. 1981. *City College and the Jewish Poor.* New Brunswick: Rutgers University Press.

Grasmuck, S. and R. Grosfoguel. 1997. "Geopolitics, Economic Niches, and Gendered Social Capital among Recent Caribbean Immigrants to New York City," *Sociological Perspectives,* 40:339–362.

Kasinitz, P. 1992. *Caribbean New York: Black Immigrants and the Politics of Race.* Ithaca: Cornell University Press.

Lisheron, M. 1997. "Rhythm and Jews," *Common Quest,* 2(1):20–33.

Lopez, D. and Y.L. Espiritu. 1989. "Panethnicity in the United States: A Theoretical Framework, " *Ethnic and Racial Studies,* 13:198–224.

Massey, D. and N. Denton. 1993. *American Apartheid: Segregation and the Making of the Underclass.* Cambridge, MA: Harvard University Press.

Mollenkopf, J., P. Kasinitz and M. Lindholm. 1995. "Profiles of Nine Immigrant Categories and their Sub-Groups and of Island-Born Puerto Ricans." In *Immigration/Migration and the CUNY Student of the Future.* New York: The City University of New York.

Oliver, M. and T. Shapiro. 1997. *Black Wealth, White Wealth: A New Perspective on Racial Inequality.* Washington, D.C.: Urban Institute Press.

Park, R.E. 1950. *Race and Culture.* Glencoe, IL: Free Press.

Pessar, P. 1999. "The Role of Gender Households, and Social Networks in the Migration Process: A Review and Appraisal." In *The Handbook of International Migration: The American Experience.* Ed. C. Hirshman, J. DeWind and P. Kasintz. New York: Russell Sage Foundation.

Portes, A. and M. Zhou. 1993. "The New Second Generation: Segmented Assimilation and Its Variants among Post-1965 Youth," *The Annals of the American Academy of Political and Social Science,* 530:74–96.

Reich, R. 1992. *The Work of Nations: Preparing Ourselves for 21st Century Capitalism.* New York: Vintage Books.

Reimers, D. 1992. *Still the Golden Door: The Third World Comes to America,* 2nd ed. New York: Colombia University Press.

Rifkin, J. and R. L. Heilbroner. 1996. *The End of Work: The Decline of the Global Labor Force and the Dawn of the Post-Market Era.* New York: Putnam Publishing Group.

Sanjek, R. 1994. "Intermarriage and the Future of Races in the United States." In *Race.* Ed. S. Gregory and R. Sanjek. New Brunswick: Rutgers University Press.

Schlesinger, A.M., Jr. 1999. *The Cycles of American History.* New York: Houghton Mifflin.

Siegel, F. 1997. *The Future Once Happened Here.* New York: Simon and Schuster.

Suro, R. 1998. "The Next Wave: How Immigration Blurs the Race Discussion, *Washington Post,* July 19.

Taylor, J.E., P.L. Martin and M. Fix. 1997. *Poverty Amid Prosperity: Immigration and the Changing Face of Rural California.* Washington, D.C.: Urban Institute Press.

Waldinger, R. 1996. *Still the Promised City? African American and New Immigrants in Postindustrial New York.* Cambridge: Harvard University Press.

———. 1997. "Beyond Nostalgia: The Old Neighborhood Revisited," *New York Affairs,* 10: 1–12.

Waters, M. 1990. *Ethnic Options.* Berkeley: University of California Press.

Wilson, W.J. 1996. *When Work Disappears: The World of the New Urban Poor.* New York: Knopf.

———. 1989. "The Underclass: Issues, Perspectives, and Public Policy," *The Annals of the American Academy of Political and Social Science,* 501:183–92.

31

Not Everyone Is Chosen

Segmented Assimilation and Its Determinants

Alejandro Portes and Rubén G. Rumbaut

Since most immigrants' children are now in school and not yet in the labour force, it is essential that the school careers and future job possibilities of these children be understood.

—Herbert J. Gans, "Second Generation Decline," p. 183

When you see someone go downtown and get a good job, if they be Puerto Rican, you see them fix up their hair and put some contact lens in their eyes. Then they fit in. And they do it! . . . Look at all the people in that building, they all turn-overs. They people who want to be white. Man, if you call them in Spanish it wind up a problem.

—Phillipe I. Bourgois, *In Search of Respect*, p. 170.

THIS CHAPTER PRESENTS THE THEORETICAL perspectives that have developed in the course of our study and that guide the analysis of data in the following chapters. The story of how a foreign minority comes to terms with its new social surroundings and is eventually absorbed into the mainstream of the host society is the cloth from which numerous sociological and economic theories have been fashioned.[1] For the most part, this story has been told in optimistic tones and with an emphasis on the eventual integration of the newcomers. In other words, increasing contact over time is expected to end in the gradual merging of foreigners and natives, and the speed of the process depends on how close descendants of immigrants come to resemble the mainstream population.

For this reason, the notion of assimilation became the master concept in both social theory and public discourse to designate the expected path to be followed by foreign groups in America. The concept conveys a factual prediction about the final outcome of the encounters between foreign minorities and the native majority and, simultaneously, an assertion of a socially desirable goal.[2]. More than half a century ago, sociologists Lloyd Warner and Leo Srole introduced their study of an American city as "part of the magnificent story of the adjustment of ethnic groups to American life" and went on to predict that "oncoming generations of new ethnics will . . . climb to the same heights."[3] In reality, the process is neither as simple nor as inevitable. To begin with, both the immigrant population and the host society are heterogeneous. Immigrants, even those of the same nationality, are frequently divided by social class, the timing of their arrival, and their generation. American society is not homogeneous either. Depending on the timing of their arrival and context of reception, immigrants can find themselves confronting diametrically different situations, and hence the course of their assimilation can lead to a number of different outcomes.

There are groups among today's second generation that are slated for a smooth transition into the mainstream and for whom ethnicity will soon be a matter of personal choice. They, like descendants of earlier Europeans, will identify with their ancestry on occasion and when convenient. There are others for whom their ethnicity will be a source of strength and who will muscle their way up, socially and economically, on the basis of their own communities' networks and resources. There are still others whose ethnicity will be neither a matter of choice nor a source of progress but a mark of subordination. These children are at risk of joining the masses of the dispossessed, compounding the spectacle of inequality and despair in America's inner cities. The prospect that members of today's second generation will join those at the bottom of society—a new rainbow underclass—has more than a purely academic interest, for it can affect the life chances of millions of Americans and the quality of life in the cities and communities where they concentrate.

Hence, while assimilation may still represent the master concept in the study of today's immigrants, the process is subject to too many contingencies and affected by too many variables to render the image of a relatively uniform and straightforward path credible. Instead, the present second generation is better defined as undergoing a process of *segmented assimilation* where outcomes vary across immigrant minorities and where rapid integration and acceptance into the American mainstream represent just one possible alternative. Why this is so is a complex story depending on a number of factors, among which four can be considered decisive: 1) the history of the immigrant first generation; 2) the pace of acculturation among parents and children and its bearing on normative integration; 3) the barriers, cultural and economic, confronted by second-generation youth in their quest for successful adaptation; and 4) the family and community resources for confronting these barriers. This chapter provides a theoretical description of each of these factors and their expected consequences as a way of fleshing out the concept of segmented assimilation and paving the way for the analysis of its diverse aspects in later chapters.

HOW IMMIGRANTS ARE RECEIVED: MODES OF INCORPORATION AND THEIR CONSEQUENCES

It stands to reason that the adaptation of second-generation youths is conditioned by what happens to their parents and that the latter's economic performance and social status are likely to vary. In contrast to journalistic and political characterizations of immigrants as a uniform population, every scholarly analysis of the subject begins by emphasizing their great diversity.[4] Today's immigrants differ along three fundamental dimensions: 1) their individual features, including their age, education, occupational skills, wealth, and knowledge of English; 2) the social environment that receives them, including the policies of the host government, the attitudes of the native population, and the presence and size of a co-ethnic community; and 3) their family structure.

The skills that immigrants bring along in the form of education, job experience, and language knowledge are referred to as their *human capital* and play a decisive role in their economic adaptation. The economic attainment of immigrants does not entirely depend on human capital, however, because its utilization is contingent on the context in which they are incorporated. Yet, by and large, educated immigrants are in a much better competitive position and are more likely to succeed occupationally and economically in their new environment. The same is true of those with extensive occupational experience.[5]

On arrival, however, immigrant workers and entrepreneurs do not confront American society as a level playing field where only their education and work experience count. Instead, a number of contextual factors shape the way in which they can put their skills to use. The policies of the receiving government represent the first such factor confronting newcomers. Although a continuum of possible governmental responses exists, the basic options are exclusion, passive acceptance, or active encouragement. When enforced, exclusion precludes immigration or forces immigrants into a wholly underground and disadvantaged existence. The second alternative is defined by the act of granting immigrants legal access to the country without any additional effort on the part of authorities to facilitate their adaptation. This neutral stance places newcomers under the protection of the law but does not grant them any special concessions to compensate for their unfamiliarity with their new environment. Most economically motivated immigration to the United States in recent years has taken place under this alternative. A third governmental option occurs when authorities take active steps to encourage a particular inflow or facilitate its resettlement. At various times during the last century, the U.S. government was directly involved in the recruitment of different categories of foreign workers and professionals deemed to be in short supply. During the last 30 years or so, active governmental support and assistance has been granted only to selected refugee flows, arriving mostly in the aftermath of communist takeovers during the cold war.[6] Government support is important because it gives newcomers access to an array of resources that do not exist for other immigrants. This edge provides refugees who have high levels of human capital with a chance for rapid upward mobility. It also improves the economic condition of those from modest backgrounds by providing job apprenticeships and direct economic assistance.

The second contextual factor is the host society and its reception of newcomers. A well-established sociological principle holds that the more similar new minorities are in terms of physical appearance, class background, language, and religion to society's mainstream, the more favorable their reception and the more rapid their integration. For this reason, educated immigrants from northwestern Europe face little difficulty in gaining access to U.S. middle- and upper-class circles and are readily able to deploy their educational and work skills to their advantage.[7] Though race is in appearance a personal trait, in reality it inheres in the values and prejudices of the culture so that individuals with the same physical appearance can be treated very differently depending on the social context in which they find themselves.

In America, race is a paramount criterion of social acceptance that can overwhelm the influence of class background, religion, or language. Regardless of their class origin or knowledge of English, nonwhite immigrants face greater obstacles in gaining access to the white middle-class mainstream and may receive lower returns for their education and work experience. A racial gradient continues to exist in U.S. culture so that the darker a person's skin is, the greater is the social distance from dominant groups and the more difficult it is to make his or her personal qualifications count.[8] the social context and its differential evaluation of newcomers account, for example, for the generally favorable reception accorded to Irish immigrants in northeastern U.S. cities and the much greater barriers faced by Haitian immigrants in the same areas, despite the fact that many Haitians are legal immigrants and many Irish are actually undocumented.[9]

The immigrant community's own compatriots represent the third and most immediate context of reception. In some cases, no such community exists, and newcomers must confront the challenges of adaptation by themselves. More common, however, is the arrival of immigrants into places where a community of their conationals already exists. Such communities can cushion the impact of a foreign culture and provide assistance for finding jobs. Help with immediate living needs, such as housing, places to shop, and schools for the children, also flow through these co-ethnic networks.[10]

This regularity in the process of adaptation conceals, however, significant differences among the ethnic communities that immigrants join. While all such communities help their own, they do so within the limits of their own information and resources. For purposes of future socioeconomic mobility, the central difference is whether the co-ethnic group is mainly composed of working-class persons or contains a significant professional and entrepreneurial element. For newcomers in working-class communities, the natural thing to do is to follow the path of earlier arrivals into the host

TABLE 3.1

Immigrant Nationalities and Their Modes of Incorporation, 1990.

Nationality	Size	Status Characteristics[a]				Family Structure	
		Median Age	College Graduates (%)[c]	Poverty Rate (%)[d]	Median Family Income ($)[d]	Both Parents Present (%)[e]	Female Head (%)[f]
Mexican	4,298,014	29.9	3.5	29.7	21,585	73	14
Filipino	912,674	38.8	43.0	5.9	47,794	78	15
Cuban	736,971	49.0	15.6	14.7	32,007	72	16
Chinese							
People's Republic	529,837	40.5	30.9	15.7	34,225	87	8
Taiwan	244,102	33.2	62.2	16.7	45,325	81	10
Hong Kong	147,131	30.3	46.8	12.7	49,618	84	10
Korean	568,397	34.9	34.4	15.6	33,406	87	11
Vietnamese	543,262	30.3	16.0	25.5	30,496	73	15
Dominican	347,858	33.6	7.5	30.0	19,694	47	41
Jamaican	334,140	35.7	14.9	12.1	34,338	53	35
Colombian	286,124	35.3	15.5	15.3	30,342	65	21
Haitian	225,393	34.6	11.8	21.7	25,556	56	28
Laotian	171,577	27.0	5.1	40.3	19,671	81	12
Nicaraguan	168,659	30.0	14.6	24.4	24,416	66	21
Cambodian	118,833	29.0	5.5	38.4	19,043	71	24

[a]U.S. Bureau of Census, *The Foreign-Born Population of the United States* (Washington, D.C.: U.S. Department of Commerce, 1993).
[b]Typology based on past studies of individual nationalities.
[c]Persons 25 years of age or over.
[d]Annual figures (1989).
[e]Children under 18 residing with both biological parents.
[f]Percent of households headed by women with no husband present.

labor market. The help that ethnic communities can offer for securing employment in these situations is constrained by the kind of jobs held by their more established members. In this fashion, immigrants with considerable human capital can be channeled to below-average occupations as a function of the co-ethnic context that they encounter and the "help" that its members can provide.[11]

On the contrary, immigrants fortunate enough to join more advantaged ethnic communities can translate their education and occupational skills into economic returns, even when still unfamiliar with the new language and culture. The main feature of this situation—where a substantial number of conationals holds professional occupations or are independent entrepreneurs—is that the support of ethnic networks does not come at the cost of accepting a working-class lifestyle or outlook. Instead, these networks open a whole range of possibilities—from employment in the outside labor market to jobs within the ethnic community—that make full use of the immigrants' potential.[12]

Jointly, these three levels of reception—governmental, societal, and communal—comprise the mode of incorporation of a particular immigrant group. These modes condition the extent to which

Mode of Incorporation[b]

Governmental[g]	Societal[h]	Co-ethnic Community[i]
Hostile	Prejudiced	Working Class, concentrated
Neutral prejudiced	Neutral to	Professional, dispersed
Favorable to hostile	Neutral to preduiced	Entrepreneurial, concentrated
Neutral	Prejudiced	Professional/entrepreneurial, concentrated
Neutral	Prejudiced	Entrepreneurial, concentrated
Favorable	Prejudiced	Entrepreneurial/working class, concentrated
Neutral	Prejudiced	Working class, concentrated
Neutral	Prejudiced	Professional/working class, dispersed
Hostile to neutral	Prejudiced	Professional/working class, dispersed
Hostile	Prejudiced	Working class, concentrated
Favorable	Prejudiced	Poor, concentrated
Hostile	Prejudiced	Professional/working class, concentrated
Favorable	Prejudiced	Poor, concentrated

[g]Favorable reception accorded to groups composed of legal refugees and asylees; neutral reception to groups of legal immigrants; hostile reception to groups suspected to harbor large numbers of unauthorized immigrants or being involved in the drug trade, becoming targets of deportation by U.S. immigrant authorities.

[h]Prejudiced reception accorded to nonwhite immigrants and to those with perceived involvement in the drug trade; neutral to groups defined as mostly white.

[i]Concentrated ethnic communities are those that have large and highly visible concentration in at least one metropolitan area.

immigrant human capital can be brought into play to promote successful economic and social adaptation. No matter how motivated and ambitious immigrants are, their future prospects will be dim if government officials persecute them, natives consistently discriminate against them, and their own community has only minimum resources to offer.

A third dimension of importance for second-generation adaptation is the composition of the immigrant family, in particular the extent to which it includes both biological parents. Immigrant family composition varies significantly across nationalities, reflecting both different cultures and

social structures in sending countries and patterns of arrival in the United States. Different modes of incorporation, in particular the outlook of authorities and strength of co-ethnic communities, can affect family composition by facilitating family reunification and reinforcing cultural norms. In turn, family contexts can be expected to affect various second-generation outcomes, even after taking parental human capital and modes of incorporation into account.

Summarizing this discussion, Table 3.1 presents a profile of the human capital, modes of incorporation, and family contexts of several of the largest immigrant groups arriving in the United States during the last two decades. These are also the groups best represented in our study, so these profiles provide a set of preliminary expectations concerning parental adaptation and subsequent second-generation outcomes. Specifically, we expect parental human capital, in the form of education and occupational skills, to positively affect their own socioeconomic attainment. In turn, achieved parental status and family composition will affect the pace and character of second-generation acculturation and subsequent adaptation outcomes. Modes of incorporation are expected to significantly affect the socioeconomic attainment of first-generation parents and to influence their family structure. The importance of these contextual variables may even extend beyond the first generation to directly affect second-generation outcomes. This is one of the main questions to be examined in the following chapters.

ACCULTURATION OF ROLE REVERSAL

In the family of José María Argüelles, a 40-year old Nicaraguan immigrant in Miami, power has drifted steadily away from him and his wife and toward their two teenage sons. José María does not speak English and has only a high school education. His and his wife's lack of permanent immigration papers means that they have been dependent on a string of odd menial jobs, like dishwashing and house cleaning, for survival. However, they have remained in the United States long enough for their children to grow up and learn the language. At 19, Pepe Argüelles already holds a waiter's job at a good restaurant and drives a better car than his parents. His younger brother, Luis, has been drifting toward a local gang dealing drugs, but the money that he brings home helps pay the rent and meet other urgent needs when his father is out of a job. José María feels powerless to discipline Luis or guide the future of their sons. "It's too late to send them back to Nicaragua," he says. "Here, they know English and know their way around far better than us . . . all that their mother and I can do is pray."[13]

One of the most poignant aspects of immigrants' adaptation to a new society is that children can become, in a very real sense, their parents' parents. This role reversal occurs when children's acculturation has moved so far ahead of their parents' that key family decisions become dependent on the children's knowledge. Because they speak the language and know the culture better, second-generation youths are often able to define the situation for themselves, prematurely freeing themselves from parental control.

Role reversal was a familiar event among offspring of working-class European immigrants at the beginning of the twentieth century, and it was often seen as part of the normal process of assimilation to America. Children of Italian, Russian, and Polish laborers raced past their parents to take jobs in the expanding industrial economy of the time, set themselves up in business, or claw their way into the corporate world.[14] Today, second-generation Latins and Asians are repeating the story but with an important twist. For reasons that we will see in detail later on, the social and economic context that allowed their Europe predecessors to move up and out of their families exists no more. In its place, a number of novel barriers to successful adaptation have emerged, making role reversal a warning sign of possible downward assimilation. Freed from parental control at a premature age, the options available to second-generation youths can be different and sometimes more dangerous than those available to children of Europeans earlier in the century.

Role reversal, like modes of incorporation, is not a uniform process. Instead, systematic differences exist among immigrant families and communities. It is possible to think of these differences as a continuum ranging from situations where parental authority is preserved to those where it is thoroughly undermined by generational gaps in acculturation. The process of acculturation is the first step toward assimilation, as both immigrant parents and children learn the new language and normative lifestyles. Yet the rates at which they do so and the extent to which this learning combines with retention of the home culture varies, with significant consequences for second-generation adaptation.[15] Table 3.2 presents a typology of possible situations depending on the acculturative

TABLE 3.2
Types of Acculturation Across Generations

Children's Learning of English and American Customs	Parents' Learning of English and American Customs	Children's Insertion into Ethnic Community	Parents' Insertion into Ethnic Community	Type	Expected Outcomes
+	+	−	−	Consonant acculturation	Joint search for integration into American mainstream: rapid shift to English monolingualism among children
−	−	+	+	Consonant resistance to acculturation	Isolation within the ethnic community; likely to return to home country
+	−	−	+	Dissonant acculturation (I)	Rupture of family ties and children's abandonment of ethnic community; limited bilingualism or English monolingualism among children
+	−	−	−	Dissonant acculturation (II)	Loss of parental authority and of parental languages; role reversal and intergenerational conflict
+	+	+	+	Selective acculturation	Preservation of parental authority; little or no intergenerational conflict; fluent bilingualism among children

Source: Adapted from Alejandro Portes and Rubén G. Rumbaut, *Immigrant America, a Portrait*, 2d ed. (Berkeley: University of California Press, 1996), p. 242.

gaps across generations and the children's insertion in the ethnic community.

Three of the outcomes portrayed in this figure are especially important. *Dissonant acculturation* takes place when children's learning of the English language and American ways and simultaneous loss of the immigrant culture outstrip their parents'. This is the situation leading to role reversal, especially when parents lack other means to maneuver in the host society without help from their children. *Consonant acculturation* is the opposite situation, where the learning process and gradual abandonment of the home language and culture occur at roughly the same pace across generations. This situation is most common when immigrant parents possess enough human capital to accompany the cultural evolution of their children and monitor it. Finally, *selective acculturation* takes place when the learning process of both generations is embedded in a co-ethnic community of sufficient size and institutional diversity to slow down the cultural shift and promote partial retention of the parents' home language and norms. This third option is associated with a relative lack of intergenerational conflict, the presence of many co-ethnics among children's friends, and the achievement of full bilingualism in the second generation.[16]

Dissonant acculturation does not necessarily lead to downward assimilation, but it undercuts parental authority and places children at risk. Consonant acculturation does not guarantee success because parents' and children's striving for acceptance into the American mainstream may be blocked by discrimination. Still, consonant acculturation lays the basis for parental guidance and mutual intergenerational support in confronting external challenges. Lastly, selective acculturation offers the most solid basis for preservation of parental authority along with the strongest bulwark against effects of external discrimination. This happens because individuals and families do not face the strains of acculturation alone but rather within the framework of their own communities. This situation slows down the process while placing the acquisition of new cultural knowledge and language within a supportive context.

Types of acculturation do not occur in a vacuum but are conditioned by the variables discussed previously, namely parental socioeconomic achievement, family composition, and modes of incorporation. When parents have greater resources—in the form of higher education, economic status, intact families, or the support of strong co-ethnic communities—intergenerational acculturation tends to shift toward the consonant or selective modes. Parent-child conflict is reduced, and children are less prone to feel embarrassed by their parents' ways. On the other hand, parents whose educational and economic resources are modest, and especially those who are socially isolated, are more likely to experience dissonant acculturation and role reversal.

NOTES

1. Alba and Nee, "Rethinking Assimilation Theory."

2. Alba and Nee, "Rethinking Assimilation Theory"; Gordon, *Assimilation in American Life.*

3. Warner and Srole, *The Social Systems of American Ethnic Groups*, p. 2.

4. For earlier European immigrants, see Kraut, *The Huddled Masses*; Rosenblum, *Immigrant Workers*. For contemporary immigrants, see Portes and Rumbaut, *Immigrant America.*

5. Jensen and Chitose, *The New Immigration*; Portes and Zhou, "Self-Employment and the Earnings of Immigrants."

6. Gold, *Refugee Communities*; Zolberg, Shurke, and Aguayo, "International Factors in the Formation of Refugee Movements"; Rumbaut, "The Structure of Refuge"; Rumbaut, "A Legacy of War."

7. By 1945, Warner and Srole were already able to design a hierarchy of American ethnic groups with white English-speaking Protestants at the top. They predicted that the more ethnic groups departed from this standard, the longer they would take to assimilate in American society. See

Warner and Srole, *The Social Systems*. See also Portes and Rumbaut, *Immigrant America*, ch. 4.

8   Portes and Rumbaut, *Immigrant America*, ch. 4; Waters, "West Indian Immigrants, African Americans, and Whites in the Workplace"; Tienda and Stier, "The Wages of Race."

9.   Stepick, *Pride against Prejudice*; Tumulty, "When Irish Eyes Are Hiding."

10.   On the role of social networks in the onset of adaptation process of immigrants, see Massey, "Understanding Mexican Migration"; Roberts, "Socially Expected Durations"; Zhou, *Chinatown*.

11.   Rumbaut, "Origins and Destinies"; Mahler, *American Dreaming*.

12.   Portes, "The Social Origins"; Gold, *Refugee Communities*.

13.   Fernández-Kelly, CILS project interview in southern Florida, 1995.

14.   Child, *Italian or American?*; Alba, *Italian Americans*; Gans, "Second Generation Decline."

15.   Gordon, *Assimilation in American Life*; Rumbaut, "Assimilation and Its Discontents"; Rumbaut, "Ties That Bind."

16.   This typology has been presented and discussed in greater detail in Portes and Rumbaut, *Immigrant America*, ch. 7.

17.   Waters, "Ethnic and Racial Identies"; Waldinger Bozorgmehr, "The Making of a Multicultural Metropolis;" Rumbaut, "Origins and Destinies."

18.   Portes and Zhou, "The New Second Generation."

19.   Jensen and Chitose, "Today's New Second Generation"; Passel and Edmonston, "Immigration and Race."

20.   On this point, see Waters, "Ethnic and Racial Identities"; Fernández-Kelly and Schauffler, "Divided Fates"; Rumbaut, "The Crucible Within."

21.   Rosenblum, *Immigrant Workers*; Marks, *Farewell—We're Good and Gone*; Fligstein, *Going North*.

22.   Sassen, *The Mobility of Labor and Capital*: Romo and Schwartz, "The Structural Embeddedness of Business Decisions"; Bluestone and Harrison, *The Deindustrialization of America*.

23.   Gans, "Second Generation Decline"; Alba and Nee, "Rethinking Assimilation Theory."

24.   Harrison and Bluestone, *The Great U-Turn*, p. 8.

25.   Harvey, *The Limits to Capital*.

26.   Gereffi, "The Organization of Buyer-Driven Global Commodity Chains"; Fernández-Kelly, *For We Are Sold*; Schoepfle and Pérez-López, "Employment Implications of Export Assembly Operations in Mexico and the Caribbean Basin."

27.   U.S. Census Bureau, *U.S. Employment Data*, 1950–1997.

28.   Karoly, "The Trend in Inequality among Families, Individuals, and Workers."

29.   Title of *Money Magazine* lead story, May 1999.

30.   Updegrave, "Assessing Your Wealth."

31.   Bean, Van Hook, and Fossett, "Immigration, Spatial and Economic Change, and African American Employment"; Wilson, "Ethnic Concentrations."

32.   Gans, "Second Generation Decline," p. 182.

33.   On this point, see Zhou and Bankston, "Social Capital and the Adaptation of the Second Generation"; Portes and MacLeod, "The Educational Progress of Children of Immigrants."

34.   While there is disagreement between advocates of mismatch theory and other positions, there is widespread consensus that the decline of America's inner-city areas is closely linked to the disappearance of industrial job opportunities in them. See Massey and Denton, *American Apartheid*; Wilson, *The Truly Disadvantaged*; Fitzpatrick, *Puerto Rican Americans*; Bonilla and Campos, "A Wealth of Poor"; Nelson and Tienda, "The Structuring of Hispanic Ethnicity."

35.   Wacquant and Wilson, "The Cost of Racial and Class Exclusion."

36. Field interview conducted for an earlier project on Miami's ethnic composition. Final results of this study are reported in Portes and Stepick, *City on the Edge.*

37. Matute-Bianchi, "Ethnic Identities and Patterns of School Success"; Bourgois, *In Search of Respect*; Waters, "Ethnic and Racial Identities."

38. Matute-Bianchi, "Situational Ethnicity."

39. Suárez-Orozco, "Towards a Psychosocial Understanding," p. 164.

40. Portes and Sensenbrenner, "Embeddedness and Immigration"; Bourgois, *In Search of Respect.*

41. Stepick, "The Refugees Nobody Wants"; Fernández-Kelly and Schauffler, "Divided Fates."

42. Waters, "Ethnic and Racial Identities," p. 191.

43. Matthei and Smith, "Women, Households, and Transnational Migration Networks"; Rother, "Island Life Not Idyllic."

44. McLanahan and Sandefur. *Growing Up with a Single Parent*; Rumbaut, "Ties That Bind"; Waters, "Immigrant Families at Risk."

45. The Indian Sikh community of California, studied by Margaret Gibson, offers a good example of this pattern of gender socialization. See Gibson, *Accommodation without Assimilation.*

46. On the significance of gender in the origins of migration and the adaptation process of immigrant families, see Hondagneu-Sotelo, *Gendered Transitions*: Grasmuck and Pessar, *Between Two Islands*; Kibria, *Family Tightrope*; Fernández-Kelly and García, "Informalization at the Core."

47. *Social capital* is defined in the literature as the ability to gain access to resources by virtue of membership in social networks and other social structures. See Coleman, "Social Capital in the Creation of Human Capital"; Portes, "Social Capital: Its Origins and Applications."

48. Bailey and Waldinger, "Primary, Secondary, and Enclave Labor Markets"; Portes, "The Social Origins."

49. Burt, *Structual Holes.*

50. This argument has been developed at greater length in Portes and Rumbaut, *Immigrant America*, ch. 7.

51. Fernández-Kelly and Schauffler, "Divided Fates."

52. Field interview conducted by Patricia Fernández-Kelly and Richard Schauffler in Miami, summer 1993.

53. Zhou and Bankston, "Social Capital and the Adaptation of the Second Generation."

54. Ibid., p. 207.

REFERENCES

Alba, Richard D. and Victor Nee. 1997. Rethinking assimilation theory for a new era of immigration. *International Migration Review* 31 (Winter), pp. 826–874.

Bailey, Thomas, and Roger Waldinger. 1991. Primary, secondary, and enclave labor markets: A training system approach. *American Sociological Review* 56 (August), pp. 432–435.

Bean, Frank D., Jennifer Van Hook, and Mark A Fossett. 1999. "Immigration, spatial and economic change, and African American employment." In *Immigration and opportunity: Race, ethnicity, and employment in the United States*, edited by Frank D. Bean and Stephanie Bell-Rose. New York: Russell Sage Foundation.

Bluestone, Barry, and Bennett Harrison. 1982. *The deindustrialization of America: Plant closings, community abandonment, and the dismantling of basic industry.* New York: Basic Books.

Bonilla, Frank, and Ricardo Campos. 1981. A wealth of poor: Puerto Ricans in the new economic order. *Daedalus* 110 (Spring), pp. 133–176.

Bourgois, Philippe I. 1995. *In search of respect: Selling crack in El Barrio.* Cambridge, U.K.: Cambridge University Press.

Burt, Ronald S. 1992. *Structural holes: The social structure of competition.* Cambridge, Mass.: Harvard University Press.

Child, Irvin L. 1970 [1943]. *Italian or American? The second generation in conflict.* New York: Russell & Russell.

Coleman, James S. 1961. Social capital in the creation of human capital. *American Journal of Sociology* 94 (supplement), pp. 95–121.

Fernández-Kelly, Patricia. 1983. *For we are sold, I and my people: Women and industry in Mexico's frontier.* Albany: State University of New York Press.

—— 1995. "Social and cultural capital in the urban ghetto: Implications for the economic sociology of immigration." In *The economic sociology of immigration: Essays in networks, ethnicity, and entrepreneurship*, edited by Alejandro Portes. New York: Russell Sage Foundation.

Fernández-Kelly, Patricia, and Ana M. García. 1989. "Informalization at the core: Hispanic women, homework, and the advanced capitalist state." In *The informal economy: Studies in advanced and less developed countries*, edited by Alejandro Portes, Manuel Castells, and Lauren Benton. Baltimore: Johns Hopkins University Press.

Fernández-Kelly, Patricia, and Richard Schauffler. 1996. "Divided fates and the new assimilation." In *The new second generation*, edited by Alejandro Portes. New York: Russell Sage Foundation.

Fitzpatrick, Joseph P. 1987. *Puerto Rican Americans: The meaning of migration to the mainland.* Englewood Cliffs, N.J.: Prentice Hall.

Fligstein, Neil. 1981. *Going North: Migration of blacks and whites from the South*, 1900–1950. New York: Academic Press.

Gans, Herbert J. 1992. "Second generation decline: Scenarios for the economic and ethnic futures of the post-1965 America immigrants. *Ethnic and Racial Studies* 15 (April), pp. 173–192.

Gereffi, Gary. 1994. "The organization of buyer-driven global commodity chains: How use retailers shape overseas production networks." In *Commodity chains and global capitalism*, edited by Gary Gereffi and Miguel Korzeniewicz. Westport, Conn.: Praeger.

Gibson, Margaret. 1989. *Accommodation without assimilation: Sikh immigrants in an American high school.* Ithaca, N.Y.: Cornell University Press.

Gold, Steven J. 1992. *Refugee communities: A comparative field study.* Newbury Park, Calif.: Sage Publications.

Gordon, Milton M. 1971. *Assimilation in American life: The role of race, religion, and national origins.* New York: Oxford University Press.

Grasmuck, Sherri, and Patricia Pessar. 1991. *Between two islands: Dominican international migration.* Berkeley: University of California Press.

Harrison, Bennett, and Barry Bluestone. 1988. *The great U-turn: Corporate restructuring and the polarizing of America.* New York: Basic Books.

Harvey, David. 1982. *The limits to capital.* Chicago: University of Chicago Press.

Hondagneu-Sotelo, Pierrette. 1994. *Gendered transitions: Mexican experiences of immigration.* Berkeley: University of California Press.

Jensen, Leif, and Yoshimi Chitose. 1996. "Today's new second generation: Evidence from the 1990 U.S. Census." In *The new second generation*, edited by Alejandro Portes. New York: Russell Sage Foundation.

Karoly, Lynn A. 1992. *The trend in inequality among families, individuals and workers in the United States: A twenty-five-year perspective.* Santa Monica, Calif.: Rand.

Kraut, Alan M. 1982. *The huddled masses: The immigrant in American society*, 1880–1921. Arlington Heights, Ill.: Harlan Davidson.

Mahler, Sarah J. 1995. *American dreaming: Immigrant life on the margins.* Princeton, N.J.: Princeton University Press.

Marks, Carole. 1989. *Farewell—We're good and gone: The great black migration.* Bloomington: Indiana University Press.

Massey, Douglas S. 1987. Understanding Mexican migration to the United States. *American Journal of Sociology* 92 (May), pp. 1372–1403.

Massey, Douglas S., and Nancy A. Denton. 1993. *American apartheid: Segregation and the making of the underclass.* Cambridge, Mass.: Harvard University Press.

Matthei, Linda M., and David A. Smith. 1996. "Women , households and transnational migration networks: The Garifuna and global economic restructuring." In *Latin America in the world- economy*, edited by Roberto Patricio Korzeniewicz and William C. Smith. Westport, Conn.: Greenwood Press.

Matute-Bianchi, María Eugenia. 1986. Ethnic identities and patterns of school success and failure among Mexican-descent and Japanese-American students in a California high school: An ethnographic analysis. *American Journal of Education* 95 (November), pp. 233–255.

McLanahan, Sara, and Gary D. Sandefur. 1994. *Growing up with a single parent: What hurts, what helps.* Cambridge, Mass.: Harvard University Press.

Nelson, Candace, and Marta Tienda. 1985. The structuring of Hispanic ethnicity: historical and contemporary perspectives. *Ethnic and Racial Studies* 8 (January), pp. 49–74.

Passel, Jeffrey S., and Barry Edmonston. 1992. Immigration and race: Recent trends in immigration to the United States. Research paper PRIP-VI-22. Washington, D.C.: Program for Research on Immigration Policy, The Urban Institute.

Portes, Alejandro. 1987. The social origins of the Cuban enclave of Miami. *Sociological Perspectives* 30 (October), pp. 340–372.

———. 1998. Social Capital: Its origins and applications in modern sociology. *Annual Review of Sociology* 24, pp. 1–24.

Portes, Alejandro, and Dag MacLeod. 1996. Educational progress of children of immigrants: The roles of class, ethnicity, and a school context. *Sociology of Education* 69 (October), pp. 255–275.

Portes, Alejandro, and Rubén G. Rumbaut. 1996. *Immigrant America: A portrait.* 2d ed. Berkeley: University of California Press.

Portes, Alejandro, and Julia Sensenbrenner. 1993. Embeddedness and immigration: Notes on the social determinants of economic action. *American Journal of Sociology* 98 (May), pp. 1320–1350.

Portes, Alejandro, and Alex Stepick. 1993. *City on the edge: The transformation of Miami.* Berkeley: University of California Press.

Portes, Alejandro, and Min Zhou. 1996. Self-employment and the earnings of immigrants. *American Sociological Review* 61 (April), pp. 219–230.

Roberts, Bryan. 1995. "Socially expected durations and the economic adjustment of immigrants." In

The economic sociology of immigration, edited by Alejandro Portes. New York: Russell Sage Foundation.

Romo, Frank P., and Michael Schwartz. 1995. The structural embeddedness of business decisions: The migration of manufacturing plants in New York State, 1960 to 1985. *American Sociological Review* 60 (December), pp. 874–907.

Rosenblum, Gerald. 1973. *Immigrant workers: Their impact on American labor radicalism.* New York: Basic Books.

Rother, Larry. 1998. Island life not idyllic for youths from U.S. *The New York Times*, 20 February.

Rumbaut, Rubén G. 1989. The structure of refuge: Southeast Asian refugees in the United States, 1975–1985. *International Review of Comparative Public Policy I* (I), pp. 95–129.

———. 1994. The crucible within: Ethnic identity, self-esteem, and segmented assimilation among children of immigrants. *International Migration Review* 28, no. 4 (Winter), pp. 748–794.

———. 1994. Origins and destinies: Immigration to the United States since World War II. *Sociological Forum* 9, no. 4 (December), pp. 583–621.

———. 1996. "A legacy of war: Refugees from Vietnam, Laos, and Cambodia." In *Origins and destinies: Immigration, race, and ethnicity in America*, edited by Silvia Pedraza and Rubén G. Rumbaut. Belmont, Calif.: Wadsworth.

———. "Assimilation and its discontents: Between rhetoric and reality." *International Migration Review* 31, no. 4 (Winter), pp. 923–960.

———. 1997. "Ties that bind: Immigration and immigrant families in the United States." In *Immigration and the family: Research and policy on U.S. Immigrants*, edited by Alan Booth, Ann C. Crouter, and Nancy S. Landale. Mahwah, N.J.: Lawrence Erlbaum Associates.

Sassen, Saskia. 1988. *The mobility of labor and capital: A study in international investment and labor flow.* Cambridge, U.K., and New York: Cambridge University Press.

Schoepfle, Gregory K., and Jorge F. Pérez-López. 1990. *Employment implications of export assembly operations in Mexico and the Caribbean Basin.* Washington, D.C.: Commission for the Study of

International Migration and Cooperative Economic Development.

Stepick, Alex. 1998. *Pride against prejudice: Haitians in the United States.* Boston: Allyn and Bacon.

Suárez-Orozco, Marcelo. 1987. "Towards a psychosocial understanding of Hispanic adaptation to American schooling." In *Success or failure? Learning the languages of minority students,* edited by Henry T. Trueba. New York: Newbury House Publishers.

Tienda, Marta, and Haya Stier. 1996. "The wages of race: Color and employment opportunity in Chicago's inner city." In *Origins and destinies: Immigration, race, and ethnicity in America,* edited by Silvia Pedraza and Rubén G. Rumbaut. Belmont, Calif.: Wadsworth.

Tumulty, Karen. 1989. When Irish eyes are hiding. *Los Angeles Times,* January 29, p. A-I.

Updegrave, Walter. 1999. Assessing your wealth. *Money* 28 (July), pp. 63–73.

U.S. Census Bureau. 1998. *U.S. employment data: 1950–1997.* Washington, D.C.: U.S. Bureau of Labor Statistics.

Wacquaint, Loïc J., and William J. Wilson. 1989. The cost of racial and class exclusion in the inner city. *Annals of the American Academy of Political and Social Science* 501, pp. 8–26.

Waldinger, Roger, and Mehdi Bozorgmehr. 1996. "The making of a multicultural metropolis." In *Ethnic Los Angeles,* edited by Roger Waldinger and Mehdi Bozorgmehr. New York: Russell Sage Foundation.

Warner. W. Lloyd, and Leo Srole. 1945. *The social systems of American ethnic groups.* New Haven, Conn.: Yale University Press.

Waters, Mary C. 1994. West Indian immigrants, African Americans, and whites in the Workplace: Different perspectives on American race relations. Paper presented at the annual meeting of the American Sociological Association, Los Angeles.

———. 1996. "Ethnic and racial identities of second generation black immigrants in New York City." In *The new second generation,* edited by Alejandro Portes. New York: Russell Sage Foundation.

———. 1997. Immigration families at risk: Factors that undermine chances for success." In *Immigration and the family: Research and policy on U.S. immigrants,* edited by Alan Booth, Ann C. Crouter, and Nancy S. Landale. Mahwah, N.J.: Lawrence Erlbaum.

Wilson, Franklin D. 1999. "Ethnic concentrations and labor market opportunities." In *Immigration and opportunity: Race, ethnicity, and employment in the United States,* edited by Frank D. Bean and Stephanie Bell-Rose. New York: Russell Sage Foundation.

Wilson, William J. 1987. *The truly disadvantaged: The inner city, the underclass, and public policy.* Chicago: University of Chicago Press.

Zhou, Min. 1992. *Chinatown: the socioeconomic potential of an urban enclave.* Philadelphia: Temple University Press.

Zhou, Min, and Carl L. Bankston III. 1996. "Social capital and the adaptation of the second generation: The case of Vietnamese youth in New Orleans." In *The new second generation,* edited by Alejandro Portes. New York: Russell Sage Foundation.

Zolberg, Aristide, Astri Shurke, and Sergio Aguayo. 1986. International factors in the formation of refugee movements. *International Migration Review* 20 (Summer), pp. 151–169.

32

Racial Antagonisms and Race-Based Social Policy

William Julius Wilson

ONE OF THE CONSEQUENCES OF THE RISE OF new poverty neighborhoods has been the souring of race relations in the city. The problems associated with high joblessness and declining social organization (for example, individual crime, hustling activities, gang violence) in inner-city ghetto neighborhoods are perceived to spill over into other parts of the city. The result is not only fierce class antagonisms in the higher-income black communities located near these deteriorated neighborhoods but, as we shall see, heightened levels of racial animosity toward blacks, especially among lower-income white ethnic and Latino groups whose communities border or are situated near jobless neighborhoods.

It is important to understand the underlying factors that have exacerbated these tensions and magnified the problem of race in America's consciousness. I shall try to demonstrate this important point by showing how the interaction between political policies and economic and social processes directly and indirectly affects racial antagonisms in urban America.

Recent books such as Andrew Hacker's *Two Nations* (1992) and Derrick Bell's *Faces at the Bottom of the Well* (1992) promote the view that racial antagonisms are so deep-seated, so primordial, that feelings of pessimism about the possibility of Americans' overcoming their racist sentiments and behaviors are justified. Media reports on a series of sensational racial attacks heightened these feelings. New York has been the scene of some of the

From *When Work Disappears: The World of the New Urban Poor* by William Julius Wilson. Copyright © 1996 by William Julius Wilson. Reprinted by permission of Alfred A. Knopf, a division of Random House, Inc.

most dramatic incidents. For example, a white jogger was raped and severely beaten in Central Park by a mob of black and Latino youths. A black teenager named Yusef Hawkins was chased and beaten to death by a mob of white youths from the neighborhood of Bensonhurst. A black man named Michael Griffin was struck and killed by a car on the Belt Parkway in Queens while fleeing a group of bat-wielding whites from Howard Beach. And a black teenager named Tawana Brawley falsely claimed that she had been kidnapped and sexually assaulted by a group of white men.

Around the nation, media reports of drive-by shootings and carjackings have fueled racial animosities and fear, as the perpetrators are frequently identified as black inner-city males. Moreover, the media coverage of a series of attacks against foreign white tourists in Florida by inner-city blacks increased awareness of the random nature of violence and further poisoned the atmosphere in terms of race relations. Although most murders and other violent crimes involve individuals who are acquainted, the sense that such crimes are being committed without provocation against strangers has heightened anxiety and fear among the general public. When victims are murdered by strangers, young people are more likely to be the perpetrators. "During 1976–1991, only 20 percent of all homicides were between strangers, whereas 34 percent of those committed by male juveniles were between strangers," states Alfred Blumstein. "Thus, the perception of the random nature of the growth in murders is reinforced by this difference in the relationship between offenders and victim."

Finally, the recent rebellion in Los Angeles, the worst race riot in the nation's history, and the events surrounding it did more to dramatize the state of American race relations and the problems in the inner city than all the other incidents combined. In the present atmosphere of heightened racial awareness, however, we forget or overlook the fact that racial antagonisms are the product of situations—economic situations, political situations, and social situations.

To understand the manifestation of racial antagonisms during certain periods is to comprehend, from both an analytic and a policy perspective, the situations that increase or reduce them. A discussion of this idea will enable me to examine the problem of race and the new urban poverty in an intergroup context. It will also set up my discussion of social policy options. Let me begin, therefore, with some thoughts on racial antagonisms and demographic changes.

Since 1960, the proportion of whites inside central cities has decreased steadily, while the proportion of minorities has grown. In 1960, the nation's population was evenly divided between cities, suburbs, and rural areas. By 1990, both urban and rural populations had declined, so that suburbs contained nearly half of the nation's population. Urban residents dipped to 31 percent of the U.S. population by 1990. As cities lost population they became poorer and darker in their racial and ethnic composition. Thus, in the eyes of many in the dominant white population, the minorities symbolize the ugly scene left behind. Today, the divide between the suburbs and the city is in many respects a racial divide. For example, whereas minorities (blacks, Hispanics, and Asians) constituted 63 percent of all the residents in the city of Chicago in 1990, 83 percent of all suburban residents in the Chicago metropolitan area were white. Across the nation in 1990, three-quarters of the dominant white population lived in suburban and rural areas, while a majority of blacks and Latinos resided in urban areas.

These demographic changes are related to the declining influence of American cities and provided the foundation for the New Federalism, an important political development that has increased the significance of race in metropolitan

areas. Beginning in 1980, the federal government drastically decreased its support for basic urban programs. In addition, the most recent economic recession further reduced the urban revenues generated by the cities themselves, thereby resulting in budget deficits that led to additional cutbacks in basic services and programs and increases in municipal taxes.

The combination of the New Federalism and the recession created a fiscal and service crisis in many cities, especially the older cities of the East and Midwest. Fiscally strapped cities helplessly watched as the problems of poverty and joblessness in the inner city multiplied, as the homeless population grew and vicious waves of crack-cocaine addiction and the violent crimes that accompanied them swept through. These problems combined to reduce the attractiveness of the city as a place to live. Accordingly, many urban residents with the economic means to relocate have left the central city for the suburbs and other areas, worsening even further the city's tax base and reducing its revenue even more.

The growing suburbanization of the population influences the extent to which national politicians will support increased federal aid to large cities and to the poor. Indeed, we can associate the sharp drop in federal support for basic urban programs since 1980 with the declining political influence of cities and the rising influence of electoral coalitions in the suburbs. Suburbs cast 36 percent of the vote in the presidential election of 1968, 48 percent in 1988, and a majority of the vote in the 1992 election.

In each of the three presidential races before the 1992 election, the Democratic presidential candidate captured huge majorities in large cities but the electoral votes went to the Republican opponent who gained an even larger number of votes from the suburban and rural residents of the states where these cities were located.

But although there is a clear racial divide between the central city and the suburbs, racial tensions in metropolitan areas continue to be concentrated in the central city. They affect relations and patterns of interaction among blacks, other minorities, and the urban whites—especially the lower-income whites—who remain.

Like inner-city minorities, lower-income whites have felt the full impact of the urban fiscal crisis in the United States. Moreover, lower-income whites are more constrained by financial exigencies to remain in the central city than are their middle-class counterparts and thereby suffer the strains of crime, higher taxes, reduced services, and inferior public schools. Furthermore, unlike the more affluent whites who choose to remain in the wealthier sections of the central city, poor or working-class whites cannot escape the problems of deteriorating public schools by sending their children to private schools, and this problem has been exacerbated by the sharp decline in the number of parochial schools (Roman Catholic) in U.S. cities.

Many of these people originally bought relatively inexpensive homes near their industrial jobs. Because of the dispersion of industry, the changing racial composition of bordering communities, rising neighborhood crime, and the surplus of central-city housing created by the population shift to the suburbs, housing values in their neighborhoods have failed to keep pace with those in the suburbs. As the industries that employ them move away to the suburbs and even to outlying rural areas, a growing number of lower-income whites in our central cities are caught in a double trap. Their devalued property cannot be sold at a price that will permit them to purchase suburban housing, and they become physically removed from their jobs and new opportunities alike. This situation increases the potential for racial tension as they compete with blacks and the rapidly growing Latino population for access to and control of the remaining decent schools, housing, and neighborhoods.

Thus, the racial struggle for power and privilege in the central city is essentially a battle of the have-nots; it is a struggle exemplified by the black-white friction over attempts to integrate working-class ethnic neighborhoods like Marquette Park on Chicago's South Side; to control local public schools, as dramatically acted out in the racial violence that followed the busing of black children from the Boston ghettos of Roxbury and Dorchester to the working-class neighborhoods of South Boston and Charlestown in the 1970s; to exercise political control of the central city, as exhibited in Chicago, Newark, Cleveland, and New York in recent years, where the mayoral races were engulfed by racial antagonism and fear.

Problems in the new poverty or high-jobless neighborhoods have also created racial antagonism among some of the high-income groups in the city. The high joblessness in ghetto neighborhoods has sapped the vitality of local businesses and other institutions and has led to fewer and shabbier movie theaters, bowling alleys, restaurants, public parks and playgrounds, and other recreational facilities. Therefore, residents of inner-city neighborhoods more often seek leisure activity in other areas of the city, where they come into brief contact with citizens of markedly different racial or class backgrounds. Sharp differences in cultural style and patterns of interaction that reflect the social isolation of both poor and middle-class neighborhoods often lead to clashes.

Some behavior on the part of residents from inner-city ghetto neighborhoods—for example, the tendency to enjoy a movie in a communal spirit by carrying on a running conversation with friends and relatives or reacting in an unrestrained manner to what they see on the screen—is considered at least inappropriate and possibly offensive by other groups, particularly black and white members of the middle class. Expressions of disapproval, either overt or with subtle hostile glances, tend to trigger belligerent responses from the inner-city ghetto residents, who then purposefully intensify the behavior that is the source of irritation. The white and even the black middle-class moviegoers then exercise their option and exit, to use Albert Hirschman's term, by taking their patronage elsewhere, expressing resentment and experiencing intensified feelings of racial or class antagonism as they depart.

The areas surrendered in such a manner become the domain of the inner-city ghetto residents. The more expensive restaurants and other establishments serving the higher-income groups in these areas, having lost their regular patrons, soon close down and are replaced by fast-food chains and other local businesses that cater to or reflect the economic and cultural resources of the new clientele. White and black middle-class citizens, in particular, complain bitterly about how certain conveniently located areas of the central city have changed—and thus become "off-limits"—following the influx of ghetto residents.

Although the focus of much of the racial tension has been on black and white encounters, in many of the urban neighborhoods incidents involve Latinos. The UPFLS ethnographic field research indicates that antagonism toward inner-city blacks is frequently expressed in the Latino neighborhoods that border the new poverty areas. An example of this appears in the following field notes made by a UPFLS research assistant:

I asked how the neighborhood was for safety in general and they said around there it was fine if you stayed in at night. They don't go out at night. They said it was the blacks that are responsible for the crime. It was a black man that took her wallet when they went to buy a sewing machine. She said that they come through the neighborhood and are even moving in to live there more. She said that they are surrounded by black neighborhoods and that it isn't safe. I asked if there weren't also Mexican gangs around that area and they said they didn't know much about that, but that it was really the blacks that caused the problems.

A Latino male in the same community expressed his bitterness toward the jobless blacks from the surrounding neighborhood:

The blacks, well, there are very few . . . who work here in Chicago. The ones who work are very nice and respectable, but the ones who don't work, well, you have to hide yourselves from them. Chicago is maybe one third pure black, like in the south and you know how they are. They are a case that you can't change until the blacks start to behave themselves or get jobs. . . . The blacks have robbed me two times. . . . I have been hit and hit with a bat and they raped a girl. How can one ever hang around with

them if they do that kind of thing? . . . They don't try to respect and they don't have the character to change. One is already afraid of them at night. One is bitter and we could never live with or associate with them.

According to several demographic projections, the Latino population, which by 1990 had exceeded 22 million in the United States, will replace African-Americans as the nation's largest minority group between 1997 and 2005. They already outnumber African-Americans in Houston and Los Angeles and are rapidly approaching the number of blacks in Dallas and New York. In cities as different as Houston, Los Angeles, and Philadelphia, "competition between blacks and Hispanic citizens over the drawing of legislative districts and the allotment of seats is intensifying." In areas of changing populations, Latino residents increasingly complain that black officials currently in office cannot represent their concerns and interests. The tensions between blacks and Latinos in Miami, to cite one example, have emerged over competition for jobs and government contracts, the distribution of political power, and claims on public services.

It would be a mistake to view the encounters between the two groups solely in racial terms, however. In Dade County, there is a tendency for the black Cubans, Dominicans, Puerto Ricans, and Panamanians to define themselves by their language and culture and not by the color of their skin. Indeed, largely because of the willingness of Hispanic whites and Hispanic blacks to live together and to mix with Haitians and other Caribbean blacks in neighborhoods relatively free of racial tension, Dade County is experiencing the most rapid desegregation of housing in the nation.

By contrast, native-born, English-speaking African-Americans continue to be the most segregated group in Miami. They are concentrated in neighborhoods characterized by high levels of joblessness and marred by pockets of poverty in the northeast section of Dade County. Although there has been some movement by higher-income groups from these neighborhoods in recent years, the poorer blacks are more likely to be trapped because of the combination of extreme economic marginality and residential segregation.

Perhaps the most intense form of racial tension among minority groups has been between inner-city blacks and Korean entrepreneurs. Following the 1965 revision of the U.S. immigration law, the flow of Asian immigrants, including Korean immigrants, increased sharply. As the Korean population in the United Staes grew, so too did the presence of Korean businesses in the inner-city ghetto. Relations between black inner-city residents and Korean store owners have been strained.

Many Korean immigrants, before entering the United States, had completed college and were employed in professional, technical, administrative, and managerial positions. Yet neither their educational nor their occupational experience in Korea is recognized in the American labor market. With their employment opportunities restricted to either low-wage manual and service occupations or self-employed small business, many opted for the latter. For example, it is estimated that 60 percent of all adult Korean immigrants in Los Angeles are self-employed in small businesses.

But "for many Koreans, small business is a bittersweet livelihood, which entails enormous physical, psychological, familial, and social costs for moderate income." Enduring racial tension in jobless inner-city neighborhoods is one of the social costs. Take, as the most dramatic example, the experiences of Korean small-business owners during the 1992 Los Angeles disruption. The most destructive riot in the nation's history, the Los Angeles melee resulted in 58 deaths, 2,383 injuries, and 17,000 arrests. Estimates of property damage ranged from $785 million to $1 billion. Approximately 4,500 businesses were either partially or totally destroyed. About half of the businesses damaged (2,300) were owned or operated by Koreans in South Central Los Angeles and nearby Koreatown.

In angry protest against the verdict that found white policemen not guilty in the beating of Rodney King, black residents of South Central Los Angeles burned and looted local property. They were joined by immigrant Hispanics and undocumented workers who, for the most part, participated in the looting of stores. Korean store owners bore the brunt of the anger and destructive behavior displayed by the local residents for several reasons. During the three days of the riot, Korean businesses were vulnerable because of their location in poor neighborhoods left unprotected by the Los Angeles police force. This same location factor meant that these businesses were easily accessible because they were located in or near the riot sites. They were also highly visible, as Korean entrepreneurs are part of a culturally and racially distinct group and their businesses are disproportionately concentrated in what turned out to be the riot area.

The factors involved in Korean and black conflicts are complex and include, in addition to prejudice, language and cultural barriers that become apparent in over-the-counter disputes. As In-Jin Yoon points out:

Merchandise sold in Korean stores is cheap and thus not built to last. Korean store owners expect that their customers accept that risk when they purchase the merchandise. In addition, due to small profit margins of their merchandise, Korean store owners either deny entirely a refund or an exchange for used merchandise or allow only a three-day or one-week warranty period. This is the most frequent source of dispute between Korean store owners and black customers. Black customers who are accustomed to a lenient refund and exchange policy in larger department stores expect the same services at smaller Korean stores. When their request for refund or exchange is rejected, they engage in verbal disputes with Korean store owners, which often develop into racial epithets between the two parties.

In Los Angeles and New York, local-based black nationalist organizations, which often perceive the pressure of Korean businesses in the inner city as a threat to the black economy, turned these over-the-counter disputes into boycotts of Korean businesses.

But if inner-city blacks have antagonistic views toward Korean store owners, the latter hold extremely negative views toward blacks, views that, even if they do not play a role in the alleged mistreatment of customers, make rapprochement difficult once a dispute begins. In a scientific survey of 198 Korean store owners in Koreatown and South Central Los Angeles, In-Jin Yoon found that 78 percent of the respondents thought blacks lazy, and 76 percent felt that blacks live off welfare. A comparison of the Korean store owners' attitudes toward blacks, whites, Asians, and Hispanics revealed that blacks were perceived to be "the least hard working, the most prone to violence, the least intelligent, and the most welfare dependent." Although Hispanics were also perceived in an unfavorable light, they were ranked higher than blacks on all of these traits. Moreover, in answer to the question "If you would hire an employee between Hispanics and blacks, whom would you hire?" 80 percent of the Korean store owners chose Hispanics over blacks, whereas only 10 percent chose blacks over Hispanics.

The Korean store owners "maintain smoother relations with Hispanics" and report fewer clashes with inner-city Hispanic customers. As Yoon puts it:

As immigrants, the two groups suffer from similar disadvantages and are not in a position to claim a nativistic sense of superiority over the other. Consequently, the Korean in small business is not perceived as a threat to the Hispanic economy, but a desirable path to success Hispanics want to follow. By contrast, the different nativity status between Koreans and blacks makes Korean store owners feel less confident in their relations with native-born blacks, who are more assertive than Hispanics toward Koreans. As long-time residents of the United States, blacks claim that they have [a right to] an economic advancement before immigrants. As a result, Korean immigrant businesses in their neighborhoods are perceived as a threat to the black economy, and as part of the white system that has been oppressing and exploiting blacks. With these attitudes, blacks resent more strongly than Hispanics any signs of disrespect and mistreatment of customers.

These racial tensions are being played out during hard economic times as most Americans struggle with the problem of declining real wages, increasing job displacement, and job insecurity in the highly integrated and highly technological global economy. During hard economic times, it is important that political leaders channel the

frustrations of citizens in positive or constructive directions. For the last few years, however, just the opposite has frequently occurred. In a time of heightened economic insecurities, the poisonous racial rhetoric of certain highly visible spokespersons has increased racial tensions and channeled frustrations in ways that severely divide the racial groups. During hard economic times, people become more receptive to simplistic ideological messages that deflect attention away from the real and complex source of their problems. Instead of associating their problems with economic and political changes, these divisive messages encourage them to turn on each other—race against race.

As the sharp increase in joblessness has drained many inner-city communities, many of these messages associate inner-city crime, outbreaks of riots, family breakdown, and welfare receipt with individual shortcomings. Arguments that blame the victim resonate with many Americans because of their very simplicity. They not only reinforce the salient belief that joblessness and poverty reflect individual inadequacies, they also discourage support for new and stronger programs to combat inner-city social dislocations.

Indeed, . . . many white Americans have turned against a strategy that emphasizes programs they perceive as benefiting only racial minorities. In the 1960s, efforts to raise the public's awareness and conscience about the plight of African-Americans helped to enact civil rights legislation and, later, affirmative action programs. The "myth of black progress," a phrase frequently invoked by black leaders to reinforce arguments for stronger race-based programs, played into the hands of conservative critics. While the strategy may have increased sympathy among some whites for the plight of black Americans, it also created the erroneous impression that federal anti-discrimination efforts had largely failed, and it overlooked the significance of the complex racial changes that had been unfolding since the mid-1960s. Perhaps most pernicious of all, it also fed a growing concern, aroused by demagogic messages, that the politicians' sensitivity to black complaints had come at the expense of the white majority.

As the turn of the century approaches, the movement for racial equality needs a new political strategy that will appeal to a broader coalition and address the many problems that originate in historical racism and afflict inner-city residents. We must recognize that these problems cannot be solved through race-based remedies alone.

REFERENCES

Bell, Derrick. 1992. *Faces at the Bottom of the Well: The Permanence of Racism.* New York: Basic Books.

Hacker, Andrew. 1992. *Two Nations: Black and White, Separate, Hostile and Unequal.* New York: Scribner's.

Part V

GENDER

—⁓—

WHEN WE LOOK AT THE UNITED STATES TODAY, we can see vast differences in power and prestige, including great inequality between men and women. A fully employed woman still earns around 70 cents for every dollar a fully employed man makes. Women occupy very few corporate boardrooms, other than in a service capacity, and few women are top corporate executives or in positions of significant political power.

Most societies in the world have strong traditions of patriarchy or other forms of male dominance. Patriarchy is the ability of men to control institutional arrangements that bestow power and privilege on men. The selections in Part V explore different aspects of gender and of male dominance.

The first section examines differences in the socialization, expectations, and social positions of males and females. Socialization refers to those social processes through which an individual learns cultural values and norms, appropriate behavior, sense of self, and social role. This section begins with an excerpt from *Gender Vertigo* by Barbara Risman. "Gender as Structure" reviews the theoretical traditions in the analysis of sex and gender and offers a useful perspective that conceptualizes gender as a structure that permeates society.

Peggy McIntosh takes a close look at the notion of privilege in "White Privilege and Male Privilege: A Personal Account of Coming to See Correspondences through Work in Women's Studies." Her personal account gives voice to some provocative and challenging insights about what it means to be a white, heterosexual, married woman in American society today. As a white person,

McIntosh had been allowed to recognize that racism disadvantages people of color, but she had been encouraged not to see the invisible advantages racism accords to white people, its privileged beneficiaries. In her article, McIntosh draws parallels between privileges accorded to whites, heterosexuals, and married people and those accorded to men. In each of these cases, the recipients of these privileges seldom perceive—let alone acknowledge or attempt to forgo—their privileges.

Maxine Baca Zinn and Bonnie Thornton Dill ask whether the predominantly white lineage of feminism can incorporate the needs of minority women. They ask whether the notion of feminism is a universal concept or whether it reflects the class and race location of those formulating it. In "Theorizing Difference from Multiracial Feminism," Zinn and Dill seek to broaden the notion of feminism in recognition of class, racial, and cultural differences.

Gender roles are learned and not instinctual, and the norms and behaviors expected of both men and women are learned. The final reading of this section examines how masculinity is learned through socialization—in this case, organized sports. In "Conceptions of Masculinity and Gender Transgression in Sports Amongst Adolescent Boys," Suzanne Laberge and Mathieu Albert examine how sport teaches boys gender roles. I am sure that all of us remember some playground or sport experience that helped form our gender identity.

The second section of Part V focuses on the ways in which gender is structured in American

291

society. Mindy Stombler's piece, "'Buddies' or 'Slutties'," describes how fraternity practices institutionalize the disempowerment of women. Her analysis gives us some insight into the complex reasons why some women accept their objectification. This selection also gives us insight into the social problem of rape.

The next reading, Elizabeth Higginbotham's "Women and Work: Exploring Race, Ethnicity, and Class," examines the workplace to conceptualize how race, class, and gender interact. She asks why important shifts in where women work have not better integrated the workplace or benefited all women. In "Why Does Jane Read and Write So Well?" Roslyn Arlin Mickelson looks at the academic achievements of women and wonders why they do so well when the payoff in the job market is not as good as it is for men. Mickelson addresses why women do well in school and attain as much education as they do in the face of limited rewards.

"Women, Men, and Work in the Twenty-First Century," by Barbara F. Reskin and Irene Padavic, describes the shape of the most important gender and workplace issues as we enter the next century. In particular, Reskin and Padavic analyze how economic restructuring affects women's employment prospects. In addition to indicating the shift from manufacturing- to service-sector jobs, noted in many other readings in this book, these authors highlight the shift from permanent, full-time employment to temporary, contingent, and part-time work. Their analysis of the kinds of jobs that will be increasingly available in the immediate future is very instructive and sobering. If you look at Table 9.1 in their article, what one big change would most advance equality?

UNDERSTANDING GENDER

33

Gender as Structure

Barbara J. Risman

THERE ARE THREE DISTINCT THEORETICAL traditions that help us to understand sex and gender, and a fourth is now taking shape. The first tradition focuses on gendered selves, whether sex differences are biological or social in origin. The second tradition . . . focuses on how the social structure (as opposed to biology or individual learning) creates gendered behavior. The third tradition emphasizes contextual issues and how doing gender re-creates inequality during interaction. The fourth, multilevel approach treats gender itself as built in to social life via socialization, interaction, and institutional organization. This new perspective integrates the previous ones; it is formed on the assumption that each viewpoint sheds different light on the same question.

From *Gender Vertigo: American Families in Transition* by Barbara J. Risman. Reprinted with permission from Yale University Press.

GENDERED SELVES

There are numerous theoretical perspectives within this tradition, but all share the assumption that maleness and femaleness are, or become, properties of individuals. . . . Research questions in this tradition focus on the development of sex differences and their relative importance for behavior.

. . . Sociobiologists have argued that such behaviors as male aggressiveness and female nurturance result from natural selection. Biosociologists stress the infant care skills in which females appear to excel. Their perspective has been criticized for its ethnocentrism and its selective use of biological species as evidence . . . .

More recent biosocial theories have posited complex interactions between environment and biological predispositions, with attention to explaining intrasex differences. This new version of biosociology may eventually help to identify the biological parameters that, in interaction with environmental stimuli, affect human behavior.

. . .

Sex role theory suggests that early childhood socialization is an influential determinant of later behavior, and research has focused on how societies create feminine women and masculine men. There is an impressive variety of sex-role explanations for gender-differentiated behavior in families. Perhaps the most commonly accepted explanation is reinforcement theory (e.g., Bandura and Walters 1963, Mischel 1966, and Weitzman 1979). Reinforcement theory suggests, for example, that girls develop nurturant personalities because they are given praise and attention for their interest in dolls and babies, and that boys develop competitive selves because they are positively reinforced for winning, whether at checkers or football. Although much literature suggests that the socialization experiences of boys and girls continue to differ dramatically, it is clearly the case that most girls raised in the 1990s have received ambiguous gender socialization: they have been taught to desire domesticity (dolls remain a popular toy for girls), as well as to pursue careers. For generations, African American girls have been socialized both for motherhood and paid work (Collins 1990).

Nancy Chodorow's (1978, 1989) feminist psychoanalytic analysis approach has also been influential, particularly in feminist scholarship. Chodorow develops an object-relations psychoanalytic perspective to explain how gendered personalities develop as a result of exclusively female mothering. . . . Chodorow notices that mothers are responsible for young children almost universally. She argues that mothers relate to their boy and girl infants differently, fusing identities with their daughters while relating to their sons as separate and distinct. As a result, according to this feminist version of psychoanalysis, girls develop selves based on connectedness and relationships while boys develop selves based on independence and autonomy. In addition, boys must reject their first love-object (mother) in order to adopt masculinity, and they do this by rejecting and devaluing what is feminine in themselves and in society. Thus, we get nurturant women and independent men in a society dominated by men and which values independence. Many feminist studies have incorporated this psychoanalytic view of gender as an underlying assumption (L. Rubin 1982; Keller 1985; Williams 1989).

. . .

Other feminist theorists, such as Ruddick (1989, 1992) and Aptheker (1989), build on the notion that the constant nature of mothering creates a certain kind of thinking, what Ruddick calls "maternal thinking." The logic of this argument does not depend on a psychoanalytic framework, but it implicitly uses one: through nurturing their children women develop psychological frameworks that value peace and justice. Therefore, if women (or men who mothered children) were powerful political actors, governments would use more peaceful conflict resolution strategies and value social justice more highly.

All individualist theories, including sex-role socialization and psychoanalytic thought, posit that by adulthood most men and women have developed very different personalities. Women have become nurturant, person oriented, and child centered. Men have become competitive and work oriented. According to individualist theorists, there are limits to flexibility. Intensely held emotions, values, and inclinations developed during childhood coalesce into a person's self-identity. Although these theorists do not deny that social structures influence family patterns, nor that notions of gender meaning are always evolving . . . they focus on how culturally determined family patterns and sex-role socialization create gendered selves, which then provide the motivations for individuals to fill their socially appropriate roles.

Historically, sex-role theorists have assumed that men and women behave differently because gender resides primarily in personality. This approach has several serious conceptual weaknesses . . . First, such theories usually presume behavioral continuity throughout the life course. In fact, women socialized for nurturance are capable of competitive and aggressive behavior, and men raised without any expectation of taking on primary responsibility can "mother" when they need to (Risman 1987; Gerson 1985, 1993; Bielby and Bielby 1984). Another weakness of these individualist-oriented theories is their oversocialized conception of human behavior—that once we know how an individual has been raised, the training is contained primarily inside his or her head (cf. Wrong 1961). Such theories might suggest, for example, that women do not revolt and are not necessarily unhappy with their subordinate status because they have been so well trained for femininity. . . .

This overdependence on internalization of culture and socialization leads to the most serious problem with sex-role theory: its depoliticization of gender inequality. Although sex-role socialization and revisionist psychoanalytic theorists often have explicitly feminist goals, their focus on sex differences has legitimated a dualistic conception of gender that relies on a reified male/female dichotomy. The very notion of comparing all men to all women without regard for diversity within groups presumes that gender is primarily about individual differences between biological males and

biological females, downplaying the role of interactional expectations and the social structure.

The sex-role socialization theory is an application of a normative role theory for human behavior. It assumes that social stability is motivated primarily by beliefs and values acquired during socialization. Individuals are assumed to use whatever resources are available to realize these values and to maintain their identities. As Stokes and Hewitt (1976) have argued, socialization cannot serve as the fundamental link between culture and action. Indeed, studies of intergenerational shifts in values suggest that economic and political conditions produce beliefs, attitudes, and preferences for action that overcome those acquired during childhood (Lesthaeghe 1980; Inglehart 1977, 1981). We cannot assume that internalization of norms—through psychoanalytic processes or sex-role socialization—is the primary means by which society organizes human conduct.

. . .

STRUCTURE VS. PERSONALITY

The overreliance on gendered selves as the primary explanation for sexual stratification led many feminist sociologists—myself included—to argue that what appear to be sex differences are really, in Epstein's terms, "deceptive distinctions" (Epstein 1988; Kanter 1977; Risman and Schwartz 1989). Although empirically documented sex differences do occur, structuralists like me have argued that men and women behave differently because they fill different positions in institutional settings, work organizations, or families. That is, the previous structural perspectives on gender assume that work and family structures create empirically distinct male and female behavior. . . . Within this perspective, men and women in the same structural slots are expected to behave identically. Epstein's (1988) voluminous review of the multidisciplinary research on gender and sex differences is perhaps the strongest and most explicit support for a social-structural explanation of gendered behavior. She suggests that there are perhaps no empirically documented differences that can be traced to the predispositions of males and females. Instead, the deceptive differences reflect women's lack of opportunity in a male-dominated society.

Gender relations in the labor force have received far more of this sort of structural analysis than have gender relations in intimate settings. Kanter's classic work *Men and Women of the Corporation* (1977) introduced this kind of structural perspective on gender in the workplace. Kanter showed that when women had access to powerful mentors, interactions with people like themselves, and the possibility for upward mobility, they behaved like others—regardless of sex—with similar advantages. These social network variables could explain success at work far better than could assumptions of masculine versus feminine work styles. Women were less often successful because they were more often blocked from network advantages, not because they feared success or had never developed competitive strategies. Men who lacked such opportunities did not advance, and they behaved with stereotypical feminine work styles. Kanter argued persuasively that structural system properties better explain sex differences in workplace behavior than does sex-role socialization.

. . .

The application of a structural perspective to gender within personal relationships has been less frequent . . . . In a series of studies (Risman 1986, 1987, 1988), I tested whether apparent sex differences in parenting styles are better attributed to sex-role socialization or to the structural contingencies of adult life. The question I asked was "Can men mother?" The answer is yes, but only if they do not have women to do it for them. The lack of sex-role socialization for nurturance did not inhibit the development of male mothering when structural contingencies demanded it. This is an important part of the story, but not all of it.

. . .

While applications of structural perspectives both to workplaces and to intimate relationships have furthered the sociological understanding of gender, there is a fundamental flaw in the logic of these arguments.

. . .

. . . Several studies (Williams 1992; Yoder 1991; Zimmer 1988) found that Kanter's hypotheses about the explanatory power of social structural variables such as relative numbers, access to mentors, and upward mobility are not, in fact, gender neutral. That is, Kanter's hypotheses are supported empirically only when societally devalued groups enter traditionally white male work environments. When white males enter traditionally female work environments, they do not hit the glass ceiling, they ride glass elevators. Reskin (1988) has suggested that we have so accepted these "structural" arguments that we sometimes forget that sexism itself stratifies our labor force. Evidence similarly points to continued existence of gendered behavior in family settings. Hertz reported that in her 1986 study of couples in which husbands and wives hold equivalent, high-status corporate jobs and brought similar resources to their marriages, the wives continue to shoulder more responsibility for family work (even if that means hiring and supervising help). Despite the importance of structural variables in explaining behavior in families, the sex category itself remains a powerful predictor of who does what kind of family work (Brines 1994; South and Spitz 1994). Gender stratification remains even when other structural aspects of work or of family life are divorced from sex category. The interactionist theory discussed below helps us to understand why.

DOING GENDER

This approach to gender was best articulated by West and Zimmerman in their 1987 article "Doing Gender.". . . West and Zimmerman suggest that once a person is labeled a member of a sex category, she or he is morally accountable for behaving as persons in that category do. That is, the person is expected to "do gender"; the ease of interaction depends on it. One of the groundbreaking aspects in this argument is that doing gender implies legitimating inequality. The authors suggest that, by definition, what is female in a patriarchal society is devalued. Within this theoretical framework, the very belief that biological males and females are essentially different (apart from their reproductive capabilities) exists to justify male dominance.

The tradition of doing gender has been well accepted in feminist sociology (West and Zimmerman's article was cited in journals more than one hundred times by 1995). West and Zimmerman articulated an insight whose time had come—that gender is not what we are but something that we do. Psychologists Deaux and Major (1990) . . . argue that interactional contexts take priority over individual traits and personality differences; others' expectations create the self-fulfilling prophecies that lead all of us to do gender. . . . They suggest that actual behavior depends on the interaction of participants' self-definitions, the expectations of others, and the cultural expectations attached to the context itself. I agree. The weakness in the doing gender approach is that it undertheorizes the pervasiveness of gender inequality in organizations and gendered identities.

Although gender is always present in our interaction, it is not present only in interaction. We must have a theoretical link from material constraints to what we do now, to who we think we are. I suggest that the doing-gender perspective is incomplete because it slights the institutional level of analysis and the links among institutional gender stratification, situational expectations, and gendered selves.

West and Fenstermaker (1995) have extended the argument from doing gender to "doing difference." They suggest that just as we create inequality when we create gender during interaction, so we create race and class inequalities when we interact in daily life. Race does not generally hold the biologically based assumption of dichotomy (as sex category does), yet in American society we constantly use race categories to guide our interactional encounters. This extension of theoretical ideas from gender to the analysis of inequalities is

perhaps the most important direction gender theorizing has taken in the past decade.

. . .

GENDER AS SOCIAL STRUCTURE

The sex-differences literature, the doing-gender contextual analyses, and the structural perspectives are not necessarily incompatible, although I, as well as others, have portrayed them as alternatives (e.g., Kanter 1977, Epstein 1988, Risman 1987, Risman and Schwartz 1989, and Ferree 1990).

. . .

My view of gender as a social structure incorporates each level of analysis.

Lorber (1994) argues that gender is an entity in and of itself that establishes patterns of expectations for individuals, orders social processes of everyday life, and is built into all other major social organizations of society. She goes further, however, to argue that gender difference is *primarily* a means to justify sexual stratification. Gender is so ubiquitous because unless we see difference, we cannot justify inequality. Lorber provides much cross-cultural, literary, and scientific evidence to show that gender difference is socially constructed and yet is universally used to justify stratification. She writes that "the continuing purpose of gender as a modern social institution is to construct women as a group to be subordinate to men as a group."

I build on this notion that gender is an entity in and of itself and has consequences at every level of analysis. And I share the concern that the very creation of difference is the foundation on which inequality rests. In my view, it is most useful to conceptualize gender as a structure that has consequences for every aspect of society.

. . .

Gender itself must be considered a structural property of society. It is not manifested just in our personalities, our cultural rules, or other institutions. Gender is deeply embedded as a basis for

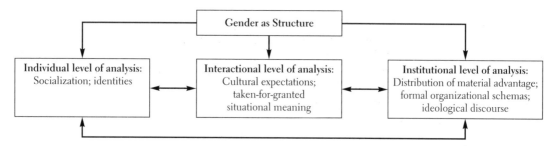

FIGURE 2.1   Gender as Structure.

stratification, differentiating opportunities and constraints. This differentiation has consequences on three levels: (1) at the individual level, for the development of gendered selves; (2) at the interactional level, for men and women face different expectations even when they fill the identical structural position; and (3) at the institutional level, for rarely will women and men be given identical positions. Differentiation at the institutional level is based on explicit regulations or laws regarding resource distribution, whether resources be defined as access to opportunities or actual material goods. (See Figure 2.1 for a schematic summary of the argument thus far.)

While the *gender structure* clearly affects selves, cultural rules, and institutions, far too much explanatory power is presumed to rest in the motivation of gendered selves. We live in a very individualistic society that teaches us to make our own choices and take responsibility for our own actions. What this has meant for theories about gender is that a tremendous amount of energy is spent on trying to understand why women and men "choose" to devote their life energies to such different enterprises. The distinctly sociological contribution to the explanation hasn't had enough attention: even when individual women and men do *not* desire to live gendered lives or to support male dominance, they often find themselves compelled to do so by the logic of gendered choices. That is, interactional pressures and institutional design create gender and the resultant inequality, even in the absence of individual desires.

. . . Choices often assumed to be based on personalities and individual preferences (e.g., conse-

quences of the gender structure at the individual level) are better understood as social constructions based on institutionally constrained opportunities and the limited availability of nongendered cognitive images.

· · ·

Even if individuals are capable of change and wish to eradicate male dominance from their personal lives, the influence of gendered institutions and interactional contexts persists. These contexts are organized by gender stratification at the institutional level, which includes the distribution of material resources organized by gender, the ways by which formal organizations and institutions themselves are gendered, and gendered ideological discourse. For example, in a society in which girls are not taught to read, we could never find a young woman who would be considered a potential international leader. Nor would men denied access to jobs with "family wages" be seen by middle-class American women as good catches for husbands.

At this moment in American society, cultural rules and cognitive images that operate at the interactional level are particularly important in the persistence of gender stratification in families. It is not that sex-role socialization or early childhood experience is trivial; gender structure creates gendered selves. But, at this point in history, sex-role socialization itself is ambivalent. In addition, it is clear that even women with feminist worldviews and substantial incomes are constrained by gender structures.

In spite of the removal of some gender discrimination in both law and organizations, gender stratification remains. That is, formal access to opportunities may be gender neutral, yet equality of results may not ensue. Therefore, neither the individual-level explanations nor those based solely on institutional discrimination can explain continued gender stratification in families. Instead, the cognitive images to which we must respond during interaction are the engines that drive continued gender stratification when individuals desire egalitarian relationships and the law allows them (cf. Ridgeway 1997).

· · ·

The social structure clearly constrains gendered action even as it makes it possible. Wives, even those who have no motivation to provide domestic service to their husbands, are constrained to do so by social expectations. A husband who has a disheveled appearance reflects poorly on his wife's domestic abilities (in real life as well as "ring around the collar" commercials). A wife will be sanctioned by friends and family for keeping a cluttered and dusty home; a husband will not be. Husbands' behaviors are constrained as well. A husband who is content with a relatively low-wage, low-stress occupation may be pressured (by his wife, among others) to provide more for his family. Few wives, however, are pressured into higher-stress, higher-wage occupations by their families. The expectations we face during ongoing interaction often push us to behave as others want us to (Heiss 1981).

Cultural images within marriage also make gendered action possible. Husbands are not free to work long hours in order to climb the career ladder or increase income unless they are superordinate partners in a system in which wives provide them the "leisure" (i.e., freedom from responsibility for self-care or family care) to do so. Some married women may leave jobs they dislike because the position of domestic wife is open to them. A husband and father unable to keep a job has few other options for gaining self-esteem and identity.

Individuals often act in a structurally patterned fashion, without much thought. Routine is taken for granted even when the action re-creates the inequitable social structure. A woman may choose to change her name upon marriage simply because it seems easier. (Some women may not even know they are making a choice, as name change is so routine in their social circle.) Yet by changing her name a woman implicitly supports and re-creates a reflective definition of wifehood. She does gender. Similarly, when a woman assents to her children carrying her husband's surname (even when she herself has retained her own), she is re-creating a patrilineal system by which family identity is traced primarily through the male line. In both these examples a couple's intention may be to create a nuclear family identity and to avoid the awkwardness of hyphenated names for children. Whatever the intention, the structure has constrained the possible choices available to them. Their purposive actions may provide them with both the desired consequences (one family name) *and* the unintended consequence of re-creating a gender structure based on reflective female identity and patrilineal family names.

· · ·

REFERENCES

Aptheker, Bettina. 1989. *Tapestries of Life: Women's Work, Women's Consciousness, and the Meaning of Daily Experience.* Amherst: University of Massachusetts Press.

Bandura, Albert, and Richard H. Walters. 1963. *Social Learning and Personality.* New York: Holt, Rinehart and Winston.

Bielby, Denise D., and William T. Bielby. 1984. "Work Commitment and Sex-Role Attitudes." *American Sociological Review* 49:234–247.

Brines, Julie. 1994. "Economic Dependency and the Division of Labor." *American Journal of Sociology* 100(3):652–688.

Chodorow, Nancy. 1978. *The Reproduction of Mothering.* Berkeley: University of California Press.

———. 1989. *Feminism and Psychoanalytic Theory.* New Haven: Yale University Press.

Collins, Patricia Hill. 1990. *Black Feminist Thought: Knowledge, Consciousness, and the Politics of Empowerment.* Boston: Unwin, Hyman.

Deaux, Kay, and Brenda Major. 1990. "A SocialPsychological Model of Gender." In *Theoretical Perspectives on Sexual Difference,* edited by Deborah Rhode. New Haven: Yale University Press.

Epstein, Cynthia Fuchs. 1988. *Deceptive Distinctions: Sex, Gender, and the Social Order.* New Haven: Yale University Press.

Ferree, Myra Marx. 1990. "Beyond Separate Spheres: Feminism and Family Research." *Journal of Marriage and the Family* 53(4):866–884.

Gerson, Kathleen. 1985. *Hard Choices.* Berkeley: University of California Press.

———. 1993. *No Man's Land.* New York: Basic Books.

Heiss, Jerold. 1981. "Social Rules." In *Social Psychology: Sociological Perspectives,* edited by Morris Rosenberg and Ralph H. Turner. New York: Basic Books.

Inglehart, Ronald. 1977. *The Silent Revolution: Changing Values and Political Styles among Western Publics.* Princeton, N.J.: Princeton University Press.

———. 1981. "Post-Materialism in an Environment of Insecurity." *American Political Science Review* 75:880–900.

Kanter, Rosabeth. 1977. *Men and Women of the Corporation.* New York: Harper and Row.

Keller, Evelyn Fox. 1985. *Reflections on Gender and Science.* New Haven: Yale University Press.

Lesthaeghe, Ron. 1980. "On the Social Control of Human Reproduction." *Population and Development Review* 4:427–548.

Lorber, Judith. 1994. *Paradoxes of Gender.* New Haven: Yale University Press.

Mischel, Walter. 1966. "A Social Learning View of Sex Differences in Behavior." In *The Development of Sex Differences,* 56–81, edited by Eleanor Maccoby. Stanford, Calif.: Stanford University Press.

Reskin, Barbara. 1988. "Bringing the Men Back In: Sex Differentiation and the Devaluation of Women's Work." *Gender and Society* 2:58–81.

Ridgeway, Cecilia. 1997. "Interaction and the Conservation of Gender Inequality: Considering Employment." *American Sociological Review* 62:218–235.

Risman, Barbara. 1988. "Just the Two of Us: Parent-Child Relationships in Single Parent Homes." *Journal of Marriage and the Family* 50:1049–1062.

———. 1987. "Intimate Relationships from a Microstructural Perspective: Mothering Men." *Gender and Society* 1:6–32.

———. 1986. "Can Men 'Mother'?: Life as a Single Father." *Family Relations* 35:95–102.

Risman, Barbara, and Pepper Schwartz. 1989. *Gender in Intimate Relationships.* Belmont, Calif.: Wadsworth.

Rubin, Lillian B. 1982. *Intimate Strangers.* New York: Harper and Row.

Ruddick, Sara. 1989. *Maternal Thinking.* Boston: Beacon Press.

———. 1992. "Thinking About Fathers." In *Rethinking the Family: Some Feminist Questions,* edited by Barrie Thorne. Boston: Northeastern University Press.

South, Scott J., and Glenna Spitz. 1994. "Housework in Marital and Nonmarital Households." *American Sociological Review* 59:327–347.

Stokes, Randall, and John Hewitt. 1976. "Aligning Actions." *American Sociological Review* 41:838–849.

Weitzman, Lenore Jacqueline. 1979. *Sex Role Socialization: A Focus on Women.* Palo Alto, Calif.: Mayfield.

West, Candace, and Don H. Zimmerman. 1987. "Doing Gender." *Gender and Society* 1(2):125–151.

West, Candace, and Sarah Fenstermaker. 1995. "Doing Difference." *Gender and Society* 9:8–37.

Williams, Christine. 1989. *Gender Differences at Work.* Berkeley: University of California Press.

———. 1992. "The Glass Escalator: Hidden Advantages for Men in the 'Female' Professions." *Social Problems* 39:253–267.

Wrong, Dennis H. 1961. "The Oversocialized Conception of Man in Modern Sociology." *American Sociological Review* 26:183–193.

Yoder, Janice. 1991. "Rethinking Tokenism: Looking Beyond Numbers." *Social Problems* 5:178–192.

Zimmer, Lynn. 1988. "Tokenism and Women in the Workplace: The Limits of Gender-Neutral Theory." *Social Problems* 35:64–77.

34

White Privilege and Male Privilege

A Personal Account of Coming to See Correspondences through Work in Women's Studies

Peggy McIntosh

THROUGH WORK TO BRING MATERIALS AND perspectives from Women's Studies into the rest of the curriculum, I have often noticed men's unwillingness to grant that they are overprivileged in the curriculum, even though they may grant that women are disadvantaged. Denials that amount to taboos surround the subject of advantages that men gain from women's disadvantages. These denials protect male privilege from being fully recognized, acknowledged, lessened, or ended.

Thinking through unacknowledged male privilege as a phenomenon with a life of its own, I realized that since hierarchies in our society are interlocking, there was most likely a phenomenon of white privilege that was similarly denied and protected, but alive and real in its effects. As a white person, I realized I had been taught about racism as something that puts others at a disadvantage, but had been taught not to see one of its corollary aspects, white privilege, which puts me at an advantage.

I think whites are carefully taught not to recognize white privilege, as males are taught not to recognize male privilege. So I have begun in an untutored way to ask what it is like to have white

Copyright © by Peggy McIntosh. Working Paper #189, Wellesley College Center for Research on Women, Wellesley, MA 02181. Permission to reprint must be obtained from the author at Wellesley College Center for Research on Women, Wellesley, MA 02181; (781) 283-2520; fax (781) 283-2504.

privilege. This paper is a partial record of my personal observations and not a scholarly analysis. It is based on my daily experiences within my particular circumstances.

I have come to see white privilege as an invisible package of unearned assets that I can count on cashing in each day, but about which I was "meant" to remain oblivious. White privilege is like an invisible weightless knapsack of special provisions, assurances, tools, maps, guides, codebooks, passports, visas, clothes, compass, emergency gear, and blank checks.

Since I have had trouble facing white privilege, and describing its results in my life, I saw parallels here with men's reluctance to acknowledge male privilege. Only rarely will a man go beyond acknowledging that women are disadvantaged to acknowledging that men have unearned advantage, or that unearned privilege has not been good for men's development as human beings, or for society's development, or that privilege systems might ever be challenged and *changed*.

I will review here several types or layers of denial that I see at work protecting, and preventing awareness about, entrenched male privilege. Then I will draw parallels, from my own experience, with the denials that veil the facts of white privilege. Finally, I will list forty-six ordinary and daily ways in which I experience having white privilege, by contrast with my African American colleagues in the same building. This list is not intended to be generalizable. Others can make their own lists from within their own life circumstances.

Writing this paper has been difficult, despite warm receptions for the talks on which it is based.[1] For describing white privilege makes one newly accountable. As we in Women's Studies work reveal male privilege and ask men to give up some of their power, so one who writes about having white privilege must ask, "Having described it, what will I do to lessen or end it?"

The denial of men's overprivileged state takes many forms in discussions of curriculum change work. Some claim that men must be central in the curriculum because they have done most of what is important or distinctive in life or in civilization. Some recognize sexism in the curriculum but deny that it makes male students seem unduly important in life. Others agree that certain *individual* thinkers are male oriented but deny that there is any *systemic* tendency in disciplinary frameworks or epistemology to overempower men as a group. Those men who do grant that male privilege takes institutionalized and embedded forms are still likely to deny that male hegemony has opened doors for them personally. Virtually all men deny that male overreward alone can explain men's centrality in all the inner sanctums of our most powerful institutions. Moreover, those few who will acknowledge that male privilege systems have overempowered them usually end up doubting that we could dismantle these privilege systems. They may say they will work to improve women's status, in the society or in the university, but they can't or won't support the idea of lessening men's. In curricular terms, this is the point at which they say that they regret they cannot use any of the interesting new scholarship on women because the syllabus is full. When the talk turns to giving men less cultural room, even the most thoughtful and

fair-minded of the men I know will tend to reflect, or fall back on, conservative assumptions about the inevitability of present gender relations and distributions of power, calling on precedent or sociobiology and psychobiology to demonstrate that male domination is natural and follows inevitably from evolutionary pressures. Others resort to arguments from "experience" or religion or social responsibility or wishing and dreaming.

After I realized, through faculty development work in Women's Studies, the extent to which men work from a base of unacknowledged privilege, I understood that much of their oppressiveness was unconscious. Then I remembered the frequent charges from women of color that white women whom they encounter are oppressive. I began to understand why we are justly seen as oppressive, even when we don't see ourselves that way. At the very least, obliviousness of one's privileged state can make a person or group irritating to be with. I began to count the ways in which I enjoy unearned skin privilege and have been conditioned into oblivion about its existence, unable to see that it put me "ahead" in any way, or put my people ahead, overrewarding us and yet also paradoxically damaging us, or that it could or should be changed.

My schooling gave me no training in seeing myself as an oppressor, as an unfairly advantaged person, or as a participant in a damaged culture. I was taught to see myself as an individual whose moral state depended on her individual moral will. At school, we were not taught about slavery in any depth; we were not taught to see slaveholders as damaged people. Slaves were seen as the only group at risk of being dehumanized. My schooling followed the pattern which Elizabeth Minnich has pointed out: whites are taught to think of their lives as morally neutral, normative, and average, and also ideal, so that when we work to benefit others, this is seen as work that will allow "them" to be more like "us." I think many of us know how obnoxious this attitude can be in men.

After frustration with men who would not recognize male privilege, I decided to try to work on myself at least by identifying some of the daily

---

[1]This paper was presented at the Virginia Women's Studies Association conference in Richmond in April, 1986, and the American Educational Research Association conference in Boston in October, 1986, and discussed with two groups of participants in the Dodge seminars for Secondary School Teachers in New York and Boston in the spring of 1987.

effects of white privilege in my life. It is crude work, at this stage, but I will give here a list of special circumstances and conditions I experience that I did not earn but that I have been made to feel are mine by birth, by citizenship, and by virtue of being a conscientious law-abiding "normal" person of goodwill. I have chosen those conditions that I think in my case *attach somewhat more to skin-color privilege* than to class, religion, ethnic status, or geographical location, though these other privileging factors are intricately intertwined. As far as I can see, my Afro-American coworkers, friends, and acquaintances with whom I come into daily or frequent contact in this particular time, place, and line of work cannot count on most of these conditions.

1. I can, if I wish, arrange to be in the company of people of my race most of the time.

2. I can avoid spending time with people whom I was trained to mistrust and who have learned to mistrust my kind or me.

3. If I should need to move, I can be pretty sure of renting or purchasing housing in an area which I can afford and in which I would want to live.

4. I can be reasonably sure that my neighbors in such a location will be neutral or pleasant to me.

5. I can go shopping alone most of the time, fairly well assured that I will not be followed or harassed by store detectives.

6. I can turn on the television or open to the front page of the paper and see people of my race widely and positively represented.

7. When I am told about our national heritage or about "civilization," I am shown that people of my color made it what it is.

8. I can be sure that my children will be given curricular materials that testify to the existence of their race.

9. If I want to, I can be pretty sure of finding a publisher for this piece on white privilege.

10. I can be fairly sure of having my voice heard in a group in which I am the only member of my race.

11. I can be casual about whether or not to listen to another woman's voice in a group in which she is the only member of her race.

12. I can go into a book shop and count on finding the writing of my race represented, into a supermarket and find the staple foods that fit with my cultural traditions, into a hairdresser's shop and find someone who can deal with my hair.

13. Whether I use checks, credit cards, or cash, I can count on my skin color not to work against the appearance that I am financially reliable.

14. I could arrange to protect our young children most of the time from people who might not like them.

15. I did not have to educate our children to be aware of systemic racism for their own daily physical protection.

16. I can be pretty sure that my children's teachers and employers will tolerate them if they fit school and workplace norms; my chief worries about them do not concern others' attitudes toward their race.

17. I can talk with my mouth full and not have people put this down to my color.

18. I can swear, or dress in secondhand clothes, or not answer letters, without having people attribute these choices to the bad morals, the poverty, or the illiteracy of my race.

19. I can speak in public to a powerful male group without putting my race on trial.

20. I can do well in a challenging situation without being called a credit to my race.

21. I am never asked to speak for all the people of my racial group.

22. I can remain oblivious to the language and customs of persons of color who constitute

the world's majority without feeling in my culture any penalty for such oblivion.

23. I can criticize our government and talk about how much I fear its policies and behavior without being seen as a cultural outsider.

24. I can be reasonably sure that if I ask to talk to "the person in charge," I will be facing a person of my race.

25. If a traffic cop pulls me over or if the IRS audits my tax return, I can be sure I haven't been singled out because of my race.

26. I can easily buy posters, postcards, picture books, greeting cards, dolls, toys, and children's magazines featuring people of my race.

27. I can go home from most meetings of organizations I belong to feeling somewhat tied in, rather than isolated, out of place, outnumbered, unheard, held at a distance, or feared.

28. I can be pretty sure that an argument with a colleague of another race is more likely to jeopardize her chances for advancement than to jeopardize mine.

29. I can be fairly sure that if I argue for the promotion of a person of another race, or a program centering on race, this is not likely to cost me heavily within my present setting, even if my colleagues disagree with me.

30. If I declare there is a racial issue at hand, or there isn't a racial issue at hand, my race will lend me more credibility for either position than a person of color will have.

31. I can choose to ignore developments in minority writing and minority activist programs, or disparage them, or learn from them, but in any case, I can find ways to be more or less protected from negative consequences of any of these choices.

32. My culture gives me little fear about ignoring the perspectives and powers of people of other races.

33. I am not made acutely aware that my shape, bearing, or body odor will be taken as a reflection on my race.

34. I can worry about racism without being seen as self-interested or self-seeking.

35. I can take a job with an affirmative action employer without having my co-workers on the job suspect that I got it because of my race.

36. If my day, week, or year is going badly, I need not ask of each negative episode or situation whether it has racial overtones.

37. I can be pretty sure of finding people who would be willing to talk with me and advise me about my next steps, professionally.

38. I can think over many options, social, political, imaginative, or professional, without asking whether a person of my race would be accepted or allowed to do what I want to do.

39. I can be late to a meeting without having the lateness reflect on my race.

40. I can choose public accommodation without fearing that people of my race cannot get in or will be mistreated in the places I have chosen.

41. I can be sure that if I need legal or medical help, my race will not work against me.

42. I can arrange my activities so that I will never have to experience feelings of rejection owing to my race.

43. If I have low credibility as a leader, I can be sure that my race is not the problem.

44. I can easily find academic courses and institutions that give attention only to people of my race.

45. I can expect figurative language and imagery in all of the arts to testify to experiences of my race.

46. I can choose blemish cover or bandages in "flesh" color and have them more or less match my skin.

I repeatedly forgot each of the realizations on this list until I wrote it down. For me, white privilege has turned out to be an elusive and fugitive subject. The pressure to avoid it is great, for in facing it I must give up the myth of meritocracy. If these things are true, this is not such a free country; one's life is not what one makes it; many doors open for certain people through no virtues of their own. These perceptions mean also that my moral condition is not what I had been led to believe. The appearance of being a good citizen rather than a troublemaker comes in large part from having all sorts of doors open automatically because of my color.

A further paralysis of nerve comes from literary silence protecting privilege. My clearest memories of finding such analysis are in Lillian Smith's unparalleled *Killers of the Dream* and Margaret Andersen's review of Karen and Mamie Fields' *Lemon Swamp*. Smith, for example, wrote about walking toward black children on the street and knowing they would step into the gutter; Andersen contrasted the pleasure that she, as a white child, took on summer driving trips to the south with Karen Fields' memories of driving in a closed car stocked with all necessities lest, in stopping, her black family should suffer "insult, or worse." Adrienne Rich also recognizes and writes about daily experiences of privilege, but in my observation, white women's writing in this area is far more often on systemic racism than on our daily lives as lightskinned women.[2]

In unpacking this invisible knapsack of white privilege, I have listed conditions of daily experience that I once took for granted, as neutral, normal, and universally available to everybody, just as I once thought of a male-focused curriculum as the neutral or accurate account that can speak for all. Nor did I think of any of these perquisites as bad for the holder. I now think that we need a more finely differentiated taxonomy of privilege, for some of these varieties are only what one would want for everyone in a just society, and others give license to be ignorant, oblivious, arrogant, and destructive. Before proposing some more finely tuned categorization, I will make some observations about the general effects of these conditions on my life and expectations.

In this potpourri of examples, some privileges make me feel at home in the world. Others allow me to escape penalties or dangers that others suffer. Through some, I escape fear, anxiety, insult, injury, or a sense of not being welcome, not being real. Some keep me from having to hide, to be in disguise, to feel sick or crazy, to negotiate each transaction from the position of being an outsider or, within my group, a person who is suspected of having too close links with a dominant culture. Most keep me from having to be angry.

I see a pattern running through the matrix of white privilege, a pattern of assumptions that were passed on to me as a white person. There was one main piece of cultural turf; it was my own turf, and I was among those who could control the turf. I could measure up to the cultural standards and take advantage of the many options I saw around me to make what the culture would call a success of my life. *My skin color was an asset for any move I was educated to want to make.* I could think of myself as "belonging" in major ways and of making social systems work for me. I could freely disparage, fear, neglect, or be oblivious to anything outside of the dominant cultural forms. Being of the main culture, I could also criticize it fairly freely. My life was reflected back to me frequently enough so that I felt, with regard to my race, if not to my sex, like one of the real people.

Whether through the curriculum or in the newspaper, the television, the economic system, or the general look of people in the streets, I received daily signals and indications that my people counted and that others *either didn't exist or must be trying, not very successfully, to be like people of my race.* I was given cultural permission not to hear voices of people of other races or a tepid cultural tolerance for hearing or acting on such voices. I was

---

[2]Andersen, Margaret, "Race and the Social Science Curriculum: A Teaching and Learning Discussion." *Radical Teacher*, November, 1984, pp. 17–20. Smith, Lillian, *Killers of the Dream*, New York: W. W. Norton, 1949.

also raised not to suffer seriously from anything that darker-skinned people might say about my group, "protected," though perhaps I should more accurately say *prohibited*, through the habits of my economic class and social group, from living in racially mixed groups or being reflective about interactions between people of differing races.

In proportion as my racial group was being made confident, comfortable, and oblivious, other groups were likely being made unconfident, uncomfortable, and alienated. Whiteness protected me from many kinds of hostility, distress, and violence, which I was being subtly trained to visit in turn upon people of color.

For this reason, the word "privilege" now seems to me misleading. Its connotations are too positive to fit the conditions and behaviors which "privilege systems" produce. We usually think of privilege as being a favored state, whether earned, or conferred by birth or luck. School graduates are reminded they are privileged and urged to use their (enviable) assets well. The word "privilege" carries the connotation of being something everyone must want. Yet some of the conditions I have described here work to systemically overempower certain groups. Such privilege simply *confers dominance*, gives permission to control, because of one's race or sex. The kind of privilege that gives license to some people to be, at best, thoughtless and, at worst, murderous should not continue to be referred to as a desirable attribute. Such "privilege" may be widely desired without being in any way beneficial to the whole society.

Moreover, though "privilege" may confer power, it does not confer moral strength. Those who do not depend on conferred dominance have traits and qualities that may never develop in those who do. Just as Women's Studies courses indicate that women survive their political circumstances to lead lives that hold the human race together, so "underprivileged" people of color who are the world's majority have survived their oppression and lived survivors' lives from which the white global minority can and must learn. In some groups, those dominated have actually become strong through *not* having all of these unearned

advantages, and this gives them a great deal to teach the others. Members of so-called privileged groups can seem foolish, ridiculous, infantile, or dangerous by contrast.

I want, then, to distinguish between earned strength and unearned power conferred systemically. Power from unearned privilege can look like strength when it is, in fact, permission to escape or to dominate. But not all of the privileges on my list are inevitably damaging. Some, like the expectation that neighbors will be decent to you, or that your race will not count against you in court, should be the norm in a just society and should be considered as the entitlement of everyone. Others, like the privilege not to listen to less powerful people, distort the humanity of the holders as well as the ignored groups. Still others, like finding one's staple foods everywhere, may be a function of being a member of a numerical majority in the population. Others have to do with not having to labor under pervasive negative stereotyping and mythology.

We might at least start by distinguishing between positive advantages that we can work to spread, to the point where they are not advantages at all but simply part of the normal civic and social fabric, and negative types of advantage that unless rejected will always reinforce our present hierarchies. For example, the positive "privilege" of belonging, the feeling that one belongs within the human circle, as Native Americans say, fosters development and should not be seen as privilege for a few. It is, let us say, an entitlement that none of us should have to earn; ideally it is an *unearned entitlement*. At present, since only a few have it, it is an *unearned advantage* for them. The negative "privilege" that gave me cultural permission not to take darker-skinned Others seriously can be seen as arbitrarily conferred dominance and should not be desirable for anyone. This paper results from a process of coming to see that some of the power that I originally saw as attendant on being a human being in the United States consisted in *unearned advantage* and *conferred dominance*, as well as other kinds of special circumstance not universally taken for granted.

In writing this paper I have also realized that white identity and status (as well as class identity and status) give me considerable power to choose whether to broach this subject and its trouble. I can pretty well decide whether to disappear and avoid and not listen and escape the dislike I may engender in other people through this essay, or interrupt, answer, interpret, preach, correct, criticize, and control to some extent what goes on in reaction to it. Being white, I am given considerable power to escape many kinds of danger or penalty as well as to choose which risks I want to take.

There is an analogy here, once again, with Women's Studies. Our male colleagues do not have a great deal to lose in supporting Women's Studies, but they do not have a great deal to lose if they oppose it either. They simply have the power to decide whether to commit themselves to more equitable distributions of power. They will probably feel few penalties whatever choice they make; they do not seem, in any obvious short-term sense, the ones at risk, though they and we are all at risk because of the behaviors that have been rewarded in them.

Through Women's Studies work I have met very few men who are truly distressed about systemic, unearned male advantage and conferred dominance. And so one question for me and others like me is whether we will be like them, or whether we will get truly distressed, even outraged, about unearned race advantage and conferred dominance and if so, what we will do to lessen them. In any case, we need to do more work in identifying how they actually affect our daily lives. We need more down-to-earth writing by people about these taboo subjects. We need more understanding of the ways in which white "privilege" damages white people, for these are not the same ways in which it damages the victimized. Skewed white psyches are an inseparable part of the picture, though I do not want to confuse the kinds of damage done to the holders of special assets and to those who suffer the deficits. Many, perhaps most, of our white students in the United States think that racism doesn't affect them because they are not people of color; they do not see "whiteness" as a racial identity. Many men

likewise think that Women's Studies does not bear on their own existences because they are not female; they do not see themselves as having gendered identities. Insisting on the universal "effects" of "privilege" systems, then, becomes one of our chief tasks, and being more explicit about the *particular* effects in particular contexts is another. Men need to join us in this work.

In addition, since race and sex are not the only advantaging systems at work, we need to similarly examine the daily experience of having age advantage, or ethnic advantage, or physical ability, or advantage related to nationality, religion, or sexual orientation. Professor Marnie Evans suggested to me that in many ways the list I made also applies directly to heterosexual privilege. This is a still more taboo subject than race privilege: the daily ways in which heterosexual privilege makes some persons comfortable or powerful, providing supports, assets, approvals, and rewards to those who live or expect to live in heterosexual pairs. Unpacking that content is still more difficult, owing to the deeper imbeddedness of heterosexual advantage and dominance and stricter taboos surrounding these.

But to start such an analysis I would put this observation from my own experience: The fact that I live under the same roof with a man triggers all kinds of societal assumptions about my worth, politics, life, and values and triggers a host of unearned advantages and powers. After recasting many elements from the original list I would add further observations like these:

1. My children do not have to answer questions about why I live with my partner (my husband).

2. I have no difficulty finding neighborhoods where people approve of our household.

3. Our children are given texts and classes that implicitly support our kind of family unit and do not turn them against my choice of domestic partnership.

4. I can travel alone or with my husband without expecting embarrassment or hostility in those who deal with us.

5. Most people I meet will see my marital arrangements as an asset to my life or as a favorable comment on my likability, my competence, or my mental health.

6. I can talk about the social events of a weekend without fearing most listeners' reactions.

7. I will feel welcomed and "normal" in the usual walks of public life, institutional and social.

8. In many contexts, I am seen as "all right" in daily work on women because I do not live chiefly with women.

Difficulties and dangers surrounding the task of finding parallels are many. Since racism, sexism, and heterosexism are not the same, the advantages associated with them should not be seen as the same. In addition, it is hard to isolate aspects of unearned advantage that derive chiefly from social class, economic class, race, religion, region, sex, or ethnic identity. The oppressions are both distinct and interlocking, as the Combahee River Collective statement of 1977 continues to remind us eloquently.[3]

One factor seems clear about all of the interlocking oppressions. They take both active forms that we can see and embedded forms that members of the dominant group are taught not to see. In my class and place, I did not see myself as a racist because I was taught to recognize racism only in individual acts of meanness by members of my group, never in invisible systems conferring racial dominance on my group from birth. Likewise, we are taught to think that sexism or heterosexism is carried on only through intentional, individual acts of discrimination, meanness, or cruelty, rather than in invisible systems conferring unsought dominance on certain groups. Disapproving of the systems won't be enough to change them. I was taught to think that racism could end if white individuals changed their attitudes; many men think sexism can be ended by individual changes in daily behavior toward women. But a man's sex provides advantage for him whether or not he approves of the way in which dominance has been conferred on his group. A "white" skin in the United States opens many doors for whites whether or not we approve of the way dominance has been conferred on us. Individual acts can palliate, but cannot end, these problems. To redesign social systems, we need first to acknowledge their colossal unseen dimensions. The silences and denials surrounding privilege are the key political tool here. They keep the thinking about equality or equity incomplete, protecting unearned advantage and conferred dominance by making these taboo subjects. Most talk by whites about equal opportunity seems to me now to be about equal opportunity to try to get into a position of dominance while denying that *systems* of dominance exist.

Obliviousness about white advantage, like obliviousness about male advantage, is kept strongly inculturated in the United States so as to maintain the myth of meritocracy, the myth that democratic choice is equally available to all. Keeping most people unaware that freedom of confident action is there for just a small number of people props up those in power and serves to keep power in the hands of the same groups that have most of it already. Though systemic change takes many decades, there are pressing questions for me and I imagine for some others like me if we raise our daily consciousness on the perquisites of being light-skinned. What will we do with such knowledge? As we know from watching men, it is an open question whether we will choose to use unearned advantage to weaken invisible privilege systems and whether we will use any of our arbitrarily awarded power to try to reconstruct power systems on a broader base.

[3]"A Black Feminist Statement," The Combahee River Collective, pp. 13–22 in G. Hull, P. Scott, B. Smith, Eds., *All the Women Are White, All the Blacks Are Men, But Some of Us Are Brave: Black Women's Studies*, Old Westbury, NY: The Feminist Press, 1982.

35

Theorizing Difference from Multiracial Feminism

Maxine Baca Zinn and Bonnie Thornton Dill

WOMEN OF COLOR HAVE LONG CHALLENGED the hegemony of feminisms constructed primarily around the lives of white middle-class women. Since the late 1960s, U.S. women of color have taken issue with unitary theories of gender. Our critiques grew out of the widespread concern about the exclusion of women of color from feminist scholarship and the misinterpretation of our experiences,[1] and ultimately "out of the very discourses, denying, permitting, and producing difference."[2] Speaking simultaneously from "within and against" both women's liberation and antiracist movements, we have insisted on the need to challenge systems of domination,[3] not merely as gendered subjects but as women whose lives are affected by our location in multiple hierarchies.

Recently, and largely in response to these challenges, work that links gender to other forms of domination is increasing. In this article, we examine this connection further as well as the ways in which difference and diversity infuse contemporary feminist studies. Our analysis draws on a conceptual framework that we refer to as "multiracial feminism."[4] This perspective is an attempt to go beyond a mere recognition of diversity and difference among women to examine structures of domination, specifically the importance of race in understanding the social construction of gender. Despite the varied concerns and multiple intellectual stances which characterize the feminisms of women of color, they share an emphasis on race as a primary force situating genders differently. It is the centrality of race, of institutionalized racism, and of struggles against racial oppression that link

Feminist Studies, Summer 1996 v22 n2 p321(11) Full text: Copyright © 1996 Feminist Studies, Inc.

the various feminist perspectives within this framework. Together, they demonstrate that racial meanings offer new theoretical directions for feminist thought.

TENSIONS IN CONTEMPORARY DIFFERENCE FEMINISM

Objections to the false universalism embedded in the concept "woman" emerged within other discourses as well as those of women of color.[5] Lesbian feminists and postmodern feminists put forth their own versions of what Susan Bordo has called "gender skepticism."[6]

Many thinkers within mainstream feminism have responded to these critiques with efforts to contextualize gender. The search for women's "universal" or "essential" characteristics is being abandoned. By examining gender in the context of other social divisions and perspectives, difference has gradually become important—even problematizing the universal categories of "women" and "men." Sandra Harding expresses the shift best in her claim that "there are no gender relations per se, but only gender relations as constructed by and between classes, races, and cultures."[7]

Many feminists now contend that difference occupies center stage as the project of women studies today.[8] According to one scholar, "difference has replaced equality as the central concern of feminist theory."[9] Many have welcomed the change, hailing it as a major revitalizing force in U.S. feminist theory.[10] But if some priorities within mainstream feminist thought have been refocused by attention to difference, there remains an "uneasy alliance,"[11] between women of color and other feminists.

If difference has helped revitalize academic feminisms, it has also "upset the apple cart" and introduced new conflicts into feminist studies.[12] For example, in a recent and widely discussed essay, Jane Rowland Martin argues that the current preoccupation with difference is leading feminism into dangerous traps. She fears that in giving privileged status to a predetermined set of analytic categories (race, ethnicity, and class), "we affirm the existence of nothing but difference." She asks, "How do we know that for us, difference does not turn on being fat, or religious, or in an abusive relationship?"[13]

We, too, see pitfalls in some strands of the difference project. However, our perspectives take their bearings from social relations. Race and class differences are crucial, we argue, not as individual characteristics (such as being fat) but insofar as they are primary organizing principles of a society which locates and positions groups within that society's opportunity structures.

Despite the much-heralded diversity trend within feminist studies, difference is often reduced to mere pluralism: a "live and let live" approach where principles of relativism generate a long list of diversities which begin with gender, class, and race and continue through a range of social structural as well as personal characteristics.[14] Another disturbing pattern, which bell hooks refers to as "the commodification of difference," is the representation of diversity as a form of exotica, "a spice, seasoning that livens up the dull dish that is mainstream white culture."[15] The major limitation of these approaches is the failure to attend to the power relations that accompany difference. Moreover, these approaches ignore the inequalities that cause some characteristics to be seen as "normal" while others are seen as "different" and thus, deviant.

Maria C. Lugones expresses irritation at those feminists who see only the problem of difference without recognizing difference.[16] Increasingly, we find that difference is recognized. But this in no way means that difference occupies a "privileged" theoretical status. Instead of using difference to rethink the category of women, difference is often a

euphemism for women who differ from the traditional norm. Even in purporting to accept difference, feminist pluralism often creates a social reality that reverts to universalizing women:

So much feminist scholarship assumes that when we cut through all of the diversity among women created by differences of racial classification, ethnicity, social class, and sexual orientation, a "universal truth" concerning women and gender lies buried underneath. But if we can face the scary possibility that no such certainty exists and that persisting in such a search will always distort or omit someone's experiences, with what do we replace this old way of thinking? Gender differences and gender politics begin to look very different if there is no essential woman at the core.[17]

WHAT IS MULTIRACIAL FEMINISM?

A new set of feminist theories have emerged from the challenges put forth by women of color. Multiracial feminism is an evolving body of theory and practice informed by wide-ranging intellectual traditions. This framework does not offer a singular or unified feminism but a body of knowledge situating women and men in multiple systems of domination. U.S. multiracial feminism encompasses several emergent perspectives developed primarily by women of color: African Americans, Latinas, Asian Americans, and Native Americans, women whose analyses are shaped by their unique perspectives as "outsiders within"—marginal intellectuals whose social locations provide them with a particular perspective on self and society.[18] Although U.S. women of color represent many races and ethnic backgrounds—with different histories and cultures—our feminisms cohere in their treatment of race as a basic social division, a structure of power, a focus of political struggle, and hence a fundamental force in shaping women's and men's lives.

This evolving intellectual and political perspective uses several controversial terms. While we adopt the label "multiracial," other terms have been used to describe this broad framework. For example, Chela Sandoval refers to "U.S. Third

World feminisms,"[19] While other scholars refer to "indigenous feminisms." In their theory text-reader, Alison M. Jagger and Paula M. Rothenberg adopt the label "multicultural feminism."[20]

We use "multiracial" rather than "multicultural" as a way of underscoring race as a power system that interacts with other structured inequalities to shape genders. Within the U.S. context, race, and the system of meanings and ideologies which accompany it, is a fundamental organizing principle of social relationships.[21] Race affects all women and men, although in different ways. Even cultural and group differences among women are produced through interaction within a racially stratified social order. Therefore, although we do not discount the importance of culture, we caution that cultural analytic frameworks that ignore race tend to view women's differences as the product of group-specific values and practices that often result in the marginalization of cultural groups which are then perceived as exotic expressions of a normative center. Our focus on race stresses the social construction of differently situated social groups and their varying degrees of advantage and power. Additionally, this emphasis on race takes on increasing political importance in an era where discourse about race is governed by color-evasive language[22] and a preference for individual rather than group remedies for social inequalities. Our analyses insist upon the primary and pervasive nature of race in contemporary U.S. society while at the same time acknowledging how race both shapes and is shaped by a variety of other social relations.

In the social sciences, multiracial feminism grew out of socialist feminist thinking. Theories about how political economic forces shape women's lives were influential as we began to uncover the social causes of racial ethnic women's subordination. But socialist feminism's concept of capitalist patriarchy, with its focus on women's unpaid (reproductive) labor in the home failed to address racial differences in the organization of reproductive labor. As feminists of color have argued, "reproductive labor has divided along racial as well as gender lines, and the specific characteristics have varied regionally and changed over time as capitalism has reorganized."[23] Despite the limitations of socialist feminism, this body of literature has been especially useful in pursuing questions about the interconnections among systems of domination.[24]

Race and ethnic studies was the other major social scientific source of multiracial feminism. It provided a basis for comparative analyses of groups that are socially and legally subordinated and remain culturally distinct within U.S. society. This includes the systematic discrimination of socially constructed racial groups and their distinctive cultural arrangements. Historically, the categories of African American, Latino, Asian American, and Native American were constructed as both racially and culturally distinct. Each group has a distinctive culture, shares a common heritage, and has developed a common identity within a larger society that subordinates them.[25]

We recognize, of course, certain problems inherent in an uncritical use of the multiracial label. First, the perspective can be hampered by a biracial model in which only African Americans and whites are seen as racial categories and all other groups are viewed through the prism of cultural differences. Latinos and Asians have always occupied distinctive places within the racial hierarchy, and current shifts in the composition of the U.S. population are racializing these groups anew.[26]

A second problem lies in treating multiracial feminism as a single analytical framework, and its principle architects, women of color, as an undifferentiated category. The concepts "multiracial feminism," "racial ethnic women," and "women of color" "homogenize quite different experiences and can falsely universalize experiences across race, ethnicity, sexual orientation, and age."[27] The feminisms created by women of color exhibit a plurality of intellectual and political positions. We speak in many voices, with inconsistencies that are born of our different social locations. Multiracial feminism embodies this plurality and richness. Our intent is not to falsely universalize women of color. Nor do we wish to promote a new racial essentialism in place of the old gender essentialism. Instead, we use these concepts to examine the structures and experiences produced by intersecting forms of race and gender.

It is also essential to acknowledge that race is a shifting and contested category whose meanings construct definitions of all aspects of social life.[28] In the United States it helped define citizenship by excluding everyone who was not a white, male property owner. It defined labor as slave or free, coolie or contract, and family as available only to those men whose marriages were recognized or whose wives could immigrate with them. Additionally, racial meanings are contested both within groups and between them.[29]

Although definitions of race are at once historically and geographically specific, they are also transnational, encompassing diasporic groups and crossing traditional geographic boundaries. Thus, while U.S. multiracial feminism calls attention to the fundamental importance of race, it must also locate the meaning of race within specific national traditions.

THE DISTINGUISHING FEATURES OF MULTIRACIAL FEMINISM

By attending to these problems, multiracial feminism offers a set of analytic premises for thinking about and theorizing gender. The following themes distinguish this branch of feminist inquiry.

First, multiracial feminism asserts that gender is constructed by a range of interlocking inequalities, what Patricia Hill Collins calls a "matrix of domination."[30] The idea of a matrix is that several fundamental systems work with and through each other. People experience race, class, gender, and sexuality differently depending upon their social location in the structures of race, class, gender, and sexuality. For example, people of the same race will experience race differently depending upon their location in the class structure as working class, professional managerial class, or unemployed; in the gender structure as female or male; and in structures of sexuality as heterosexual, homosexual, or bisexual.

Multiracial feminism also examines the simultaneity of systems in shaping women's experience and identity. Race, class, gender, and sexuality are not reducible to individual attributes to be measured and assessed for their separate contribution in explaining given social outcomes, an approach that Elizabeth Spelman calls "popbead metaphysics," where a women's identity consists of the sum of parts neatly divisible from one another.[31] The matrix of domination seeks to account for the multiple ways that women experience themselves as gendered, raced, classed, and sexualized.

Second, multiracial feminism emphasizes the intersectional nature of hierarchies at all levels of social life. Class, race, gender, and sexuality are components of both social structure and social interaction. Women and men are differently embedded in locations created by these cross-cutting hierarchies. As a result, women and men throughout the social order experience different forms of privilege and subordination, depending on their race, class, gender, and sexuality. In other words, intersecting forms of domination produce both oppression and opportunity. At the same time that structures of race, class, and gender create disadvantages for women of color, they provide unacknowledged benefits for those who are at the top of these hierarchies—whites, members of the upper classes, and males. Therefore, multiracial feminism applies not only to racial ethnic women but also to women and men of all races, classes, and genders.

Third, multiracial feminism highlights the relational nature of dominance and subordination. Power is the cornerstone of women's differences.[32] This means that women's differences are connected in systematic ways.[33] Race is a vital element in the pattern of relations among minority and white women. As Linda Gordon argues, the very meanings of being a white woman in the United States have been affected by the existence of subordinated women of color: "They intersect in conflict and in occasional cooperation, but always in mutual influence."[34]

Fourth, multiracial feminism explores the interplay of social structure and women's agency. Within the constraints of race, class, and gender oppression, women create viable lives for themselves, their families, and their communities. Women of color have resisted and often undermined the forces of power that control them. From acts of quiet dignity and steadfast determination to involvement in revolt and rebellion, women struggle to shape their own lives. Racial oppression has been a common focus of the "dynamic oppositional agency" of women of color. As Chandra Talpade Mohanty points out, it is the nature and organization of women's opposition which mediates and differentiates the impact of structures of domination.[35]

Fifth, multiracial feminism encompasses wide-ranging methodological approaches, and like other branches of feminist thought, relies on varied theoretical tools as well. Ruth Frankenberg and Lata Mani identify three guiding principles of inclusive feminist inquiry: "building complex analyses, avoiding erasure, specifying location."[36] In the last decade, the opening up of academic feminism has focused attention on social location in the production of knowledge. Most basically, research by and about marginalized women has destabilized what used to be considered as universal categories of gender. Marginalized locations are well suited for grasping social relations that remained obscure from more privileged vantage points. Lived experience, in other words, creates alternative ways of understanding the social world and the experience of different groups of women within it. Racially informed standpoint epistemologies have provided new topics, fresh questions, and new understandings of women and men. Women of color have, as Norma Alarcon argues, asserted ourselves as subjects, using our voices to challenge dominant conceptions of truth.[37]

Sixth, multiracial feminism brings together understandings drawn from the lived experiences of diverse and continuously changing groups of women. Among Asian Americans, Native Americans, Latinas, and Blacks are many different national cultural and ethnic groups. Each one is engaged in the process of testing, refining, and reshaping these broader categories in

its own image. Such internal differences heighten awareness of and sensitivity to both commonalities and differences, serving as a constant reminder of the importance of comparative study and maintaining a creative tension between diversity and universalization.

DIFFERENCE AND TRANSFORMATION

Efforts to make women's studies less partial and less distorted have produced important changes in academic feminism. Inclusive thinking has provided a way to build multiplicity and difference into our analyses. This has led to the discovery that race matters for everyone. White women, too, must be reconceptualized as a category that is multiply defined by race, class and other differences. As Ruth Frankenberg demonstrates in a study of whiteness among contemporary women, all kinds of social relations, even those that appear neutral, are, in fact, racialized. Frankenberg further complicates the very notion of a unified white identity by introducing issues of Jewish identity.[38] Therefore, the lives of women of color cannot be seen as a variation on a more general model of white American womanhood. The model of womanhood that feminist social science once held as "universal" is also a product of race and class.

When we analyze the power relations constituting all social arrangements and shaping women's lives in distinctive ways, we can begin to grapple with core feminist issues about how genders are socially constructed and constructed differently. Women's difference is built into our study of gender. Yet this perspective is quite far removed from the atheoretical pluralism implied in much contemporary thinking about gender.

Multiracial feminism, in our view, focuses not just on differences but also on the way in which differences and domination intersect and are historically and socially constituted. It challenges feminist scholars to go beyond the mere recognition and inclusion of difference to reshape the basic concepts and theories of our disciplines. By attending to women's social location based on race, class, and gender, multiracial feminism seeks to clarify the structural sources of diversity. Ultimately, multiracial feminism forces us to see privilege and subordination as interrelated and to pose such questions as: How do the existences and experiences of all people—women and men, different racial-ethnic groups, and different classes—shape the experiences of each other? How are those relationships defined and enforced through social institutions that are the primary sites for negotiating power within society? How do these differences contribute to the construction of both individual and group identity? Once we acknowledge that all women are affected by the racial order of society, then it becomes clear that the insights of multiracial feminism provide an analytical framework, not solely for understanding the experiences of women of color but for understanding all women, and men, as well.

NOTES

1. Maxine Baca Zinn, Lynn Weber Cannon, Elizabeth Higginbotham, and Bonnie Thornton Dill, "The Costs of Exclusionary Practices in Women's Studies," *Signs* 11 (winter 1986): 290–303.

2. Chela Sandoval, "U.S. Third World Feminism: The Theory and Method of Oppositional Consciousness in the Postmodern World," *Genders* (spring 1991): 1–24.

3. Ruth Frankenberg and Lata Mani, "Cross Currents, Crosstalk: Race, 'Postcoloniality,' and the Politics of Location," *Cultural Studies* 7 (May 1993): 292–310.

4. We use the term "multiracial feminism" to convey the multiplicity of racial groups and feminist perspectives.

5. A growing body of work on difference in feminist thought now exists. Although we cannot cite all the current work, the following are representative: Michele Barrett, "The Concept of Difference," *Feminist Review* 26 (July 1987): 29–42; Christina Crosby, "Dealing with Difference," in *Feminists Theorize the Political*, ed. Judith Butler and Joan W. Scott (New York: Routledge, 1992), 130–143; Elizabeth Fox-Genovese, "Difference, Diversity, and Divisions in an Agenda for the Women's Movement," in *Color, Class, and Country: Experiences of Gender*, ed. Gay Young and Bette J. Dickerson (London: Zed Books, 1994), 232–248; Nancy A. Hewitt, "Compounding Differences," *Feminist Studies* 18 (summer 1992): 313–326; Maria C. Lugones, "On the Logic of Feminist Pluralism," in *Feminist Ethics*, ed. Claudia Card (Lawrence: University of Kansas Press, 1991), 35–44; Rita S. Gallin and Anne Ferguson, "The Plurality of Feminism: Rethinking 'Difference,'" in *The Woman and International Development Annual* (Boulder: Westview Press, 1993), 3: 1–16; and Linda Gordon, "On Difference," *Genders* 10 (spring 1991): 91–111.

6. Susan Bordo, "Feminism, Postmodernism, and Gender Skepticism," in *Feminism/Postmodernism*, ed. Linda J. Nicholson (London: Routledge, 1990), 133–156.

7. Sandra G. Harding, *Whose Science? Whose Knowledge? Thinking from Women's Lives* (Ithaca: Cornell University Press, 1991), 179.

8. Crosby, 131.

9. Fox-Genovese, 232.

10. Faye Ginsberg and Anna Lowenhaupt Tsing, Introduction to *Uncertain Terms, Negotiating Gender in American Culture*, ed. Faye Ginsberg and Anna Lowenhaupt Tsing (Boston: Beacon Press, 1990), 3.

11. Sandoval, 2.

12. Sandra Morgan, "Making Connections: Socialist-Feminist Challenges to Marxist Scholarship," in *Women and a New Academy: Gender and Cultural Contexts*, ed. Jean F. O'Barr (Madison: University of Wisconsin Press, 1989), 149.

13. Jane Rowland Martin, "Methodological Essentialism, False Difference, and Other Dangerous Traps," *Signs* 19 (spring 1994): 647.

14. Barrett, 32.

15. bell hooks, *Black Looks: Race and Representation* (Boston: South End Press, 1992), 21.

16. Lugones, 35–44.

17. Patricia Hill Collins, Foreword to *Women of Color in U.S. Society*, ed. Maxine Baca Zinn and Bonnie Thornton Dill (Philadelphia: Temple University Press, 1994), xv.

18. Patricia Hill Collins, "Learning from the Outsider Within: The Sociological Significance of Black Feminist Thought," *Social Problems* 33 (December 1986): 514–532.

19. Sandoval, 1.

20. Alison M. Jagger and Paula S. Rothenberg, *Feminist Frameworks: Alternative Theoretical Accounts of the Relations between Women and Men*, 3d ed. (New York: McGraw-Hill, 1993).

21. Michael Omi and Howard Winant, *Racial Formation in the United States: From the 1960s to the 1980s*, 2d ed. (New York: Routledge, 1994).

22. Ruth Frankenberg, *The Social Construction of Whiteness: White Women, Race Matters* (Minneapolis: University of Minnesota Press, 1993).

23. Evelyn Nakano Glenn, "From Servitude to Service Work: Historical Continuities in the Racial Division of Paid Reproductive Labor," *Signs* 18 (autumn 1992): 3. See also Bonnie Thornton Dill, "Our Mothers' Grief: Racial-Ethnic Women and the Maintenance of Families," *Journal of Family History* 13, no. 4 (1988): 415–431.

24. Morgan, 146.

25. Maxine Baca Zinn and Bonnie Thornton Dill, "Difference and Domination," in *Women of Color in U.S. Society*, 11–12.

26. See Omi and Winant, 53–76, for a discussion of racial formation.

27. Margaret L. Andersen and Patricia Hill Collins, *Race, Class, and Gender: An Anthology* (Belmont, Calif.: Wadsworth, 1992), xvi.

28. Omi and Winant.

29. Nazli Kibria, "Migration and Vietnamese American Women: Remaking Ethnicity," in *Women of Color in U.S. Society*, 247–261.

30. Patricia Hill Collins, *Black Feminist Thought: Knowledge, Consciousness, and the Politics of Empowerment* (Boston: Unwin Hyman, 1990).

31. Elizabeth Spelman, *Inessential Women: Problems of Exclusion in Feminist Thought* (Boston: Beacon Press, 1988), 136.

32. Several discussions of difference make this point. See Baca Zinn and Dill, 10; Gordon, 106; and Lynn Weber, in the "Symposium on West and Fenstermaker's 'Doing Difference,'" *Gender & Society* 9 (August 1995): 515–519.

33. Glenn, 10.

34. Gordon, 106.

35. Chandra Talpade Mohanty, "Cartographies of Struggle: Third World Women and the Politics of Feminism," in *Third World Women and the Politics of Feminism*, ed. Chandra Talpade Mohanty, Ann Russo, and Lourdes Torres (Bloomington: Indiana University Press, 1991), 13.

36. Frankenberg and Mani, 306.

37. Norma Alarcon, "The Theoretical Subject(s) of This Bridge Called My Back and Anglo-American Feminism," in *Making Face, Making Soul, Haciendo Caras: Creative and Critical Perspectives by Women of Color*, ed. Gloria Anzaldua (San Francisco: Aunt Lute, 1990), 356.

38. Frankenberg. See also Evelyn Torton Beck, "The Politics of Jewish Invisibility," *NWSA Journal* (fall 1988): 93–102.

36

Conceptions of Masculinity and Gender Transgressions in Sport Among Adolescent Boys

Hegemony, Contestation, and the Social Class Dynamic

Suzanne Laberge and Mathieu Albert

CASES OF WOMEN VENTURING INTO MEN-dominated fields and of men venturing into women-dominated ones constitute rich social facts that can shed light on key issues about the dynamics peculiar to the construction of gendered social life and gendered identities. Various social processes are particularly enacted in these experiences, such as (a) the complex interaction between patriarchal culture, gendered social organization, and gender identity; (b) the asymmetry of gender relations; and (c) the dynamics of change and resistance in a given social order. Modernization, the progression of capitalism, and the feminist movement that marked the first quarter of the 20th century led to a mass entry of women into "male preserves" (Dunning, 1986: Theberge, 1995), such as the workplace and sport, thereby fostering the study of gender relations with a particular focus on the integration of women in "nontraditional" domains. Hence, fem-

AUTHORS' NOTE: This research was supported by the Social Sciences and Humanities Research Council of Canada. We thank the editors for their constructive comments. We also are indebted to Michael Gilson and Yvan Girardin for their invaluable help in editing the English version of this chapter. Address correspondence to Suzanne Laberge, Department of Kinesiology, Université de Montréal, P.O. Box 6128, Station Centre-Ville, Montréal (Québec), CANADA H3C 3J7; phone: (514) 343-7934 (office); fax: (514) 343-2181; e-mail: suzanne.laberge@umontreal.ca

inist scholars scrutinized many social processes that previously had gone unchallenged or were only marginally questioned, such as men's oppression of women (patriarchal power) and the sexual division of labor. The upheavals in social organization and the turbulence in gender ideologies that eventually occurred fueled the gender self-consciousness and "crisis" then experienced by some men (Kimmel, 1987b) and influenced the rise of scholarship on masculinity. The primary concerns of these scholars were mainly oriented toward deconstructing and theorizing masculinity, that is, discovering the sociohistorical construction of masculinity and its cultural and internal differentiations (Brod, 1987; Carrigan Connell, & Lee, 1985; Connell, 1993; Kimmel, 1987a; Hearn & Morgan, 1990; Morgan, 1992). It is only somewhat recently that we have witnessed a growing number of empirical studies addressing the issue of men venturing into nontraditional occupations (e.g., Poole, 1996) or into so-called women's sporting activities (Adams, 1993; Davis, 1990). We believe that this avenue can provide a fruitful means to further our understanding of the internal differentiation of maleness and the dynamics of gender relations.

This chapter seeks to explore and interpret (a) the various meanings that male adolescents give to masculinity, intermale tensions, and oppositions; and (b) their differential and contradictory appraisals of men who participate in so-called women's sports—that is, men who transgress the rules of gender order in sport. The chapter aims ultimately to identify and understand the links and the contradictions between conceptions of masculinity and expressed judgments of men's transgressions of the gender order. Particular attention is paid to how conceptions of masculinities and judgments of men's transgressions interact with the structure of social classes.

CONCEPTUAL FRAMEWORK

Some of the main research questions were inspired by the theorizing of Harding (1986) regarding the social construction of gender. According to Harding, gendered social life is produced through three distinct processes. First, there is *gender symbolism,* which refers to "assigning dualistic gender metaphors to various perceived dichotomies that rarely have anything to do with sex differences" (p. 17). Cultural expressions of gender symbolism are to be found in the binary oppositions masculine/feminine and the various gender stereotypes (e.g., delicate/sturdy, gracious/powerful, sensitivity/toughness) that are quite illusive and exclude a majority of men and women. The process *gender structure* consists of "appealing to these gender dualisms to organize social activity" (p. 17); this results in social interactions that are constructed according to a dualistic division of activities based on gender. The third process, which Harding calls *individual gender,* refers to "a form of socially constructed individual identity only imperfectly correlated with either the 'reality' or the perception of sex differences" (p. 18). In this chapter, we consider the understandings of masculinity expressed by adolescents as an interaction between individual gender and gender symbolism. We attempt to discern the extent which they personally integrate or contest masculine stereotypes or dominant symbols of masculinity. We conceptualize sport as a gender structure that is organized according to a dualistic understanding of gender. We also examine agency by addressing individual reactions to gender symbols (personal opinions about masculinity) and individual beliefs about gender transgressions in sport.

Our analysis relies heavily on Connell's (1995) conceptualization of masculinity as "simultaneously a place in gender relations, the practices through which men and women engage that place in gender, and the effects of these practices in bodily experience, personality and culture" (p.71). We believe that his approach meshes well with Harding's (1986) formulation, because both stress that genders are simultaneously cultural forms, structures of social activities, and identities. Following Connell (1987), we distinguish between the local or microlevel dimensions of gender relations (e.g., in sport, religion, work, the state, the media, family life), which he calls "gender regimes," and the abstract or macrolevel "gender order," which refers to "the structural inventory of an entire society" (pp. 98–99, 111). We also employ recent feminist and profeminist research that emphasizes the need to acknowledge the existence of multiple masculinities and the complex intersections and tensions among gender, class, race, and sexuality (Brod, 1987; Carrigan et al., 1985; Connell, 1993, 1995; Hearn & Collinson, 1994; Messner, 1990b, 1993).

METHOD

This chapter reports on the qualitative portion of a larger study on coeducation, somatic culture, and gender relations undertaken among Québec adolescents. The qualitative part of the research was designed to address the following questions:

1. What are the current referents for masculinity and femininity among male and female adolescents? To what extent do they reproduce, resist, or transform dominant gender symbols or sterotypes?

2. What are adolescents' judgments vis-à-vis transgression of a gendered social activity like sport? Is the acceptance or discrediting gender-symmetric?

3. Is there a relation between conceptions of masculinity and femininity and the approval or stigmatization of gender transgression?

4. What do the previously stated processes suggest regarding the reproduction or the transformation of gender hierarchies?

In previous research, we noted that it was difficult to get adolescents to articulate their genuine opinions in face-to-face interviews. Adolescents are often reticent to express themselves, either because they are afraid that they might give a wrong answer, or because they feel uncomfortable in this artificial form of interaction. As a result of informal talks with some adolescents, we decided that essays on an issue of concern to their age-group would be a more suitable strategy for eliciting responses. Accordingly, we asked students in three French secondary 5 grade schools (i.e., 15- to 16-year-olds) in the Montréal area to write essays. We included students from two public high schools, one in a working-class (WC) district and the other in a middle-class (MC) suburb, as well as another group from a private high school in an affluent neighborhood (UC).

At our first meeting, the students were asked to write an essay about gender and sport. They were encouraged to think about their compositions and to discuss them with their friends. The essay was presented as an opportunity to express their opinions on a debatable subject. They were told that their essays would be handled in a confidential manner and that their anonymity would be preserved. They were given four topics that were presented in colloquial language and in ways that stressed there was no right or wrong answer and that they should feel comfortable about expressing their highly personal opinions. Students also were encouraged to relate any of their own sport experiences that were relevant to the following four topics:

1. Describe what a "masculine" or a "virile" boy means to you, if such a category exists. How would you characterize a person who is said to be masculine? In other words, how would you define masculinity?

2. Describe what a "feminine" girl means to you, if such a category exists. How would

you characterize a person who is said to be feminine? In other words, how would you define femininity?

Assume that men's sports are those mainly played by men (e.g., football, boxing, ice hockey) and women's sports are those primarily participated in by women (e.g., figure skating, aerobic dance, ringette[1]).

3. How would you perceive a man who plays a women's sport? In your opinion, does this make him less masculine?

4. How would you perceive a woman who plays a men's sport? In your opinion, does this make her less feminine?

A few days after our first meeting, we returned and allowed students a full class period (usually 75 minutes) to write the essays. They were asked to write about half a page on each topic and to indicate their gender and their country of origin at the top of the page (there were quite a few immigrants in the MC and WC schools). This research strategy exceeded our expectations, as the students were surprisingly expressive in their opinions and appraisals of our questions.

We undertook a content analysis of the essays using a computer program called *Content Analysis Tool*, designed especially for this study by a computer technician using Macintosh HyperCard language. After rejecting a dozen essays either because the handwriting was illegible or because the text was incomprehensible, we ended up with a total of 354 valid essays, 174 by boys and 180 by girls, which were quite evenly issued from the three social milieus (see Table 12.1).

In this chapter, we examine only the boys' essays and only the sections that contained their ideas about masculinity (Topic 1) and about men's transgressive behavior (Topic 3). The boys' appraisals of girls' transgressions and the girls' appraisals of boys' trespasses are briefly considered to highlight the significance of the findings.

Our analysis is composed of three sections. We begin by exploring conceptions of masculinity (Topic 1), using Connell's (1990) concept of

TABLE 12.1
Type of School Students Attended, by Gender

Type of School Attended	Boys	Girls
Public school in working-class neighborhood	55	63
Public school in middle-class neighborhood	54	63
Private school in affluent neighborhood	65	54
Total	174	180

hegemonic masculinity, which refers to the "culturally idealized form of masculine character," which associates masculinity with "toughness and competitiveness," the "subordination of women," and "the marginalization of gay men" (pp. 83, 94). We also relate this approach of hegemonic masculinity to Connell's (1995) triad of *reproduction, resistance, and transformation* (pp. 76–77). The second part focuses on judgments of men's transgressions, to find out whether boys endorse or critique the gendered organization of sport. Finally, we look into possible links or contradictions between conceptions of masculinity and appraisals of men's transgressions of the gender regime of sport.

RESULTS

Conceptions of Masculinity

Reproducing hegemonic masculinity. The boys' understandings of masculinity approximated the hegemonic form, as they stressed physical and moral strength, seductive power, heterosexuality, control over one's own emotions, leadership, and masculine display. The following quotation[2] is typical of the form of masculinity exalted by a significant proportion of boys from the three social milieus:

A virile guy is one who is tall, has wide shoulders, and who, above all, is strong. He plays a lot of sports, mainly men's sports such as ice hockey and football. He's got to be macho[3] because if he isn't, he will not be successful with girls. Usually, a virile guy is successful with all the girls because, whether we like it or not, girls

like manly guys. He is also someone who impresses others and commands respect. He is not afraid of others. (UC, No. 03532)

This type of masculinity also was expounded in relational terms, with a great many boys positioning masculinity in opposition to femininity and/or other types of men—typically, physically smaller, "lower-profile" men, or homosexuals:

A normal guy, a real guy, is a guy who has character, who won't be henpecked by a girl. (WC, No. 43212)

A virile guy, a "real one," can be any guy that is really built or who rides around on a Harley-Davidson. Not necessarily a Hell's Angels. A guy like Arnold or Sylvester Stallone, who are strong physically and also mentally. A real man has few feminine manners. Thus, he can't be too soft. Or, not too timid or a loner. They are not "fags." A gay is neither a man nor a woman, he is garbage, waste. He may be muscular, but, he is surely a sado-masochist, therefore not a "real man." (MC, No. 27022)

In summary, boys' descriptions of maleness consistently articulated hegemonic principles such as domination over women and the subordination and marginalization of men who did not possess their masculine ideals.

Class Background Hegemonic Masculinity

Further examination showed that the boys' understandings of hegemonic masculinity differed according to their class milieus. For example, leadership and sociability were more exalted among boys in the private high school:

A virile guy is a guy that is not shy, who is the "leader" of his group, who expresses his opinions, without being ridiculous, who is not embarrassed to talk to anybody. He distinguishes himself from others because he imposes himself much more. (UC, No. 08732)

Boys from the public school in an MC suburb extolled intelligence and sociability: "[A virile guy] is an intelligent person, who has self-confidence and high self-esteem. A man who respects others, and expects others to respect him" (MC, No. 32022). Insouciant bravado, male chauvinism, and masculine showing-off were more exalted among the boys from the public school in a WC district:

> A virile guy is physically fit, is tall enough and has a deep voice. He must look "cool" when he walks. He must look good to be noticed when he wanders about in the street. Sometimes, he is a "showoff." He is always ready to fight to show he is the strongest. . . . He should have a knack with girls. Also, a real man should have many women because it is inconceivable that a man have only one woman. (WC, No. 19712)

To understand these differences, we need to look into the differential living conditions under which they arise and assess what is at stake for members of the various classes. Conceptions of masculinity are shaped by the range of possibilities, interests, and the experiences of everyday life. UC boys are most often socialized with the aim of occupying management or leadership positions in the labor force. Thus, to become a man means developing the qualities that characterize a future position associated with administering people. Their class position means that they are unlikely to aspire to occupations requiring physical strength, thereby lessening the importance of physical sturdiness in the evaluation of maleness. For the MC boys, upward social and economic mobility is one of their major goals; thus, a diploma and academic capital are perceived as the major means available for achieving that end. This possibly explains the emphasis they placed on intelligence in their descriptions of a "real man." The masculine showoff and the perceived necessity of being fearless associated with maleness in the WC boys' essays is con-

sonant with the violence that often surrounds their lives. Most telling in this regard was the statement of one of them:

> For me a real guy is someone athletic, someone who is not afraid to be hurt and not afraid to protect his girlfriend. A real guy is also someone who can go out late at night and come back home without any harm. (WC, No. 21612)

This class-distinctive valorization of "fearless" persona among the WC boys also was evidenced by Goodey (1997), as seen in his study on adolescents and crime:

> At its extreme, "fearlessness" can be expressed as physical aggression among working-class boys in their attempt to assert their masculinity. In comparison, middle-class boys, while also having to take on the masculine criteria of fearlessness, are able to and tend to project their masculine hegemony through different channels, such as academic success. (p. 410)

Hondagneu-Sotelo and Messner (1994) and Messner (1990b) shed light on this hypermasculine style. On the basis of their study of Mexican immigrant men, they found, "Marginalized and subordinated men tend to overtly display exaggerated embodiments and verbalizations of masculinity that can be read as a desire to express power over others within a context of relative powerlessness" (1994, p. 214). They share, with Collinson's (1988) understanding of the sexually aggressive and misogynist humor of Australian male blue-collar workers, and with Majors and Billson's (1992) reading of the "cool pose" of young black men, the insight that subordinated men tend to use specific masculine displays as a way to resist, at least symbolically, the various forms of oppression that they face within hierarchies of intermale dominance. Hypermasculine style thus can be read as a gender-class affirmation and an oppositional politics to the "discreet masculine charm" favored by men of the bourgeoisie. For instance, one boy from the UC milieu enunciated, with a certain contempt, his stereotyped representation of WC masculinity:

> Listen, for me, a virile man is the typical worker with big arms working in the factory all week long to provide

TABLE 12.2

Boys' Conceptions of Hegemonic Masculinity, by Type of School Attended (in Percentages)

Type of School Attended	Conceptions of Hegemonic Masculinity		
	Reproductive	Resistant	Transformative
Public school in working-class neighborhoods (*n* = 55)	55	27	18
Public school in middle-class neighborhood (*n* = 54)	48	19	33
Private school in affluent neighborhood (*n* = 65)	54	21	25
Total (N = 174)	52	23	25

for this family, who plays hockey with his buddies on Wednesday night, who goes to get drunk with them on Saturday night at the corner pub, who loves his wife but he does not let her know very often because he doesn't know how, who lives a rather boring life that makes him happy. In short, as cliché as it may seem, that is my definition of a virile man. Please note, this not the type of man I admire. (UC, No. 12932)

In sum, we suggest that hegemonic conceptions of masculinity are oriented toward dominance over women and the subordination of other configurations of masculinity. We also submit that the exercise of power is culturally produced through the strategic use of signifiers associated with this form of masculinity. Furthermore, we have argued that hegemonic masculinity interacts with class background, as a component of class politics.

Contesting hegemonic masculinity. Although hegemonic, the mode of masculinity just discussed also was contested and confronted strongly with alternative versions among the adolescents. Indeed, the content analysis of the writings relating to the first topic showed two opposing tendencies: one that endorsed the hegemonic form of masculinity (the reproduction process presented previously) and others that critiqued or challenged it (resistance process), sometimes with a call for alternative versions to it (transformation process).

Although the aim here is not to count heads, we present in Table 12.2 the findings that emerged from the content analysis according to the categories of reproduction, resistance, and transformation of hegemonic masculinity within each social milieu. As we can see, reproductive elements were prominent in all three social groups. However, nearly equal numbers of respondents enunciated resistant or transformative views.

Resisting hegemonic masculinity. Recalcitrant views were roughly similar across social class. Many boys criticized overt and exaggerated masculine displays and also strongly voiced their own oppressive experiences:

A virile guy is a guy who always shows that he is not scared and who always takes up challenges of force and who always shares his sexual adventures with his friends. He walks like a "showoff" and he is not himself. Guys like that bug me! (MC, No 37922)

In a manner similar to that seen in the writings endorsing hegemonic forms of masculinity, oppositional stances had some class-specific links. UC and MC boys usually challenged hegemonic masculinity, theoretically by advocating a disruption of gender categories:

A virile guy is a stereotype. . . . The important thing is to be well-balanced, not virile nor feminine. We must attain a balance between our feminine and our masculine sides. To feel well within ourselves. Not be stuck in a stereotype or make up stories. We shouldn't constantly try to distinguish ourselves from girls. Between the two sexes, there are similarities. After all, we are all human. There are also some differences, and here too, there is no harm. (UC, No. 01732)

By contrast, WC boys tended to critique the social problems that hegemonic masculinity raised for them in everyday life (e.g., violence, rejection of school, family problems):

A virile guy or a real guy, I believe is a person who is somewhat stuck up. It is a guy who thinks of his image a lot. It is someone who may also wear tattoos on his body to show his "tough" side. He has long hair and a pretty "tough" look. A virile guy is also someone who doesn't care about others nor about school. He always wants to party. (WC, No. 19812)

A kind of resigned oppositional politics vis-à-vis the breadth sway of hegemonic masculinity was also evident in some of the WC boys' writings:

Virility is a behavior that has always existed, only recently have we begun to abolish this behavior. . . . Being virile is playing for the gallery, showing off. I do not like virility because in my mind, it leads to violence. My grandfather was a "virile man," he could not show his emotions towards my mother. Instead of showing his love for her, he was harsh and behaved like a man raised by wolves. Virile men are well accepted in society's lower classes but they will never make it with normal people because as soon as a person is slightly more intelligent and refined, he becomes humane, has emotions, and has actions which are more thought-out than simply scratching one's balls. I say "up yours" to all macho guys. (WC, No. 43612)

This young man bitterly expressed the dual oppression that he, like many others in his environment, suffered as a result of hegemonic masculinity and class oppression. We speculate that oppositional politics to the hegemonic form of masculinity would be more difficult to sustain in the working class due to more overt masculine displays, the threat of violence that might be encountered, and the comprehension that possibilities for

upward social mobility are very slight. On the other hand, these boys are also the most common victims of other men's violence and exploitation, so they have a material basis for opposing hegemonic masculinity.

Transforming hegemonic masculinity. A significant proportion of all boys (about 25%) communicated transformative views about hegemonic masculinity in their essays. Such tendencies usually were related to having the capacity to develop intimate and respectful relationships with others, particularly with women:

What is a virile guy? An intelligent guy who knows how to use his brains. A polite guy who knows how to be discreet. A sociable guy who knows how to weigh his words. A guy who knows how to court a lovely young woman without rushing her. A romantic guy. Not too much of a boaster. (MC, No. 29822)

We again found differences across the three social classes. Thoughtfulness, peacefulness or nonviolence, and respect for women were emphasized among some WC boys, who asserted an oppositional politics to the prevailing style of hegemonic masculinity:

He is an understanding guy with whom we can have fun. A guy who does not have [a] macho style. . . . He is rather the kind of guy who likes to mingle with good people, who, instead of using his muscles, will use his head and think before acting. He is the type of guy that a girl will say of him, he is decent, he has never harmed me in any way or done anything I did not want. (WC, No. 23812)

The larger proportion of MC boys (33% as opposed to 25% overall) explicating new definitions of the "real man" should be viewed cautiously, because many of them showed some ambivalence, especially with regard to gender equality. Although they advocated equality between the sexes, they also insisted on the necessity of maintaining differences and, furthermore, refrained from granting too much liberty:

A virile guy is a guy who can express his feelings and not physical strength. Because a man's real strength is not in his muscles but in his heart. . . . and he lets girls assume the place they deserve, *without however allowing them too much freedom.* (MLC, No. 31822, italics added)

One possible explanation for this ambivalence or apparent contradiction concerning gender relationships may come from the impression that women represent a threat to boys' longing for social advancement, especially because MC girls often do better in school than their male classmates (Bouchard & St-Amand, 1996). Because social and economic achievement are key factors in the construction of their masculine identity, the egalitarian values of the MC boys are mitigated by fear of competition from MC girls.

Emotional expressivity and greater concern for family life were more often advanced by UC boys (a masculine pattern often labeled *"homme rose"* [pink men] in the Francophone community):

He is a sensitive and affectionate guy; he can easily express his feelings. He respects people of his sex as well as those of the opposite sex. . . . He has much respect for women without being afraid of them. Family is very important for him. He respects his parents and pays attention to the advice of his friends (males and females). . . . He solves all his problems without physical intervention. . . . He solves all his problems without physical intervention. . . . He must be faithful to his girlfriend. (UC, No. 15132)

On one hand, it is possible that such expressions signify that a genuine shift is occurring among some of these boys in appraisals of what it is to be a man. On the other hand, it is feasible that their statements are merely an attempt to appear "politically correct." For instance, Hondagneu-Sotelo and Messner (1994) and Messner (1993) argued that recent emotionally expressive manifestations of masculinity are not a sign of counter hegemonic gender politics, but rather

a shift in personal styles and lifestyles of privileged men that eliminate or at least mitigate many of the aspects of "traditional masculinity" that men have found unhealthful or emotionally constraining. . . . These shifts in styles of masculinity do little, if any-

thing, to address issues of power and inequality raised by feminist women. (Messner, 1993, p. 728)

This interpretation is apposite to our UC group, although it would be necessary to conduct an in-depth field study of the boys' everyday practices to verify this thesis. Thus, we would concur with Messner's (1993) observation:

[Some men] would like to stop paying the "cost" of the hegemonic form of masculinity, but it does not necessarily signal a desire to cease benefiting from what Connell (1995) calls the "patriarchal dividend." Because the new, softer symbols of masculinity do not substantially address issues of gender inequality and men's power over women, it would rather suggest they represent a "modernization of hegemonic masculinity" (Carrigan et al., 1985, p. 596) rather than a real desire for transformation in the structure of power. (p. 730)

In this first section, we have explored the symbols or signifiers that adolescents from different social classes associate with masculinity. A content analysis based on the categories of reproduction, resistance, and transformation of the hegemonic masculinity has shown that the gender symbols of masculinity are contradictory and that the differing conceptions of maleness serve as ground for oppositions and power relations between the adolescent boys. Moreover, we found that social class and gender interacted. Indeed, distinctive emphases on particular signifiers of masculinity showed different stakes according to social class and diverse positions in the power structure.

Transgressing the Gender Regime of Sport

This section focuses on the second process identified by Harding (1986), gender structure. The gendered structure of sport is conspicuously evident in "sport typing" (Kane, 1995), by which some activities are defined as exclusively male (e.g., football, boxing) or female (e.g. synchronized swimming, rhythmic gymnastic), or, within the same sport, different rules or modalities of play are set up (e.g., tennis, figure skating). What happens when this dualistic gender structure is challenged, as in the case of men venturing into so-called women's sports and vice versa? To what extent does overstepping gender boundaries contest or transform the binary structure of sport and eventually erode gender stereotypes? The third and fourth topics suggested for the student essays were aimed at investigating such issues. We first examine the boys' appraisals of men participating in women's sports to ascertain whether they believe that transgressions of the gender regime affect masculinity. Second, we contrast their judgments about men's transgressions with their beliefs about women's trespasses. Third, we briefly consider the girls' appraisal of men's transgressive acts. Finally, we examine connections between the opposing conceptions of masculinity and the contrasting appraisals of transgressions. This allows us to analyze the links between gender symbolism and gender structure, as well as the internal contradictions that surround masculinity.

Boys' Judgments of Men's Trangresssions

To highlight the wide range of stances with regard to men playing a women's sport, we classified the boys' comments into those that were perceived to be threatening and nonthreatening to masculinity. The argument most frequently used to support perceived threats to masculinity was that participating in a women's sport prevented men from developing their inherent physical prowess:

A guy who plays women's sports looks less virile. A real guy must be sturdy and strong. He cannot develop these characteristics in the majority of sports for girls. Strength is THE characteristic of men, while beauty is THE characteristic of the feminine girl. . . . For me, a guy who plays football or ice hockey will always be more virile than one who figure skates or does aerobic dance. Figure skating is a very nice and difficult sport; however, guys who play it look less virile. (UC, No. 16832)

Similarly, other boys felt that it was simply unnatural for men to engage in such unorthodox behavior:

But I cannot deny that they are less virile since they are more gracious and less "brutal." We try to get rid of

stereotypes and that is why we do sports of the other sex. *However, we forget that these stereotypes were created by nature which has made guys larger and more sturdy and girls smaller and more gracious.* (UC, No. 05732, italics added)

Moreover, men who crossed over gender boundaries were assigned an inferior status:

When I see a guy who figure skates, I have ideas much more pejorative than when I see a guy who dances. I don't know why it is like that but in general, *I have a tendency to treat men who do women's sports as inferior to others.* (UC, No. 14332, italics added)

With regard to the nonthreatening stance to masculinity, two main arguments were invoked. First, men participating in women's sports were nonetheless perceived to display physical prowess:

A guy who figures skates is a virile guy because he must be in as good a shape as a guy who plays ice hockey, and maybe more because when he has a partner, he must be careful not to drop her when he "throws" her in the air: A lot of power is needed to catch her. I find seeing this quite fantastic. It is very virile. (MC, No. 36722)

Second, some boys claimed that each individual has the right to do what he wants:

It does not mean that because he is involved in a sport "reserved" for girls, that he does [it like] a girl. I do not find him more "queer" than me or than another guy because it is what he likes to do and I do not have the right to stop him from doing what he likes to do, like he does not have the right to stop me from mountain biking. (MC, No. 32422)

Table 12.3 shows that here are class differences between stances of the WC, MC, and UC boys toward transgressive acts, with two thirds of the WC boys believing that involvement in women's sport threatens masculinity, whereas MC and UC boys were split almost equally between a positive and a negative appraisal.

Two out of three of the WC boys considered women's sports to be inappropriate for men. The main reasons given for this view were that these

TABLE 12.3

Boys' Judgments of Men's Transgressions in Sport as a Threat to Masculinity, by Type of School Attended (in Percentages)

	Judgments of Men's Transgressions in Sport as a Threat to Masculinity	
Type of School Attended	Threatening	Nonthreatening
Public School in working-class neighborhood (*n* = 55)	67	33
Public School in middle-class neighborhood (*n* = 54)	48	52
Private School in affluent neighborhood (*n* = 65)	46	54
Total (N = 174)	53	47

sports either did not require physical strength or did not have competitive objectives:

A guy who does women's sports looks totally ridiculous. When I watch him in action, I cannot stop laughing at him. If we take, for example, aerobic dance, this type of sport does not work for guys as girls do this sport to maintain their figure or to look pretty. (WC, No. 24312)

The dominant logic here was that men participating in a women's sport were associated with women, "queers," or "fags":

For me, a guy who participates in women's sports is a fag who cannot express himself in men's sports like ice hockey where one must use one's physique. Women's sports are for girls and guys who take part in them look less virile because a virile guy is one who has character and physical strength, and who would never dare play a women's sport where there is hardly any physical contact or challenge. (WC, No. 24112)

A guy who plays women's sports is less virile because he ruins his male image. For me he is only a fag and he disgraces our reputation. (WC, No. 19712)

WC boys expressed a considerable amount of verbal violence against homosexuals. This might be due to the fact that their previously noted hyper-

masculine style makes breaches of gender boundaries in sport particularly formidable for them. We also might speculate that (as Messner, 1992b, has demonstrated) the social significance that men attach to sport varies by social class, so it is possible that sport plays an especially potent role in the construction of masculinity among WC boys.

Despite some boys' endorsement of a dualistic gendering of sport, about half of the MC and the UC boys asserted that masculinity was not affected by transgressive acts in sport. However, the reason most frequently put forward was different for the two social groups. MC usually gave a "freedom of choice" account:

I believe a guy who likes his sport (whatever it may be) has the right to play it without being called a homosexual. In fact, he is not less virile, because a sport is a sport and anybody who wants to play it may do so without being finger pointed. (MC, No 29222)

This statement suggests a desire to depart from the conventional gender dualism in sport. Yet, it might also constitute what some feminists have termed "a liberal 'gloss' on a generally more conventional outlook" (Kraus, as quoted in Messner, 1993, p. 726), as Hearn and Morgan (1990) contend:

Even when men are developing a consciousness of their gender identity and a desire to challenge gender ideologies, the basis of these desires often appears to be more in terms of abstract principles or general political programmes than direct experience. (p. 15)

Because the boys' open-mindedness does not seem to lie within the scope of the feminist project of social transformation, we would be more inclined to interpret it as a liberal veneer that does not seriously challenge the status quo between men, and between men and women in the gender structure.

The main argument supporting men's transgressive behavior among UC boys consisted of connected ideas about corporeal and moral strength:

Fag, wimp, sissy are only some of the insulting names that guys practicing women's sports must sustain. Figure skating, gymnastics, and aerobic dance are sports that are physically demanding. I support a hundred percent the guys who have the courage to undertake those sports. It is only machos who laugh at the men who play these sports. I would like to see them doing only half of what the others do. (UC, No. 03832)

These accounts suggest a kind of "ideological recycling" of symbols associated with hegemonic masculinity. Moral strength (in this case for facing stigmatization and discrediting by peers) and physical prowess are used as proof of masculinity, thereby "legitimating" transgressive behavior. This reinforces rather than contests the hierarchical and dualistic gender configuration of sport, as men are still considered both different and superior even when they are involved in a traditionally women's arena. Moreover, the reference to physical and mental strength to support a positive appraisal of transgressions may be construed as a strategy for the members of the dominant class to overcome the paradox of maintaining and reconstructing their cultural and structural dominance over women while preserving their image of gender equality promoter. Once again, boys' assessments of transgressions demonstrate that social class contributes to the construction of various masculinities: The strong stigmatization of transgressions among WC boys is congruent with the hypermasculine style prevailing in this milieu; the "neutral-safe" rhetoric of the MC boys is consonant with a logic of individual rights; and the ideological recuperation of traditional markers of hegemonic masculinity by the UC respondents is congruent with their affirmation of greater gender equality while still clinging to the status quo.

Boys' Judgments of Men's and Women's Transgressions

As noted, we also compared (a) the boys' appraisals of men participating in women's sports with their evaluations of women taking part in men's sports and (b) the boys' and girls' assessments of men's transgressions. Because of space limitations, we give only a brief account of these two sets of data.

Sixty percent of the boys indicated that transgressive sportswomen did not threaten femininity, compared with 47% who claimed that transgressive men threatened masculinity (see Table 12.4). Argument supporting women's transgressions included items like "She is as feminine as any other woman"; "She will even be more sexy, because she will be in better shape"; "It's OK if she's still feminine after playing sports"; and "She has the right to do what she wants, without any harm to her femininity." Forty percent of the boys considered women's trangressions to be a threat to femininity, compared with 53% who believed that transgressions by men threatened masculinity. Arguments against women transgressors were mainly posed in terms of "It's not their place," "They behave like men," "It depends on the sport," and outright sexism.

Because the judgments on men and on women may not necessarily be symmetric for the same individual, we examined the symmetry/asymmetry within each boy's writing in more depth. Table 12.4 indicates that, overall, a higher percentage (22%) were asymmetric in being negative for men and positive for women, compared with only 9% asymmetry in the reverse sense. Lamar and Kite (1998) found similar asymmetry in men's attitudes toward

TABLE 12.4

Symmetry/Asymmetry in Boys' Judgments of Men's and Women's Transgressions in Sport, by Type of School Attended (in Percentages)

| | Judgments of Men's and Women's Transgressions in Sport | | | |
Type of School Attended	Positive for Men and for Women	Negative for Men and for Women	Positive for Men/Negative for Women	Negative for Men/Positive for Women
Public school in working-class neighborhood (*n* = 55)	27	47	6	20
Public school in middle-class neighborhood (*n* = 54)	43	26	9	22
Private school in affluent neighborhood (*n* = 65)	43	23	11	23
Total (N = 174)	38	31	9	22

gay men and toward lesbians, the former being more negative than the latter.

The following comments were typical of boys from all three social classes:

Men's transgression: A guy who plays a women's sport is not a "real" guy. Women's sports are finesse sports mostly based on movement. Men's sports are mostly rough, with physical contact and strategy. A guy who plays a women's sport is, therefore, weak, a weakling who does not want to hurt himself. He is less virile than others. . . . Men's sport is contact, strategy, fast thinking. Therefore, I believe that a guy who does women's sports is less intelligent.

Women's transgression: A girl who does men's sports is not the same. She is less feminine but there is a place for them. . . . *Girls can dare participate in men's sports because they are weaker than boys but guys cannot do women's sports. This is degrading oneself!* (MC, No. 27022, italics added)

This gender asymmetry in the boys' appraisal of sportive transgressions highlights their valorization of so-called men's sports and their trivialization of so-called women's sports. Men's transgressions would signify an erosion of male superiority, whereas women's transgressions would signify tran-

scending women's weakness. This logic contributes largely to the resistance to a "degendering" (Connell, 1995; Harding, 1986) process among men and is a crucial issue in the politics of changing men.

One shortcoming of some feminist claims for equity is that they ask women to "exchange major aspects of their gender identity for the masculine version—without prescribing a similar 'degendering' process for men" (Harding, 1986, p. 53). Promoting a degendering process among men in sport would have to be effected via an undermining of the cultural supremacy of men's sports and of the forms of bodily practices associated with hegemonic masculinity, while enhancing the status of women's sports and of bodily practices associated with femininity. Indeed, masculine hegemony is not simply a product of the things men do but also of the meanings their activities acquire through unequal social interactions.

Boys' and Girls' Appraisals of Men's Transgressions

There were striking differences between the boys and girls, especially in attending the school in the

TABLE 12.5

Boys' and Girls' Judgments of Men's Transgressions in Sport as a Threat to Masculinity, by Type of School Attended (in Percentages)

Type of School Attended	Judgments of Men's Transgressions in Sport as a Threat to Masculinity	
	Threatening	Nonthreatening
Public school in working-class neighborhood		
Boys ($n = 55$)	67	33
Girls ($n = 63$)	36	64
Public school in middle-class neighborhood		
Boys ($n = 54$)	48	52
Girls ($n = 63$)	26	74
Private school in affluent neighborhood		
Boys ($n = 65$)	46	54
Girls ($n = 54$)	22	78

NOTE: The gender difference was statistically significant at $p < .001$.

WC district, with respect to how men's transgressions affected masculinity (see Table 12.5).

Following is a girl's telling expression of valorization of men's participation in women's sports:

As far as I am concerned, there is no difference between boys who play women's sports and those who play men's sports. It's great if, in spite of the various prejudices, a boy has a positive attitude in this regard. I would be proud of him, and I would be proud to show to the other guys that he is not a "sissy" because he wants to engage in a women's sport. We need equality between genders, and to obtain it we [need to] begin by involving men in our sports. (WC, No. 40511)

The greater openness displayed by girls in all three schools toward men's transgressions represents what Bourdieu (1979/1984) terms a "logic of equality" commonly found in subordinated groups.

Interestingly, in a survey we conducted within the current research program, we also found a stronger positive attitude among the girls toward coeducation in physical education classes (Laberge, 1969). Although gender integration in sport is still a controversial issue among feminist scholars (Birrell, 1984; Kane, 1995), we speculate that it can constitute a worthwhile avenue for the degendering of sport and other gendered bodily practices, as well as for the transformation of unequal gender relations.

Nonetheless, we cannot ignore the substantial proportion of girls in every school (36%, 26%, and 22%, respectively) who believed that men's participation in women's sports affected masculinity in a negative fashion, thereby contributing to the maintenance of hegemonic masculinity in sport. The reconstruction of the larger gender order depends to some extent on the collusion of certain women with hegemonic masculinity and their endorsement of dualistic gender stereotypes. In this regard, women, like other dominated groups, sometimes actively participate in their own subordination.

Relationships Between Boys' Conceptions of Masculinity and Men's Transgressions

In the final stage in our analysis, we explore a possible connection between the boys' different conceptions of masculinity and their opinions of

TABLE 12.6
Boys' Judgments of Men's Transgressions in Sport, by Their Conception of Masculinity
(in Percentages)

Conception of Hegemonic Masculinity	Judgments of Men's Transgressions in Sport as a Threat to Masculinity	
	Threatening	Nonthreatening
Reproductive ($n = 91$)	69	31
Resistant ($n = 39$)	33	67
Transformative ($n = 44$)	39	61
Total ($N = 174$)	53	47

NOTE: The relation was statistically significant at $p < .001$.

men's transgressions. As expected, there were relatively strong differences with respect to how "reproductive," "resistant," and "transformative" boys viewed the threats that men's transgressions posed to hegemonic masculinity (see Table 12.6). This may indicate the intimate connections between the processes of gender symbolism and gender structure that construct gendered social life. But this pattern does not seem to be systematic within individuals, as there were differences among the boys.

In the case of the boys who endorse hegemonic masculinity, just fewer than one third claimed that transgressions did not threaten masculinity. Closer scrutiny of their appraisals revealed that physical and moral strength were the two main arguments that they invoked:

For me, that has nothing to do with virility, because I know that most so-called "women's sports" are at least as demanding as the so-called "men's sports." For example, ballet dancing is one of the most demanding sports at the muscular level, and so are figure skating and gymnastics. I, myself, did some aerobic dance and believe me, when I started, I found it as exhausting as the physical conditioning I had done for football. (UC, No. 08732)

A guy who does women's sports is as masculine as he would be if he practiced men's sports. In fact, he could even be more masculine that the other guys who participate in men's sports because he must have a strong character in order to play a women's sport because other guys could see him as "inferior." (UC, No. 13432)

As noted, this appeal to physical and moral strength is in line with the hegemonic form of masculinity, thereby suggesting and "ideological recycling" with regard to gender politics. Therefore, the contradiction found here seems to be more apparent than substantive.

However, the data also showed a contradiction among the boys who either mentioned resisting or transforming hegemonic masculinity and their claims that men's transgressions threatened masculinity (33% and 39%, respectively). For the boys who showed some resistance to hegemonic masculinity, this contradiction appeared more frequently in the WC group:

I find that guys that do women's sports are not respected by the other guys. It's true, they look less virile. So what? It is their choice. They have the right to do as they wish, they must learn not to listen to what other guys tell them, like for example, when they are called fag, idiot, girlie. (WC, No. 22312)

This ambivalent appraisal shows both a denunciation of prejudices, alongside a relative compliance with the gender regime that fosters these prejudices. Although the boy believes that this sport practice makes the boys "look less virile," he also seems to approve of, and encourage, boys' participation in women's sports, the latter view being more in line with his contestation of the hegemonic form of masculinity. Given the hypermasculine ethos of the working class, participation in women's sports is unlikely to be viewed as an enticing proposition for men.

For the boys who sought a transformation of hegemonic masculinity, this contradiction appeared more often in the MC and UC groups. In reading the following excerpts, one should keep in mind that the boys did propose counterhegemonic interpretations of masculinity in previous lines of their essays:

Writing high-class moral principles would be very nice, very elegant, but would be very hypocritical. Excuse the expression, but a guy who does women's sports is a fag, a queer, a brown pusher. Why? I find it impossible to explain. This idea was instilled in me by the people in my social environment; society carved it in my head. For a long time, this idea has been deeply carved in my skull and the worst part of it is that I really believe that a guy who does a women's sport is a faggot; what can I say! The power of society's pressures on us! Incredible but true! (UC, No. 03132)

I do not want to be sexist, but I will not perceive as virile a guy who plays women's sports; it is my first impression. If I had known a guy for a long time and he started to do women's sports, I would ask myself some questions but I would respect his choice.
(MC, No 36422)

These tensions suggest that (a) gendered practices, particularly bodily ones, are more resistant to change than are gender symbols; and (b) gendered practices play a pivotal role in the construction of social life.

Gender symbolism worked at a general and abstract level, whereas gender structure immediately affects the meanings of one's experience and one's social interaction. Moreover, these findings attest to the complexity of the articulation of gender symbolism and gender structure within individual subjectivity and the contradictory layerings of an individual's gender identity.

CONCLUSION

This study has shown that the construction of hegemonic masculinity is neither seamless nor unproblematic but a relational and conflictive process that is marked by differences, power relations, and ambivalence. In summing up, we emphasize two major points.

First, the differences and tensions we observed among the three groups of boys suggest that class milieus interweave with gender at both the symbolic and structural levels. Beyond a core of similarities, the image of hegemonic masculinity propounded by the three groups revealed nuances that were closely linked to the specific material conditions in which they arose: Leadership was valued more highly in the UC setting, sociability was more important for MC boys, and hypermasculine displays were prominent in the WC Group. Reciprocally, gender symbolism was found to contribute to class politics, in that class-specific signs of hegemonic masculinity were used by the UC boys to reassert their cultural dominance. Likewise, resistance to hegemonic masculinity was shaped by intraclass gender politics, as the UC and MC boys stood mainly on classic liberal grounds, and the WC group was more concerned with deploring the social problems caused by hegemonic patterns of masculinity in their daily lives. Neither did the purportedly transformative and progressive versions of masculinity escape class influences—their emphases were congruent with specific class interests and intraclass gendered power relationships.

Appraisals of transgresssions of the gender regime of sport showed the interaction between class and gender more conspicuously. For instance, the pronounced stigmatization of transgressions by the WC boys is congruent with the hypermasculine style that prevails in this context. Although MC and UC boys showed comparably greater openness to men's transgressions in sport, their reasonings were based on a distinctive social logic that was clearly grounded in class interest. The liberal stance that generally predominates in the middle class likely inspired the boys' stronger appeal to individual rights in support of their positive assessment of men's transgressions, a position that is not at odds with their concern for social and economic mobility. As for the UC group, the ideological recycling of the symbols of hegemonic masculinity, which legitimized men's transgressions, points to their contradictory stakes as a dominant group—maintaining the status quo in gender and class relations while adopting the image of gender equality promoter.

Our findings confirm the contribution that a materialist analysis can make to the understanding of the social construction of gender. As Messner (1996) put it, "[M]aterialist analysis reveals how differential access to resources, opportunities, and different relationship to structural constraints shape the contests in which people think, interact and construct political practice and discourse" (p. 228). It must be stressed that we are not privileging class over gender in our analysis. To the contrary, we are advocating a nonhierarchical theorizing, one "that allow[s] us to conceptualize varied and shifting forms of domination in such a way that we do not privilege one at the expense of distorting or ignoring the others" (Messner & Sabo, 1990, p. 10). In this regard, it seems important to examine how interactions between gender and other hierarchical symbols and structures (e.g., race, ethnicity, and sexuality) shape our beliefs and practices about gender. This approach might cast light on the complexity observed in the gender-class dynamic and, hence, provide further evidence against a theory that would advocate the autonomy of gender relations.

A second key finding relates to the boys' appraisal of men's transgressive behavior in sport. The strong negative appraisal of men's transgressions appeared both in their contrasts with women's transgressions and via those boys who contested hegemonic masculinity but perceived men's transgressions as a threat to masculinity. These results point to the boy's reluctance toward degendering

and, hence, the development of any meaningful transformative potential.

Nonetheless, we concur with Connell (1995) and Harding (1986), and with many feminist scholars, in asserting that a strict degendering strategy may involve important flaws—one being that it means sameness and the loss of positive elements of both men's and women's culture. Degendering also could result in the disparagement of transgressors and a failure to dismantle either the binary opposites of gender hierarchies or the intramale pecking order. To counter the first shortcoming, Connell (1995) proposed a "degendering-recomposing" strategy that is intimately linked to a project of social justice (p. 234). Another shortcoming of a simplistic degendering strategy, given how many boys (and significant numbers of girls) held negative attitudes toward men who participated in women's sports, is that it can underplay the crucial importance of "meaning" in gender politics. As we have stressed, masculine hegemony is not simply a product of men's practices but is closely linked with the connotations their activities acquire through unequal social interactions.

Thus, we argue that a necessary condition for a degendering strategy to work in a transformative fashion in sport is for it to be grounded in a collective project that contests naturalized assumptions about sportsmen's alleged superiority and sportswomen's purported inferiority. Moreover, we believe that a degendering strategy inspired by a "politics of meaning" must be implemented not only at the symbolic and structural levels but also, and perhaps primarily, at the level of the body, the material basis of individual identity—"the ground chosen by defenders of patriarchy, where the fear of men being turned into women is most poignant" (Connell, 1995, p. 232). In this regard, sport practices may represent a powerful site of contestation. Ultimately, what is at stake in a degendering strategy is power in a context of inequality. Indeed , to the extent that genders structure our perceptions and organize social life, they also serve to distribute power, that is, differential control over, and/or access to, material and symbolic resources.

NOTES

1. Ringette is a relatively recent sport that originated in Ontario and was designed as an alternative to ice hockey for girls. Although it was played almost exclusively by girls, there is now a growing interest among boys to try the game.

2. All quotations have been translated from French. Because most of the essays were written in vernacular language, close attention has been paid to ensuring that the students' comments correspond as closely as possible to their original meaning.

3. The term *macho* has long been part of the vernacular French of Québec, although its users are not necessarily familiar with its ethnic reference to Latino and Latin American men. It has become a hackneyed word whose referent varies greatly among users. However, it generally conforms to Klein's (1995b) definition: men's propensity to "dominate and control through sexuality, fighting, and other forms of competitive behavior" (p. 371).

REFERENCES

Adams, M. L. (1993). To be an ordinary hero: Male figure skaters and the ideology of gender. In T. Haddad (Ed.), *Men and masculinities* (pp. 163–181). Toronto: Canadian Scholars Press.

Birrell, S. (1984). Separatism as an issue in women's sports. *Arena Review, 8,* 21–29.

Bouchard, P., & St-Amand, P. (1996). *Garçons et filles: Stéréotypes et réussite scolaire* [Boys and girls: Stereotypes and academic success]. Montréal, Canada: Les Editions du remue-ménage.

Bourdieu, P. (1984). *Distinction: A social critique of the judgment of taste* (R. Nice, Trans.). Cambridge, MA: Harvard University Press. (Original work published 1979.)

Brod, H. (Ed.). (1987). *The making of masculinities: The new men's studies.* Boston: Allyn & Bacon.

Carrigan, T., Connell, B., & Lee, J. (1985). Toward a new sociology of masculinity. *Theory and Society, 14,* 551–604.

Collinson, D. L. (1988). Engineering humor: Masculinity, joking and conflict in shop-floor relations. *Organization Studies, 9,* 181–199.

Connell, R. W. (1987). *Gender and power: Society, the person, and sexual politics.* Stanford, CA: Stanford University Press.

Connell, R. W. (1990). An iron man: The body and some contradictions of hegemonic masculinity. In M. Messner & D. Sabo (Eds.), *Sport, men, and the gender order: Critical feminist perspectives* (pp. 83–96). Champaign, IL: Human Kinetics.

Connell, R. W. (1993). The big picture: Masculinities in recent world history. *Theory and Society, 22,* 597–625.

Connell, R. W. (1995). *Masculinities.* Berkeley: University of California Press.

Davis, L. R. (1990). Male cheerleaders and the naturalization of gender. In M. Messner & D. Sabo (Eds.) *Sport, men and the gender order: Critical feminist perspectives* (pp. 153–161). Champaign, IL: Human Kinetics.

Dunning, E. (1986). Sport as a male preserve: Notes on the social sources of masculinity and its transformations. In N. Elias & E. Dunning (Eds.), *Quest for excitement: Sport and leisure in the civilizing process* (pp. 267–283). Oxford, UK: Basil Blackwell.

Goodey, J. (1997). Boys don't cry: Masculinities, fear of crime and fearlessness, *British Journal of Criminology, 37,* 401–418.

Harding. S. (1986). *The science question in feminism.* Ithaca, NY: Cornell University Press.

Hearn, J., & Collinson, D. L. (1994). Theorizing unities and differences between men and between masculinities. In H. Brod & M. Kaufman (Eds.), *Theorizing masculinities* (pp. 97–118). Thousand Oaks, CA: Sage.

Hearn, J., & Morgan, D. (1990). Men, masculinities and social theory. In J. Hearn & D. Morgan (Eds.), *Men, masculinities and social theory* (pp. 1–18). Winchester, MA: Unwin Hyman.

Hodagneu-Sotelo, P., & Messner, M. A. (1994). Gender displays and men's power: The "new man" and the Mexican immigrant man. In H. Brod & M. Kaufman (Eds.), *Theorizing masculinities* (pp. 200–218). Thousand Oaks, CA: Sage.

Kane, M. J. (1995). Resistance/transformation of the oppositional binary: Exposing sport as a continuum. *Journal of Sport and Social Issues, 19*, 191–218.

Kimmel, M. S. (1987a). *Changing men: New directions in research on men and masculinity.* Newbury Park, CA: Sage.

Kimmel, M. S. (1987b). Men's responses to feminism at the turn of the century: 1880–1920. *Gender and Society, 1*, 261–283.

Klein, A. (1995b). Tender machos: Masculine contrasts in the Mexican baseball league. *Sociology of Sport Journal, 12*, 370–388.

Laberge, S. (1996, September). *La mixité dans les cours d'éducation physique au secondaire: Un contexte émancipatoire ou aliénant pour les adolescentes* [Coeducation in high school physical education classes: An emancipating or alienating context for adolescent girls]. Paper presented at the International Symposium on Feminist Research, Université Laval, Québec, Canada.

Lamar, L., & Kite, M. (1998). Sex differences in attitudes toward gay men and lesbians–A multidimensional perspective. *Journal of Sex Research, 35*, 189–196.

Majors, R., & Billson, J. M. (1992). *Cool pose: The dilemmas of black manhood in America.* Lexington, MA: Lexington Books.

Messner, M. A. (1990b). Masculinities and athletic careers: Bonding and status differences. In M. Messner & D. Sabo (Eds.), *Sport, men and the gender order: Critical feminist perspectives* (pp. 97–108). Champaign, IL: Human Kinetics.

Messner, M. (1990d). When bodies are weapons: Masculinity and violence in sport. *International Review for the Sociology of Sport, 25*, 203–218.

Messner, M. A. (1993). Changing men" and feminist politics in the United States. *Theory and Society, 22*, 723–737.

Messner, M. (1994). Women in the men's locker room? In M. Messner & D. Sabo (Eds.), *Sex, violence and power in sport* (pp. 42–52). Freedom, CA: Crossing.

Messner, M. A. (1996). Studying up on sex. *Sociology of Sport Journal, 13*, 221–237.

Messner, M. A., & Sabo D. (Eds.). (1990). *Sport, men and the gender order: Critical feminist perspectives.* Champaign, IL: Human Kinetics.

Morgan, D. (1992). *Discovering men.* Boston: Routledge & Kegan Paul.

Poole, M. (1996). Being a man and becoming a nurse: Three men's stories. *Journal of Gender Studies, 5*, 39–47.

Theberge, N. (1995). Gender, sport, and the social construction of community: A case study from women's ice hockey. *Sociology of Sport Journal, 12*, 389–403.

37

"Buddies" or "Slutties"

The Collective Sexual Reputation of Fraternity Little Sisters

Mindy Stombler

FRATERNITY LITTLE SISTERS, SOMETIMES CALLED "sweethearts," are undergraduate women affiliated with a men's social fraternity; they typically serve the fraternity in a "hostess" or "booster" capacity. Fraternity men select women to be little sisters on the basis of beauty and sociability, following a rush process modeled after fraternity men's rush.[1] Rushees attend parties or interest meetings for several days and, if selected, go through a pledge period and are subsequently initiated as quasi-members of the fraternity (Stombler and Martin 1994).

In general, women say they join little sister groups for social reasons—to meet men, make friends, attend parties and other social activities, feel like a member of a "family," connect to campus life, and have fun. Compared to sororities, little sister organizations provide a less structured social environment and are substantially less expensive; yet they still allow women to be part of the Greek system (Stombler and Martin 1994).[2] Fraternity members sponsor many social events, maintain a high level of status on campus, and publicly display their affection and "respect"[3] for the women in their little sister program. Because fraternity men often dominate the top positions of student government, service organizations, and intramural sports, women affiliated as fraternity

From *Gender and Society*, Vol. 8, #3, September 1994, pp. 297–323. Copyright © 1994 by Sage Publications. Reprinted by permission of Sage Publications, Inc.

little sisters may gain valued resources through their association with a fraternity (Stombler and Martin 1994).

For the first two decades they were in existence, fraternity little sister programs received little scrutiny on college campuses. In recent years, however, such programs gained notoriety after the national media began associating them with gang and acquaintance rapes by fraternity men in the late 1980s (see Martin and Hummer 1989; Sanday 1990; Stombler and Martin 1994); consequently, many university administrators and national and local fraternity organizations have disbanded little sister programs. National fraternity organizations cite increased insurance rates, possible loss of legal gender-segregated organizational status, diversion of resources away from chapter operations, disharmony among brothers, and distraction of chapter members from the performance of essential duties as reasons to disband little sister programs. Nevertheless, according to national fraternity and sorority organizations and university administrators, each semester thousands of women on college campuses across the country continue to "rush" these organizations.

Little sisters participate in selected activities and certain rituals of a specific fraternity, but they enjoy neither full membership status in the fraternity nor the privileges and levels of participation that accompany it. Fraternity men's denial of the individual and collective rights that accompany full membership is at the core of the system of exploitation in fraternity little sister organizations (Martin and Stombler 1993). Fraternity organizational structures and the practices of members institutionalize the disempowerment of women on campus (Martin and Stombler 1993; Stombler and Martin 1994). Among the consequences of this exploitation are the sexual objectification, exploitation, and abuse of little sisters.

THEORETICAL ISSUES

An analysis of sexual dynamics is central to understanding the creation and maintenance of gender inequality. In general, men develop the rules or scripts for both men's and women's interaction as gendered, sexual beings. Men set the standards for interaction and valued behavior (French 1985; MacKinnon 1987; Millett 1970) and define femininity as (1) women's sexual attractiveness and availability to men and (2) women's sexuality in general (Bartky 1990; Jaggar 1983; MacKinnon 1989; Millett 1970). Both definitions of femininity are essential to creating and maintaining gender inequality (MacKinnon 1989).

Sexual objectification is a fundamental process in maintaining male dominance (Bartky 1990; MacKinnon 1989; Schur 1988). Sexual objectification, as a "ritual of subjugation" (Bartky 1990), is a "material reality" in women's lives (MacKinnon 1989; Schur 1988). Men expect women to titillate them, even under circumstances that are not overtly sexual. Men negatively sanction women who fail to express their sexuality in ways that please them. This sets the stage for a structurally induced sense of powerlessness and dependency and for women's acceptance of their own sexual objectification; indeed, some women seem to enjoy and even cultivate the object role.

Both on and off the college campus, women's everyday lives and peer relationships are subject to male domination. More pernicious than sexist school authorities, policies, and materials in the transmission of male privilege, the heterosexual peer group plays a crucial role in transmitting traditional gender relations (Cowie and Lees 1981;

Gwartney-Gibbs and Stockard 1989; Handler 1993; Holland and Eisenhart 1990; Lees 1986; Martin and Hummer 1989; Sanday 1990). Through their peer associations, college women come to value sex and love over scholarly goals. They learn that their attractiveness to men—and the status that accompanies attaining a "boyfriend"—is an integral part of their self-worth (Holland and Eisenhart 1990). For these reasons, a focus on organizational sites where traditional peer relations thrive and where the sexual objectification of women is a naturalized part of organizational structure and ideology is an important one.

Campus organizations have the ability to structure the informal peer culture that promotes a male definition of women's identity. Fraternity little sister programs are formal organizations in the sense that many women participate, elect officers, and hold meetings; yet most campus officials and national fraternity officials do not formally recognize them.

METHODS AND DATA

Data for this article come from open-ended in-depth interviews, participant observation, official reports and documents, and newspaper articles. Interview and participant observation data come from the campuses of five public universities in three states in the Southeast.

I interviewed 21 women of traditional college age who were little sisters from eight men's social fraternities.

I conducted participant observation at one fraternity, where I observed little sister rush, several parties and social events, and an orientation meeting of newly chosen little sisters. Because I played a "naive student role," I had several little sisters act as tour guides through their world. To observe little sister/fraternity brother interaction on another campus, I also attended intramural sports events where fraternity members participate.

Archival data consist of official inquiry and commission reports about fraternities, sororities, and little sister organizations; local and national fraternity and sorority publications; local and national newspaper articles; and nationally televised reports of and talk show transcripts on sexual assault involving fraternity little sisters.

I used the grounded theory method to analyze these data, organizing the findings around the concepts generated using this specific method (Glaser 1978, 1992; . . . Martin and Turner 1986; Strauss and Corbin 1990; Turner 1981).

COLLECTIVE SEXUAL REPUTATION

Although women were aware of some negative images of the little sister program before they rushed, they decided to rush anyway. Aside from feeling unappreciated, little sisters cited their collective sexual reputation as the most troublesome aspect of their participation in the program. *Collective sexual reputation* refers to the negative characterization of women who participate in little sister programs as sexually active and available to fraternity men. Fraternity little sisters and fraternity brothers used words like "slut," "whore," "loose," and "promiscuous" to describe women who supposedly had sex with multiple fraternity men or who consented "too easily" or "too quickly" to having sex, according to respondents' standards.

A nearly universal aspect of the little sister collective sexual reputation was that little sisters were required to or chose to become sexually active with one or more fraternity brother. Virtually all women were aware of this reputation before they joined little sister organizations:

I remember hearing that you had to sleep with a brother to get in, which wasn't true. I heard [I would have to sleep with] a brother, all the brothers, everything. The reputation of the sweethearts is the same on both campuses. Wherever you go, I don't care, they say the same thing, "y'all have to sleep with the brothers" or "how many brothers have you slept with," all that stuff. It's always sexual.

Little Sisters' Explanation of Their Negative Reputation

Women in little sister programs identified several sources of their collective sexual reputation. Some claimed it was the result of non-Greek or non-little sisters' distorted view of reality; thus the negative little sister reputation was either a result of outsiders' active imagination or their jealousy:

If you're not inside an organization, you don't know what the hell is going on, and people talk because they're jealous because they didn't get picked or because their friends didn't get picked. The brothers tell us that now that you're in this organization a lot of other girls aren't going to like you because you got picked over their friend or them. It's just jealousy. They're going to start making up rumors. They won't look at the whole picture, the organization as a whole.

Some women in little sister programs cited historical antecedents to their collective reputation in order to explain it. They spoke of an ancient past when little sisters had unsavory motivations for joining the program (i.e., solely to have sex with the brothers) or when women were abused by fraternity men. One little sister explained:

Maybe a long time ago girls got into this because it was either the thing to do or they want to get with [have sex with] brothers. Our brothers are known for being playboys or "pretty boys." That is their reputation. Yes, some of them are very cute. Maybe a lot of the girls in the past joined so that they could always be around them or so they can try and date one.

In addition to attributing their current reputation to the dishonorable motivations of past little sisters, little sisters explained the content of the little sister reputation by mentally reworking past events that may have tainted their collective image. One little sister dismissed an incident in her fraternity where a brother filmed a woman, without her knowledge, in a sex act, and later sent the videotape to her mother. An important part of her story was her conviction that the woman was not a little sister. Little sisters denied the premeditation inherent in videotaping and interpreted it as an incident that "got out of hand"; moreover, by portraying the incident as an event of the distant past, the woman who recounted the story trivialized it. By conceptualizing events such as tapes or filmed sex as part of an unsavory distant history, little sisters denied the possibility that the structure of fraternities continued to facilitate such unacceptable and illegal behavior (cf. Martin and Hummer 1989).

Other little sisters too, clung to the familial title of "little sister" and the protective assumptions that accompanied it, even if this meant denying fraternity men's unscrupulous motivations. Some women denied the existence of a negative collective sexual reputation altogether, as did this one:

On our campus little sisters are not viewed as whores. I know on some campuses that is the reputation. Every now and then maybe a whore does get it [chosen as a little sister] but that's just because on campus one out of every one hundred girls is a whore, so one of them is bound to get a jersey [be picked as a little sister].

Strategies Men and Women Use to Resist the Collective Sexual Reputation

Fraternity men and little sisters practiced various forms of damage control relating to the collective sexual reputation. One way little sisters in particular, and fraternities in general, combated their negative reputation was through community service and other "good press" activities. The women participated in fund-raising and community service events with the fraternity men. Some fraternity men and little sisters used linguistic strategies to resist the collective sexual reputation, the most obvious being the members' use of familial language to describe relationships within fraternities (e.g., little sisters, big brothers, line mommies and daddies).

Another strategy fraternity brothers and little sisters used was to disseminate information to potential little sister recruits that contradicted the "sluts" label. One fraternity staged a meeting where men and women confronted the reputation issue in an effort to invalidate the collective sexual reputation in the minds of potential little sister recruits. The brothers' (and veteran little sisters') strategy was effective because the women rushees who were skeptical continued to move forward in the little sister rush process at this fraternity.

A strategy that some women used to combat the collective sexual reputation was to monitor their own behavior and that of other women. Most little sisters were not sexually irresponsible and

they tried to downplay the actions of those few who were. Many ignored or ostracized women they defined as "promiscuous," priding themselves on their own nonpromiscuity. By castigating others, women cooperated with fraternity men by participating in the social control of other women.

Once in a fraternity, little sisters emphasized the importance of their own reputations as individual women. Women who did not comply with the fraternity men's unspecified standards were often tossed aside by both little sisters and fraternity brothers, victims of a "bad reputation." Women were put in a compromising situation where they needed men's approval and affection to gain and maintain status among their peers. Their ultimate value as women rested on protecting their individual reputation, which was formed by men in the fraternity.

In their efforts to preserve the integrity of their little sister organization's reputation, little sisters reacted strongly to the brothers' selection of women they labeled as "promiscuous." Little sisters recognized only a small group of little sisters as "bad." Fraternity men must carefully select the different types of little sisters they recruit.[4] If they choose too many women with bad individual reputations, they risk tarnishing their fraternity reputation.

SEXUAL OBJECTIFICATION: WOMEN AS COMMODITIES

One way fraternity brothers contributed to the collective sexual reputation of women in little sister programs was by sexually objectifying and commodifying them. The commodity form ignores the individual, making the commodification of women necessary for a negative collective reputation to exist. Without women's objectification and commodification, little sisters would become individual, identifiable, knowable women, each having an individual reputation; yet brothers were unwilling to have each woman regarded individually as promiscuous because individual little sisters dated individual brothers.

Evidence of the sexual objectification of little sisters was most vivid in the recruitment of male pledges to the fraternity (see Martin and Hummer 1989). Women were one form of fraternity "capital," who were valued as commodities—both in terms of quality and quantity. Fraternity men used pictures of little sisters and their presence at fraternity events, especially during rush week, to entice potential male pledges to their fraternity. By using these women as a resource in their recruitment strategy, fraternity men depersonalized and commodified them. Women became pieces of advertising for the fraternity, either in pictures or in the flesh. A fraternity little sister coordinator echoed the notion that little sisters attract male rushees to fraternities: "Guys come in and say, 'That larger chapter has all these women over there. I'm going to pledge there.'" Although this was in the fraternity men's best interest to sexually objectify and commodify women to do this, they could not allow this message to become too distasteful, discouraging potential little sister rushees or harming their fraternity reputation regarding their ability to attract what one fraternity man described as "classy" women.

Because women were a fraternity resource that drew men to a particular fraternity in much the same way that keg parties did, the message fraternity rushees received was that both beer and women were available for their consumption. One fraternity president, upset with the recent disbanding of little sister programs on his campus, compared alcohol to the power of little sisters to attract male pledges: "If you can't drink and can't have bands, the only thing you're looking for is girls, so it's a good thing if you've got girls" ("Dropping little sisters" 1990).

Little Sisters as Commodified Labor

Fraternity men often asked and even required little sisters to attend rush week at their fraternity. Some women accepted this request as legitimate and provided this and other services to the fraternity brothers in exchange for their own enhanced status and for male companionship. The currency of exchange was not monetary. Instead, this commodity form had special features: exchange value for little sisters was not a wage relation, but rather

status or access to men, whereas the use value for fraternities was a variety of supportive labor. Although not all little sisters accepted this arrangement willingly, those who did not rarely had the power to fight it (Stombler and Martin 1994). One woman complained about the expectation that she serve as a companion to men in a geishalike capacity and her lack of power to contest it within the fraternity culture:

Something that made me so mad was that when they would tell us to go up to the would-be pledge and make sure that he is having a good time. . . . [The brothers would say] "You know, dance with him or give him a drink or something or walk outside with him." I wouldn't complain about this in front of everybody. I wouldn't stand up at a little sister meeting and say, "They're using us." I didn't feel like I had the power to do that.

In several fraternities, the little sisters participated in an annual fund-raiser called "Slave Auction," in which brothers encouraged them to get intoxicated and dance seductively on stage in front of them. Brothers bid on the women for their services (such as baking, cleaning, and chauffeuring) as "slave for a week." Brothers bid more money and cheered louder for women who simulated sex on a pole erected in the middle of the stage. Although some women acknowledged the potential for this event to be interpreted as sexist, they failed to recognize its inherently racist nature and they rarely fought it. Those who did object to the event expressed their discontent by participating in a lackluster way.

Advertising the Commodity: Fetishized Bodies

Archival data included advertisements for little sister lingerie shows during fraternity pledge week and close-up pictures of little sisters' buttocks in bathing suits used in conjunction with the fraternity name. One fraternity presented male rushees with a glossy booklet complete with a full-color centerfold layout of their little sisters, most of whom posed in bathing suits. Printed in the middle of the centerfold was the following message:

"Our Little Sister organization is composed of the most beautiful women at State University. Chosen on the basis of beauty, charm, and loyalty to [fraternity name], they remember our birthdays, host parties for us, and generally take pretty good care of the Brothers."

Fraternity men advertised their stock of women who were little sisters in many ways. They gave or sold shirts, key chains, or mugs with fraternity letters on them to the women. Not all women, however, were allowed to advertise for fraternities. A little sister coordinator explained why two women were not chosen as little sisters:

Last rush we were in the process of picking little sisters. Two of the girls were pretty heavy girls. They were nice girls. I gave them a yes vote, but the majority of the chapter didn't want them to wear our letters around campus because they didn't want that image to come across. They didn't get bids. Now they won't come around the house anymore.

Women were aware of the beauty requirements of little sisterhood. According to one, "[Her fraternity] once went to go get a girl they had voted for and when they saw how good-looking her roommate was they gave her a jersey, too." The brothers at one fraternity required prospective little sisters to attach photographs to their letters of intent and used these to determine which women to interview. One little sister described how a little sister was expelled during a revamping of the little sister program because of her "plain" looks. Clearly beauty was a major selection criterion.

Fraternity men expected little sisters not to resist and even to be flattered by their sexual objectification. Feeling flattered is a recurrent response among women to their disempowerment in society and in their peer groups. Flattered little sisters were reacting to the male-dominated, capitalist character of society. Sex and sexual imagery sell. Fraternity men depersonalized and "thingified" their little sister commodities to the point of only representing them as parts, for example as buttocks or as breasts. They fetishized women's bodies; they used them as pieces of advertising. Although not all little sisters were flattered by their objectification, few fought it. Those who objected to it instead became inactive, quit the organization, or ignored the objectification. Women's sexual objectification has become naturalized. These attitudes and this atmosphere contributed to both the campuswide and nationwide reputations of little sister programs.

CONFLICTING SEXUAL EXPECTATIONS

Although the collective reputation of little sisters was that of women who sexually service the fraternity brothers, individual women resisted being perceived as sexually available. Despite fraternity advertising that suggested little sisters were sexually available, some little sisters did not have sex with fraternity brothers. Fraternity men tempered the harsh collective sexual reputation of women in little sister programs by promoting a picture of some as "buddies" or "sisters," a familial, nonsexual characterization that appealed to many women. In this way, fraternity men benefited both from having sexually available women ("slutties") to entertain them and buddies to protect the fraternity reputation and to provide legitimate dates and mates.

Fraternity men, as full members in the fraternity, were the only people empowered to define expectations of little sister program participants (Stombler and Martin 1994), but their expectations about sexual activity were vague and conflicting. By failing to delineate clear sexual expectations, fraternity men contributed to the reputation of little sisters as women sexually available for the brothers' consumption. Many different types of relationships with brothers were acceptable. Although some fraternity men expected little sisters to date or have sexual relations with fraternity brothers, it was also the brothers who deemed whether or not women's behavior was "promiscuous." On the other hand, many little sisters dated fraternity brothers or joined little sister programs because their boyfriends were fraternity brothers. Little sister "buddies" often went on casual dates with the brothers; some of these were platonic and some were not. At one fraternity, the women counted eight upcoming brother/little sister marriages in their fraternity. Fraternity men needed more than one "type" of woman (in terms of quality) and controlled the number of each type of woman they chose (in terms of quantity).

Fraternity brothers and little sisters characterized some little sister organizations as comprised mostly of "buddies" and others mostly of "slutties" or "sluts." Most fraternities solicited both types of women, allowing individual fraternity members choices regarding the type of little sisters with whom they formed relationships. One fraternity newsletter included an invitation requesting fraternity brothers to bring both their "buddies and slutties" to the next fraternity party ("Fraternity songs" 1993).

Undermining Fraternity Men's Solidarity

Not only were "overly" sexually active women at risk of losing their status and membership in the little sister program, even women who were sexually involved with only one fraternity brother within a serious relationship risked their membership. Many little sisters who severed romantic relationships with long-term fraternity brothers became inactive; others were punished for the disloyal act of dating a man in another fraternity. One woman, who had ended a relationship with a brother, was traumatized by a "jersey pulling," in which three fraternity brothers visited her apartment without notice and delivered the news that she was discharged from the little sister program. Although she was treated poorly after she and her fraternity boyfriend ended their relationship, she never anticipated being discharged:

When me and my boyfriend were dating, I felt pretty comfortable going around the house but after we broke up it got a little tense. I still hung around the house, but they [the brothers] didn't treat me the same. [It was like] they were broken up with me, too, and they wouldn't talk to me. They were very childish, like if you broke up with one of *their* brothers you were just trash or something.

This woman's dating experiences indicated that if a little sister dated a fraternity brother it was an individual decision. A breakup, however, was a collective event, subject to collective punishment.

Under some circumstances, friendships between brothers could be threatened and fraternity solidarity undermined if a little sister had sex with more than one brother. The usual result was that the fraternity men blamed the woman; thus little sisters were punished for threatening group cohesion among the fraternity brothers. Fraternity men, however, organized rituals where multiple men had sex with one woman. The difference was who made the choice—men or women. One woman was reacting to several little sisters being kicked out of her fraternity—one of whom had sex with two different fraternity brothers within a short period of time, making the brothers jealous—when she said: "They are supposed to be brothers, and you can't beat up on your brother. The best thing for them to do is to take it out on a little sister."

How Women Cope with Vague and Conflicting Sexual Expectations

At least some fraternity members expected sexual services from little sisters. The dilemma for these women was that in order to protect their own reputations, they had to decide which behavior would please which category of brothers and which behavior would be self-destructive. Most were convinced that the brothers did not want promiscuous women to participate as little sisters. It is common to hear, "The guys do not want sluts"; yet other little sisters believed that some women were accepted just because they were "easy sex for the guys." When asked how the little sisters were able to strike a balance, one succinctly replied, "discreet sex" (Moffatt 1989; Risman 1982). The desirability of sexually available women varied within and across fraternities. The ambiguous nature of correct sexual behavior endangered something that little sisters held dear—their value as a quality commodity to men. Their dilemma lay in maintaining their individual reputations within an organization that put individual reputations at risk due to its collective sexual reputation.

When asked what fraternity men wanted from little sister program participants, fraternity little sisters described a multifaceted and often conflicting reality. Some believed that fraternity men chose a certain number of little sisters solely for their sexual availability. A group of little sisters referred to these women as the "token ten" of the newly selected pledge class. Others believed that the fraternity brothers purposely refused membership to women with bad reputations because it hurt the fraternity's collective reputation. The data presented here supported both scenarios: men wanted both types of women. Often, fraternity men would choose women with "bad reputations," sexually abuse them, and then treat them discourteously enough to discourage their continuing participation in the program. How did women know how to respond to brothers' conflicting expectations? One particularly introspective little sister claimed that most brothers do not want "loose" little sisters but that some do so that they could use them to satisfy themselves sexually. The answer, for the brothers, was left with the women who were little sisters who were held *individually* responsible for their collective sexual reputation.

SEXUAL ABUSE

Sexual expectations that fraternity men left contradictory and purposely vague, the sexual objectification and commodification of little sisters, and the structure and values inherent in fraternities all contributed to an environment that exacerbated women's risk of sexual abuse and sexual assault (Boeringer, Shehan, and Akers 1991; Boswell and Spade 1993; Copenhaver and Grauerholz 1991; Gwartney-Gibbs and Stockard 1989; Martin and Hummer 1989). Because they blamed little sisters for their own assaults, men who sexually abused and assaulted little sisters contributed to the collective sexual reputation of little sisters. The threat of sexual abuse, as well as its actual incidence, contributed to fraternity men's control over women—enhancing their power to define and evaluate little sister actions. Their evaluation in turn validated the collective sexual reputation of little sisters. Researchers have provided powerful evidence regarding the prevalence of fraternity gang rape, including the rape of fraternity little sisters (Ehrhart and Sandler 1985; Martin and Hummer 1989; O'Sullivan 1991; Sanday 1990). Some fraternity men have admitted that fraternity gang rape is a common occurrence ("They never call it rape" 1990). One little sister told me she believed that each weekend, at her fraternity alone, about three women were victims of acquaintance rape.

Most little sisters conceptualized sexual abuse with a "victim blaming" mentality by claiming that little sisters who were abused failed to control their own actions. Some viewed fraternity brothers as men with uncontrollable sexual urges and were fearful while at the fraternity, but others described their fraternity as a safe haven, a place where they could "let their guard down," and where they trusted the men. The women used different strategies for dealing with the perceived potential for sexual abuse, for maintaining their personal safety, and for fighting their collective reputation. At one fraternity, veteran little sisters instructed new ones to remain "composed" and "act like a lady" at all times, including (but not limited to) avoiding intoxication. Others described a safe atmosphere, yet were instructed by fellow little sisters to carry weapons, such as mace. Most little sisters created a distinction between "good" and "bad" brothers, failing to categorize the organization as a whole as dangerous (see Boswell and Spade 1993 for a discussion of different fraternity cultures). One common strategy was to avoid potentially harmful brothers: "Even the guys told us, you know, 'Just watch your step,' because like I said, all brothers aren't like dogs or something. Some are, some aren't. Some are good, some are bad."

Fraternity men told the little sisters that "acting like a lady" and remaining in control or knowing "when to say when" would prevent sexual abuse, implying that those who were sexually abused brought it on themselves. Women who did not follow these guidelines and were abused or were promiscuous remained silent—a strategy that may have helped combat a collective sexual reputation but hurt individual women in the process.

Many women who put rapes of little sisters "in perspective" drew comparisons between Greeks (members of fraternities, sororities, and fraternity little sister programs) and non-Greeks and emphasized the prevalence of non-Greek rape. Denying Greek exceptionalism was another strategy for dealing with the reality of sexual assault and combating the little sister reputation.

DISCUSSION

Because the relationship of domination between little sisters and fraternity men is institutionalized, sexual exploitation seems natural to most little sisters. Just as there is no shortage of candidates for Playmate of the Month (Bartky 1990), there is no shortage of women on college campuses willing to rush fraternity little sister programs. Many of these women participate enthusiastically in their own sexual objectification and sexual exploitation. Holland and Eisenhart (1990) emphasized the importance of peer groups in the transmission of traditional gender relations and the importance women place on having a boyfriend; fraternity little sisterhood symbolizes the affirmation of personal womanhood not by a single male power, but by 30 to 150 high-status men.

Many little sisters consistently work to reverse their collective sexual reputation as "slutties" and maintain their personal reputations as "buddies." Fraternity brothers validate the collective sexual reputation through their behavior when it benefits them. They dismiss it when they try to attract women recruits and campus support. Fraternity brothers send conflicting messages regarding sexual expectations that confuse little sisters and their understanding of the collective reputation. Paradoxically, women join fraternity little sister organizations to enhance their reputations by attaching themselves to high-status men, while at the same time they jeopardize themselves by acquiring the collective sexual reputation that is inherently negative. A woman's reputation is on the line throughout her experiences in the fraternity. At the same time that she must accept the public negative definition of little sisters by becoming one, she must struggle to preserve her private reputation within an organization whose structure, dynamics, and ideology make this goal difficult. She may be called a "buddy," but men often continue to apply sexual pressure. The woman must decide when to comply and when to refuse—not always aware that it is the men who will decide if and when she has crossed the line they deliberately blur. Little sisters tend to blame individual women for any sexual abuse they endure and for the "soiled" little sister reputation their actions reinforce. Because women attribute the negative collective reputation to individuals rather than to a collective (the fraternity), it is logical to them that individual women are to blame for sexual abuse. Little sisters assume that if they are not promiscuous and if they negatively sanction fellow little sisters who are, they can maintain some degree of control over their collective reputation and their likelihood of sexual abuse. Fraternity men walk a fine line between their desire to promote the collective sexual reputation of little sisters enough to draw men recruits and their fear of discouraging women recruits. Ambiguous and contradictory sexual expectations help them maintain that delicate balance.

Women's sexual availability is implicit in little sister commodification. It is characterized not by a monetary exchange (as in the classic sense of the term "commodity") but by status or access to men as the exchange value for little sisters. The use value for fraternities is comprised of a variety of little sister labor that includes supporting the brothers by acting as rush hosts, displaying themselves to attract recruits, serving food, organizing cheerleading for sports events, giving advice to individual brothers, providing a "woman's touch" in party decorations, and organizing social activities. Whereas some of the men's practices and strategies for commodifying little sisters are obvious, others are more subtle. The commodification of women, however, is a necessary component of the collective sexual reputation of little sisters.

Women are doubly disempowered. First, they are excluded from the fraternity's hierarchy and any formal claim to power and second, they are substantively disempowered when fraternity men use them for advertising or for sex and then discard them. Confusion over expectations of what the little sister role is in the realm of sexuality creates ideal conditions for exploitation. When the women are uncertain of the expectations, or when the expectations conflict, they are kept perpetually off balance.

The little sister role is not only ambiguous, it is often dangerous. Many fraternity men want women who will "put out" but they do not want women who will soil the organization's "white bread" reputation—a perpetuation of some men's desire for a Madonna in the living room and a whore in the bedroom. Little sisters often describe their relationship as a "buddy" relationship; yet most had had sexual relations with at least one brother. Little sisters are aware of the negative component of the collective sexual reputation. They are willing to rush despite this by defining themselves differently. It is ironic that concern for individual reputations occurs simultaneously with the acquisition of a public persona that coveys a bad reputation.

Fraternity men mask the relationship between brothers and little sisters even more by using familial terms to describe fraternity relations. Upon joining, little sisters are assigned to choose "big brothers" and "little brothers." The result is a seemingly innocuous—yet incestuous—string of relationships. Much like victims in incestuous families, little sisters walk a line between potential exposure and public shame or suffering through a conspiracy of silence.

Although little sisters and fraternity brothers participate in little sister programs to meet one another, once women and men begin to date, their relationship to the fraternity is allegedly removed from the realm of organizational interest and becomes a private affair; yet "jersey pulling" and ostracism provide dramatic evidence that the organization is still involved. Similarly, sexual relations such as "one-night stands" are framed as occurring outside of the organizational realm, while clearly occurring within it. Brothers sometimes offer advice to one another, but each brother has the right to control women as he sees fit, according to the unwritten rules of the organization.

Many little sisters deny the possibility of rapes occurring within their organization and describe their fraternity brothers as "safe." Their characterizations may be disingenuous. Veteran little sisters tell new ones that "boys will be boys" and that they should carry weapons. Veteran little sisters and fraternity men expend substantial effort to promote an image of the fraternity as a safe haven where friends hang out—in the face of a much harsher reality. Some fraternities may be safe places where an ethic exists among fraternity brothers that sexual assault is not acceptable, but not all fraternities are safe. Because they arrange the organizational structure, fraternity men are inoculated against the unpleasant consequences their behavior could have in the "real" world (see Martin and Hummer 1989). Some women realize the inherent danger within the fraternity's organizational structure and dynamics. This does not, however, usually taint their evaluations of their experiences in the fraternity.

Little sisters are disempowered through their use by men as sexual commodities, through their sexual exploitation, through their lack of control over their sexual reputations (both individual and collective), and through the threat and reality of sexual abuse. Fraternity little sister organizations systematize the reproduction of gender inequality on the college campus and put women at risk. Although some women are capable, in some settings, of resisting some fraternity men's exploitation, the fact remains that not all women can do so. Because little sister organizations reside in an educational institution, it is possible to alter them. Perhaps with administrative involvement and institutional support, some of the worst excesses of these oppressive relationships between men and women can be controlled.

NOTES

Author's Note: I thank Patricia Yancey Martin, Debra Street, Irene Padavic, James D. Orcutt, Chris S. O'Sullivan, Susan P. Morgan, Amber Ault, Stefan Timmermans, Larry Isaac, Beth E. Schneider, Margaret Andersen, and two anonymous reviewers for advice on earlier drafts of the paper. I thank Patricia Yancey Martin for collaborating on data collection. The larger project was supported by grants to Patricia Yancey Martin from the President's Small Grant Program of the Florida State University Foundation and the Florida State University Committee on Creativity and Research through its Faculty Research Support Program.

1. This is more the case in predominantly Euro–American fraternities than in predominantly African American ones (Stombler and Padavic 1994).

2. Both "Greek," or sorority, and "independent," or non-sorority, women become little sisters. An informal in-class survey of 53 women identified 24 as little sisters. Of those 24, 14 were not in sororities; 10 of the women participated in both fraternity little sister programs and sororities.

3. Fraternity men flattered women who were little sisters by performing what they consider to be acts of respect, such as standing when a woman entered the room or allowing women to be the first to eat at the fraternity meal. Men also displayed their affection for little sisters by presenting them with flowers and serenading them. Gwartney-Gibbs and Stockard (1989) documented a dialectical system of exploitation within fraternities where women were honored, then degraded, and then honored again, as causing the women to feel indebted to fraternity men, thus leading them to succumb to sexual pressure.

4. A man I interviewed who was privy to the brothers' interactions during secret meetings described how they discuss each potential little sister's attributes, including individual sexual reputations, before choosing program participants.

REFERENCES

Bartky, Sandra Lee. 1990. *Femininity and domination: Studies in the phenomenology of oppression.* New York: Routledge.

Boeringer, Scot B., Constance L. Shehan, and Ronald L. Akers. 1991. Social contexts and social learning in sexual coercion and aggression: Assessing the contribution of fraternity membership. *Family Relations* 40:58–64.

Boswell, Ayres A., and Joan Z. Spade. 1993. Fraternities, gender relations, and rape culture on college campuses. Unpublished manuscript, Department of Sociology and Anthropology, Lehigh University.

Bryan, William A. 1987. Contemporary fraternity and sorority issues. In *Fraternities and sororities on the contemporary college campus.* New Directions for Student Services, no. 40, edited by R. B. Winston, Jr., W. R. Nettles III, and J. H. Opper, Jr., 37–56. San Francisco: Jossey-Bass.

Copenhaver, Stacey, and Elizabeth Grauerholz. 1991. Sexual victimization among sorority women: Exploring the link between sexual violence and institutional practice. *Sex Roles* 24:31–41.

Cowie, C., and S. Lees. 1981. Slags or drags. *Feminist Review* 9:17–31.

Dropping "little sisters": Fraternities ending much criticized programs. 1990, 25 January. *Atlanta Journal and Constitution* pp. A10, A11.

Dworkin, Andrea. 1981. *Pornography: Men possessing women.* New York: Perigee.

Ehrhart, Julie K., and Bernice R. Sandler. 1985. *Campus gang rape: Party games?* Washington, DC: Association for American Colleges.

Fraternity songs and writings: Coming under criticism. 1993. *About Women on Campus* 2 (2):9.

French, Marilyn. 1985. *Beyond power: On women, men, and morals.* New York: Summit.

Glaser, Barney G. 1978. *Theoretical sensitivity: Advances in the methodology of grounded theory.* Mill Valley, CA: Sociology Press.

——. 1992. *Basics of grounded theory analysis.* Mill Valley, CA: Sociology Press.

Gwartney-Gibbs, Patricia, and Jean Stockard. 1989. Courtship aggression and mixed-sex peer groups. In *Violence in dating relationships: Emerging social issues,* edited by Maureen A. Pirog-Good and Jan E. Stets. New York: Praeger.

Handler, Lisa. 1993. In the fraternal sisterhood: Sororities as gender strategy. Paper presented at the annual meeting of the American Sociological Association, Miami Beach.

Holland, Dorothy C., and Margaret A. Eisenhart. 1990. *Educated in romance: Women, achievement, and college culture.* Chicago: University of Chicago Press.

Jaggar, Alison M. 1983. *Feminist politics and human nature.* Sussex: Harvester.

Karlof, Linda, and Timothy Cargill. 1991. Fraternity and sorority membership and gender dominance attitudes. *Sex Roles* 25:417–23.

Lees, Sue. 1986. *Losing out: Sexuality and adolescent girls.* London: Hutchinson.

MacKinnon, Catherine A. 1987. *Feminism unmodified: Discourses on life and law.* Cambridge, MA: Harvard University Press.

——. 1989. *Towards a feminist therapy of the state.* Cambridge, MA: Harvard University Press.

Martin, Patricia Yancey, and Robert A. Hummer. 1989. Fraternities and rape on campus. *Gender & Society* 3:457–73.

Martin, Patricia Yancey, and Mindy Stombler. 1993. Gender politics in fraternity little sister groups: How men take power away from women. Unpublished manuscript. Department of Sociology, Florida State University.

Martin, Patricia Yancey, and Barry A. Turner. 1986. Grounded theory and organizational research. *Journal of Applied Behavioral Science* 22:141–57.

McKee, C. William. 1987. Understanding the diversity of the Greek world. In *Fraternities and sororities on the contemporary college campus.* New Directions for Student Services, no. 40, edited

by R. B. Winston, Jr., W. R. Nettles III, and J. H. Opper, Jr. San Francisco: Jossey-Bass.

Millett, Kate. 1970. *Sexual politics.* Garden City, NY: Doubleday.

Moffatt, Michael. 1989. *Coming of age in New Jersey: College and American culture.* New Brunswick, NJ: Rutgers University Press.

O'Sullivan, Chris S. 1991. Acquaintance gang rape on campus. In *Acquaintance rape: The hidden crime,* edited by A. Parrot and L. Bechhofer. New York: Wiley.

Riker, Hal C. 1983. Programming for personal development. In *The eighties: Challenges for fraternities and sororities,* edited by William A. Bryan and Robert A. Schwartz. Carbondale: Southern Illinois University Press.

Risman, Barbara. 1982. College women and sororities: The social construction and reaffirmation of gender roles. *Urban Life* 11:231–52.

Sanday, Peggy Reeves. 1990. *Fraternity gang rape: Sex, brotherhood, and privilege on campus.* New York: New York University Press.

Schur, Edwin M. 1988. *The Americanization of sex.* Philadelphia: Temple University Press.

Stombler, Mindy, and Irene Padavic. 1994. Getting a man or getting ahead: A comparative analysis of African-American and EuroAmerican fraternity little sister programs on college campuses. Paper presented at the annual meeting of the American Sociological Association, Los Angeles.

Stombler, Mindy, and Patricia Yancey Martin. 1994. Bringing women in, keeping women down: Fraternity "little sister" organizations. *Journal of Contemporary Ethnography* 23.

Strauss, Anselm L., and Juliet Corbin. 1990. *Basics of qualitative research: Grounded theory procedures and techniques.* Newbury Park, CA: Sage.

They never call it rape. 1990, 13 April. Segment on "20/20."

Turner, Barry A. 1981. Some practical aspects of qualitative data analysis: One way of organizing the cognitive processes associated with the generation of grounded theory. *Quality and Quantity* 15: 225–47. . . .

38

Women and Work

Exploring Race, Ethnicity, and Class

Elizabeth Higginbotham

PERHAPS NO AREA OF SOCIAL LIFE HAS CHANGED so profoundly for women in the United States in the last half of the 20th century as the area of employment. Patterns of employment for women—that is, who is involved in paid employment, how long women work over their lifetimes, and the types of work that women do—have shifted. If one takes a picture of employment for women in 1947, when, after World War II, women were being pushed out of war industries and other factories and back into the home and traditionally female occupations, and compares that with the scene in 1997, one can learn a great deal.

Current patterns of education and employment for women are sharply different from those of the past. In the 1960s and 1970s, women had made substantial progress in closing the education gap that separated them from men (Bianchi 1995). In fact, women in the late baby boom cohort have levels of educational attainment very similar to those of men in the same group. Gains in educational attainment have opened new occupations for women and enhanced women's earnings relative to men's (Bianchi 1995).

In 1948, the labor force participation rate for women 20 years and older was 31.8%; in 1994, the rate was 59.3% (U.S. Department of Labor 1995). As a whole, this group spends more years in the labor force than did the earlier same age cohort. For some women, employment begins in high

school; a recent U.S. Department of Labor (1995) report indicates that two-fifths of high school seniors have jobs. Furthermore, even contemporary women who have school-age children and children under 3 years of age are more likely to be employed than earlier cohorts. In looking at the enhanced diversity among families in the United States, Sara McLanahan and Lynne Casper (1995) found that since 1960, married mothers have increased their participation in paid employment. They conclude: "By 1990, currently married mothers were nearly as likely to be in the labor force (59%) as formerly married single mothers (64%), and they were more likely to be employed than never-married mothers (48%)" (pp. 12–13).

In the 1940s and 1950s, most women worked within a narrow range of occupations. Today, traditional female occupations for women at all levels of educational attainment are still their major source of employment, even though thousands more men have entered these work spheres (Reskin and Roos 1990). Thus women are still subject to sex segregation in the labor market.

Women's increasing long-term involvement with paid labor has consequences for shifting patterns in other areas of social life, especially the family. Working outside the home means that women who are married, have children, or both, face double duty, as they are still primarily responsible for the home and the care of children. These stresses have implications for all involved. Although we can celebrate increases in consumer goods and services, we are still facing an era when few new institutions have developed to help with family reproductive labor. Thus it is up to families, often

From *Women and Work: Exploring Race, Ethnicity, and Class*, edited by Elizabeth Higginbotham and Mary Romero. Copyright © 1997 by Sage Publications, Inc. Reprinted by permission of Sage Publications, Inc.

the wives and mothers, to coordinate, monitor, and oversee the new services and products that are available.

Women do not receive financial rewards for all the labor they perform outside the homes. Women in the United States have long been involved in volunteer work that ranges from church activities, social reform efforts, and the support of civic and cultural institutions to direct outreach and delivery of social services that improve the lives of members of their communities. Women's volunteer work, while often invisible, has been the topic of recent research that addresses how gender as well as race and class shape the motivations of women volunteers, the types of work these women do, and how such work is received (Daniels 1988; Shaw 1996). Through the century, nonpaid work for women has also changed. The demands of paid employment have led some women to reduce their volunteer work. New social movements have shifted the nature of the nonpaid work that women do. As new populations face various stages of racial oppression, women may continue to feel a critical urgency to work for their communities and families, but these changes may take them into new arenas. Also, as members of disadvantaged communities, women of color and working-class women might feel the need to continue such work along with paid employment, even if it means facing triple duty as they work on the job, in the home, and in the community.

There have clearly been critical changes over the past 50 years in how women work during their lifetimes, in both paid and nonpaid work. In the face of these dramatic changes, critical differences have persisted within the population of employed women. Major inequalities in U.S. society shape where women work, their working conditions, their wages and salaries, their abilities to control their work environments, and how they see themselves and their options in the workplace. Inequalities also shape their sense of urgency to add community work to their other weekly tasks.

. . .

. . . We want not only to address race and ethnicity, but to investigate the role of nativity and citizenship. Citizenship is a privilege that many native-born U.S. citizens take for granted. Yet inequalities in work options and political resources among native-born citizens and many levels of naturalized citizens and resident aliens have been expressed in several ways in historical and contemporary life. In the 19th century, and earlier in the 20th century, whether or not an immigrant was eligible for citizenship was key in shaping his or her employment options as well as political rights. Chinese, Japanese, and Korean immigrants faced legislation that limited their employment options, taxed them on the work that they could do, and limited where they could live. Because they were denied the right to become citizens, they were limited to the use of the courts and protests by their native governments as the means of challenging discrimination and their disadvantaged status (McClain 1994; Takaki 1990). Although many immigrants faced hard times, the option of citizenship meant that at some point they could enter the political system. Like African Americans, denied the right to vote for decades in the South, Asian immigrants and even second-generation Asian Americans used the courts and general social and economic betterment in their own communities to advance within the system. In the contemporary United States, recent immigration laws have also structured narrow employment options for new immigrants, especially those who are not documented. The rights and access to resources of those legal immigrants who do not become naturalized citizens are also at risk. Thus, increasingly, scholars addressing the issues surrounding women and their employment cannot avoid looking at the varied circumstances of recent immigrants.

When we look at this complex web of rights, privileges, and disadvantages, we learn much about how the matrix of domination works to create or limit employment options and how people are often forced to struggle in and outside work settings to shift the balance of power in society. An exploration of these dimensions of inequality is critical to an understanding of women's situations in paid employment and volunteer work.

CONCEPTUALIZING RACE, ETHNICITY, AND SOCIAL CLASS

Race, ethnicity, and social class shape distinctive circumstances for women throughout the life cycle; given that most women in the United States spend many years in the workforce, this has dramatic implications for their lives. In examining this area, it is central to consider that race, ethnicity, and social class are recognized as critical dimensions of analysis for all women, not just women who lack privileges with regard to these social categories. Thus they are critical for understanding the lives of women who are privileged with regard to race, ethnicity, or both, and those who are members of the upper or middle classes. In the arena of women and work, race, ethnicity, and social class can be critical tools for analysis . . . we can learn much about the current levels of inequality in our society by focusing on the interaction of gender with race, ethnicity, and social class.

Traditional approaches to research on employment that address race and ethnicity often assume that the male experience speaks for the group. For example, in *The Declining Significance of Race*, William J. Wilson (1978) used data on the employment patterns of Black men to reach his conclusions about the increasing number of Black people employed in middle-class occupations and thus the enhanced stratification within the Black community. However, looking at the experiences of women from various racial, ethnic, and social class groups can shed needed light on critical dimensions of the experiences of groups exposed to racial and/or ethnic privileges or disadvantages. For example, in the past 20 years, many middle- and working-class families have responded to the decline in male wages, relative to the cost of living, by sending married women into the labor force (Timmer, Eitzen, and Talley 1994). Thus we find large increases in the percentages of married women in the labor market. Looking at both male and female employment patterns is critical to understanding central changes in the U.S. economy and their impacts on workers. We cannot understand how individuals and families have faced deindustrialization and downsizing by looking only at male employment patterns.

Examining women's employment patterns within racial and ethnic groups is also important for understanding how individuals and families respond to shifts in the larger political economy. For example, in conducting comparative research on professional and managerial women in the Memphis, Tennessee, area, Lynn Weber and I found important racial differences among college-educated women in the baby boom cohort. We found that most of the raised working-class and raised middle-class African American women had mothers who were involved with paid employment. Thus, when asked about having working mothers, these respondents did not think it was a big deal. A minority of the raised working-class and raised middle-class White women in the same study had mothers who worked outside the home. Many of the White women reported feeling very different from other children in their neighborhoods because their mothers worked outside the home.

In the 20th century, the percentages of women working outside the home have not been the same for all racial groups. According to 1990 data, it is now very common for mothers to work in the labor market (McLanahan and Casper 1995). However, this trend represents major increases in the proportions of working mothers among White women, but not very significant increases among Black women, because Black women have had a long-established pattern of involvement in work outside the home, even when they are married and have children (Dill 1988; Jones 1985; Shaw 1996). This trend also tells us that a pattern of coping with economic marginality among Black families has expanded to other groups, as the wages of the male breadwinners are insufficient to meet all family needs.

. . .

Ethnicity entails more than simply cultural patterns or characteristics of national origin; it also speaks to persistent ties that connect people to each other and shape how they may interact with people from different ethnic groups. Again, there is a power dimension involved in these relationships. For example, people from the majority group define what is and is not appropriate and limit the terms employed to judge who is allowed to join the majority.

A social stratification model of race and ethnicity has received less attention than class in the social sciences, but it is important for understanding what happens when people come together in a workplace, where they clearly are different in terms of their power in that environment and the overall society. The role of power is plainly evident in institutionalized racism, a dynamic feature of the modern U.S. labor market. Many scholars are familiar with the legacy of colonial labor markets in the 18th and 19th centuries, but in the 20th century job ceilings and other forms of institutionalized discrimination ensured that men of color were barred from industrial work, so that they were available for other work, often agricultural, service, and preindustrial types of labor (Barrera 1979; Takaki 1990; Nee and Nee 1973; Harris 1982). These jobs were lower in pay, more dangerous, and had fewer benefits than the industrial jobs reserved for White males. The ill treatment faced by men of color jeopardized their ability to provide for their families and also pushed women of color into paid employment (Amott and Matthaei 1991; Dill 1988; Jones 1985).

Patterns of institutionalized racism are also found in the experiences of women in U.S. labor markets. Clerical and sales jobs, which are clearly recognized as women's work, would be better classified for most of the 20th century as White women's work, as women of color have gained significant access to white-collar positions only since the 1970s. Evelyn Nakano Glenn (1992) argues that the overrepresentation of women of color in paid reproductive labor, particularly domestic work, is evidence of racial and gender barriers in the labor market. Regional differences are apparent, but race and gender have operated to keep women of color in domestic work as other options have not been available, due to level of industrial development or the fact that other work was reserved for White women. Glenn documents the complex factors that have restricted employment options for women of color: the need to work because male earnings were insufficient to support their families; the limitations they faced in educational opportunities that could lead to other work; and the limitations on legal and civil rights, making it difficult for them to make demands on the system. A legacy of domestic work is found among Mexican American women in the Southwest, African American women in the South, and Japanese men and women in California and Hawaii. Glenn and other scholars who explore the ways that women of color are pushed into the labor market (Amott and Matthaei 1991; Dill 1988; Higginbotham 1983; Jones 1985) have also documented the consequences for their families. However, we need more investigations into the intersection of work and family with an eye to racial, ethnic, and social class differences.

During World War II, women of color found new employment options, especially in industrial work, but—like White women at the time—many were pushed out of these jobs as soldiers returned following the war. Many working-class women and women of color returned to a narrow range of occupations, because employment was still critical for family survival (Marks 1989; Jones 1985). However, as the sociologists Michael Omi and Howard Winant (1994) note, the political gains made during the New Deal and World War II gave people of color new leverage for challenging political economic arrangements and thus the racial hierarchy. People of color made inroads, often the men first, into manufacturing and service industries that offered better pay. Many more men of color were unionized, especially in Congress of Industrial Organizations (CIO) drives. Political and economic gains provided the backdrop for additional challenges to the racial hierarchies of the 1950s, 1960s, and 1970s. These struggles were played out in the workplace, as people strived to improve their individual and groups' positions. There were also struggles within communities around issues of housing, schools, public service accommodations, and other areas, as racial hierarchies were also challenged in these spheres (Massey and Denton 1993; Omi and Winant 1994; Pohlmann 1990).

The years since the end of World War II have witnessed successes in some arenas. The nation's racial/ethnic populations have become more economically diverse, as members have moved into business and professional and managerial occupations. Even during the regressive policies of the Reagan-Bush era in the 1980s and the early 1990s, the communities of color in the United States developed middle-class segments, following patterns of polarization among the general population. Although the majority of middle-class people in this nation continue to be White, there are increasing numbers of people of color in this group. Yet we cannot assume that their entrance into the middle class or even professional and managerial occupations means these groups are like the majority group in terms of their experiences in the world of work and in their communities. We have to explore how race and ethnicity may shape their experiences as they enter the more privileged social classes.

There is also a downside to this increased polarization. In this period of slow economic growth, the economic stability of many middle- and working-class people is threatened; thus we need to know more about how race and ethnicity, as well as gender, will shape the impacts of these trends (Marks 1989; Timmer et al. 1994; Wilson 1978). Central questions revolve around how people cope with structural inequalities in work, the nature of their resistance, and consequences for their families and communities. These questions take on particular significance in an era of shrinking government and civic responsibility for those who face major structural barriers to full participation in U.S. life.

The political era after World War II was a time of loosened immigration restrictions, and eventually the United States passed a new law in 1965 that ended national differences in quotas for entrance. This legislation has meant dramatic increases in Asian immigration, the group most targeted by previous restrictions (Takaki 1990). However, the implementation of quotas in the Western Hemisphere has meant that national groups that had not previously been subjected to quotas, such as persons from Mexico and the nations of the Caribbean, now have quotas lower than the numbers of people who previously immigrated annually. These immigration changes have meant new expressions of privileges and disadvantages that have had impacts on many residents of the United States. As Sylvia Pedraza (1991) notes, we need to look at women's participation in migration and the consequences for them, especially the impact of new work roles on family life.

In the United States we are often comfortable thinking about social classes as status groups that are arranged in some sort of hierarchy. Working within a distributional framework, social classes become defined as job categories, qualities of jobs, or specific levels of income. Such approaches enable people to avoid discussions of power and many of the complexities of modern social life (Lucal 1994). There is coexisting tradition in which scholars employ a relational model that seeks to explore how social class relates to social relationships. People are not set only in some rankings along a scale, but in relationships with each other.

Increasingly popular is the use of a professional-managerial/working-class dichotomy that builds on the work of Braverman (1974) and Poulantzas (1974). This perspective, notes Reeve Vanneman and Lynn Weber Cannon (1987), is in line with the views of most Americans, who do recognize social class divisions that relate to power: "To be middle class in America is to own productive property, or to have supervisory authority, or to perform mental labor at the expense of manual workers" (p. 61).[1] Throughout this volume, the contributors employ different definitions of social class divisions, depending upon their disciplines. However, several direct attention to the implications of social class membership for interactions across social class lines and how people in working-class jobs survive in the face of exploitation.

Issues of power for women, as they relate to control and supervision, encourage us to ask many new questions. Scholars can move beyond examining how securing a professional occupation enables one to attain a certain middle-class lifestyle and attend to how power dynamics might give women more or less flexibility on the job and how that relates to the integration of work with other roles, especially those of spouse and mother. What are the implications of women's moving into new roles in the workplace? Does a woman's employment in middle-class occupations alter the balance of power within the family? How do coworkers adjust to having women in professional and managerial occupations? Does the reception of women in new roles vary by race, ethnicity, and social class background? Also, social class can shape the inhabitants of jobs, so that middle- and working-class people bring different perspectives to the workplace and to their work in their communities.

As we conceptualize race, ethnicity, social class, and gender in the workplace, we also have to think about how individuals consider these issues in their day-to-day interactions. In particular, race, ethnicity, and social class involve membership in specific communities, with particular legacies and sets of resources for political and social action and webs of family obligations. To explore these issues, I borrow from the key concepts of human recognition, social space, and social time that Joe Feagin, Hernan Vera, and Nikitah Imani (1996) employ in their research on Black students in colleges and universities.

We know that the major ideology with regard to race among White Americans is color blindness—that is, a willingness to ignore the reality of race and just see people as people (Omi and Winant 1994; Frankenberg 1993). Indeed, in our study of professional and managerial women in Memphis, Lynn Weber and I found middle-class White women who claim not to notice race . . . As a stance, this "color-blind" perspective can be a powerful force for the preservation of the racial status quo. Adoption of this position means that people of color are not seen when they enter new work settings—they are invisible as full human beings as coworkers and supervisors work not to notice their race. Employers, fellow workers, and clients might fail to see them as unique

human beings with "distinctive talents, virtues, interests and problems" (Feagin et al. 1996, p. 14). As individuals enter work settings, they can be appreciated for themselves, including the unique perspectives they bring to the work group. Ignoring these qualities or pretending that race does not matter is a way of silencing them as individuals. Further, this is not the path to ending racial discrimination. We can also see this problem with interactions across social class lines, where social class origins might not be very clear. We have to work to address the sources of material differences in people's lives and what that means for the different parties.

As social pressures and legislation have opened many doors for individuals, women of color and members of the working class might enter middle-class work settings and find the atmosphere chilling, which then influences the interactions in those spaces. We have to recognize that as people of color and working-class persons enter spaces that were formerly middle-class and all White, there is a cost for them. These settings might be hostile and alien and, in their physical reality, not welcoming to people who are different. There are also places where interactions can be scripted by race, ethnicity, and social class, with people playing their appropriate roles. Legislation and social movements have meant new occupations for many previously disadvantaged groups, so it is not unusual now for coworkers to come from widely varying groups. However, when people move out of their previous prescribed roles and come together in new ways without their old scripts, there can be tensions and problems. It is important that employers, administrators, and those responsible for justice in the workplace hold supervisors accountable for ensuring that tensions are not translated into new structures of inequality.

In terms of social time, there is a historical memory among "outgroups" that is rarely recognized by members of the majority group, because they are often taught sanitized histories of oppression (Feagin et al. 1996). Stories of biased treatment and exploitation are kept alive in the families and communities of the disadvantaged, where the legacy of oppression is validated by others. For example, as a young Chicana enters domestic work, she may be very clear that this job is the type of work that her mother and perhaps her grandmother did before her (Romero 1992). Thus she might view and interpret her interactions on the job with White employers through that collective history, whereas the White employer may look only to the immediate interaction for clues to what is happening.

We have to keep in mind that as members of any group enter new social settings, those individuals might carry with them and understand their present experiences in terms beyond their personal experiences because they are conscious of familial and communal racial and social class histories. Thus women and men carry more than just visible signs of their race, ethnicity, and possibly social class origins with them into a workplace. They use their communal and personal histories as lenses through which they view the racial, ethnic, and social class privileges and disadvantages they find on the job. Rather than pretending that differences do not exist, we can learn to appreciate the histories and perspectives of individuals who have faced disadvantages in the past. Such insights can help us to revamp work settings to make them welcoming for all.

. . .

THE PERSISTENCE OF GENDER INEQUALITY

Attention to the differences among women should not divert political attention and social science research from exploring the persistence of gender differences. Comparisons of women with men indicate that there are major inequalities. Women's earnings still lag behind men's in the United States. In 1996, women who usually work full time had median earnings of $415 a week, or 75.2% of the $552 median for men (U.S. Department of Labor 1996b). This earnings gap is indicative of the fact that women still face discrimination in gaining access to employment and also on the job, especially in traditional male occupations across the spectrum, from mining and other industrial work to the professions and corporate boardrooms.

We cannot attribute the earnings gap to lack of educational attainment on the part of women. An analysis of U.S. Census data by the Economic Policy Institute found great similarities in the earnings of college-educated Black and White women who had been in their jobs for 1–5 years: Black women had slightly higher earnings, with an average hourly rate of $11.41, whereas White women's average rate was $11.38 per hour in 1991 (U.S. Department of Labor 1996c). College-educated Black males' rate was slightly lower than those of the women at $11.26 per hour, but White males' average hourly rate was the highest at $12.85.

When this information was reported in the *New York Times* (Roberts 1994), the article's author highlighted the earnings difference between college-educated Black men and Black women and pondered the impact on marital options, even though nothing in the data addressed issues of marriage. However, the real story is the gap between White men and Black men and all women. Although it is a matter of cents that distinguishes the earnings differential between Black women and White women and Black men, the *New York Times* article did not give attention to the $1.44 gap between Black women's earnings and those of White men. We could all appreciate a headline that notes "College-Educated White Males Still Ahead in Hourly Earnings." At least that would expose the way much of the public still takes for granted the higher earnings of White males and shifts the discussion to who among the previously disadvantaged is improving over the others.

Natalie Sokoloff (1992), in a comparative study of occupational segregation among Black and White women in professional occupations, also brings the persistence of White male privilege into view. She notes that the decades from 1960 to 1980 witnessed the creation of many new middle-class jobs. Many of these positions went to women and Black men, but the majority went to White men. Thus it is important to look at the data from various perspectives, and to be critical of mainstream approaches. Biased presentation of statistical data can drive a political wedge between oppressed groups and leave White male privilege unexamined. The quest should be to remove barriers for all people. To do so, we have to look at all groups and their complexities of privileges and disadvantages.

In the 1990s, we find that the range of occupations in which women are employed is more varied than in 1947, although the majority of women are still in sex-segregated occupations. In 1995, 16.9 million women were employed in professional and managerial specialties (U.S. Department of Labor 1996a), but the majority were in traditionally female occupations (Sokoloff 1992): 24.1 million in technical, sales, and administrative support positions, and another 10.2 million in service occupations (U.S. Department of Labor 1996a).

However, women can now be found tending bar, baking bread outside the home, selling real estate, and in positions in banking other than behind tellers' windows. As scholars have explored the trend of women's moving into many traditionally male occupations, they have identified significant patterns. Barbara Reskin and Patricia Roos (1990) have found that women may have gained particular occupational titles, but where they work in formerly predominantly male fields can be different from where the men work. For instance, women might be clustered into certain segments of an occupation, or limited in their areas of specialty or task. It is also common for women to practice their occupations or professions in the public sector rather than the private sector; this is often the case for educated Black women (Reskin and Roos 1990; Higginbotham 1987, 1994).

Reskin and Roos (1990) also found that women are likely to enter fields as men abandon them in response to structural changes and/or earnings decline. Polly Phipps (1990) documents the case of pharmacy, where small, entrepreneurial, independent drugstores are in decline as most prescriptions drugs are dispensed either by large firms (Walmart, Walgreen, Rite Aid, Osco, and other major stores) or in hospitals. We also see that this field has shifted from 87.9% male in 1970 to 76% male in 1980 and then 68% male in

1988.[2] As men have left pharmacy and the actual demand for pharmacists has grown, women have attended pharmacy schools and taken an increasing percentage of the positions in the field.

The changes in where women work, although they challenge the dominant pattern of sex segregation of the workplace, have not given us genuine integration of workplaces that benefits all women. As women enter new fields, they rarely close the wage gap. However, they have increasingly entered jobs that pay better than many traditionally female occupations. Yet the general national decline in wages means that women's benefits are limited. Also, the payoff for women of additional training and higher education may be minimal rather than the major rewards they expect as they enter professions and other formerly predominantly male occupations. What is critical here is the way that gender bias is still evident in the decline of wages in these fields.

Public action and advocacy against gender inequality are necessary to redress women's blocked access to jobs and mobility within traditionally male occupations and professions, and to promote equal pay for comparable work, higher wages for traditionally female professions, and other efforts that seek to address important differences in employment prospects for men and women. Yet, to further these efforts, particularly as they involve building coalitions among women, it is equally important to address the varied circumstances among women.

. . .

NOTES

1. In *The American Perception of Class*, Vanneman and Weber Cannon (1987) build on class divisions as specified by Nicos Poulantzas (1974) and then use quantitative analysis to explore the validity of these divisions with respect to the U.S. public.
2. I calculated these percentages based on Table 1.6 in Reskin and Roos (1990, pp. 17–18).

REFERENCES

Amott, Teresa L. and Julie Matthaei. 1991. *Race, Gender, and Work: A Multicultural Economic History of Women in the United States.* Boston: South End.

Barrera, Mario. 1979. *Race and Class in the Southwest.* South Bend, IN: University of Notre Dame Press.

Bianchi, Suzanne. 1995. "Changing Economic Roles of Women and Men." Pp. 107–54 in *State of the Union: America in the 1990s, Vol. 1, Economic Trends,* edited by R. Farley. New York: Russell Sage Foundation.

Braverman, Harry. 1974. *Labor and Monopoly Capital.* New York: Monthly Review Press.

Daniels, Arlene Kaplan. 1988. *Invisible Careers: Women Civic Leaders from the Volunteer World.* Chicago: University of Chicago Press.

Dill, Bonnie Thornton. 1988. "Our Mothers' Grief: Racial Ethnic Women and and the Maintenance of Families." *Journal of Family History* 13:415–31.

Feagin, Joe R., Hernan Vera, and Nikitah Imani. 1996. *The Agony of Education.* New York: Routledge.

Frankenberg, Ruth. 1993. *White Women, Race Matters: The Social Construction of Whiteness.* Minneapolis: University of Minnesota Press.

Glenn, Evelyn Nakano. 1992. "From Servitude to Service Work: Historical Continuities in the Racial Division of Paid Reproductive Labor." *Signs: Journal of Women in Culture and Society* 18:1–43.

Harris, William. 1982. *The Harder We Run: Black Workers since the Civil War.* New York: Oxford University Press.

Higginbotham, Elizabeth. 1983. "Laid Bare by the System: Work and Survival for Black and Hispanic Women." Pp. 200–215 in *Class, Race and Sex: The Dynamics of Control,* edited by A. Swerdlow and H. Lessinger. Boston: G. K. Hall.

———. 1987. "Employment for Professional Black Women in the Twentieth Century." Pp. 73–91 in *Ingredients for Women's Employment Policy,* edited by C. Bose and G. Spitze. Albany: State University of New York Press.

———. 1994. "Black Professional Women: Job Ceiling and Employment Sectors." Pp. 113–31 in *Women of Color in U.S. Society,* edited by M. Baca Zinn and B. T. Dill. Philadelphia: Temple University Press.

Jones, Jacqueline. 1985. *Labor of Love, Labor of Sorrow: Black Women, Work, and Family from Slavery to the Present.* New York: Basic Books.

Lucal, Betsy. 1994. "Class Stratification in Introductory Textbooks: Relational or Distributional Models?" *Teaching Sociology* 22:139–50.

Marks, Carole C. 1989. *Farewell—We're Good and Gone: The Black Labor Migration.* Bloomington: Indiana University Press.

Massey, Douglas S. and Nancy A. Denton. 1993. *American Apartheid: Segregation and the Making of the Underclass.* Cambridge, MA: Harvard University Press.

McClain, Charles J. 1994. *In Search of Equality: The Chinese Struggle against Discrimination in Nineteenth-Century America.* Berkeley: University of California Press.

McLanahan, Sara and Lynne Casper. 1995. "Growing Diversity and Inequality in the American Family." Pp. 1–45 in *State of the Union: America in the 1990s, Vol. 2, Social Trends,* edited by R. Farley. New York: Russell Sage Foundation.

Nee, Victor and Brett DeBary Nee. 1973. *Longtime Californ': A Documentary Study of an American Chinatown.* Boston: Houghton Mifflin.

Omi, Michael and Howard Winant. 1994. *Racial Formation in the United States: 1960–1990.* 2nd ed. New York: Routledge.

Pedraza, Sylvia. 1991. "Women and Migration: The Social Consequences of Gender." Pp. 303–25 in *Annual Review of Sociology,* Vol. 17, edited by W. R. Scott and J. Blake. Palo Alto, CA: Annual Reviews.

Phipps, Polly A. 1990. "Industrial and Occupational Change in Pharmacy: Prescription for Feminization." Pp. 111–27 in *Job Queues, Gender Queues: Explaining Women's Inroads into Male Occupations,* edited by B. F. Reskin and P. A. Roos. Philadelphia: Temple University Press.

Pohlmann, Marcus D. 1990. *Black Politics in Conservative America.* New York: Longman.

Poulantzas, Nicos. 1974. *Classes in Contemporary Capitalism.* London: New Left.

Reskin, Barbara F. and Patricia A. Roos, eds. 1990. *Job Queues, Gender Queues: Explaining Women's Inroads and Male Occupations.* Philadelphia: Temple University Press.

Roberts, Sam. 1994. "Black Women Graduates Outpace Male Counterparts." *New York Times*, October 31, pp. A8, A12.

Romero, Mary. 1992. *Maid in the U.S.A.* New York: Routledge.

Shaw, Stephanie J. 1996. *What a Woman Ought to Be and to Do: Black Professional Women Workers during the Jim Crow Era.* Chicago: University of Chicago Press.

Sokoloff, Natalie. 1992. *Black Women and White Women in the Professions.* New York: Routledge.

Takaki, Ronald. 1990. *Strangers from a Different Shore: A History of Asian Americans.* Boston: Little, Brown.

Timmer, Doug, D. Stanley Eitzen, and Kathryn D. Talley. 1994. *Paths to Homelessness: Extreme Poverty and the Urban Housing Crisis.* Boulder, CO: Westview.

U.S. Department of Labor. 1995. *Report on the American Workforce.* Washington, DC: Government Printing Office.

U.S. Department of Labor. 1996a. *20 Facts on Women Workers* (Women's Bureau Fact Sheet No. 96-2, September). Washington, DC: Government Printing Office.

U.S. Department of Labor. 1996b. *Usual Weekly Earnings of Wage and Salary Workers, Third Quarter of 1996* (Bureau of Labor Statistics release, October 24). Washington, DC: Government Printing Office.

U.S. Department of Labor. 1996c. *Black Women in the Labor Force* (Women's Bureau Fact Sheet No. 96-4, November). Washington, DC: Government Printing Office.

Vanneman, Reeve and Lynn Weber Cannon. 1987. *The American Perception of Class.* Philadelphia: Temple University Press.

Wilson, William J. 1978. *The Declining Significance of Race: Blacks and Changing American Institutions.* Chicago: University of Chicago Press.

39

Why Does Jane Read and Write So Well?

The Anomaly of Women's Achievement

Roslyn Arlin Mickelson

THE EVIDENCE IS IN AND THE CONCLUSION IS clear: Women can and do achieve academically as well as do men. The myth of female underachievement has been exposed by many studies that have indicated that women's motivation and behavior to achieve not only equal but often surpass that of men (Klein 1985; Maccoby and Jacklin 1974; National Center for Educational Statistics 1986; Stockard 1985; Stockard and Wood 1984; U.S. Bureau of the Census 1987). Today, as in the past, more girls than boys graduate from high school and more women than men

From *Sociology of Education* 1989, Vol. 62 (January): 47–63. Reprinted with permission from American Sociological Association.

receive baccalaureate degrees, and nationwide, women now outnumber men in master's degree programs. More men than women are enrolled only in professional and Ph.D. programs, but even here, the gaps between women and men are closing (National Center for Educational Statistics 1986; Stockard et al. 1980). Fields of specialization continue to be gender linked—mathematics, engineering, and the physical and biological sciences are dominated by males, and the social sciences and humanities are dominated by females—but evidence from a study of undergraduates indicates that differences are disappearing here, too (Hafner and Shaha 1984).

If the picture of women's achievement and attainment is so positive, why do educators and researchers pay so much attention to the subject? One obvious answer lies in the different areas of achievement. Because high-paying careers (those with the best pay, benefits, working conditions, and career ladders) usually require strong backgrounds in mathematics and science, the fact that women continue to lag behind men in these areas is important. A second answer involves the links among schooling, work, and income. Even though women have all but closed the overall gap in educational attainment between the sexes, the occupational world fails to reward women equitably for their accomplishments. Research suggests strongly that the inequalities faced by women in the occupational world cannot be linked, except in the most tenuous ways, to differences in educational achievement and attainment (Stockard 1985, p. 320).

The issue of structural inequality in the work world raises another question that is the focus of this reading. In view of the limited rewards that women are likely to receive from education, why do they do as well and attain as much education as they do? In this society, in which educational credentials purportedly are linked to jobs, promotions, wages, and status, women's educational accomplishments appear anomalous because women continue to receive far fewer rewards for their educational credentials than do men with compara-

ble credentials. One might expect that if women knew of the diminished opportunities that lay ahead, they would put less effort into school because these efforts are likely to yield smaller returns to them than to males who make similar efforts. Yet, this is not the case. This reading explores why gender stratification in the opportunity structure appears to be of little relevance to young women's academic achievement and attainment. It examines the anomaly of females' achievement in light of four hypotheses and presents empirical evidence to assess each hypothesis. Finally, drawing on emerging feminist theory, it suggests directions for future research.

BASIS OF THE ANOMALY

The academic achievement of female students is a curious reversal of a dynamic found among minority and working-class students. A study conducted by the author in 1983 indicated that both working-class and minority youths underachieve, in part, because of the poor returns they are likely to receive from education (Mickelson 1984, 1990). This research was inspired largely by the work of Ogbu (1979), which examined the American opportunity structure and its possible influence on the scholastic achievement of minority students. Ogbu argued that members of a social group that faces a job ceiling know that they do so, and this knowledge channels and shapes their children's academic behavior. The term "job ceiling" refers to overt and informal practices that limit members of castelike minority groups (such as blacks and Chicanos) from unrestricted competition for the jobs for which they are qualified. Members of these groups are excluded from or not allowed to obtain their proportionate share of desirable jobs and hence are overwhelmingly confined to the least desirable jobs in the occupational structure. Ogbu contended that because the job ceiling faced by black adults prevents them from receiving rewards that are commensurate with their educational credentials, education is not the same bridge to adult status for blacks as it is for whites. Black children see that efforts in school often do not have the same outcomes for them as do similar efforts for members of socially dominant groups, such as middle-class white men. Thus, they tend to put less effort and commitment into their schoolwork and hence perform less well, on average, than do middle-class white youths. As Ogbu (1979, p. 193) stated:

I think their perception of the job ceiling is still a major factor that colors [minority] attitudes and school performance. . . . Given the premise that what motivates Americans to maximize their achievement efforts in school is their belief that the better education one has, the more money and more status [one will acquire] . . . is it logical to expect Blacks and Whites to exert the same energy and perform alike in school when the job ceiling consistently underutilizes the black talent and ability and underrewards Blacks for their education?

The author's study tested Ogbu's thesis on minority underachievement but expanded the research to include class and gender—two additional social forces that are strongly related to differential occupational returns on education—by examining students' attitudes toward education in relation to their high school grades. In 1983, 1,193 seniors in nine comprehensive public high schools in the Los Angeles area completed a questionnaire that ascertained their attitudes toward education, family background, and educational and occupational aspirations, as well as various measures of school outcomes. The results showed that all students hold two sets of attitudes toward education, but only one set predicts their achievement in school. The first set of attitudes is composed of beliefs about education and opportunity, as found in the dominant ideology of U.S. society. These attitudes, which the author calls *abstract* attitudes toward education, embody the Protestant Ethic's promise that schooling is a vehicle for upward mobility and success (for example, "Education is the key to success in the future"). These beliefs are widely shared and vary little at this level of abstraction. Abstract attitudes, therefore, cannot predict achievement behavior. The second set of

beliefs about education consists of *concrete* attitudes, which reflect the diverse material realities that people experience with regard to returns on education from the opportunity structure ("Based on their experiences, my parents say people like us are not always paid or promoted according to our education"). Agreement or disagreement with statements of concrete attitudes closely follow class and racial divisions in society. The overall findings indicate that concrete attitudes, not abstract ones, predict achievement in high school (see Mickelson forthcoming for a complete presentation of the research).

This research demonstrates that the effort that students put into their schoolwork and their academic achievement is influenced by students' accurate assessments of the class- and race-linked occupational returns their education is likely to bring them as they make the transition to adulthood. It suggests that middle-class white youths correctly interpret their parents' experiences in the labor market as evidence that they, too, can expect returns commensurate with their educational attainment; therefore, it is not surprising that they generally earn high grades and are likely to attend college. Following this same logic, working-class and black youths put less effort into their schoolwork because they judge that for people like themselves, the payoffs for schooling are limited; hence, they receive lower grades and go to college less often than do middle-class whites (Mickelson 1984, 1990).

Consequently, individuals who are reasonably aware of the realities of the opportunity structure that lie ahead should put more effort or less effort into schoolwork, depending on the occupational returns they are likely to receive. It is in this context that the achievement and attainment of females appear anomalous. If occupational opportunities help shape students' educational goals and achievements, as Ogbu and this author believe, women should not achieve as well or attain as much education as do men in comparable racial and class subgroups.

Yet women do not achieve as one might predict on the basis of gender inequalities in the opportunity structure. In other words, the relatively poor occupational return on educational investments does not appear to depress either their school performance or their willingness to earn advanced degrees. The anomaly considered in this article, then, is not "Why can't Jane read and write?" because she certainly does, but "Why does Jane read and write so well?"

EXTENT OF THE ANOMALY

To capture the anomalous quality of women's educational achievement in light of the gender-linked job ceiling women face, the following discussion reviews the research on women's educational and occupational outcomes, with special attention to racial and class variations in each. It is important to note that most sociological studies, including those that compare the educational attainment of blacks and whites, tended, until recently, either to ignore women or to treat them as persons whose social status was a function of their father's or husband's positions (Acker 1973, 1980; Bernard 1981; Oakley 1974). Turner's (1964) was a classic study in this tradition; it measured women's goals and ambitions by the occupation they expected their husbands to attain. During the past two decades, however, many social scientists have turned their attention to women's unique experiences in achievement, education, and the labor market. It is these studies that are reviewed in this section.

Academic Achievement

Differences in the academic achievement of males and females involve issues of both performance and motivation. Differences in performance are mediated by age and by type of cognitive activity (Kaufman and Richardson 1982). For example, girls generally do better in school until puberty (Klein 1985). The new learning climate of the junior high school, which is more competitive and more individualistic than is the elementary school, works against girls' strengths, such as working cooperatively in groups (Eccles and Hoffman

1985; Steinkamp and Maehr 1984). Although the grade-point averages of boys and girls are comparable in high school, girls tend to outperform boys in verbal tasks, while boys do better in visual-spatial and quantitative activities. Boys and girls differ, however, in the kind of elective courses they choose in high school (there are few gender differences in the enrollment in mandatory high school courses). These gender differences appear particularly in vocational education, where the sex segregation of the work world is mirrored in the students' enrollment. Thus, boys are still more likely than are girls to enroll in higher level mathematics and science courses (National Center for Educational Statistics 1984). Many researchers have attributed the gender differences in quantitative achievement to the different courses in which boys and girls enroll (Berryman 1983; Pallas and Alexander 1983).[1] Although the domains of academic achievement continue to differ by gender, once-popular stereotypes of girls as under- or nonachievers are now considered more mythical than factual (Stockard and Wood 1984).

Gender differences in the motivation to achieve are complex. Earlier research attributed differences in attainment and alleged achievement to girls' lower motivation to achieve. More recent studies, however, have confirmed Maccoby and Jacklin's (1974) conclusions that levels of motivation to achieve among women, including intellectual achievement, continue to equal or surpass

---

[1] Whether gender differences in quantitative achievement are due to sociobiological or environmental factors, such as socialization and exposure to different curricula, remains controversial. However, recent work by Professor Harold Stevenson and his colleagues in the Department of Psychology, University of Michigan, Ann Arbor (personal communication, 1987) strongly supports the idea that gender differences in the performance of American students in mathematics achievement of American schoolchildren with that of children from Japan, Taiwan, and China. They found that there are no significant gender differences in mathematics achievement among Asian students.

those of men (Klein 1985; Lueptow 1980, 1984; Stockard 1985; Stockard and Wood 1984).[2]

Educational Attainment

Until recently, men and women differed in how much schooling they acquired. Alexander and Eckland (1974) showed that female status depressed educational attainment. Nevertheless, today, more women than men graduate from high school (National Center for Educational Statistics 1986; Stockard et al. 1980; U.S. Bureau of the Census 1987). Differences in the subjects in which women and men major at the undergraduate level contribute to differences at the graduate and professional levels (Berryman 1983). On the graduate level, gender differences in attainment appear both in the types of degrees that are sought (women are less likely to be found in science departments and professional schools) and in the completion of advanced degree programs (Astin 1969; Berryman 1983; Klein 1985). Structural factors, such as curricular placement and counseling practices in elementary and high schools, are likely contributors to these patterns in higher education. For example, Hallinan and Sorensen (1987) reported that among equally able girls and boys in elementary school, boys are more likely than girls to be placed in high-ability mathematics groups. However, in a personal communication (1987), Jeannie Oakes, a social scientist with the RAND Corporation, noted that she found no systematic evidence of gender differences in track placement among secondary students; girls are just as likely as boys to be found in academic tracks,

although they are less likely to choose additional mathematics and science courses when they have fulfilled the minimum requirements for entrance into college.

Racial and Class Differences

Historically, white working-class women generally did not seek education beyond high school because they thought that the home and family were their careers and that their husbands' "family wage" would provide them with a decent life (Rubin 1986). Bernard (1981) noted that among working-class women, the lack of a job was evidence of their husbands' abilities as providers. Today, when working-class women work outside the home, they do so in the secondary labor market, in which advanced educational credentials are not necessary (Howe 1977; Rubin 1976). Nevertheless, they often have more education than their husbands because when they work, they work in clerical or service occupations that require writing and spelling skills. Although white middle-class women often went to college in the past, most of those who sought a higher education did not necessarily plan careers because work outside the home was not intrinsically desired or financially necessary. However, they might attempt to start careers after the children left home (Bernard 1981). Only since the 1970s, with the decline of the "family wage," have middle- and working-class white women faced the economic and social realities that make employment and the concomitant educational credentials seem necessary.

The case of black women is strikingly different from that of white women. Black women from all classes have always worked outside their homes (Davis 1981). Because the labor market was highly segregated by gender and class, the vast majority of black women were excluded from all but the most menial domestic and service jobs. Nevertheless, black women were more likely than were black men to obtain an education, especially a higher education. This gender pattern of educational achievement represents a reversal of the pattern found historically among whites.

---

[2]Although gender differences exist in vocational tracks, they are rooted in differences in the lived cultures of adolescent boys and girls, as well as in certain structural aspects of schooling, such as counseling practices. Valli's (1986) research on clerical education and Lee and Bryk's (1986) study of girls' achievement and attitudes in single-sex secondary schools suggest the importance of lived cultures for the achievement of females.

Consequently, the small cadre of educated middle-class blacks was composed primarily of women. Middle-class black women did not view their education as a credential for a desirable marriage or as "social finishing," as did many of their white counterparts. Instead, they believed that education was a bona fide credential for entry into the middle-class occupational structure. Although the vast majority of these women were confined to careers in teaching and, to a lesser degree, nursing or social work, they worked in their chosen occupations for which they were trained, albeit their careers were constrained severely by a race- and sex-segregated occupational structure. Today, black women, unlike white women, do not face the relatively new experience of having to work to survive, they have always had to do so (Davis 1981; Simms and Malveaux 1987; Wallace 1980).

Today, class differences in black women's educational attainment remain. Teenage motherhood, epidemic among poor blacks, has a devastating effect on educational outcomes (Children's Defense Fund 1985, 1988; Rumberger 1983).[3] Black women from working- and lower-class backgrounds continue to attain less schooling than any ethnic group except Hispanics and Native Americans (Children's Defense Fund 1988; U.S. Bureau of the Census 1987).

Differences in Returns on Education

Members of the working-class, women, and minorities continue to receive lower returns on their education than do middle-class white men. In 1982, the U.S. Commisssion on Civil Rights reported that at every level of training, blacks, Hispanics, and women receive lower pay and have higher levels of under- and unemployment than do white middle-class men. Moreover, in many instances, the disparities are greater among female

and minority workers with the most education (Treiman and Hartman 1981).

Treiman and Hartman (1981, p. 16) reported that "minority males employed full time earned 75.3 percent of the salary of similarly employed majority males; majority females earned 58.6 percent and minority females 55.8 percent." These disparities were present even after the authors controlled for differences in seniority, education, age, specific vocational training, local pay rates, average number of hours worked, number of weeks worked per year, and other characteristics.

A primary reason for the persistence of unequal returns is that men and women continue to work in sex-segregated labor markets that have different career ladders (Sewell, Hauser, and Wolf 1980). Rosenfeld (1980) examined career trajectories (the job histories of socioeconomic status and income over an individual's work life) by sex and race. She found that white men have a general advantage over all other groups in many aspects of their careers, including wages and status, and that women and nonwhite men have similar career profiles. Kanter (1977) described the problems faced by women in the corporate world: White men gain more status than does any other group and nonwhite women gain the least, and the differences between white men and other groups increase over time. The exception to this trend is the small number of black women with extremely high levels of education (Carrigan 1981; Jones 1987; Rosenfeld 1980; Wilkerson 1987). Among black women managers with MBAs, the evidence is mixed. Although their career mobility rates were nearly identical to those of men, personal and institutional factors affected their promotions differently than they did for men (Nkomo and Cox 1987). For example, mentors were more available to men than to women and men were more likely to be promoted if they had line positions, while women were more likely to be promoted if they worked in large, rather than small, firms.

Why do women continue to achieve and value education in the face of limited potential returns on their efforts? A review of the literature reveals at least four hypotheses as possible explanations for

---

[3]The "epidemic" is not confined to the black community; the rate of increase in teenage pregnancies is higher among white girls than among black girls (Children's Defense Fund 1985, 1988).

this anomaly. The following sections discuss these hypotheses and assess each in the light of some relevant research.

DIFFERENTIAL REFERENCE GROUPS

The first hypothesis is drawn from reference-group theory, which Nilson (1982, p. 1) summarized as follows:

"[M]entally healthy" individuals realistically assess their statuses in comparison to others who are perceived to be fairly similar on at least one important, visible dimension of actual or expected rewards or resources. It is only within a range of meaningful comparison that satisfaction or dissatisfaction is felt.

From reference-group theory, one can deduce that women are aware of their diminished status in relation to men but when they evaluate what a fair and just return on education might be, they look to other women, not to men, as a point of reference. Women's evaluations of whether returns on schooling are equitable are based on their awareness that there are two occupational structures, one for them and one for men (Treiman and Terrell 1975).[4] In this context, women are likely to believe that their education is rewarded. Empirical research indicates that women's incremental return on education is similar to men's, but the intercept of the regression equation is lower for women than for men. That is, year for year and credential for credential, both men and women receive more returns on more education but they start in different places in the opportunity structure. In addition, the internal career ladders in the female occupational structure are much more limited than are those in the male sector (England et al. 1988; Sewell, Hauser, and Wolf 1980).

Reference-group theory may explain why women do not consider their mothers', aunts', and

---

[4]Waite (1981) confirmed that 75 percent of women work in occupations whose incumbents are more than 50 percent female and that 32 percent are in occupations whose incumbents are more than 90 percent female.

older sisters' poor returns on education to be unfair. The returns are fair in terms of a sex-segregated occupational structure, particularly if a woman sees that her role model's education enabled her to move from an unskilled, tedious, dangerous laboring position to a higher-status, clean, pink-collar job. This is exactly what educational credentials have done for many women in the past 20 years: With education, a woman can move from cafeteria worker to secretary, from secretary to teacher, and from clerk to registered nurse.

. . .

THE POLLYANNA HYPOTHESIS

According to this explanation, the typical young woman who graduates from high school is likely to be optimistic about her future. Although she may be aware of the sexism that her mother and aunts experienced in the workplace, she interprets it as the problem of the "older generation," which the women's movement has already addressed. Such a view is likely to be a product of this historical moment and of the limited world of high school seniors. Young women today have been exposed to 15 years of rhetoric from the women's movement. They have heard of affirmative action and Title IX. They see that society is changing; women can run for the vice-presidency of the United States. The major social institutions that they experience beyond the nuclear family are the mass media and the high school, where women appear to be moving toward gender equity. The rhetoric and the reality of their world outside the family converge into a picture in which women seemingly can achieve their potentials, largely unencumbered by sexism.

Adolescent girls have not yet faced situations that conflict with the rhetoric of equal opportunity for women. They are not yet in the job market, and they have yet to enter close relationships with men in whch they may face the choice of subordinating their goals and ambitions to save the family unit. It will be two or three years before these young women achieve adult status and face these possibilities. In the Pollyannaish world of adolescent girls, their education will be treated just like a man's and their careers will not be compromised by family responsibilities because their husbands will be equal partners in a dual-career marriage. For these Pollyannas, sexism is a thing of the past; they need not worry about it because the battle for equality has been won.

. . .

The Pollyanna hypothesis suggests that today young women believe they have "come a long way"—that barriers to successful careers in both the marketplace and the home have fallen by the wayside. This belief may explain the anomaly of women's achievement: Women do well in school because they have no doubt that they will be able to take their rightful places in industry and the professions next to their comparably educated brothers. To explode the myth that the battle has been won, more comparable worth cases must make headlines and more Elizabeth Hishons, Christine Crafts, and Theda Skocpols may have to sue their employers for sexism.[5] Perhaps young women must encounter the gender-segregated occupational structure, the gap in the salaries of men and women, and the problems that most women face in "happily integrating" the career-husband-children "triad" before their attitudes toward education, career, and family reflect, to a greater degree, the realities of modern society.

---

[5]Elizabeth Hishon is the lawyer who won permission from the U.S. Supreme Court to sue her former employer, Atlanta's prestigious law firm King and Spalding, for sex discrimination because it failed to grant her or any other woman partnership in the 100-partner firm. Christine Craft is the television anchor who was fired because her employers thought she was not sufficiently attractive to report the news. Theda Skocpol is the sociologist who received tenure from Harvard University after winning a sex-discrimination suit against the university, which originally failed to grant her tenure.

SOCIAL POWERLESSNESS

Theories of the social powerlessness of women are the basis of the third explanation for the apparent failure of sexism in the opportunity structure to affect women's motivations to achieve in school. This explanation posits that marriage is a consciously sought alternative to a career. Aware of the structural inequalities in the occupational world, women know that they cannot expect equitable returns on their education, no matter how well they have done in school, and realize that they must seek a husband if they wish to be socially and financially secure. In addition, they are aware of the economic plight of those who attempt to be independent of a male partner (breadwinner) or of those who are left to support young children alone. Thus, young women strive for future status and success by choosing a "promising" husband rather than by focusing on a career. Education still has a role; it is essential for acquiring an appropriate husband.

Educational achievement in high school allows a woman to attend college, where she can meet men who are likely to have suitable futures as breadwinners. Accordingly, the primary evaluation of social returns on her educational achievement and attainment will not be made in the labor market, but in marriage. This hypothesis applies to the middle-class woman who must marry a college-educated man simply to maintain the social status and lifestyle of her childhood and to the working-class woman who aspires to upward mobility.

. . .

For both middle- and working-class women, black and white, education and marriage have different meanings for potential social status. Arguably, white adolescent girls are aware of the less-than-favorable occupational options that await them and know that for most women (at least for white women), the safest and most reliable route to high status as an adult may be through a good marriage. Although the situation is more ambiguous for young black women, marriage remains important to the economic survival of black families. Wilson (1988) made this point as well in his discussion of the structural origins of the underclass.[6] As Featherman (1978, p. 53) commented:

[V]icarious achievement (through a spouse) remains a major mechanism for intergenerational continuity or change in status for women, supplementing or complementing the opportunities for achievement through independent pursuits outside marriage and the home economy.

SEX-ROLE SOCIALIZATION

The fourth hypothesis with regard to the anomaly of women's achievement comes from the literature on sex-role socialization. According to the asymmetry model described by Kaufman and Richardson (1982), boys' achievement is motivated by the desire for mastery and other intrinsic rewards, while girls' achievement is directed toward winning social approval and other extrinsic rewards. Little girls want to please and be "good" so they will earn love and approval. Women's motivation for achievement, it is suggested, evolves from early childhood needs for love and the approval of others, more than for mastery and self-reliance, which underlies the motivation of men. Clearly, this distinction is rigidly simplistic. Marciano (1981) suggested a subtler explanation: The "center of gravity" of women's motivation to achieve is an orientation to others, while the "center of gravity" of men's motivation is a desire for mastery and self-gratification. Girls perform well in school because good performance is compatible with affiliative motives and consistent with the

---

[6]Wilson (1988) has been criticized by those who interpret his discussion of the unavailability of marriageable men for underclass women as an argument that poor women are but a husband away from economic insolvency. Although he denies that this was his intent, the relative lack of a detailed discussion of the effects of the sex-segregated occupational structure lends support to his critics.

"good girl" role into which they are socialized (Kaufman and Richardson 1982; Maccoby and Jacklin 1974; Weitzman 1979, 1984).

The sex-role socialization hypothesis actually has two aspects. First, girls do well in school because they are socialized to be good. Being a "good girl" in school means dutifully following orders and instructions from teachers, being decorous and compliant, and accepting rules with little protest. This is the kind of behavior that is more compatible with female than with male sex roles. Weitzman (1984, p. 172) explained how girls' early sex-role socialization produces a particular kind of motivation to achieve that is not found in boys:

The dependence and affection-seeking responses seen as normal for both boys and girls in early childhood become defined as feminine in older children. . . . [G]irls are not separated from their parents as sources of support and nurturance, and they are therefore not forced to develop internal controls and an independent sense of self. Instead, the self they value is the one that emanates from the appraisals of others. Consequently, girls develop a greater need for the approval of others . . . than do boys.

The second part of this argument revolves around the male sex role and achievement. Although the female sex role demands that girls be good and do well in school, the male sex role, particularly among working-class white boys, requires a degree of resistance to authority figures like teachers and a certain devaluation of schoolwork because it is "feminine" (Stockard et al. 1980; Willis 1977). The lived culture of working-class men glorifies manual labor, which involves physical strength, a willingness to get dirty, and an attitude of rebellion against and independence from superiors, as distinguished from the attitudes of submission and appeasement associated with women (Bologh 1986). Thus, the high achievement of female students may be due to two separate sex-role processes: Girls do well because they are socialized to be good and they do better than some boys because the sex-role socialization of boys requires a degree of academic under-achievement.

As Stockard et al. (1980) noted, good students display behavior that is generally sex typed as feminine. Therefore, it is understandable if boys do not conform to the role of good student because being a good student would mean acting feminine. Boys do not refuse to learn, but they may not reflect learning in the ways that are required for high grades. Until this century, even elite white men tempered their achievement in college to receive a "gentleman's C."[7]

. . .

DISCUSSION

The anomaly with which this article began remains essentially unresolved. Why do women do so well in school when they can expect only relatively limited returns on their educational achievements? The rationale underlying the educational attainment of most men—gaining credentials that will bring higher pay, better jobs, and promotions—is, in many ways, inadequate for women. The academic achievement and attainment of women defy this logic because women continue to match (and often surpass) men without the same occupational returns from schooling that men receive.

The four hypotheses explored in the previous section offered a variety of perspectives on the question of why women achieve in school. The first three hypotheses examined how young women view the connection between education and the occupational structure, while the fourth ignored structure altogether. Although these hypotheses offer some insight into the question of women's achievement, all four hypotheses suffer from certain problems:

---

[7]An interesting twist on this was reported by Fordham and Ogbu (1986), who described how able black students consciously hide their ability and temper their achievement lest they be labeled as "acting white." The similarities and differences between labeling achievement as either feminine or white behavior, an implication of pariahlike status in both cases, need further exploration.

- Reference-group theory assumes that women are aware of the greater returns from education that men receive but do not care. This idea requires a major leap of faith.

- If one accepts the reference-group premise that young women are aware of a sex-segregated occupational structure, one must deny the Pollyanna and the social powerlessness hypotheses. The Pollyanna theory presumes that the basis of the reference-group hypothesis—a sex-segregated occupational structure—is a thing of the past. The social powerlessness hypothesis denies the direct relevance of occupational returns on education for women's decisions and proposes that good marriages, not careers, are the fundamental motivation behind women's educational attainment. If this is true, then a sex-segregated occupational structure is less relevant than is women's primarily dependent status in society.

- Furthermore, the Pollyanna theory and the social powerlessness theory are mutually exclusive. One denies that young women perceive sexism as a factor in the status-attainment process, but the other identifies sexism as such a prominent component of the status-attainment process that marriage appears to be the most reasonable alternative for women who seek social and financial security.

- The sex-role socialization hypothesis focuses completely on the individual and her early socialization experiences. It fails to link her behavior in school to such broad social-structural phenomena as those discussed in the other hypotheses. Any account of social behavior that fails to incorporate structure is limited in its explanatory power.

A final shortcoming of all the hypotheses discussed in this article is the uneven ability of the theories to explain the achievement and attainment behavior of women from diverse racial and class backgrounds. It is likely, for example, that the Pollyanna phenomenon is more characteristic of middle-class women, while reference group is a more likely explanation of working-class experiences. Social powerlessness theory is also relevant mainly to middle-class white women; it is especially inadequate for poor and working-class black women.

. . .

REFERENCES

Acker, J. 1973. "Women and Social Stratification: A Case of Intellectual Sexism." *American Journal of Sociology* 78(4):936–945.

———. 1980. "Women and Stratification: A Review of Recent Literature." *Contemporary Sociology* 9:25–39.

Alexander, K. L., and B. K. Eckland. 1974. "Sex Differences in the Educational Attainment Process." *American Sociological Review* 39:668–682.

Astin, H. 1969. *The Female Doctorate in America.* New York: Russell Sage Foundation.

Bernard, J. 1981. *The Female World.* New York: Free Press.

Berryman, S. E. 1983. *Who Will Do Science?* New York: Rockefeller Foundation.

Bologh, R. W. 1986. "Dialectical Feminism: Beyond Marx, Weber, and Masculine Theorizing." Paper presented at the Annual Meetings of the American Sociological Association, New York.

Carrigan, S. P. 1981. "Income Variation: A Comparison of Determinants for Men and Women." Unpublished doctoral dissertation, University of California at Los Angeles.

Children's Defense Fund. 1985. *Black Children, White Children.* Washington, DC: Children's Defense Fund.

———. 1988. *Children's Defense Budget FY 1989.* Washington, DC: Children's Defense Fund.

Davis, A. 1981. *Women, Race, and Class.* New York: Random House.

Eccles, J. S., and I. W. Hoffman. 1985. "Sex Roles, Socialization, and Occupational Behavior." Pp. 367–420 in *Research in Child Development and Social Policy,* vol. 1, edited by H. W. Stevenson and A. E. Siegel. Chicago: University of Chicago Press.

England, P., G. Farkas, B. Kilbourne, and T. Dou. 1988. "Explaining Occupational Sex Segregation and Wages: Findings from a Model with Fixed Effects." *American Sociological Review* 53(4):528–543.

Featherman, D. O. 1978. "Schooling and Occupational Careers: Constancy and Change in Worldly Success." Madison: Center for Demography and Ecology, University of Wisconsin.

Fordham, S., and J. U. Ogbu. 1986. "Black Students' School Success: Coping with the Burden of 'Acting White.'" *Urban Review* 18:176–206.

Hafner, A. I., and S. Shaha. 1984. "Gender Differences in the Prediction of Freshman Grades." Paper presented at the Annual Meeting of the American Educational Research Association, New Orleans (April).

Hallinan, M. T., and A. B. Sorensen. 1987. "Ability Grouping and Sex Differences in Mathematics Achievement." *Sociology and Education* 60(2): 63–73.

Howe, L. K. 1977. *Pink Collar Workers.* New York: Avon Books.

Jones, B. A. P. 1987. "Black Women and Labor Force Participation: An Analysis of Sluggish Growth Rates." Pp. 11–32 in *Slipping Through the Cracks: The Status of Black Women,* edited by M. C. Simms and J. Malveaux. New Brunswick, NJ: Transaction Books.

Kanter, R. M. 1977. *Men and Women of the Corporation.* New York: Basic Books.

Kaufman, D. R., and B. Richardson. 1982. *Achievement and Women: Challenging the Assumptions.* New York: Free Press.

Klein, S., ed. 1985. *Handbook for Achieving Sex Equity through Education.* Baltimore, MD: Johns Hopkins University Press.

Lee, V. E., and A. S. Bryk. 1986. "Effects of Single-Sex Secondary Schools on Student Achievement and Attitudes." *Journal of Educational Psychology* 78(5):381–395.

Lueptow, L. B. 1980. "Social Change and Sex Role Change in Adolescent Orientation toward Life, Work, and Achievement: 1967–1975." *Social Psychology Quarterly* 43(1):48–59.

———. 1984. *Adolescent Sex Roles and Social Change.* New York: Columbia University Press.

Maccoby, E., and C. Jacklin. 1974. *The Psychology of Sex Differences.* Palo Alto, CA: Stanford University Press.

Marciano, T. D. 1981. "Socialization and Women at Work." *National Forum* 71:24–25.

Mickelson, R. A. 1984. "Race, Class, and Gender Differences in Adolescent Academic Achievement Attitudes and Behaviors." Unpublished doctoral dissertation, University of California at Los Angeles.

———. 1990. The Attitude-Achievement Paradox among Black Adolescents." *Sociology of Education.*

National Center for Educational Statistics. 1984. "Science and Mathematics Education in American High Schools: Results from the High School and Beyond Study." *Bulletin of the U.S. Department of Education.* Washington, DC: U.S. Government Printing Office.

———. 1986. *Earned Degrees Conferred, Department of Education.* Washington, DC: U.S. Government Printing Office.

Nilson, L. B. 1982. "The Perceptual Distortions of Social Distance: Why the Underdog Principle Seldom Works." Paper presented at the meetings of the American Sociological Association, San Francisco.

Nkomo, S. M., and T. Cox. 1987. "Gender Differences in the Upward Mobility of Black Managers." Paper presented at the meetings of the National Academy of Management, New Orleans.

Oakley, A. 1974. *The Sociology of Housework.* New York: Pantheon Books.

Ogbu, J. U. 1979. *Minority Education and Caste.* New York: Academic Press.

Pallas, A. M., and K. Alexander. 1983. "Sex Differences in Quantitative SAT Performance: New Evidence on Differential Course Work Hypothesis." *American Educational Research Journal* 20(2):165–182.

Rosenfeld, R. 1980. "Race and Sex Differences in Career Dynamics." *American Sociological Review* 45: 583–609.

Rubin, L. 1976. *Worlds of Pain.* New York: Basic Books.

Rumberger, R. 1983. "Dropping Out of High School: The Influence of Race, Sex, and Family Background." *American Educational Research Journal* 20(2):199–220.

Sewell, W., R. Hauser, and W. Wolf. 1980. "Sex, Schooling, and Occupational Status." *American Journal of Sociology* 86(3):551–583.

Simms, M. C., and J. Malveaux. 1987. *Slipping Through the Cracks: The Status of Black Women.* New Brunswick, NJ: Transaction Books.

Steinkamp, M. W., and M. L. Maehr. 1984. "Gender Differences in Motivational Orientation toward Achievement in School Science: A Quantitative Synthesis." *American Educational Research Journal* 21(1):39–59.

Stockard, J. 1985. "Education and Gender Equality: A Critical View." Pp. 299–326 in *Research in Sociology of Education and Socialization,* vol. 5. Greenwich, CT: JAI Press.

Stockard, J., P. A. Schmuck, K. Kempner, P. Williams, S. K. Edson, and M. A. Smith. 1980. *Sex Equity in Education.* New York: Academic Press.

Stockard, J., and J. W. Wood. 1984. "The Myth of Female Underachievement: A Reexamination of Sex Differences in Academic Underachievement." *American Educational Research Journal* 21(4): 825–838.

Treiman, D. W., and H. Hartman. 1981. *Women, Wages, and Work: Equal Pay for Equal Value.* Washington, DC: National Academy Press.

Treiman, D. W., and K. Terrell. 1975. "Sex and the Process of Status Attainment: A Comparison of Working Men and Women." *American Sociological Review* 40(20):174–200.

Turner, R. 1964. *The Social Context of Ambition.* San Francisco: Chandler Publishing Co.

U.S. Bureau of the Census. 1987. Educational Attainment in the United States: March 1982–1985. *Current Population Reports,* Series P-20, No. 415. Washington, DC: U.S. Department of Commerce.

Valli, L. 1986. *Becoming Clerical Workers.* Boston: Routledge & Rogan-Paul.

Waite, L. J. 1981. *U.S. Women at Work.* Santa Monica, CA: The RAND Corp.

Wallace, P. A. 1980. *Black Women in the Labor Force.* Cambridge, MA: MIT Press.

Weitzman, L. J. 1979. *Sex-Role Socialization.* Palo Alto, CA: Mayfield Publishing Co.

———. 1984. "Sex-Role Socialization: A Focus on Women." Pp. 157–237 in *Women. A Feminist Perspective*, edited by J. Freeman. Palo Alto, CA: Mayfield Publishing Co.

Willis, P. 1977. *Learning to Labor.* New York: Columbia University Press.

Wilson, W. J. 1988. *The Truly Disadvantaged.* Chicago: University of Chicago Press.

40

Women, Men, and Work in the Twenty-First Century

Barbara F. Reskin and Irene Padavic

TRENDS IN WORK AT THE END OF THE TWENTIETH CENTURY

Four major workplace changes are currently underway in America: the restructuring of the economy toward decreased employment in manufacturing and increased employment in services; the polarization of jobs into simpler, deskilled jobs and upgraded, more complex ones; the increasing importance of part-time and temporary workers; and the growing diversity in the workforce. The first three trends—economic restructuring, upgrading and deskilling, and increasing part-time and temporary work—are occurring as a result of employers' attempts to compete profitably in an increasingly global economy. The increasing diversity in the workplace is a result of changes in this country's demography.

Economic Restructuring

Economic restructuring is the ongoing transformation of a nation's economy, in which some indus-

tries and jobs grow and others decline. For several decades, the proportion of U.S. workers employed in production industries has been dropping and the proportion employed in services has been growing. The manufacturing sector is projected to employ only about 13 percent of workers by the year 2005, down from a high of 24 percent in 1940 (Kutscher 1991:7). Many U.S. firms have been exporting manufacturing jobs to lower-wage parts of the world, such as Asia and Mexico.[1] The loss of these jobs has contributed to the decline in American men's earnings. . . .

While the U.S. industrial base has been crumbling, the growth of the service sector has created millions of new jobs. This trend, too, will continue. Experts project that almost 90 percent of new jobs created between 1988 and the year 2000 will be in the service sector (National Commission on Working Women 1990) and that 81 percent of all jobs in the year 2005 will be in service industries (Carey and Franklin 1991).

From *Women and Men at Work* by Barbara F. Reskin and Irene Padavic. Copyright © 1994 by Pine Forge Press. Reprinted by permission of Sage Publications, Inc.

[1]Many of these jobs in developing countries go to women, drawing them into the labor force and providing them with pay and autonomy that they would not otherwise have. But this employment also subjects women to sweatshop working conditions, extremely low pay, and hazardous jobs.

TABLE 9.1

Occupations with the Largest Projected Job Growth, 1990 to 2005

Occupation	Number of Projected New Jobs	Percent Female (1992)	Median Weekly Wages for Both Sexes (1992)
Retail sales clerks	887,000	54.5	$270
Registered nurses	767,000	93.5	662
Cashiers	685,000	75.7	219
General office clerks	670,000	84.1	356
Truck drivers	617,000	3.3	418
Managers and administrators	598,000	43.6	650
Janitors and cleaners	555,000	22.0	291
Nursing aides, orderlies	552,000	87.9	266
Food-counter and related workers	550,000	60.9	204
Waiters, waitresses	449,000	72.9	222
Secondary school teachers	437,000	53.9	610
Information clerks and receptionists	422,000	88.6	319

Source: Data from Silvestri and Lukasiewicz 1991:table 4; U.S. Bureau of Labor Statistics 1992a:table 5.

The decline of the manufacturing sector and explosion of the service sector matter because these sectors provide very different kinds of jobs. Wages tend to be substantially lower in the service sector: For every dollar an employer paid in manufacturing wages in 1991, a retail-trade worker or personal-services worker earned 63 cents (U.S. Bureau of the Census 1992). In addition, service-sector jobs have twice the turnover rate of those in manufacturing and are substantially more likely to be part time, hence lacking benefits.

Many of the fastest-growing service occupations are in well-paying fields like law, medicine, and computers. However, the occupations predicted to supply the most new jobs (with the exceptions of registered nurses and general managers) are low-skilled, low-paying ones such as waiter, janitor, and food-counter worker (see Table 9.1). In fact, low-skilled, low-paying jobs are predicted to employ eight times more workers than highly

skilled service-sector jobs are (Silvestri and Lukasiewicz 1987).

Upgrading and Deskilling

The second trend is change in the level of skills that jobs demand. Economic restructuring is *up-grading* some jobs and *deskilling*—or reducing the complexity, skill, and knowledge—of others. The decline in manufacturing jobs has cost the economy many skilled and semiskilled blue-collar jobs. At the same time, the growth of the service sector has created both skilled and unskilled jobs. As Table 9.1 shows, however, low-skill service-sector jobs will predominate.

One way that employers have deskilled jobs is through new technologies (Levin and Rumberger 1987). This sort of deskilling has occurred in secretarial work, bookkeeping, printing, and insurance adjusting and underwriting, to name a few occupations. According to Randy Hodson and Robert Parker (1988:25), "Increasingly, whether the context is manufacturing or the automated office, control and discretion are being removed from workers and placed directly in automated equipment." The occupation of butcher, for example, has been deskilled by the introduction of boxed beef (in which central processing plants do many of the early stages of processing); as a result, cutters need less technical competence (Walsh 1989). Deskilling is also common at fast-food restaurants. Burger King can now train workers to operate the cash register with nine minutes of training, and it is trying to cut two minutes off this time (Hodgkinson 1988). Twenty years ago, a McDonald's counter worker needed the ability to work a cash register and make change; today counter workers need only identify the picture of a hamburger on the register. Moreover, many modern cash registers now are programmed to take over part of the selling job: When a McDonald's counter worker punches the keys for a hamburger and a shake, the keys for apple pie, cookies, and ice cream light up to remind the worker to suggest them (Leidner 1991). In clerical work, the secretary of 20 years ago was a generalist, performing a wide variety of tasks; that worker has been replaced by the word-processing operator, whose sole task is to manually strike a keyboard, often under electronic surveillance (Sweeney and Nussbaum 1989).

At the same time, new technology—especially computerization—is upgrading some jobs (Zuboff 1988). Some innovative companies have redesigned jobs to provide workers with more autonomy, because autonomy is critical for a quick response to a rapidly changing business environment. These upgraded jobs tend to offer high wages and advancement potential. Workers in upgraded jobs can also develop their skills and expertise in a variety of areas.

Researchers are debating whether deskilling or upgrading predominates in today's workplace. They agree, however, that advanced technology in itself does not determine the skill level of a job. Instead, employers and workers determine what effect new technology has on work: If workers have no power and if employers do not seek the advantages of a more skilled workforce, then new technology is likely to lead to deskilling (Hodson and Parker 1988).

The Rise of the Contingent Workforce

The third trend is the expansion of the contingent workforce. *Contingent work* is any job in which workers lack an explicit or implicit contract for long-term employment or in which the minimum hours vary unsystematically (Polivka and Nardone 1989:11). In short, contingent workers lack job security and income security. Their jobs depend on the employer's need for workers. Contingent workers include temporary workers, many part-time workers, and some independent contractors.

Employers rely on contingent workers so they can expand and contract their workforce in response to changing circumstances. The economic rationale behind a contingent workforce is cost savings. Not having to pay for health insurance, sick leave, unemployment insurance, workers' compensation, Social Security, pensions, and vacations saves employers 20 to 40 percent of the cost of regular employees (Sweeney and Nussbaum 1989; Callaghan and Hartmann 1991). The same factors that make contingent work attractive to employers—the lack of job security and benefits—make it unattractive to workers. Not surprisingly, contingent employment has been concentrated in industries where workers have little power to combat the practice through unions (Cornfield 1987).

Contingent workers include three groups:

• *Temporary workers.* Temporary employment grew 3 to 10 times faster than overall employment between 1982 and 1992 (Ansberry 1993; Hartmann 1993). In 1992, two-thirds of new private-sector jobs were temporary (Ansberry 1993). Many of these contingent workers hold a series of jobs punctuated by unemployment; they often find jobs through temporary-employment agencies, which have burgeoned in recent years. Clerical work has been the mainstay of temporary work, but increasingly employers are hiring professional and technical workers on this basis (Christensen 1989). For example, some computer programmers, accountants, and managers now work on a contingent basis.

• *Part-time workers.* Part-time employment has been growing fastest in the retail-trade and service sectors (Tilly 1991). Among all employed non-agricultural workers, 18.9 percent worked part time in 1992, but the proportion of part-time workers in services was 23.6 percent (U.S. Bureau of Labor Statistics 1993). Most part-time jobs provide few fringe benefits and no opportunity for advancement. Their greatest disadvantage, however, is the low pay. The average part-time worker earned only 58 percent of the hourly pay of a full-time worker in 1989 (Tilly 1991:12); the hourly pay was even less for workers employed part time and for part of the year (Institute for Women's Policy Research 1993). As you might guess, turnover is high. The U.S. Bureau of Labor Statistics classifies part-time employment as being either voluntary or involuntary. Between 1970 and 1990, almost 90 percent of the growth in part-time employment was due to the growth of involuntary part-time employment (Callaghan and Hartmann 1991). Thus it seems that the growth of part-time employment is largely driven by employer needs, not workers' choices.

• *Independent contractors.* . . . Independent contractors are workers whom employers hire on a freelance basis to do work that regular employees otherwise would do in-house (Christensen 1989). According to the Internal Revenue Service, the number of independent contractors grew by over 50 percent between 1985 and 1988, to 9.5 million workers (U.S. General Accounting Office 1991). Employers have switched many workers to independent-contractor status to save on fringe benefits, reduce the permanent payroll, and reduce tax requirements. Many textbook editors, real estate agents, and building cleaners, for example, now work on this basis, whereas in the past they were regular employees. Even professionals are subject to becoming independent con-

tractors (Zachary and Ortega 1993). Aetna Life & Casualty Company cut 2,600 jobs in 1992 and then rehired many laid-off workers to do the same job as independent contractors, at lower pay and without benefits (Zachary and Ortega 1993).

The numbers of independent contractors, temporary workers, and part-time workers—the contingent workforce—are growing and undoubtedly will continue to grow. It is difficult to measure contingent employment, because some contingent workers fall in more than one category, but one estimate is that in 1988 about 25 to 30 percent of the workforce was made up of contingent workers (Belous 1989).

Workforce Diversity

According to the U.S. Bureau of Labor Statistics, women, minorities, and immigrants make up a growing segment of the workforce, and their share is predicted to continue growing at least through the year 2005 (Kutscher 1991). Whites are expected to remain the majority of workers, but their share of the labor force is expected to drop from 78.6 percent in 1990 to 73 percent in 2005. African Americans will expand their share of the workforce from 10.7 percent in 1990 to 11.6 percent in 2005. Hispanics will increase even more rapidly, from 7.7 percent of the workforce to 11.1 percent, exceeding the projected growth in labor force participation of African Americans. Asians and others are expected to increase from 3.1 percent of the labor force to 4.3 percent.

Immigration has fueled recent population growth in the United States. Whereas in the 1960s immigration was responsible for only 11 percent of population growth, in the 1970s it accounted for 33 percent, and in the 1980s it accounted for 39 percent (Johnston and Packer 1987). Legal and undocumented immigrants are also likely to be the fastest-growing group in the labor market. Recent immigrants, most of whom are from Asia and Latin America, tend to be either high-skilled, well-educated workers or low-skilled, little-educated ones ("The Immigrants" 1992). The rising number of immigrants and their historical tendency to be active in the labor force means that they will make up an increasing share of the labor force.

IMPLICATIONS FOR WORKING WOMEN AND MEN

These economic changes will have a substantial effect on progress toward equality between women and men in the workforce. The impact will be felt in five areas: labor force participation, sex segregation, the pay gap, the gendering of work, and the relationship between work and family.

Labor Force Participation

Society has come to take women in the workforce for granted. Women will account for 62 percent of net labor force growth between 1990 and 2005, and men's labor force participation will decline slightly. As a result, in 2005, 47.4 percent of the civilian labor force will be female (U.S. Women's Bureau 1992). The labor force participation rates of women of color are projected to outpace white women's: Hispanic and Asian women's participation rate will grow 80 percent between 1900 and 2005, African-American women's will grow 34 percent, and white women's will grow 23 percent (U.S. Women's Bureau 1992).

By the turn of the twenty-first century, 61 percent of all working-age women are projected to be in the labor force (Fullerton 1987), up from 57.8 percent in 1992 (U.S. Women's Bureau 1993). Just 30 years ago, researchers were asking whether working mothers caused juvenile delinquency. Now most young women college graduates expect to work full time. As a result, researchers and federal agencies are asking how society can accommodate women's labor force participation, and employers are exploring ways to facilitate their increasing dependency on women workers.

Sex Segregation

The preface to this book described a prospective employer's unequal treatment of male and female applicants for the position of manager for a lawn-care firm. Can we expect prospective employers in the year 2005 to treat women and men more equally than the Cincinnati employer did in the summer of 1993? In this section we consider the ways in which economic restructuring and the changing nature of work may indeed affect the degree of sex segregation at the beginning of the twenty-first century.

The overall level of segregation in the future will depend partly on trends in the occupations that are already heavily segregated. The growth of female-dominated jobs—such as information clerk, nurses' aide, and food-counter worker—will tend to increase sex segregation in the workplace.[2] On the other hand, the loss of heavily male skilled and semiskilled manufacturing jobs will help offset the segregative effect of the growth of predominantly female jobs. Obviously, segregation that stems from the loss of desirable jobs is not in anyone's interest. The kind of integration that will benefit women and society will result from women's expanded access to all jobs—the good ones and the not-so-good ones.

Two factors point to the continuation of a sex segregated workforce. Although the trend toward upgrading will help highly educated, computer-literate women, minorities, and immigrants, deskilling is likely to consign others to low-skill jobs. Moreover, as economic restructuring shrinks the number of well-paying, male-dominated jobs, men

---

[2]Part of the increase in sex segregation will be due to the growth of contingent jobs that are female-dominated (Callaghan and Hartmann 1991). Employers seeking contingent workers rely heavily on groups concentrated at the bottom of the labor hierarchy: women, minorities, youth, and the elderly (Sweeney and Nussbaum 1989). Consider temporary and part-time workers: In the late 1980s, women were about 45 percent of total workers but about two-thirds of all temporary and part-time workers (Tilly 1991). African Americans are also overrepresented among temporary workers: In the mid 1980s, they were 10.4 percent of the labor force but 12 percent of temporary workers (Howe 1986).

are likely to resist women's entry into customarily male jobs.

On the bright side, the credentials and lifetime work expectations that women bring to the job increasingly resemble men's, so employers may be more likely to treat the sexes similarly. Additionally, as employers gain more experience with competent women in nontraditional jobs, competitive pressure to hire the best available workers may induce employers to hire more women.

In the workplace of the year 2000, the increased presence of women, nonwhites, and immigrants in the labor force may mean that the good jobs will not be reserved for "people with white skins . . . and wing tips" (White 1992:35). For example, if a lawn-care service seeks to hire 10 people and women are 6 of the 10 best-qualified applicants, the chances are good that the company will hire some women. Given the present concentration of women, minorities, and immigrants in the lower echelons of the labor market, however, a great deal of change will be necessary for them to move to the top.

The increased numbers of ethnic minorities in the labor force does not mean that they will find enhanced employment opportunities. These workers are concentrated in declining occupations and are underrepresented in rapidly growing skilled occupations (Kutscher 1991:9; Silvestri and Lukasiewicz 1991:92). In addition, minorities' relative disadvantages in education and training—along with discrimination—will restrict their access to the higher-paying new jobs. In 1990, for example, African Americans made up only 7 percent and Hispanics only 3 percent of workers in the fast-growing occupation of mathematical and computer scientist (Silvestri and Lukasiewicz 1991). Yet these two minority groups were each 14 percent of the workers in the declining occupation of machine operators, assemblers, and inspectors.

The Promotion Gap Will economic restructuring enhance women's chances of promotion? Not likely. Employers are eliminating many middle-management jobs as part of the retrench-

ment that has accompanied growing international competition. This economizing is likely to hamper women's and minorities' promotion chances for three reasons. First, the glass ceiling has trapped many women and minorities in exactly those mid-level management jobs that are slated for elimination, putting them at risk of unemployment; similarly, women's and minorities' concentration in staff positions that are not central to the organization's primary mission—such as personnel, public relations, and affirmative action—puts them at greater risk of unemployment. Second, the elimination of middle-management jobs will destroy job ladders out of the lower-level jobs in which women and minorities have been concentrated. Third, because higher-level jobs will require up-to-date training and skills, employers are likely to prefer newly trained graduates from outside the firm over current employees (Acker 1992).

The Authority Gap The changing economy is not likely to improve women's and minorities' access to authority on the job either. Of course, some women will be found in those new upgraded, autonomous jobs where workers can exercise authority. Currently, however, the service-sector jobs that most women hold are the type that employers are most likely to deskill or shift to contingent status (Eitzen and Baca-Zinn 1992). Most female workers are unlikely to overcome the authority gap unless the government enforces laws designed to protect women's and minorities' access to jobs with authority. The U.S. Department of Labor's recent initiative to enforce the Glass Ceiling Act of 1991 provides a basis for cautious optimism.

Polarization between jobs that offer considerable decision-making authority and those that offer little may be under way within traditionally female jobs (Acker 1992). This split is between routine, low-wage, closely supervised jobs and relatively nonroutine, high-paying, autonomous jobs. Within nursing, for example, nurses and nurses' aides are moving further apart (Glazer 1991). New technology has upgraded the jobs of registered nurses, whereas the work of nurses' aides is low skilled and is paid at near-minimum wage. Women of color are concentrated disproportionately in the least desirable of the traditionally female occupations, so that polarization within these jobs is likely to raise yet another barrier to minority women's chances to exercise authority on the job.

Computerization is another force that may exacerbate the authority gap. Computerization allows bosses to more closely supervise lower-level workers, who disproportionately are women and ethnic minorities. In 1987, one study showed, employers used computers to monitor the work of 4 million to 6 million workers (Sweeney and Nussbaum 1989:155). One telephone company, for example, allowed operators 20 seconds per call. An employee claimed that operators have so little time to assist customers that they sometimes give out wrong numbers just to get customers off the line (Sweeney and Nussbaum 1989:155).

Research hints that the trend toward upgrading workers' skills and responsibilities benefits women less often than men. When Swedish banks assigned female tellers to tasks that managers had formerly done, such as approving loans and providing customers with investment and tax advice, they did not recognize the change as increasing the tellers' skill levels (Acker 1992). Whether skill upgrading increases authority depends partly on employers' willingness to acknowledge work as skilled when women perform it.

The Pay Gap   Economic and demographic trends may improve the pay gap, although the gap is likely to shrink mostly because of men's declining pay rather than women's increasing pay. Five of ten jobs predicted to expand most by the year 2000 pay below-poverty wages (Silvestri and Lukasiewicz 1987). Thus, according to many observers, the overall impact of restructuring on the wages of ordinary working people has been negative and is likely to remain so (Harrison and Bluestone 1988; Phillips 1990). The risk of unemployment has also increased in the new economy as jobs have been exported overseas to countries where workers command much lower pay than U.S. workers.

The decline in industrial jobs has been particularly destructive for people of color, some of whom had succeeded in moving into the middle class through unionized jobs in heavy industry (Wilson 1991; Higginbotham 1992). These jobs are being replaced by lower-paying jobs or no jobs (Higginbotham 1992:187). Women who had found jobs in traditionally male blue-collar industries have watched their jobs disappear. In general, though, white men have suffered greater earnings losses from industrial decline than women, because men had more to lose in the first place. They earned higher pay than women and minorities and were more likely to work in heavy industry, the sector hardest hit by the transformation of the economy (Acker 1992).

At the same time, the service sector has grown. If you look back at Table 9.1, you can see that some of the growth in the service sector will continue to be in higher-level professional, managerial, and technical fields where salaries are high (Acker 1992). But a great deal of the growth will be in low-wage service-sector jobs, where women, minorities, and immigrants are currently concentrated.

Overall, then, the pay gap should shrink as women increase their work experience. It will shrink further if women increase their representation in male jobs. The decline of men's average wages, through the loss of industrial jobs and the shift to a service economy, will help to narrow the pay gap but will not improve women's or men's economic condition.

The Gendering of Work

Employers and female and male workers all contribute to the gendered nature of work. One particularly troublesome outcome of gendered work is sexual harassment. The future on this score looks promising. Most large companies have implemented sexual harassment policies and training programs. Most important, however, are court decisions that have held employers responsible for workplace harassment. A unanimous 1993 ruling by the U.S. Supreme Court (*Teresa Harris v. Forklift*

Systems) now gives workers a basis for claiming sexual harassment without having to prove that they have suffered psychological damage. Forcing employers to examine how workplace environments foster sexual harassment and holding them accountable is a major step forward.

We note with dismay, however, indications of how deep-seated the gendering of jobs is. Arthur Ochs Sulzberger, Jr., of *The New York Times*, a supporter of equal opportunities for women, has said that he wants to leave his son a more egalitarian paper than the one he inherited. From someone who will shape public opinion in the next century, this statement is encouraging—until we learn that Sulzberger also has a daughter (N. Robertson 1992:252). Even well-intentioned men may have difficulty seeing their own gender biases—in this case, the belief that sons, not daughters, inherit family businesses.

The fact remains that workers gender jobs both because gender is an important element of the larger culture and because those workers want to protect their material interests. To the extent that the four work trends discussed in this chapter—particularly deskilling and the decline of the manufacturing sector—hurt men as a group, male workers will continue to use gendering to preserve their stake in traditionally male jobs and their grip on authority.

The Relationship Between Work and Family

. . . Employers have organized work based on the presumption that workers are men who have few, if any, outside demands on their time. Implicitly, in conflicts between work and family, employers have long assumed that the family should take the back seat. Will the workplace of the future assume that work has absolute primacy in workers' lives? We think not.

For several years, employers have been gradually—and often grudgingly—accommodating to the reality of workers' lives, and momentum for more change is building. Some employers instituted family policies as early as 1965, and many such policies have been incorporated into workplace bureaucracies. Although government policies on family are not as far-reaching in the United States as in other industrialized nations, over 60 percent of employers now have personnel policies that help some workers juggle work and family. Few employers, however, have family policies that provide the most useful kinds of help. Congress took a step toward addressing the conflict between family and work by passing the 1993 Family and Medical Leave Act. This law requires employers to give some workers, both female and male, the right to keep their jobs when family crises or normal life events compel workers to take time from paid work. The Family and Medical Leave Act thus formally recognizes that workers have a right to meet family demands without sacrificing their jobs.

Employers' growing reliance on home workers and the growth of small home-based businesses are likely to perpetuate the unequal sexual division of labor between husbands and wives. Expectations that women should have near-exclusive responsibility for housework and childcare have not changed substantially. In 1975, among employed people, men spent 46 percent as much time as women on housework; in 1987 they spent 57 percent as much time. However, most of the improvement was due to couples' leaving tasks undone or hiring others to do them rather than men's doing more (Shelton 1992:74–5). The speed with which the domestic division of labor becomes more equal will depend on women's ability and willingness to insist that their partners share housework. And their ability to insist on more equal sharing will in turn depend on how fast women catch up to men in their paychecks and job status.

CONCLUSION

Women have made enormous progress in the last 30 years. Many employers treat the sexes more fairly than in the past. Consider the story of one organization. In 1993 the National Institutes of Health commissioned a self-study to learn if it treated its female and male employees equally. The study revealed that men outearned women at almost every rank and that women were less likely than men with the same credentials to be promoted. The director and her subordinates immediately took action: They instituted a formal policy regarding sex discrimination in job ladders, implemented a family-leave policy, vowed to bring women's salaries in line with men's, and formed a commission to recommend ways to discipline employees who engaged in discrimination or sexual harassment (Watson 1993:889). Both the self-study and the agency's response would have been inconceivable 30 years ago. Today the organization takes equality seriously. But the passage of time is not the only explanation for this agency's concern with sex inequality. Note that a woman was at the helm when the self-study was undertaken and when the agency reacted to the study's findings.

Few organizations have women at the top with the power to implement such change. Therefore, how quickly women achieve equality with men at work will largely depend on how much pressure ordinary working women put on employers, legislators, and policymakers. Not until the late 1960s, with the huge influx into the labor force of highly educated women who sought both careers and families, did women mount an attack on sex inequality at work. They sued employers for discrimination and pressured federal agencies to enforce laws against sex discrimination. They demanded and sometimes won flexible work schedules and led the appeal for accessible and affordable childcare. And they organized for pay equity, a concept—like sexual harassment—that was not even in the dictionary 20 years ago.

Opponents to sex equality have not taken these gains lying down, and the 1980s brought an effective counteroffensive. Conservative politicians tried to dilute federal affirmative action regulations, derailed efforts to enforce discrimination rules, and for a time made it harder to prove discrimination in court. They replaced appellate and Supreme Court judges who supported equal rights with opponents of equality. A series of Supreme Court decisions relieved employers of the obligation to desegregate jobs, although the

Civil Rights Act of 1991 will help undo the courts' actions.

This backward march has taught us that constant enforcement is crucial in reducing inequality in the workplace. The important laws are in place: Compared to other industrialized countries, our antidiscrimination laws stand alone in providing for serious financial penalties (Bergmann 1986). The challenge is ensuring that regulatory agencies enforce them. Laws like Title VII of the 1964 Civil Rights Act are only as strong as the muscle behind them. Moreover, prohibitive costs of litigation prevent most discrimination victims from turning to the courts. Even a victory in court does not guarantee change. Court decisions that require employers to pay money damages often leave intact underlying discriminatory policies and practices (Bergmann 1986).

Enforcement is crucial, because it can make the cost of discrimination prohibitively high for employers. An attorney offered an analogy between the cost of discrimination and business costs:

The only reason why we have seat belts or airbags in cars, the only reason why we have protectors on [industrial] presses for people who work on the assembly line is because it was costing the manufacturer of those goods too much money in payments stemming from successful lawsuits by injured people. (White 1992:201)

The prognosis for equality in the workplace depends on what Americans demand of their employers and government. It is encouraging to note that women and men workers have allied to further their rights as citizens and workers, as when the township of Ypsilanti, Michigan, sued General Motors in 1993 for accepting community incentives to remain in the town and then moving to a lower-wage area. Women workers at U.S.-owned factories just over the border in Mexico have organized the *Comite Fronterizo de Obreras* (Border Committee of Women Workers), which has fought successfully to gain higher pay, to protect workers from industrial chemicals, and to force employers to obey the Mexican labor laws. These workers have broadened their influence by forming alliances with churches and sympathetic unions in the United States. They are now investigating ways to permanently change their factories. These examples show that workers who fight can win.

The media and employers often claim that sex discrimination is all but dead. They insist that the barriers are gone: Women, like men, can now succeed through their own individual efforts. If pushed, these authorities may admit that women lag behind men in access to good jobs, promotions, and equal pay. But, they remind us, the American Dream says that if you are number two, like Avis Car Rental, you simply have to try harder. If you are Avis, this strategy may work, because Hertz is not making the rules. Women, however, are still competing in an economic world where men make the rules. Hard work pays off only for some fortunate women with the right class background, educational credentials, skin color, weight—and with good luck. For most women, however, hard work is not enough, because the system of sex inequality has beneficiaries as well as victims and those beneficiaries have a stake in not seeing the problem and minimizing real change.

To work for progress, we must see through the media's message. In a society that applauds its commitment to justice, recognizing injustice is the first step for the social pressure that progress requires. New regulations and better enforcement of existing ones are essential to reducing inequities in work processes and outcomes. Equally important, however, are policies that will improve the overall quality of work. The trends discussed in this chapter indicate the possibility of a deteriorating future, with a growing proportion of workers in low-paid and contingent jobs. Many analysts argue that our society is at a critical juncture where we must consciously break with past policies. A number of these analysts call for federal industrial policies that give employers tax incentives to create good jobs, for workplace policies that promote greater worker control, and for employment policies that provide equal opportunities and rewards regardless of workers' color or sex (see, for example, Harrison and Bluestone 1988; Reich 1991; Thurow 1992). For a better social and eco-nomic future, in which greater equity in employment accompanies better jobs for all workers, we must choose a new direction.

REFERENCES

Acker, Joan. 1992. "The Future of Women and Work: Ending the Twentieth Century." *Sociological Perspectives* 35:53–68.

Ansberry, Claire. 1993. "Workers Are Forced to Take More Jobs with Few Benefits." *Wall Street Journal* (March 11):A1.

Belous, Richard S. 1989. *The Contingent Economy: The Growth of the Temporary, Part-Time, and Subcontracted Workforce.* McLean, VA: National Planning Association.

Bergmann, Barbara R. 1986. *The Economic Emergence of Women.* New York: Basic Books.

Callaghan, Polly and Heidi Hartmann. 1991. *Contingent Work: A Chart Book on Part-Time and Temporary Employment.* Washington, DC: Economic Policy Institute.

Carey, Max L. and James C. Franklin. 1991. "Industry Output, Job Growth Slowdown Continues." *Monthly Labor Review* 114:45–63.

Christensen, Kathleen. 1989. "Flexible Staffing and Scheduling in U.S. Corporations." *Research Bulletin No. 240.* New York: The Conference Board.

Cornfield, Daniel. 1987. *Workers, Managers, and Technological Change.* New York: Plenum Press.

Eitzen, D. Stanley and Maxine Baca-Zinn. 1992. "Structural Transformation and Systems of Inequality." Pp. 178–82 in Margaret L. Anderson and Patricia Hill Collins (eds.), *Race, Class, and Gender.* Belmont, CA: Wadsworth.

Fullerton, Howard N. 1987. "Labor Force Projections: 1986–2000." *Monthly Labor Review* 110:10–29.

Glazer, Nona Y. 1991. "'Between a Rock and a Hard Place': Women's Professional Organizations in Nursing and Class, Racial, and Ethnic Inequalities." *Gender & Society* 5:351–72.

Harrison, Bennett and Barry Bluestone. 1988. *The Great U-Turn.* New York: Basic Books.

Hartmann, Heidi. 1993. "Profits and Losses of Temps in the Workplace." *Washington Times* (June 6):B4.

Higginbotham, Elizabeth. 1992. "We Were Never on a Pedestal: Women of Color Continue to Struggle with Poverty, Racism, and Sexism." Pp. 183–90 in Margaret L. Anderson and Patricia Hill Collins (eds.), *Race, Class, and Gender.* Belmont, CA: Wadsworth.

Hodgkinson, Harold. 1988. Presentation to the Florida Task Force on Improving Math, Science, and Computer Education, Orlando, FL. (May 14).

Hodson, Randy and Robert E. Parker. 1988. "Work in High Technology Settings: A Review of the Empirical Literature." *Research in the Sociology of Work* 4:1–29.

Howe, Wayne. 1986. "Temporary Help Workers: Who They Are, What Jobs They Hold." *Monthly Labor Review* 109:45–7.

"The Immigrants: How They're Helping to Revitalize the U.S. Economy." 1992. *Business Week* (July 13): 114, 116–120, 154.

Institute for Women's Policy Research. 1993. "State Pay Equity Programs Raise Women's Wages." News release, May 20. Washington, DC: Institute for Women's Policy Research.

Johnston, William B. and Arnold H. Packer. 1987. *Workforce 2000: Work and Workers for the 21st Century.* Indianapolis: Hudson Institute.

Kutscher, Ronald E. 1991. "New BLS Projections: Findings and Implications." *Monthly Labor Review* 114:3–12.

Leidner, Robin. 1991. "Serving Hamburgers and Selling Insurance: Gender, Work, and Identity in Interactive Service Jobs." *Gender & Society* 5: 154–77.

Levin, Henry M. and Russell W. Rumberger. 1987. "Educational Requirements for New Technologies: Visions, Possibilities and Current Realities." *Educational Policy* 1:333–54.

National Commission on Working Women. 1990. *Women and Work: Workforce 2000 Trends.* Washington, DC: Wider Opportunities for Women.

Phillips, Kevin. 1990. *The Politics of Rich and Poor.* New York: Random House.

Polivka, Anne E. and Thomas Nardone. 1989. "On the Definition of 'Contingent Work.'" *Monthly Labor Review* 112:9–16.

Reich, Robert B. 1991. *The Work of Nations: Preparing Ourselves for 21st Century Capitalism.* New York: Knopf.

Robertson, Nan. 1992. *The Girls in the Balcony.* New York: Random House.

Shelton, Beth Anne. 1992. *Women, Men, and Time: Gender Differences in Paid Work, Housework, and Leisure.* New York: Greenwood.

Silvestri, George and John Lukasiewicz. 1987. "A Look at Occupational Employment Trends to the Year 2000." *Monthly Labor Review* 110:46–63.

———. 1991. "Occupational Employment Projections." *Monthly Labor Review* 114:64–94.

Sweeney, John J. and Karen Nussbaum. 1989. *Solutions for the New Work Force.* Cabin John, MD: Seven Locks.

Teresa Harris v. Forklift Systems, Inc. U.S. Supreme Court Slip Opinion 92–1168. Unpublished.

Thurow, Lester C. 1992. *Head-to-Head: The Coming Economic Battles among Japan, Europe, and America.* New York: Morrow.

Tilly, Chris. 1991. "Reasons for the Continuing Growth of Part-Time Employment." *Monthly Labor Review* 114:10–18.

U.S. Bureau of the Census. 1992. *Statistical Abstracts of the United States: 1992.* Washington, DC: U.S. Government Printing Office.

U.S. Bureau of Labor Statistics. 1992. *Workers on Flexible and Shift Schedules.* News release 92-491 (August 14). Washington, DC: U.S. Department of Labor.

———. 1993. *Employment and Earnings* 40 (January). Washington, DC: U.S. Department of Labor.

U.S. General Accounting Office. 1991. *Workers at Risk: Increased Number in Contingent Employment Lack Insurance, Other Benefits.* GAO Report No. HRD-91-56. Washington, DC: U.S. Government Printing Office.

U.S. Women's Bureau. 1992. *Facts on Working Women.* Report No. 92-1. Washington, DC: U.S. Government Printing Office.

———. 1993. *Facts on Working Women.* Report No. 93-2. Washington, DC: U.S. Government Printing Office.

Walsh, John P. 1989. "Technological Change and the Division of Labor: The Case of Retail Meat-cutters." *Work and Occupations* 16:165–83.

Watson, Traci. 1993. "Glossy Strategic Plan Hits the Streets." *Science* 260:888–9.

White, Jane. 1992. *A Few Good Women: Breaking the Barriers to Top Management.* Englewood Cliffs, NJ: Prentice-Hall.

Wilson, William J. 1991. "Studying Inner-City Social Dislocations." *American Sociological Review* 56:1–14.

Zachary, G. Pascal and Bob Ortega. 1993. "Workplace Revolution Boosts Productivity at Cost of Job Security." *Wall Street Journal* (March 10):A1, A8.

Zuboff, Shoshanna. 1988. *In the Age of the Smart Machine: The Future of Work and Power.* New York: Basic Books.

Part VI

CLASS, RACE, AND GENDER IN AN INSTITUTIONAL CONTEXT: EDUCATION AND THE ENVIRONMENT

—⁓—

CLASS, RACE, AND GENDER DIMENSIONS OF INequality do not function in isolation. Rather, their dynamic interaction is highly complex. Class, race and ethnicity, and gender are simultaneous, intersecting, and sometimes crosscutting systems of relationships and meanings. We have a tendency to debate what status is more important and powerful in structuring inequality: Class, race and ethnicity, or gender? Rather than abstractly ordering oppressing statuses, I think it is far more analytically useful to examine race, class, and gender within specific institutional contexts. Not only does this approach facilitate a better understanding of how inequality operates in these contexts, but it also shows more clearly how race, class, and gender interact in specific settings. The last part of this reader, then, examines the powerful dynamic in two different institutional contexts: education and the environment.

In the United States, public education is the one institution charged with preparing young people for careers, adulthood, and the future. It has the historic mission of providing an avenue for social mobility. In schools, students' talents, skills, hard work, and motivation are the currency for determining, at least in theory, who gets ahead and who falls behind in the competition for success. Part VI examines how educational environments and opportunities still reflect inequality in this country; how various groups attempt to influence social change or to maintain the status quo;

and how the dynamics of class, race, and gender intersect in an institutional context.

Education offers the potential to better our lives as it provides all of us with the common elements of language, culture, values, and a national identity. Arguably, the great post–World War II expansion of the American middle class was made possible by state-sponsored opportunities for higher education. The readings in this part describe some views on how institutional processes reinforce the existing structure of racial, class, and gender stratification. For instance, schools make available differing educational opportunities, which maintain and reinforce societal inequalities. The first reading indicates how schools prepare the children of the upper class to gain and hold power, the second illustrates how schools keep the children of poverty powerless, and, the third looks at whether educational reforms can reduce inequality. We can only hope that the experiences of the past provide some inspiration, as well as cautionary lessons for the future.

One of the readings from Part II, the article by Ralph Turner, bears directly on the issues addressed in this part, as it examined two theoretically different systems of mobility: In one system, the power elite perpetuates itself by sponsoring a few selected persons to enter the elite; in the other, elite status and training are available to any person who wins such status via an open contest. In "The Vital Link: Prep Schools and Higher Education,"

Peter W. Cookson and Caroline Hodges Persell explore one mechanism for sponsored mobility, describing how elite schools confer special privilege and status on their students by facilitating students' admission to prestigious colleges, from which the students may be recruited for top positions of political, professional, financial, and business leadership. America's upper class is replenished and maintained by this institutional process. This essay recalls some of the themes set forth in the contribution by G. William Domhoff in Part III regarding how elites recruit and rule.

"The Savage Inequalities of Public Education in New York," by Jonathan Kozol, offers a poignant contrast to Cookson and Persell's article. Kozol reviews what sorts of educational opportunities are available in school districts that are unwilling or financially unable to provide adequate resources for education. Not surprisingly, disadvantaged students find little to help them overcome their economic and other deprivations in broken-down, overcrowded, understaffed schools that lack even the most fundamental resources requisite for an effective education. Instead of lifting them up out of poverty, such schools further ensure these children's position at the bottom of the socioeconomic heap. Kozol's book has demonstrated how far Americans still have to go before reaching, or even approaching, equal educational opportunity for all.

It is fitting to conclude the educational section with Roslyn Mickelson and Stephen Smith's essay "Can Education Eliminate Race, Class, and Gender Inequality?" A good education and the doors it can open are the heart of the American dream and economic success. Mickelson and Smith measure contemporary educational opportunity against its promise. Is educational opportunity enough to reduce inequality?

The environment has become one of the foremost concerns at the beginning of the twenty-first century. In contrast, hardly anyone was concerned about environmental justice just a few decades ago. And, as the articles in this section powerfully demonstrate, a comprehensive understanding of environmental dangers, risks, and remedies is woefully incomplete without examining how fundamental dimensions of inequality connect to environmental conditions. One can even make an argument that understanding the roadmap of inequality is indispensable to examining the pattern of environmental damage and dangers. The articles in the last part of this reader set the framework for, and provide illustrations of, this approach.

Robert Bullard's article, "Environmental Justice for All," presents a framework for environmental justice. From local zoning to global dumping, Bullard argues that broad powerful dynamics of inequality shape environmental conditions and crisis. He invites us to think about which populations face graver environmental harms and risks, then he challenges us to tackle the structures and policies that produce differential risks. "Toxic Waste and Race in the United States" by Charles Lee continues this theme by discussing why minorities confront more severe environmental dangers. Lee also explains why minority communities and organizations have been at the forefront of the environmental justice movement.

The last article by Regina Austin and Michael Schill, "Black, Brown, Red, and Poisoned," illustrates how class, race, and gender are integral features of toxic exposure and environmental danger. They pose serious challenges to the traditional way of seeing environmental concerns that focus exclusively on trees and water and tend to leave people out of the equation. This is a fitting final article because it analyzes a phenomenon—topic exposure—that seemingly places everyone at risk equally and shows how and why the burden falls on vulnerable groups.

41

The Vital Link

Prep Schools and Higher Education

Peter W. Cookson, Jr. and Caroline Hodges Persell

LIKE YOUTHS UNDERGOING A TRIBAL RITE OF passage in which the badge of manhood is killing their first lion, prep youths have historically sought to bag an Ivy League college acceptance. But, like lions, Ivy League acceptances have become more difficult to obtain. Their growing scarcity means that prep schools need to convince many students and parents that X, Y, and Z colleges are as good as Harvard, Yale, and Princeton, and therefore as worthy a prize for undergoing the grueling period of preparation.

The students whose families are seeking their socialization for power, however, are skeptical. Virtually everyone in prep school is going to college, so whether or not one goes is not the critical question; *where* one goes is what matters. Going to the right college is "part of the formula for their lives," as a select 16 college advisor phrased it.[1] As we shall discuss in this chapter, the students' collective identity functions in their collective

aspiration for similar colleges, including those with relatively modest academic or social backgrounds.

Many students come to boarding school with the hope that it will enable them to get into a better college. The prep schools know that this promise poses certain problems for them, given the changes that have occurred in college admissions during the last twenty-five years. In the past most of their graduates could easily get into the college of their choice, but today it is not so easy. Prep schools have responded by honing their very professional college advisory operation and by exercising what political clout they can in relation to the colleges. The result is a higher—though not perfect—payoff for elite prep school graduates, compared to other applicants.

COLLECTIVE ASPIRATION

Prep school parents are undoubtedly the first source of pressure urging prep school students to attend the "right" college. Among freshmen, 51 percent said that they thought that ten years from now the most valuable part of their boarding school experience would be "where it helped you get into college." Many students enter boarding school with high expectations about how it will help them get into a prestigious college.

Parents and students are not totally divorced from reality. Where one goes to college is related to occupational and financial success. Researchers have found significant relationships between the particular colleges people attend and career success in a variety of fields. For example, the social prestige and selectivity of one's college is related

From *Preparing for Power: America's Elite Boarding Schools* by Peter W. Cookson, Jr. and Caroline Hodges Persell. Copyright © 1985 by Peter W. Cookson, Jr., and Caroline Hodges Persell. Reprinted by permission of Basic Books, a member of Perseus Books, L.L.C.

[1] *Editor's note:* The authors use Baltzell's (1964) list from 1964: Phillips Academy, Phillips Exeter Academy, Episcopal High School, Hill School, St. Paul's School, St. Mark's School, Lawrenceville School, Groton School, Woodbury Forest School, Taft School, Hotchkiss School, Choate School, St. George's School, Middlesex School, Deerfield Academy, and Kent School.

to the prestige of the graduate or professional school one attends (Crane 1965; Brint 1980), to a person's professional occupational attainment (Brint 1980; Tinto 1980), to attaining a high rank in business (Pierson 1969; Useem and Karabel 1984), and to becoming an editor with a major publishing house (Coser, Kadushin, and Powell 1982). Half of Ronald Reagan's "sagebrush" cabinet have an Ivy League connection.

The opinions of parents and preps alike help to forge a collective sense of what is an appropriate prep college. The parental and student "vision of what constitutes a 'good' college is very narrow," said a college advisor at a select 16 school, and "acceptance at lesser known colleges is equivalent to failure." "Parents keep resuscitating dreams, which die hard," says another advisor. "The worst parents are those who didn't go to the top colleges themselves." And part of the problem originates with "the admissions office [of the boarding school] which keeps admitting kids from high-achieving families."

One college advisor said a student told him that he thought he would "make better contacts" at the major university in the state than at a nationally respected liberal arts college in a neighboring state. While the student may be right, what is notable is that a seventeen-year-old was articulating the importance of making the right contacts.

If students have not focused on where they want to go to college, the other students in a boarding school will readily offer opinions about the prestige of various colleges, and peer opinions play an important role in shaping the collective view of what is an acceptable college. This helps to explain why a student would tell his college advisor, "I'd be happy at any of the Ivy League colleges," despite the fact that the advisor knows they are such very different places.

One of the most visible indicators that prep school students share a collective identity is the similarity in their aspirations for college, despite the range of competence among them. With a third having combined SAT scores of 1,050 or below, and some with *combined* scores in the 500s (a perfect combined score is 1,600), they apply in overwhelming numbers to the most selective private colleges in the United States. They have what one college advisor in a select 16 school called, "a strong sense of entitlement about them."

While nationally 78 percent of college students attend public institutions, only 58 percent of boarding school students even apply to public institutions. Similarly, while 2 percent of the national college population attends the most highly selective colleges and universities, fully 84 percent of boarding school students apply to such colleges. Finally, while less than one percent of college students attend the Ivy League colleges, 46 percent of boarding school students apply to one or more of the eight Ivy League colleges.

A handful of colleges receive a significant share of their applications from prep school students. Five colleges received a total of 647 applications (or 13 percent of those filed), and ten schools received 1,110 applications (or 22 percent of all the applications these seniors filed). This convergence of taste suggests that certain colleges are much more likely than others to be perceived as appropriate by prep school students. Exhibit 9.1 lists the fifty colleges receiving the most applications, grouped in terms of whether they received more than 100, 51 to 99, or 26 to 50 applications from prep school students. These colleges are almost all private.

This convergence of aspirations contributes to the pressures felt by prep school students over the issue of college acceptance. They feel that their collective membership is at stake, not just their individual egos. How else can we explain the otherwise mystifying statement that students "feel like failures when they get accepted at Brown, Bowdoin, or Amherst, instead of Harvard, Yale, or Princeton," as one select 16 college advisor noted. The pain of rejection is intensified by its immediate public nature in boarding school. Unlike public high-school and day school students, boarding school students must undergo acceptance or rejection in full public view at their adjacent mail boxes. There is precious little physical or psychic space in the total institution for face saving; everybody knows the score, and the body count as well.

EXHIBIT 9.1
Colleges Receiving the Most Prep Applications (1982–83)

More Than 100 Applications

[a]Princeton	[a]Brown	[a]Harvard	[a]Yale

51–99 Applications

[a]Dartmouth	U. of Virginia	U. of California	Northwestern
Tufts	Middlebury College	(Berkeley)	Boston University
Georgetown	Williams College	Denison	Colby College
Duke	U. of Vermont	Connecticut College	Bowdoin College
[a]Cornell	Amherst	Colgate	Hamilton College
Stanford	U. of North Carolina	Vanderbilt	[a]Columbia
U. of Michigan	(Chapel Hill)	Boston College	

25–50 Applications

[a]U. of Pennsylvania	Wellesley	U. of Richmond	Dickinson College
Skidmore College	Bucknell	Holy Cross	Michigan State
Trinity College	Pomona College	Tulane	Lewis and Clark
Wesleyan University	U. of New Hampshire	Kenyon	College
St. Lawrence	Ohio Wesleyan	Hobart & William Smith	Johns Hopkins
Bates College	University	College	U. of Rochester

[a]Ivy League colleges
Note: Based on the college destinations of 1,035 seniors in our sample; data provided by the boarding schools. Colleges are listed within groups by the number of applications received.

Part of the promise of the prep rite of passage is that it will help students traverse this last trial successfully. But the potency of the prep magic has been weakened in the last few decades, leaving the schools with the problem of being less effective than in the past, although they are still more effective than most other secondary schools. . . .

PROFESSIONALISM AND PRIVATE POLITICS

The college advisors at most elite boarding schools are well attuned to the world of private college admissions. They organize the process so as to smooth as many kinks as possible out of it and to present their students in the most favorable light. They have responded to the increasingly competitive college admissions scene with two major

strategies—professionalizing their operation and using their political networks.

The resources most leading boarding schools devote to college advisement are considerable, and they enable advisors to manage the process in a competent and effective manner. Advisors at most of the leading schools are savvy and highly organized. Most do not teach because of their travel schedules, frequent visits by college admissions officers, and numerous phone calls. Especially at the select 16 schools, they have been doing the job for a number of years, and learned the ropes by assisting an experienced college advisor for several years. Many have visited sixty, seventy, or more colleges.

Each advisor is responsible for from 65 to 140 students, a contrast to many public high schools in which college advisors may have as many as 400 to 500 students in their care, although the average is 323 (Coleman, Hoffer, and Kilgore 1982, 179). Most boarding schools have substantial clerical and, increasingly, computerized support services. All college advisors seem to have unlimited long-distance telephone access. With fewer facilities, big public high schools often limit students to a fixed number of college applications, say six or seven. Boarding school students may file as many as fifteen or twenty applications, although the average number is 4.8.

The contrast between the professional operations of the elite schools which are socializing their students for power and the more relaxed attitude of, for example, a progressive school is dramatic. For example, in one of the latter schools, the college advisor was new, and had not visited any colleges, and had himself attended a minor state college. His office was located in a remote building a good distance from the center of campus. The office was a single room, with one counselor, a secretary who came in two half days per week, a typewriter that was shared with several other departments, and a filing system that reposed in a single desk drawer.

The difference in the focus of the college advisory program in a girls school was also apparent. The advisor said, "There is almost more anxiety about the process of applying to college than the result." At a boys or coed school, no one would suggest that there was no anxiety about the result.

The highly professional operations of the prep schools engaged in socializing their students for power is evident in three activities: the organization of the timetable, written materials, and letters of recommendation. College advisors at these schools have rationalized the admissions process through time and can readily rattle off the timetable of events in the process. . . . It is designed to assuage the worries of students and parents about the process. Don't worry, the message is, everything is under control; there is a time and a place for all the necessary steps, and we will guide you through the process.

Many college advisors prepare voluminous materials to help students and their families through the process. Many have questionnaires for students and parents to obtain information about what they want in a college; particular colleges they are considering; where relatives attended college (to know what legacy factors they have); whether or not they need financial aid; and what summer work, travel, volunteer, athletic, student government, club, publications, or debate activities they have been involved in. Other questionnaires ask what books they have read in the last six months, what musical, artistic, or theatrical involvement they have had, and ask about independent study and research. Often advisors ask students to prepare a written autobiography or self-evaluation. They might ask students to say how they are unique, what they do best, or how particular experiences have affected them.

Some advisors at elite schools prepare guidebooks for students to help them make their college selections. Aside from providing the timetable for tests, early admissions, application deadlines, and so forth, they may suggest factors to consider about colleges—such as their size, location, program, quality of undergraduate life, facilities, instruction, or financial factors. The guidebook will explain how to arrange visits and interviews, what might be asked in an interview and ways to respond, how to dress, how to prepare questions to ask the interviewer, and how to complete an application, including checking the spelling. The guidebook is an effective way of sharing the advisor's experience and wisdom.

College advisors also use their knowledge when writing letters of recommendation. All secondary schools are asked to write letters of recommendation for their applicants, but differences exist in the effort and backup support that various schools are able to provide. Given the small number of students boarding school advisors have to supervise, they are able to write a well-reasoned letter for each student.

At one boarding school, where about half the graduating class goes to Harvard, Yale, or Princeton, the advisor interviews the entire faculty on each member of the senior class. He tapes all their comments and has them transcribed. This produces a "huge confidential dossier which gives a very good sense of where each student is." In addition, housemasters and coaches write reports. Then the advisor interviews each senior. After each interview, he makes verbal notes on a dicta-phone. After assimilating all these impressions of each student, the college advisor writes his letter of recommendation, which he is able to pack with corroborative details illustrating a candidate's strengths. The thoroughness, thought, and care that goes into this process insures that anything and everything positive that could be said about a student is included, thereby maximizing his or her chances for a favorable reception.

Some advisors include their assessment of the difficulty of the academic course load a student is taking in their letters of recommendation. Where possible, they may try to compare the applicant with others from the school who have attended the college and been successful there.[2]

We saw some of the letters of recommenda-tion, without the students' names on them. They were beautifully crafted, one-page presentations. One advisor said his goal in the letter was "to pre-sent the student as accurately and fully as possible to the college." He was relatively new to the job and wanted to be seen as "trustworthy and holding nothing back," to establish credibility for future dealings with the colleges. College admissions officers had told him that "the quotes from the teachers are the things they respected most" in his letters.

The importance of well-designed letters of recommendation is underscored by James W. Wickenden, Jr., director of admissions at Prince-ton University, in his letter to Princeton alumni:

In evaluating each applicant the admission staff also takes into account the supporting documents from col-lege counselors and teachers. These materials can vary greatly in quality: while most are good, and some ex-ceptional, about 25 percent do little to help the appli-cants. For example, the entire secondary school report on one applicant was: "Real fine candidate." Another teacher prepared the same report for *all* applicants, made a xerox copy of the report with blank spaces left for the names of students who might ask for recommen-dations, and simply filled in the blanks before sending these statements off to the various colleges. Obviously, candidates with this type of counseling and support are at a real disadvantage in the admission race. (Wickenden 1979, 1)

Such a policy indeed favors schools with the re-sources and personnel to write good letters.

The help the elite prep schools give their stu-dents extends beyond the curriculum and teach-ing they offer and the highly professional formal procedures they follow in getting them into col-lege. Their help reaches into the informal, inter-personal world of "horsetrading" that exists in friendly phone calls, beers, and dinner with col-lege admissions officers.

The close social relationships between col-lege advisors, especially those in select 16 schools, and admissions officers, particularly those in Ivy League colleges, rest on social similarities, fre-quent contact over an extended time, a sense of trust, shared information, and mutual coopera-tion. The existence and operation of these ties may well improve a boarding school student's chances for admission to a highly desired college. College advisors at select 16 prep schools are much more likely to be Harvard, Yale, or Princeton graduates than other schools' advisors. Among the eleven select 16 school college advisors on whom data were available, ten were Harvard, Yale, or Prince-ton graduates, while among the twenty-three other schools' advisors on whom data were available, only three were Ivy League graduates, and none were from Harvard, Yale, or Princeton, suggesting that the select 16 prep schools consider such a connection to be important.

---

[2]This assumes they know how their graduates do once they get to college. The Ivy League colleges used to send transcripts back to the prep schools so they could see how they did, but recent concerns about privacy have stopped that practice. Several college advisors said they had sent a questionnaire to their graduates, or would like to do one, to see how they were faring. In general, this is an area where many feel they could do more than they are doing.

The close personal relationships between select 16 college advisors and college admissions officers have been built up over a considerable number of years. College advisors at select 16 schools tend to have longer tenures (ten, fifteen, or even more years is not unusual) than college advisors at other schools (who are more likely to have recently assumed the job). Given the "importance of continuity on both sides of the relationship" that was stressed by an advisor at one select 16 school, the greater continuity at select 16 schools is one of several factors in their favor.

Often prep school college advisors are invited to sit in on admissions committee decisions, to see how a college puts its class together. By doing this, they can see the makeup of the applicant pool. Such information helps them to see the competition their students face and may suggest strategies they can use in putting their candidates forward. They learn other useful information from personal contacts as well, such as which colleges are having an "admissions pinch," and hence might be receptive to somewhat weaker candidates, and that it is important for a student who has taken a year off between high school and college to document what was done during that year.

One advisor knew of a student who had enhanced his chances for admission to an elite college by writing a journal of a trip to Mozambique. Another knew that a borderline student could try for admission in February rather than September at an elite college, and might have a better chance then. This kind of inside lore about the admissions process helps boarding school college advisors sell their students more effectively than advisors without such knowledge can.

The close relationship between elite schools and colleges is reflected in another indicator. At least one Ivy League college (Harvard) puts the applications from certain boarding schools into different colored folders (Karen 1985). Hence, the admissions committee knows immediately which applicants are from certain boarding schools. Moreover, sociologist David Karen found that being from one of those select boarding schools was positively related to admission to Harvard,

even when academic and personal factors were comparable.

College advisors cooperate with the colleges in several ways. They try to screen out hopeless prospects, or as one advisor tactfully put it, "I try to discourage unproductive leads." They also "try to shape up different applicant pools for different colleges." They push students to choose which of the Ivy League colleges they want, rather than applying to all of them. A student's first choice is information they often use in their bartering sessions with colleges to clinch the promise of an acceptance. In these ways, college advisors anticipate the colleges' reactions and do some of the pre-screening of applicants for them.

In addition to cooperating with the colleges, a group of select 16 school college advisors cooperate among themselves, sharing information and developing common strategies for dealing with colleges. They meet together regularly and share college admissions statistics within their group. This organization began as an informal group of friends that played poker together. As they were comparing statistics and discussing common problems, they agreed that the practice of class ranking hurt their students, since most of them were in the top quarter of their class before coming to boarding school, but invariably half of the students ended up in the bottom half of their prep school class.[3]

Colleges had indicated to them that "it didn't look good on their profiles to have students who ranked low in their class." The group of select 16 school advisors agreed to stop providing an absolute class rank to colleges, but instead to indicate the decile or quintile rank of each student. Colleges can put such students in a "not ranked" category or can report the decile or quintile rank. No entering student from such a secondary school is labeled as the bottom person in the class. No other

---

[3]Seniors at some of the elite schools suggested their awareness of this situation when they said, in effect, "If only I'd stayed home in my public school, I would have gotten into Harvard easily."

eight schools in the country would have had the political clout to modify admissions rules like this.

College advisors, especially those at the select 16 schools, use their close personal relationships with college admissions officers to lobby for their students. "We want to be sure they are reading the applications of our students fairly, and we lobby for our students," said one select 16 school college advisor. "The colleges make their best decisions on our students and those from [another select 16 school], because they have the most information on these students." "When I drive to the [Ivy League] colleges, I give them a reading on our applicants. I let them know if I think they are making a mistake." Another said, "I don't very often tell a college they are making a mistake, but when I do, that case is often reconsidered."

Select 16 school advisors do not stop with simply asking elite college admissions officers to reconsider a decision, however. They try to barter, and the colleges leave this possibility open when they say, "Let's talk about your group." One select 16 school college advisor stresses that if his school recommends someone and he or she is accepted, that student will come. While not all colleges heed this warranty, some do and it may help the process.

Another select 16 school advisor said, "It is getting harder than it used to be to say to an admissions officer, 'take a chance on this one,' especially at Harvard which now has so many more applications." But it is significant that he did not say that it was impossible to make such a statement. If all else fails in a negotiation, a select 16 advisor said, "We lobby for the college to make him your absolute first choice on the waiting list." Such a compromise represents a chance for both parties to save face.

Most public high-school counselors do not know elite college admissions officers, nor do they have the resources to call them up or drive over to talk with them. One counselor from the Midwest, however, did come to an eastern Ivy League college to sit in on the admissions committee decision for his truly outstanding candidate—SATs in

the 700s, top in his class, class president, star athlete, and nevertheless a friendly, modest person. An advisor from an elite eastern prep school was also there, lobbying on behalf of his candidate— a nice, undistinguished fellow with SATs in the 600s, middle of his class, average athlete, and no strong signs of leadership. After hearing both the counselors, the Ivy League college chose the latter candidate. The public school counselor walked out in disgust. Afterwards, the Ivy League admissions officer said to the prep school advisor, "We may not be able to have these open meetings anymore." Even in the unusual case where a public school counselor did everything that a select 16 boarding school college advisor did, it was not enough to help the applicant to gain admittance. Despite today's competitive admissions environment, the elite prep school advisors are still listened to more closely by college admissions officers than public school counselors, suggesting that the prep school advisor is known to consistently offer the colleges a steady supply of socially elite and academically prepared students.

"YOU HAVE TO GO TO ONE OF THOSE PREP SCHOOLS. . . ."

The collegiate destinations of prep school students are very different from those of high-school students in the United States. Nationally, only seven out of ten eighteen-year-olds graduate from high school (Plisko 1984, 13). Of those seven, less than three have taken a strong academic curriculum (Fiske 1983, C8) and are prepared for four-year liberal arts colleges in the country. So by the time they reach the starting block for college, three-quarters of American young people are already considerably behind prep school students.

Even among American young people who go to college, vast differences exist; 78 percent go to public institutions and 38 percent attend two-year colleges or universities (U.S. Bureau of the Census 1984, 161). Nationally, only 2 percent of all college students attend the most highly selective colleges in the United States (that is, those whose entering freshmen have an average combined verbal and mathematics SAT score of 1,175 or better, as determined by Astin, King, and Richardson 1981), and much less than one percent nationally attend one of the eight eastern Ivy League colleges.

Almost all boarding school students attend four-year colleges immediately after graduation. Three-quarters of them attend private colleges or universities, half attend the most highly selective colleges in the United States, and one in five attends an Ivy League college. The colleges they attend are heavily concentrated on the East Coast and in California.[4]

Prep school students are also likely to attend colleges that have large numbers of their graduates from the upper class or who have otherwise achieved high status. A college's social prestige and social achievement were measured by Gene R. Hawes in his *Comprehensive Guide to Colleges* (1979); the more graduates a college has listed in the *Social Register*, the higher its social prestige, and the more graduates it has listed in *Who's Who*, the higher its social achievement. Thirty-seven percent of the seniors in our sample were bound for colleges in the top two social prestige categories established by Hawes, and 59 percent of the seniors were bound for colleges in the top two categories for social achievement.

Public high-school students do not fare so well, even when they have similar aspirations. An article in the *New York Times* captured the poignant case of a very strong public school applicant (eleventh in his class, 790/800 on his SATs) who was rejected by Harvard. After hearing the news his father said, "To get into Harvard . . . you have to go to one of those prep schools" (Winerip, 20 April, 1984, B4).

The father's perceptions are not completely off the mark. When four sets of application pools to Ivy League colleges are compared (see Table 9.1),

the acceptance rate is highest for select 16 boarding school applicants, followed by other leading boarding school applicants, then by students who graduate from an academically selective public high school,[5] and finally by the entire national application pool.

Is this higher rate of acceptance due to the superior academic credentials or the higher social family backgrounds of prep school students compared to public school students? Cookson (1981) addressed this question when he compared the college destinations of prep school students with those of suburban high-school students. He found that public school students who were similar to prep school students in terms of their SAT scores and family backgrounds were accepted at less selective colleges and generally planned to attend less prestigious colleges than their prep school peers. He also found that in the transition from secondary school to college, public schools had much less organizational clout than did prep schools. This was indicated by the fact that the personal qualities (for example, SAT scores and family backgrounds) of public school students play a larger role in where they go to college than do the personal qualities of prep school students, who apparently benefit from the reputation of their schools when college admissions officers select freshmen. In effect, prep schools themselves are able to place "floors" under their less able students and thus insure that in the transition from school to college there are fewer casualties.

We explored this issue further by comparing students from select 16 and other leading prep schools, while holding their SAT scores constant. In Table 9.2, SAT scores are related to being accepted at both Ivy League and other very highly selective colleges, for both select 16 and other boarding school students who applied to those colleges. Select 16 school students, however, are

---

[4]The top six states, in order, where more than 50 preps attended college are: Massachusetts (129), New York (127), California (93), North Carolina (61), Connecticut (58), and Pennsylvania (55).

[5]To be admitted to this particular science high school, which is in a large northeastern city, students must be recommended by their junior high school and score high on math and verbal admissions tests.

TABLE 9.1

Acceptance Rates of Ivy League Colleges from Four Application Pools

College	Select 16 Boarding Schools (1982–83)[a]	Other Leading Boarding Schools (1982–83)[a]	Selective Public High School (1984)[b]	National Group of Applicants (1982)[c]
Brown University				
% accepted	35	20	28	22
Number of applications	95	45	114	11,854
Columbia University				
% accepted	66	29	32	41
Number of applications	35	7	170	3,650
Cornell University				
% accepted	57	36	55	31
Number of applications	65	25	112	17,927
Dartmouth College				
% accepted	41	21	41	22
Number of applications	79	33	37	8,313
Harvard University				
% accepted	38	28	20	17
Number of applications	104	29	127	13,341
Princeton University				
% accepted	40	28	18	18
Number of applications	103	40	109	11,804
University of Pennsylvania				
% accepted	45	32	33	36
Number of applications	40	19	167	11,000
Yale University				
% accepted	40	32	15	20
Number of applications	92	25	124	11,023
Overall % accepted	42	27	30	26
Total number of applications	613	223	960	88,912

[a]These 836 applications from prep school seniors were made by the 1,035 seniors in our sample who applied to one or more Ivy League colleges.

[b]Based on data supplied by college advisor at the school.

[c]Figures available as of November 1984, *National College Databank.*

TABLE 9.2

Acceptance at Ivy League and Highly Selective* Colleges by Boarding School Status and SAT Scores

	High SATs (1,220–1,580)		Medium SATs (1,060–1,216)		Low SATs (540–1,050)	
	Select 16 Schools	Other Leading Prep Schools	Select 16 Schools	Other Leading Prep Schools	Select 16 Schools	Other Leading Prep Schools
Accepted at Ivy League College (%)	66	45	39	27	19	27
Number of students applying (Total: 471)	(271)	(64)	(99)	(37)	(31)	(26)
Accepted at most highly selective colleges (%)	90	71	81	70	57	39
Number of students applying (Total: 870)	(265)	(86)	(190)	(114)	(85)	(130)

*Highly selective colleges are classified in Alexander W. Astin, Margo R. King, and Gerald T. Richardson, *The American Freshman: National Norms for Fall 1981* (Los Angeles: University of California, Laboratory for Research in Higher Education, 1981).

Note: Based on our sample of 1,035 prep school seniors.

more likely to be accepted than students from other leading boarding schools with similar scores, for every category of scores except one (low SATs at Ivy League colleges). This exception may be due to the large numbers of high-scoring select 16 school students who apply to Ivy League colleges. But in general, select 16 school students do very well in their quest for admission to elite colleges. Among those with high SATs (1,220–1,580 combined verbal and math scores), 90 percent of those who applied to the most highly selective colleges were accepted, and 66 percent of those who applied to Ivy League colleges were accepted.

The vital link between prep schools and elite colleges results in one of three discernible outcomes for students. Some, specifically those with good academic credentials and SAT scores, appear to be "turbocharged" by the prep rite of passage, especially if it occurs in a select 16 school. These students are easy for college advisors to place because the colleges are delighted to admit highly qualified students who have flourished in a prep school. They are strong students who would, undoubtedly, have gone to elite colleges in good numbers anyway, but attending a select 16 prep school magnifies their chance for success.

A second group of students benefit from what might be called the "knighting effect" of attending an elite prep school. As Table 9.3 indicates, 89 percent of students who scored between 1,220 and 1,580 on their SAT exams, and who came from families in the bottom third of the socioeconomic status range in our sample, were accepted by a highly selective college. For the

TABLE 9.3

Acceptances at Most Highly Selective Colleges by Socioeconomic Status and SAT Scores

Socioeconomic Status	SATs (Combined Scores)		
	1,220–1,580	1,060–1,216	540–1,050
Top Third (%)	83	74	57
N	(126)	(109)	(64)
Middle Third (%)	85	81	38
N	(128)	(112)	(69)
Bottom Third (%)	89	75	42
N	(97)	(83)	(82)

academically talented but less affluent student, prep schools provide a route for upward mobility. A similar trend is evident for minorities and girls. Ralph Turner's belief (1966) that private schools offer no special mobility opportunities to students is not supported by these findings. In fact, for a few outstanding individuals, attending a prep school may be a critical first step in upward mobility. These findings give credence to Digby Baltzell's claim (1964) that prep schools integrate new brains with old wealth to revitalize the upper classes.

Table 9.3 also indicates that a high percentage of those with weak SATs (540 to 1,050 combined scores) do manage to gain admission to the highly selective colleges. Fifty-nine percent of the high socioeconomic status–low SATs group gain acceptance to a selective college, an indicator that the schools not only serve mobility functions, but maintenance functions as well. These are the students who have had floors placed under them by attending prep school.

When we view the college admissions process in general, it becomes clear that prep schools, especially the select 16 schools, offer strong and relatively weak students alike a tremendous boost in gaining acceptance to the colleges of their choice. For girls, minorities, and students from modest family backgrounds, the schools provide educational mobility, and for upper- and upper-middle-class students with good academic records, the schools help with their connections to prestigious colleges.

The organizational support that the schools offer to students is matched by few, if any, public schools, or, for that matter, matched by few private day schools. From the moment prep school students enter their schools, they know they are expected to enter a selective college, and they have been given the tools to gain acceptance. They also know that the college admissions environment is highly competitive. To fail to go to a selective college is considered by most prep school students a serious detour on the road to social and economic success. Where you go to college defines in good measure who you are, and the days when preps could automatically expect to go to an Ivy League or other highly selective college are over. They have to earn their way—or at least part of their way. Prep schools open doors for students, but then they must know how to walk through the doors themselves. Yet compared to their public school peers, prep school students start the race for college with substantial advantages. The safety net of organizational support is wide and strong, and should a student fall from academic grace there is somebody to help them get up.

In a college admissions system that stresses merit, the advantages prep school students enjoy raise some complex and disturbing issues. How fair is it to public school students to allow prep school students to be consistently given the competitive edge so that they win a disproportionately high number of coveted acceptances? What is really being rewarded when students are accepted at the best private colleges—personal achievement or institutional affiliation? For the prep school student, the first major dividend that he or she collects from surviving the prep rite of passage is acceptance to a suitable college, and the feeling that the acceptance is a deserved one.

REFERENCES

Astin, Alexander W.; King, Margo R.; and Richardson, Gerald T. *The American Freshman: National Norms for Fall 1981.* Los Angeles: University of California, Laboratory for Research in Higher Education, 1981.

Baltzell, E. Digby. *The Protestant Establishment.* New York: Random House, 1964.

Brint, Steven G. "Intra-occupational Stratification in Six High Status Occupations: An Analysis of Status and Status Attainment in Academe, Science, Law, Corporate Management, Engineering and Medicine." Photocopy, Yale University, New Haven, 1980.

Coleman, James S.; Hoffer, Thomas; and Kilgore, Sally. *High School Achievement.* New York: Basic Books, 1982.

Cookson, Peter Willis, Jr. "Private Secondary Boarding School and Public Suburban High School Graduation: An Analysis of College Attendance Plans." Ph.D. diss., New York University, 1981.

Coser, Lewis A.; Kadushin, Charles; and Powell, Walter W. *Books: The Culture & Commerce of Publishing.* New York: Basic Books, 1982.

Crane, Diana. "Scientists at Major and Minor Universities: A Study of Productivity and Recognition." *American Sociological Review* 30 (October 1965): 699–714.

Fiske, Edward B. "High Schools Stiffen Diploma Requirements." *New York Times,* 9 October 1983, 1, 68.

Hawes, Gene R. *Hawes Comprehensive Guide to Colleges.* New York: New American Library, 1979.

Karabel, Jerome. "Status-Group Struggle, Organizational Interests, and the Limits of Institutional Autonomy: the Transformation of Harvard, Yale, and Princeton 1918–1940." *Theory and Society* (January 1984): 1–40.

Karen, David. "Who Gets into Harvard? Selection and Exclusion." Ph.D. diss., Department of Sociology, Harvard University, 1985.

The National College Databank. Princeton, N.J.: Peterson's Guides, 1984. Bibliographic Retrieval Service electronic database.

Pierson, George W. *The Education of American Leaders.* New York: Frederick A. Praeger, 1969.

Plisko, Valena White. *The Condition of Education, 1984 Edition.* Washington, D.C.: U.S. Government Printing Office, 1984.

Thomas, Evan. "Choosing the Class of '83." *Time,* 9 April 1979, 63–74.

Tinto, Vincent. "College Origin and Patterns of Status Attainment." *Sociology of Work and Occupations* 7 (November 1980): 457–86.

Turner, Ralph H. "Sponsored and Contest Mobility and the School System." In *Class, Status and Power,* edited by Reinhard Bendix and Seymour Martin Lipset. 2d ed. New York: Free Press, 1966.

U.S. Bureau of the Census. *Statistical Abstract of the United States: 1984.* Washington, D.C.: U.S. Government Printing Office, 1983.

Useem, Michael, and Karabel, Jerome. "Educational Pathways through Top Corporate Management: Patterns of Stratification Within Companies and Differences among Companies." Paper presented at the American Sociological Association annual meeting, San Antonio, Texas, August 1984 (Revised November 1984).

Wickenden, James W., Jr. "Letter to All Princeton Alumni." Princeton, N.J.: Princeton University, October 1979.

Winerip, Michael. "Moments of Truth Come by Mail for Seniors at Great Neck South." *New York Times,* 20 April 1984, B1, B4.

42

The Savage Inequalities of Public Education in New York

Jonathan Kozol

"IN A COUNTRY WHERE THERE IS NO DISTINC-tion of class," Lord Acton wrote of the United States 130 years ago, "a child is not born to the sta-tion of its parents, but with an indefinite claim to all the prizes that can be won by thought and labor. It is in conformity with the theory of equality . . . to give as near as possible to every youth an equal state in life." Americans, he said, "are unwilling that any should be deprived in childhood of the means of competition."

It is hard to read these words today without a sense of irony and sadness. Denial of "the means of competition" is perhaps the single most consis-tent outcome of the education offered to poor chil-dren in the schools of our large cities; and nowhere is this pattern of denial more explicit or more ab-solute than in the public schools of New York City.

Average expenditures per pupil in the city of New York in 1987 were some $5,500. In the high-est spending suburbs of New York (Great Neck or Manhasset, for example, on Long Island) funding levels rose above $11,000, with the highest districts in the state at $15,000. "Why . . . ," asks the city's Board of Education, "should our students receive less" than do "similar students" who live else-where? "The inequity is clear."

But the inequality to which these words refer goes even further than the school board may be eager to reveal. "It is perhaps the supreme irony,"

———————

From *Savage Inequalities* by Jonathan Kozol. Copy-right © 1991 by Jonathan Kozol. Reprinted by permis-sion of Crown Publishers, Inc., a division of Random House, Inc.

says the nonprofit Community Service Society [CSS] of New York, that "the same Board of Edu-cation which perceives so clearly the inequities" of funding between separate towns and cities "is perpetuating similar inequities" right in New York. And, in comment on the Board of Educa-tion's final statement—"the inequity is clear"— the CSS observes, "New York City's poorest . . . districts could adopt that eloquent statement with few changes."

New York City's public schools are subdivided into 32 school districts. District 10 encompasses a large part of the Bronx but is, effectively, two separate districts. One of these districts, Riverdale, is in the northwest section of the Bronx. Home to many of the city's most sophisticated and well-educated families, its elementary schools have rela-tively few low-income students. The other section, to the south and east, is poor and heavily nonwhite.

The contrast between public schools in each of these two neighborhoods is obvious to any visi-tor. At Public School 24 in Riverdale, the princi-pal speaks enthusiastically of his teaching staff. At Public School 79, serving poorer children to the south, the principal says that he is forced to take the "tenth-best" teachers. "I thank God they're still breathing," he remarks of those from whom he must select his teachers.

Some years ago, District 10 received an allo-cation for computers. The local board decided to give each elementary school an equal number of computers, even though the schools in Riverdale had smaller classes and far fewer students. When it was pointed out that schools in Riverdale, as a result, had twice the number of computers in proportion to their student populations as the schools in the poor neighborhoods, the chairman of the local board replied, "What is fair is what is determined . . . to be fair."

The superintendent of District 10, Fred Goldberg, tells the *New York Times* that "every effort" is made "to distribute resources equitably." He speculates that some gap might exist because some of the poorer schools need to use funds earmarked for computers to buy basic supplies like pens and paper. Asked about the differences in teachers noted by the principals, he says there are no differences, then adds that next year he'll begin a program to improve the quality of teachers in the poorer schools. Questioned about differences in physical appearances between the richer and the poorer schools, he says, "I think it's demographics."

Sometimes a school principal, whatever his background or his politics, looks into the faces of the children in his school and offers a disarming statement that cuts through official ambiguity. "These are the kids most in need," says Edward Flanery, the principal of one of the low-income schools, "and they get the worst teachers." For children of diverse needs in his overcrowded rooms, he says, "you need an outstanding teacher. And what do you get? You get the worst."

In order to find Public School 261 in District 10, a visitor is told to look for a mortician's office. The funeral home, which faces Jerome Avenue in the North Bronx, is easy to identify by its green awning. The school is next door, in a former roller-skating rink. No sign identifies the building as a school. A metal awning frame without an awning supports a flagpole, but there is no flag.

In the street in front of the school there is an elevated public transit line. Heavy traffic fills the street. The existence of the school is virtually concealed within this crowded city block.

In a vestibule between the outer and inner glass doors of the school there is a sign with these words: "All children are capable of learning."

Beyond the inner doors a guard is seated. The lobby is long and narrow. The ceiling is low. There are no windows. All the teachers that I see at first are middle-aged white women. The principal, who is also a white woman, tells me that the school's "capacity" is 900 but that there are 1,300 children here. The size of classes for fifth and sixth grade children in New York, she says, is "capped" at 32, but she says that class size in the school goes "up to 34." (I later see classes, however, as large as 37.) Classes for younger children, she goes on, are "capped at 25," but a school can go above this limit if it puts an extra adult in the room. Lack of space, she says, prevents the school from operating a prekindergarten program.

I ask the principal where her children go to school. They are enrolled in private school, she says.

"Lunchtime is a challenge for us," she explains. "Limited space obliges us to do it in three shifts, 450 children at a time."

Textbooks are scarce and children have to share their social studies books. The principal says there is one full-time pupil counselor and another who is here two days a week: a ratio of 930 children to one counselor. The carpets are patched and sometimes taped together to conceal an open space. "I could use some new rugs," she observes.

To make up for the building's lack of windows and the crowded feeling that results, the staff puts plants and fish tanks in the corridors. Some of the plants are flourishing. Two boys, released from class, are in a corridor beside a tank, their noses pressed against the glass. A school of pinkish fish inside the tank are darting back and forth. Farther down the corridor a small Hispanic girl is watering the plants.

Two first grade classes share a single room without a window, divided only by a blackboard. Four kindergartens and a sixth grade class of Spanish-speaking children have been packed into a single room in which, again, there is no window. A second grade bilingual class of 37 children has its own room but again there is no window.

By eleven o'clock, the lunchroom is already packed with appetite and life. The kids line up to get their meals, then eat them in ten minutes. After that, with no place they can go to play, they sit and wait until it's time to line up and go back to class.

On the second floor I visit four classes taking place within another undivided space. The room has a low ceiling. File cabinets and movable black-boards give a small degree of isolation to each class. Again, there are no windows.

The library is a tiny, windowless and claustro-phobic room. I count approximately 700 books. Seeing no reference books, I ask a teacher if ency-clopedias and other reference books are kept in classrooms.

"We don't have encyclopedias in classrooms," she replies. "That is for the suburbs."

The school, I am told, has 26 computers for its 1,300 children. There is one small gym and children get one period, and sometimes two, each week. Recess, however, is not possible because there is no playground. "Head Start," the princi-pal says, "scarcely exists in District 10. We have no space."

The school, I am told, is 90 percent black and Hispanic; the other 10 percent are Asian, white or Middle Eastern.

In a sixth grade social studies class the walls are bare of words or decorations. There seems to be no ventilation system, or, if one exists, it isn't working.

The class discusses the Nile River and the Fertile Crescent.

The teacher, in a droning voice: "How is it useful that these civilizations developed close to rivers?"

A child, in a good loud voice: "What kind of question is that?"

In my notes I find these words: "An uncom-fortable feeling—being in a building with no win-dows. There are metal ducts across the room. Do they give air? I feel asphyxiated. . . ."

On the top floor of the school, a sixth grade of 30 children shares a room with 29 bilingual sec-ond graders. Because of the high class size there is an assistant with each teacher. This means that 59 children and four grown-ups—63 in all—must share a room that, in a suburban school, would hold no more than 20 children and one teacher.

There are, at least, some outside windows in this room—it is the only room with windows in the school—and the room has a high ceiling. It is a relief to see some daylight.

I return to see the kindergarten classes on the ground floor and feel stifled once again by lack of air and the low ceiling. Nearly 120 children and adults are doing what they can to make the best of things: 80 children in four kindergarten classes, 30 children in the sixth grade class, and about eight grown-ups who are aides and teachers. The kindergarten children sitting on the worn rug, which is patched with tape, look up at me and turn their heads to follow me as I walk past them.

As I leave the school, a sixth grade teacher stops to talk. I ask her, "Is there air conditioning in warmer weather?"

Teachers, while inside the building, are re-luctant to give answers to this kind of question. Outside, on the sidewalk, she is less constrained: "I had an awful room last year. In the winter it was 56 degrees. In the summer it was up to 90. It was sweltering."

I ask her, "Do the children ever comment on the building?"

"They don't say," she answers, "but they know."

I ask her if they see it as a racial message.

"All these children see TV," she says. "They know what suburban schools are like. Then they look around them at their school. This was a roller-rink, you know. . . . They don't comment on it but you see it in their eyes. They understand." . . .

Stark as the inequities in District 10 appear, educators say that they are "mild" in comparison to other situations in the city. Some of the most stunning inequality, according to a report by the Community Service Society, derives from alloca-tions granted by state legislators to school districts where they have political allies. The poorest dis-tricts in the city get approximately 90 cents per pupil from these legislative grants, while the rich-est districts have been given $14 for each pupil.

Newspapers in New York City have reported other instances of the misallocation of resources.

"The Board of Education," wrote the *New York Post* during July of 1987, "was hit with bombshell charges yesterday that money earmarked for fighting drug abuse and illiteracy in ghetto schools was funneled instead to schools in wealthy areas."

In receipt of extra legislative funds, according to the *Post*, affluent districts were funded "at a rate 14 times greater than low-income districts." The paper said the city's poorest areas were underfunded "with stunning consistency."

The report by the Community Service Society cites an official of the New York City Board of Education who remarks that there is "no point" in putting further money "into some poor districts" because, in his belief, "new teachers would not stay there." But the report observes that, in an instance where beginning teacher salaries were raised by nearly half, "that problem largely disappeared"—another interesting reminder of the difference money makes when we are willing to invest it. Nonetheless, says the report, "the perception that the poorest districts are beyond help still remains. . . ." Perhaps the worst result of such beliefs, says the report, is the message that resources would be "wasted on poor children." This message "trickles down to districts, schools, and classrooms." Children hear and understand this theme—they are poor investments—and behave accordingly. If society's resources would be wasted on their destinies, perhaps their own determination would be wasted too. "Expectations are a powerful force . . . ," the CSS observes.

Despite the evidence, the CSS report leans over backwards not to fuel the flames of racial indignation. "In the present climate," the report says, "suggestions of racism must be made with caution. However, it is inescapable that these inequities are being perpetrated on [school] districts which are virtually all black and Hispanic. . . ." While the report says, very carefully, that there is no "evidence" of "deliberate individual discrimination," it nonetheless concludes that "those who allocate resources make decisions over and over again which penalize the poorest districts." Analysis of city policy, the study says, "speaks to systemic bias which constitutes a conspiracy of effect. . . . Whether consciously or not, the system writes off its poorest students."

. . .

It is not only at the grade-school level that inequities like these are seen in New York City. Morris High School in the South Bronx, for example, says a teacher who has taught here more than 20 years, "does everything an inanimate object can do to keep children from being educated."

Blackboards at the school, according to the *New York Times*, are "so badly cracked that teachers are afraid to let students write on them for fear they'll cut themselves. Some mornings, fallen chips of paint cover classrooms like snow. . . . Teachers and students have come to see humor in the waterfall that courses down six flights of stairs after a heavy rain."

One classroom, we are told, has been sealed off "because of a gaping hole in the floor." In the band room, "chairs are positioned where acoustic tiles don't fall quite so often." In many places, "plaster and ceramic tile have peeled off" the walls, leaving the external brick wall of the school exposed. "There isn't much between us and the great outdoors," the principal reports.

A "landscape of hopelessness"—"burnt-out apartments, boarded windows, vacant lot upon garbage-strewn vacant lot"—surrounds the school. Statistics tell us, says the *Times*, that the South Bronx is "the poorest congressional district in the United States." But statistics cannot tell us "what it means to a child to leave his often hellish home and go to a school—his hope for a transcendent future—that is literally falling apart."

The head of school facilities for the Board of Education speaks of classrooms unrepaired years after having been destroyed by fire. "What's really sad," she notes, "is that so many kids come from places that look as bad as our schools—and we have nothing better to offer them."

A year later, when I visit Morris High, most of these conditions are unchanged. Water still cascades down the stairs. Plaster is still falling from the walls. Female students tell me that they shower after school to wash the plaster from their hair. Entering ninth grade children at the school, I'm told, read about four years behind grade level.

From the street, the school looks like a medieval castle; its turreted tower rises high above the devastated lots below. A plaque in the principal's office tells a visitor that this is the oldest high school in the Bronx.

The first things that one senses in the building are the sweetness, the real innocence, of many of the children, the patience and determination of the teachers, and the shameful disrepair of the surroundings. The principal is unsparing in her honesty. "The first floor," she tells me as we head off to the stairwell, "isn't bad—unless you go into the gym or auditorium." It's the top two floors, she says, the fourth and fifth floors, that reveal the full extent of Morris High's neglect by New York City's Board of Education.

Despite her warning, I am somewhat stunned to see a huge hole in the ceiling of the stairwell on the school's fourth floor. The plaster is gone, exposing rusted metal bars embedded in the outside wall. It will cost as much as $50 million to restore the school to an acceptable condition, she reports.

Jack Forman, the head of the English department, is a scholarly and handsome gray-haired man whose academic specialty is British literature. Sitting in his office in a pinstripe shirt and red suspenders, his feet up on the table, he is interrupted by a stream of kids. A tiny ninth grade student seems to hesitate outside the office door. Forman invites her to come in and, after she has given him a message ("Carmen had to leave—for an emergency") and gone to her next class, his face breaks out into a smile. "She's a lovely little kid. These students live in a tough neighborhood, but they are children and I speak to them as children."

Forman says that freshman English students get a solid diet of good reading: *A Tale of Two Cities*, *Manchild in the Promised Land*, Steinbeck's *The Pearl*, some African fiction, a number of Greek tragedies. "We're implementing an AP course ["advanced placement"—for pre-college students] for the first time. We don't know how many children will succeed in it, but we intend to try. Our mission is to stretch their minds, to give them every chance to grow beyond their present expectations.

"I have strong feelings about getting past the basics. Too many schools are stripping down curriculum to meet the pressure for success on tests that measure only minimal skills. That's why I teach a theater course. Students who don't respond to ordinary classes may surprise us, and surprise themselves, when they are asked to step out on a stage.

"I have a student, Carlos, who had dropped out once and then returned. He had no confidence in his ability. Then he began to act. He memorized the part of Pyramus. Then he played Sebastian in *The Tempest*. He had a photographic memory. Amazing! He will graduate, I hope, this June.

"Now, if we didn't have that theater program, you have got to ask if Carlos would have stayed in school."

In a sun-drenched corner room on the top floor, a female teacher and some 25 black and Hispanic children are reading a poem by Paul Laurence Dunbar. Holes in the walls and ceiling leave exposed the structural brick. The sun appears to blind the teacher. There are no shades. Sheets of torn construction paper have been taped to windowpanes, but the glare is quite relentless. The children look forlorn and sleepy.

I know why the caged bird sings. . . .
It is not a carol of joy. . . .

"This is your homework," says the teacher. "Let's get on with it."

But the children cannot seem to wake up to the words. A 15-year-old boy, wearing a floppy purple hat, white jersey and striped baggy pants, is asked to read the lines.

I know what the caged bird feels . . .
When the wind stirs soft through the springing grass,
And the river flows like a stream of glass. . . .

A 15-year-old girl with curly long red hair and many freckles reads the lines. Her T-shirt hangs down almost to her knees.

I know why the caged bird beats his wing
Till its blood is red on the cruel bars.

A boy named Victor, sitting at my side, whispers the words: "I know why the caged bird beats his wing. . . . His blood is red. He wants to spread his wings."

The teacher asks the children what the poet means or what the imagery conveys. There is no response at first. Then Victor lifts his hand. "The poem is about ancient days of slavery," he says. "The bird destroys himself because he can't escape the cage."

"Why does he sing?" the teacher asks.

"He sings out of the longing to be free."

At the end of class the teacher tells me, "Forty, maybe 45 percent out of this group will graduate."

The counseling office is the worst room I have seen. There is a large blue barrel by the window. "When it rains," one of the counselors says, "that barrel will be full." I ask her how the kids react. "They would like to see the rain stop in the office," she replies.

The counselor seems to like the kids and points to three young women sitting at a table in the middle of the room. One of them, an elegant tall girl with long dark hair, is studying her homework. She's wearing jeans, a long black coat, a black turtleneck, a black hat with a bright red band. "I love the style of these kids," the counselor says.

A very shy light-skinned girl waits by the desk. A transfer from another school, she's with her father. They fill out certain transfer forms and ask the counselor some questions. The father's earnestness, his faith in the importance of these details, and the child's almost painful shyness stay in my mind later.

At eleven o'clock, about 200 children in a top-floor room are watching Forman's theater class performing *The Creation* by James Weldon Johnson. Next, a gospel choir sings—"I once was lost and now am found"—and then a tall black student gives a powerful delivery of a much-recited speech of Martin Luther King while another student does an agonizing, slow-paced slave ballet. The students seem mesmerized. The speaker's voice is strong and filled with longing.

"One day, the sons of former slaves and the sons of former slave-owners will be able to sit down together at the table of brotherhood."

But the register of enrollment given to me by the principal reflects the demographics of continued racial segregation: Of the students in this school, 38 percent are black, 62 percent Hispanic. There are no white children in the building.

The session ends with a terrific fast jazz concert by a band composed of students dressed in black ties, crimson jackets and white shirts. A student with a small trimmed beard and mustache stands to do a solo on the saxophone. The pianist is the same young man who read the words of Martin Luther King. His solo, on a battered Baldwin, brings the students to their feet.

Victor Acosta and eight other boys and girls meet with me in the freshman counselors' office. They talk about "the table of brotherhood"—the words of Dr. King that we have heard recited by the theater class upstairs.

"We are not yet seated at that table," Victor says.

"The table is set but no one's in the chairs," says a black student who, I later learn, is named Carissa.

Alexander, a 16-year-old student who was brought here by his parents from Jamaica just a year ago, says this: "You can understand things better when you go among the wealthy. You look around you at their school, although it's impolite to do that, and you take a deep breath at the sight of all those beautiful surroundings. Then you come back home and see that these are things you do not have. You think of the difference. Not at first. It takes a while to settle in."

I ask him why these differences exist.

"Let me answer that," says Israel, a small, wiry Puerto Rican boy. "If you threw us all into some different place, some ugly land, and put white children in this building in our place, this school would start to shine. No question. The parents would say: 'This building sucks. It's ugly. Fix it up.' They'd fix it fast—no question.

"People on the outside," he goes on, "may think that we don't know what it is like for other students, but we *visit* other schools and we have eyes and we have brains. You cannot hide the differences. You see it and compare. . . .

"Most of the students in this school won't go to college. Many of them will join the military. If there's a war, we have to fight. Why should I go to war and fight for opportunities I can't enjoy—for things rich people value, for their freedom, but I do not *have* that freedom and I can't go to their schools?"

"You tell your friends, 'I go to Morris High,'" Carissa says. "They make a face. How does that make you feel?" she points to the floor beside the water barrel. "I found wild mushrooms growing in that corner."

"Big fat ugly things with hairs," says Victor.

Alexander then begins an explanation of the way that inequality becomes ensconced. "See," he says, "the parents of rich children have the money to get into better schools. Then, after a while, they begin to say, 'Well, I have this. Why not keep it for my children?' In other words, it locks them into the idea of always having something more. After that, these things—the extra things they have—are seen like an *inheritance*. They feel it's theirs and they don't understand why we should question it.

"See, that's where the trouble starts. They get used to what they have. They think it's theirs by rights because they had it from the start. So it leaves those children with a legacy of greed. I don't think most people understand this."

One of the counselors, who sits nearby, looks at me and then at Alexander. Later he says, "It's quite remarkable how much these children see. You wouldn't know it from their academic work. Most of them write poorly. There is a tremendous gulf between their skills and capabilities. This gulf, this dissonance, is frightening. I mean, it says so much about the squandering of human worth. . . ."

I ask the students if they can explain the reasons for the physical condition of the school.

"Hey, it's like a welfare hospital! You're getting it for free," says Alexander. "You have no power to complain."

"Is money really everything?" I ask.

"It's a nice fraction of everything," he says.

Janice, who is soft-spoken and black, speaks about the overcrowding of the school. "I make it my business," she says, "to know my fellow students. But it isn't easy when the classes are so large. I had 45 children in my fifth grade class. The teacher sometimes didn't know you. She would ask you, 'What's your name?'"

"You *want* the teacher to know your name," says Rosie, who is Puerto Rican. "The teacher asks me, 'Are you really in this class?' 'Yes, I've been here all semester.' But she doesn't know my name."

All the students hope to go to college. After college they have ambitious plans. One of them hopes to be a doctor. Two want to be lawyers. Alexander wants to be an architect. Carissa hopes to be a businesswoman. What is the likelihood that they will live up to these dreams? Five years ago, I'm told, there were approximately 500 freshman students in the school. Of these, only 180 survived four grades and made it through twelfth grade to graduation; only 82 were skilled enough to take the SATs. The projection I have heard for this year's ninth grade class is that 150 or so may graduate four years from now. Which of the kids before me will survive?

Rosie speaks of sixth grade classmates who had babies and left school. Victor speaks of boys who left school during eighth grade. Only one of the children in this group has ever been a student in a racially desegregated school.

"How long will it be," I ask, "before white children and black and Hispanic children in New York will go to the same schools?"

"How long has the United States existed?" Alexander asks.

Janice says, "Two hundred years."

"Give it another two hundred years," says Alexander.

"Thank you," says Carissa.

. . .

New York City has a number of selective high schools that have special programs and impressive up-to-date facilities. Schools like Morris High, in contrast, says the *New York Times*, tend to be "most overcrowded" and have "the highest dropout rates" and "lowest scores." In addition, we read, they receive "less money" per pupil.

The selective schools, according to the *Times*, "compete for the brightest students, but some students who might qualify lose out for lack of information and counseling." Other families, says the paper, "win admission through political influence."

The *Times* writes that these better-funded schools should not be "the preserve of an unfairly chosen elite." Yet, if the experience of other cities holds in New York City, this is what these special schools are meant to be. They are *intended* to be enclaves of superior education, private schools essentially, within the public system.

New York City's selective admissions program, says the principal of nonselective Jackson High, "has had the effect of making Jackson a racially segregated high school. . . . Simultaneously, the most 'difficult' and 'challenging' black students [have been] *encouraged* to select Jackson. . . ." The plan, she says, has had the effect of "placing a disproportionate number" of nonachieving children in one school. Moreover, she observes, students who do not meet "acceptable standards" in their chosen schools are sent back to schools like Jackson, making it effectively a dumping ground for children who are unsuccessful elsewhere.

"The gerrymandered zoning and the high school selection processes," according to a resident of the Jackson district, "create a citywide skimming policy that we compare to orange juice—our black youngsters are being treated like the sediment." The city, she says, is "not shaking the juice right." But she may be wrong. In the minds of those who have their eyes on an effective triage process—selective betterment of the most fortunate—this may be exactly the right way to shake the juice.

Unfairness on this scale is hard to contemplate in any setting. In the case of New York City and par-

ticularly Riverdale, however, it takes on a special poignance. Riverdale, after all, is not a redneck neighborhood. It has been home for many years to some of the most progressive people in the nation. Dozens of college students from this neighborhood went south during the civil rights campaigns to fight for the desegregation of the schools and restaurants and stores. The parents of those students often made large contributions to support the work of SNCC [Student Nonviolent Coordinating Committee] and CORE [Congress of Racial Equality]. One generation passes, and the cruelties they fought in Mississippi have come north to New York City. Suddenly, no doubt unwittingly, they find themselves opposed to simple things they would have died for 20 years before. Perhaps it isn't fair to say they are "opposed." A better word, more accurate, might be "oblivious." They do not want poor children to be harmed. They simply want the best for their own children. To the children of the South Bronx, it is all the same. . . .

A 16-year-old student in the South Bronx tells me that he went to English class for two months in the fall of 1989 before the school supplied him with a textbook. He spent the entire year without a science text. "My mother offered to help me with my science, which was hard for me," he says, "but I could not bring home a book."

In May of 1990 he is facing final exams, but, because the school requires students to pass in their textbooks one week prior to the end of the semester, he is forced to study without math and English texts.

He wants to go to college and he knows that math and English are important, but he's feeling overwhelmed, especially in math. He asked his teacher if he could come in for extra help, but she informed him that she didn't have the time. He asked if he could come to school an hour early, when she might have time to help him, but security precautions at the school made this impossible.

Sitting in his kitchen, I attempt to help him with his math and English. In math, according to a practice test he has been given, he is asked to solve the following equation: "$2x - 2 = 14$. What is x?" He finds this baffling. In English, he is told he'll have to know the parts of speech. In the sentence "Jack walks to the store," he is unable to identify the verb.

He is in a dark mood, worried about this and other problems. His mother has recently been diagnosed as having cancer. We leave the apartment and walk downstairs to the street. He's a full-grown young man, tall and quiet and strong-looking; but out on the street, when it is time to say good-bye, his eyes fill up with tears.

In the fall of the year, he phones me at my home. "There are 42 students in my science class, 40 in my English class—45 in my home room. When all the kids show up, five of us have to stand in back."

A first-year English teacher at another high school in the Bronx calls me two nights later: "I've got five classes—42 in each! We have no textbooks yet. I'm using my old textbook from the seventh grade. They're doing construction all around me so the noise is quite amazing. They're actually *drilling* in the hall outside my room. I have more kids than desks in all five classes.

"A student came in today whom I had never seen. I said, 'We'll have to wait and see if someone doesn't come so you can have a chair.' She looked at me and said, 'I'm leaving.'"

The other teachers tell her that the problem will resolve itself. "Half the students will be gone by Christmastime, they say. It's awful when you realize that the school is *counting* on the failure of one half my class. If they didn't count on it, perhaps it wouldn't happen. If I *began* with 20 students in a class, I'd have lots more time to spend with each of them. I'd have a chance to track them down, go to their homes, see them on the weekends. . . . I don't understand why people in New York permit this."

One of the students in her class, she says, wrote this two-line poem for Martin Luther King:

He tried to help the white and black.
Now that he's dead he can't do jack.

Another student wrote these lines:

America the beautiful,
Who are you beautiful for?

"Frequently," says a teacher at another crowded high school in New York, "a student may be in the wrong class for a term and never know it." With only one counselor to 700 students system-wide in New York City, there is little help available to those who feel confused. It is not surprising, says the teacher, "that many find the experience so cold, impersonal and disheartening that they decide to stay home by the sad warmth of the TV set."

According to a recent study issued by the State Commissioner of Education, "as many as three out of four blacks" in New York City "and four out of five Latinos fail to complete high school within the traditional four-year period." The number of students of all races who drop out between ninth and twelfth grades, and do not return, and never finish school, remains a mystery in New York City. The *Times* itself, at various points, has offered estimates that range from 25 percent to nearly twice that high—a range of numbers that suggests how inconsistent and perplexing school board estimates appear even to seasoned journalists. Sara Rimer of the *New York Times* pegged the rate of those who do not graduate at 46 percent in 1990—a figure that seems credible because it is consistent with the numbers for most other cities with large nonwhite student populations. Including those who drop out during junior high—numbers not included in the dropout figures offered by the New York City Board of Education—it may be that roughly half of New York City's children do not finish school.

The school board goes to great extremes to understate these numbers, and now and then the press explains why numbers coming from the central office are not necessarily to be believed. Number-juggling by school boards—for example, by devising "a new formula" of calculation to appease the public by appearing to show progress—is familiar all over the nation. The *Times*, for instance, notes in another article that, while the "official" dropout rate "has fallen from 45 percent to 29.2 percent," watchdog groups say that the alleged "improvement" stems from "changes in the way the number has been calculated." School boards, moreover, have a vested interest in low-balling dropout figures since the federal and state aid that they receive is pegged to actual attendance.

Listening to children who drop out of school, we often hear an awful note of anonymity. "I hated the school. . . . I never knew who my counselor was," a former New York City student says. "He wasn't available for me. . . . I saw him once. . . . One ten-minute interview. . . . That was all."

Chaos and anonymity overtake some of the elementary schools as well. "A child identified as a chronic truant," reports an official of the Rheedlen Foundation, a child welfare agency in New York City, "might be reported by the teacher—or he might not. Someone from the public school attendance office might try to contact the parents and might be successful, or he might not. The child might attend school again. Probably not." Several children of my acquaintance in the New York City schools were truant for eight months in 1988 and 1989 but were never phoned or visited by school attendance officers.

"We have children," says one grade-school principal, "who just disappear from the face of the earth."

This information strikes one as astonishing. How does a child simply "disappear" in New York City? Efficiency in information transfer—when it comes to stock transactions, for example—is one of the city's best-developed skills. Why is it so difficult to keep track of poor children? When the school board loses track of hundreds of poor children, the explanations given by the city point to "managerial dilemmas" and to "problems" in a new computer system. The same dilemmas are advanced as explanations for the city's inability to get books into classrooms in sufficient numbers for

the class enrollments, or to paint the walls or keep the roofs from leaking. But managerial dilemmas never quite suffice to justify these failures. A city which is home to some of the most clever and aggressive and ingenious men and women in the world surely could devise more orderly and less humiliating ways to meet the needs of these poor children. Failure to do so rests in explanations other than a flawed administration, but the city and, particularly, its press appears to favor the administrative explanation. It defuses anger at injustice and replaces it with irritation at bureaucracy.

New York City manages expertly, and with marvelous predictability, whatever it considers humanly important. Fax machines, computers, automated telephones and even messengers on bikes convey a million bits of data through Manhattan every day to guarantee that Wall Street brokers get their orders placed, confirmed, delivered, at the moment they demand. But leaking roofs cannot be fixed and books cannot be gotten into Morris High in time to meet the fall enrollment. Efficiency in educational provision for low-income children, as in health care and most other elementals of existence, is secreted and doled out by our municipalities as if it were a scarce resource. Like kindness, cleanliness and promptness of provision, it is not secured by gravity of need but by the cash, skin color and class status of the applicant.

At a high school in Crown Heights, a neighborhood of Brooklyn, "bathrooms, gymnasiums, hallways and closets" have been converted into classrooms, says the *New York Times*. "We have no closets—they're classrooms now," says the principal of another school. "We went to a school," says Robert Wagner, former president of the city's Board of Education, "where there were five Haitian youngsters literally [having classes] in a urinal."

At P.S. 94 in District 10, where 1,300 children study in a building suitable for 700, the gym has been transformed into four noisy, makeshift classrooms. The gym teacher improvises with no gym. A reading teacher, in whose room "huge pieces of a ceiling" have collapsed, according to the *Times*, "covering the floor, the desks and the books," describes the rain that spills in through the roof. "If society gave a damn about these children," says the teacher, "they wouldn't let this happen." These are the same conditions I observed in Boston's segregated schools a quarter-century ago. Nothing has changed.

A class of third grade children at the school has four different teachers in a five-month span in 1989. "We get dizzy," says one child in the class. The only social worker in the school has 30 minutes in a week to help a troubled child. Her caseload holds the names of nearly 80 children. The only truant officer available, who splits her time between this and three other schools in District 10—the district has ten truant officers, in all, for 36,000 children—is responsible for finding and retrieving no less than 400 children at a given time.

When a school board hires just *one* woman to retrieve 400 missing children from the streets of the North Bronx, we may reasonably conclude that it does not particularly desire to find them. If 100 of these children startled us by showing up at school, moreover, there would be no room for them in P.S. 94. The building couldn't hold them.

Many of these problems, says the press again, may be attributed to inefficiency and certain very special bureaucratic difficulties in the New York City system. . . . However, comparable problems are apparent in Chicago, and the same conditions are routinely found in other systems serving mainly nonwhite children. The systems and bureaucracies are different. What is consistent is that all of them are serving children who are viewed as having little value to America. . . .

The differences between school districts and *within* school districts in the city are, however, almost insignificant compared to those between the city and the world of affluence around it—in Westchester County, for example, and in largely prosperous Long Island.

Even in the suburbs, nonetheless, it has been noted that a differential system still exists, and it may not be surprising to discover that the differences are once again determined by the social class, parental wealth, and sometimes race, of the schoolchildren. A study, a few years ago, of 20 of the wealthiest and poorest districts of Long Island, for example, matched by location and size of enrollment, found that the differences in per-pupil spending were not only large but had approximately doubled in a five-year period. Schools, in Great Neck, in 1987, spent $11,265 for each pupil. In affluent Jericho and Manhasset the figures were, respectively, $11,325 and $11,370. In Oyster Bay the figure was $9,980. Compare this to Levittown, also on Long Island but a town of mostly working-class white families, where per-pupil spending dropped to $6,900. Then compare these numbers to the spending level in the town of Roosevelt, the poorest district in the county, where the schools are 99 percent nonwhite and where the figure dropped to $6,340. Finally, consider New York City, where, in the same year, $5,590 was invested in each pupil—less than half of what was spent in Great Neck. The pattern is almost identical to that which we have seen outside Chicago.

Again, look at Westchester County, where, in the same year, the same range of discrepancies was found. Affluent Bronxville, an attractive suburb just north of the Bronx, spent $10,000 for each pupil. Chappaqua's yearly spending figure rose above $9,000. Studying the chart again, we locate Yonkers—a blue-collar town that is predominantly white but where over half the student population is nonwhite—and we find the figure drops to $7,400. This is not the lowest figure, though. The lowest-spending schools within Westchester, spending a full thousand dollars less than Yonkers, serve the suburb of Mount Vernon, where three quarters of the children in the public schools are black.

"If you're looking for a home," a realtor notes, "you can look at the charts for school expenditures and use them to determine if your neighbors will be white and wealthy or, conversely, black or white but poor."

Newsday, a Long Island paper, notes that these comparisons are studied with great interest by home-buyers. Indeed, the paper notes, the state's exhaustive compilation, "Statistical Profiles of Public School Districts," has unexpectedly become a small best-seller. People who want to know if public schools in areas where they are planning to buy homes are actually as good as it is claimed in real-estate brochures, according to *Newsday,* now can use the "Statistical Profiles" as a more authoritative source. Superintendents in some districts say the publication, which compares student performance, spending, staff, and such in every state school system, "will be useful for home-buyers." For real-estate agents in the highest-rated districts, the appearance of this publication is good news. It helps to elevate the value of the homes they have for sale.

In effect, a circular phenomenon evolves. The richer districts—those in which the property lots and houses are more highly valued—have more revenue, derived from taxing land and homes, to fund their public schools. The reputation of the schools, in turn, adds to the value of their homes, and this, in turn, expands the tax base for their public schools. The fact that they can levy lower taxes than the poorer districts, but exact more money, raises values even more; and this, again, means further funds for smaller classes and for higher teacher salaries within their public schools. Few of the children in the schools of Roosevelt or Mount Vernon will, as a result, be likely to compete effectively with kids in Great Neck and Manhasset for admissions to the better local colleges and universities of New York state. Even fewer will compete for more exclusive Ivy League admissions. And few of the graduates or dropouts of those poorer systems, as a consequence, are likely ever to earn enough to buy a home in Great Neck or Manhasset.

The New York State Commissioner of Education cautions parents not to make "the judgment that a district is good because the scores are good, or bad because the scores are bad." This, we will find, is a recurrent theme in public statements on this issue, and the commissioner is correct, of course, that overemphasis on test scores, when the differences are slight, can be deceptive. But it may be somewhat disingenuous to act as if the larger differences do not effectively predict success or failure for large numbers of schoolchildren. Certainly home-buyers will be easily convinced that schools in Jericho, third-highest-spending district on Long Island, where the dropout rate is an astonishing and enviable "zero" and where all but 3 percent of seniors go to college, are likely to be "good" compared to those of New York City, which spends only half as much per pupil and where only half the students ever graduate.

An apparent obligation of officials in these situations is to shelter the recipients of privilege from the potential wrath of those who are less favored. Officials manage, in effect, to broadcast a dual message. To their friends they say, in private, "This is the best place to buy a home. These are the best schools. These are the hospitals. These are the physicians." For the record, however, they assure the public that these numbers must not be regarded as implying any drastic differentials.

"The question," says the New York State Commissioner, is not how good the test scores look, but "how well is the district doing by the children it enrolls?" This will bring to mind the statement of New Trier High School's former head of student services. ("This school is right," he said, "for this community." It wouldn't, however, be "right" for everyone.) It does not require much political sophistication to decode these statements—no more than it requires to discern what is at stake when scholars at conservative foundations tell us that black and white children may have "different learning styles" and require "different strategies" and maybe "different schools."

The commissioner's question—"How well is the district doing by the children it enrolls?"—sounds reasonable. But the answers that are given to that question, as we know, will be determined by class expectations. The schools of the South Bronx—not many, but a few at least—are "doing well" by future typists, auto mechanics, office clerks and factory employees. The schools of Great Neck are "doing well" by those who will someday employ them.

There is a certain grim aesthetic in the almost perfect upward scaling of expenditures from poorest of the poor to richest of the rich within the New York City area: $5,590 for the children of the Bronx and Harlem, $6,340 for the non-white kids of Roosevelt, $6,400 for the black kids of Mount Vernon, $7,400 for the slightly better-off community of Yonkers, over $11,000 for the very lucky children of Manhasset, Jericho and Great Neck. In an ethical society, where money was apportioned in accord with need, these scalings would run almost in precise reverse.

. . .

The point is often made that, even with a genuine equality of schooling for poor children, other forces still would militate against their school performance. Cultural and economic factors and the flight of middle-income blacks from inner cities still would have their consequences in the heightened concentration of the poorest children in the poorest neighborhoods. Teen-age pregnancy, drug use and other problems still would render many families in these neighborhoods all but dysfunctional. Nothing I have said within this book should leave the misimpression that I do not think these factors are enormously important. A polarization of this issue, whereby some insist upon the primacy of school, others upon the primacy of family and neighborhood, obscures the fact that both are elemental forces in the lives of children.

The family, however, differs from the school in the significant respect that government is not responsible, or at least not directly, for the inequalities of family background. It *is* responsible for inequalities in public education. The school is the creature of the state; the family is not. To the degree, moreover, that destructive family situations may be bettered by the future acts of government, no one expects that this could happen in the years immediately ahead. Schools, on the other hand, could make dramatic changes almost overnight if fiscal equity were a reality.

If the New York City schools were funded, for example, at the level of the highest-spending suburbs of Long Island, a fourth grade class of 36 children such as those I visited in District 10 would have had $200,000 *more* invested in their education during 1987. Although a portion of this extra money would have gone into administrative costs, the remainder would have been enough to hire two extraordinary teachers at enticing salaries of $50,000 each, divide the class into *two classes* of some 18 children each, provide them with computers, carpets, air conditioning, new texts and reference books and learning games—indeed, with everything available today in the most affluent school districts—and also pay the costs of extra counseling to help those children cope with the dilemmas that they face at home. Even the most skeptical detractor of "the worth of spending further money in the public schools" would hesitate, I think, to face a grade-school principal in the South Bronx and try to tell her that this "wouldn't make much difference."

It is obvious that urban schools have other problems in addition to their insufficient funding. Administrative chaos is endemic in some urban systems. (The fact that this in itself is a reflection of our low regard for children who depend upon these systems is a separate matter.) Greater funding, if it were intelligently applied, could partially correct these problems—by making possible, for instance, the employment of some very gifted, high-paid fiscal managers who could assure that money is well used—but it probably is also true that major structural reforms would still be needed. To polarize these points, however, and to argue, as the White House has been claiming for a decade, that administrative changes are a "better" answer to the problem than equality of funding and real efforts at desegregation is dishonest and simplistic. The suburbs have better administrations (sometimes, but not always), and they also have a lot more money in proportion to their children's needs. To speak of the former and evade the latter is a formula that guarantees that nothing will be done *today* for children who have no responsibility for either problem.

To be in favor of "good families" or of "good administration" does not take much courage or originality. It is hard to think of anyone who is opposed to either. To be in favor of redistribution of resources and of racial integration would require a great deal of courage—and a soaring sense of vision—in a president or any other politician. Whether such courage or such vision will someday become transcendent forces in our nation is by no means clear.

The train ride from Grand Central Station to suburban Rye, New York, takes 35 to 40 minutes. The high school is a short ride from the station. Build of handsome gray stone and set in a landscaped campus, it resembles a New England prep school. On a day in early June of 1990, I enter the school and am directed by a student to the office.

The principal, a relaxed, unhurried man who, unlike many urban principals, seems gratified to have me visit in his school, takes me in to see the auditorium, which, he says, was recently restored with private charitable funds ($400,000) raised by parents. The crenellated ceiling, which is white and spotless, and the polished dark-wood paneling contrast with the collapsing structure of the auditorium at Morris High. The principal strikes his fist against the balcony: "They made this place extremely solid." Through a window, one can see the spreading branches of a beech tree in the central courtyard of the school.

In a student lounge, a dozen seniors are relaxing on a carpeted floor that is constructed with a number of tiers so that, as the principal explains, "they can stretch out and be comfortable while reading."

The library is wood-paneled, like the auditorium. Students, all of whom are white, are seated at private carrels, of which there are approximately 40. Some are doing homework; others are looking through the *New York Times*. Every student that I see during my visit to the school is white or Asian, though I later learn there are a number of Hispanic students and that 1 or 2 percent of students in the school are black.

According to the principal, the school has 96 computers for 546 children. The typical student, he says, studies a foreign language for four or five years, beginning in the junior high school, and a second foreign language (Latin is available) for two years. Of 140 seniors, 92 are now enrolled in AP classes. Maximum teacher salary will soon reach $70,000. Per-pupil funding is above $12,000 at the time I visit.

The students I meet include eleventh and twelfth graders. The teacher tells me that the class is reading Robert Coles, Studs Terkel, Alice Walker. He tells me I will find them more than willing to engage me in debate, and this turns out to be correct. Primed for my visit, it appears, they narrow in directly on the dual questions of equality and race.

Three general positions soon emerge and seem to be accepted widely. The first is that the fiscal inequalities "do matter very much" in shaping what a school can offer ("That is obvious," one student says) and that any loss of funds in Rye, as a potential consequence of future equalizing, would be damaging to many things the town regards as quite essential.

The second position is that racial integration—for example, by the busing of black children from the city or a nonwhite suburb to this school—would meet with strong resistance, and the reason would not simply be the fear that certain standards might decline. The reason, several students say straightforwardly, is "racial" or, as others say it, "out-and-out racism" on the part of adults.

The third position voiced by many students, but not all, is that equity is basically a goal to be desired and should be pursued for moral reasons, but "will probably make no major difference" since poor children "still would lack the motivation" and "would probably fail in any case because of other problems."

At this point I ask if they can truly say "it wouldn't make a difference" since it's never been attempted. Several students then seem to rethink their views and say that "it might work, but it would have to start with preschool and the elementary grades" and "it might be 20 years before we'd see a difference."

At this stage in the discussion, several students speak with some real feeling of the present inequalities, which, they say, are "obviously unfair," and one student goes a little further and proposes that "we need to change a lot more than the schools." Another says she'd favor racial integration "by whatever means—including busing—even if my parents disapprove." But a contradictory opinion also is expressed with a good deal of fervor and is stated by one student in a rather biting voice: "I don't see why we should do it. How could it be of benefit to us?"

Throughout the discussion, whatever the views the children voice, there is a degree of unreality about the whole exchange. The children are lucid and their language is well chosen and their arguments well made, but there is a sense that they are dealing with an issue that does not feel very vivid, and that nothing that we say about it to each other really matters since it's "just a theoretical discussion." To a certain degree, the skillfulness and cleverness that they display seem to derive precisely from this sense of unreality. Questions of unfairness feel more like a geometric problem than a matter of humanity or conscience. A few of the students do break through the note of unreality, but, when they do, they cease to be so agile in their use of words and speak more awkwardly. Ethical challenges seem to threaten their effectiveness. There is the sense that they were skating over ice and that the issues we addressed were safely frozen underneath. When they stop to look beneath the ice they start to stumble. The verbal competence they have acquired here may have been gained by building walls around some regions of the heart.

"I don't think that busing students from their ghetto to a different school would do much good," one student says. "You can take them out of the environment, but you can't take the environment out of *them*. If someone grows up in the South Bronx, he's not going to be prone to learn." His name is Max and he has short black hair and speaks with confidence. "Busing didn't work when it was tried,"

he says. I ask him how he knows this and he says he saw a television movie about Boston.

"I agree that it's unfair the way it is," another student says. "We have AP courses and they don't. Our classes are much smaller." But, she says, "putting them in schools like ours is not the answer. Why not put some AP classes into *their* school? Fix the roof and paint the halls so it will not be so depressing."

The students know the term "separate but equal," but seem unaware of its historical associations. "Keep them where they are but make it equal," says a girl in the front row.

A student named Jennifer, whose manner of speech is somewhat less refined and polished than that of the others, tells me that her parents came here from New York. "My family is originally from the Bronx. Schools are hell there. That's one reason that we moved. I don't think it's our responsibility to pay our taxes to provide for *them*. I mean, my parents used to live there and they wanted to get out. There's no point in coming to a place like this, where schools are good, and then your taxes go back to the place where you began."

I bait her a bit: "Do you mean that, now that you are not in hell, you have no feeling for the people that you left behind?"

"It has to be the people in the area who want an education. If your parents just don't care, it won't do any good to spend a lot of money. Someone else can't want a good life for you. You have got to want it for yourself." Then she adds, however, "I agree that everyone should have a chance at taking the same courses. . . ."

I ask her if she'd think it fair to pay more taxes so that this was possible.

"I don't see how that benefits me," she says.

It occurs to me how hard it would have been for anyone to make that kind of statement, even in the wealthiest suburban school, in 1968. Her classmates would have been unsettled by the voicing of such undisguised self-interest. Here in Rye, in 1990, she can say this with impunity. She's an interesting girl and I reluctantly admire her for being so straightforward.

Max raises a different point. "I'm not convinced," he says, "that AP courses would be valued in the Bronx. Not everyone is going to go to college."

Jennifer picks up on this and carries it a little further. "The point," she says, "is that you cannot give an equal chance to every single person. If you did it, you'd be changing the whole economic system. Let's be honest. If you equalize the money, someone's got to be shortchanged. I don't doubt that children in the Bronx are getting a bad deal. But do we want *everyone* to get a mediocre education?"

"The other point," says Max, "is that you need to match the money that you spend to whether children in the school can profit from it. We get twice as much as kids in the South Bronx, but our school is *more* than twice as good and that's because of who is here. Money isn't the whole story. . . ."

"In New York," says Jennifer, "rich people put their kids in private school. If we equalize between New York and Rye, you would see the same thing happen here. People would pull out their kids. Some people do it now. So it would happen a lot more."

An eleventh grader shakes her head at this. "Poor children need more money. It's as simple as that," she says. "Money comes from taxes. If we have it, we should pay it."

It is at this point that a boy named David picks up on a statement made before. "Someone said just now that this is not our obligation, our responsibility. I don't think that that's the question. I don't think you'd do it, pay more taxes or whatever, out of obligation. You would do it just because . . . it is unfair the way it is." He falters on these words and looks a bit embarrassed. Unlike many of the other students who have spoken, he is somewhat hesitant and seems to choke up on his words. "Well, it's easy for me to be sitting here and say I'd spend my parents' money. I'm not working. I don't earn the money. I don't need to be conservative until I do. I can be as open-minded and unrealistic as I want to be. You can be a liberal until you have a mortgage."

I ask him what he'd likely say if he were ten years older. "Hopefully," he says, "my values would remain the same. But I know that having money does affect you. This, at least, is what they tell me."

Spurred perhaps by David's words, another student says, "The biggest tax that people pay is to the federal government. Why not take some money from the budget that we spend on armaments and use it for the children in these urban schools?"

A well-dressed student with a healthy tan, however, says that using federal taxes for the poor "would be like giving charity," and "charitable things have never worked. . . . Charity will not instill the poor with self-respect."

Max returns to something that he said before: "The environment is everything. It's going to take something more than money." He goes on to speak of inefficiency and of alleged corruption in the New York City schools. "Some years ago the chancellor was caught in borrowing $100,000 from the schools. I am told that he did not intend to pay it back. These things happen too much in New York. Why should we pour money in, when they are wasting what they have?"

I ask him, "Have we *any* obligations to poor people?"

"I don't think the burden is on us," says Jennifer again. "Taxing the rich to help the poor— we'd be getting nothing out of it. I don't understand how it would make a better educational experience for me."

"A child's in school only six hours a day," says Max. "You've got to deal with what is happening at home. If his father's in the streets, his mother's using crack . . . how is money going to make a difference?"

David dismisses this and tells me, "Here's what we should do. Put more money into preschool, kindergarten, elementary years. Pay college kids to tutor inner-city children. Get rid of the property tax, which is too uneven, and use income taxes to support these schools. Pay teachers more to work in places like the Bronx. It has to come from taxes. Pay them extra to go into the worst schools. You could forgive their college loans to make it worth their while."

"Give the children Head Start classes," says another student. "If they need more buildings, given them extra money so they wouldn't need to be so crowded."

"It has got to come from taxes," David says again.

"I'm against busing," Max repeats, although this subject hasn't been brought up by anybody else in a long while.

"When people talk this way," says David, "they are saying, actually—" He stops and starts again: "They're saying that black kids will never learn. Even if you spend more in New York. Even if you bring them here to Rye. So what it means is—you are writing people off. You're just dismissing them. . . ."

"I'd like it if we had black students in this school," the girl beside him says.

"It seems rather odd," says David when the hour is up, "that we were sitting in an AP class discussing whether poor kids in the Bronx deserve to get an AP class. We are in a powerful position."

. . .

In his earnestness and in his willingness to search his conscience, David reminds me of some of the kids I knew during the civil rights campaigns of the mid-1960s. Standing here beside him and his teacher, it occurs to me that many students from this town, much like those in Riverdale, were active in those struggles. Hundreds of kids from neighborhoods like these exposed themselves to all the dangers and the violence that waited for young volunteers in rural areas of Mississippi.

Today, after a quarter of a century, black and white children go to the same schools in many parts of Mississippi—the public schools of Mississippi are, in fact, far more desegregated now than public schools in New York City—but the schools are very poor. In 1987, when a child in Great Neck or Manhasset was receiving education costing some $11,000, children in Neshoba County,

Mississippi, scene of many of the bloodiest events during the voter registration drives of 23 years before, received some $1,500 for their education. In equally poor Greene County, Mississippi, things got so bad in the winter of 1988 that children enrolled at Sand Hill Elementary School had to bring toilet paper, as well as writing paper, from their homes because, according to the *Jackson Daily News*, "the school has no money for supplies." In the same year, *Time* magazine described conditions in the Mississippi town of Tunica. The roof of a junior high school building in the district had "collapsed" some years before, the magazine reported, but the district had no money for repairs. School desks were "split" and textbooks were "rotting," said *Time*. "Outside, there is no playground equipment."

At Humphreys County High School, in the Mississippi Delta, the science lab has no equipment except a tattered periodic table. "The only air conditioning," says a recent visitor, "is a hole in the roof." In June and September, when the temperature outside can reach 100 degrees, the school is "double hot," according to the principal. Children graduating from the school, he says, have little to look forward to except low-paid employment at a local catfish plant.

Until 1983, Mississippi was one of the few states with no kindergarten program and without compulsory attendance laws. Governor William Winter tried that year to get the legislature to approve a $60-million plan to upgrade public education. The plan included early childhood education, higher teacher salaries, a better math and science program for the high schools, and compulsory attendance with provisions for enforcement. The state's powerful oil corporations, facing a modest increase in their taxes to support the plan, lobbied vigorously against it. The Mid-Continent Oil and Gas Association began a television advertising campaign to defeat the bill, according to a *Newsweek* story.

"The vested interests are just too powerful," a state legislator said. Those interests, according to *Newsweek*, are "unlikely" to rush to the aid of public schools that serve poor children.

It is unlikely that the parents or the kids in Rye or Riverdale know much about realities like these; and, if they do, they may well tell themselves that Mississippi is a distant place and that they have work enough to do to face inequities in New York City. But, in reality, the plight of children in the South Bronx of New York is almost as far from them as that of children in the farthest reaches of the South.

All of these children say the Pledge of Allegiance every morning. Whether in the New York suburbs, Mississippi, or the South Bronx, they salute the same flag. They place their hands across their hearts and join their voices in a tribute to "one nation indivisible" which promises liberty and justice to all people. What is the danger that the people in a town like Rye would face if they resolved to make this statement true? How much would it really harm their children to compete in a fair race?

REFERENCES

Allen, M. 1986. "Asbestos in Chicago Housing Authority Apartments Poses Possible Health Hazards." *Chicago Reporter* 15: 1–4.

Asher, J. 1984. "A Warning to Employers: Unique Charge of Murder." *Philadelphia Inquirer*, February 26.

Bullard, R. D. 1984. "Unplanned Environs: The Price of Unplanned Growth in Boomtown Houston." *California Sociologist* 7: 85–101.

———. 1987a. "Environmentalism, Economic Blackmail, and Civil Rights: Competing Agendas Within the Black Community." Paper presented at the Annual Meeting of the Society for the Study of Social Problems, August 14–16.

———. 1987b. "Implications of Toxics in Minority Communities." *Proceedings of Conference on Community Toxic Pollution Awareness for Historically Black Colleges and Universities.* Tallahassee, FL: Legal Environmental Assistance Foundation.

———. 1988. *Environmentalism and HBCU's: Forging an Agenda for Change.* Unpublished paper. New York: United Church of Christ.

Bullard, R. D. and B. H. Wright 1986. "The Politics of Pollution: Implications for the Black Community. *Phylon* 47: 71–8.

Center for the Biology of Natural Systems. 1987a. *Prospectus.* Flushing, NY: Queens College.

———. 1987b. *Research and Educational Activities, 1986–1987.* Flushing, NY: Queens College.

Conyers, J. 1987. Personal Communication. Member, U.S. House of Representatives, Washington, DC, May 2, 1987.

Debro, T. 1987. "Federal Government Funding Opportunities." *Proceedings of Conference on Community Toxic Pollution Awareness for Historically Black Colleges and Universities.* Tallahassee, FL: Legal Environmental Assistance Foundation.

Editorial. 1987. "Dumping on Black America." *Atlanta Constitution*, April 27.

———. 1989. "A Walk for Toxic Justice." *Environmental Action* January/February.

Freudenberg, N. 1984a. "Citizen Action for Environmental Health: Report on a Survey of Community Organizations." *American Public Health Journal* 74: 444–48

———. 1984b. "Not In Our Backyards: Community Action for Health and the Environment." *Monthly Review Press* 22: 34–9.

Greenhouse, S. 1985. "Business and the Law: Responsibility for Job Safety." *New York Times*, June 25.

Gunter, B. and Williams, M. 1984. "Alabama: The Nation's Dumping Ground—A Special Report on Hazardous Wastes and Toxic Chemicals in Alabama." *Montgomery Advertiser* (June and December): Two-part special supplement.

Hoagland, D. 1987. "Church Persists as Farmworker Advocate." *Fresno Bee*, August 16.

Hopkins, D. R. 1987. Correspondence to Benjamin F. Chavis, Jr. July 31.

Human Environment Center. 1981a. *Minority Education for Environmental and Natural Resource Professions: Before College.* Washington, DC: Human Environment Center.

———. 1981b. *Minority Education for Environmental and Natural Resource Professions: Higher Education.* Washington, DC: Human Evnironment Center.

Lee, C. 1987a. "Toxic Wastes and Race: Developing A National Agenda." Keynote Speech at the Center for Third World Organizing Toxics and Minorities Conference, August 5.

———. 1987b. Toxic Wastes and Race: Its Significance for Historically Black Colleges and Universities." *Proceedings of Conference on Community Toxic Pollution Awareness for Historically Black Colleges and Universities.* Tallahassee, FL: Legal Environmental Assistance Foundation.

Murray, L. R. 1987. Personal Communication. Former Director of Occupational and Environmental Medicine, Meharry Medical College, Nashville, TN, May 12, 1987.

National Council of Churches. 1987/88. "The Lumbee River, Lumbee Indians and GSX, Inc." *The Egg: National Journal of Eco-Justice* (Winter): 10–1.

Nelson, D. 1987. "Our Toxic Trap: Crisis on Far South Side." *Chicago Sun-Times*, May 31–June 5. Six-part series.

Porter, J. W. 1987. Correspondence to Benjamin F. Chavis, Jr., July 1.

Puerto Rico Industrial Mission. 1986. *General Proposal.* San Juan, PR: Puerto Rico Industrial Mission.

Ruffins, P. 1989. "Blacks Suffer Health Hazards Yet Remain Inactive on Environment." *Los Angeles Times*, August 27.

Russell, D. 1989. "Environmental Racism: Minority Communities and Their Battle Against Toxics." *Amicus Journal* (Spring): 22–32.

Shuey, C. 1984. "Uranium Mill Tailings: Toxic Waste in the West." *Engage/Social Action* (October): 40–5.

Sidel, V. W. 1987. Personal Communication. Former President, American Public Health Association, New York, NY, May 18, 1987.

Southern Organizing Committee for Economic and Social Justice. 1989. "New Anti-Toxics Drive Taking Root." *Southern Fight Back* 14: 22.

Southwest Organizing Committee. 1989. *The Southwest Organizing Project Community Environmental Program.* Albuquerque, NM: Southwest Organizing Committee.

Student Environmental Health Project. 1987. *1987 Summer Internship Sites.* Personal correspondence with Maria Shutt, November 20.

———. 1985. *Annual Report: 1984–1985.* Nashville, TN: Vanderbilt University Center for Health Services.

———. 1986. *Annual Report: 1985–1986.* Nashville, TN: Vanderbilt University Center for Health Services.

Stults, K. 1988. "Roulette, Southern Style." In *Everyone's Backyard.* Arlington, VA: Citizen's Clearinghouse for Hazardous Wastes.

Taylor, R. A. 1984. "Do Environmentalists Care about the Poor?" *U.S. News & World Report* 96: 51–2.

United Church of Christ Commission for Racial Justice. 1987. *Toxic Wastes and Race in the United States: A National Report on the Racial and Socio-Economic Characteristics of Communities Surrounding Hazardous Waste Sites.* New York: United Church of Christ.

United Farm Workers. 1985. *Vineyard Pesticides More Dangerous than Watermelon Poison; Check Grape Pesticides Before Placing on Market, Chavez Demands.* Press Release July 17.

———. 1986. "The Wrath of Grapes: The Tragedy of Pesticide Poisoning." Food and Justice (February/March): 4–7.

U.S. Department of Health and Human Services. 1985. *Report of the Secretary's Task Force on Black and Minority Health.* Washington, DC: U.S. Department of Health and Human Services.

U.S. General Accounting Office. 1983. *Siting of Hazardous Waste Landfills and Their Correlation with the Racial and Socio-Economic Status of Surrounding Communities.* Washington, DC: U.S. General Accounting Office.

Vanderbilt, University Center for Health Services. 1987. *Mission Statement.* Personal correspondence with Maria Shutt, November 20.

Wasserstrom, R. F. and R. Wiles. 1985. *Field Duty: U.S. Farmworkers and Pesticide Safety.* Washington, DC: World Resources Institute.

Weisskopf, M. 1987. "Rights Group Finds Racism in Dump Siting." *Washington Post*, April 16.

43

Can Education Eliminate Race, Class, and Gender Inequality?

Roslyn Arlin Mickelson and Stephen Samuel Smith

INTRODUCTION

Parents, politicians, and educational policy makers share the belief that a "good education" is *the* meal ticket. It will unlock the door to economic opportunity and thus enable disadvantaged groups or individuals to improve their lot dramatically.[1] This belief is one of the assumptions that has long been part of the American Dream. According to the putative dominant ideology, the United States is basically a meritocracy in which hard work and individual effort are rewarded, especially in financial terms.[2] Related to this central belief are a series of culturally enshrined misconceptions about poverty and wealth. The central one is that poverty and wealth are the result of individual inadequacies or strengths rather than the results of the distributive mechanisms of the capitalist economy. A second misconception is the belief that everyone is the master of his or her own fate. The dominant ideology assumes that American society is open and competitive, a place where an individual's status depends on talent and motivation, not inherited position, connections, or privileges linked to ascriptive characteristics like gender or race. To compete fairly, everyone must have access to education free of the fetters of family background, gender, and race. Since the middle of this century, the reform policies of the federal government have been designed, at least officially, to enhance individuals' opportunities to acquire education. The question we will explore in this essay is whether expanding educational opportunity is enough to reduce the inequalities of race, social

class, and gender which continue to characterize U. S. society.

We begin by discussing some of the major educational policies and programs of the past forty-five years that sought to reduce social inequality through expanding equality of educational opportunity. This discussion highlights the success and failures of programs such as school desegregation, compensatory education, Title IX, and job training. We then focus on the barriers these programs face in actually reducing social inequality. Our point is that inequality is so deeply rooted in the structure and operation of the U.S. political economy, that, at best, educational reforms can play only a limited role in ameliorating such inequality. In fact, there is considerable evidence that indicates that, for poor and many minority children, education helps legitimate, if not actually reproduce, significant aspects of social inequality in their lives. Finally, we speculate about education's potential role in individual and social transformation.

First, it is necessary to distinguish among equality, equality of opportunity, and equality of educational opportunity. The term *equality* has been the subject of extensive scholarly and political debate, much of which is beyond the scope of this essay. Most Americans reject equality of life conditions as a goal, because it would require a fundamental transformation of our basic economic and political institutions, a scenario most are unwilling to accept. As Ralph Waldo Emerson put it, "The genius of our country has worked out our true policy—opportunity."

The distinction between equality of opportunity and equality of outcome is important.

Printed by permission of the authors.

Through this country's history, equality has most typically been understood in the former way. Rather than a call for the equal distribution of money, property, or many other social goods, the concern over equality has been with equal opportunity in pursuit of these goods. In the words of Jennifer Hochschild, "So long as we live in a democratic capitalist society—that is, so long as we maintain the formal promise of political and social equality while encouraging the practice of economic inequality—we need the idea of equal opportunity to bridge that otherwise unacceptable contradiction."[3] To use a current metaphor: If life is a game, the playing field must be level; if life is a race, the starting line must be in same place for everyone. For the playing field to be level, many believe education is crucial because it gives individuals the wherewithal to compete in the allegedly meritocratic system. In America, then, *equality* is really understood to mean *equality of opportunity*, which itself hinges on *equality of educational opportunity*.

THE SPOTTY RECORD OF FEDERAL EDUCATIONAL REFORMS

In the past forty-five years, a series of educational reforms initiated at the national level has been introduced into local school systems. All of the reforms aimed to move education closer to the ideal of equality of educational opportunity. Here we discuss several of these reforms, and how the concept of equality of educational opportunity has evolved. Given the importance of race and racism in U.S. history, many of the federal education policies during this period attempted to redress the most egregious forms of inequality based on race.

School Desegregation

Although American society has long claimed to be based on equality of opportunity, the history of race relations suggests the opposite. Perhaps the most influential early discussion of this disparity was Gunnar Myrdal's *An American Dilemma*, published in 1944. The book vividly exposed the

contradictions between the ethos of freedom, justice, equality of opportunity and the actual experiences of African Americans in the United States.[4]

The links among desegregation, expanded educational opportunity, and the larger issue of equality of opportunity are very clear from the history of the desegregation movement. This movement, whose first phase culminated in the 1954 *Brown* decision outlawing *de jure* segregation in school, was the first orchestrated attempt in U.S. history to directly address inequality of educational opportunity. The NAACP strategically chose school segregation to be the camel's nose under the tent of the Jim Crow (segregated) society. That one of the nation's foremost civil rights organizations saw the attack on segregated schools as the opening salvo in the battle against society-wide inequality is a powerful example of the American belief that education has a pivotal role in promoting equality of opportunity.

Has desegregation succeeded? This is really three questions: First, to what extent are the nation's schools desegregated? Second, have desegregation efforts enhanced students' academic outcomes? Third, what are the long term outcomes of desegregated educational experiences?

Since 1954, progress toward the desegregation of the nation's public schools has been uneven and limited. Blacks experienced little progress in desegregation until the mid-1960s when, in response to the civil rights movement, a series of federal laws, executive actions, and judicial decisions resulted in significant gains, especially in the South. Progress continued until 1988, when the effects of a series of federal court decisions and various local and national political developments precipitated marked trends toward the resegregation of black students. Nationally, in 1944-1995, 33 percent of Black students attended majority White schools compared with the approximately 37 percent who attended majority White schools for much of the 1980s.[5]

Historically, Latinos were relatively less segregated than African Americans. However, from the mid-1960s to the mid-1990s there was a steady increase in the percentage of the Latino students who attended segregated schools. As a result, education for Latinos is now more segregated than it is for Blacks.

Given the long history of legalized segregation in the south, it is ironic that the South's schools systems are now generally the country's most *de*segregated, while those in the northeast are the most intensely segregated. However, even desegregated schools are often resegregated at the classroom level by tracking or ability grouping. There is a strong relationship between race and social class, and racial isolation is often an outgrowth of residential segregation and socio-economic background.

Has desegregation helped to equalize educational outcomes? A better question might be which desegregation programs under what circumstances accomplish which goals? Evidence from recent desegregation research suggests that, overall, children benefit academically and socially from well-run programs. Black students enjoy modest academic gains, while the academic achievement of White children is not hurt, and in some cases is helped, by desegregation. In school systems which have undergone desegregation efforts, the racial gap in educational outcomes has generally been reduced, but not eliminated.

More important than short-term academic gains are the long-term consequence of desegregation for Black students. Compared to those who attended racially isolated schools, Black adults who experienced desegregated education as children are more likely to attend multiracial colleges and graduate from them, work in higher-status jobs, live in integrated neighborhoods, assess their abilities more realistically when choosing an occupation, and to report interracial friendships.[6]

Despite these modest, but positive, outcomes, in the last decade of the twentieth century, most American children attend schools segregated by race, ethnicity, and social class. Consequently, forty-five years of official federal interventions aimed at achieving equality of educational opportunity through school desegregation have only made small steps toward achieving that goal; children from different race and class backgrounds continue to receive segregated and, in many respects, unequal educations.

The Coleman Report

Largely because evidence introduced in the 1954 *Brown* case showed that resources in segregated Black and White schools were grossly unequal, Congress mandated in 1964 a national study of the "lack of availability of equality of educational opportunity for individuals due to race, color, religious, or national origin in public schools." The authors of the subsequent study, James Coleman and his associates, expected to find glaring disparities in educational resources available to African-American and White students and that these differences would explain the substantial achievement differences between majority and minority students.

Instead, the Coleman Report, released in 1966, produced some very unexpected findings which became the underpinning for many subsequent educational policies and programs. The researchers found that twelve years after *Brown*, most Americans still attended segregated schools but that the characteristic of Black and White schools (e.g., facilities, books, labs, teacher experience, and expenditures) were surprisingly similar. Apparently, segregated Southern districts had upgraded Black educational facilities in the wake of the *Brown* decision. Coleman and his colleagues also found that variations in school resources had relatively little to do with the variations in students' school performance. Instead, they found that family background influenced an individual's school achievement more than any other factor, including school characteristics.[7] Subsequent research has provided a better understanding of when, where, and how resources and school characteristics influence student outcomes.

However, at the time, the Coleman Report had dramatic and long-lasting effects. The report tended to deflect attention away from how schools operated and instead focused public policy upon poor and minority children and their families as the ultimate sources of unequal school outcomes.

Numerous observers concluded incorrectly that schools had little to do with Black-White educational differences because they paid insufficient attention to another of the report's findings that implicated schools in inequality of educational outcomes. That finding showed that African-American and White achievement differences increased with every year of schooling. That is, the achievement gap between Black and White first graders was much smaller than the gap between twelfth graders. This finding suggested that, at best, schools reinforce the disadvantages of race and class and, at worst, are themselves a major source of educational inequality.

Although published over thirty years ago, the Coleman Report remains one of the most important and controversial pieces of social research ever completed in the United States. One of its many lasting results was a redefinition of the concept of equality of educational opportunity. The report made it clear that putting greater resources into schools, in and of itself, was not necessarily associated with greater student achievement or with eliminating the racial gap in school outcomes. In other words, resource levels alone were no longer considered a satisfactory measure of equality of educational opportunity. As a result, the Coleman Report helped reconceptualize the notion of equality of educational opportunity. It became a matter of equality of educational outcomes, measured in terms of academic achievement (performance) and attainment (amount of schooling completed) irrespective of race, gender, and socioeconomic background. This goal has yet to be reached in the United States.

Compensatory Education

A second outcome of the Coleman Report was widespread support for compensatory education. Policy makers interpreted the finding that family background was the strongest predictor of students' achievement as evidence of "cultural deprivation" among poor and minority families. This interpretation gave impetus to an education movement designed to compensate for the al-

leged cultural deficiencies of families that were neither middle class nor White, so that when so-called disadvantaged children came to school, they could compete without the handicaps of their background.

Beginning with the passage of the Elementary and Secondary Education Act in 1965, a series of educational programs offered low-income and underachieving children developmental preschool followed by a host of individualized programs in math, reading, and language arts once they arrived in elementary school. Examples of compensatory education programs include:

- Early childhood education such as Head Start

- Follow Through, where Head Start children, now in elementary school, continue to receive special programs

- Title I (formerly called Chapter I), which provides language arts and math programs plus food, medicine, and clothing to needy children in primary schools

- Guidance and counseling in secondary schools

Compensatory education programs have had a controversial history. Critics from the left charge that the underlying premise of compensatory education—that poor and minority families are deficient relative to middle-class White families—is racist and elitist. Critics on the right argue that compensatory education is a waste of time and money because the lower achievement scores of minority and poor children are due to their inferior intelligence. Policy critics charge that it is impossible to judge the effectiveness of compensatory education programs unless they are fully funded and implemented so that all eligible children receive services. Since the inception of compensatory education programs, less than half of eligible students have received services.

Despite criticism from such diverse quarters, the compensatory education movement survived the past thirty years. The Head Start program, for example, is currently embraced by a wide range of Americans who consider it a cost-effective strategy to help poor children do better in school. A growing body of research demonstrates the existence of both cognitive and social benefits from early childhood education for low-income and minority children. However, the achievement gaps between minority and White, and between working-and middle-class, children remain. Furthermore, evaluations of Title I and Follow Through have been unable to demonstrate unambiguous benefits. One must conclude that compensatory education, like desegregated education, has neither leveled the playing field nor eliminated racial or social class inequality in educational outcomes.

Human Capital Theory and Workforce Education Programs

The widely held belief that a good education is *the* meal ticket to reducing inequality receives its most sophisticated exposition in human capital theory, which holds that greater levels of education are investments in human beings' productive capacities. People who are poor, according to this theory, have had inadequate investments in their education. Over many decades, numerous education and training programs have been implemented, but the school-to-work transition remains problematic for many noncollege-bound youth. During the last third of this century, specific programs linked to anti-poverty efforts were implemented and eventually scrapped for failing to provide low-income youth with what they needed. While the Comprehensive Education and Training Act (CETA) and its successor, the Job Training and Partnership Act (JPTA), two of the best known programs, gave skill training to low-income youth, the jobs needed to employ them were simply not there. Moreover, JPTA graduates were no more likely to obtain a job than those without such training.

A variety of workforce education programs exist today in America's schools. These are attempts to provide broad-based technical skills to students, although they have not completely displaced the more traditional vocational education programs. However, current programs are of questionable value for reducing inequality for a number of reasons. First, there is a striking absence of bridges from schools to workplaces. Other than tapping into their personal networks, youth usually do not know alternative options for obtaining jobs. Schools rarely have outreach programs, and employers who hire entry-level workers only occasionally check grades and transcripts. The federal government's initiative for community-based one-stop job centers, where potential workers and employers can match their availabilities via computerized databases, may prove useful in the future by providing the necessary bridges and pathways from school to work. But they are only in their infancy.

A second reason to question the utility of these programs is that the human capital approach views the problem of inequality as a lack of worker skill, not a paucity of well-paying jobs. The poor often have a great deal of skills and education. What they lack are well-paying jobs in which to invest their skills. In fact, many studies indicate there is an adequate match between skill requirements of current jobs and those possessed by the workforce. Rather, the complaints of most employers are that entry-level new hires lack a strong work ethic, a problem human capital theory does not address.

The third reason to question the utility of workforce development education for reducing inequality has to do with the changing nature of the post-industrial economy. There is little certain knowledge of what the restructuring and globalization of the economy will mean for future workers. It is entirely possible that workforce education will prepare people for jobs which have been relocated to Mexico, Thailand, or India. Certainly, there is already evidence of such a trend. And the relocation of these jobs has more to do with the cost of labor in these nations than with the education or skill levels of Americans. It is not surprising, then, that educational reforms based on human capital theory have not, and cannot, substantially narrow race, class, and gender differences in equality of opportunity in this society.

Title IX

Title IX of the 1972 Higher Education Act is the primary federal law prohibiting sex discrimination in education. It states, "No person in the United States shall, on the basis of sex, be excluded from participation in, be denied benefit of, or be subjected to discrimination under any program or activity receiving Federal financial assistance." Until Title IX's passage, gender inequality in educational opportunity received minimal legislative attention. The act mandates gender equality of treatment in admission, courses, financial aid, counseling services, employment, and athletics.

The effect of Title IX upon college athletics has been especially controversial. While women constitute 53 percent of undergraduates, they are only 37 percent of college athletes. This is undoubtedly due to the complex interaction between institutional practices and gender-role socialization over the life course. Certainly, the fact that the vast majority of colleges spend much more money on recruiting and scholarships for male athletes contributes to the disparities.

In spring 1997, the U.S. Supreme court refused to review a lower court's ruling in *Brown v. Cohen* that states in essence that Title IX requires universities to provide equal athletic opportunities for male and female students regardless of cost. Courts have generally upheld the following three-pronged test for compliance: (1) the percentage of athletes who are females should reflect the percentage of students who are female; (2) there must be a continuous record of expanding athletic opportunities for female athletes; and (3) schools must accommodate the athletic interests and abilities of female students. As of the ruling, very few universities were in compliance with the law.

Gender discrimination exists in other areas of education where it takes a variety of forms. For example, in K–12 education official curricular materials frequently feature a preponderance of male characters. Male and female characters typically exhibit traditional gender roles. Vocational education at the high school and college level remains gender-segregated to some degree. School ad-

ministrators at all levels are overwhelmingly male although most teachers in elementary and secondary schools are female. In higher education, the situation is more complex. Faculty women in academia are found disproportionately in the lower ranks, are less likely to be promoted, and continue to earn less than their male colleagues.

Like the laws and policies aimed at eliminating race differences in school processes and outcomes, those designed to eliminate gender differences in educational opportunities have, at best, only narrowed them. Access to educational opportunity in the United States remains unequal for people of different gender, race, ethnic, and socioeconomic backgrounds.

EQUALITY OF EDUCATIONAL OPPORTUNITY AND EQUALITY OF INCOME

Despite the failures of these many programs to eliminate the inequality of educational opportunity over the past 45 years, there is one indicator of substantial progress: measured in median years, the gap in educational attainment between Blacks and Whites, and between males and females, has all but disappeared. In 1997, the median educational attainment of most groups was slightly more than twelve years. In the 1940s, by contrast, White males and females had a median educational attainment of just under nine years, African American males about five years, and African American women about six.

However, the main goal of educational reform is not merely to give all groups the opportunity to receive the same quality and quantity of education. According to the dominant ideology, the ultimate goal of these reforms is to provide equal educational opportunity in order to facilitate equal access to jobs, housing, and various other aspects of the American dream. It thus becomes crucial to examine whether the virtual elimination of the gap in educational attainment has been accompanied by a comparable decrease in other measure of inequality.

Of the various ways inequality can be measured, income is one of the most useful. Much of a person's social standing and access to the good things in life depends on his or her income.[8] Unfortunately, the dramatic progress in narrowing the gap in educational attainment has not been matched by a comparable narrowing of the gap in income inequality. Median individual earnings by race and gender indicate that White men still earn significantly more than any other group. Black men trail White men, and all women earn significantly less than all men. Even when occupation, experience, and level of education are controlled, women earn less than men, and Black men earn less than White men. It is only Black and White women with comparable educational credentials in similar jobs who earn about the same.

The discrepancy between the near elimination of the gap in median educational attainment and the ongoing gaps in median income is further evidence that addressing the inequality of educational opportunity is woefully insufficient for addressing broader sources of inequality throughout society.

This discrepancy can be explained by the nature of the U.S. political economy. The main cause of income inequality is the structure and operation of U.S. capitalism, a set of institutions which scarcely have been affected by the educational reforms discussed earlier. Greater equality of educational opportunity has not led to a corresponding decrease in income inequality because educational reforms do not create good-paying jobs, affect gender-segregated and racially segmented occupational structures, or limit the mobility of capital either between regions of the country or between the United States and other countries. For example, no matter how good an education White working-class or minority youth may receive, it does nothing to alter the fact that thousands of relatively good paying manufacturing jobs have left northern inner cities for northern suburbs, the sunbelt, or foreign countries.

Many argue that numerous service jobs remain or that new manufacturing positions have been created in the wake of this capital flight. But

these pay less than the departed manufacturing jobs, are often part-time or temporary, and frequently do not provide benefits. Even middle-class youth are beginning to fear the nature of jobs which await them once they complete their formal education. Without changes in the structure and operation of the capitalist economy, educational reforms alone cannot markedly improve the social and economic position of disadvantaged groups. This is the primary reason that educational reforms do little to affect the gross social inequalities that inspired them in the first place.

. . .

CONCLUSION

In this [essay] we have argued that educational reforms alone cannot reduce inequality. Nevertheless, education remain important to any struggle to reduce inequality. Moreover, education is more than a meal ticket; it is intrinsically worthwhile and crucially important for the survival of democratic society. Many of the programs discussed in this essay contribute to the enhancement of individuals' cognitive growth and thus promote important non-sexist, nonracist attitudes and practices. Many of these programs also make schools somewhat more humane places for adults and children. Furthermore, education, even reformist liberal education, contains the seeds of individual and social transformation. Those of us committed to the struggle against inequality cannot be paralyzed by the structural barriers that make it impossible for education to eliminate inequality. We must look upon the schools as arenas of struggle against race, gender, and social class inequality.

NOTES

1. This essay draws on an article by Roslyn Arlin Mickelson that appeared as "Education and the Struggle Against Race, Class and Gender Inequality," *Humanity and Society* 11(4) (1987): 440–64.

2. Ascertaining whether a set of beliefs constitutes the dominant ideology in a particular society

involves a host of difficult theoretical and empirical questions. For this reason we use the term *putative dominant ideology*. For discussion of these questions, see Nicholas Abercrombie et al., *The Dominant Ideology Thesis* (London: George Allen & Unwin, 1980); James C. Scott, *Weapons of the Weak* (New Haven: Yale University Press, 1985); Stephen Samuel Smith, "Political Acquiescence and Beliefs About State Coercion" (unpublished Ph.D. dissertation, Stanford University, 1990).

3. Jennifer Hochschild, "The Double-Edged Sword of Equal Educational Opportunity." Paper presented at the meeting of the American Education Research Association, Washington, D. C., April 22, 1987.

4. Gunnar Myrdal, *An American Dilemma: The Negro Problem and Modern Democracy* (New York: Harper & Row, 1944).

5. Gary Orfield, Mark D. Bachmeier, David R. James, and Tamela Eitle, "Deepening Segregation in American Public Schools" (Cambridge, MA: Harvard Project on School Desegregation, 1997).

6. Amy Stuart Wells and Robert L. Crain, "Perpetuation Theory and the Long-Term Effects of School Desegregation," *Review of Educational Research* 64(4) (1994): 531–55.

7. J. S. Coleman et al., *Equality of Educational Opportunity* (Washington, D.C.: Government Printing Office, 1966).

8. To be sure, income does not measure class-based inequality, but there is a positive correlation between income and class. Income has the additional advantage of being easily quantifiable. Were we to use another measure of inequality, e.g., wealth, the disjuncture between it and increases in educational attainment would be even larger. Although the distribution of wealth in U.S. society has remained fairly stable since the Depression, the gap between rich and poor increased in the 1980s and 1990s. Although accurate data are difficult to obtain, a 1992 study by the Federal Reserve found that in 1989 the top one-half of one percent of households held 29 percent of the wealth held by all households.

44

Environmental Justice for All

Robert D. Bullard

PEOPLE OF COLOR HAVE ALWAYS RESISTED ACtions by government and private industry that threaten the quality of life in their communities. Until recently, this resistance was largely ignored by policymakers. This activism took place before the first Earth Day in 1970; however, many of these struggles went unnoticed or were defined as merely part of the "modern" environmental movement. This chapter outlines a framework that can be used to address disparate impact, unequal protection, and environmental discrimination.

ANATOMY OF EARLY STRUGGLES

In 1967, students at predominantly African American Texas Southern University in Houston were involved in a campus riot triggered by the death of an eight-year-old African American girl, who had drowned at a garbage dump. Student protest-ers questioned why a garbage dump was located in the middle of the mostly African American Sunnyside neighborhood.[1] The protests got out of hand. Police were met with rocks and bottles. Gunshots were fired. A police officer, struck by a ricocheting bullet, was killed. Nearly 500 male students were cleared from the dormitories, and many of the leaders were arrested. The Kerner Commission classified the disturbance at Texas Southern University as a "serious disorder."[2]

In 1968, Reverend Martin Luther King, Jr., went to Memphis on an environmental justice mission—better working conditions and pay for striking African American garbage workers. King was killed in Memphis before he could complete this mission. Nevertheless, garbage and landfills did not disappear as an environmental justice issue.

In 1979, residents of Houston's Northwood manor subdivision (a suburban neighborhood of African American home owners) filed the first lawsuit charging environmental discrimination. More than 83 percent of the Northwood Manor residents owned their homes. In *Bean v. Southwestern Waste Management*, Houston residents charged Browning-Ferris Industries with locating a municipal solid waste landfill in their commu-nity. An early attempt to place a similar facility in the same area in 1970—when the area was mostly white—had been defeated by the Harris County Board of Supervisors.

Houston has a long history of locating its solid waste facilities in communities of color, especially in African American neighborhoods. From the early 1920s through the late 1970s, all five of the city-owned sanitary landfills and six of its eight mu-nicipal solid waste incinerators were located in mostly African American neighborhoods. Simi-larly, three of the four privately owned solid waste landfills were located in mostly African American communities during this period. African Ameri-cans, however, made up only 28 percent of the city's population. Despite the overwhelming statis-tical evidence, the plaintiffs lost their lawsuit, and the Whispering Pines landfill was built in North-wood Manor.[3]

Some proponents of the Whispering Pines landfill suggested that the African American neighborhood would benefit from the waste facil-ity by way of the jobs and taxes it would provide. However, Charles Streadit, president of Houston's Northeast Community Action Group, addressed the benefits and liabilities associated with the landfill in his neighborhood:

Sure, Browning-Ferris Industries [owner of the Whis-pering Pines landfill] pays taxes, but so do we. We need all the money we can to upgrade our school sys-tem. But we shouldn't have to be poisoned to get im-provements for our children. When my property values go down, that means less for the schools and my children's education. . . . A silent war is being waged against black neighborhoods. Slowly, we are being picked off by the industries that don't give a damn about polluting our neighborhood, contaminating our water, fouling our air, clogging our streets with big garbage trucks, and lowering our property values. It's hard enough for blacks to scrape and save enough money to buy a home, then you see your dream shattered by a garbage dump. That's a dirty trick. No amount of money can buy self-respect.[4]

The aforementioned examples show a clear link between civil rights and environmental jus-tice. However, it was not until the early 1980s that a national movement for environmental justice took root in several mainstream civil rights orga-nizations. The environmental justice movement took shape out of the 1982 protests in Warren County, North Carolina. This mostly African American and rural county had been selected as the burial site for 30,000 cubic yards of soil cont-aminated with highly toxic PCBs (polychlori-nated biphenyls). Oil laced with PCBs had been illegally dumped along roadways in fourteen North Carolina counties in 1978; the roadways were cleaned up in 1982.[5]

More than 500 protesters were jailed over the siting of the Warren County PCB landfill. Dem-onstrations were led by a number of national civil rights advocacy groups, including the United Church of Christ Commission for Racial Justice, the Southern Christian Leadership Conference, and the Congressional Black Caucus. African American civil rights activists, political officials, religious leaders, and local residents marched in protest against "Hunt's Dump" (named for Texas's governor at that time, James Hunt). Why had Warren County been selected for the PCB landfill? Opponents contend that the decision made more political sense than environmental sense.[6]

Although the demonstrations were unsuccessful in halting construction of the landfill, the protests marked the first time African Americans had mobilized a national, broad-based group to oppose what they defined as environmental racism. The demonstrations also prompted District of Columbia delegate Walter Fauntroy, who was chairman of the Congressional Black Caucus, to initiate the 1983 U.S. General Accounting Office (GAO) study of hazardous waste landfill siting in the Environmental Protection Agency's Region IV.[7] Fauntroy had been active in the protests and was one of the many who went to jail over the landfill.

The 1983 GAO study found a strong relationship between the location of off-site hazardous waste landfills and the race and socioeconomic status of the surrounding communities. The study identified four off-site hazardous waste landfills in the eight states (Alabama, Florida, Georgia, Kentucky, Mississippi, North Carolina, and Tennessee) that constitute the EPA's Region IV. The four sites included Chemical Waste Management (Sumter County, Alabama); SCA Services (Sumter County, South Carolina); Industrial Chemical Company (Chester County, South Carolina), and the Warren County PCB landfill (Warren County, North Carolina).

African Americans made up the majority of the population in three of the four communities where off-site hazardous waste landfills were located. In 1983, African Americans were clearly overrepresented in communities with waste sites, since they made up only about one-fifth of the region's population, yet African American communities contained three-fourths of the off-site landfills. These ecological imbalances have not been re-

versed a decade later. In 1992, African Americans constituted about one-fifth of the population in Region IV. However, the two operating off-site hazardous waste landfills in the region were located in zip code regions where African Americans made up the majority of the population.

A new form of environmental activism has emerged in communities of color. Activists have not limited their attacks to well-publicized toxic contamination issues but have begun to seek remedial action on neighborhood disinvestment, housing discrimination and residential segregation, urban mass transportation, pollution, and other environmental problems that threaten public safety.

Activist groups of color have begun to build a national movement for justice. In October 1991, the First National People of Color Environmental Leadership Summit was held in Washington, DC. The Summit demonstrated that it is possible to build a multi-issue, multiracial environmental movement around *justice*. Environmental activism was shown to be alive and well in African American, Latino American, Asian American, and Native American communities.

The four-day Summit was attended by more than 650 grass-roots and national leaders representing more than 300 environmental groups of color. The Summit was planned *by* people of color. Delegates came from all fifty states, including Alaska and Hawaii, as well as from Puerto Rico, Chile, Mexico, and the Marshall Islands. Delegates attended the Summit to share their action strategies, redefine the environmental movement, and develop common plans for addressing environmental problems affecting people of color in the United States and around the world.

Grass-roots groups organized themselves around a number of environmental issues, ranging from the siting of landfills and incinerators to lead pollution. At the Summit, delegates adopted the "Principles of Environmental Justice," which they are using as a guide for organizing, networking, and relating to other groups. The common thread that runs throughout the grass-roots groups of color is their demand for a *just* environment.

People of Color Grassroots Environmental Groups

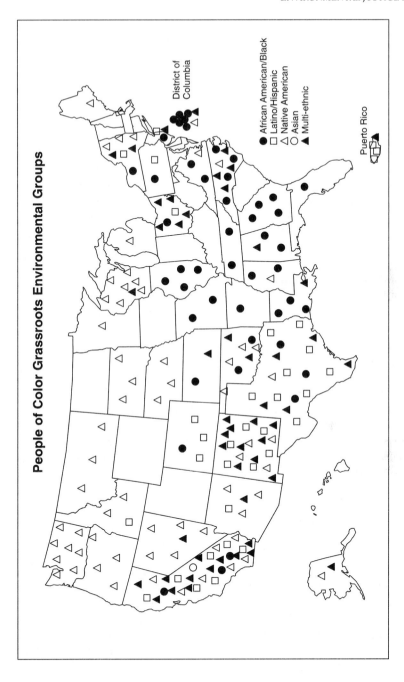

THE ENVIRONMENTAL JUSTICE FRAMEWORK

There is general agreement that the nation's environmental problems need immediate attention. The head of the U.S. Environmental Protection Agency, writing in the agency's *EPA Journal*, stressed that "environmental protection should be applied fairly."[8] However, the nation's environmental laws, regulations, and policies are not applied uniformly across the board, resulting in some individuals, neighborhoods, and communities being exposed to elevated health risks.

Environmental decision making operates at the juncture of science, technology, economics, politics, and ethics. A 1992 study by staff writers from the *National Law Journal* uncovered glaring inequities in the way the federal EPA enforces its laws. The authors write:

There is a racial divide in the way the U.S. government cleans up toxic waste sites and punishes polluters. White communities see faster action, better results and stiffer penalties than communities where blacks, Hispanics and other minorities live. This unequal protection often occurs whether the community is wealthy or poor.[9]

After examining census data, civil court dockets, and the EPA's own record of performance at 1,177 Superfund toxic waste sites, the *National Law Journal* report revealed the following:

1. Penalties under hazardous waste laws at sites having the greatest white population were 500 percent higher than penalties with the greatest minority population, averaging $335,566 for white areas, compared to $55,318 for minority areas.

2. The disparity under the toxic waste law occurs by race alone, not income. The average penalty in areas with the lowest income is $113, 491, 3 percent more than the average penalty in areas with the highest median incomes.

3. For all the federal environmental laws aimed at protecting citizens from air, water, and waste pollution, penalties in white communities were 46 percent higher than in minority communities.

4. Under the giant Superfund cleanup program, abandoned hazardous waste sites in minority areas take 20 percent longer to be placed on the national priority list than those in white areas.

5. In more than half of the 10 autonomous regions that administer EPA programs around the country, action on cleanup at Superfund sites begins from 12 percent to 42 percent later at minority sites than at the white sites.

6. At minority sites, the EPA chooses "containment," the capping or walling off of a hazardous waste dump site, 7 percent more frequently than the cleanup method preferred under the law, permanent "treatment," to eliminate the waste or rid it of its toxins. At white sites, the EPA orders treatment 22 percent more often than containment.[10]

These findings suggest that unequal environmental protection places communities of color at special risk. The environmental justice framework attempts to uncover the underlying assumptions that may influence environmental decision making. It also rests on an analysis of strategies to eliminate unfair, unjust, and inequitable conditions and decisions. The basic elements of the framework consists of five basic characteristics:.

1. Incorporates the principle of the right of all individuals to be protected from environmental degradation,

2. Adopts a public health model of prevention (elimination of the threat before harm occurs) as the preferred strategy,

3. Shifts the burden of proof to polluters and dischargers who do harm or discriminate or who do not give equal protection to racial and ethnic minorities and other "protected" classes,

4. Allows disparate impact and statistical weight, as opposed to "intent," to infer discrimination,

5. Redresses disproportionate risk burdens through targeted action and resources.

The goal of an environmental justice framework is to make environmental protection more democratic. More important, it brings to the surface the *ethical* and *political* questions of "who gets what, why, and in what amount."[11] Who pays for, and who benefits from, technological expansion?

Environmental and health laws have not provided equal protection for all Americans. Most of the nation's environmental policies distribute the costs in a regressive pattern while providing disproportionate benefits for whites and individuals who fall at the upper end of the education and income scale.[12] Numerous studies, dating back to the 1970s, reveal that communities of color have borne greater health and environmental risk burdens than has society at large.[13]

Nationally based conservation and environmental groups have played an instrumental role in shaping this nation's environmental laws and regulations. It was not until recently, however, that these nongovernmental organizations (NGOs) paid attention to environmental and health threats to poor, working-class persons and to communities of color.

The environmental justice movement attempts to address environmental enforcement, compliance, policy formulation, and decision making. It defines environment in very broad terms, as the places where people live, work, and play. The question of environmental justice is not anchored in a scientific debate but rests on an ethical analysis of environmental decision making.

Current decision-making models have proven to be inadequate in protecting at-risk communities. Emphasis on defining risk as the probability of fatality addresses only part of the health threats. Should endangered communities have to wait for a "body count" for government to act? Many communities would say no to this question.

Often, environmental stressors result in adverse health effects short of death. The health effects might be developmental, reproductive, respiratory, neurotoxic, or psychological in nature. As a consequence, the assignment of "acceptable" risk, use of averages, and siting of risky technologies (i.e., incinerators, landfills, chemical plants, smelters, etc.) often result from value judgements that serve to legitimate the imposition of inequitable social policies.

ENDANGERED COMMUNITIES

Millions of Americans live in housing and physical environments that are overburdened with environmental problems including older housing with lead-based paint, congested freeways that criss-cross their neighborhoods, industries that emit dangerous pollutants into the area, and abandoned toxic waste sites.

Virtually all of the studies of exposure to outdoor air pollution have found significant differences in exposure by income and race.[14] African Americans and Latino Americans are more likely than whites to live in areas with reduced air quality. For example, National Argonne Laboratory researchers D. R. Wernette and L. A. Nieves found the following:

In 1990, 437 of the 3,109 countries and independent cities failed to meet at least one of the EPA ambient air quality standards. . . . 57 percent of whites, 65 percent of African Americans, and 80 percent of Hispanics live in 437 counties with substandard air quality. Out of the whole population, a total of 33 percent of whites, 50 percent of African Americans, and 60 percent of Hispanics live in the 136 counties in which two or more air pollutants exceed standards. The percentage living in the 29 counties designated as nonattainment areas for three or more pollutants are 12 percent of whites, 20 percent of African Americans, and 31 percent of Hispanics.[15]

The public health community has very little information to explain the magnitude of some of the health problems related to air pollution. However, we do know that persons suffering from asthma are particularly sensitive to the effects of carbon monoxide, sulfur dioxides, particulate matter, ozone, and nitrogen oxides.[16] African Americans, for example, have a significantly higher prevalence of asthma than does the general population.[17]

In the heavily populated Los Angeles air basin, more than 71 percent of African Americans and 50 percent of Latino Americans live in areas with the most polluted air, while only 34 percent of whites live in highly polluted areas.[18] For a few days in 1992, the attention of the entire world was affixed on the flames of Los Angeles. Even before the uprising, however, *San Francisco Examiner* reporter Jane Kay described the zip code region in which the now riot-torn South Central Los Angeles neighborhood is located as the "dirtiest" zip code (90058) in California.[19] This 1-square-mile area is saturated with abandoned toxic waste sites, freeways, smokestacks, and wastewater pipes from polluting industries.

Efforts to rebuild South Central Los Angeles and other neighborhoods scarred by the uprising will need to incorporate environmental justice initiatives—rebuilding will need to encompass more than replacing the burned-out liquor stores, pawnshops, check-cashing centers, and fast food operations.

A "green" initiative will need to incorporate strategies employing incumbent residents in cleanup and rebuilding efforts that adopt environmentally sound technologies. Moreover, redlining practices must be vigorously attacked if any serious rebuilding of South Central Los Angeles is to take place. A partnership is needed between community institutions and businesses and the various government agencies (environmental protection, housing, public health, public works, human services, job training, education, business development, law enforcement, etc.) to create sustainable neighborhoods.

Threatened communities in southeastern Louisiana's petrochemical corridor (the 85-mile stretch along the Mississippi River from Baton Rouge to New Orleans) typify the industrial madness that has gone unchecked for too long. The corridor has been dubbed "Cancer Alley" by some environmentalists.[20] Health concerns raised by residents and grass-roots activists who live in Alsen, Saint Gabriel, Geismer, Morrisonville, and Lions, all of which are located in close proximity to polluting industries, have not been adequately addressed by local, state, and federal agencies, including the federal EPA and the Agency for Toxic Substances and Disease Registry (ATSDR).

A few contaminated African American communities in Cancer Alley have been bought out or are in the process of being bought out by industries under their "good neighbor" programs. Dow Chemical, the state's largest chemical plant, is buying out residents of mostly African American Morrisonville.[21] The communities of Sunrise and Reveilletown (founded by former slaves) no longer exist. The buyout settlements are often sealed. Few of the recent settlement agreements allow for health monitoring or surveillance of affected residents once they are dispersed.[22]

Some settlements have even required the "victims" to sign waivers that preclude them from bringing any further lawsuits against the polluting industry. These practices have resulted in the scattering of residents, making it difficult to carry out follow-up or long-term health monitoring.

A few health assessments have been conducted by federal agencies, but few of these reports have found their way into the hands of residents of the affected communities. An environmental justice framework could assist communities in Cancer Alley as they negotiate buyout agreements or contemplate litigation or some other risk reduction strategy.

Industrial encroachment into Chicago's South Side neighborhoods is yet another example of endangered communities. Chicago is the nation's third largest city and one of the most racially segregated cities in the country. More than 92 percent of the city's 1.1 million African American residents live in racially segregated areas. The Altgeld Gardens housing project, located on the city's Southeast Side, is one of these segregated enclaves.

Altgeld Gardens is encircled by municipal and hazardous waste landfills, toxic waste incinerators, grain elevators, sewer treatment facilities, smelters, steel mills, and a host of other polluting industries. Because of the physical location, Hazel Johnson, a community organizer in the neighborhood, has dubbed the area a "toxic doughnut." Others see their community as a "toxic soup," where residents perform the role of human guinea pigs.

The Southeast Side neighborhood is home to 150,000 residents, of whom 7 percent are African American and 11 percent are Latino American. It also has 50 active or closed commercial hazardous waste landfills, 100 factories (including seven chemical plants and five steel mills), and 103 abandoned toxic waste dumps.[23] Currently, health and risk assessment data collected by the state of Illinois and the federal EPA for facility permitting have failed to take into account the cumulative and synergistic effects of having so many "layers" of poisons in one community.

Altgeld Gardens residents wonder at what point government will declare a moratorium on permitting any new noxious facilities in their neighborhood. Can a "saturation threshold" be determined without the necessary studies (one such study would be mandated under the proposed Environmental Justice Act of 1992) that delineate the cumulative health impacts of all of the polluting industries in the area? All of the polluting industries (lead smelters, landfills, incinerators, steel mills, foundries, metal-plating and metal-coating operations, grain elevators, etc.) imperil the health of nearby residents and should be factored into any future facility permitting decision.

Environmental justice advocates have sought to persuade the various levels of government (federal, state, and local) to adopt a framework that addresses distributive impacts, concentration, enforcement, and compliance concerns. They have taken their fight to city halls, state capitals, and the U.S. Congress.

In 1990, New York City adopted a "fair share" legislative model designed to ensure that every borough and every community within each borough bear its fair share of noxious facilities. Public hearings have begun to address risk burdens in New York City's boroughs. Proceedings from a hearing on environmental disparities in the Bronx point to concerns raised by African Americans and Puerto Ricans who see their neighborhoods threatened by garbage transfer stations, salvage yards, and recycling centers. The report reveals the following:

On the Hunts Point peninsula alone there are at least thirty private transfer stations, a large-scale Department of Environmental Protection (DEP) sewage treatment plant and a sludge dewatering facility, two Department of Sanitation (DOS) marine transfer stations, a citywide privately regulated medical waste incinerator, a proposed DOS resource recovery facility and three proposed DEP sludge processing facilities.

That all of the facilities listed above are located immediately adjacent to the Hunts Point Food Center, the biggest wholesale food and meat distribution facility of its kind in the United States, and the largest source of employment in the South Bronx, is disconcerting. A policy whereby low-income and minority communities have become the "dumping grounds" for unwanted land uses works to create an environment of disincentives to community-based development initiatives. It also undermines existing businesses.[24]

In 1992, Chicago congresswoman Cardiss Collins offered an amendment to the bill reauthorizing the Resource Conservation and Recovery Act (RCRA), requiring "community information statements" that assess the demographic makeup of proposed waste site areas and the cumulative impact a new facility would have on the existing environmental burden.

In a similar vein, in 1992 Georgia congressman John Lewis, a longtime civil rights activist, and former senator Al Gore (former vice president) introduced their version of an Environmental Justice Act. (The 1993 version of the Environmental Justice Act was introduced in the House by John Lewis and in the Senate by Max Baucus, a Democrat from Montana.) The act (S. 2806 and H.R. 5326) was designed to "establish a program to ensure nondiscriminatory compliance with environmental, health, and safety laws and to ensure equal protection of the public health."

Some communities form a special case for environmental justice and risk reduction. Because of more stringent state and federal environmental regulations, Native American reservations, from New York to California, have become prime targets for risky technologies. Native American nations are quasi-sovereign and do not fall under state jurisdiction. Similarly, reservations are "lands the feds forgot," and their inhabitants "must contend with some of America's worst pollution."[25]

Few reservations have infrastructures to handle the risky technologies that are being proposed for their communities, and more than 100 waste disposal facilities have been proposed for Native American lands.[26] Reservation inhabitants have among the worst poverty, unemployment, education, and health problems of all Americans. Targeting Native American land for disposal of wastes is a form of "garbage imperialism."

TOXIC WASTE BOMBS

The hazardous waste problem continues to be one of the most "serious problems facing the industrial world,"[27] Toxic time bombs are not randomly scattered across the urban landscape. In New Jersey (a state with one of the highest concentrations of uncontrolled toxic waste dumps), hazardous waste sites are often located in communities that have high percentages of poor, elderly, young, and minority residents.[28]

Few national studies have been conducted on the sociodemographic characteristics of populations living around toxic waste sites. Although the federal EPA has been in business for more than two decades, it has yet to conduct a national study of the problems of toxic wastes in communities of color. In fact, the United Church of Christ Commission for Racial Justice, a church-based civil rights organization, conducted the first national study on the topic.[29]

The Commission for Racial Justice's landmark study, *Toxic Wastes and Race in the United States*, found race to be the single most important factor (i.e., more important than income, home ownership rate, and property values) in the location of abandoned toxic waste sites.[30] The study also found that (1) three out of five African Americans live in communities with abandoned toxic waste sites; (2) 60 percent (15 million) African

Americans live in communities with one or more abandoned toxic waste sites; (3) three of the five largest commercial hazardous waste landfills are located in predominantly African American or Latino American communities and account for 40 percent of the nation's total estimated landfill capacity; and (4) African Americans are heavily overrepresented in the populations of cities with the largest number of abandoned toxic waste sites.[31]

In metropolitan Chicago, for example, more than 81.3 percent of Latino Americans and 76 percent of African Americans live in communities with abandoned toxic waste sites, compared with 59 percent of whites. Similarly, 81.3 percent of Latino Americans and 69.8 percent of African Americans in the Houston metropolitan area live in communities with abandoned toxic waste sites, compared with 57.1 percent of whites. Latino Americans in the Los Angeles metropolitan area are nearly twice as likely as their Anglo counterparts to live in a community with an abandoned toxic waste site.[32]

The mounting waste problem is adding to the potential health threat to environmental high-impact areas. Incineration has become the leading technology for disposal of this waste. This technology is also becoming a major source of dioxin, as well as lead, mercury, and other heavy metals released into the environment. For example, millions of pounds of lead per year will be emitted from the nation's municipal solid waste incinerators in the next few years. All of this lead is being released despite what we know about its hazards to human health.

Hazardous waste incinerators are not randomly scattered across the landscape. A 1990 Greenpeace report, *Playing with Fire*, found that (1) the minority portion of the population in communities with existing incinerators is 89 percent higher than the national average; (2) communities where incinerators are proposed have minority populations 60 percent higher than the national average; (3) average income in communities with existing incinerators is 15 percent less than the national average; (4) property values in communities that are hosts to incinerators are 38 percent

TABLE 1.1

Estimated Percentages of Children (Living in Cities with Population over 1 Million) 0.5–5 Years Old with Blood Levels Greater than 15 µg/dl, by Race and Income (1988)

RACE	Income		
	<$6,000	$6,000–$15,000	>$15,000
African American	68%	54%	38%
White	36%	23%	12%

Source: Agency for Toxic Substances and Disease Registry, *The Nature and Extent of Lead Poisoning in Children in the United States: A Report to Congress* (Atlanta: U.S. Department of Health and Human Services, 1988).

lower than the national average; and (5) average property values are 35 percent lower in communities where incinerators are proposed.[33]

Environmental scientists have not refined their research methodologies to assess the cumulative and synergistic effects of all of society's poisons on the human body. However, some health problems cannot wait for the tools to catch up with common sense. For example, the nation's lead contamination problem demands urgent attention. An environmental strategy is needed to address childhood lead poisoning. It is time for action.

THE POLITICS OF LEAD POISONING

Why has so little been done to prevent lead poisoning in the United States? Overwhelming scientific evidence exists on the ill effects of lead on the human body. However, very little has been done to rid the nation of lead poisoning—a preventable disease tagged the "number one environmental health threat to children" by the federal Agency for Toxic Substances and Disease Registry.[34]

Lead began to be phased out of gasoline in the 1970s. It is ironic that the "regulations were initially developed to protect the newly developed catalytic converter in automobiles, a pollution-control device that happens to be rendered inoperative by lead, rather than to safeguard human health."[35] In 1971, a child was not considered at risk for lead poisoning unless he or she had

400 micrograms of lead per liter of blood (or 40 micrograms per deciliter [µg/dl]). Since that time, the amount of lead that is considered safe has continually dropped. In 1991, the U.S. Public Health Service changed the official definition of an unsafe level to 10 µg/dl. Even at that level, a child's IQ can be slightly diminished and physical growth stunted. Lead poisoning is correlated with both income and race (see Table 1.1).[36]

A coalition of environmental, social justice, and civil libertarian groups are now joining forces to address the lead problem. The Natural Resources Defense Council, the NAACP Legal Defense and Education Fund, the American Civil Liberties Union, and the Legal Aid Society of Alameda County, California, won an out-of-court settlement worth $15 million to $20 million for a blood lead–testing program. The lawsuit, *Matthews v. Coye*, involved the failure of the state of California to conduct federally mandated testing for lead of some 557,000 poor children who receive Medicaid. This historic agreement will probably trigger similar actions in other states that have failed to live up to federally mandated screening requirements.[37]

CONCLUSION

Despite the recent attempts by federal environmental and health agencies to reduce risks to all Americans, environmental inequities still persist.

Some children, workers, and communities are disproportionately affected by unhealthy air, unsafe drinking water, dangerous chemicals, lead, pesticides, and toxic wastes.

If this nation is to achieve environmental justice, the environment in urban ghettos, barrios, reservations, and rural poverty pockets must be given the same protection as that provided to the suburbs. All communities—African American or white, rich or poor—deserve to be protected from the ravages of pollution.

The current emphasis on waste management and pollution control regulations encourages dependence on disposal technologies, which are themselves sources of toxic pollution. Pushing incinerators and risk technologies off on people under the guise of economic development is not a solution to this nation's waste problem. It is imperative that waste reduction programs mandated by federal, state, and local government be funded that set goals for recycling, composting, and using recycled materials.

An environmental justice framework needs to be incorporated into a national policy on facility siting. In addition to the standard technical requirements, environmental justice proposals will need to require implementation of some type of "fair share" plan that takes into account sociodemographic, economic, and cultural factors of affected communities. It is clear that current environmental regulations and "protectionist" devices (zoning, deed restrictions, and other land use controls) have not had the same impact on all segments of society.

The federal EPA needs to take the lead in ensuring that all Americans are protected. It is time for this nation to clean up the health-threatening lead contamination problem and prevent future generations from being poisoned. No segment of society should be allowed to become a dumping ground or be sacrificed because of economic vulnerability or racial discrimination.

In order for risk reduction strategies to be effective in environmental high-impact areas and for vulnerable populations, there needs to be sweeping changes in key areas of the science model and environmental health research. At minimum, these changes must include a reevaluation of attitudes, biases, and values of the scientists who conduct environmental health research and risk assessment and the officials who make policy decisions.

Acceptance of the public as an active and equal partner in research and environmental decision making is a first step toward building trust within affected communities. Government agencies and other responsible parties need to incorporate principles of environmental justice into their strategic planning of risk reduction.

We need a holistic methodology in documenting, remediating, and preventing environmental health problems. Prevention is the key. Environmental justice demands that lead poisoning—the number one environmental health problem affecting children—be given the attention and priority it deserves. It is the poorest among the nation's inhabitants who are being poisoned at an alarming rate. Many of these individuals and families have little or no access to regular health care.

The solution lies in leveling the playing field and protecting all Americans. Environmental decision makers have failed to address the "justice" questions of who gets help and who does not, who can afford help and who cannot, why some contaminated communities get studied while others are left off the research agenda, why some communities get cleaned up at a faster rate than others, why some cleanup methods are selected over others, and why industry poisons some communities and not others.

Finally, a national environmental justice action agenda is needed to begin addressing environmental inequities that result from procedural, geographic, and societal imbalances. Federal, state, and local legislation is needed to target resources for those areas where societal risk burdens are the greatest. States that are initiating fair share plans to address interstate waste conflicts need also to begin addressing intrastate environmental siting imbalances. It is time for environmental justice to become a national priority.

NOTES

1. Robert D. Bullard, *Invisible Houston: The Black Experience in Boom and Bust* (College Station: Texas A & M University Press, 1987), pp. 110–111.

2. National Advisory Commission on Civil Disorders, *Report of the National Advisory Commission on Civil Disorders* (New York: Dutton, 1968), pp. 40–41.

3. See Robert D. Bullard, *Dumping in Dixie: Race, Class, and Environmental Quality* (Boulder, CO: Westview Press, 1990), chap. 3.

4. Interview with Charles Streadit, president of the Houston Northeast Community Action Group, May 30, 1988.

5. Ken Geiser and Gerry Waneck, "PCBs and Warren County," *Science for the People* 15 (July–August 1983): 13–17.

6. Ibid.

7. General Accounting Office, *Siting of Hazardous Waste Landfills and Their Correlation with Racial Economic Status of Surrounding Communities* (Washington, DC: General Accounting Office, 1983), p. 1.

8. William K. Reilly, "Environmental Equity: EPA's Position," *EPA Journal* 18 (March–April 1992): 18.

9. Marianne Lavelle and Marcia Coyle, "Unequal Protection," *National Law Journal*, September 21, 1992, pp. S1–S2.

10. Ibid., p. S2.

11. See Robert D. Bullard and Beverly H. Wright, "The Politics of Pollution: Implications for the Black Community," *Phylon* 47 (March 1986): 71–78; Bullard, *Dumping in Dixie*, pp. 25–43.

12. See R. B. Stewart, "Paradoxes of Liberty, Integrity, and Fraternity: The Collective Nature of Environmental Quality and Judicial Review of Administrative Action," *Environmental Law* 7 (1977): 474–476; Leonard Gianessi, H. M. Peskin, and E. Wolff, "The Distributional Effects of Uniform Air Pollution Policy in the U.S.," *Quarterly Journal of Economics* 56 (May 1977): 281–301.

13. See W. J. Kruvant, "People, Energy, and Pollution," pp. 125–167 in *The American Energy Consumer*, ed. D. K. Newman and Dawn Day (Cambridge, MA: Ballinger, 1975); Robert D. Bullard, "Solid Waste Sites and the Back Houston Community," "Sociological Inquiry 53 (Spring 1983): 273–288; United Church of Christ Commission for Racial Justice, *Toxic Wastes and Race in the United States: A National Study of the Racial and Socioeconomic Characteristics of Communities with Hazardous Waste Sites* (New York: United Church of Christ Commission for Racial Justice, 1987); Michel Gelobter, "The Distribution of Air Pollution by Income and Race" (paper presented at the Second Symposium on Social Science in Resource Management, Urbana, Illinois, June 1988); Dick Russell, "Environmental Racism," *Amicus Journal* 11 (Spring 1989): 22– 32; Bullard, *Dumping in Dixie*; Paul Ong and Evelyn Blumenberg, "Race and Environmentalism" (Los Angeles: University of California, Los Angeles, Graduate School of Architecture and Urban Planning, March 1990); Eric Mann, *L.A.'s Lethal Air: New Strategies for Policy, Organizing, and Action* (Los Angeles: Labor/ Community Strategy Center, 1991); Leslie A. Nieves, "Not in Whose Backyard? Minority Population Concentrations and Noxious Facility Sites" (paper presented at the annual meeting of the American Association for the Advancement of Science, Chicago, February 1991); D. R. Wernette and L. A. Nieves, "Breathing Polluted Air: Minorities Are Disproportionately Exposed," *EPA Journal* 18 (March–April 1992): 16–17; Robert D. Bullard, "In Our Backyards: Minority Communities Get Most of the Dumps," *EPA Journal* 18 (March– April 1992): 11–12; Bunyan Bryant and Paul Mohai, eds., *Race and the Incidence of Environmental Hazards* (Boulder, CO: Westview Press, 1992).

14. See Gelobter, "The Distribution of Air Pollution."

15. Wernette and Nieves, "Breathing Polluted Air," pp. 16–17.

16. See Mann, *L.A.'s Lethal Air.*

17. See H. P. Mak, H. Abbey, and R. C. Talamo, "Prevalence of Asthma and Health Service Utilization of Asthmatic Children in an Inner City," *Journal of Allergy and Clinical Immunology* 70 (1982): 367–372; I. F. Goldstein and A. F. Goldstein and A. L. Weinstein, "Air Pollution and Asthma: Effects of Exposure to Short-Term Sulfur Dioxide Peaks," *Environmental Research* 40 (1986): 332–345; J. Schwartz, D. Gold, D. W. Dockey. S. T. Weiss, and F.E. Speozer, "Predictors of Asthma and Persistent Wheeze in a National Sample of Children in the United States," *American Review of Respiratory Disease* 142 (1990): 555–562.

18. Ong and Blumenburg, "Race and Environmentalism"; Mann, *L.A.'s Lethal Air.*

19. Jane Kay, "Fighting Toxic Racism: L.A.'s Minority Neighborhood Is the 'Dirtiest' in the State," *San Francisco Examiner*, April 7, 1991.

20. Conger Beasley, "Of Pollution and Poverty: Keeping Watch in 'Cancer Alley,'" *Buzzworm* 2 (July–August 1990): 39–45.

21. James O'Byrne, "Death of a Town," *Times Picayune*, February 20, 1991.

22. Bullard, *Dumping in Dixie*, pp. 65–69; James O'Byrne and Mark Schleifstein, "Invisible Poisons," *Times Picayune*, February 18, 1991.

23. Greenpeace, "Home Street, USA," *Greenpeace* (October–November 1991): 8–13.

24. Fernando Ferrer, "Testimony by the Office of Bronx Borough President," *Proceedings of the Public Hearing on Minorities and the Environment: An Exploration into the Effects of Environmental Policies, Practices, and Conditions on Minority and Low-Income Communities* (Bronx, NY: Bronx Planning Office, September 20, 1991), p. 27.

25. Robert Tomsho, "Dumping Grounds: Indian Tribes Contend with Some of the Worst of America's Pollution," *Wall Street Journal,* November 29, 1990; Jane Kay, "Indian Lands Targeted for Waste Disposal Sites," *San Francisco Examiner*, April 10, 1991; Bradley Angel, *The Toxic Threat to Indian Lands: A Greenpeace Report* (San Francisco: Greenpeace, 1992).

26. Angel *Toxic Threat to Indian Lands.*

27. Samuel S. Epstein, Lester O. Brown, and Carl Pope, *Hazardous Waste in America* (San Francisco: Sierra Club Books, 1983), pp. 33–39.

28. Michael R. Greenberg and Richard F. Anderson, *Hazardous Waste Sites: The Credibility Gap* New Brunswick, NJ: Rutgers University, Center for Urban Policy Research, 1984), pp. 158–159; Bullard, *Dumping in Dixie*, pp. 4–5.

29. United Church of Christ Commission for Racial Justice, *Toxic Wastes and Race.*

30. Ibid., pp. xiii–xiv.

31. Ibid., pp. 18–19.

32. United Church of Christ Commission for Racial Justice, *Toxic Wastes and Race.*

33. Pat Costner and Joe Thornton, *Playing with Fire* (Washington, DC: Greenpeace, 1990).

34. Agency for Toxic Substances and Disease Registry, *The Nature and Extent of Lead Poisoning in Children in the United States: A Report to Congress* (Atlanta: U.S. Department of Health Human Services, 1988).

35. Peter Reich, *The Hour of Lead* (Washington, DC: Environmental Defense Fund, 1992), p. 42.

36. Agency for Toxic Substances and Disease Registry, *Nature and Extent of Lead Poisoning.*

37. *Bill Lann Lee, "Environmental Litigation on Behalf of Poor, Minority Children; Matthews v. Coye: A Case Study"* (paper presented at the annual meeting of the American Association for the Advancement of Science, Chicago, April 1992).

45

Toxic Waste and Race in the United States

Charles Lee

I HAVE BEEN ASKED TO WRITE ON THE "SITUA-tion regarding hazardous wastes and race since the United Church of Christ study." In so doing, I must necessarily touch upon the interrelationships between many sectors of society as they relate to this subject, including government, academia, grass-roots communities, and the environmental and civil rights movements. Moreover, I must necessarily provide information on the background and events leading up to the study as well as the factors motivating it. This charge is broad in nature and I attempt to present both our perspectives on the study's place in issues of environment and race as well as its specific impact on these issues.

The study referred to in my charge is "Toxic Wastes and Race in the United States: A National Report on the Racial and Socio-Economic Characteristics of Communities Surrounding Hazardous Waste Sites." This study, published by the United Church of Christ Commission for Racial Justice and released at the National Press Club in Washington, D.C. on April 15, 1987, is the first comprehensive national study of the demographic patterns associated with the location of hazardous waste sites. At that time, Dr. Benjamin F. Chavis, Jr., Executive Director of the United Church of Christ Commission for Racial Justice, coined the phrase "environmental racism."

In response to the Commission for Racial Justice report, Dr. Linda Rae Murray, former Director of Occupational and Environmental Medicine at Meharry Medical College, said the report was the "first time anyone has looked at the placement of toxic dumps nationally. It proves that issues of race and class are most important determinants of where hazardous waste facilities are placed" (1987). Dr. Victor W. Sidel, former President of the American Public Health Association, called it "an extremely important contribution to the discussion both of toxic wastes and of selective health risks to minority communities" (1987). Rep. John Conyers (D-MI) called the report "a powerful indictment of those who argue that poor health and other problems in black, Hispanic, and minority communities are self-inflicted" (1987).

The *Atlanta Constitution* editorialized that "the United Church of Christ Commission for Racial Justice put an end last week to speculation that white America has been dumping its garbage in Black America's backyard. . . . [T]hat puts an extra burden of responsibility on public health and environmental inspectors to spot potential problems before they become health hazards. Where to look? The Commission report points the way" (Editorial, 1987).

Before proceeding, I must caution the readers of this article regarding the perspective of the author of this article. As the individual who directed this study and authorized this report, I am

---

Charles Lee is the Director of Research for the Commission for Racial Justice for the United Church of Christ. One of the most publicized works of the commission is its report, "Toxic Waste and Race in the United States: A National Report on the Racial and Social-Economic Characteristics of Communities with Hazardous Waste Sites."

From *Race and the Incidence of Environmental Hazards: A Time for Discourse* Bunyan Bryant & Paul Mohai, editors, Boulder: Westview Press. 1992.

necessarily not in the best position to critique it. Nor is the United Church of Christ Commission for Racial Justice a disinterested party; we clearly see ourselves as an advocacy organization on issues of "environmental racism."

In addition, I want to emphasize that this paper gives only a partial review of the developments since the publication of "Toxic Wastes and Race in the United States." There is a need to do an in depth study of this study of this subject, something which has begun to take place. In addition, theoretical models for analyzing such developments also need to be developed.

BACKGROUND

We do, however, bring a unique perspective as a national organization which has done pioneering work in the area of environment and race. It should come as no surprise that the United Church of Christ Commission for Racial Justice study is, rather than the starting point, a culmination of nearly five years of work in this area. A brief description of this background will help to answer an often asked set of questions, i.e.; "Why is a civil rights organization like the United Church of Christ Commission for Racial Justice working around issues of the environment?" and "What does race have to do with environment?"

The Commission for Racial Justice is the national civil rights agency of the United Church of Christ, a 1.7 million member Protestant denomination which has its roots among the Congregationalist forefathers of this nation. Long active in social advocacy causes such as the Abolitionist Movement, the United Church of Christ, along with its predecessor denominations, has always been proud of its outspoken social witness. The Commission for Racial Justice was formed during the 1960s, at the height of the civil rights movement, and at the present time, remains the only national denominational entity solely devoted to racial justice advocacy. This history alone merits an entire discussion, one which by itself would be quite lengthy and is not central to this essay. We

allude to it, however, to provide background for the institutional basis for our work in environment and race.

In 1982, residents of predominantly African American, Warren County, North Carolina approached the Rev. Leon White, then director of the Commission's North Carolina/Virginia Field Office, regarding the proposed siting of a polychlorinated biphenyl (PCB) landfill. For nearly four years, the residents had been protesting the State of North Carolina's plan to take soil laden with PCBs which had been illegally dumped along 210 miles of highway, for disposal in a landfill near Afton, North Carolina.

Although White had no background in environmental issues, he was a veteran of the civil rights struggles in the South and quickly saw the potential for applying these lessons to this struggle. White catalyzed a series of events which culminated in a campaign of non-violent civil disobedience to block the PCB trucks. Over five hundred arrests took place, including White, Chavis, Dr. Joseph Lowery of the Southern Christian Leadership Conference, and Congressman Walter E. Fauntroy (D-DC). For the first time since the late sixties, African American and white activists in the deep South joined together in protest. White and others were responsible for what some describe as a "merger of the environmental and civil rights movements." Clearly, without this intervention, Warren County could easily have remained another passing incident rather than evolving into the significant event that it has become.

As dramatic as they were, the events in Warren County were unsuccessful in preventing the unwanted landfill from being sited. If one were to use that criterion as a measure of the grassroots community's opposition, one would have to conclude that the community's efforts amounted to little. The struggle was significant, however, in many other different ways.

First, it prevented the state from making the Warren County site anything other than a nonactive PCB landfill. Although the State of North

Carolina used the PCB crisis to publicly rationalize the landfill's siting, there were documents which clearly stated the state's intention to use it for other hazardous wastes. Second, it caused the State of North Carolina to reexamine its entire perspective on the siting issue, beginning with Governor James Hunt's declaration of a two year moratorium on hazardous waste landfill siting.

Finally, it focused national attention on this issue and generated further investigation of the relationship between pollution and minority communities. Subsequent to his arrest, Fauntroy requested a study on the racial demographics of hazardous waste sites. This report, produced by the U.S. General Accounting Office (GAO), found three out of the four landfills in the Southeast to be located in predominantly poor African American communities. Although it examined only four off-site landfills in the U.S. Environmental Protection Agency's Region IV, the GAO study was unique as one of the only studies to date on the relationship between race and toxics (U.S. General Accounting Office, 1983). Moreover it was a predecessor to "Toxic Wastes and Race in the United States":

The GAO study, while important, was limited by its regional scope. It was not designed to examine the relationship between the location of hazardous waste facilities throughout the United States and the racial and socio-economic characteristics of persons residing near them. Nor, prior to our current report, had there been a study to ascertain whether the GAO finding was indicative of any national patterns (United Church of Christ Commission for Racial Justice, 1987: 3).

This statement aptly describes the void in research around pollution problems in minority communities when the Commission for Racial Justice first came across this issue. Due to the lack of research focused on environmental problems confronting racial minority communities, we needed to do first hand investigation. Our initial work consisted primarily of traveling across the country and conducting locally based, educational, organizational and mobilizational efforts in African American, Hispanic and Native American communities impacted by environmental problems, many of which have led to ongoing work by participants. Besides this fact-finding, we wanted to highlight the most prominent examples of this problem, some of which included the following:

1. The nation's largest hazardous waste landfill, receiving toxic materials from 45 states and several foreign countries, is located in predominantly African American and poor Sumter County, in the heart of the Alabama Black Belt (Gunter and Williams, 1984);

2. The predominantly African American and Hispanic Southside of Chicago, Illinois, has the greatest concentration of hazardous waste sites in the nation (Nelson, 1987);

3. In Houston, Texas, six of the eight municipal incinerators and all five of the municipal landfills are located in predominantly African American neighborhoods. One of the two remaining incinerators is located in a predominantly Hispanic neighborhood (Bulklard, 1984: 95);

4. African American residents of a West Dallas neighborhood whose children suffered irreversible brain damage from exposure to lead from a nearby smelter won a $20 million out of court settlement (Bullard, 1987a: 12);

5. Pesticide exposure among predominantly Hispanic farm workers causes more than 300,000 pesticide-related illnesses each year. A large percentage of farm workers are women of childbearing age and children. This may be directly related to the emergence of childhood cancer clusters in McFarland and Delano, California (Wasserstrom and Wiles, 1985);

6. Navajo Indians were used as the primary workforce for the mining of uranium ore, leading to alarming lung cancer mortality rates. In addition, the Navajo community in Shiprock, New Mexico, where 1,100 tons of

radioactive sands and nearly 100 tons of radioactive waste water flooded the Rio Puerco River, is one of numerous Native American communities near uranium mills and nuclear facilities (Shuey, 1984: 42);

7. Three executives in Illinois were convicted of murder in the death of a Polish immigrant worker from cyanide poisoning. This plant employed mostly Hispanic and Polish immigrants who spoke and read little English. The skull and crossbones warning labels were erased from the cyanide drums (Asher, 1984: Greenhouse, 1985);

8. Fraying asbestos was discovered in the housing projects of Chicago. Asbestos, a ticking time bomb which cause crippling lung diseases and cancer, is an especially serious problem in substandard housing common to most of the nation's inner cities (Allen, 1986); and

9. Puerto Rico is one of the most heavily polluted regions of the world. For example, Puerto Rico's underground aquifer's have been contaminated by massive discharges from pharmaceutical companies, oil refineries and petrochemical plants. La Ciudad Christiana, a small community near Humacao, is the only community in North America which has been relocated due to mercury poisoning (Puerto Rico Industrial Mission, 1986).

Although we began to uncover numerous instances of racial minority communities impacted by environmental pollution, there was no research comprehensive enough to counter the claim that the above stated cases were merely exceptions and not the rule. This pointed to the clear need for new research.

We believed that much of the work of the Commission for Racial Justice consisted of helping to "continually define and redefine" the various forms of racial injustice in the context of rapid and ever-changing political, social, economic conditions. Chavis reiterated this concept in his preface to "Toxic Wastes and Race in the United States."

We realize that involvement in this type of research is a departure from our traditional protest methodology. However, if we are to advance our struggle in the future, it will depend largely on the availability of timely and reliable information (United Church of Christ Commission for Racial Justice, 1987).

SUMMARY OF FINDINGS

The findings of the Commission for Racial Justice's research was compiled in the report, "Toxic Wastes and Race in the United States." The racial composition of a community was found to be the single variable best able to explain the existence or non-existence of commercial hazardous waste facilities in a given community area. Minorities, mostly African and Hispanic Americans, are strikingly overrepresented in communities with such facilities. Communities with a single hazardous waste facility were found to have twice the percentage of minorities as communities without such a facility (24 percent vs. 12 percent). Communities with two or more facilities have more than three time the minority representation than communities without any such sites (38 percent vs. 12 percent). Although, as expected, communities with hazardous waste sites generally proved to have lower socio-economic status, the economic status of residents was not as good a predictor of a facilities existence as race itself.

The study found that more than fifteen million African Americans and eight million Hispanic Americans lived in communities with one or more hazardous waste sites. The locations of uncontrolled toxic waste sites also a display a disproportionate impact on racial minority communities. The study has conclusively shown that African Americans in particular are overrepresented in the populations of metropolitan areas with the largest number of uncontrolled toxic waste sites. Although African Americans comprise 11.7 percent of the general population, the percentage of African Americans is markedly higher in those six cities that top the hazardous waste list:

TABLE 1
Six Cities Which Lead the Hazardous Waste List

Cities	No. of Sites	Percent African Americans
Memphis, TN	173	43.3
St. Louis, MO	160	27.5
Houston, TX	152	23.6
Cleveland, OH	106	23.7
Chicago, IL	103	37.2
Atlanta, GA	94	46.1

The study further shows that three of the five largest commercial hazardous waste landfills in the United States, accounting for approximately 40 percent of the total commercial landfill capacity, are located in overwhelmingly African or Hispanic American communities. The largest of these, the site at Emelle, Alabama, accounts for one quarter of this total capacity (United Church of Christ Commision for Racial Justice, 1987).

In discussing a context for examining toxic wastes and race, we identified three key issues:

1. A major obstacle to engendering much needed awareness and action around environmental concerns within racial minority communities is lack of information. As a whole, community activists have found the acquisition of information to be a difficult task. One recent survey found that nearly "nine out of every ten groups (88 percent) perceived obstacles to obtaining information" (Freudenberg, 1984a). The information necessary tends to be highly technical or legal in nature. Moreover, institutional resistance to providing information is likely to be greater for groups such as racial minorities;

2. The hazardous waste issue, as well as other environmental problems, has become very much linked to the state of the economy in a given community. These communities have been, and continue to be, beset by poverty, unemployment and problems related to poor housing, education, and health. These communities cannot afford the luxury of being primarily concerned about the state of their environment when confronted by a plethora of pressing problems related to their day-to-day survival. Within this context, racial minority communities become particularly vulnerable to those who advocate the siting of a hazardous facility as an avenue for employment and economic development. Thus, proposals that economic incentives be offered to mitigate local opposition to the establishment of new hazardous facilities raise disturbing social policy questions; and

3. Consideration of the racial and socioeconomic status of a community when dealing with hazardous wastes is critical from a public health perspective. Many reports, such as the Report of the Secretary's Task Force on Black and Minority Health, have documented the lower health status of minority populations (U.S. Department of Health and Human Services, 1985). This status needs to be considered when priorities are set for cleanup of hazardous waste sites. Furthermore, consideration of existing health status needs to be incorporated into the decision-making process for location of new facilities. Lacking this, there is the risk of compounding serious preexisting health problems in these communities.

The report concludes with 25 specific recommendations, geared toward federal, state and municipal governments, churches and community organizations, academic institutions, philanthropies and others. It should be noted that this study focused upon hazardous waste sites. This was not meant, however, to imply that hazardous waste sites are necessarily a more widespread or dangerous environmental problem than others. The primary reason for looking at hazardous waste sites was the existence of nationally comprehensive data, i.e., the Comprehensive Environmental

Response, Compensation and liability Act Information System (CERCLIS) and national directories on commercial facilities. Many other problems in minority communities, such as air pollution, workplace exposure, pesticides, lead poisoning, asbestos, municipal waste and others, are either equally or more serious.

GRASSROOTS AND POLITICAL ACTIVISM

The most significant and long-lasting set of developments during the past several years has been the increasing activism of minority communities. Since the Warren County incident, there has been a remarkable upsurge in minority communities taking up the struggle around environmental concerns. This upsurge can be measured in terms of the number and the diversity of communities involved, their geographic distribution, their varied racial and ethnic backgrounds, and the different kinds of environmental problems addressed. However, grassroots and political activism can be also be measured in terms of the maturity, level of organization and the strategic perspectives of many organizers involved in this issue. As some of the following examples show, many of the communities working to combat environmental threats have developed highly sophisticated organizing strategies.

In 1987, residents of Los Angeles, California successfully blocked the construction of a garbage incinerator, the Los Angeles City Energy Recovery Project (LANCER), in a predominantly African American inner-city neighborhood. This resulted from a five-year struggle which involved the repeated mobilization of hundreds of residents for demonstrations and hearings. Their struggle was complicated by the fact that Los Angeles' mayor, Tom Bradley, and other elected officials were African American. During this process, local activists used tactics such as making public the waiver of Los Angeles' South Africa Divestiture Ordinance. This was done to accommodate Ogden-Martin, the facility's private operator, which had yet to sever its commercial ties

in South Africa. A University of California/Los Angeles study concluded that the incinerator's environmental impact report and other key documents contained serious inconsistencies. Even though he had already committed $12 million towards LANCER, Bradley asked the city council to withdraw the project (Russell, 1989).

In Robeson County, North Carolina, a predominantly African and Native American area, the Center for Community Action spearheaded a campaign encompassing four counties along the Lumbee River in Southeast North Carolina to resist the siting of two facilities. The first facility, a commercial low-level radioactive waste incinerator, was rejected by the state after a concerted campaign which involved demonstrations of approximately 4,000 people. The second involved a regional chemical waste treatment plant. In 1988, the state legislature passed a water quality bill much more stringent than the national bill and would have derailed this facility. However, the EPA has sought to void North Carolina's statute (National Council of Churches, 1987/1988).

In Albuquerque, New Mexico , as the result of a workshop conducted in December, 1984, by the United Church of Christ Commission for Racial Justice, the Southwest Organizing Committee (SWOC) began to focus on the environmental problems of the area. SWOC employed a strategy which linked voter registration with education around environmental problems. This strategy was combined with action campaigns in specific neighborhoods. For example, the Albuquerque area has especially serious problems with groundwater contamination. SWOC conducted water testing sessions in local communities and was successful in getting new water lines laid in certain neighborhoods. It also conducted city-wide environmental tours, for the purposes of educating residents as well as holding accountability sessions for political candidates and elected officials. This project had the support of the National Council of Churches, which SWOC in holding an "Interdenominational Hearing on Toxics in Minority Communities" in September, 1989 (Southwest Organizing Committee, 1989).

In Louisiana, a bi-racial coalition of community, environmental and labor groups joined together to focus attention on the environmental problems associated with a corridor between Baton Rouge and New Orleans. The coalition, called the Louisiana Toxics Project, is composed of the Gulf Coast Tenants Association, the Delta Chapter of the Sierra Club, the Louisiana Environmental Action Network and the Oil, Chemical, and Atomic Workers Union. It started when a group of tenants attended a national environmentalist meeting early in 1988 in Atlanta, Georgia and realized that they could do something about the poisoning of their communities. In November, 1988, the coalition conducted and eighty-mile, ten-day march along the Mississippi River between Baton Rouge and New Orleans. According to Pat Bryant, the project's director, "the myth that African Americans are not interested in protecting the earth has been proven a lie in Louisiana" (Southern Organizing Committee for Economic and Social Justice, 1989: 3).

The United Farm Workers Union (UFW), after the 1985 finding of aldicarb-contaminated watermelon from California, began to focus upon pesticide problems affecting farmworkers (United Farm Workers union, 1985). This led to their "Wrath of Grapes" national boycott. This boycott was meant to focus national attention on the plight of migrant farmworkers and demanded the banning of five pesticides (United Farm Workers Union, 1986). One tactic used to further this boycott was a month long fast by Cesar Chavez. Chavez's fast was carried on by others, including the Rev. Jesse Jackson and Dr. Benjamin Chavis. By the beginning of 1989, the boycott had caused a serious decline in grape sales in the New York metropolitan area, the single largest table grape marketing area in the nation. Along with a national boycott, the UFW worked in conjunction with the National Farm Worker Ministry, a church-based support group, to work with childhood cancer victims in the San Joaquin Valley (Hoagland, 1987).

These are but a few of the emerging and ongoing grassroots communities active around environmental issues. They reflect the significant growth in public awareness of toxic pollution in racial minority communities. While the Commission for Racial Justice report may have played a part in engendering this awareness, the upsurge in minority-based community activism generally has its own dynamics and reflects the overdue recognition of a social reality, i.e., the disparate distribution of environmental contaminants in their communities.

The report, however, did provide, for the first time, a nationally comprehensive study that gives credence to those who want to focus on these issues, either for overall public policy development or for grassroots activists addressing specific problems in racial minority communities. Because of this report and others, "sufficient evidence of the impact of toxics in racial and ethnic communities has come to the fore to silence anyone who would argue that there is no connection between pollution and race" (Lee, 1987a).

No example serves to illustrate this better than the following article regarding the successful campaign of residents of Hancock County, Georgia, spearheaded by Cynthia Smith, to prevent the siting of an incinerator in their county:

They talked about the 'blackness' of the issue, quoting from the United Church of Christ's study on toxic wastes and race to the residents of this 78% black county. When Hancock residents started coming together to oppose the facility in September 1987, they called themselves Citizens Against Hazardous Wastes in Hancock County. Prayer vigils, rallies, public meetings, and lots of door-to-door talking with folks paid off in generating a unified base of support and a strong voice. CAHW used that voice to successfully block the facility. They spoke of racism, planned to sue the county for several instances of barring residents from a public meeting, and considered recalling their county commissioners from office (Stults, 1998: 3).

Although other communities in the South do not seem to be fundamentally different from Hancock County, few of them which confront environmental issues for the first time are likely to have the stunning success of Hancock County.

Many of the issues which were raised in "Toxic Wastes and Race in the United States," particularly those related to economics and the hazardous waste issue, present major obstacles.

For example, the proponents of the LANCER project approached Gilbert Lindsay, an African American city councilman who represented the district surrounding the proposed plant, and offered a $10 million community development fund to finance improvements in a community center, to be named after his wife (Russell, 1989: 26). Another example involves a plan to rehabitate the Love Canal, New York, area. A bill was envisioned that would allow the construction of low income housing in the area. Among the persons most willing to relocate in such an area of questionable safety would be African Americans in a neighboring housing project, whose situation had never been addressed throughout the many years of controversy over the Love Canal landfill.

The interrelated issues of economics, politics and the lack of community environmental consciousness have exerted a powerful influence in Sumter County, Alabama, site of the nation's largest hazardous waste landfill. Originally a smaller landfill owned in part by the son-in-law of former Governor George Wallace, the facility was purchased and expanded by Chemical Waste Management, Inc. Throughout this process, Sumter County residents were not aware of the site's real purpose. For example, one commonly held belief was that the plant was involved in the production of fertilizer , a logical use of the dolomite chalk formation (otherwise known as Selma chalk) upon which the area rests. If anything, the facility provided much needed employment for this highly depressed area. Not until workers began to complain about working conditions and health problems did the truth about the facility begin to emerge.

The landfill, through a surcharge on each barrel of waste transported to the site, also provides revenues to the area, particularly the school system. This has been labeled by local activist, John Zieppert, as "blood money." However, the area does suffer from a low tax base and lack of economic development. At the same time, the

Alabama Black Belt remains a particularly contentious battleground for African American political rights. One example of these continuing struggles during recent years is the persecution of African American leadership for alleged voting fraud. Indeed, such issues have taken precedence over environmental problems, which correctly or incorrectly, are viewed as luxury concerns.

In many ways, Sumter County is illustrative of the dichotomy between traditional civil rights and environmental agendas. Traditional civil rights organizations have focused on traditional issues such as employment, housing, education, economic development and political participation to the exclusion of environmental concerns. Moreover, there exists a historical enmity between these two movements. Since its inception, the environmental movement has in the main viewed problems in racial minority communities as an unwelcome stepchild. For example, during Earth Day activities in 1970 at San Jose College, organizers bought a brand new Cadillac and buried it. The Black Student Union demonstrated in protest, contending that such money could have been better spent on the problems of the inner cities. Several years later, the membership of the National Sierra Club was polled on the question of whether it should increase involvement in urban poor and minorities. The proposal was rejected three to one (Freudenberg, 1984b; 212-213). In 1984, Ronald Taylor, in *U.S. News and World Report*, asked in an article by the same name, "Do environmentalists care about the poor?" For these and other reasons, traditional civil rights organizations have long viewed "environmentalism" with distrust and hostility.

On the other hand, the civil rights movement has also been faulted for its lack of concern over environmental issues. In a recent commentary, Paul Ruffins, Executive Director of Black Network News, said that despite the growing evidence of minority exposure to toxins,

such organizations as the NAACP and the Urban League—exquisitely sensitive to threats to minorities in areas such as education, housing, jobs, AIDS, and drugs, have almost completely ignored environmental hazards. For example, the program for a recent Urban League Conference offered more than 20 forums, from child care to the lack of minority teachers. Not one was dedicated to environmental issues (Ruffin, 1989).

Much has been made of the perception that environmentalists and minority-based organizations, whose support has come from corporations and labor unions, have fundamentally divergent interests. Whereas this schism is reflected in very real and intractable issues such as "economic blackmail" (Bullard, 1987a), there are indications that this alone cannot fully explain the inaction of civil rights organizations on environmental issues. For example, the Congressional Black Caucus has been rated to be among the most progressive voting blocks on environmental issues (Taylor, 1984). An issue that has yet to be fully examined is simply the lack of familiarity on the part of civil rights community with such issues. In many respects, environmental issues are difficult to grasp, being highly technical and regulatory in nature. Poorer communities, lacking readily available pool of residents, such as doctors, lawyers, and scientists, who are familiar with the nomenclature of environmental protection, are at a distinct disadvantage.

Accessibility to persons trained in environmental fields has been found to be a major element of success by communities confronting environmental problems. The article entitled "Citizen Action for Environmental Health: Report on a Survey of Community Organizations," reports the findings of a nationwide survey with grassroots environmental organizations:

Identification and control of environmental health hazards have depended primarily on two strategies: scientific research and government regulation. In the last decade, a third strategy has emerged. In communities across the country, concerned citizens have banded together to attempt to force government or industry to reduce or eliminate a suspected hazard in their neighborhood (Freudenberg, 1984a).

As important and viable as this strategy has proven to be, it is only beginning to be recognized and used in African American and other racial/ethnic communities. There have been major developments, since the United Church of Christ Commission for Racial Justice study, on the part of both the environmental and civil rights movements that begin to address these issues. In early 1988, the National Sierra Club and the National Toxics Coalition co-sponsored the Southern Environmental Assembly in Atlanta, Georgia, the event which gave rise to the formation of the Louisiana Toxics Project. The event was aimed at impacting the 1988 presidential political campaign. While the organizers of this conference hired an African American organizer and sought to involve African Americans and showcase African American leaders such as Rep. John Lewis (D-GA), Lowery and Chavis, it was largely unsuccessful in obtaining African American participation. The delegation from Louisiana represented the bulk of the conference's African American participation. Nonetheless, as seen by developments in Louisiana and other areas, the conference did have a significant impact. An ongoing project, the African American Environmental Services project, based in Atlanta, Georgia, now exists, The Natural Resources Defense Council (NRDC) has devoted several articles of the *Amicus Journal* to minority issues, as will Environmental Action, which is planning to publish a major issue on minorities and the environment. NRDC is also beginning a project on environmental problems in minority communities in New York City.

Progressive African American leadership has begun to make the link between environment and civil rights. Besides the United Church of Christ Commission for Racial Justice's efforts, Jesse Jackson made the environment a major issue in his 1988 campaign. At the time, growing restiveness around environmental concerns such as global warming have combined with the commemoration of the twentieth anniversary of Earth Day to create an upsurge of public interest in recent years. The approach of environmentalists today have some significant difference from that of 1970. Among the board members of the 1990 Earth Day committee was Jesse Jackson. A tour by Jackson of minority communities with environmental problems in early 1990 was conducted.

There is an important ripple effect from this upsurge of activism around environmental issues in minority communities. The issue is now a highly visible one, reflected in the accompanying upsurge in press coverage. Such visibility not only aids the work of local activists by making industry and government agencies take their interests more seriously, but will cause political leaders to begin to see the value of this issue as a part of their political platforms.

46

Black, Brown, Red, and Poisoned

Regina Austin and Michael Schill

The economics of poverty in combination with the presence of industrial pollution combine to result in poor people being much more exposed to toxins than the rest of society. The environmental movement must give more attention to disadvantaged humans than to nonhuman environments.

PEOPLE OF COLOR THROUGHOUT THE UNITED States are receiving more than their fair share of the poisonous fruits of industrial production. They live cheek by jowl with waste dumps, incinerators, landfills, smelters, factories, chemical plants, and oil refineries whose operations make them sick and kill them young. They are poisoned by the air they breathe, the water they drink, the fish they catch, the vegetables they grow, and, in the case of children, the very ground they play on. Even the residents of some of the most rural hamlets of the South and Southwest suffer from the ill effects of toxins.

The disproportionate location of sources of toxic pollution in communities of color is the result of various development patterns. In some

The Humanist, July–August 1994 v54 n4 p9(8). Copyright © 1994 American Humanist Association. Reprinted with permission. Additional copying is prohibited.

cases, the residential communities where people of color now live were originally the homes of whites who worked in the facilities that generate toxic emissions. The housing and the industry sprang up roughly simultaneously. Whites vacated the housing (but not necessarily the jobs) for better shelter as their socioeconomic status improved, and poorer black and brown folks who enjoy much less residential mobility took their place. In other cases, housing for African Americans and Latino Americans was built in the vicinity of existing industrial operations because the land was cheap and the people were poor. For example, Richmond, California, developed downwind from a Chevron oil refinery when African Americans migrated to the area to work in shipyards during World War II.

In yet a third pattern, sources of toxic pollution were placed in existing minority communities. The explanations for such sitings are numerous; some reflect the impact of racial and ethnic discrimination. The impact, of course, may be attenuated and less than obvious. The most neutral basis for a siting choice is probably the natural characteristics of the land, such as mineral content of the soil. Low population density would appear to be a similar criterion. It has been argued, however, that in the South, a sparse concentration of inhabitants is correlated with poverty, which is, in turn, correlated with race. As Conner Bailey and Charles Faupel have noted in the Proceedings of the Michigan Conference on Race and the Incidence of Environmental Hazards: "It follows that criteria for siting hazardous waste facilities which include density of population will have the effect of targeting rural black communities that have high rates of poverty."

Likewise, the compatibility of pollution with preexisting uses might conceivably make some sites more suitable than others for polluting operations. Pollution tends to attract other sources of pollutants, particularly, those associated with toxic disposal. For example, Chemical Waste Management, Inc., has proposed the construction of a toxic waste incinerator outside of Kettleman City, California, a community composed largely of Latino farm workers. Chem Waste also has proposed to build a hazardous waste incinerator in Emelle, a predominantly African American community located in the heart of Alabama's "black belt." The company already has hazardous waste landfills in Emelle and Kettleman City.

According to the company's spokesperson, quoted in the Los Angeles Times for February 24, 1991, Chem Waste placed the landfill in Kettleman City "because of the area's geographical features. Because the landfill handles toxic waste . . . it is an ideal spot for an incinerator"; the tons of toxic waste ash that the incinerator will generate can be "contained and disposed of at the installation's landfill." Residents of Kettleman City face a "triple whammy" of threats from pesticides in the fields, the nearby hazardous waste landfill, and a proposed hazardous waste incinerator. This case is not unique.

After reviewing the literature on hazardous waste incineration, Harvey White has concluded

in the Proceedings of the Michigan Conference that "minority communities represent a "least cost" option for waste incineration . . . because much of the waste to be incinerated is already in these communities." Despite its apparent neutrality, the siting based upon compatibility may be related to racial and ethnic discrimination, particularly if such discrimination influenced the siting of preexisting sources of pollution.

Polluters know that communities of low-income and working-class people with no more than a high-school education are not as effective at marshaling opposition as communities of middle- or upper-income people. People of color in the United States have traditionally had less clout with which to check legislative and executive abuse or to challenge regulatory laxity. Private corporations, moreover, can have a powerful effect on the behavior of public officials. Poor minority people wind up the losers to them both.

People of color are more likely than whites to be economically impoverished, and economic vulnerability makes impoverished communities of color prime targets for "risky" technologies. Historically, these communities are more likely than others to tolerate pollution-generating commercial development in the hope that economic benefits will inure to the community in forms of jobs, increased taxes, and civic improvements. Once the benefits start to flow, the community may be reluctant to forgo them even when they are accompanied by poisonous spills or emissions. According to Robert D. Bullard in his book *Dumping in Dixie: Class, and Environmental Luality*, this was the case in Emelle, in Sumter County, Alabama, site of the nation's largest hazardous waste landfill.

Sumter County's population is roughly 70 percent African American, and 30 percent of its inhabitants fall below the poverty line. Although the landfill was apparently leaking, it was difficult to rally support against the plant among African American politicians because its operations contributed an estimated $15.9 million to the local economy in the form of wages, local purchases of goods and service, and per-ton landfill user fees.

Of course, benefits do not always materialize after the polluter begins operations. For example, West Harlem was supposed to receive, as a trade-off for accepting New York City's largest sewage treatment plant, an elaborate state park to be built on the roof of the facility. The plant is functioning, fouling the air with emissions of hydrogen sulfide and promoting an infestation of rats and mosquitoes. The park, however, has yet to be completed, the tennis courts have been removed from the plans completely, and the "first-rate" restaurant has be scaled down to a pizza parlor.

In other cases, there is no net profit to distribute among the people. Dana Alston, in the Panos Institute report "Taking Back Our Lives," observes that new jobs created by the poisonous enterprises are "filled with highly skilled labor from outside the community," while the increased tax revenues go not to "social services or community development projects, but . . . toward expanding the infrastructure to better serve the industry."

Once a polluter has begun operations, the victims' options are limited. Mobilizing a community against an existing polluter is more difficult than organizing opposition to a proposed toxic-waste-producing activity. Resignation sets in, and the resources for attacking ongoing pollution are not as numerous, and the tactics not as potent, as those available during the proposal stage. Furthermore, though some individuals are able to escape toxic poisoning by moving out of the area, the flight of others will be blocked by limited incomes, housing discrimination, and restrictive land-use regulations.

THREAT TO BARRIOS, GHETTOS, AND RESERVATIONS

Pollution is no longer accepted as an unalterable consequence of living in the "bottom" (the least pleasant, poorest area minorities can occupy) by those on the bottom of the status hierarchy. Like anybody else, people of color are distressed by accidental toxic spills, explosions, and inexplicable patterns of miscarriages and cancers—and they are beginning to fight back, from Maine to Alaska.

To be sure, people of color face some fairly high barriers to effective mobilization against toxic threats, such as limited time and money; lack of access to technical, medical, and legal expertise; relatively weak influence in political and media circles; and ideological conflicts that pit jobs against the environment. Limited fluency in English and fear of immigration authorities will keep some of those affected, especially Latinos, quiescent. Yet despite the odds, poor minority people are responding to their poisoning with a grass-roots movement of their own.

Activist groups of color are waging grass-roots environmental campaigns all over the country. Although they are informally connected, these campaigns reflect shared characteristics and goals. The activity of these groups is indicative of a grass-roots movement that occupies a distinctive position relative to both the mainstream movement and the white grass-roots environmental movement. The environmental justice movement is anti-elitist and anti-racist. It capitalizes on the social and cultural differences of people of color as it cautiously builds alliances with whites and persons of the middle class. It is both fiercely environmental and conscious of the need for economic development in economically disenfranchised communities. Most distinctive of all, this movement has been extremely outspoken in challenging the integrity and bona fides of mainstream establishment environmental organizations.

People of color have not been mobilized to join grass-roots environmental campaigns because of their general concern for the environment. Characterizing a problem as being "environmental" may carry weight in some circles, but it has much less impact among poor minority people. It is not that people of color are uninterested in the environment—a suggestion the grass-roots activists find insulting. In fact, they are more likely to be concerned about pollution than are people who are wealthier and white. Rather, in the view of many people of color, environmentalism is associated with the preservation of wildlife and wilderness, which simply is not more important than the survival of people and the communities in which they live; thus, the mainstream movement has its priorities skewed.

The mainstream movement, so the critique goes, embodies white, bourgeois values—values that are foreign to African-Americans, Latino Americans, Asian Americans, and Native Americans. Environment sociologist Dorceta Taylor has characterized the motivations of those who make donations to mainstream organizations as follows:

[In part, the] motivation to contribute is derived from traditional Romantic and Transcendental ideas—the idea of helping to conserve or preserve land and nature for one's own present and future use, or for future generations. Such use involves the ability to get away from it all; to transcend earthly worries, to escape, to commune with nature. The possibility of having a transcendental experience is strongly linked to the desire to save the places where such experiences are likely to occur.

Even the more engaged environmentalists— those whose involvement includes participation in demonstrations and boycotts—are thought to be imbued with romantic and transcendental notions that favor nature over society and the individual's experiences of the natural realm over the collective experience.

There are a number of reasons why people of color might not share such feelings. Their prospects for transcendental communion with nature are restricted. Parks and recreational areas have been closed to them because of discrimination, inaccessibility, cost, their lack of specialized skills or equipment, and residence requirements for admission. They must find their recreation close to home. Harm to the environment caused by industrial development is not really their responsibility because they have relatively little economic power or control over the exploitation of natural resources. Since rich white people messed it up, rich white people ought to clean it up. In any event, emphasis on the environment in the abstract diverts attention and resources from the pressing, concrete problems that people of color—especially those with little or no income—confront every day.

Nonetheless, communities of color have addressed environmental problems that directly threaten them on their own terms. The narrowness of the mainstream movement, which appears to be more interested in endangered nonhuman species and pristine, undeveloped land than at-risk humans, makes poor minority people think that their concerns are not "environmental." Cognizant of this misconception and eschewing terminology that artificially compartmentalizes people's troubles, minority grass-roots environmental activists take a multidimensional approach to pollution problems. Thus, the sickening, poisonous odors emitted by landfills and sewage plants are considered matters of public health or government accountability, while workplace contamination is a labor issue, and lead-based paint in public-housing projects is a landlord-tenant problem.

The very names of some of the organizations and the goals they espouse belie the primacy of environmental concerns. The Southwest Organizing Project of Albuquerque has been very successful in mobilizing people around issues of water pollution and workplace contamination. For example, SWOP fought for the rollback of charges levied against a group of home owners who were forced to hook up with a municipal water system because nitroglycerine had contaminated private wells. SWOP then campaigned to make the federal government assume responsibility for the pollution, which was attributed to operations at a nearby military installation. Yet in a briefing paper entitled "Major National Environmental Organizations and the Problem of the 'Environmental Movement,'" SWOP describes itself as follows:

SWOP does not consider itself an "environmental" organization but, rather, a community-based organization which addresses toxics issues as part of a broader agenda of action to realize social, racial, and economic justice. We do not single out the environment as necessarily having a special place above all other issues; rather, we recognize that issues of toxic contamination fit within an agenda which can (and in our practical day-to-day work does) include employment, education, housing, health care, and other issues of social, racial, and economic justice.

In some ways, minority grass-roots environmentalism reflects the interrelationship among various forms of subordination, about which Daniel Zwerdling wrote in the Progressive (January 1973), in an early attack on the parochialism of the mainstream environmental movement:

Pollution, poverty, and worker security reflect three different ways that American corporations express themselves as they exploit people and resources for maximum profits. When corporations need raw materials, they strip them from public lands as cheaply as possible and leave behind great scars on the earth. When they need labor, they hire workers as cheaply as possible and leave behind women and men broken by industrial injuries, diseases, and debt. When corporations produce their goods they use the cheapest and fastest methods available and leave behind vast quantities of waste. The corporations dump the wastes in the poorest and most powerless parts of town. And when they earn their profits, the corporations divide them among company executives and investors, leaving behind poor people who cannot afford medical care or food or decent homes.

Ordinary, plain-speaking people who are the casualties of toxic poisoning articulate the critique somewhat more pointedly. As Cancer Alley resident Amos Favorite put it:

We are victims . . . Not just blacks. Whites are in this thing too. We're all victimized by a system that puts the dollar before everything else. That's the way it was in the old days when the dogs and whips were masters, and that's the way it is today when we got stuff in the water and the air we can't even see that can kill us deader than we ever thought we could die.

In the estimation of the grass-roots folks, however, race and ethnicity surpass class as explanations for the undue toxic burden heaped on people of color. Activists see these environmental inequities as unfair and unjust—practices that many feel should be illegal. Of course, it is hard to prove that racial discrimination is responsible for siting choices and government inaction in the

environmental area, particularly in a court of law. One need only point to the examples of Bean v. Southwestern Waste Management (Houston, Texas), Bordeaux Action Committee v. Metropolitan Nashville (Nashville, Tennessee), and RISE v. Kay (King and Queen counties, Virginia) to see the limited utility of current antidiscrimination doctrine in redressing the plight of poisoned communities of color.

Environmental activists of color draw a good deal of their inspiration from the modern civil-rights movement of the 1960s. That movement was advanced by hardwon Supreme Court decisions. These organizers hope that a civil-rights victory in the environmental area will validate their charges of environmental racism, help to flesh out the concept of environmental equity, serve as a catalyst for further activism, and, just possibly, force polluters to reconsider siting in poor minority communities.

CAPITALIZING ON THE RESOURCES OF COMMON CULTURE

For people, of color, social and cultural difficulties such as language are not handicaps but the communal resources that facilitate mobilization around issues like toxic poisoning. As members of the same race, ethnicity, gender, and even age cadre, would-be participants share cultural traditions, modes, and mores that encourage cooperation and unity. People of color may be more responsive to organizing efforts than whites because they already have experience with collective action through community groups and institutions such as churches, parent-teacher associations, and town watches or informal social networks. Shared criticisms of racism, a distrust of corporate power, and little expectation that government will be responsive to their complaints are common sentiments in communities of color and support the call to action around environmental concerns.

Grass-roots environmentalism is also fostered by notions that might be considered feminist or womanist. Acting on a realization that toxic poisoning is a threat to home and family, poor minority women have moved into the public realm to confront corporate and government officials whose modes of analysis reflect patriarchy, white supremacy, and class and scientific elitism. There are numerous examples of women of color whose strengths and talents have made them leaders of grass-roots environmental efforts.

The organization Mothers of East Los Angeles illustrates the link between group culture and mobilization in the ethnic grass-roots environmental movement. Persistent efforts by MELA defeated proposals for constructing a state prison and a toxic waste incinerator in the group's mostly Latin American neighborhood in East Los Angeles.

Similarly, the Lumbee Indians of Robeson County, North Carolina, who attached spiritual significance to a river that would have been polluted by a hazardous waste facility proposed by the GSX Corporation, waged a campaign against the facility on the grounds of cultural genocide. Throughout the campaign, as Richard Regan and M. Legerton report in the anthology Communities in Economic Crisis: Appalachia and the South, "Native American dance, music, and regalia were used at every major public hearing. Local Lumbee churches provided convenient meeting locations for GSX planning sessions. Leaflet distribution at these churches reached significant minority populations in every pocket of the county's nearly 1,000 square miles."

Concerned Citizens of Choctaw defeated a plan to locate a hazardous waste facility on their lands in Philadelphia, Mississippi. The Good Road Coalition, a grass-roots Native American group based on the Rosebud Reservation in South Dakota, defeated plans by a Connecticut-based company to build a 6,000-acre garbage landfill on the Rosebud. Local residents initiated a recall election, defeating several tribal council leaders and the landfill proposal. The project, dubbed "dances with garbage," typifies the lengths the Lakota people and other Native Americans will go to preserve their land, which is an essential part of their religion and culture.

Consider, finally, the Toxic Avengers of El Puente, a group of environmental organizers based in the Williamsburg section of Brooklyn, New York. (Their name is taken from the title of a popular, low-budget horror movie.) The group attacks not only government racism but also "adultism—adult superiority and privilege. The members, whose ages range from nine to 28, combine their activism with programs to educate themselves and others about the science of toxic hazards.

The importance of culture in the environmental justice movement seems not to have produced the kind of distrust and misgivings that might impede interaction with white working-class and middle-class groups engaged in grass-roots environmental activism. There are numerous examples of ethnic-based associations working in coalitions with organizations from the mainstream. There are also localities in which antagonism and suspicion that are the legacy of white racism have kept whites and African-Americans from uniting against a common toxic enemy. The link between the minority groups and the majority groups seems grounded in material exchange, not ideological fellowship. The white groups attacking toxins at the grass-roots level have been useful sources of financial assistance and information about tactics and goals.

. . .

BRIDGING THE JUSTICE-ENVIRONMENT GAP

At the same time that environmental justice activists are battling polluters, some are engaged on another front in a struggle against the elitism and racism that exist within the mainstream environmental movement. There are several substantive points of disagreement between grass-roots groups of color and mainstream environmental organizations. First, communities of color are tired of shouldering the fallout from environmental regulation. A letter sent to ten of the establishment environmental organizations by the Southwest Organizing Project and numerous activists of color engaged in the grass-roots environmental struggle illustrates the level of exasperation:

Your organizations continue to support and promote policies which emphasize the clean-up and preservation of the environment on the backs of working people in general and people of color in particular. In the name of eliminating environmental hazards at any cost, across the country industrial and other economic activities which employ us are being shut down, curtailed, or prevented while our survival needs and cultures are ignored. We suffer the end results of these actions, but are never full participants in the decision-making which leads to them.

Although the indictment, standing alone, seems fairly broad, it is backed up with specific illustrations of the adverse impact mainstream environmentalism has had on poor minority people. In response to pressure from environmentalists concerned about saving wildlife and protecting the health of the general population, pesticides of great persistence but low acute toxicity—such as DDT and chlordane—have been restricted or banned. They have been replaced by pesticides that degrade rapidly but are more acutely toxic, such as parathion. The substitutes, of course, pose a greater risk to farm workers and their children, who are for the most part people of color. Baldemar Velasquez of the Farm Labor Organizing Committee characteristics the mainstream's failings in regard to pesticides as follows:

The environmental groups are not responding to try to right the wrongs and change the motivation of industry, which is greed and profit at the expense of everyone. When you start dealing with that issue, you're dealing with structural change in terms of how decisions are made and who benefits from them. The agenda of the environmental movement seems to be focused on getting rid of a particular chemical. This is not enough, because they'll replace it with something else that's worse.

Another threat to communities of color is the growing popularity of NIMBY (not in my backyard) groups. People of color have much to fear from these groups because their communities are the ones most likely to lose the contests to keep the toxins out. The grass-roots environmentalists argue that, rather than trying to bar polluters who will simply locate elsewhere, energies should be directed at bringing the amount of pollution down to zero. In lieu of NIMBY, mainstream environmentalists should be preaching NIABY (not in anyone's backyard).

Finally conservation organizations are making "debt-for-nature" swaps throughout the so-called Third World. Through swaps, conservation organizations procure ownership of foreign indebtedness (either by gift or by purchase at a reduced rate) and negotiate with foreign governments for reduction of the debt in exchange for land. Grass-roots environmental activists of color complain that these deals—which turn conservation organizations into creditors of so-called Third World peoples—legitimate the debt and the exploitation on which it is based.

The positions staked out by environmental justice activists regarding fallout from environmental regulation are consistent with the values that are ingrained in the rest of the movement's activities. The fallout critique is not opposed to environmentalism or environmental regulation. In attacking the political conservatism of the mainstream, the grass-roots environmentalists are not themselves lapsing into environmental conservatism. In fact, the fallout from which communities of color suffer can be cured with more, not less, environmentalism, provided it is anti-elitist, anti-racist, sensitive to the cultural norms and mores of people of color, mindful of the impact of domestic regulation on brothers and sisters abroad, and cognizant of the substantial need for economic development in disenfranchised countries.

Unlike those in the mainstream organizations, people involved in the environmental justice movement cannot afford to lose sight of the material circumstances of the black, brown, red and yellow folks who are their compatriots and constituents. Nor do the grass-roots activists intend to abandon their environmental agenda. The "eco" in eco-justice stands as much for "economic" as for "ecological." For many communities of color, it is too late for NIMBY. They already have a dump, an incinerator, a smelter, a petrochemical plant, or a military base in their neighborhood. And according to one environmental-justice advocate (quoted by Conger Beasley in the July/August 1900 issue of Buzzworm), they do not necessarily want the polluters "to pack up and move away. That's not what we're asking for. We just want them to clean up the mess they've made. They can do it. It's only fair." What they do want is accountability from existing polluters.

The dual environmental-economic agenda of the minority grass-roots movement is reflected in two items of the Bill of Rights drafted by the Southwest Organizing Project's Community Environmental Program:

Right to Clean Industry: We have the right to clean industry; industry that will contribute to the economic development of our communities and that will enhance the environment and beauty of our landscape. We have the right to say "No" to industries that we feel will be polluters and disrupt our life-styles and traditions. We have the right to choose which industries we feel will benefit our communities most, and we have the right to public notice and public hearings to allow us to make these decisions.

Right to Prevention: We have the right to participate in the formulation of public policy that prevents toxic pollution from entering our communities. We support technologies that will provide jobs, business opportunities, and conservation of valuable resources. As residents and workers, we have the right to safe equipment and safety measures to prevent our exposure in the community and the workplace.

Prevention of toxic accidents and communal participation in risk allocation decisions should be the key components of future negotiations regarding industrial sites in poor minority communities. It is hard to envision a world without trade-offs, and it is too soon to tell what sort of compromises enlightened minority communities might be willing to make (or, more likely, might feel compelled to make) when presented with proposals from industries that are mostly clean but a little bit dirty. They might be willing to accept some exposure in exchange not for cash or credit but for control. To the extent that communities do not create and carry out their own plans for economic development, their right to reject poisonous enterprises will be limited. Therein lies the next hurdle for environmental activists of color.

The struggle to contain the poisoning of poor minority communities requires resources which the grass-roots environmentalists do not have and the mainstream environmentalists do. Environmental justice advocates reject the romantic view of the mainstream and stress that its power is material, not transcendental. As Vernice Miller, co-founder of West Harlem Environmental Action put it: "They're going to have to get off the stick of preserving birds and trees and seals and things like that and talk about what's affecting real people. . . . Organizations of color are forcing the issue."

In addition to challenging some of the goals of the mainstream movement, environmental justice activists are going after the mainstream for failing to integrate their staffs and boards, for failing to enlarge their agendas to include the concerns of poor minority communities, and for failing to share their bountiful resources with poorer grass-roots groups. These challenges strike a nerve in organizations that view themselves as being faithful to the liberalism of the 1960s. Whether their guilt, concern, or embarrassment will translate into greater cooperation between minority environmental groups and the mainstream or the integration of the organizations' bureaucracies remains to be seen. The grass-roots folks seem to think that, if they achieve the second goal, they will be closer to achieving the first. They may be fooling themselves. Some consideration should be given to devices for ensuring the accountability of people of color who find positions in mainstream organizations as a result of complaints from the grass-roots.

People of color have provided the crucial leadership for the growing environmental justice movement in the United States. This movement, in all aspects of its operations, is anti-elitist, class conscious, populist, and participatory. It attacks environmental problems as being intertwined with other pressing economic, social, and political ills. It capitalizes on the social and cultural strengths of people of color and demands in turn that their life-styles, traditions, and values be respected by polluters and mainstream environmental organizations alike.

The environmental justice movement is still in its embryonic stages. Its ideology has yet to be fully developed, let alone tested. Moreover, it is too easy for outsiders to criticize the trade-offs and compromises poor people and people of color bearing toxic burdens have made. It is important to understand the movement on its own terms if one hopes to make policy proposals that will be of use to those struggling to save themselves. Grass-roots people have proven that they are capable of leading, speaking, and doing for themselves.